ATM

solutions for enterprise internetworking

Data Communications and Networks Series
Consulting Editor. Dr C. Smythe, University of Sheffield

Selected titles in the Data Communications and Networks Series

Other Related Addison Wesley Longman Titles

ATM

solutions for enterprise internetworking

David Ginsburg

Addison-Wesley

Harlow, England • Reading, Massachusetts • Menlo Park, California
New York • Don Mills, Ontario • Amsterdam • Bonn • Sydney • Singapore
Tokyo • Madrid • San Juan • Milan • Mexico City • Seoul • Taipei

© Addison Wesley Longman 1996

Addison Wesley Longman Limited
Edinburgh Gate
Harlow
Essex CM20 2JE
England

and Associated Companies throughout the world.

Cover designed by Op den Brouw, Design & Illustration, Reading
and printed by The Riverside Printing Co. (Reading) Ltd.
Typeset by Wyvern Typesetting Ltd., Bristol
Printed and bound by T.J. Press, Padstow, Cornwall.

First printed 1996

ISBN 0-201-87701-5

British Library Cataloguing-in-Publication Data
A catalogue record for this book is available from the British Library.

Library of Congress Cataloguing-in-Publication Data is available.

Dedication

To my mother, who has taught three generations that nothing is impossible.

Trademarks

MS-DOS is a registered trademark and Windows is a trademark of Microsoft Corporation.

DEC, DECnet, LAT and Ultrix are trademarks of the Digital Equipment Corporation.

Sun Microsystems is a registered trademark and Sun, SunOS, Solaris and Solstice are trademarks of Sun Microsystems Inc.

OSF is a trademark of the Open Software Foundation Inc.

AppleTalk and QuickTime are registered trademarks and Macintosh is a trademark of Apple Computers Inc.

Xerox is a registered trademark and Ethernet is a trademark of Xerox Corporation.

Novell, Netware, Internet Packet Exchange (IPX) and UNIX are trademarks of Novell Inc.

AIX, RS/6000, IBM, SNA, NetBIOS and Token Ring are trademarks of International Business Machines Corporation.

CompuServe is a trademark of CompuServe, Inc.

Intel and Indeo are trademarks of Intel Corporation.

HP is a registered trademark and Hewlett-Packard and Open View are trademarks of Hewlett-Packard Company.

Sniffer is a trademark of Network General.

Thomflex is a trademark of Thompson-CSF.

Netscape Navigator is a trademark of Netscape Communications Corporation.

Contents

Preface

Why the intense interest in ATM? Reasons are many, but most relate to the increasing role which internetworks play in our society and their effect. During the past year or two, the global computer network known as the Internet has been popularized to an extent hard to predict even a few short years ago. Does a day pass when we don't see a reference in the paper to the Net or catch the Web reference at the end of a TV commercial? On a more somber note, will the various communities connected to this network be able to retain their identities, and will the basic premise of the Internet, the free exchange of ideas, survive under the growing weight of government and commercial pressures? When we start mentioning 'effect on society', we are far removed from the nuts and bolts of a technology; and implications are much greater. A decade or two from now, we may look back on the growth of this global information infrastructure as one of the four turning points in the evolution of human society, on par with fire, the printed word, and the telephone.

With popularization and increasing use comes a demand for more sophisticated services; the integration of voice and video along with the traditional text traffic. Thus the requirement for a technology capable of meeting these requirements in a scalable way. Over the past 25 years, the Internet has evolved, using the technology most appropriate for the time. Along the way, we have seen leased lines, packet data services, satellites, and now ATM. But is ATM only limited to the Internet, or is it applicable to other services and networks as well? For the first time, we have a single technology capable of supporting the various voice, video, and data services to the home or business, supplanting existing dedicated networks. Even today, we see digitized broadcasts distributed to TV-top decoders and Enterprise voice and data wide-area networks all based on ATM. In 1996, ATM is rightfully becoming the technology of choice for a number of environments, including workgroups in small and large businesses, high-speed trunking within the service providers, and even video and information distribution to the residence. Over the next decade, ATM technology will increasingly provide the backbone for the evolving Global Information Infrastructure, the Net.

Is 'ATM: Solutions for Enterprise Internetworking' just another ATM book, or does it break new ground? Beginning in about 1990, a number of books have addressed ATM. Until recently, those focusing solely on ATM have devoted most of their efforts to looking at the technology and standardization, with the latter emphasis focusing on the ITU, where in reality organizations such as the ATM Forum and the Internet Engineering Task Force should be placed on-par. Other publications have treated ATM in passing; maybe a chapter or two on the technology and how it will one day be suitable for implementation. But none have covered the technology and services from the standpoint of the implementor: Which standards are truly relevant and have they been implemented? What devices should I deploy for a given application environment? How do I configure these devices? What caveats should I be aware of? This book answers these questions, by first looking at business drivers within the industry and comparing these to reality. We then look at standards, focusing on work within the ATM Forum and the IETF in addition to the ITU. Next, we look at ATM as a technology, first looking at the physical layer, then the ATM layer, and finally higher layer services including signaling and traffic management. With this understanding, we then look at the infrastructure of an ATM network: the switches, routers, and end-systems, along with how they interact and provide user services. Finally, and most critical, we present a number of implementation examples based on a combination of private and public networks and combining the various data, voice, and video models. The book is internetworking oriented, focusing on the deployment within an enterprise internetwork. At the same time, it does not ignore the integration of voice and video traffic into this environment.

Some of the standardization information reflects work-in-progress within the ATM Forum and the Internet Engineering Task Force. Thus, it details ways of solving some very difficult problems as of Winter, 1996, and may be subject to change. Nevertheless, the general approaches and directions as outlined in the book should remain valid for some time.

Credits

Special thanks to Arthur Lin, George Swallow, Allan Leinwand, Roland Acra, John Doyle, Guy Fedorkow, Anthony Alles, Jim Forster, Francois Le Faucher, Matt Barletta, and Steve Simlo, all from Cisco Systems.

To Eckhart Eichler from ProIn Consulting in Austria, George Howat from the University of Edinburgh, and Jon Crowcroft from University College London.

To Ian Henning, Jeremy Barnes, Dave Newson, and Dave Pratt at the BT Futures Testbed – thanks.

To Max Hall, and most of all, Catherine Joseph (biz).

Finally, a special thanks to my employer, Cisco Systems, for providing support over the last 18 months. Many of the figures are also adapted from Cisco Systems presentations.

Other figures have been adapted from ATM Forum, ITU, and IETF documents.

1

ATM background and business drivers

In looking at any new technology, one may wonder why some have succeeded while others, perhaps just as suitable from a technological standpoint, have failed. The last two decades are littered with LAN and WAN technologies; some, given up as dead, have made remarkable resurgences recently. The success of a technology is dependent upon: building the proper business case; a bottom line analysis of why 'this' technology is superior to 'that'; and most importantly, communicating this analysis not only to the technical network planners but also to their managers who make the purchasing decisions. Looking at ATM, the case has been made exceptionally well, helped in great part by the media. Corporations, even some traditionally distrustful of the latest and greatest, are willing to make this move to a new technology because they perceive that it will have a fundamental impact on the way they do business and the way their employees interface. Hopefully, this impact will result in increased productivity from an individual and a corporate standpoint. But, with all its support (hype) in the media, we sometimes need to take a step back and look at ATM in the context of actual requirements. Is it really the ultimate end-to-end technology, or should it be deployed in stages? Why choose ATM rather than competing high-bandwidth technologies? How mature are the standards and how will any changes affect equipment?

1.1 ATM: what and why?

Asynchronous Transfer Mode, commonly known as ATM, is a networking technology capable of transporting all higher forms of intelligence – voice, video, and data, from one user to another over a local or wide area. This universality is the 'why' of ATM, a single platform and technology resulting in cost savings and quality of service improvements for both end users and service provider. This is not saying that ATM is the ideal technology on which to base any one of these services. Many alternatives exist, but none are suitable for use in both the local and wide area, or have the widespread vendor and service provider support which ATM has gathered. In any case, within a production networking environment, ATM will find its place among other networking technologies as part of an end-to-end solution.

The term 'ATM' is used to describe the **Broadband Integrated Services Digital Network (B-ISDN)**, having been adopted by the internetworking and computer industry, as well as by the world press, to designate what is actually a combination of technologies and services. The B-ISDN was and is a concept providing integrated services to the user, an outgrowth of 64 Kbps-ISDN (sometimes called Narrowband ISDN).

ATM is a technology which resides directly above the physical infrastructure: the fiber, copper, or wireless transmission system. In fact, ATM operates at the physical layer, providing connection-oriented MAC-like service to voice transport between PABXs, video transport between video CODECs, and of course data transport. However, this forced classification usually breaks down in reality since ATM exhibits many characteristics of higher-layer protocols under actual deployment. Looking at the data environment, the International Standardization Organization (ISO) has defined a layered internetworking reference model known as the Open Systems Interconnect (OSI) reference model. This model is a method by which interactions between various processes within end-systems (that is, PCs, workstations, and routers) and intermediate-systems (that is, ATM switches) may be mapped to each other in a logical way, helping to guarantee interoperability. An idea of where ATM fits within this reference model (Figure 1.1) helps in its understanding and capabilities, and though the model is more relevant to the data networking world, its concepts may be applied to voice and video as well.

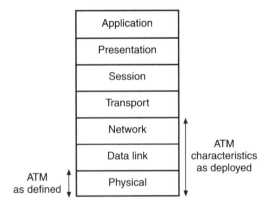

Figure 1.1 ATM and the OSI reference model.

ATM is capable of utilizing most deployed physical media types and transmission infrastructures. In the case of data networking, higher-layer services are based on well-defined data link, network, transport, session, and presentation layers, while video and voice support may rely on more of a direct mapping between the application (if one exists), the video or voice encoding, and the ATM layer. Layer 3, the network layer, is sometimes known as the internetwork layer based on its relevance for end-to-end internetworking. This is one area where ATM does not map effectively to the layering model, since the ATM layer will contain many features commonly associated with the network layer, such as hierarchical addressing and routing.

The most basic concept of ATM, and what differentiates it from past technologies, is the equal length cell structure. All higher-layer traffic, be it voice, video, or data, is broken into ATM 'cells', 53-byte packets containing a header and data payload. The header contains information identifying a particular virtual circuit, with many virtual circuits sharing a single physical interface, while the payload is normally available for user data. This concept, where multiple user data flows share a physical interface, is no different than that found within X.25 and Frame Relay. Unlike these two technologies, an equal length packet allows switches with very high throughput with almost all processing taking place in hardware. The ATM cell on its own, however, does not guarantee higher performance. This requires proper switch design, network design, and software within the ATM network supporting higher-layer services. In fact, ATM may have just the opposite effect on data traffic unless these guidelines are adhered to.

As user traffic arrives at the ATM interface within a computer, router, video CODEC, or PABX, it is segmented into the 53-byte cells described above. Over a single interface, these cells are interleaved and sent over the interface as they are generated. This contrasts to traditional **Time Division Multiplexing (TDM)** architectures where time slices are pre-allocated for the various traffic types. Thus, the term **Asynchronous Time Division Multiplexing** may more adequately describe ATM.

A second fundamental concept behind ATM is that it is connection-oriented. Unlike shared LAN technologies or the router-based segment of the Internet, where data is packetized and sent to its destination along a route calculated on a hop-by-hop basis, systems participating in ATM will signal a connection across the network. Once the connection has been established, it is expected to be able to support the **Quality of Service (QoS)** requirements of the sources and destinations, to include parameters such as bandwidth, probability of discarded data, and delay. This QoS support is critical when ATM is used as a transport for services to include PABX interconnect or even reliable data transmission.

⌈ Though a datagram-oriented network may support QoS by making use of various queuing and resource reservation techniques in the support of voice and video, it will not support the large installed base of more traditional voice and video equipment. Time division multiplexers support these services, but are not usually deployed in the local area. Thus, ATM is the only technology which truly supports these requirements over both the local and wide area.

A commonly asked question is whether or not ATM is the most efficient and cost effective solution for data networking, if in fact alternative technologies exist which are capable of providing QoS support. The deployment of ATM must really be looked at in the context of multiple services: data, voice, and video. In many environments, such as a high-speed campus backbone or high-performance workgroup, ATM will have definite advantages. It is the first networking technology which allows users to economically deploy a common physical infrastructure and signaling mechanism from end-station to end-station over intervening local- and wide-area ATM network segments. Whereas existing networks translate from Ethernet, Token Ring, or **Fiber Distributed Data Interface (FDDI)** in the local area to X.25, Frame Relay, ISDN, or leased lines in the wide area, with inherent complexity, ATM provides for a single end-to-end architecture where appropriate. 'Appropriate' is defined by the network architect after an analysis of applications and of available local- and wide-area services, and though this end-to-end transparency is a promise of ATM, actual implementations will combine many of the above technologies. The 'why' of ATM therefore is probably best answered by looking at the business drivers behind its implementation and then comparing the promise of ATM with reality. ⌉

1.2 Business drivers

Having introduced the fundamentals of ATM as a technology, the next step is to look at why ATM is so popular in the presence of so many competing technologies. The business case for ATM includes applications, technology, and user perceptions. Within a continuum, the advent of new applications and the deployment of new hardware often leads to the requirement for new network designs. Implemementors see ATM as a technology that can deliver integrated services and end-to-end scalability, while at the same time supporting existing applications.

1.2.1 Applications

Applications differ in their network requirements. As real-time and multimedia applications are deployed alongside existing text-oriented systems, the networking infrastructure must reflect these changes; shared Ethernets or Token Ring will no longer suffice. Figure 1.2 shows an

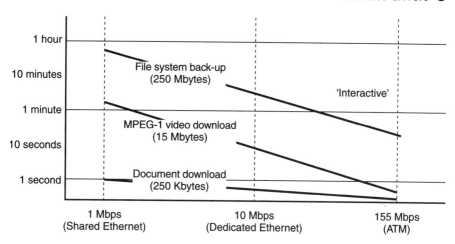

Figure 1.2 Application wait times.

example of application bandwidth requirements, comparing typical data transfer requirements with resulting wait times at various bandwidths. Although most applications will function at speeds lower than that provided by ATM, they may not appear 'interactive' to the user. This word has different meanings for different people, and here we use one minute as a guideline as to how long a user should be required to wait for a transaction to complete. Thus, application throughput requirements to the end-system do not necessarily mandate ATM. It is the aggregate across the backbone which mandates this technology. Consider 500 users on dedicated LAN segments using a mix of the applications depicted in Figure 1.2. Even assuming a 20% utilization, this equates to 1 Gbps of traffic over the backbone. At 1 or even 2 Gbps, a case may be made for Fast Ethernet or FDDI switching; anything greater, and we require ATM. High-performance servers may also be considered as part of the campus or high-rise core. These devices, when equipped with ATM interfaces at 155 or 622 Mbps and above will be better capable of serving user data requests. The demand for additional bandwidth extends to the wide area as well, for as network planners deploy bandwidth-hungry applications across the corporation, users will demand an acceptable QoS. ATM is one way to guarantee this expected QoS across both the local and wide areas, first through static configuration and then by working together with QoS-aware applications such as those described later in this book.

1.2.2 Hardware

The applications described above have come about only through the deployment of high-performance clients and servers. These new end-systems have the capability of overloading many shared-media LANs as well as some switched networks. For comparison purposes, the computation capability of a PC or workstation in **Millions of Instructions per**

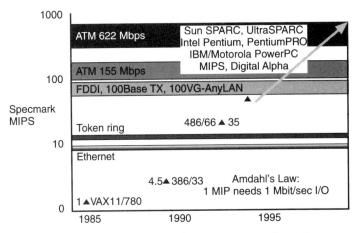

Figure 1.3 End-station bandwidth utilization. Source: Cisco Systems.

Second (MIPS) may be roughly equated to its ability to fully utilize a given network bandwidth in Mbps. As depicted in Figure 1.3, whereas an Intel 486-based PC is only capable of saturating an Ethernet or Token Ring segment, current generation PCs, workstations, and Internet terminals will be capable of utilizing the full 100 Mbps bandwidth of ATM, switched high-speed Ethernet, or FDDI. This fact sometimes catches network planners unaware, and they, along with their end users, suddenly notice that a single LAN segment which in the past serviced 10–20 users will no longer suffice under the offered load from these new devices. The deployment of higher-performance end-systems has in fact degraded network responsiveness. As a first step, each user will be provided with a dedicated 10/16/100 Mbps LAN connection. This is microsegmentation, and is the reason why LAN switching is so popular at present. In this environment, ATM to the desktop is also well positioned in the form of high-performance servers or workstations which should be connected directly to the backbone.

1.2.3 Integrated services

The application- and hardware-oriented business case made for ATM in the preceding paragraphs may be applied equally well to alternative technologies such as switched FDDI or high-speed Ethernet. A more convincing argument is therefore needed. ATM's promise of providing a single integrated network is this justification, and holds the most allure for network planners hoping to minimize cost and complexity. Consider a 'pre-ATM' infrastructure as depicted at the bottom of Figure 1.4. A single user will have multiple service connections, each with associated cost, end-

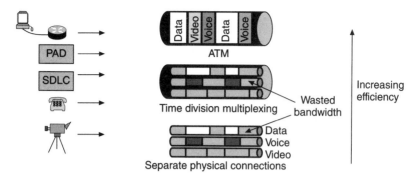

Figure 1.4 Increases in efficiency.

systems, and reliability concerns. In replacing these multiple services, the total integration of data and voice introduces some new concerns and design rules to those familiar with data networking but new to the voice world. Questions surrounding the deployment of PC-based voice and video, and its relationship to 'legacy' voice will arise as well. Some early adopters of ATM as a true multiservice platform may be branch offices wishing to minimize their monthly tariffs or corporations replacing their existing TDM backbones. Still, 'legacy' phonesets will remain well into the future, and interworking from voice over ATM to Narrowband-ISDN within a corporation or at the telephone company's central office will not occur overnight. ATM will be firmly entrenched in the data environment before it is universally accepted for voice transport.

1.3 Promise and reality

Though ATM holds much promise as a universal networking technology, and the business drivers regarding scalability and integrated services are sound, what factors will really influence its acceptance? Though public service providers will help further the technology across the wide area, it will be users in the local area who may determine its level of success. They evaluate cost, potential cost savings, standards, and manageability in the face of alternatives. On a more subjective level, they attempt to determine whether ATM is a 'safe' technology; whether its potential advantages outweigh perceived risks. Finally, the network planner will of course be 'helped' in the decision process by numerous trade journals, vendor claims, analyst reports, and possibly a desire not to be left behind in the deployment of a new technology. Sometimes, it is these intangibles which will drive the decision to adopt ATM.

1.3.1 Public service providers, consumers, and vendors

ATM deployment and factors contributing to its success may be looked at from two angles. The first is the public service provider (sometimes called **Public Telephone and Telegraph (PTT)**, where a government agency; or Telco in the United States), and the second is the consumer. Tying both together are the vendors. The service providers in fact were the early driving forces behind what was then known as B-ISDN as a method of combining the existing parallel networks – Plain Old Telephone Service (POTS), packet data, cable, circuit data – into a single integrated network (see Figure 1.5). Many early studies as to the expected traffic profiles over B-ISDN were conducted in conjunction with the central office switch vendors, to the extent of predicting traffic flows for the various types of service planned which then went into switch design (see Goode, 1990). Though this single integrated network is still the ultimate goal, the early growth of ATM in the data networking environment was unanticipated. This growth has resulted in an earlier than expected demand for ATM in the wide area, with the service providers all faced with the situation that if they do not offer the service, a competitor will. In addition, it has tended to slant the results of the above mentioned studies, shifting demand towards data. The demand is not only due to bandwidth requirements, but results from cost considerations as well. Where a large business will today subscribe to multiple services for voice, video, and data, each with an associated tariff, ATM will provide the same user with a single interface into the public network. Note that this aggregation assumes that the service provider, be it a Telco or some alternative, is permitted to offer the full range of integrated services over the link. In many places, this is not yet the case due to regulatory restrictions. Therefore, one of the enabling factors which will lead to the wide deployment of ATM will be the relaxing of existing regulations concerning who may offer a given service or provide content in an area.

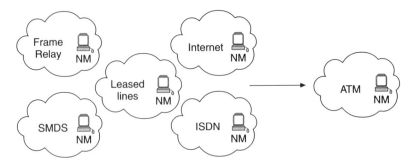

Figure 1.5 Integration of services within ATM.
NM: Network Management (Operation & Support Systems)

In deploying ATM, service providers will take note of the end-user requirements in planning services and provisioning bandwidth. These end users may be divided into three categories: residential, small business, and medium/large business. Each of these three will have a different traffic profile and therefore will require a different mix of services. For example, the residential customer will primarily require TV and voice, while video conferencing and data will be required intermittently. In contrast, although video distribution may be a factor for business customers, the bulk of their needs are for data; the larger the business size, the higher the volume and complexity of the data transfers. These differences will have a real impact in how a service is deployed, to include advertising, the choice of customer premises equipment, bandwidth required in the local loop, and switching capabilities at the central office. A potential problem in designing a service is that some of these profiles may change over time due to new technologies or unforeseen applications. For example, in the early 1990's most people would not have foreseen the potential impact of the Internet on residential customers and their use of data services (that is, Mosaic or Netscape). As an example of just how difficult it is to predict future requirements, many of the ATM traffic studies conducted at the beginning of the 1990s, and used to size central office ATM switches, are now effectively obsolete. This is due to the residential data deployment described above along with fundamental changes in video distribution profiles due to compression. Examples of current ATM residential and commercial deployments are described in a later chapter.

1.3.2 Costs

Another factor leading to ATM's acceptance will be the price it can be delivered at and how this price compares to alternative technologies. The introduction of ATM into a corporate or public network requires a substantial up-front investment for all but the smallest of pilot installations. For the business customer, ATM switches, router interfaces, and network interface cards for PCs must all be procured. Costs are even greater when ATM is deployed in parallel with LAN switching, which is often the case. Service providers planning residential installations are faced with even greater costs: switches, video servers, distribution systems, and user terminals (also known as set-top boxes). In the wide area, the infrastructure cost will play a major role, be it leased lines as part of a private WAN or a tariffed public ATM service. For example, in the WAN, international links will not drop in price as fast as national connections. Given these up-front costs, the reverse side of this cost analysis must then be answered: what cost savings will ATM provide or what additional revenues will it generate?

Equipment costs

An interesting observation relates to the pricing of ATM equipment. When introducing new technologies to the marketplace, two pricing models may be invoked (see Phelan, 1994). The first, termed 'standard pricing', places a premium on the cost charged to early adopters in a possible attempt to recoup initial development and marketing expenses. As volumes increase, the prices will decrease, resulting in gradual growth. This has been the pricing structure used for most technologies in the past, to include personal computers and internetworking devices. In contrast, a 'forward pricing' model will set prices at below cost for these same early adopters. Because of this, equipment prices will fall more gradually, but at the same time the quantity shipped will experience a steeper growth curve. ATM technology combines the two pricing models, as evidenced by the cost of local-area ATM devices in contrast to equipment positioned for use in the wide area. In the end, this forward pricing will be advantageous to the customer if the firms competing for market presence are able to maintain their investment in new features while operating with sub-optimal returns on investment.

ATM equipment costs have experienced further drops as new entrants have entered the switching, ATM chipset, and even the ATM signaling software markets. This abundance of ATM technology has resulted in competition, leading to lower costs for ATM hardware. As an example, the cost per 155 Mbps ATM connection, which includes the **Network Interface Card (NIC)** and the switch port, dropped below $2000 by mid-1995. This is in fact lower than that for FDDI. At the same time, ATM NICs were available at retail prices of under $700 for 155 Mbps **Unshielded Twisted Pair (UTP)** 5 and under $900 for multimode fiber and, by 1996, prices had dropped to below $500. At this price, ATM becomes a viable alternative for server or high-performance workstation/PC connectivity, where NICs should not exceed 25% of the system price. In the coming year or two, ATM, FDDI/**Copper Distributed Data Interface (CDDI)**, and LAN switching will all compete in the sub-$1000 price range per port (with desktop LAN switching in fact approaching the cost of hubs). Maybe more obvious is the cost per megabit of performance between ATM and other technologies. Using this barometer, ATM, FDDI, CDDI, 100 Mbps Ethernet, and switched 10 Mbps Ethernet all share a range between $10 and $20 per Mbps, with ATM at the centerpoint. Looking at the WAN, users compare ATM equipment costs against the competing TDM technologies which are currently used for private corporate backbones. Once the price-per-port reaches parity, operational cost savings in the wide area must then be evaluated. With equipment costs then no longer a factor, the evaluation shifts to feature comparison and an evaluation of the maturity of the various technologies.

The same cost considerations apply when ATM is deployed within the small business or residential environment. Though some elements of the existing infrastructure such as the installed cable plant may be reutilized, the initial investment in ATM switching, video servers, set-top boxes, and system software will be substantial. Current estimates place the cost per customer in the range of $1000 for integrated services (voice, video, and data) to under $500 for video only. This does not, however, cover the costs of the switches and servers at the service provider's point of presence. The tradeoff here is return on investment: whether the additional cost of integrated services will be recovered by voice and data traffic. One element of this debate is whether it is worthwhile to spend more initially in the hope of greater returns on investment in the future. Since the greatest cost of the fiber or coaxial installation may be the installation itself, it may be more logical to go with a technology capable of delivering more in the future. In this case, fiber clearly wins.

Operational costs

Operational costs may be divided into two areas. The first is the initial cost of deploying the technology, the cost of re-training, installation, and changes in networking paradigms. These functions are known as **Operations, Administration, and Maintenance (OAM)**. The introduction of ATM often results in major changes to the networking architecture, changes in end-system connectivity, and a requirement for training of both end users and administrators. Even the deployment of services such as LAN emulation over ATM, designed to be transparent to the end users, will require major changes in the network and a great deal of up-front management. Over time, although OAM must still be considered in the wide area, the cost of connectivity will have the greatest impact. In fact, WAN costs will often exceed 75% of the year-to-year operational cost of a network. This is due to differences in local-area ATM (L-ATM) and wide-area deployments.

In contrast to localized ATM networks, where end users own and operate the cable plant, in effect making tariffing a non-issue, a major factor influencing the acceptance of ATM over the wide area will be the price of connectivity. Whereas the majority of wide-area connections at present do not exceed 1.5 or 2 Mbps, with most connectivity at 64 Kbps, ATM requires at least these data rates. In the future, most connectivity will be at 34, 45, or even 155 Mbps and above. Since 155 Mbps is over 2000 times greater than 64 Kbps, it is obvious that the wide-area tariff structure must change for ATM to be accepted by end users. This retariffing will be even more critical among residential customers. Though consumers will be provided with 6 Mbps and above as an access speed, they will not be expected to pay as if this were a business data connection. One favorable sign is increasing competition between the traditional public service providers and a new wave of **Competitive Service Providers (CSP)** from the cable, energy, and transportation sectors. In Europe, deregulation of the PTTs will also help to make a more realistic tariff structure a reality. Consider differences in wide-area circuit costs between those countries which have deregulated PTTs and those which have not. For example, whereas a New York to San Francisco 45 Mbps was tariffed at $216,000 at the beginning of 1995, a connection in France at just over half that rate (25 Mbps) required an annual payment of $240,000, not including data transmitted. Assuming a user wanted to actually send data over the connection, the yearly tariff could easily double. Since that time, circuit costs in the United States and Great Britain, both countries with competitive Telco environments, have decreased even further.

Cost savings

The cost of deploying ATM, either within the corporation or to the home, will be balanced by the expected cost savings or expected revenue generated. Except for the smallest of pilot and demonstration installations, the difficult cost questions must be answered. Within a corporation, this will include changes in the way of doing business made possible by the technology. This is a broad area, and may include gains due to quicker access to information, more effective training, and closer contact with suppliers and customers. One area within a corporation where there is a constant search for efficiencies is the networking organization. In contrast to centrally controlled and maintained mainframe-based networks, with the advent of client-server architectures, computing resources became decentralized. This decentralization may in fact cost more than a centralized architecture, in that higher-skilled individuals are acting as system administrators and performing backups. Many corporations are therefore reversing the trends of recent years by redeploying their servers to the computer room where they will have greater control over security and maintenance. Also, the hardware itself, and therefore software licensing costs, may be consolidated into fewer, higher-performance systems. The deployment of ATM into the backbone will act as the enabling technology for this change in architecture and associated cost savings. An organization spread over multiple sites will expect to see savings in connectivity costs, either by integrating all traffic flows onto a single public service or by more efficiently utilizing bandwidth within a private WAN.

ATM as a public service must generate revenues acceptable to the public service providers (and to the stockholders as well). Although a great deal of money has been spent in deploying pilot ATM data and video distribution networks, universal deployment will depend upon whether the new revenues generated from these services outweigh the costs. For example, if more money can be made by opening corner video rental stores than by deploying an ATM-based **Video-on-Demand**

(VoD) network, the service provider would be wise to consider the former. The argument in favor of ATM, and the reason for the pilot networks with no guarantee of an early return on investment, is that it has a potential far beyond the video store in providing a base for voice and data services as well.

The cost savings or new revenues outlined above must be quantified, and then balanced against the equipment and operational costs outlined in the previous paragraphs. The case will be made if ATM can be shown to result in the best return on investment when compared with the alternatives.

1.3.3 ATM end-to-end

Perhaps the greatest potential promise of ATM relates to its applicability in both the local and wide area. An end-to-end technology, identical whether on a PC or on a central office switch, promising desktop to desktop QoS support, is the networking Holy Grail of administrators and users alike. Within a corporation, headquarters and branch offices are all served by a single technology at bandwidths ranging from $N \times 64$ Kbps to 622 Mbps and above. Internal to each location, ATM would provide 155 Mbps to each and every desktop. Will an all-ATM world someday be reality, or is it hype? Assuming that over the next few years ATM will be the dominant wide-area networking architecture, the area for greatest debate is then local area ATM. Within the local area, the greatest deployment of ATM will be as a backbone technology, connecting LAN switches, routers, and hubs, as opposed to providing ubiquitous connectivity to the desktop. This is not to say that these same network planners will not deploy ATM to the desktop where required or justified. What it does say is that the investment in existing LAN technologies, the Ethernets, Token Rings, and FDDIs, will be of major concern when deploying ATM.

This reliance on existing LANs may seem a contradiction to the scalability and QoS support described above. In fact it is not, for the majority of high-performance users will use applications, including 'killer' applications such as multiple compressed video sessions, which only require the bandwidth provided by LAN switching. A logical deployment will be more of a hybrid between ATM and existing LAN technologies, with ATM providing the contentionless high bandwidth required by servers and LAN switching providing connectivity to clients. This hybrid architecture is borne out by studies showing ATM NIC sales accounting for anywhere from 0.5% to 25% (Terdoslavich, 1994) of the overall NIC market in 1997. Ultimately, ATM, Fast Ethernet, and LAN switching will all compete for a share of local-area traffic. Technologies with less appeal over time will be FDDI/CDDI to the desktop and intelligent hubs.

One may assume that, towards the end of the decade, ATM to the desktop will comprise the majority of new installations, but this is not a foregone conclusion. In any case, universal deployment will only occur after the wide acceptance of ATM as a local-area backbone and as a wide-area technology. The above analysis of course concentrates on ATM as a data technology (including packet-based voice and video). Deployment of ATM as a universal voice and video technology into the home will proceed at a much slower pace and may never (at least in our lifetimes) totally replace existing technologies.

1.3.4 User acceptance

Ultimately, the success of ATM will be determined in part by the willingness of network managers to stake their enterprise networks, budgets, and reputations on this technology. In addition to the factors described above, adoption of ATM will depend on the state of standardization, user perception, and user demands upon network administrators. Standardization plays a major role in that managers are only willing to introduce proprietary or pre-standard products into their production environments if they can demonstrate tangible added value over open standards. Many of the early questions asked about the suitability of ATM dealt with standards, either the lack thereof or implementation complexity, as opposed to pricing or underlying technology. Network planners require multivendor interoperability and stable specifications, for they can no longer be locked into a single vendor. This is one reason why production networks could not be installed until 1995; interoperable switches and end-systems just did not exist. By mid-1995 many of the most critical aspects affecting ATM scalability had been tackled by the ATM Forum (as described in Chaper 2). However, even in 1996 there is still concern as to the stability of the standards as released by the Forum.

  User perception is also a factor, with networking journals and vendor contacts playing an advertising role no different from commercial television. The perception has been quickly generated that those who don't join the rush to use ATM will be left behind. This is borne out by ATM's place as the most highly reported and hotly contested networking technology of the last few years. There are very few network planners out there who are not aware of ATM and its advantages and disadvantages (at least according to the press). This has been reinforced by a more or less united front in support of ATM from the carriers, the LAN internetworking vendors, WAN equipment suppliers, and system integrators. Those opposing ATM or even questioning its universal applicability are in the minority and mostly ignored. Though the average network planner rightly realizes that ATM must be considered in making architecture or purchasing decisions, the disadvantage of this intense publicity is that undue pressure may be exerted to deploy ATM in those environments where it is not entirely suited.

may be left untouched in the face of new applications, hardware, and technologies. The point at which this threshold is crossed may be totally unplanned, resulting from the installation of one new client, server application or platform. Just as network planners who built their LANs based on hubs never would have predicted the requirement for LAN switching, those same planners are a bit more forward looking the second time around, and realize that LAN switching will many times result in the overload of existing backbone technologies.

Major concerns among network planners include the cost of ATM equipment, migration strategies, the use of LAN emulation to interconnect ATM with existing networks, and the acceptance of 25 Mbps ATM to the desktop (see Business Wire, 1994). The cost of ATM equipment and installation is a driving factor behind incremental migration strategies as opposed to the total replacement of existing networking equipment. This phased migration is not just a marketing ploy from the router and LAN vendors – it is reality. In any case, even a partial migration must be cost-justified, resulting in quantifiable improvements in performance and functionality. During migration, users need a seamless transition path, which is often based on LAN switching technologies. Driving forces behind ATM implementation include the deployment of new messaging and database applications, problems with congestion on the backbone, transaction processing, and the emergence of multimedia to the desktop (see Business Wire, 1994). Ultimately, network planners faced with upgrading their networks may travel two paths: one based on early adoption of ATM, the other based on more conventional router and multiplexer technologies. In either case, ATM takes its place as a part of a final networking architecture, as shown in Figure 1.6.

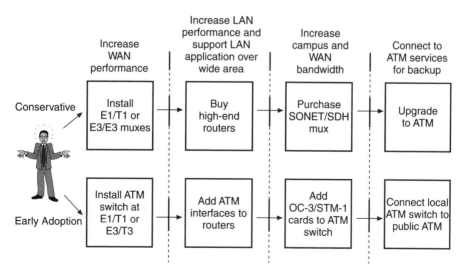

Figure 1.6 Internetwork upgrade paths.

By 1995, a growing realism concerning the deployment of ATM was apparent. In contrast to earlier forecasts of end-to-end ATM networks, in effect making all existing LAN and WAN technologies obsolete, users and vendors had adopted an approach based on a combination of ATM and existing LANs in enterprise internetworks. A survey conducted at the Next Generation Networks conference in Washington DC resulted in a realistic view which justified ATM based on the need to integrate LAN and WAN traffic as opposed to an earlier analysis listing multimedia as the 'killer application' for ATM. Major problems identified with early ATM implementations, besides interoperability and the availability of standards, included network management and security. These results were confirmed in a more recent study (Focus Data, 1995) showing that users were requesting the following from ATM: increased backbone capacity, bandwidth to the desk, more choice in application server placement, accommodation of network growth, virtual workgroups, and capacity to the desk. Once installed, the network is expected to offer interoperability, scalability, manageability, congestion management, legacy LAN support, and virtual LAN support. A treatment of implementing ATM must therefore take into account interworking with existing LAN and WAN technologies, while at the same time providing solutions to these concerns. Before delving into the details of ATM standardization and architecture, we look at a final business driver – ATM revenues based on the predicted installed base both in the LAN and WAN (see Figure 1.7). The large differences in installed base are due to differences in opinion as to ATM uptake.

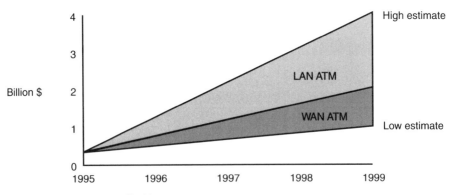

Figure 1.7 ATM installed base.

2

Standardization

Standards allow multiple vendors to develop to a common set of specifications and, hopefully, upon deployment, these devices will interoperate. In reality, a great deal of testing is sometimes required before an end user can be assured of interoperability. By the same token, standards allow service providers and end users to request equipment conforming to certain characteristics, no longer bound to the offerings of a single vendor. This results in an open market and, ultimately, lower costs due to competition among vendors and economies of scale. There are two types of standard: those originally developed by a single vendor or consortium and then accepted by the marketplace (*de facto*), and those generated through consensus within a national or international standards body (*de jure*). In looking at ATM, we are more interested in the latter, for it would be very difficult for an individual vendor to develop and then attempt to market a system which was not interoperable.

Over the last hundred years, telecommunications standards development on a global scale has been the responsibility of the International Telecommunications Union (ITU), formed by representatives from the various national service providers and standards organizations. The ITU is a truly international organization, whose standards have permitted interoperability within the global telephone and data (Telex, X.25, and so on) networks to name just two examples. Note that the ITU has only recently had vendor or end-user representation to any great extent. Whether this change will affect the standardization process is yet to be seen. This is especially true in relation to ATM, where a strong independent organization exists. Parallel to standardization on the national and global scale, an entire set of proprietary networking standards was introduced within the computer industry, those from IBM and DEC being the most widely deployed.

It was only during the 1980s that the first open standard for computer networking – TCP/IP – became a major factor in decision making. In contrast to the efforts of the ITU (which also resulted in the OSI networking environment) and those proprietary efforts of single vendors, developments within TCP/IP resulted from efforts within a new type of standards body consisting of end users, vendors, and service providers. This organization, the **Internet Engineering Task Force (IETF)**, relies on early implementations of draft standards (Internet Drafts, Draft-Standard **Requests for Comments (RFCs)**, and Proposed-Standard RFCs) in contrast to the ITU's approach of waiting until publication of the International Standard for any wide implementation. This consensus within the IETF is documented in the form of RFCs, general implementation guidelines which vendors may code to. Where multiple RFCs exist in response to a specific networking problem to be solved, the marketplace would determine which (if any) proposals will succeed in the long term.

Towards the end of the 1980s, new networking technologies were on the horizon, and many vendors felt that these new technologies could be brought to market quicker if implementation bodies structured on the same model as the IETF could be formed. This line of thinking led to the formation of both the Frame Relay Forum and the **Switched Multimegabit Data Services (SMDS)** Interest Group. Both of these groups draw on ITU standards where available, only creating or modifying where essential. This in particular contrasts with standardization efforts within the IETF. As with Frame Relay and SMDS, end users and vendors considering ATM saw a need for an organization capable of developing implementation agreements from ITU standards, even spurring on the ITU where required. This led to the formation of the ATM Forum. In some instances, the ATMF would develop standards on its own if the ITU did not address a specific set of requirements or if it looked as if the ITU would not meet perceived time-to-market requirements. Since that time, the various end users, vendors, and service providers within the ATMF have devoted an increasing amount of effort to defining standards which will lead to early deployment of large ATM networks. In fact, some feel that momentum within the ATM standardization process may have actually shifted from the ITU to the ATMF due to the fast pace of technological developments and time-to-market requirements. This may be due to the fact that the ATMF more closely models the actual decision-making processes within the internetworking industry.

Within the traditional ITU standardization process, companies usually generate contributions which they then submit to national technical coordination bodies, resulting in national standards when required. These coordination bodies may also pass on contributions to regional organizations (that is, ETSI) or directly to the ITU, which may result in regional or world standards respectively. This hierarchical procedure has changed somewhat with the ATMF. Now, contributions are submitted directly to one of the Sub-Working Groups (SWGs) within the ATMF, debated and altered, and then passed on to the plenary for approval. Since the ATMF meets six times a year (with the SWGs often meeting in

the interim), the reaction time of the ATMF is much shorter in comparison to the ITU. Still, any agreements generated by the ATMF have in
reality just as much weight (or even more) as those from the ITU since
vendor and service provider input is integral to the design phase. Thus,
the time between standardization and implementation may be shortened
substantially; the time between implementation and deployment is
shortened as well.

The emergence of the ATMF, along with other technology forums
including the Frame Relay Forum and the SMDS Interest Group, has
marked a major shift in the furthering of internetworking standards.
Parallel to the growth of these organizations has been the increasing
importance of the IETF due to the wide implementation within the internetworking community of the standards outlined in the RFCs. The
impact of decisions made within the IETF, not only on end users, but also
on vendors and service providers, was most evident during the debates
leading up to the acceptance of a proposal for IP Next Generation (IPv6).
In much the same way, the decision as to which avenue of approach
should be taken for ATM congestion control was heavily debated within
the ATMF.

The perceived gulf between the two types of standards organization – the ITU and the various forums which include the ATM Forum,
Frame Relay Forum, IETF, and Network Management Forum to name a
few – began to be addressed in 1995 with the ITU beginning to recommend and reference standards from these groups. This is in contrast to
the former method of rewriting non-ITU standards. One advantage of
this new approach is the quicker development of standards and a change
to eliminate duplication of effort. Still, the major differences between
the two types of organization remain, the ITU being more general and
platform-oriented, consisting of permanent study groups, while the ATM
Forum and others, consisting of temporary or semi-permanent working
groups, are better placed to solve near-term problems (see Evagora,
1995). In fact, the ITU is seriously investigating the creation of project
groups cutting across a number of the study groups to complement the
existing structure. As an additional sign of change, the pace of standardization within the ITU has increased over the last 10 years, and is now of
the order of 10 months compared to 4–6 years on average.

In developing standards it is important to note that while some
features are desirable, others are critical in making hardware and services available. One company's views on this theme (Engel and Mobasser,
1990) judges standards on three criteria: whether they are relevant,
whether they are evolutionary, and whether they are universal. For relevance, standards organizations must be able to prioritize contributions
and ideas in terms of their commercial applicability and practicality.
This is very true within the ATMF, faced with upwards of 1000 contributions in a given year. In terms of evolution, a given set of standards
should have some compatibility with current standards as well as being

able to draw on past effort and experience. This is quite true with B-ISDN signaling, for example, making use of ISDN concepts and structures. Universality is critical to being able to offer systems to a global market. Problems resulting from the previous broadcast systems (NTSC, PAL, SECAM) and transmission hierarchies (North American and European) should not be repeated in broadband networking or service deployment. A recently formed organization, the **Digital Audio Visual Council (DAVIC)**, is addressing these concerns. Sadly, on the physical transmission side, there are already some differences between SONET and **Synchronous Digital Hierarchy (SDH)** which require localization of equipment.

For a closer look at standards, we first focus on the current status of efforts within the ITU, and then relate them to the implementation agreements generated by the ATMF. We then detail the workings of the ATMF and the IETF by looking at each of the committees and working groups, their functions, and recent efforts.

2.1 Decision for ATM versus fast packet and TDM

Though ATM was selected as the basis for B-ISDN, at least three competing technologies – fast packet, TDM/SONET, and fast circuit switching – are also capable of meeting most if not all the criteria intended for ATM. With the deployment of more powerful hardware and techniques for handling voice over high-delay connections, **Fast Packet Switching (FPS)** has become a reality for the support of not only data, but voice and video as well. A successful architecture developed by one vendor is described in a later chapter. The next alternative, actually implemented in a number of places, uses SONET/SDH as the common underlying infrastructure. ATM in this case is just one user of the service, on a par with N-ISDN trunking and TDM channels. In fact, some central office switches have been extended to provide for switching and trunking at multiples of 64 Kbps. A variant of this scheme would be to map the higher-layer data directly into SONET frames without the addition of the ATM sublayer. This alternative is described in Chaper 6. A switching technique very suitable for bursty traffic requiring strong QoS guarantees is 'fast circuit' switching, where the end-to-end connection is established in the order of milliseconds. With this speed, the circuit may be created as needed for bursts. As described in a later chapter, proposed changes to ATM signaling may enable this mode of switching over existing ATM networks.

The two broadband contenders, FPS and **Asynchronous Time Division (ATD)**, first made their move from the laboratory to the standardization and vendor communities around 1983. FPS, proposed by Bell

Laboratories, grew out of packet-switching concepts (that is, X.25) but moved protocol processing from software to hardware. This was made possible by moving many of the packet-switching functions (that is, error and flow control) to end-systems within the network. A decision was made, though, to allow for variable length packets (averaging 100 bytes) in keeping with the intent that FPS would be data oriented. Note that many of these concepts have been adopted within Frame Relay and also within some proprietary broadband networking architectures. In contrast to FPS, early ATD research took place on the other side of the Atlantic at France Telecom's research laboratories, CNET. This had evolved from the TDM concept with one important addition. Instead of assigning data to fixed channels on a per-connection basis, a header containing a logical connection identifier allowed data to be multiplexed dynamically. Interestingly, ATD was defined at layer 1 of the OSI reference model in keeping with its multiplexing basis. Also, proponents of ATD had proposed a fixed packet size of between 8 and 32 bytes, more suitable for voice, but also capable of supporting data (Dupraz and de Prycker, 1990).

In 1985, the ITU (CCITT Study Group XVIII) began investigating these alternatives under the term **Packet Transfer Mode (PTM)**. Then in 1988, a decision was made to select one variant as the technological basis for B-ISDN. The ATD alternative based on fixed-length packets (now known as cells) was selected and renamed ATM due to its versatility in being able to support both voice and data.

Why a short fixed-length cell? If we look at the queuing latency of a link running at 155 Mbps, a 53-byte ATM cell will require 2.7 μsec for transmission onto the physical medium. This contrasts to 1.2 ms for a 1500 octet Ethernet frame on a 10 Mbps LAN segment. If one attempts to interleave these frames, the possible variance in queuing delays would not permit the support of real-time data.

Many times, a user will be faced with the dilemma of whether to adopt a pre-standard or proprietary implementation by a vendor or hold out and wait for a standards-based solution. This is a difficult question, and the answer relates to what capabilities are required and when. Looking back at the cost analysis, if the capabilities which ATM can provide are required, and if the cost analysis considers a possible future upgrade to allow operation in a multivendor environment (if required), then use of vendor-specific solutions is desirable. In fact, the only viable wide area ATM solutions until well into 1996 were based on proprietary solutions. Though local area ATM was a bit simpler, large networks in the same timeframe also depended upon vendor-specific protocols at the core of the network. With this said, the user should always have an ultimate goal of compliance.

2.2 International Telecommunication Union (ITU)

The ITU is the United Nations agency which deals with telecommunications, with membership by country. It is chartered to create two types of standards: regulations which are binding and recommendations which are guidelines. This contrasts to the ATM Forum's charter of creating specifications based on existing standards where available. Within the ITU, the Telecommunications Standards Sector (ITU-T, formerly CCITT) has responsibility for standards relating to computing and networking. For example, V.32, X.25, and H.261 are just some of the recommendations published by this organization. Often associated with the ITU, but in fact a separate agency, is the International Organization for Standardization, known as the ISO (not an acronym but derived from the Greek 'isos' meaning 'equal'). This organization comprises representatives from the various national and regional standardization bodies, for example: American National Standards Institute (ANSI), Deutsches Institut fuer Normung (DIN), British Standards Institute (BSI), and the Association Française de Normalisation (AFNOR). The purpose of the ISO is to integrate the various national standards and then publish the results as ISO standards. Some of the more well-known standards include those dealing with computer systems (Open Systems Interconnection, or OSI), computer networking (8802 series), and production quality (9000 series). The OSI standards also define the seven-layer reference model, familiar to all involved with internetworking. As will be seen during the discussion of ATM data models, this reference model has presented problems at times. Other standards of interest to the Internet community, derived from vendor organizations other than the ATM Forum, are summarized in Appendix A. Within the ISO, a Joint Technical Committee with the IEC (JTC1) deals with information technology. A good overview of the various standards organizations, contacts, and procedures is given in Kuhn, 1994. Some of this information is summarized in Appendix A as well.

2.2.1 Background

It was only in 1988 that ATM was chosen over alternative technologies such as Fast Packet Switching (SONET/SDH was not a contender at the time) to provide the basis for B-ISDN. This selection was included as part of the CCITT's Blue Book of Recommendations. The starting point for B-ISDN standardization is currently the ITU-T Study Group 13, formerly the CCITT Study Group XVIII. A second group, Study Group 11, has responsibility for signaling protocols. National and continental standardization groups are represented at the ITU, including the North American ANSI T1S1.5 and the European ETSI. Due to the expected complexity of the signaling standard, a series of releases was planned. In keeping with a desire for expediency, Group 11 went ahead and based Release 1 on existing N-ISDN protocols which included Q.931 and ISUP. In retrospect, this may not have been the proper course of action due to the complexities of adapting N-ISDN standards for ATM. Possible causes for the delay in releasing the standard include the need to support previously unidentified additional features as well as a view by some that the service providers and vendors themselves prolonged the standardization process in an attempt to delay the commercial availability of ATM.

This delay may also have been due to the service providers recognizing that, with the advent of ATM, a fundamental structural change would occur in their networks. In fact, this change has been ongoing for some time, with the network intelligence migrating from the core of the traditional public network to the periphery; from large central office (CO) switches to smaller CO access switches, user-operated switches, and higher-layer terminating equipment such as routers. This distributed intelligence threatens the basic services which public service providers have provided in the past, for operators may be relegated to becoming nothing more than providers of high-bandwidth transport services unless they are creative with service offerings. This concern was summed up by statements implying that the cost of future bandwidth would be minimal with services such as video conferencing, database backup, and Internet connectivity providing value added and acting as a basis for differentiation between providers. Standards also allow multiple vendors to supply equipment to a given service provider, affecting the sometimes close relationships between these providers and the traditional preferred vendor(s).

2.2.2 Recommendations

The ITU has defined the ATM protocol stack in its I.360 series of recommendations. These cover each layer, including physical, ATM, adaptation, and service support. This latter topic is addressed in the I.364 recommendation, approved by Study Group 13. It provided a starting point for the development of detailed implementation specifications. Study Group 13 is also involved with the definition of standards for Frame Relay over ATM. Another group within the ITU, Study Group 1, addresses connection-oriented services. This group completed a detailed service definition for ATM Virtual Paths/Virtual Channels in anticipation of native ATM-based services.

The first release of B-ISDN standards, published at the end of the 1984–88 study period, was not very detailed in its technical coverage of broadband networks. Recommendation I.121 did specify ATM as the switching system at the expense of detailing specifics of B-ISDN signaling, switching, and services. In fact, most of its focus was on defining SDH as the transmission system of choice, detailed in the G.707,

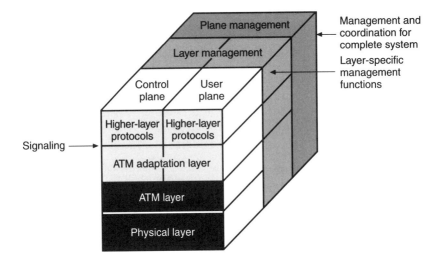

Figure 2.1 B-ISDN reference model.

G.708, and G.709 series of recommendations. These early standards, though incomplete did result in the first generation of ATM switching equipment.

Recommendation I.320 (*ISDN Protocol Reference Model*) defines the B-ISDN reference model, shown in Figure 2.1. This document introduces the concept of planes, relating to a system as a whole, in addition to the familiar layer terminology. The model is three dimensional, with interactions occurring between layers in three domains: the user plane, responsible for user information transfer with control; the control plane, responsible for call control and connection to include signaling; and the management plane, containing network supervision as well as layer and plane management.

The various B-ISDN standards as referenced by *Broadband Aspects of ISDN (I.121)* are summarized in Appendix A. As we will see in the discussion on signaling, there is a great deal of compatibility between efforts within the ITU and those within the ATM Forum.

2.3 ATM Forum

Though the original business case for ATM was driven by the public service providers, the early deployment and acceptance of the technology would have been in doubt without the support of the internetworking industry and without end-user input to the standardization process. Basically, the B-ISDN recommendations under development were public networking-oriented, and somewhat paralleled in scope the work done on OSI. Continuing the analogy, an organization was needed for the ATM community in the same way that the IETF functions in the internet-working community to foster the early deployment of standards-based technology. This turning point in the 'popularization' of ATM was the formation of the ATM Forum in 1991 by Cisco Systems, Northern Telecom, Sprint, and Adaptive. This organization is composed of end users, vendors, and service providers, and aims to generate interoperability agreements based on existing ITU standards with a goal to ensure the early availability of standards-based interoperable equipment. As representation grew to include most internetworking, computing equipment, central office switch vendors, as well as service providers, this goal has become a reality.

The ATM Forum, an 'international non-profit organization formed with the objective of accelerating the use of ATM products and services through a rapid convergence of interoperability specifications,' was founded in 1991 and has grown to over 800 members including vendors, operators, and users. The popularity of the Forum is based on realities of the marketplace. Traditional consensus-oriented standards bodies such as the ITU-T must accommodate many differing and conflicting needs, often resulting in general specifications. Also, in the internetworking field, and looking at broadband technologies in particular, time-to-market is a driving factor. To accomplish this, while matching standards with user requirements, users must be involved in the standardization process. This involvement is evident in the success of other user-driven interest groups including the Frame Relay Forum and SMDS Interest Group (SIG, ESIG). The ATMF did not set out to be a standards body, and initially drew on subsets of international standards, most notably those of the ITU-T, to generate implementation specifications. This is often a two-way process, with the ATMF identifying items in the standards which may be changed or fulfilling a proactive role by submitting ATMF-generated extensions to the standards back to the ITU via the national standards bodies (ANSI, ETSI, and so on). More recently, the Forum has taken the initiative in developing new standards where existing ones do not yet exist, and has opened more direct lines of communications to the ITU (described later). This is especially true in regard to trunking, congestion avoidance, and physical media, but has also expanded to include almost every aspect of ATM. The fundamental reason for this is the synergy achieved by bringing together the user and vendor communities in an organization capable of taking fundamental research and turning it into multivendor standards in less than a year.

Whether the ATM Forum will continue to enjoy the success that it has had during the first few years is yet to be seen. A parallel may be drawn with the IETF, which has managed to remain dynamic despite explosive growth in terms of individual involvement and visibility. As the Forum grows to possibly 1000+ vendors and end-users, it must manage this growth. In addition, the ATM Forum is considered to be 'closed' by some people, since it requires membership to take part, and thus obtain access to the various contributions. A concern sometimes raised relates to the Forum's decision-making process. In comparison to the ITU, which requires consensus even if it results in less-defined standards, the Forum relies on votes by participants. This sometimes results in the losing camp regrouping for a second attempt (for example, 25 Mbps) or striking out on their own (for example, Quantum Flow Control). In either case, this results in confusion within the marketplace.

In describing the efforts of the Forum, we first look at its various committees, with the focus on the Technical Committee, and then introduce the ATMF's released works. This is only a brief introduction, as the practical aspects of these documents are detailed in Chapter 3. Finally, we briefly describe liaisons with external standardization bodies such as the ITU, ANSI, ETSI, and the IETF. This last organization is then described in greater detail.

2.3.1 Committees

The ATM Forum consists of a Technical Committee, three Marketing and Awareness Committees for North America, Europe, and Asia-Pacific, and an Enterprise Network Roundtable (ENR) attended by end users. Most documents (known as contributions) relating to proposed and finished standards are first submitted to the Technical Committee, and then to the Forum plenary as a whole. The Technical Committee works with other standards organizations (for example, ANSI, ITU) to select appropriate standards, resolve differences between standards, and recommend new standards. The Marketing and Awareness Committees are responsible for the coordination of the development of technical papers and educational presentations, the facilitation of information exchange between the ENR and the Technical Committee, and the publication of the ATM Forum newsletter, *53 Bytes*. Finally, the Enterprise Network Roundtable acts as a forum for user ideas and concerns. Current efforts within the ENR have included academic networking. The first meeting of this Academic Roundtable (ART) at the 1995 Spring Interop set out to address how educational institutions can help accelerate the deployment of ATM as an enabling technology for new methods of learning.

2.3.2 Technical Committee working groups: goals and efforts

Within the ATM Forum, the Technical Committee's Sub-Working Groups (SWGs, sometimes shortened to 'Working Groups' by those involved with the process) are responsible for addressing and then finding solutions to those concerns which will affect the successful implementation of ATM. The documents issued by these groups are the ones with which we are most familiar: the User–Network Interface (UNI), Private Network–Network Interface (PNNI), Traffic Management, and LAN Emulation specifications to name a few. These Sub-Working Groups (SWGs) may change over time depending upon needs and if they have completed their task, although some cases, the efforts of a group may be extended if future work is required after the initial release of a standard. In what is a very streamlined process, ATM Forum members submit proposals electronically to each of these SWGs. These contributions are then discussed and modified during regular meetings, between meetings via E-mail, and at special SWG sessions. Once members have agreed on a given proposal, the completed work is released for a ballot within the SWG. Assuming all goes well, the Forum plenary will approve the document. As of mid-1996, the major SWGs and their responsibilities and accomplishments include:

- **Physical layer (PHY)**, responsible for defining the various physical interface types and data rates in both the local and wide area. These include fiber, twisted pair, coaxial cable, wireless, and residential. In fact, wireless may break off into a new group.

- **Private Network–Network Interface (PNNI)**, with the aim of developing an open ATM trunking interface capable of QoS support, topology discovery, and global hierarchy. The SWG has also specified an interim trunking protocol known as the **Interim Interswitch Signaling Protocol (IISP)** and is now addressing public to private internetworking, as well as new ATM routing models.

- **Broadband Inter-Carrier Interface (B-ICI)**, with the aim of defining the interface connecting multiple management domains (that is, different service providers). This contrasts with the UNI connecting an end-system and a switch or the PNNI defining trunking usually between two switches.

- **Signaling**, responsible for defining the procedures to be used when establishing connections over both the interface between the end user and the ATM switch. This, in combination with the PNNI, will allow us to deploy scalable ATM networks. The SWG's efforts are probably the most well known within the ATM community, resulting in the UNI 2.0, 3.0, 3.1, and most recently 4.0. Their efforts are also very closely aligned with those of the ITU, drawing on that body's signaling work (that is, Q.2931) for use as part of the UNI. The UNI 4.0 also includes capabilities such as proxy signaling, the support of multiple signaling channels across the UNI (that is, within VPs), and some introductory work on application layer usage of third-party call setup.

- **Traffic Management (TM)**, defining the various ATM traffic classes and methods of supporting them. This is a very complex area, and requires close liaison with both Signaling and PNNI. Some of the greatest debates within the Forum occurred during the selection of an adaptive congestion avoidance mechanism in support of **Available Bit Rate (ABR)** traffic.

- **Service Aspects and Applications (SAA)**, looking at the whole range of higher-layer services and applications which may be offered by the underlying ATM network. The group has evaluated ATM functionality required to support voice, resulting in the **Circuit Emulation Standard (CES)** and more recently **Voice and Telephony over ATM (VTOA)**. Work within SAA aimed at supporting LAN applications led to the formation of the LAN Emulation SWG. Other work areas include **Audio Visual Multimedia Services (AMS)**, where the group seeks to define methods of supporting multimedia data transport over ATM, Directory Services, focusing on the identification and registry of resources across an ATM network, Frame Relay/ATM interworking (IW), and SMDS/ATM interworking (in cooperation with the SMDS Interest Group and ESIG). The group has also addressed extensions to the ATM-DXI, including data rates of $N \times 64$ Kbps and DS1/E1 which resulted in the **Frame-UNI (FUNI)**, and has developed a semantic definition which will allow other bodies (X/OPEN, Winsock, and so on) to develop **ATM Applications Programming Interfaces (APIs)**. This will allow end applications to use the ATM network more efficiently. New work areas include a Next Phase API and AMS, and the cellular infrastructure.

- **LAN emulation (LANE)**, resulting in a method of supporting traditional LAN applications across the ATM backbone. This group is still active, defining v2 of the specification which will also be used as part of MPOA (see below).

- **Multiprotocol over ATM (MPOA)**, building upon work within the IETF and within the LANE SWG to develop a model for multiprotocol Layer 2 and Layer 3 networking across ATM. This includes defining the various servers, protocols, and encapsulations. MPOA maintains an active liaison with the IETF. Efforts to interwork the IETF's RSVP with ATM also take place within this group.

- **Residential Broadband (RBB)**, defining a service and physical infrastructure for delivery of ATM to homes and small businesses. Unlike the other SWGs which focus on business customers and service providers, RBB must closely liaise with external organizations involved in this area. These include DAVIC which develops architectures and standards for distributing video to the residence, the Forum's AMS, and the ITU.

- **Network management**, an often overlooked factor in successfully deploying an ATM network. This group is responsible for developing requirements and interface specifications for network management information flows between management systems and the network as well as between management systems across administrative boundaries (that is, private-to-public and public-to-public). The group carries out a large part of its effort through liaisons with other standards bodies (Network Management Forum, IETF, ITU, ETSI) to integrate the various network management proposals and schema with a goal of ensuring that the SNMP **Management Information Bases (MIBs)** and management interfaces are compatible. This liaison has resulted in the ATMF network management framework, summarizing the various network management protocols, interfaces, and MIBs used at both public and private UNIs and **Network–Network Interfaces (NNIs)**. The group addresses end-to-end management issues through cooperation with other ATMF SWGs, and has responsibility for ATM MIB registration.

- **Testing**, which considers issues including diagnostic, interoperability, and conformance tests with a goal of producing a set of testing specifications which may be used to ensure that ATM products are compliant and interoperable.

- **Security**, aiming to define a comprehensive architecture for ATM network security from the user, signaling, and management perspectives. Both authentication and encryption will be addressed in three environments: switch to switch, user to switch, and user to user.

In Chapter 3, we detail the protocols and develop the concepts introduced in the above points.

2.3.3 Released works

Completed works of the committees described above are published as ATM Forum specifications. Since the release of the original UNI 2.0 and 3.0, these documents have addressed trunking via the PNNI and the B-ICI, traffic management, physical interfaces, LAN emulation, and service aspects of ATM. All completed specifications are summarized in Appendix A; the more well-known specifications are listed in Table 2.1.

The most well known of the Forum's documents is the User-Network Interface (UNI), first published by the ATM Forum in June 1992 as the UNI 2.0. This early UNI focused on **Permanent Virtual**

Table 2.1 Major ATM Forum released specifications.

Specification	Name	Document number	Date
UNI 3.1	User–Network Interface Version 3.1	UNI 3.1	1995
UNI 4.0	Signaling Version 4.0	(95-1434)	1996
PNNI	Private Network-to-Network Interface		
	Phase 1	AF-PNNI-0055	1996
B-ICI	Broadband Inter-Carrier-Interface (V.2)	AF-BICI-0013	1996
IISP	Interim Interswitch Signaling Protocol	AF-PNNI-0026	1995
LANE	LAN Emulation Version 1	AF-LANE-0021	1995
TM	Traffic Management 4.0	AF-TM-0056	1996
DXI	Data Exchange Interface	DXI	1993
FUNI	Frame User–Network Interface	AF-SAA-0030	1995
CES	Circuit Emulation Service	AF-SAA-0032	1995
AMS	Audio Visual Multimedia Services	AF-SAA-0049	1995

Circuits/Connections (PVCs) only, while the UNI 3.0 release included major increases in functionality. Some major features of the UNI 3.0 included

- **Switched Virtual Circuit/Connection (SVC)** support via a signaling channel

- Addressing (both **Network Services Access Point (NSAP)** format and E.164)

- **pt-mpt** (point-to-multipoint) connections

- **Interim Local Management Interface (ILMI).**

At the beginning of 1995, the Forum completed work on the UNI 3.1, bringing UNI signaling into alignment with the ITU. No major increases in functionality were added, and as noted later in the book, some vendors, having implemented the UNI 3.0, are opting to incrementally deploy UNI 4.0 functionality. The latest release of the UNI, Signaling 4.0, includes support for ABR service as well as leaf-initiated-joins for multipoint connections, frame discard, anycasting (group addressing), proxy signaling, and some supplementary services. This was ratified during the first half of 1996. Future versions of the UNI are expected to include ATM 'calls' as well as renegotiation of parameters for established connections. This book describes technical aspects of the UNI, to include various physical interface types, congestion avoidance, signaling, and network management, as part of the respective sections on ATM architecture.

Closely aligned with the UNI is the recent Traffic Management specification, defining the various traffic classes supported by an ATM network. This document also addresses an ABR service in support of data traffic.

Just as the UNI defines the interface between an end-system and an ATM switch, trunk interfaces between switches are defined in the

PNNI and the B-ICI. The first is applicable to private ATM networks, though unlimited in geographic extent, while the second is applicable to trunks interconnecting public networks.

The LAN Emulation specification defines a LAN Emulation Service across an ATM network providing support for Virtual LANs. Release 1 of this service is intended for initial deployment of Ethernet and Token Ring emulated LANs, while a planned second release will address redundancy and QoS issues.

To help speed the deployment of ATM and alleviate lingering concerns as to the stability of the technology and standards the ATM Forum, at the Spring 1996 Anchorage meeting, produced a document known as the 'Anchorage Accord' (Dobrowski, 1996). This document outlines the various Core and Service Foundation Specifications on which users can deploy ATM, mostly outlined in Table 2.1, as well as standards expected within the next 12–18 months to complete the basic service environment, including MPOA, LANE v2, RBB, ANS, and VTOA. Most importantly, the accord states clearly that changes to the basic specifications will be made only to bring their features into alignment (i.e., PNNI with Signaling 4) or based on changes by the ITU-T.

2.3.4 Liaisons with external standards bodies

Since both the ITU and the ATM Forum work closely on ATM-related issues, it is only logical that the two organizations should have close relationships. During the course of 1995, official liaisons were created between a number of the ITU-T's Study Groups and the SWGs under the Forum's Technical Committee. These liaisons include: Study Group 7, Data Communication Networks; Study Group 9, Television and Sound Transmission; Study Group 11, Signaling and Switching; Study Group 13, General Network Aspects; and Study Group 15, Transmission Systems and Equipment. As work within the ATM Forum and the ITU sometimes complements each other, procedures are now in place to allow both organizations to officially accept contributions from the other, leading to their acceptance as ATM Forum Specifications or ITU Recommendations. The Forum-developed ABR specification is an example of this. In the future we should see even greater cooperation, to include a freer exchange of documentation between the Forum and the ITU. Current restrictive policies present problems for many. In Spring 1996, the ATM Forum initiated closer relationships with ETSI with the goal of speeding standards development and avoiding duplication of effort (Sass, 1996). This cooperation includes document exchange and committee participation. Within ETSI, the specific work areas addressed include: Network Aspects, Signaling, Protocols, and Switching, Methods for Testing and Specifications, and Radio Equipment and Systems.

The ATM Forum also maintains close communications with the IETF, particularly in the the area of internetworking: to include the classical model, multicasting and Multiprotocol over ATM. This ensures that efforts do not overlap and that the Forum's specifications align to the IETF's RFCs. In fact, many individuals participate in both organizations.

2.4 Internet Engineering Task Force (IETF)

The IETF has the responsibility to develop Internet standards. This group operates under the **Internet Architecture Board (IAB)**, which in turn falls under the **Internet Society (ISOC)**, an incorporated non-profit-making professional society. The charter of the ISOC is to oversee the architecture of the worldwide multiprotocol Internet. The **Internet Research Task Force (IRTF)** also falls under the jurisdiction of the IAB. Whereas the IETF deals with current Internet protocol and standardization issues, the IRTF takes more of a long-term view. Management of the standardization process comes from the **Internet Engineering Steering Group (IESG)**. The IETF is divided into topic-based areas, including applications, transport services, routing and addressing, and security, to name a few. The various working groups with responsibility for standards development and RFC preparation fall under an area. Decisions by the IETF resulting in Internet standards are published as freely available RFCs. Publication of an RFC does not imply standards status for a given proposal; an RFC may be informational, experiential, or may specify a standards-track effort. In the latter case, if the RFC does gain standards status, it will be assigned an STD number. An additional side of the IETF, the Secretariat, provides the full-time planning and administrative support. The Secretariat is administered by the **Corporation for National Research Initiatives (CNRI)** in the United States. The RFCs most relevant to ATM deployment are listed in Table 2.2.

Due to overlapping interests (and membership) between some of the IETF working groups and the ATM Forum, liaisons are quite close

Table 2.2 IETF RFCs relevant to ATM.

Number	Title
RFC-1209	The Transmission of IP Datagrams over the SMDS Service
RFC-1483	Multiprotocol Encapsulation over ATM Adaptation Layer 5
RFC-1490	Multiprotocol Interconnect over Frame Relay
RFC-1577 (+)	Classical IP and ARP over ATM and extensions
RFC-1626	Default IP MTU for use over ATM AAL5
RFC-1695	ATM MIB
RFC-1755	ATM Signaling Support for IP over ATM
RFC-1932	IP over ATM: A Framework Document
RFC-NHRP	NBMA Next Hop Resolution Protocol (NHRP)
RFC-Mcast	Multicasting across Classical ATM
RFC-PIM	Protocol Independent Multicasting (PIM): Motivation and Architecture

between the two bodies. As we will see within the section on ATM services, protocols and architectures defined by both groups complement each other and are both essential for the continued success of ATM. One example is MPOA, where the IETF outlined very early (Laubach, 1995a) what it considered essential if this protocol was to see wide acceptance. In fact, MPOA uses two IETF protocols – Next Hop Resolution Protocol (NHRP) and Multicast Address Resolution Server (MARS)/Media Access Control (MAC) – as part of its architecture.

In contrast to the *de jure* standards resulting from world standards bodies such as the ISO, IETF standards are *de facto*, made legitimate by virtue of vendor and end-user support. Though sometimes criticized, *de facto* standards are often more successful than *de jure* standards in that they require support to come into being in the first place. The process by which the IETF operates is known as open development, where anyone may contribute (either in person at a meeting or on-line) to the development of a specification. This contrasts to organizations open to all but requiring membership (for example, the ATM Forum) or the publication by a single vendor of a proprietary technology in the hope that it will become an accepted standard. One area in which the IETF excels is in being able to balance the desire for the best technology, possibly at the expense of a large installed base, and the best compromise, resulting in 'design by committee' if taken to an extreme. The core of the IETF's success is in its charter to solve specific and immediate problems in contrast to wide-ranging and long-term goals. Thus, results are more applicable to immediate implementation (see Crocker, 1993).

2.5 Digital Audio Visual Council (DAVIC)

The DAVIC is a relatively new organization focusing on the transmission of video to the home by developing interoperability standards for the transmission of broadcast and interactive digital audio visual applications. Of prime concern is that standardization will result in economies of scale, finally resulting in low costs to the consumer. The organization also seeks to avoid confusion in the marketplace due to a potential proliferation of standards. Over the last year or so, the ATM Forum has had a liaison with DAVIC with the intent of harmonizing the methods of delivering video to the home with work within the Forum's RBB and AMS groups. Any developments within DAVIC will be made available to all interested parties and will be contributed to international standards bodies for further action. Just as with the ATM Forum, the organization attempts to use existing interfaces, protocols, and architectures, augmenting standards or developing new ones as required. As of mid-1995, DAVIC was divided into five technical committees:

1   Set-Top Unit, specifying a reference set-top unit and relevant interfaces

2   Server, specifying video server interfaces (and only interfaces)

3   Network, specifying a reference model for delivery systems, interfaces, and methods

4   System and Applications, specifying an overall reference model to include copyright management, broker functions, and application portability

5   Technology, with the aim of interfacing with external organizations about standards and technological issues.

The organization produced a core services document, covering Video on Demand, at the end of 1995 (Digital Audio Visual Council, 1995) which will be refined based on interoperability testing during 1996.

The **Digital Video Broadcasting (DVB)** Project within the European Broadcasting Union also plays a part in the standardization of video delivery, although with originally more of a European perspective. The project is defining a video solution suitable for all media, including cable, satellite, and traditional broadcast, and some specifications have already been adopted as standards by ETSI (DVB Project Office, 1995). The Project's efforts are not directly tied into ATM, and in fact rely on the MPEG-2 transport stream (described later). This is based on existing marketplace requirements and vendor capabilities, as well as an appreciation that ATM in the home is not widespread at present. Therefore, in many cases, a native ATM service will not be provided and, when it is, it may be encapsulated in some other framing structure. Over the next few years, these two philosophies will hopefully converge. We describe these different architectures and their implications on ATM deployment in further detail later. One important role of DVB has been to define various MPEG-2 profiles in terms of quality. In deploying MPEG-2 over ATM, these have relevance in their effect on the amount of bandwidth required to the home or business. We detail these profiles in Chapter 4.

2.6 IEEE

Though the IEEE is involved on the periphery of ATM for the most part, recent efforts in the 802.14 committee (see IEEE, 1995a) have resulted in closer coordination with the IETF and the ATM Forum. The committee is looking at ways to use the cable TV infrastructure as a transport for broadband communications services. The networking technology of choice, or at least one alternative, will be ATM. We look at the use of cable and HFC systems for ATM transport in the Section 3.1, while the possible services to be offered across such a network are covered in Section 4.4.

3

Architecture

The architecture of a system is the method of construction as well as the functions performed by each element. A completed system is documented by a set of blueprints or functional diagrams. In the same way, in discussing the architecture of an ATM network, we rely on the OSI reference model to provide a blueprint for mapping the various functions performed by end-systems and intermediate systems and their interactions. This will include a close look at the physical ATM network, including the transmission technologies and interfaces, the ATM layer, and the **ATM Adaptation Layer (AAL)**. This physical network includes standardized interfaces, providing support for the creation of end-to-end SVCs and PVCs within the logical network. Within this logical ATM network, we look at the various methods of signaling, addressing, routing, and managing traffic. This will lead into a discussion of the various ATM models over which we may offer data, voice, and video services. As data-oriented networks will comprise the bulk of initial ATM implementations, especially in the workgroup and campus environment, these data models are described in greater detail. Figure 3.1 depicts these various ATM network planes: the physical, logical, and service networks.

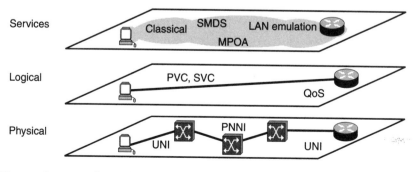

Figure 3.1 ATM logical layering.

3.1 The physical ATM network

Standards exist for encapsulating higher-layer services, adapting this information for transmission over the ATM network, segmenting it into ATM cells, and finally placing the cells on a physical medium for transmission. Referencing the OSI model, the physical layer (Layer 1) is actually divided into two sublayers: **Physical Media Dependent (PMD)** and **Transmission Convergence (TC, or Physical Media Independent)**. A direct correlation between the data link layer (Layer 2) and the ATM layer is a bit more difficult due to the functions carried out within the ATM and ATM Adaptation layers. Although these functions are performed at Layer 2, the ATM sublayer is often associated with the physical layer. The AAL is divided into a **Convergence Sublayer (CS)** and a **Segmentation and Reassembly (SAR)** sublayer, with the CS partitioned even further into a **Common Part Convergence Sublayer (CPCS)** and a **Service-Specific Convergence Sublayer (SSCS)**. We will describe all of these in the following sections. Above the ATM-AAL, the 'traditional' Layer 2 MAC header as found in Ethernet or Token Ring is preserved within the **LAN Emulation (LANE)** service or as part of alternative bridging mechanisms which rely on encapsulation. The existence of this MAC header lends credence to the argument that ATM is a 'sub'-Layer 2 technology. Figures 3.2 and 3.3 list the various functions performed at the physical, ATM, and ATM Adaptation layers.

In looking at the ATM protocol, we first focus on the physical layer with its many media and data rate variations. As part of the physical layer, we describe SDH/SONET, the underlying transmission structure proposed by the ITU for ATM, in greater detail. Next is the ATM layer, where we look at the cell structure across both the User–Network

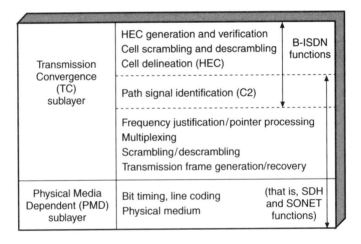

Figure 3.2 ATM layering – physical layer.

ATM Adaptation Layer (AAL)	Convergence Sublayer (CS):	Message identification, clock recovery (may also include CPCS and SSCS for some AAL types)
	Segmentation and Reassembly (SAR) sublayer:	Segmentation and reassembly of higher-layer information
ATM layer	Flow control, VPI/VCI translation, cell multiplexing/demultiplexing, QoS, F4 and F5 management	

Figure 3.3 ATM layering – ATM and adaptation layers.

Interface (UNI) and Network–Node Interface (NNI). Finally, the function and method of operation for each of the ATM Adaptation Layers (AALs) is described in depth.

3.1.1 Interfaces

As with any networking technology, ATM defines a number of standardized interfaces which will allow the interconnection of switches and ATM-connected routers and workstations from multiple vendors. This is no different from the DTE-DCE definitions within X.25 and Frame Relay's UNI and NNI. The UNI defined as part of ATM provides for interconnection of end-systems to an ATM switch, while an NNI connects ATM switches. Within ATM, different types of UNI and NNI have been defined. Users connecting to a private ATM network, forexample in a corporation or university, will use the **Private UNI (UNI)**.

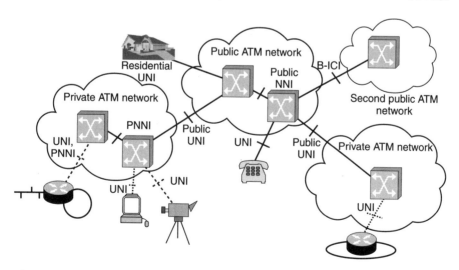

Figure 3.4 ATM public and private interfaces.

Table 3.1 ATM public and private interfaces.

Between:	End-systems	Private ATM network	Public ATM network
End-systems	Private UNI	Private UNI	Public UNI
Private ATM network	Private UNI	IISP, PNNI	Public UNI
Public ATM network	Public UNI	Public UNI	B-ICI

This interface has been defined in great detail by the ATM Forum within the UNI 3.0, 3.1, and 4.0 specifications. A different class of user, connecting directly to a public ATM service, will connect via the public UNI. This interface has been primarily defined by the Forum as well, though its roots lie in earlier ITU specifications. A third UNI has been standardized for the interconnection of residential end-systems such as set-top units and the ATM service. This is known as the Residential UNI.

ATM switches are interconnected via one of three NNIs. The first, the **Private NNI (PNNI)**, is for deployment as part of a private ATM network. The public NNI is for the interconnection of ATM switches within a single service provider, while the Broadband Inter-carrier Interface, or B-ICI, will trunk multiple ATM service providers. The PNNI is of course under the jurisdiction of the ATM Forum, while the latter two interfaces, though aligned with the ITU, also see most standardization activity from within the Forum. NNIs are covered in greater detail in the section *ATM trunking and routing*. We depict these various interfaces in Figure 3.4 and Table 3.1.

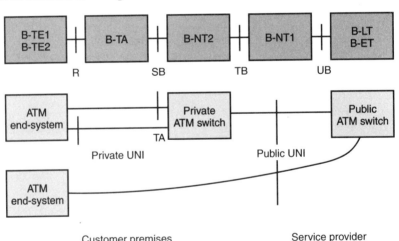

Figure 3.5 B-ISDN terminations.

B-NT1	Layer 1	Provides line termination and transmission interface
B-NT2	Layers 1 and 2	Adaptation for different media types, cell delineation, buffering, multiplexing and demultiplexing, UPC, and the signaling protocol
B-TE	End-system	
B-TA	Connected non-B-ISDN devices	

Looking more closely at these interfaces, the ITU has defined a number of reference points which are worth mentioning. In Figure 3.5, we compare the UNI and NNI as defined by the ATM Forum to this reference configuration for B-ISDN defined by the ITU and based upon that used for narrowband ISDN. When describing the UNI and PNNI, these reference points are rarely used.

Virtual Paths (VPs) and Virtual Channels (VCs)

Fundamental to the discussion of interfaces into ATM are the concepts of **Virtual Paths (VPs)** and **Virtual Channels (VCs)**. Individual VPs and VCs (sometimes called Virtual Channel Links, VCLs) form end-to-end **Virtual Path Connections (VPCs)** and end-to-end **Virtual Channel Connections (VCCs)**. We identify these VPCs and VCCs via unique end-to-end **VPC Identifiers (VPCIs)** and **VCC Identifiers (VCCIs)**. A single ATM physical interface may support multiple VPCs, each of which will contain multiple VCCs. In most cases, multiple VPs will be used between switches, while the UNI will default to a single VP. The reason for implementing VPs is due to manageability of the ATM network, where a great number of VCCs may be aggregated across ATM trunks. Traffic management, rerouting, and even switching may be based on these VPCs. The rationale behind this can be shown by considering a large ATM core switch aggregating trunks. From a network management perspective, control of each and every VCC would be impossible. We identify individual VPCs and VCCs via fields within the ATM cell header, described in Section 3.1.6. Consider Figure 3.6, where multiple VPCs and VCCs share a single physical interface. VPI=2 is switched as a VP by the switch between ports 2 and 5, while VPI=1 is split into its individual VCCs within the switch. Though both originate at port 2, one VCC is directed to port 4 while the other leaves the switch via port 3. This will be common in deployed networks, with switches capable of both VP and VC switching. We describe these different types of switch later. Note that some early ATM switches, commonly known as cross-connects, were only capable of VP switching.

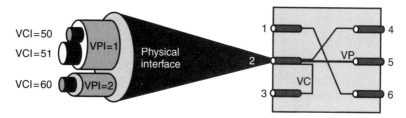

Figure 3.6 ATM VP and VC switching.

Virtual path 1 is switched intact between ports 2 and 5
Virtual path 2 is split into its component virtual channels for switching

Private User–Network Interface (UNI)

Possibly the most well-known of the ATM interfaces is the UNI used to connect ATM end-systems to a private ATM network. If part of an MIS staff, and deploying ATM in the workgroup, campus, or as part of an international corporate backbone, the degree to which the various ATM-connected routers, LAN switches, PCs, and workstations support a given release of the UNI will determine the overall functionality available as part of that deployment. During the first year or two of ATM implementation, there was sometimes a great deal of confusion as to which NIC or switch supported which elements of the ATM Forum UNI. Luckily, this has changed for the better with wider interoperability testing and greater vendor experience. The first UNI was Version 2.0, providing for PVC-based connections between end-systems and switches. Most implementations during 1994 and into the first half of 1995 were based on these PVCs or a proprietary UNI supporting SVCs. By summer 1995, the UNI 3.0 was widely supported, allowing implementors to deploy multi-vendor production networks based on SVCs. The latest release, Signaling 4.0, provides additional functions and some vendors may skip the UNI 3.1 and instead deploy Signaling 4.0. UNI differences and features are described in Section 3.2.3. Private ATM implementations will use an addressing structure based on NSAP format addresses, while routing and signaling between ATM switches is based on the PNNI. Both of these topics are described later in this chapter.

Public UNI

In contrast to the private UNI, used when connecting to private ATM networks, an end-system attached directly to a public ATM service will use a public UNI. In reality, the major difference between these two interfaces is the addressing structure. Whereas the private UNI is based on NSAPs, E.164 addresses are used on the public interface. In many instances, a private ATM network dispersed over multiple locations may use this UNI to connect to a public service, with the private network trunking tunneled via the public UNI.

Residential UNI

A more recent UNI is defined to provide cost-effective connectivity between residences or small businesses and a local service provider. This may be considered a variant of the public UNI, in that it is deployed in the public setting, though signaling, transmission speed, and physical media requirements may be quite different. Typical end-systems include intelligent set-top boxes such as those used in many previously referenced **VoD** trials or specialized hardware and software incorporated in a PC. The goal of the group defining this interface within the Forum is to 'define/extend the public UNI for two-way (symmetrical and asymmetrical) digital information transport between a customer premises end-station and a distribution network.'

Network-to-Node or Network–Network Interface (NNI)

Switches comprising a private ATM network will implement the PNNI on their trunks. This protocol provides for support of ATM signaling and routing. Likewise, the public NNI, or just NNI, and the B-ICI, provide these functions between public switches or service providers. We describe the PNNI and B-ICI in greater detail in Section 3.3.

3.1.2 Physical

The lowest layer of the OSI seven-layer protocol model is the physical layer, which includes the underlying transmission and switching infrastructure used to support ATM's various data models and services. This physical layer is further divided into two sublayers. The lower sublayer, Physical Media Dependent (PMD), is directly associated with a given media type and transmission speed. Layered above the PMD, the Transmission Convergence (TC) sublayer is independent of the underlying physical media, and provides the necessary framing and convergence for the transmission medium. After introducing transmission systems in general, we will describe the various options which ATM users have in both the local and wide area in greater detail.

Transmission hierarchies

Phone networks, TV stations, and mobile radios all use transmission systems, be it copper-based, fiber, or wireless. With the introduction of data LANs and multiservice WANs, network planners have become familiar with the terminology associated with these systems: singlemode or multimode fiber, **Unshielded Twisted Pair (UTP) or Shielded Twisted Pair (STP)**, and so on. Due to the bandwidths over which ATM may be deployed, an awareness of the possible transmission technologies in both the local and wide area is essential. Whereas local-area deployments span a few kilometers at most, a wide-area ATM deployment must span metropolitan, regional, and even international distances. These deployments must therefore use public transmission technologies, either owned and operated by the user or provided as part of a public carrier-based transmission system. A transmission system is required when the distance between two locations exceeds that possible with a direct fiber or coaxial link. This distance may vary, and is dependent upon the type of physical media, the bandwidth, and the types of device used to terminate the media. As an example, point-to-point fiber connections are limited in distance depending upon the type of fiber deployed and terminating equipment. Whereas singlemode fiber is capable of direct runs of up to 60 km, multimode fiber is usually limited to 2 km and below, based on transmission speed.

For links exceeding these distances, the public service provider must deploy transmission equipment which will regenerate the signal. Early systems were based on analog technology, with its inherent loss and distortion, but at present the two primary backbone transmission technologies are SDH/SONET and the earlier PDH. Under both technologies, high-bandwidth trunks are created by aggregating multiple lower bandwidth connections. The way in which these connections are built up is shown in Figure 3.7. Other technologies, including wireless and ADSL, will see deployment to residences and small businesses. The PDH and SDH transmission infrastructure will be operated by a public service provider or may be deployed by an end user. In the latter case, this user may procure 'dark fiber' from a primary (that is traditional phone company) or competitive (that is, cable, energy, transport) service provider and run PDH or SDH without the requirement for a carrier-operated transmission infrastructure. Within a metropolitan area, the SDH interfaces on ATM switches may connect to this 'dark fiber' without use of an active transmission system. It is not expected that end users will deploy ADSL, as this technology is more suitable for residential or small business oriented deployments by service providers.

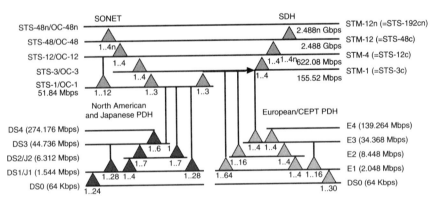

Figure 3.7 Transmission hierarchies.

Note Japanese PDH also includes J3 rate of 32.064 Mbps

Physical Media Dependent (PMD) and Transmission Convergence (TC) layers

When deploying ATM, the lowest layer of the protocol stack is the PMD layer, a sublayer providing for the physical infrastructure and including specifications for encoding techniques, optical wavelengths, fiber or cable types, timing and connectors. ATM is extremely versatile, and in comparison to other technologies such as Ethernet or Frame Relay, may be deployed over almost every local- and wide-area transmission technology with the exception of low-speed WAN links (that is, sub-64 Kbps). From a practical standpoint, the ATM cell structure will not normally be implemented at speeds below T1/E1. Physical media standardized by the ATM Forum include SDH/SONET, PDH, and ADSL in the wide area. ADSL, as opposed to being deployed as a backbone technology such as PDH and SDH, is not hierarchical and will see strong acceptance only as part of residential deployments. Local-area standards include 4B/5B (the FDDI physical technique, commonly referred to by the chipset name, TAXI), the Fiber Channel, SDH/SONET, and Desktop ATM25. Over time, the ATM Forum will standardize additional physical interface types and data rates. We summarize the wide variety of transmission technologies capable of providing support for ATM is summarized in Table 3.2.

Table 3.2 Representative physical media.

Standard	Bit rate (Mbps)	Physical media	Wavelength or resistance (Note 5)	Encoding technique	Connector type
Public interfaces:					
SDH STM-4 (Notes 1, 2)	622.080	9 µm SM	1300µm nominal 2-60km	NRZ	SC (FC)
SDH STM-1 (Note 1)	155.520	9 µm SM	1300µm nominal C 15-60km	NRZ	SC
SDH STM-1 (Note 1)	155.520	62.5 µm MM	1300µm nominal 2km	NRZ	SC (FC)
SDH STM-1	155.520	Coaxial pair	75 ohm	CMI	BNC
SONET STS-1	51.840	SM	1310 µm 15 km	NRZ	SC (FC)
PDH E4	139.264	Coaxial pair	75 ohm	CMI	BNC
PDH DS3	44.736	Coaxial pair	75 ohm	B3ZS	BNC
PDH E3	34.368	Coaxial pair	75 ohm	HDB3	BNC
PDH E2	8.448	Coaxial pair	75 ohm	HDB3	BNC
PDH J2	6.312	TP/coaxial	110/75 ohm	B6ZS/B8ZS	RJ-45/BNC
PDH E1	2.048	TP/coaxial	120/75 ohm	HDB3	8pin/BNC
PDH DS1	1.544	Twisted pair	100 ohm DSX-1	AMI/B8ZS	RJ-45/RJ-48
Inverse mux	nx1.544	Twisted pair	100 ohm DSX-1	AMI/B8ZS	RJ-45/RJ-48
Inverse mux	nx2.048	TP/coaxial	120/75 ohm	HDB3	8pin/BNC

(continued)

Standard	Bit rate (Mbps)	Physical media	Wavelength or resistance (Note 5)	Encoding technique	Connector type
Private interfaces: (Note 3)					
SDH/STM-4	622.08	MM (LED)	1300 nm nominal (Note 4)	NRZ	SC (ST)
SDH/STM-4	622.08	MM (Laser)	780 nm nominal (Note 4)	NRZ	SC (ST)
SDH/STM-1	155.52	UTP5	100 ohm	NRZ	RJ-45
SDH/STM-1	155.52	STP (Type 1)	150 ohm	NRZ	MIC/9pinD
SDH/STM-1	155.52	UTP3	100 ohm	64-CAP	RJ-45
SDH/STM-1	155.52	Plastic fiber	650 nm nominal	NRZ	PN (JIS F07)
Fiber channel	155.52	62.5 μm MM	1300 nm	8B/10B	SC
TAXI (FDDI)	100	62.5 μm MM	1300 nm	NRZ/4B/5B	MIC
SONET STS1	51.84	SM, MM, coax	1310 nm/75 ohm	NRZ/CMI	SC (ST), BNC
SONET STS1	51.84	Plastic fiber	650 nm nominal	NRZ	PN (JIS F07)
SONET STS1	51.84	UTP3	100 ohm	16-CAP	RJ-45
SONET STS1	25.92	UTP3	100 ohm	4-CAP	RJ-45
SONET STS1	12.96	UTP3	100 ohm	2-CAP	RJ-45
Desktop ATM25	25.6	UTP3	100 ohm	NRZI	RJ-45
Cell stream	25.6	UTP3	100 ohm	NRZI/4B/5B	Varies
Cell stream	155.52	MM, STP	Varies	8B/10B	Varies

Note 1: Also for private use

Note 2: STM-1 includes SONET STS-3c; both use OC-3 (Optical Carrier 3)
STM-4 includes SONET STS-12c; both use OC-12

Note 3: Refer to text for the various residential access network interfaces

Note 4: 622 Mbps SM is 1274–1356 nm for intermediate reach and 1261–1360 nm for short reach
622 Mbps MM LED is 1270–1380 nm
622 Mbps MM laser is 770–860 nm

Note 5: G.957 defines the physical optical interface; G.652 defines wavelengths

Encoding techniques [G.703]:

AMI – Bipolar.

B3ZS (also designated HDB2 – High Density Bipolar Two Zeros) – Each block of three (or four for HDB3) successive zeros is replaced by 00V (or 000V) or B0V (B00V). The choice is made so that the number of B pulses between consecutive V pulses is odd. Thus, the code introduces no dc component. A B is an inverted pulse conforming to AMI, while a V represents an AMI violation.

B8ZS (Bipolar with Eight Zeros Substitution) – Each block of eight successive zeros is replaced by 000VB0VB.

B6ZS (Bipolar with Six Zeros Substitution) – Each block of six successive zeros is replaced by 0VB0VB.

CMI (Coded Mark Inversion) – Two-level non-return-to-zero code where binary 0 is coded so that both amplitude levels are attained consecutively, each for half a unit time interval. Binary 1 is coded by either of the amplitude levels for one time interval such that the level alternates for successive binary 1s. CMI is used for SDH.

NRZ – 1 bit is + and 0 bit is –RS232 or V.24.

NRZI – 0 is change of state and 1 is no change; used by SDLC/HDLC and FDDI.

Differential Manchester – Token Ring

4B/5B encoding – 125 Mbaud for 100 Mbps data coding originally used for FDDI.

Each of the above interface standards relies on a combination of bit rate, physical media type, encoding scheme, and connector type. The bit rate is usually associated with the transmission rate of a given level within the SDH or PDH hierarchy. This differs in the local area, where additional interfaces based on existing hardware have also been defined. Fiber actually exists in two variants, singlemode, able to carry data over longer distances but traditionally more expensive to deploy, and multimode, less expensive but limited to a few kilometers. For this reason, singlemode fiber has traditionally been deployed as part of public transmission systems while multimode fiber is deployed in the local area. The encoding scheme is the method by which the actual data is coded in different bit patterns for transmission, and usually seeks to minimize the potential for errors while at the same time minimizing coding overhead. Finally, connector types are standardized as well. These physical elements are described in greater detail as part of Chapter 5.

The upper half of the physical layer is the Transmission Convergence (TC) sublayer. This sublayer provides for HEC generation and verification, cell scrambling and descrambling, cell delineation, path signal identification, pointer processing, multiplexing, and transmission frame generation and recovery if a frame-based system is implemented (that is, STM-1 or E3 G.804). For DS3- and E3-based transmission based on the **Physical Layer Convergence Protocol (PLCP)**, the TC sublayer includes PLCP framing, timing, and cell delineation instead.

SDH/SONET

The **Synchronous Digital Hierarchy (SDH)** and **Synchronous Optical Network (SONET)** are transmission and multiplexing standards developed to replace the existing **Plesiosynchronous Digital Hierarchy (PDH)**. The two standards, SDH and SONET, are deployed in the wide area at data rates from 155 Mbps to 9.6 Gbps. At 155 Mbps, the implementation is based on a framing structure known as **STM-1** for SDH and **STS-3c** for SONET. The basic mapping of ATM cells onto the STM repeats for higher data rates. With the introduction of local-area ATM networks, network administrators are faced with having to gain a knowledge of these wide-area transmission terms for the first time, as the majority of ATM deployments in the campus are based on SDH/SONET. Looking back at the original recommendations from the ITU, ATM in fact was always intended to be deployed over SDH/SONET, with PDH as an interim solution. As more and more service providers upgrade their systems, deployment of SDH/SONET in both trunking and in the local loop (the 'last mile' between customer and local exchange) should become ubiquitous.

The SDH as defined by the ITU is an outgrowth of the North American SONET standard developed by Bellcore in the United States. Because of their similarities, the transmission equipment deployed in both environments is very similar but, as will be seen shortly, not exactly alike. Vendors developing SDH or SONET transmission systems must therefore produce both European and North American variants of the various multiplexers and cross-connects. The versatility of the technology in terms of bandwidth aggregation, reliability, and manageability has implications for ATM, and is revisited in Chapter 6. Figure 3.8 depicts a typical SONET or SDH network.

When SDH/SONET is deployed in a protection ring topology, an important consideration is the total bandwidth available within the system. Within a 622 Mbps system, a total of four 155 Mbps channels are available. Thus, three ATM switches connected via **Add-Drop**

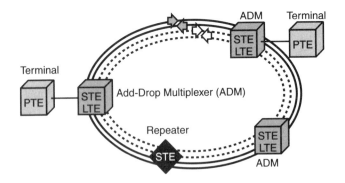

Figure 3.8 SDH/SONET network.

————Normal path
··········Protection path

PTE   Path Terminating Equipment
LTE   Line Terminating Equipment
STE   Section Terminating Equipment

Multiplexers (ADMs) into a triangle will use three of these channels. If an additional switch were to be deployed, only a single trunk would be possible. Any additional switches would require additional bandwidth in the ring, either a second 622 Mbps requiring additional fiber or installation of 2.4 Gbps ADMs. This limitation of the protection ring is one reason why many ATM trunks across SDH/SONET are deployed over point-to-point links, relying on ATM layer rerouting across failed physical connections.

Both SDH and SONET standardize a bit-synchronous method of building high-speed transmission paths by aggregating multiple lower-speed connections, in contrast to the bit-stuffing mechanisms used in creating higher-speed links under the older PDH standard. Due to this PDH bit stuffing, a given lower-speed data stream, 64 Kbps for example, may not be recovered from a 34 Mbps E3 trunk without first demultiplexing this stream through E1 at 2 Mbps. In contrast, pointers within SDH/SONET allow one to identify the 64 Kbps connection described above from even a 155 Mbps link. This has major implications for the deployment of low cost add-drop multiplexing equipment, and provides a basis for a scalable and manageable infrastructure. Network management is supported via reserved bit patterns within the data frames. These patterns allow management to occur at the three sublayers of SDH: the **regenerator section level**, the **digital section level**, and the **transmission path level**. Details of these bit patterns will only be covered as far as their relationship to ATM network management is concerned. Though SDH, and especially SONET, leads one to believe that only fiber may be used, coaxial cable may also be used as physical media for SDH in the wide area. This is the first of a number of differences between the two technologies. Whereas SDH may be (and has been) deployed over electrical interfaces, SONET (true to its name – Synchronous *Optical* Network) makes no provision for anything other than fiber except for local interconnects. This affects the types of ATM interface that may be deployed, and thus which interfaces the switch vendors must develop.

In the campus environment, SDH is the transmission technique of choice for connecting ATM-equipped workstations to workgroup switches and for the trunking between these same switches. At present, the vast majority of installations are at 155. During 1996, 622 Mbps installations and above should be widely available for connecting high-performance servers and trunking ATM switches. Extremely versatile, SDH technology in the local area is deployed over single and multimedia fiber, coaxial cabling, and twisted pair. Although singlemode fiber is of most interest in the wide area, some large manufacturing campuses have deployed this type due to the distance limitations of multimode fiber. The less common coaxial cable has also seen some deployment in large campuses. The majority of installations are based on multimode fiber both due to its lower deployment cost and wide support on PCs and work-stations. Finally, UTP may also be used as a transmission medium for 155 Mbps.

A concern often voiced regarding the installation of SDH and SONET is interoperability between the two standards. The differences between the two systems play a role in the design of ATM end-systems and intermediate systems as well as in the interconnection of European and North American networks. Initial differences relate to terminology between SONET and SDH. SONET, only defined across optical fiber in the wide area, is based on an optical signal known as the **Optical Carrier-Level 1 (OC-1)** at 51.84 Mbps. Its electrical equivalent for interconnecting non-optical end-systems and multiplexers is the **Synchronous Transport Signal-Level 1 (STS-1)** at the same data rate. There is a distinction between the mappings for the lowest level of the SDH, based on the **Synchronous Transport Module-1 (STM-1)** and the SONET **Synchronous Transport Signal-3c (STS-3c)**, derived from the concatenation of three STS-1 signals each at 51.84 Mbps (the lowest SONET transmission rate). This concatenated signal is required for interoperation between SONET and SDH; the simple aggregation of 3xSTS-1, known as STS-3, is not compatible. Other terms used to describe the various tributaries within SONET and SDH, such as the **Virtual Tributary (VT)**, the **Virtual Container (VC)**, and the **Administrative Unit (AU)** are not visible to the end user implementing the technology. Both schemes use ADMs, where individual tributaries at data rates down to T1/E1 may be added or removed from a higher order trunk without the need for demultiplexing (a requirement under the PDH described in the next section).

Though the SDH/SONET frame headers are almost identical, they do differ in the assignment of some fields. For all practical purposes, this will not affect interoperation of ATM devices, though some ATM switches are very particular about what bit patterns they wish to see in each field. More relevant is the procedure used for cell rate decoupling. This is the method by which a variable input cell rate is padded at the physical interface rate by the insertion of filler cells. These filler cells are iden-tified via certain bit patterns in the ATM cell header. The method varies between SDH, where unassigned cells (CLP=0) are inserted, and SONET, which uses idle cells (CLP=1). This has implications for the configuration of ATM CPE and switches, for the methods used by each device must match. Most devices must be manually configured for one of these two modes of operation. Luckily, this is only a software option.

When mapping ATM into SONET/SDH, the PMD layer is further divided into three sublayers: the **transmission path level**, the **digital section level**, and the **regenerator section level**. These three sublay-ers are related to a SONET-specific five-layer reference model, based on a photonic layer providing bit transmission and lightwave multiplexing, a section layer providing for signal regeneration, framing, and scrambling, and a span layer providing for add-drop multiplexing and cross-connects enabling STS-n transport. ATM is mapped into SONET at this last layer. Above the span layer is an STS-n network layer for the mapping of wideband (DS-3 and above) signals into the STS and a sub-STS network layer for the mapping of narrowband (DS0, DS1) into the STS. The 'n' just refers to the level within the SONET hierarchy. Of note are the 155.52 Mbps (SONET STS-3c or STM-1) and 622.08 Mbps (STS-12c or STM-4) transmission rates originally defined within B-ISDN. After accounting for the above overhead, the actual ATM payload rates are 149.76 and 599.04 Mbps respectively, with 135.631 and 542.524 Mbps available at the AAL.

The SONET/SDH frame structure consists of '**rows**' and '**columns**.' Each frame occupies 125 μs, with the bytes transmitted in row sequence. Section and path overhead occupy the first columns of the frame. Frames contain nine rows and, in the case of STM-1, 270 columns, of which 10 are reserved for network management. In a non-ATM environment, lower-order signals are mapped directly into columns. For example, a DS-1 signal will be mapped to three columns, with each position in the frame representing 64 Kbps. This mapping is not the case with ATM, where the entire span layer is treated as a single payload. For STM-1, this span delivers 149.76 Mbps and is also known as the Virtual Container (VC)-4. An ATM cell mapped into the payload may wrap around at the end of one row. In addition, the SDH frame is scrambled between devices. The polynomial used for this is $1 + x^{\wedge 6} + x^{\wedge 7}$, detailed in G.709.

We map ATM cells directly into the STM-1 frame (see Figure 3.9), with the start of the initial cell identified via one of two mechanisms. The first (defined in ITU-T, 1993a) relies on a byte (H4) in the path overhead field explicitly identifying the offset of the ATM cell. A simpler method

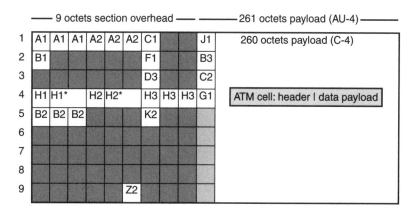

Figure 3.9 SDH/SONET mapping at 155 Mbps.

* VC-4 and VC-3 path overheard (POH)

Other SONET/SDH overhead function, national use or undefined making use of the **Head Error Check (HEC)** field pattern in the ATM cell header has replaced this. Using the HEC, a receiver will examine the incoming flow of bits and will check if a given 8 bits comprise a valid **Cyclic Redundancy Check (CRC)** for the preceding 32 bits. If this is the case, this octet may be the HEC of an ATM cell. This process is repeated six times, after which framing is assumed. Under this technique, unused bandwidth is always occupied with 'unassigned' ATM cells which have a VPI and VCI both set to zero. As with the SDH frame, the ATM payload is in turn scrambled based on the polynomial function $x^{43} + 1$ (ITU-T, 1993/a).

Moving up a layer in the SONET/SDH hierarchy, three 622.08 Mbps PMDs exist, including singlemode fiber and two variants of multimode fiber. In practice, a public UNI or NNI will use only singlemode while a private interface may use either singlemode or multimode. If singlemode fiber is deployed, it will be terminated with either lasers or LEDs for short reach (2 km), while intermediate reach (15 km) will be based on lasers only. A multimode PMD is also based on LEDs or lasers, though the two are not interoperable over a single link. As opposed to singlemode, this interface is intended for a maximum link length of 300 meters (see ATM Forum, 1995d). For both SM and MM, the Transmission Convergence (TC) sublayer is as defined in (ANSI, 1995) for SONET STS-12c and in (ITU-T, 1993a) for the SDH AU-4-4c. When mapped into either SDH or SONET, the ATM cell payload is first scrambled and then mapped into the **Synchronous Payload Envelope (SPE)**. This SPE is then placed into the SDH or SONET frame using the H1-H2 pointer, at which point the entire frame is once again scrambled. In the reverse direction, the H1-H2 pointer is used to locate the SPE. Figure 3.10 describes the STS-12c/STM-4 frame. In Appendix A we

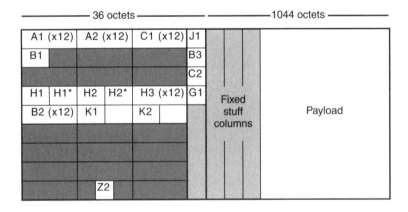

Figure 3.10 SDH/SONET mapping at 622 Mbps.

Other SONET/SDH overhead function, national use or undefined

Table 3.3 ATM to PDH PLCP mapping for E3.

PLCP framing		POI	POH	PLCP payload
1 octet	**1 octet**	**1 octet**	**1 octet**	**53 octets**
A1	A2	P8	Z3	1st DQDB slot
A1	A2	P7	Z2	2nd slot
A1	A2	P6	Z1	3rd slot
A1	A2	P5	F1	4th slot
A1	A2	P4	B1	5th slot
A1	A2	P3	G1	6th slot
A1	A2	P2	M2	7th slot
A1	A2	P1	M1	8th slot
A1	A2	P0	C1	9th slot
				Trailer: 18–20 octets

A1, A2	Framing 11110110 00101000	B1	Bit Interleaved Parity (BIP-8)
P8–P0	Path overhead integrity	G1	PLCP path status
Z1–Z3	Growth octets	M1, M2	DQDB layer management information
F1	PLCP path user channel	C1	Cycle/stuff counter

summarize the differences between the SDH and SONET overhead fields at 155 and 622 Mbps.

PDH

Though ATM was originally defined for operation over SONET/SDH data rates, many initial deployments use the existing PDH infrastructure. This is not only due to the lack of SONET/SDH in the local loop and tariffing considerations (that is, the cost of 155 Mbps in comparison to 34 or 45 Mbps), but also based on the fact that many smaller corporations and their branch offices will not require 155 Mbps or greater bandwidth due to more efficient use of lower-speed connection due to the deployment of more efficient video and data compression algorithms. ATM over PDH is deployed at both E3/DS3 and at E1/DS1. Although the ITU-T in G.804 (see ITU, 1994a) defines ATM mappings at higher data rates of 97.728 (NA/Japan 4th Level, based on 6.312 and 32.064 Mbps hierarchies) and 139.264 (E4) Mbps, these are not widely deployed; therefore, these rates are not described here.

ATM over PDH is most widely deployed at E3, so this standard should be considered first. Two methods exist for mapping ATM cells into the E3 frame. The original mapping uses the **Physical Layer Convergence Protocol (PLCP)** as defined in G.851 for mapping the **Distributed Queue Dual Bus (DQDB)** into 34.368 Mbps (Table 3.3). This is based on 9 × 57 octet G.751 E3 frame followed by an 18–20 octet trailer. The first four octets in each row provide for framing overhead and management, while the remaining 53 octets map directly to an ATM cell. Though this method is capable of passing timing from the physical layer to the original DQDB layer in support of isochronous services, this capability, adding additional overhead, is not required for

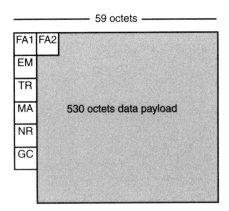

Figure 3.11 ATM to PDH G.832 mapping.

FA1, 2	Framing
EM	Error monitoring (BIP-8)
TR	Trail trace
MA	Maintenance (FERF, and so on)
NR	Network operator octet
GC	General-purpose communications

ATM. Therefore, a more recent method based on HEC-based mapping and adopted by ATM equipment vendors has become the standard. This HEC mapping, standardized as G.804 (see ITU, 1994a) and G.832 (see ITU, 1994b), is in fact more closely aligned with the mapping of cells over

680 bits

M frame	1 bit	84 bits	1 bit	84 bits	1 bit	84 bits	1 bit	84 bits	1 bit	84 bits	1 bit	84 bits	1 bit	84 bits	1 bit	84 bits
1	X1		F1		C1		F2		C2		F3		C3		F4	
2	X2		F1		C1		F2		C2		F3		C3		F4	
3	P1		F1		C1		F2		C2		F3		C3		F4	
4	P2		F1		C1		F2		C2		F3		C3		F4	
5	M1		F1		C1		F2		C2		F3		C3		F4	
6	M2		F1		C1		F2		C2		F3		C3		F4	
7	M3		F1		C1		F2		C2		F3		C3		F4	

Notes
4760 bits total; 680 bits per M frame
X1, X2, P1, and P2 are defined in ANSI T1.107
M1= 0, M2 =1, M3 = 0, F2 = 0, F3 = 0, F4 = 1
C1, C2, and C3 should be assigned IAW ANSI T1.404-1994 for C-bit parity

▉ ▨ ATM cells (data)

Figure 3.12 ATM direct mapping for DS3.

STM-1. ATM cells are mapped into a 530 octet data payload, with overhead functions concatenated to the start of the 9×59 octet frame (see Figure 3.11). Though this newer mapping is eventually expected to totally replace G.851, there are still many transmission systems using the former mapping. This has implications for ATM deployment. The same two methods exist for mapping into E4 (139.264 Mbps), although neither are widely implemented. Over the next year or two, this higher data rate is expected to all but disappear.

The DS3 mapping is based on a direct mapping of ATM cells into the DS3 payload IAW ANSI T1.646 (see ANSI, 1995), as shown in Figure 3.12. This mapping supersedes the PLCP-based mapping as defined in the UNI 3.0/3.1 (also ANSI T1.624), though this latter format is still acceptable for backwards compatibility (ATM Forum, 1995e). The direct mapping provides 44.21 Mbps of ATM cell transfer capability, with ATM cells aligned to nibble (half-byte) boundaries within the 84 bit fields. Where implemented, the older PLCP mapping (equivalent to the E3 PLCP and a subset of that defined in IEEE, 1990) includes overhead octets for the PLCP, framing, a Path Overhead Indicator (POI), and Path Overhead (POH) (Table 3.4). These are responsible for frame alignment, parity, counters, and path status. Within the 12 DS3 rows, each of these fields occupies a byte. The DS3 PLCP frame may begin anywhere within the DS3 payload. Under the PLCP, the available bit rate for the transport of ATM cells is 40.704 Mbps (payload of 36.864 Mbps) – thus the trend towards direct mapping.

Although transmission systems at intermediate rates between DS3/E3 and DS1/E1 are not widely deployed, they do exist. In Japan, an interface at 6.312 Mbps known as J2 has seen wide acceptance, while in Europe, we find E2 at 8.448 Mbps in some countries. The ITU-T has defined ATM cell mappings for both of these data rates, while the ATM

Table 3.4 ATM PDH PLCP mapping for DS3 (125 US).

PLCP framing		POI	POH	PLCP payload
1 octet	**1 octet**	**1 octet**	**1 octet**	**53 octets**
A1	A2	P11	Z6	1st cell
A1	A2	P10	Z5	2nd cell
A1	A2	P9	Z4	3rd cell
A1	A2	P8	Z3	4th cell
A1	A2	P7	Z2	5th cell
A1	A2	P6	Z1	6th cell
A1	A2	P5	F1	7th cell
A1	A2	P4	B1	8th cell
A1	A2	P3	G1	9th cell
A1	A2	P2	M2	10th cell
A1	A2	P1	M1	11th cell
A1	A2	P0	C1	12th cell

Trailer: 13-14 nibbles

Forum has more recently based work on these recommendations. If we consider J2 to have 98 timeslots, the last two are reserved for signaling, frame alignment, and OAM.

The ATM Forum has also defined access via both DS1 and E1 physical interfaces. These rates are finding wide deployment in branch locations or as part of WAN backbones, where cost is the driving factor. The DS1 UNI operates at 1.544 Mbps with an ATM data rate of 1.536 Mbps (ATM Forum, 1994a) and a cell payload rate of 1.391 Mbps. Mapping into the DS1 is based on the 24-frame **Extended Super-frame Format (ESF)** which provides for PDH level OAM (Figure 3.13).

As with other physical layers, the interface adapts the cell rate to the DS1 payload by inserting unassigned or idle cells, while cell delineation is based on the HEC.

E1 mapping at 2.048 Mbps is based on the 32 timeslot frame structure as defined in (ITU, 1991a). Timeslot 0 contains F3 OAM (equivalent to that defined for T1), while timeslot 16 is reserved for signaling. This leaves timeslots 1–15 and 17–31 for ATM cells. Unlike the T1 mapping, there is no superframe structure. For a physical interface, E1 ATM relies on either 120 ohm (ISO/IEC 10173) or 75 ohm coaxial (DIN 47295 or 47297) as a physical connector, while electrical characteristics should comply with G.703 (ITU, 1991b). Although ATM cells are octet aligned with the 30 available slots, there is no relationship between the ATM cell and the E1 frame (Hoelzle, 1994). E1 overhead at the ATM layer reduces available bandwidth to 1.92 Mbps while the AAL overhead further reduces this to 1.738 Mbps.

An ATM access at an intermediate rate between T1/E1 and T3/E3 will play an important role in the wide deployment of ATM, since many users will require speeds in excess of T1/E1 but may not be able to justify the costs of T3/E3. In both the US and Europe, the breakeven point is about $8 \times T1/E1$ before the higher-speed connection becomes justifiable. We summarize this $N \times T1/E1$ access in the section *ATM Inverse Multiplexing (AIMUX)*, below.

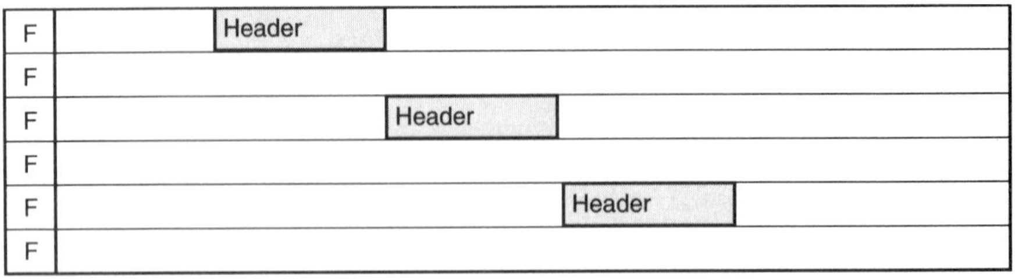

Figure 3.13 ATM to PDH DS1 mapping.

Notes
ATM cell mapping field is 24 octets; length of frame is 193 bits or 125 μsec
F = F3 OAM: detection of LOF, performance monitoring, transmission of FERF and LOC, and performance reporting

N×64 Kbps

At data rates below 1.544 or 2 Mbps, the ATM cell interface suffers from an unacceptable level of overhead due to the ATM cell header introduced during frame segmentation. In addition, the SAR delay also plays a major part at these low rates. Just as a frame-based interface has been deployed for DQDB-based SMDS at these rates, a frame-based ATM interface known as the **Frame UNI (FUNI)** is now deployed. This interface eliminates the segmentation process, but as opposed to an older frame interface known as the ATM-DXI, the FUNI supports signaling, QoS, and network management. This FUNI is described in greater detail in a later section. As an aside, due to some of the delay characteristics associated with the transport of $N{\times}64$ Kbps **Constant Bit Rate (CBR)** traffic within an E1/DS1 ATM link, a variant of the standard UNI has been proposed which would combine facets of time division multiplexing and ATM. Each 64 Kbps channel would be assigned via network management to either non-ATM CBR or ATM data.

ATM Inverse Multiplexing (AIMUX)

Inverse multiplexing is a means of combining multiple physical connections into a higher-bandwidth logical link. Consider an organization requiring multiples of DS1/E1 across the wide area. Currently deployed services are at either DS1/E1, too little, or DS3/E3, many times too much in terms of bandwidth and cost. A middle ground is therefore required. Previous to the ATM Inverse Multiplexer Standard (AIM) (Vallee, 1995), this could only be accomplished through the use of multiple ATM trunks if the switches were capable of load balancing. This load balancing is not totally dynamic, however, and can only be performed on a per-VCC basis due to cell ordering. AIM allows a single $N{\times}$DS1/E1 ATM trunk to be split among multiple physical connections on a per-cell basis, preserving both cell order and QoS. An important feature of the AIMUX is its ability to add or delete DS1/E1 links on demand due to changing load requirements or physical faults. Note that this has some parallels with the BONDing standard used within N-ISDN for load balancing. The ATM switch now sees a single trunk, when in reality the data flows over multiple, possibly diverse links. Hardware supporting the AIM.

Under AIMUX operation, a single ATM stream will pass through the ATM multiplexing function which will perform the necessary functions to divide this cell stream among multiple links (Figure 3.14). The inverse of this occurs at the destination. A new type of OAM cell is defined which is used to synchronize the links as well as identify added or deleted connections. This **Sequence Number (SN)** OAM cell contains a sequence number used by the receiver during reconstruction of the original cell stream. Though this SN is used to implicitly derive a sequence number for each incoming cell, no change in the normal cell

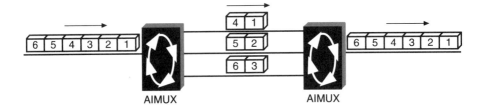

Figure 3.14 ATM inverse multiplexing (AIMUX).

structure is required as the receiver knows to accept one cell from each link in turn. The AIM function also compensates for differential link delays and will eliminate links which do not meet a determined QoS. These links may include dial-up services. During link establishment, the AIM will first check link quality, and then add any qualifying links to the group through the use of SN OAM cells. Adding or deleting links from the group without affecting operation of the remaining connections is also carried out by these management cells.

Note that alternatives to the AIM do exist for trunking at rates between T1/E1 and T3/E3. Many deployments use external inverse multiplexers based on switch interfaces between T1/E1 and about 8 Mbps in the case of V.35, RS-449 or T3/E3. In the former case, the trunk will be split into between two and four T1/E1 links at the physical layer, with the inverse mux responsible for tracking synchronization, error recovery, and activating/deactivating the individual links. Alternatively, a T3/E3 switch interface will feed into an inverse mux which will also split the trunk. We assume that the trunk is transmitting at a cell rate much below the physical interface speed (that is, a cell rate equivalent to a data rate of 10 Mbps). The mux will recognize the difference between data and idle cells, forwarding only the former onto $N{\times}$T1/E1 link. Note that this capability is very close to the actual AIM function. This is true, and will be a way for vendors to implement AIM equivalent as a standalone feature for switches incapable of supporting the standard.

Access and home area networks: ADSL, HFC, FTTC, VDSL, and FTTH

The requirements for connectivity in the residential sector are different from those in the commercial environment in three major ways. Though cost is a factor in the latter, it plays a primary role in providing low-cost access to homes and small businesses. Next, service providers deploying services to the home must use the existing fiber, coaxial, and twisted pair infrastructures due to economics. Finally, the predicted data profile of these users is often asymmetric in that they may be provided with high downstream and limited upstream bandwidth. In the following section, we look at the various physical interfaces relevant to the home and small business. These interfaces are under discussion within various organizations including the ATM Forum, the ITU, and DAVIC. We divide the problem domain into two areas, the access network connecting to an ATM core network, and the **Home-Area Network (HAN, or Home ATM Network)** providing services within the home. Later in the book, we look at the various services which may be offered across these technologies.

Alternatives for the access network include, in how close fiber reaches to the home, **Fiber to the Home (FTTH)**, **Fiber to the Curb (FTTC)**, the **Very high-speed Digitial Subscriber Line (VDSL)**, **Hybrid Fiber/Coax (HFC)**, and the **Asymmetic Digital Subscriber Line (ADSL)** (Figure 3.15). This fiber termination point is known as the **Optical Network Termination (ONT)**, at which point the signal will be distributed in a star (ADSL, VDSL, FTTH) or bus (HFC, FTTC) topology. Under these various technologies, broadcast video may be introduced at this ONT or closer to the headend. Depending upon the type of distribution technology deployed, the equipment used at this headend and at the customer side will of course differ, and the broadcast video will be analog (HFC) or digital (ADSL, VDSL, FTTC, FTTH). For example, within an HFC environment, originating traffic may pass through an **ATM Digital Terminal (ADT)** which will have control over the 802.14 access layer. At the downstream end of the HFC network, an **ATM Interface Unit (AIU)** will terminate the HFC and provide the ATM **Home UNI (HUNI)** into the home or business. At this HUNI, we replace

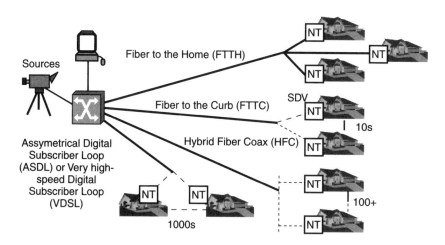

Figure 3.15 Residential access options.

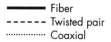
Fiber
Twisted pair
Coaxial

the incoming VPI field with the AIU station address. Although we have considered HFC, the architecture of the headend and customer devices should not be too different for other technologies (see Wojnaroski, 1995a).

Stepping back from the transmission architecture, the Residential Broadband Group within the ATM Forum has defined a number of reference interfaces to be used when describing VoD. These include the **ATM Network Interface (ANI)** connecting an external ATM network to the service provider's delivery network. At the downstream end of this delivery network a UNIw (technology-specific UNI) based on one of the access technologies described in the previous paragraph will connect via a **Network Termination (NT)** to an HAN. This NT may be passive, whereby access network protocols are propagated into the HAN, or active, capable of protocol and transmission technology conversion. The reference interface within this HAN is the HUNI, still undergoing definition. A typical HAN will include HUNI-compliant devices, non-ATM devices connected via **ATM Termination Equipment (ATE)**, and possibly UNI compliant devices as well (see Figure 3.16). An HAN must be simple, low cost, accommodate non-ATM devices, allow intra-HAN communication in the absence of the access network, and support bandwidths up to 155 Mbps. Clearly, this is a totally new area for standardization, management, and hardware.

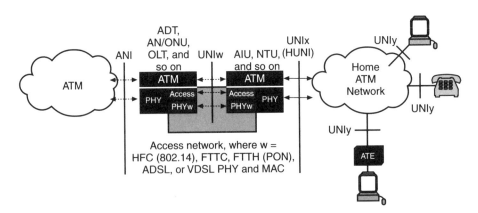

Figure 3.16 Residential reference configuration. Source: ATM Forum (Wojnaroski, 1995a).

ANI	ATM Network Interface	ADT	ATM Digital Terminal for HFC
OLT	Optical Line Terminal for FTTH PON	AIU	ATM Interface Unit for HFC
NTU	Network Termination Unit for PON, FTTC	AN	Access Node for FTTC
		UNIx or UNIy	Subset of standard UNI
UNIw	Technology-specific UNI	FTTC	Fiber to the Curb
HFC	Hybrid Fiber Coax	ADSL	Asymmetric Digital Subscriber Line
FTTH	Fiber to the Home		
VDSL	Very high-speed Digital Subscriber Line	ONU	Optical Network Unit for FTTC

As introduced above, standards for each of these technologies are generated within the IEEE, DAVIC, and the ATM Forum. IEEE 802.14, specifying a physical layer and MAC for use over HFC networks, is expected to be standardized during early 1997. FTTC is further along within DAVIC, where a detailed draft specification was available at the end of 1995, and in fact was adopted as a baseline by the ATM Forum. DAVIC is now addressing SDV and HFC.

ADSL is based on an asymmetrical division of the link, with 2 to 6 Mbps or greater available in the downstream direction but only 64 or 640 Kbps towards the service provider. If we look at the frequency spectrum of the copper wire, POTS resides in the baseband, while the ADSL equipment modulates the upstream and downstream digital signal at higher frequencies. Although the upstream bandwidth is limited, and the reasoning behind the term 'asymmetric', this should not present a problem as the technology is positioned for the residential market where most data relationships are oriented towards data or video downloads. In a typical configuration, an ATM access adapter will interface the ADSL line to both the ATM and PSTN networks, while the reverse occurs at the **ADSL Network Termination (ANT)** within the residence. This ANT is the active interface between the access network and the HAN. When used for the transport of ATM, the ADSL modem is considered to be part of the physical medium sublayer, with ATM residing over an ADSL-specific TC sublayer. This TC–PM interface, defined by the ADSL Forum, may be compliant with the UTOPIA specification (to be detailed in a later section). Signaling across ADSL may be accomplished via either the ADSL control channel or within ATM signaling cells. When deployed, the former may be used by MPEG2 for control, while the latter may provide UNI functionality.

ADSL technology may be most widely deployed in those places where there is not a large installed base of coaxial cable, and is expected to see wide use by the traditional service providers. However, one potential problem is that ADSL is still limited to a single MPEG2 channel (6 Mbps) at a link distance of 4 km. If this bandwidth can be increased to 8 Mbps or more at the same distance, the technology will be capable of supporting two or more video channels of 4 Mbps each, one for viewing and another for recording, for example. In fact, higher-speed variants of the ADSL are now appearing, extending the downstream bandwidth into the broadband range. This B-ADSL technology, now known as VDSL, offers data rates up to 55 Mbps downstream and, currently, 1.6 Mbps upstream, at the expense of distance. For example, 26 Mbps to the subscriber is limited to 1000 meters while 55 Mbps shortens this distance to 300 meters. Nevertheless, this still avoids the expense of having to lay fiber into the home (Sweeney, 1995a). In the future, higher upstream data rates of 19.2 Mbps and above may also be possible. Note that these VDSL data rates effectively align to STS-1 and its sub-rates, important from the transmission perspective.

As with ADSL, VDSL distributes the signal spectrum of the copper wire, placing POTS/ISDN in the baseband below 80 Khz, upstream data between 300 and 700 Khz, and downstream data at 1000 Khz and above. If we operate VDSL over coaxial cable, this upstream/ downstream split may in fact be reversed to allow broadcast video to occupy the higher frequency space (as in the DAVIC specification). Both active and passive NT architectures are possible. In the former case, end devices connect over point-to-point or shared media to a hub, which then connects to the VDSL termination. Upstream bandwidth is accessed via a MAC protocol between these devices and the NT. If we deploy passive NTs, the VDSL unit may be integral to the end-system and we extend the MAC protocol to the upstream end of the VDSL link. Ultimately, Telcos and PTTs may line up in favor of VDSL, with the cable providers well positioned to use FTTC, FTTH, and HFC. At present, a number of organizations are investigating VDSL, including ANSI T1E1.4, ETSI, DAVIC, the ATM Forum, and the ADSL Forum (1995). Note the bandwidth versus distance continuum formed by ADSL and VDSL technologies.

As opposed to wide-area solutions based on traditional PDH and SDH infrastructures, HFC relies on the existing cable TV environment to provide broadband connectivity. The IEEE's 802.14 committee is standardizing ways in which the existing coaxial and fiber cable plant may be adapted to support two-way communications for a number of residential and business services. The standard supports both symmetrical and asymmetrical transmission, OAM, low delay, and a very large number of users on the same system. Just as with other networking technologies, the 802.14 provides a MAC service to end-systems under control of the ADT. Alternative protocol architectures include an 'ATM friendly' model which peers the 802.2 LLC with the ATM layer. Here, each interfaces to the 802.14 MAC and physical layers. An 'all ATM' variant would be to layer all 802 MAC layers over ATM, while still using the 802.14 physical layer (Laubach, 1995b)

This service includes the concept of connectionless and connection-oriented service along with QoS. Predictable delay is a factor of a fair access method to the media. The network itself is based on an HFC reference model providing service to 500 households on average, although some vendors have designed HFC to serve on the order of 140 homes with increases in upstream bandwidth available. The topology is therefore designed around a cable infrastructure of fiber for trunking and coax for feeders and drops. Looking back once again at the reference interface (UNI_w, or in this case UNI_{HFC}), 1996 will see the definition of a number of critical issues surrounding the delivery of services across this interface. This includes traffic management, VCI/VPI mapping, signaling support, minimum and maximum bandwidth (both downstream and upstream), and how we can guarantee a **Cell Delay Variation (CDV)** capable of supporting future voice services. In fact, these concerns apply to all residential access networks currently undergoing definition.

HFC should be deployed over enhanced cable plant which provides a maximum bandwidth of 750 Mhz to 1 Ghz. Allowing for 50–550 Mhz of analog TV traffic, up to 400 Mhz is potentially available for data and VoD. Based on a data rate of 43 Mbps per 6 Mhz channel, this 400 Mhz space equates to a potential bandwidth of over 2.8 Gbps of throughput shared among the 500 subscribers. In the upstream direction, an individual user's bandwidth as controlled by the headend may be dedicated in support of CBR or ABR, or shared, possibly relying on a contention protocol such as Slotted ALOHA. With reference to Figure 3.16, an HFC network will include an ADT where it interfaces into the service provider's internal ATM network and an AIU at each residence. Wojnaroski (1995a) describes these devices in detail. Probably the most critical part of HFC deployment is the availability of CPE with the proper functionality and price point to make this a viable service. Based on testing conducted by Cable Labs during Fall, 1995, the current generation of cable modems will require a great deal of reworking during 1996 to make low-cost interoperable networks a reality.

FTTC is the next step in connectivity, bringing fiber to a maximum of 1000 feet (typical) from a home where it is converted to copper. These distances are based on the use of passive or active NTs. An active NT will provide for greater bandwidth within the HAN, while the use of a passive NT may result in a possible re-use of in-home wiring. The technology will serve about 10–30 homes at a maximum bandwidth of 51.84 Mbps downstream. In the reverse direction, the technology supports a maximum of 19.44 Mbps if deployed over coaxial cable and 1.62 Mbps over twisted pair (see DAVIC, 1995). This last value is more realistic since the majority of installations will re-use the existing twisted pair.

In one deployment, voice, video, and data services are transported to a device known as the **Host Digital Terminal (HDT)** and then into a **Passive Optical Network (PON)**. This HDT facilitates SVC connections from the ATM switch to the CPE. It contains both ATM and STM elements, the first for on-demand services and the latter for digital broadcast. Both signals are multiplexed into a single downstream signal for output onto the PON. The FTTC portion terminates at the **Optical Network Unit (ONU)** in the upstream direction, where it is converted into either coaxial cable or twisted pair. At this point, demultiplexing of the ATM and SDH signals occurs.

Devices now exist for this last link in the FTTC solution, capable of supporting data rates of up to 51.84 Mbps downstream (16CAP) and 1.6 Mbps upstream (QPSK) at distances of 300 meters and less. This **Switched Digital Video (SDV)** architecture is sufficient bandwidth for voice, data, and multiple video streams. In a typical configuration, the downstream signal is carried as a series of 125µs STS-1 frames, while users access upstream bandwidth in increments of 16 Kbps up to a maximum of 1 Mbps (assuming all TDMA slots are used). This requires a MAC layer analogous to that provided within HFC by 802.14, with the

ONU controlling media access. Sharing the same physical media with the data (which is modulated at 6–26 Mhz) is voice traffic at frequencies below 1 Mhz and broadcast video at higher frequencies. Using this technique, an ONU directs downstream ATM cells to the appropriate SDV links (and therefore set-top boxes) while reframing the upstream QPSK data. The set-top box at the customer receives this SDV stream and separates the ATM data streams from the MPEG2 video (AT&T News Release, 1995). Note that although this FTTC architecture supports ATM, it need not be a native ATM service.

Extending upon FTTC, FTTH brings the fiber into the home itself where a service provider may not have a large installed base of coaxial cable. As with FTTC, the delivery mechanism for FTTH will commonly be a PON at a data rate of 155 or 622 Mbps, supporting video, ISDN/POTS, and Internet services. At the lower data rate, users would select broadcast channels on demand while at the higher rate all could be delivered simultaneously. A typical user would be provided with anywhere from 3 to 15 Mbps in the upstream direction depending upon requirements. All data over the ATM-PON is digitized, with ATM cells encapsulated within a 7 octet PON layer header (Takigawa et al, 1995). Both FTTC and FTTH are point-to-multipoint architectures, where the signal travels over the same physical media from a splitter to multiple NTs. Therefore, an access method much like FTTC is required for FTTH. The architecture of the ATM-PON system is compatible with many ATM devices due to physical media and coding. This contrasts with HFC where signals must be modulated onto the system.

The technologies described in the preceding paragraphs are summarized in Table 3.5 which outlines data rates, the length of the copper segment of the network, and the number of users served per **Optical Network Termination (ONT)**. This ONT (or ONU) is the termination point for the fiber portion of the network. The different technologies are bound by a basic observation: the longer the copper feed, the

Table 3.5 Residential access technologies. Source: ATM Forum (Gibbons et al, 1995, and ADSL Forum, 1995).

Technology	Downstream data rate	Upstream data rate	Copper distance	Homes per ONT
ADSL	2–9 Mbps	640 Kbps	18 000–4 000 ft	0(10^3)
HFC	18 Mbps	280 Kbps	<5 000 ft	100–500
VDSL	13–55 Mbps	1.6 Mbps	4 500–1 000 ft	0(10^2)
FTTC	13–55 Mbps	1.6 Mbps	<= 3 000 ft	0(10)
		19 Mbps	<= 300 ft	
FTTH	<=622 Mbps	<=155 Mbps	n/a	0(1)

Note 0(10^3)=100–999; 0(10^2)=10–99. VDSL is sometimes referred to as ADSL3. HFC assumes 150 users, 2.8 Gbps downstream capacity, 43 Mpbs total upstream, and transport of existing analog TV traffic

greater the re-use of existing cable plant, while the longer the fiber feed, the higher the bandwidth deliverable (Gibbons *et al*, 1995).

Complementing technologies such as HFC and ADSL which provide connectivity to the home or small business are proposals for media and data rates internal to these environments. The HAN will interconnect the various home ATM and non-ATM devices in a bus or star topology, while also allowing interconnectivity to one or more network providers. Although some of the local-area technologies described below are suitable, service providers require low-cost alternatives based on either fiber, coaxial cable, or twisted pair.

Parallel to efforts within the ATM Forum to identify and standardize the use of ATM in the home is work in progress within the IEEE to define a generalized home network. IEEE 1394 (IEEE, 1995a) describes a home network capable of interconnecting the various video, telephony, and computing devices as well as appliances found within a home. The IEEE 1394 serial bus interface standard, which includes standard interfaces, data rates up to 400 Mbps, and operation over both fiber (glass or plastic) and twisted pair (UTP-3 or -5) at distances between 4.5 and 500 meters, may be a serious contender to ATM in the home. It is considered 'plug-and-play', allowing isochronous connectivity for up to 63 peripheral devices. This **Home Audio Visual Digital Network (HAVDN)** is initially a bus, but the standard provides for repeaters, bridges, and even routing when required. Vendors are already developing open device driver interfaces, APIs, and host controller interfaces for this standard. In a 1394 environment, an incoming ATM stream will be terminated at the 1394/ATM **Network Interface Unit (NIU)**. This device also terminates the wide-area transmission technology such as ADSL or HFC. Note that this architecture requires ATM end-systems to connect upstream from the 1394 NIU. A second proposal will utilize UTP-5 at 50 Mbps or greater (Whitby Strevens, 1995a). This physical layer would use 5B4TP encoding and is under consideration as part of IEEE 1355. Non-ATM traffic could be carried across this technology through the use of typed packets (described in Section 3.1.5).

Wireless

Although most ATM installations will be based on fiber, coaxial cable, or twisted pair, there is an increasing need for wireless ATM deployments in both LANs and WANs. Consider mobile users local to a building requiring ATM bandwidth, or remote users where only satellite connections exist. In looking at wireless technology, four configurations are most common: satellite, dedicated microwave, fixed wireless, and dynamic (or mobile) wireless. Each of these technologies poses different demands on network designs and protocols. The first three technologies may present a standard interface to the ATM user, with error correction and shared access provided as part of the service. Satellite links have an additional requirement in terms of delay, but this is handled through adjustment of buffer sizes. Mobile networks create additional challenges in terms of authentication and security, reliability, subscriber hand-off, and, probably most critically, interoperability. Reliability of the link is a major concern due to a bit error profile which makes the use of **Forward Error Correction (FEC)** ineffective due to the amount of coding required. Thus, we require a form of selective retransmission at the cell level, an area to be addressed as part of any wireless UNI. We look at this mechanism in greater detail when discussing traffic management, and at security in Section 3.6. In actual deployment, a new wireless data link control and MAC sublayer within the ATM network layer will provide the necessary functions described above. One proposal in fact uses TDMA to provide support for the multiple ATM traffic classes. Towards the end of 1996 and into 1997, the wireless UNI is expected to address most if not all of these issues, leading to the deployment of inter-operable wireless ATM systems (Raychaudnuri *et al*, 1995).

Local area only

The local area includes workgroup, high-rise, and campus environments. As the cabling infrastructure is user-owned in the vast majority of cases, driving factors in the local area include the cost of the transmission tech-nology and compatibility with the installed cable plant. Though inter-faces based on variants of existing local-area transport technologies, such as TAXI and fiber channel, were expected to capture the majority of the market, in reality SDH-based interfaces, derived from the public domain, have received greatest success. This has been driven by the availability of low-cost multimode and UTP hardware. In addition, users perceive SDH/SONET at 155 Mbps to be preferable to TAXI at 100 Mbps. Where distances exceed that possible with multimode interfaces, users also deploy singlemode SDH. More recently, a low-cost 25 Mbps ATM interface has also been deployed in the local area.

SDH over UTP and STP

Although SDH is more widely known in WANs or LANs across fiber, the ATM Forum has defined SDH-based physical interfaces at 155 Mbps or sub-rates of this speed across both UTP and STP. These copper interfaces play an important role by allowing the re-use of existing twisted pair for ATM. Though distance limited, this does not usually present a problem in the workgroup, while the lower cost of copper interfaces in comparison to fiber tends to make up for any inconveniences. To date, the Forum has defined three SDH-derived twisted-pair physical layers: 155 Mbps over UTP-5 and STP (ATM Forum, 1994b), 51 Mbps and below over

UTP-3 (ATM Forum, 1994c), and 155 Mbps over UTP-3 (ATM Forum, 1995f).

The 155 Mbps UTP interface is based on the SONET STS-3c (SDH STM-1) frame with mapping equivalent to the fiber interface as described in the previous section. Although the standard is most closely associated with UTP cable, STP Type 1 also complies. In both cases, a connection is limited to 100 meters, which includes 10 meters for patch cords and a maximum of four connectors. Components will comply with EIA/TIA Standards Proposal 2840-A, EIA/TIA-568-A (1994) and ISO/IEC DIS 11801 (1992) for UTP-5 and STP. The connector for UTP-5 is the 8-pin RJ-45 (defined in ISO 8877 (1987)) while users deploying STP have two options. The first is based on the traditional STP four-contact MIC, while a 9-pin D-type connector for active interfaces may also be deployed.

If UTP-5 is unavailable, users may also deploy ATM over UTP-3 at speeds ranging from 12.96 to 155 Mbps based on the same SONET/SDH frame structure. The ATM Forum (1994c) addresses a primary data rate of 51.84 Mbps over UTP-3, with optional sub-rates at 25.92 and 12.96 Mbps, while the ATM Forum (1995f) extends this to 155.52 Mbps. The lower rates will support longer distances or may be used with non-UTP-3-compliant components. Encoding at each of the rates is as follows: 64-CAP for 155.52 Mbps, 16-CAP for 51.84 Mbps, 4-CAP for 25.92 Mbps, and 2-CAP for 12.96 Mbps. Note that each progressively lower data rate requires simpler encoding. The lower rates come at an advantage of distance, and where the baseline data rate of 51.84 Mbps is limited to 100 meters (including patches as above), sub-rates allow the distances outlined in Table 3.6. Connectors are always the 8-pin RJ-45, as used for UTP-5. The specification also mentions the use of UTP-5 at these lower data rates, resulting in longer possible distances.

Although the UTP-3 and UTP-5 specifications rely on the SONET/SDH frame, there is one notable difference in comparison to the fiber-based physical layers. Columns 30 and 59 of the 87 columns comprising the STS-1 frame are designated as fixed stuff, and the bandwidth available to the user is 48.384 Mbps.

Within a workgroup, ATM over twisted pair will become popular for the reasons outlined above. In fact, interworking between fiber and twisted pair is also possible via converters, enabling the use of fiber-only switches in the workgroup or copper-only switches connected via in-ground fiber.

Table 3.6 Category 3 and 5 UTP distance versus bandwidth.

Cable type	155.52 Mbps	51.84 Mbps	25.92 Mbps	12.96 Mbps
Category 3	100 meters	100 meters	170 meters	200 meters
Category 5	150 meters	160 meters	270 meters	320 meters

More recently, the Forum has begun to look seriously at low-cost physical interfaces based on plastic optical fiber. This includes both 155 Mbps (ATM Forum, 1995g) and 51.8 Mbps (ATM Forum, 1995h) variants, the first intended for commerical use and the second applying mainly to the residence. Both take advantage of the superior emission and security characteristics of fiber in comparison to twisted pair and the re-use of optical components developed for the consumer electronics industry. In addition, in some parts of the world the penetration of UTP to the desktop is not as widespread as in Europe or North America. At 155 Mbps over **Plastic Optical Fiber (POF)**, the LEDs operate at 650 nm and the links are terminated with what are known as **Premises Network (PN)** connectors. Greater attenuation across the relatively short link (up to 13 dB) is compensated for by a receiver power budget of 17 dB (7 dB larger than conventional MM fiber). A variant of this interface is based on **Plastic Clad Silica Fiber (PFC)**, capable of extending the distance to 300 m. We now look at the 51.8 Mbps interface intended for the HAN. This also operates at 650 nm, with the same power budget as the 155 Mbps interface.

4B/5B (TAXI)

The 4B/5B interface, equivalent to that standardized for FDDI, was the first ATM interface to be deployed in the local area. This 100 Mbps interface is often known as TAXI due to the chipset used. The standard is based on a scheme whereby 4 data bits are coded into 5 bits for transmission, yielding a signaling rate of 125 Mbaud, and allowing for various overhead patterns. With overhead taken into account, the standard yields 88.89 Mbps of cell payload. Since the 4B/5B is based on multimode fiber only, unlike the singlemode FDDI variant, the standard is limited to 2 km between devices. Therefore, it is not really suited for use as part of a metropolitan deployment unless external multimedia to singlemode converters are installed. In addition, the TAXI interface does not provide the scalability in data rates available under SDH/SONET. Higher-speed FDDI variants have of course been proposed (see Chapter 6) and even standardized, but it is unlikely that any of these will see acceptance within ATM. The 4B/5B frame structure is shown in Table 3.7, where the first four octets contain overhead functions.

Table 3.7 4B/5B coding.

Synchronization	J (11000)	K (10001)
Start of frame	T (01101)	T (01101)
ATM cell	53-byte ATM cell	

25 Mbps

An interesting story regarding the standardization process within the ATM Forum (and in the industry in general) relates to the eventual acceptance by the Forum, in January 1995, of the 25.6 Mbps standard. Originally submitted in February 1993 by IBM and Chipcom (among others), it was first passed-over in July 1993 in favor of 51 Mbps but finally selected in preference to an alternative low-speed proposal known as UNI-PHY-25 due to the efforts of the Desktop ATM25 alliance. This alliance, formed in Fall 1994, included over 25 vendors and basically standardized the proposal external to the Forum. When resubmitted, members included implementation examples. 25 Mbps ATM was developed in an attempt to bring affordable ATM to the desktop, made possible by the re-use of the Token Ring physical layer but with 4B/5B encoding based on two-level NRZI. Thus, the proposal, specifying a mid-range user interface, drew on available and low-cost technology. A driving force behind this proposal was research showing that corporations place more importance on cost, interoperability, and network management when evaluating ATM as opposed to making decisions based on sheer bandwidth. The question of bandwidth is dealt with by the full-duplex nature of ATM in contrast to existing shared media systems. When contrasted to dedicated (non-full-duplex) Ethernet, it offers a five-fold performance improvement. Supporters also point out the advantages in providing end-to-end ATM solutions in comparison to hybrid LAN switching to ATM systems.

A feature of this standard is the prepending of the 53-byte ATM cell with a command byte within the TC sublayer. This byte, used to identify the start of cells, also is used to transmit the 8 kHz timing marker, critical in supporting isochronous traffic. This marker, generated when an 8 kHz sync pulse is detected, will actually interrupt the ATM cell on an octet boundary (Sourbes *et al*, 1993). Though now a standard, potential obstacles facing 25.6 are the quick deployment of 155 Mbps over UTP-5 and, most importantly, the wide deployment of Ethernet and Token Ring LAN switching requiring no changes in end-systems. In favor of 25 Mbps, a possible future success factor will be through the re-use of a large UTP-3 cabling base, incapable of supporting 155 Mbps. Potentially, a single workstation or PC interface could be software selectable to operate at 25 Mbps over UTP-3 or 155 Mbps over UTP-5.

As mentioned above, a consortium of vendors proposed a 25.92 Mbps physical interface based on a sub-rate of SONET/SDH in counter to the Desktop ATM25 proposal. This interface, termed UNI-PHY-25, grew out of work conducted as part of the Saturn (SONET/SDH-ATM User Network) group, an alliance formed in 1992 to promote the development of interoperable ATM chips. Members of Saturn include founders Sun Microsystems and PMC/Sierra, and over 30 computer, internetworking, and switch vendors. Academia and research are also well represented. The specification called for use of the ATMF-approved transmission convergence protocol for fractional SONET STS-1, logically equivalent to the 155 Mbps standard. **Non-Return to Zero (NRZ)** encoding over UTP-3 would provide the physical connectivity. Because of this re-use of higher-speed technology, chipsets, software, and interface designs originally developed for 155 Mbps may be re-used at 25.92 Mbps. As with the IBM proposal, the PMC/Sierra alternative would have faced competition from higher-speed interfaces, though it may have greater acceptance as a residential interface.

The selection of Desktop ATM25 in preference to UNI-PHY-25 demonstrates the power of vendor alliances in influencing the standardization process. Potential difficulties with this approach, though, include scenarios where a certain course of action is first taken within a committee leading to a standard. One or more companies dissatisfied with this outcome gather support outside of the standardization process, more or less in an attempt to reverse previous decisions. The eventual result is user confusion and a delay in eventual product availability. Luckily, 25 Mbps was just an additional interface alternative and not a potential change to a standard.

8B/10B (fiber channel)

The fiber channel standard was adopted by the ATM Forum as one method of transporting local-area ATM data. Though standardized early, it has not seen wide support among network planners and implementors. The standard itself is a product of the ANSI X3T9.3 committee, and is capable of supporting various higher-layer services to include the **Intelligent Peripheral Interface (IPI)**, **Small Computer System Interface (SCSI)**, and **High Performance Parallel Interface (HIPPI)**. Distances may range from 2 m to 2 km at a data rate of 100 Mbps to over 4 Gbps. The fiber channel is divided into six layers, to include a transmission protocol (FC-1) based on 8B/10B coding, a signaling protocol (FC-2), a service interface for stripping and multicast (FC-3), and a channel protocol which interacts with the higher-layer command sets of IPI or SCSI (FC-4). Within the ATMF, the fiber channel is standardized at 155.52 Mbps over 1300 nm fiber, and the maximum permissible distance is 2 km. The ATM Forum coding is shown in Table 3.8, where a block consists of 27 cells, the first of which contains overhead information.

Table 3.8 8B/10B (fiber channel) coding.

Cell 1	Synchronization × 4
Physical layer overhead	Synchronization 2
(53 bytes)	Physical layer OAM
Cells 2–27	ATM cells

Cell-based clear channel

The 'clear channel' interface is capable of supporting multiple physical media and data rates (ATM Forum, 1995i). Consider a local interface based on V.35, EIA/TIA 449/530 (old RS232), EIA/TIA 612/613 (HSSI), or unframed E1/G.703 which has no requirements on higher-layer framing or bitstream coding. An ATM cell stream may be directly transported over any of these interfaces at any supported data rate. In contrast to most other local- and wide-area ATM interfaces, physical layer OAM cells (F1 and F2) do not exist. Cell rate decoupling may be based on either idle or unassigned cells, while cell delineation is performed using the HEC mechanism. Finally, the interface may or may not support scrambling. Though this interface is quite easy to implement, it is unknown just how widely it will be deployed in comparison to SDH/SONET or Desktop ATM 25.

Analysis

With the various physical layer options in both the local and wide area, the choice for implementation can be confusing. Depending upon installed cable plant, plans for expansion, and budget, one or another of the technologies may be correct. Also, nothing precludes combining two or more of the technologies. The various standards are summarized in Table 3.9, with comments on expected acceptance.

Internal system interfaces

On a different level from the external interfaces described in the sections above are interconnects internal to a system. These interfaces are at the board or chip level, allowing standardization between vendors. The most well known of these, the **Universal Test and Operations PHY Interface for ATM (UTOPIA)**, provides a standardized interface between the physical and ATM layers. This is important in board design, where a common logic 'motherboard' may support different **Physical Layer Interface Modules (PLIMs)**. A second type of interface at the component level is the **Workable Interface Requirements Example (WIRE)**.

UTOPIA

UTOPIA is a data path interface between the ATM physical layer and the ATM layer itself as well as an interface for management and control. Two levels of UTOPIA have been defined: Level 1, based on an 8-bit wide data path, operates at up to 25 MHz and supports data rates up to 155 Mbps (ATM Forum, 1994d). Though a 16-bit wide data path supporting

Table 3.9 Physical media deployment.

Technology	Distance	Cost	Deployment status	Deploy?
622 Mbps SM	Unlimited	High	Predicted wide deployment	Yes
622 Mbps MM	300 M	High	Predicted deployment in local area	Yes
155 Mbps SM	Unlimited	High	Wide deployment	Yes
155 Mbps MM	2 km	Moderate	Wide deployment in local area	Yes
155 Mbps UTP-5	100 m	Low	Wide deployment in local area	Yes
155 Mbps UTP-3	100 m	Low	Predicted deployment in local area	Yes
155 Mbps plastic	50 m	Low	Predicted deployment	TBD
50 Mbps plastic	50 m	Low	Predicted residential deployment	TBD
E4 copper	Unlimited	High (Note 1)	Very limited deployment in Europe	No
E3/DS3 copper	Unlimited	High (Note 1)	Wide deployment in wide area	Yes
E2/J2 copper	Unlimited	High (Note 1)	Niche deployment in wide area – E2 for UK and others, J2 for Japan	Yes
E1/DS1 copper	Unlimited	High (Note 1)	Wide deployment in wide area	Yes
N×64 Kbps	Unlimited	High (Note 1)	Growing deployment in wide area	Yes
155 Mbps fiber channel	Variable	High (Note 2)	Limited deployment in local area	No
100 Mbps TAXI	2 km	Moderate	Declining deployment in local area	No
51 Mbps UTP-3	100 m	High (Note 2)	Very limited deployment in local area	No
25.6 Mbps UTP-3	100 m	Low	Wide deployment in local area	Yes
Cell-based clear channel	Variable	Unknown	Unknown	TBD
HFC, ADSL, FTTC, and so on	Variable	Moderate	Residential access networks	Yes
Home (internal)	Variable	Low	Based on public operators	TBD

Note 1   PDH-based interfaces are listed as having a high cost due to the cost of the transmission systems and their use exclusively in the wide area

Note 2   Fiber channel and 51 Mbps SONET are not inherently high-cost technologies. Currently, costs are high due to lack of economies of scale.

data rates of up to 622 Mbps was described, the Level 2 specification (ATM Forum, 1994e) actually defines this. Level 2 provides for two additional clock rates, 33 MHz and 50 MHz, while also defining a reference model capable of supporting multiple ATM physical layers in connection with multiple ATM layers. The 33 MHz clock, most suitable for PC-based designs, may operate over both the 8- and 16-bit data paths, while the 50 MHz clock is intended for use only over 16-bit.

The purpose of the UTOPIA is to define a standardized interface between the two layers defined above, providing for greater interoperability between devices of multiple vendors along with decoupling the physical layer and its many variants from the ATM layer. With the release of Level 2, the following interface rates are supported: 622 Mbps and 155 Mbps SONET/SDH, 155 Mbps 8B/10B, 100 Mbps 4B/5B (TAXI), 44.736 Mbps DS3, and 51.84 Mbps OC-1. One area which the standard

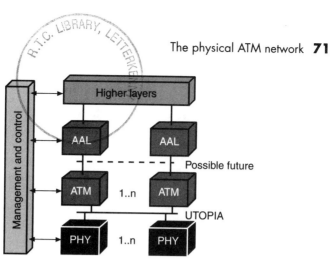

Figure 3.17 UTOPIA reference configuration. Source: ATM Forum.

addresses is the processing of the ATM cell HEC. Although this is considered to be a physical layer function, UTOPIA does provide for the transfer of the HEC to the ATM layer for processing. Within the UTOPIA cell, the HEC is known as the UDF, for User DeFined. While a single cell is sent over the 8-bit path, two ATM cell octets are sent in parallel over the 16-bit data path. An interesting feature is that this Level 2 UTOPIA cell is 54 octets, containing two UDF fields capable of carrying the HEC.

Although the UTOPIA is currently defined only between the physical and ATM sublayers, it may be extended at some point in the future to include the interface between ATM and AAL. More interesting are the various possibilities for combining multiple physical layers with multiple ATMs. Consider an end-system distributing data across multiple physical interfaces. This allows for economies at the ATM layer and above. Figure 3.17 depicts the UTOPIA references configuration along with possible extensions.

More recently, a serial UTOPIA has been proposed as a lower-cost alternative to the parallel UTOPIA. This interface, known as NIRVANA (Whitby-Strevens, 1995b), would be suited for use in the residential environment where cost is a major factor. Based on IEEE 1355 (ISO/IEC 14575), non-ATM traffic (that is, non-cell-based MPEG) could be multiplexed onto the same interface as ATM cells at data rates up to 200 Mbps. This is accomplished through the use of a packet format as defined in the above specification which includes a format type. The format field is used to identify ATM cells, LLC packets, and MPEG-2, to name a few.

WIRE

Looking within the physical layer, vendors have set out to reduce the possibility of electromagnetic radiation (EMI) caused by high-speed circuitry. This has resulted in the publication of the **Workable**

Interface Requirements Example (WIRE) (Wurster *et al*, 1995), a method by which the interfaces between the PMD-based **Line Interface Unit (LIU)** on a card and the TC sublayer are kept below 20 MHz. This is accomplished by creating serial or, in most cases, parallel data paths between the devices. For example, at data rates up to the mid-range PMD, a simple serial-mode interface would suffice, while at 155 Mbps an 8-bit path would be recommended, limiting the frequency to 19.44 MHz with inherent EMI advantages. Both 4×8-bit and 32-bit allow rates of up to 622 Mbps for UTP-5, with the STS-12c/STM-4 demultiplexed at the TC into four parallel STS-3c/STM-1 streams at the same internal data rate as above. Finally, the 32-bit parallel interface allows connectivity across optical fiber at 622 Mbps and above.

3.1.3 ATM layer

The purpose of the ATM layer is to provide for the transparent transfer of ATM cells, technically known as **ATM Service Data Units (ATM-SDUs)**, across pre-established connections in accordance with a specified traffic contract. This layer focuses on the basic unit of data within the ATM network – the 53-octet cell. (A quick clarification on octets and bytes: for practical purposes, an octet is equivalent to a byte, though the former is more common within data communications while the latter is found in computing.) The structure of this cell is dependent upon whether an ATM connection is between an end-system – an ATM-equipped router, LAN switch, PC, or workstation – and the ATM switch, or between two switching systems. As introduced earlier, in the former case this interface is known as the UNI, while the interface between switching systems is known as the NNI. An additional function of the ATM layer is cell rate decoupling, whereby unassigned cells are inserted into the cell stream to create a continuous flow of ATM cells. This is required for interfaces such as SONET/SDH and PDH which operate with synchronous cell streams; it is not required for the 4B/5B interface. Some confusion may arise when speaking of this decoupling function since the ITU-T specifies the insertion of idle cells into the cell stream at the physical layer.

UNI cell structure

A discussion of the ATM UNI should begin with the basic ATM cell structure. An interesting story relates to how the 53-byte ATM cell was chosen by the ITU (the CCITT at the time). In discussing the proposed cell length, the CCITT was basically divided into two camps – the Europeans, favoring 36 (32+4) bytes, and the US promoting 70 (64+6) bytes. The 32-octet payload favored by the Europeans grew out of a desire to optimize the future ATM network for voice traffic. Specifically, a

64 Kbps voice channel requires 4 ms for conversion into a 32-octet cell, while it would require twice that long for 64 octets. As the end-to-end delay should be limited to 25 ms to avoid the need for echo cancellation and suppression, this additional delay was deemed unacceptable at the time. The view from the US contingent was that echo cancellation would be required in any case as opposed to the European networks which had not implemented this. Another view of the differences is based on origin – the Europeans were more telephony oriented, stressing delay, connection-oriented networks, and QoS guarantees, while the Americans were more concerned with data issues such as connectionless networks and capacity sharing. In the end, a 48-octet payload was chosen by splitting the difference. The size of the ATM cell header was also under contention, where tradeoffs were made on the size of the VPI/VCI fields as well as which ATM functions should be actually identified by bits in the header.

The cell header at the UNI is responsible for identifying the VC to which the cell belongs, as well as whether user or maintenance information is contained within and whether or not the cell has a greater chance of being discarded if the network experiences congestion. Header fields are defined in Figure 3.18.

If implemented, the **Generic Flow Control (GFC)** is not carried end-to-end and has local significance for the user (that is, flow control). This field will be overwritten by the network. In UNI 3.0, two modes of operation were defined: uncontrolled and controlled access.

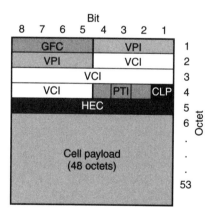

Figure 3.18 ATM cell structure at the UNI. Source: ATM Forum, 1995a.

GFC	Generic Flow Control
VPI	Virtual Path Identifier
VCI	Virtual Channel Identifier
PTI	Payload Type Identifier
CLP	Cell Loss Priority
HEC	Header Error Check

Controlled access implied that the hosts should modify their transmission behavior in accordance with this field. Since the time of UNI 3.0 publication, the future use of the GFC has been called into question even though some vendors have proposed sometimes proprietary uses for this field.

The **Virtual Path Identifier/Virtual Channel Identifier (VPI/VCI)** fields identify the VC across the physical interface, and have only local significance between the end-system and the ATM switch. Though the number of bits assigned to the VPI and VCI are normally fixed, the boundary between the two may be altered by end-system and switch software to provide for a greater number of VPs or VCs. For example, in a strict VC switching environment, the VPI field may be set to a minimum. Likewise, in a public network relying on VP switching only, the VCI may be minimized.

The **Payload Type Identifier (PTI)** is a 3-bit field used to identify whether the cell contains user data or a management (F5) flow. In addition, it is used to indicate whether or not a cell has experienced congestion. It may also be used for resource management, and is used by AAL5 to identify the final cell of a higher-layer data frame. In this latter case, the last bit, signifying ATM user-to-user information, is set to a '1'. The possible PTI values are summarized in Table 3.10.

The **Cell Loss Priority (CLP)** one-bit field is used by the user to indicate whether a cell should have a higher (CLP=1) or lower (CLP=0) chance of discard when the network is congested. This field is used by switches implementing the 'leaky bucket' mechanism for traffic policing.

The **Header Error Check (HEC)** is used for detecting errors in the cell header, and may also be used to synchronize a receiver to an incoming cell stream. Note that this HEC is only partially effective since an incorrect header will have a 1 in 256 chance of passing. In this case, the result will be an unused VPI/VCI combination which is discarded by the switch. However, if a valid combination results then the cell will be forwarded to the given destination where it will fail reassembly. An example of the second use of the HEC is within SDH. The receiver will

Table 3.10 Payload type indicator values. Source: ATM Forum, 1995a.

PTI coding	Description
000	User data cell; no congestion
001	User data cell; no congestion; end of AAL5 SDU
010	User data cell; congestion experienced
011	User data cell; congestion experienced; end of AAL5 SDU
100	Segment OAM F5 flow
101	End-to-end OAM F5 flow
110	RM cell
111	Reserved

check incoming bytes in groups of five until finding a valid header, repeating this for a defined number until cell synchronization.

In all, these cell header fields occupy 5 bytes of the 53-byte ATM cell. For an idea of the resulting overhead, refer to the SONET frame described as part of the physical layer above. From the 155.52 Mbps physical bandwidth, 135.63 Mbps is now available to the ATM payload after SONET and ATM overheads. This loss is sometimes known as the 'cell tax'.

As defined in the ATM Forum UNI, the ATM layer is responsible for:

- VC multiplexing (via the VPI/VCI fields),

- Cell rate decoupling for unassigned cells (via pre-assigned header values),

- Cell discrimination (also via pre-assigned values),

- Payload type identification (via the PT field),

- Loss priority indication (via the CLP), and

- Traffic shaping (not carried in the header but part of the traffic profile for a given VC).

Cell rate decoupling is a function whereby unassigned cells are inserted into a cell stream which is not filled. This is required by physical layers which use synchronous cell time slots (that is, SDH, DS3/E3). Note that views differ within the ITU and the ATM Forum as to how this should be accomplished. The Forum specifies use of the unassigned cells, while the ITU calls for physical layer decoupling based on idle cells. For UNI compliance, E3/E4 interfaces may use this latter definition. The means by which the identification of unassigned cells, along signaling, OAM or resource management, occurs is via a pre-defined header field value. Combinations of these values are summarized in Table 3.11.

Detailing Table 3.11, meta-signaling cells are used by a meta-signaling protocol (when implemented) for the establishment and release of signaling VCs, while broadcast signaling is used to broadcast signaling information independent of service profiles. Point-to-point signaling is self-explanatory, and is the type implemented between end-systems and switches or between switches at present. The various OAM cells are used for the exchange of network management data at the physical layer as well as part of the VP and VC, and resource management cells are used for ABR, as one example. Finally, **Interim Local Management Interface (ILMI)** cells are exchanged across the UNI between end-systems and ATM switches for management.

Table 3.11 Pre-allocated VPI/VCIS. Source: ATM Forum, 1995a.

Type	VPI	VCI	VCI	PTI	CLP
Idle cell identification	0000 0000	0000 0000	0000 0000	000	1
Unassigned cell	0000 0000	0000 0000	0000 0000	bbb	0
Meta-signaling	xxxx xxxx	0000 0000	0000 0001	0a0	c
General broadcast signaling	xxxx xxxx	0000 0000	0000 0010	0aa	c
Point-to-point signaling	xxxx xxxx	0000 0000	0000 0101	0aa	c
LANE Configuration Direct	xxxx xxxx	0000 0000	0001 0001	aaa	c
Physical layer OAM (F3)	0000 0000	0000 0000	0000 0000	100	1
Virtual path OAM (F4)	yyyy yyyy	0000 0000	0000 0011	0a0	a
Virtual path end-to-end OAM	yyyy yyyy	0000 0000	0000 0100	0a0	a
Virtual channel OAM (F5)	yyyy yyyy	zzzz zzzz	zzzz zzzz	100	a
Virtual channel end-to-end OAM	yyyy yyyy	zzzz zzzz	zzzz zzzz	101	a
ILMI	0000 0000	0000 0000	0001 0000	aaa	0
IFMP/GSMP	0000 0000	0000 0000	0000 1111	aaa	0
PNNI PTSP	yyyy yyyy	0000 0000	0011 0000	aaa	0
RM cells for VPCs	yyyy yyyy	0000 0000	0000 0110	110	a
RM cells for VCCs	yyyy yyyy	zzzz zzzz	zzzz zzzz	110	a

Notes

a May be set by the ATM layer to 0 or 1

b Don't care

c The originating entity should set to 0; the network may change this value

x Any valid VPI: VPI=0 and VCI<>0 used for user signaling with the local exchange, VPI<>0 and VCI<>0 used for signaling with other entities

y Any valid VPI (user data cell VPI)

z Any valid VCI (user data cell VCI)

NNI cell structure

The interface between ATM switching systems is referred to as the Network-to-Node (sometimes known as Network–Network) Interface, or NNI. This NNI may be further divided into two types – public and private. In either case, the interface makes use of the basic ATM cell header structure with one exception. The VPI field is expanded by four additional bits at the expense of the GFC which had significance only between an end-system and its nearest switch. Between switching systems, the large number of VCs defined will probably be aggregated into VPs. Thus the 255 possible VPs defined at the UNI may not prove sufficient in this case. A major work area within the ATMF is that of defining the protocol to be used for topology discovery and flow control between ATM switches. This PNNI protocol, described later, may also be extended to support Layer 3 (IP, and so on) routing over the ATM network. This possibility is addressed in Section 4.1.

3.1.4 Adaptation

Above the ATM layer, the ATM Adaptation Layer (AAL) provides for the transformation of the higher-layer services – voice, video, and data – into a form suitable for transmission over the ATM infrastructure. The AAL preserves timing relationships for traffic requiring it (constant bit rate data, for example). The AAL may also add additional header information which will allow the emulation of a connectionless service over ATM. AALs are commonly associated with the ATM service classes which they provide service for, though in the L-ATM environment especially, the use of AAL terminology has in the past been more prevalent than references to these service classes.

The standard divides the AAL into two sublayers: the **Convergence Sublayer (CS)** and the **Segmentation and Re-assembly (SAR)** sublayer. The CS is further partitioned into a **common part CS** and a **service-specific CS** for some AALs. The common part is responsible for packet framing and error detection, while the service-specific part provides for connection-oriented or connection-less service. The SAR is of course responsible for the actual segmentation of a user data frame into ATM cells and vice versa.

As stated above, the AAL is in effect a protocol designed to meet the needs of a given class of service. In this, it relates closely to the ATM service categories as described in the ATM Forum Traffic Management Specification (ATM Forum, 1996b). The specification references **Constant Bit Rate (CBR)**, **real-time Variable Bit Rate (rt-VBR)**, **non-real-time Variable Bit Rate (nrt-VBR)**, **Unspecified Bit Rate (UBR)**, and **Available Bit Rate (ABR)** services, described in greater detail as part of Section 3.5. In the internetworking community, these traffic classes have mostly replaced use of the ITU bearer capabilities (A, B, C, D, and X) as described in ITU F.811 and F.812, and then the service classes (A, B, C, and D) as documented in ITU I.362. In fact, the ITU has defined **Deterministic Bit Rate (DBR)**, **Statistical Bit Rate (SBR)**, and **ATM Block Transfer (ABT)** to replace these bearer capabilities. We may map DBR to CBR, SBR with timing to rt-VBR, and finally SBR without timing to nrt-VBR. In the context of our discussion, the traffic designators as defined by the ATM Forum are probably more appropriate. For completeness, we map them to the service classes in Table 3.12. Note that the ATM Forum only uses classes A, C, X, and what is known as VP. This last class is used to offer a virtual path service across the network. BCOB-B, intended for VBR with synchronization, and BCOB-D, for connectionless traffic, are either undefined or not implemented.

The remainder of the discussion will focus on the AALs and how they provide for the support of the different types of user services. In addition, we will evaluate whether all AALs are relevant in designing ATM networks.

Table 3.12 ATM service classes.

Attribute	Class A, X, VP (Notes 1, 2)	C, X, VP, (B – Note 3)	C, X, VP	(D – Note 3)
Applications	Circuit Emulation (CBR)	Real-time VBR	CO data; user-network signaling messages Non-real-time VBR	CL data Non-real-time
Adaptations Traffic profile	AAL1 (Note 4) CBR (DBR)	AAL5, AAL2 rt-VBR (SBR)	AAL5, AAL3/4 nrt-VBR (SBR) UBR, ABR (ABT)	AAL5, AAL3/4 ABR (ABT), UBR
Timing relation between source and destination	Related		Non-related	
Connection mode	Connection oriented			Connectionless

Note 1   Class X also proposed for user-identified constant or variable bit rate, timing, and whether connection oriented or connectionless. This is not UBR.
Note 2   VP service is different from BCOB-X since we transport the VCI and PT field transparently across the network.
Note 3   Undefined within the ATM Forum's UNI 4.0.
Note 4   AAL1 is also used in some instances for VBR traffic, though this has not yet been standardized.

AAL1

AAL1, or class A, supports constant bit rate connections across the ATM network in support of the **Circuit Emulation Service (CES)**. This AAL is further divided into structured or unstructured service depending upon the type of CES to be supported. The incoming synchronous sample is segmented, and placed in an ATM cell along with a 3-bit sequence number (SN) for detecting lost or inserted cells. The error detection and correction field is 4 bits (CRC), able to correct a single bit error in the overhead byte or detect multiple bit errors. The most interesting field is the **CS Indication (CSI)**, used to carry timing recovery information or an indication of structured data. In every odd sequence numbered cell, this field indicates whether synchronous clocking is available. If not, it is used to convey the four bits of **Synchronous Residual Timestamp (SRTS)** information every eight cells (see Section 4.2). In every even cell, this field contains an indication as to whether the frame is structured or unstructured. If structured, an additional byte of overhead is required every eight cells. This is the P format cell depicted in Figure 3.19.

Structured AAL1 uses fixed-length blocks of data, with each of these blocks some number of octets. A block size of 1 octet corresponds to a single DS0 (64 Kbps) stream, while the pointer is used to identify block sizes greater than one. The actual layout of the $N \times 64$ Kbps data within the blocks depends on the type of service supported. For example, encoding $N \times 64$ without signaling (that is, in the presence of **Common Channel Signaling (CCS)**) involves collecting one octet from each

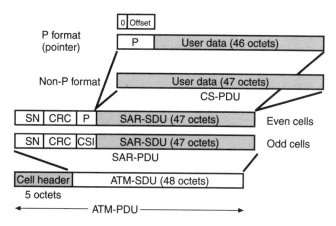

Figure 3.19 ATM Adaptation Layer (AAL) 1.

timeslot and then grouping them in sequence. With **Channel Associated Signaling (CAS)**, the AAL1 block is divided into two sections. The first carries the $N \times 64$ Kbps payload, while the second carries the signaling bits. The payload part of the structure is one multiframe in length, $N \times 24$ octets for DS1 and $N \times 16$ octets for E1. The signaling substructure contains the ABCD signaling bits for each timeslot. As an example, six channels will result in a structure size of 147 octets for DS1 and 99 octets for E1 (ATM Forum, 1995b).

The CES introduced above in effect allows the ATM network to emulate a TDM-like connection. In practice, an ATM switch capable of adapting PABX voice traffic to ATM will interconnect these devices at T1/E1 or multiples of 64 Kbps. If techniques such as compression and silence suppression are deployed, then the ATM bandwidth is efficiently used. This is not necessarily the case for video, where the data rate varies greatly over time. For efficient use of bandwidth for video, individual bandwidth slices (that is, 64 Kbps) would need to be allocated and deallocated dynamically. This is one reason for the selection of AAL5 for video within the ATM Forum.

Recently, some vendors have implemented VBR across AAL1. Though originally not intended for this traffic profile, the AAL1 is capable of supporting this. The use of AAL1 for VBR may be standardized in the future, at the expense of AAL2. Finally, the Forum is now investigating whether a separate adaptation is desirable for low speed ($N \times 64$ Kbps) voice.

AAL2

AAL2, mapped to ITU service class B, is optimized for the transport of variable bit rate, time-dependent traffic over ATM. As with AAL1, the SAR provides for a sequence number but, in addition, a given cell will

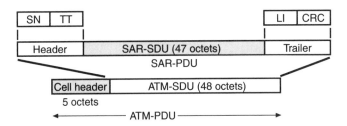

Figure 3.20 ATM Adaptation Layer (AAL) 2.

contain a designator as to whether it is the beginning, middle, or end of a higher-layer information frame (see Figure 3.20). Appended to the SAR-SDU is a **Length Indication (LI)** and a CRC. The resultant SAR-PDU is delivered to the ATM layer where it forms the payload (ATM-SDU) of the ATM cell (ATM-PDU). An AAL2 cell may also be partially filled, in which case unused bytes will be padded. The most obvious use is for the transfer of video, though momentum is shifting to AAL5 for this application. In any case, the ATM Forum may specify the use of AAL2 in conjunction with video at some point in the future based on an as yet undefined service-specific convergence sublayer. If timing can be recovered at the destination, and if another AAL5 can provide a requisite QoS for the video traffic, then is a separate AAL really useful? This will become more obvious when we discuss possible service definitions for use over AAL5. Also, with some vendors implementing VBR over AAL1 for variable rate voice, AAL2 may no longer be needed.

AAL3/4

AAL3/4, mapped to ITU service classes C and D, is the first of the data adaptations and provides for the transport of connectionless as well as connection-oriented data over ATM. AAL3/4 is usually implemented in conjunction with a **Connectionless Server Function (CLSF)** as part of the ATM network. The CLSF is a physical device or process closely coupled with an ATM switch which will accept AAL3/4 data from multiple users. In turn, the CLSF resequences and retransmits this data, while at time same time providing the broadcast and multicast functionality associated with connectionless networking. The resulting ATM service, SMDS or CBDS over ATM, will be discussed in greater detail in the next section.

AAL3/4 includes additional overhead which provides for the multiplexing of messages from multiple users connected over the same VC between the ATM end-system and the CLSF. A higher-layer data frame from 0 to 65535 octets, the **Common Part Convergence Sublayer Service Data Unit (CPCS-SDU)**, is prepended with a header consisting of a **Common Part Indicator (CPI)**, a **Beginning Tag (BTAG) field**, and a **buffer allocation size (BA-size)** to be used by the destination for allocating memory. In addition, a trailer including padding, an alignment field, an **End Tag (ETAG) field** identical to the BTAG, and the length of the SDU is also included. The resulting CPCS-PDU is delivered to the SAR sublayer where it is segmented into four types of SAR-PDU. Each of these four PDU types includes a **Segment Type (ST)** indication as to whether the cell is the BOM, COM, or EOM. The fourth type of PDU, SSM, provides for data frames which may fit in a single cell. After the ST, the PDU includes an SN allowing for resequencing of out-of-order cells at the CLSF and a **Multiplexing Identification (MID)** field providing for the interleaving of PDUs from multiple end users. This allows for cell level retransmission and support for the 'fan-in' of cells into a single VCC, in effect the reverse direction of a multicast connection. Each PDU also includes a trailer consisting of an LI and a CRC (see Table 3.13 and Figure 3.21). These SAR-PDUs are then delivered to the ATM layer as an ATM-SDU. The cell header is prepended, and the ATM-PDU is created.

The cost of the additional functionality provided by the SN and MID is additional overhead, with AAL3/4 SAR using 4 bytes of the ATM cell payload to perform its job. Thus, 44 bytes (or possibly less for EOM and SSM) out of the original 53 bytes remain, a loss approaching 20%. AAL 3/4 is therefore used only where required and in conjunction with the CLSF. A problem with AAL3/4 is its lack of wide support from the SAR chip vendors. In addition, the value of the MID in providing a method to identify out-of-sequence cells has not really been taken advantage of since no accepted scheme of assigning this field has yet been deployed. Therefore, the CLSF must implement resequencing, applicable to both AAL3/4 and AAL5. For this reason, AAL5 will probably be the adaptation of choice for SMDS/CBDS over ATM in the future and AAL3/4 should slowly die out.

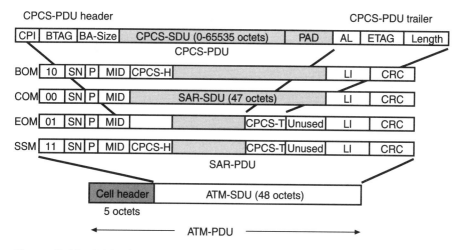

Figure 3.21 ATM Adaptation Layer (AAL) 3/4.

Table 3.13 AAL3/4 SDU and PDU details.

Field	Abbr.	Length (octets)	Description
AAL3/4 SAR PDU frame = 48 bytes (ATM cell payload)			
Segment Type	ST	2 bits	Beginning of message 10
			Continuation of message 00
			End of message 01
			Single segment message 11
Sequence Number	SN	4 bits	To verify that all SAR–PDUs of the CPCS–PDU have been received and correctly sequenced
Message Identifier	MID	10 bits	Associates an SAR–PDU with a given CPCS–PDU; all SAR–PDUs belonging to the CPCS–PDU will have the same MID (this MID from 1–1023 is assigned in order to each CPCS–PDU)
SAR–PDU payload		44	User information – up to 44 CPCS octets –PDU Pad – to fill out the 44 octets
Length Indication	LI	6 bits	How many of the 44 octets are user information: for BOM and COM, this will equal 44 octets; for EOM 4, 8,..., 44, and for SSM 8, 12,..., 44 octets
Cyclic Redundancy Check	CRC	10 bits	Detects errors in the SAR–PDU
AAL3/4 CPCS PDU frame = $N \times 44$ bytes			
Common Part Indicator	CPI	1	Indicates the type of message within the CPCS–PDU and defines the counting unit for the BA–size and length fields
Beginning Tag	BEtag	1	Used in conjunction with the End Tag to form an association between the BOM and EOM
Buffer allocation size	BA-size	2	Length of the user information subfield of the CPCS payload
Payload		Variable	User Information – CLS–PDU PAD – 0–3 octets for 4-octet alignment
Alignment	AL	1	Provides 4-octet alignment for the trailer
End Tag	BEtag	1	See above
Length		2	Length of user information subfield
AAL3/4 CLS–PDU fields			
Destination and source address	DA/SA	8	First 4 bits identify the address type – 1100 for public individual addresses and 1110 for group addresses; remaining 60 bits identify the E.164 address
Higher Layer Protocol Identifier	HLPI	6 bits	ICIP–CLS–PDU to ICIP L3–PDU (CLNIP) alignment; ø otherwise
Pad Length	PL	2 bits	00 – ICIP–CLS–PDU to ICIP L3–PDU alignment
Quality of Service	QoS	4 bits	same as above
CRC32 Indicator Bit	CIB	1 bit	0[CLNAP] or 1[CLNIP]
Header Extension Length	HEL	3 bits	011
Bridging	BRI	2	
Header extension	HE	12	
Service-Specific Information	SSI	8	Used to support SMDS over the B-ICI (CLNIP only)
Cyclic Redundancy Check			CRC32 0/4 Uded if CIB=1
ICIP user data		Variable	End-user data; contains the SIP L3–PDU (99188 max) without its SIP L3–PDU trailer

AAL5

Unlike AALs 1 to 4, originally specified by the ITU, AAL5 is an outgrowth of the data communications industry, and thus is optimized for data transport. Originally introduced by IBM, and known as the 'IBM AAL', it was later proposed to the newly-formed ATM Forum and has now been fed into the ITU standardization process. Intended for the point-to-point (or point-to-multipoint) transport of data traffic, it eliminates the overhead (SN, MID) found in AAL3/4. Thus, the entire ATM Cell payload (48 bytes) is available for user data with one exception. Where the resequencing capabilities of AAL3/4 at the expense of four additional overhead bytes are not required, the increase in efficiency is substantial. Note that this lack of interleaving may present problems in some environments. Consider multicasting, where point-to-multipoint connections are established. If these connections were bi-directional, leaf nodes could transmit PDUs into the connection which would be replicated to other leafs, probably intermixed with PDUs from other senders. For this reason, an AAL5 point-to-multipoint connection must be unidirectional. Though the interleaving capabilities of AAL3/4 may be proposed as a solution to this limitation, a second problem is created in that all nodes participating in the group would be required to use unique MIDs. The limited length of the MID field would then limit the number of nodes in a multicast group. In local-area ATM, AAL5 is the adaptation of choice for data transmission; in the WAN, AAL5 is also universally deployed with the exception of some SMDS/CBDS services which use AAL3/4.

As with the other AALs, the higher-layer data frame is first encapsulated in a CPCS-PDU consisting of the data payload (CPCS-SDU) along with a padding field and a trailer consisting of a user-to-user information field (CPCS-UU), a CPI, a length field, and a CRC (Figure 3.22). This length of the initial data frame is limited by the AAL to 65535 octets; in reality, it may be lower in actual implementation (Classical IP over ATM or LANE, for example). But unlike AAL3/4, no additional overhead is added to this PDU at the SAR sublayer. The SAR-PDUs – BOM, COM, and EOM – still have meaning, but instead of explicitly identifying each type of SAR-PDU, the cell containing the EOM is identified by setting a bit within the PTI in the cell header (the ATM user-to-user bit – bit 3). Thus, no additional overhead is required within the ATM-SDU other than that taken by the CPCS-PDU trailer in the cell containing the EOM.

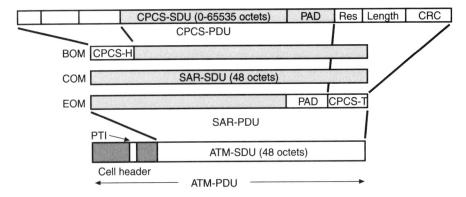

Figure 3.22 ATM Adaptation Layer (AAL) 5.

ATM error correction including forward error correction

Before we delve into higher-layer services within an ATM network, we should first look at error correction within ATM. One method proposed is **Forward Error Correction (FEC)**, a function which may be implemented just above the AAL as a new SSCS, and a subject of debate within the ATM Forum. Consider a data frame segmented into 10, 100, or even 1000 ATM cells. Since ATM itself contains no inherent error correction mechanism other than the HEC, as the AAL CRC is for error detection only, the loss of a single cell due to congestion or a line error will result in the retransmission of the entire data frame by the end-system. In some cases, an entire transmission window as opposed to a single packet must be retransmitted. Techniques to counter this include ABR and **Early Packet Discard (EPD)**. Thus, the problem is mainly with high BER paths such as wireless LANs, where these two techniques may only be partially effective, leading to unacceptable overhead. For example, on a link with a BER or 10^{-9}, the probability for error at an MTU of 9180 bytes is 1×10^{-4}, not very good odds at all. If we look at the CLR, transmission of an 8 Kbyte packet over a link with a CLR of 10^{-6} will have a 2×10^{-4} chance of failing. One class of applications very intolerant to this level of loss is guaranteed multicasting, where the potential for retransmission increases linearly with the number of receivers. A second is VBR service where data may be dropped due to the lack of a reactive flow control capability (such as that which exists within ABR). The problem is therefore serious, leading to an investigation of the various means of error correction.

Esaki *et al*, 1995a, propose a new ATM SSCS implementing FEC. This proposal complements work underway within the ITU-T to define an FEC scheme oriented to continuous bit stream audio-visual traffic, assuming the use of CBR, resulting in a low CLR, and not mandating error-free transmission. The proposed FEC-SSCS allows for a higher CLR, less strict demands on latency, asynchronous data streams (packets), a requirement for error-free transmission, and operation with a transport layer. An ATM FEC does not preclude the use of an application FEC. The proposed FEC-SSCS is designed for variable length AAL5 and AAL3/4 SDUs, and supports error recovery due to both cell loss and bit errors (see Esaki *et al*, 1995b). This SSCS is located in the upper part of the AAL above the CPCS. When an error is detected by the CPCS entity at a destination, the FEC-SSCS entity will attempt to recover the original data via the FEC algorithm. This algorithm is based on three operational modes, one capable of correcting only bit errors (**symbol error correction**, where a symbol is 8 or 16 bits), one used for cell loss (**symbol loss correction**), and a mode capable of both (**symbol error and loss correction**). A feature of the FEC is its ability to signal to the upper layer (that is, TCP) if it has detected cell loss or a bit error. The transport layer may use this information for flow or congestion control.

During FEC negotiation, the source will indicate how much redundant data should be sent. Note that this is a tradeoff between a higher overhead and better error correction capabilities. Under operation, an IP packet, for example, will generate an FEC-SSCS-SDU which is segmented into a series of FEC frames containing user data and the FEC code. The FEC-SSCS-PDU will contain this SDU along with a header (SSCS-UU) containing user-to-user control information. Esaki *et al*, 1995b, detail possible contents of the data and FEC code fields along with the algorithms used (for example, Reed-Solomon) to generate the redundant data. In short, if amount 'M' data is transmitted with amount 'S' in the FEC code, then amount 'S' missing data may be recovered from the original data stream. Thus the tradeoff described above. The relationship for bit error correction is a little more complicated.

However appealing the deployment of FEC may be, questions have been raised as to its performance in practice, especially in the presence of other congestion avoidance schemes (Ikeda *et al*, 1995, and Ratta *et al*, 1995). One area of concern is the relationship of FEC with EPD, the first optimized for random cell loss while the second is more efficient for bursty cell loss. In fact, most cell loss is bursty, resulting in better performance with EPD as opposed to FEC since encoding for this type of loss profile must include extra redundancy to handle bursty loss, adding to delay for all traffic (and especially at low bandwidths) and bandwidth overhead when there is no cell loss. Probably more critical is the operation of FEC in conjunction with ABR. If we consider ABR networks to have minimal cell loss, the FEC mechanisms will only add additional overhead. The one potential area of deployment, then, is within UBR, though the performance of UBR with EPD has been shown to be better than that possible with FEC. On the physical level, we expect the implementors of wireless technology, generally assumed to have a high BER in comparison to fiber, to implement lower-layer FEC providing a higher-reliability bit pipe to ATM. The one application environment in which FEC is assumed to have real advantages – multicasting where receivers do not ask for retransmission – may be solved through the introduction of more robust techniques based on error handling or FEC at the application layer. This also has an advantage in media independence but requires each application to implement the required function, placing an additional burden on the end-system. These applications will also benefit from ABR, though support for pt-mpt connections is still in development. In fact, it may be kept to below 1 in 10^{-6}, in which case the packet loss rate will be 1 in 10^{-4}.

Although FEC work is not an ATM Forum priority at present, ultimately, ATM users may find various error correction and recovery techniques deployed, on the physical layer as part of the transmission system, within ATM, at the transport layer, and within end applications. Within a single network, different systems may co-exist, and the challenge will be to ensure that techniques implemented at one layer do not counteract or adversely affect those implemented at another.

3.2 Signaling

In all but the smallest of ATM networks, users must have the capability of signaling a connection across the network. The type of VCC created via this signaling mechanism is known as a **Switched Virtual Circuit (SVC)**, contrasting to the **Permanent Virtual Circuit (PVC)** established via network management. Efforts to define ways of signaling SVCs began within the ITU (the CCITT at the time) while, more recently, the ATM Forum has used these recommendations and sometimes expanded upon them to generate the UNI. Three versions of the UNI support SVCs – 3.0, 3.1, and the most recent, 4.0. As of the UNI 3.1, ATM Forum signaling aligned with the ITU's Q.2931 protocol.

Q.2931 signaling may almost be looked at as an application running on top of the lower (physical, ATM, and AA) layers. In the case of ATM, signaling occurs over a **Signaling ATM Adaptation Layer (SAAL)** residing between the ATM layer and the Q.2931 signaling protocol. The SAAL provides for the reliable transport of signaling messages between two ATM systems, to include the recovery of multiple gaps in the data stream. This contrasts to the single recovery available within LAPB and TCP, and is therefore very suitable for the transport of signaling information across ATM due to its robustness. The SAAL is composed of two sublayers: the common part and a service-specific part. The service-specific part is subdivided into a **Service-Specific Coordination Function (SSCF)** and a **Service-Specific Connection Oriented Protocol (SSCOP)**. The SSCF maps Q.2931's requirements into the SSCOP, while the SSCOP includes mechanisms for establishing, releasing, and monitoring signaling information exchange between signaling

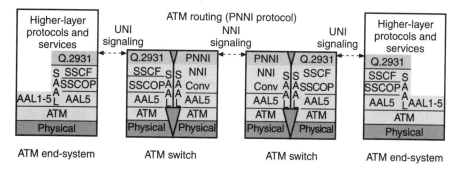

Figure 3.23 ATM signaling.

entities. It is here that we recover lost or corrupted signaling SDUs. ITU-T Recommendations Q.2130 and Q.2110 describe the SSCF and the SSCOP. The common part, based on the AAL5's SAR and CPCS, ensures information transfer and detection of corrupt SDUs. Between ATM switches, an NNI convergence over the SAAL is used for PNNI signaling, which is described later. The interrelationship between the various signaling sublayers is depicted in Figure 3.23.

Signaling between the end-system and the ATM switch usually takes place over VPI=0/VCI=5, although this is not always the case. If we implement a feature such as SVC tunneling (described later), the signaling channel will often be over a VPI other than zero. Also, some proprietary UNI and NNI protocols use a VCI other than five for signaling. Note that the use of more than one VP at an interface does not imply that we require multiple signaling connections, since a single signaling link may service multiple VPCs.

Within both the ITU and the ATM Forum, work has focused on implementing signaling over the private and public UNIs, the PNNI, and the B-ICI with separate signaling documents applying to the UNI, the PNNI, and the B-ICI. In looking at ATM signaling, we first review the ways of creating VCCs – PVCs and SVCs – along with their connection types. This leads into a brief description of public ATM signaling, over which the ATM Forum has developed its specifications, leading us into a description of ATM Forum signaling procedures.

3.2.1 Connection types

We begin the discussion of ATM signaling with a comparison of the two VC establishment mechanisms: PVCs based on preconfiguration via network management and SVCs based on real-time signaling. These two mechanisms relate to all ATM models, with a combination of PVCs and SVCs deployed depending upon application. Related to the mode of connection establishment is the type of connection. This is to the number of senders and receivers participating in a given connection, and may be grouped into **point-to-point (pt-pt)**, **point-to-multipoint (pt-mpt)**, and **multipoint-to-multipoint (mpt-mpt)** PVCs or SVCs.

An ATM network will support SVCs, PVCs, or a combination of the two. In establishing a path between two SVC-based private ATM domains, a public ATM segment based on a PVC service may be common, in which case the SVCs may be tunneled. We introduce this technique later. The concept of SVCs and PVCs within ATM is analogous to that of X.25 and, more recently, Frame Relay. PVC-based networks rely on network management to configure all connections between ATM end-systems and ATM switches as well as between ATM switches. As with SVCs, the network administrator may set QoS parameters for each VC, to include a **Peak Cell Rate (PCR)**, a **Sustainable Cell Rate (SCR/A)**, a **Burst Length (BL)**, and a **Cell Loss Priority (CLP)**. At the UNI, PVCs may be grouped into one or more VPs. Between switches, the network administrator will often configure multiple VPs. These VPs may be permanent (PVP), or in the future Switched (SVP). As each PVC is assigned a unique VPI/VCI at the UNI and at each NNI, the network management overhead may become quite substantial in anything beyond a small network. Thus, the PVC concept only scales so far. PVC-based networks will support Classical IP, LAN emulation (difficult), SMDS/CBDS, and Frame Relay. In many cases, even a private ATM network based primarily on SVCs may use PVCs for the exchange of Layer 3 routing information. In both private and public ATM domains, ATMF signaling based on any of the UNI releases (3.0, 3.1, or 4.0) may be used to establish SVCs. Public signaling may also use the ITU B-ISDN standard (compatible with UNI 3.1 and 4.0). Between ATM switches, signaling in a private domain will be handled by the PNNI while signaling in the public domain will use the ITU NNI within a single service provider's domain and the B-ICI between domains.

ATM supports different types of connection across these SVCs and PVCs. One important concept is that ATM VCCs are in fact composed of two unidirectional connections, one in each direction. The most basic is a bi-directional point-to-point (pt-pt) VCC, connecting two parties. Although bandwidth may be specified separately in both directions, in many cases the bandwidth allocated will be symmetric. This pt-pt connection is defined as Type 1 within the ITU-T, and requires both directions of the VCC to traverse the same physical route. A more complex connection type is the unidirectional point-to-multipoint (pt-mpt), defined as Type 2 within the ITU. Under a pt-mpt VCC, one party is the root and the destinations are known as **leaves**. Signaling must provide for adding and deleting these leaves on demand, either at the initiation of the root or of individual leaves. This connection type supports multicast services across ATM. Unidirectional multipoint-to-point VCCs (Type 3) are the opposite of the above, requiring resequencing of cells at the root since they arrive from different leaves over the same VPI/VCI. Currently, only AAL3/4 with its MID field supports this.

It is expected that this connection type will see use in the residential environment, where data from different servers is merged at a central distribution point. This would be preferable to using multiple pt-pt VCCs for the same purpose. Finally, multipoint-to-multipoint (mpt-mpt) VCCs support true multipoint conferencing. These Type 4 connections require some type of conferencing server, which will also solve the re-sequencing problem of mpt-pt VCCs. Later, when we discuss multicast-ing across ATM, this server will appear as one solution to the problem. In the absence of such a device, each user may open a pt-mpt VCC, in effect simulating a mpt-mpt VCC.

A second important concept when looking at ATM connections is the relationship between a single pt-pt or pt-mpt VCC and an ATM call. A call may include multiple connections (or no connection at all), each with its own QoS. Consider a multimedia call combining video-conferencing, file transfers, and a shared whiteboard. Each part of this integrated application will be best served by a VCC optimized for the most efficient use of resources. Although this could be accomplished by setting up the VCCs one by one, it is preferable to be able to group them into a single connection request. In the wide area, the concept of a call is required for efficient billing. One type of call, consisting of no active VCCs, whereby resources at each end of the proposed connection are first identified, may be useful. This prevents the pre-allocation of network resources for a call which may fail. Calls also support what is known as a **Common Routing Group (CRG)**. A potential problem with the use of different VCCs is the use of multiple routes to a destination, each with different latencies (Kwok, 1995). A CRG will force all VCCs over the same physical path, a feature which may also be useful as part of the AIMUX standard described in Section 3.1.4.

3.2.2 Public signaling

The initial public signaling standard includes a UNI defined in ITU-T Recommendation Q.2931 and a NNI defined in B-ISUP. Q.2931 is based on the Q.931 used in N-ISDN but with major modifications, while the latter standard provides for control of the ATM service between public networks and is based on the N-ISDN Signaling System Number 7 (SS7). An earlier draft standard known as Q.93B was used as the basis for the UNI 3.0. One thing to note is that this well-known ITU-T document, which the ATM Forum references for signaling (Q.2931), in fact applies only to point-to-point VCCs, while a companion, Q.2971, covers point-to-multipoint connections. As with Q.931, the signaling protocol makes use of messages which consist of **Information Elements (IEs)**. An interest-ing field is the IE instruction indicator, which will allow an end-station which does not understand the meaning of a given IE to either continue processing or abort the signaling request.

At first release, public signaling was limited to point-to-point connections (Type 1), in contrast to the point-to-multipoint connections (Type 2) supported by later versions of the UNI. In addition, the bandwidth as specified by the calling party cannot be altered by the called party and may not be adjusted after the connection is established. Nevertheless, this level of service is sufficient for most basic circuit emulation and data transport services. It is not sufficient, however, for multimedia, with its demands for multipoint connectivity and variable data rates. Finally, the initial Q.2931 does not provide for QoS support. Though specified in the signaling, it does not interface to actual service parameters. Why is this lack of support a potential problem? In selecting the proper route for a call, the NNI protocol must determine whether or not a given path will support a requested QoS. This has been a major design goal in the development of a private NNI within the ATMF. Further work on signaling is in the direction of a 'transaction-oriented' protocol which will separate connection and call signaling, thus providing better support for complex calls. For example, if multiple devices share a UNI, or if multiple signaling VCs should be established, a meta-signaling VC will be established to create these individual VCs. This is described in greater detail below.

During the next few years, signaling will be enhanced by adding additional **Capability Sets (CSs)**. These are aligned with the release; for example, CS1 is part of Release 1. CS2 has been further divided into Step 1 and 2, with the first available in 1994 and the second in 1995, while CS3 should be available in 1997 at the latest. In CS2 Step 1, the calling party can specify a range of bandwidths to be accepted by the destination. This feature is lacking in the first release. Also, the QoS may be altered during the course of a connection. Point-to-multipoint connections are also supported, based initially on the 'add party' mechanism used by the UNI. In the future, a quicker method making use of a multi-party identifier to group parallel connections may also be implemented. Along these same lines, a single call may consist of multiple point-to-point connections, each assigned a given QoS. Note that a potential problem with these multiple connections is the possibility that they may be diversely routed across the ATM network resulting in possible synchronization problems. This is solved via a **common route connection group**, forcing the network to use the same path for these connections. CS2 will also support the separation of call and bearer control protocols. These build upon the **Application Service Elements (ASEs)** available as part of B-ISUP by using the **Transaction Capability Action Part (TCAP)** and the **Signaling Connection Control Part (SCCP)** for transport. Functions available will include 'look-ahead' where one exchange can check downstream to find out whether a call is likely to be accepted. Even more useful may be the **Call Without Connection (CWC)** function which will permit a call to be established before resources are actually reserved in the network.

CS2 Step 2 includes support for a combination of point-to-point and point-to-multipoint connections in the same call, as well as support for multipoint-to-point (Type 3) connections providing feedback. This may be useful in data gathering, for example, in the case of multiple video sources relaying data to a central monitoring center. The most complex type of connection is the multipoint-to-multipoint (Type 4) connection, useful in conferencing and LAN emulation. As part of multicasting, a new party should be able to join an existing multicast session. This is known as a **leaf-initiated join**. Finally, Step 2 may include support for third-party initiated actions, where one party may request a connection between two others.

Upon release of CS3, interworking between B-ISDN and **Intelligent Networks (INs)** will be possible. This will provide for the deployment of value-added services (some analogous to those available under N-ISDN) along with more sophisticated multimedia, database, and cable TV services. Many of these new services are discussed in Chapter 5. As is obvious, these capabilities will require the deployment of a sophisticated control and signaling architecture. In furthering this goal, work is underway to define a **Telecommunications Information Network Architecture (TINA)** based on the distributed computing environment.

Even with the deployment of the PNNI Phase 1, there is still a gap in providing interoperability between private and public signaling. One reason for this is due to the lack of support by many public ATM networks for any type of signaling at all due to technical or administrative reasons. In any case, some method must be provided by which an end user connected to the public ATM cloud at various points may transport signaling requests from one point to another across public PVCs. One method of accomplishing this is via SVC tunneling, described below. Eventually, service providers should implement interworking between the PNNI and the NNI. This interworking, now being addressed within the ATM Forum, includes the injection of reachability information from the public network into the private network as well as transporting NSAP format addresses across the E.164-based public network.

A solution to the above problem may be to deploy a variant of an exterior routing protocol (for example, the inter-domain routing protocol) at the boundary of the public and private networks. The PNNI, capable of accepting external routes, would consider reachability information from the public network as such. An alternative would be to look at the entire public network as a single PNNI peer group. In the interim, the private network could tunnel signaling requests across the public network by carrying out address translation at the boundary. The egress switch from the private network would transfer the destination NSAP format address to the destination subaddress field and then replace the standard destination field with the E.164 address corresponding to the public UNI of the switch providing connectivity to the distant private network. The public network, presented with an E.164 address, could then route the request using its NNI. The translation procedure is repeated at the ingress to the destination private network. A question arises as to how private networks will obtain destination E.164 information in the first place. Initially, this may occur in the same way that dialer lists are established on routers – via manual configuration. A more elegant future solution could use directory services along the line of the domain name system or X.500 directory system.

3.2.3 ATM Forum UNI

The ATM Forum has adapted the ITU's recommendations and crafted these into multivendor implementation agreements. In doing this, the Forum has sometimes deleted or added capabilities based on requirements. The first version of the signaling agreement, the UNI 2.0, only supported PVCs. The first SVC-capable revision, the UNI 3.0, was based on a pre-standard ITU signaling recommendation, Q.93B. Changes by the ITU resulted in the requirement for a new UNI, version 3.1. These changes included a minor change, the redesignation of the signaling protocol itself from Q.93B to Q.2931, and a more major change, an alteration of the SSCOP from Q.SAAL1, Q.SAAL2, and Q.SAAL3 to Q.2110, Q.2120, and Q.2130. Further refinements resulted in the Signaling 4.0 document, usually known as UNI 4.0. The UNI 3.1 was the last unified document. With the release of what is usually called the UNI 4.0, the various aspects of an ATM network have been split into Signaling 4.0, Traffic Management 4.0, the PNNI, the ILMI, and the various physical interface documents.

Since the ATM Forum UNI addresses both the private and public UNI, it must be capable of supporting private and public ATM addressing formats. The format for the private ATM address, known as an **ATM end-system address**, is based on the OSI Network Service Access Point as defined in ISO 8348 and ITU-T X.213. This 20-octet address uses the same structure, semantics, and encoding as the OSI NSAP. As part of this structure, the low-order part containing the ESI and SEL conforms to ISO 10589. An ATM end-system using any one of the three IDI formats, DCC, ICD, or E.164, must be capable of signaling a connection to a system independent of the format used by the destination. ATM systems connected to a public network may use either NSAP format addresses, or, in addition, native E.164 addresses. In the latter case, these addresses will be administered by a public network. We describe the structure and use for each of these address formats later.

With the release of Signaling 4.0, end-systems now have the ability to join an already established point-to-point or point-to-multipoint VCC. This capability is known as a **Leaf Initiated Join (LIJ)**, and includes two types of connection, root-prompted and leaf-prompted. For the former, the leaves must notify the root of their intent to join an existing call, in which case the root may accept or reject the request, while in the latter case the network will add leaf nodes automatically. Although new users may join this multipoint connection, its QoS remains unchanged. Dynamic QoS renegotiation for pt-pt and pt-mpt connections will need to wait for a future release of the UNI, although it is close to approval within the ITU as Q.2964. This would allow PCR renegotiation for CBR/DBR or VBR/SBR as well as dynamic changes in SCR and BT for SBR/VBR. On a side note, although we usually consider UBR as having no guaranteed PCR, we may still police this value (that is, as part of a public ATM offering) and thus it is possibly subject to renegotiation as well.

Signaling 4.0 also identifies a new address format known as **Anycast**, used to identify services available across an ATM network. An application on an end-system will signal the group address of a particular service. The ATM switch, having knowledge of registered services via the **Interim Local Management Interface (ILMI)**, will route the request across the network to the nearest instance of this service. The source may then establish a pt-pt connection to the destination. We may limit the extent of these connection requests to a local area, a campus, or a region by specifying a scope within the signaling message. The UNI 4.0 also supports the ABR traffic class for the first time, though at present only pt-pt ABR VCCs are detailed. Support for pt-mpt ABR is left to individual vendor implementations. Finally, signaling messages may now indicate whether or not a switch will support frame discard. Both this and ABR are detailed in Section 3.5.

An optional feature of Signaling 4.0 is the ability for a user to perform signaling for one or more other users who do not support signaling. This first user is known as the **Proxy Signaling Agent (PSA)**, and will have one or more signaling VCs, each VC associated with a set of VPs located on different UNIs which it will control. This may be useful when an ATM host connects to a switch over multiple physical UNIs, all sharing the same ATM address. The PSA will then be capable of establishing connections over these interfaces. Another situation results when multiple users connect to an ATM mux. UNI 4.0 supports a remapping feature where we may translate the individual user signaling channels (VPI=0, VCI=5) to unique VPIs for transport into the network. Once again, a single signaling channel may control these multiple VPs. Other supplementary services supported by the UNI (and defined as Capability Set 1), which we do not describe in any detail, include (ITU-T, 1995a, 1995b, and 1995c):

- Direct Dialing In (DDI)

- Multiple Subscriber Number (MSN)

- Calling Line or Connected Line Identification Presentation and Restriction (CLIP/CLIR, COLP/COLR)

- Subaddressing (SUB)

- User–User Signaling (UUS).

For completeness, we also list the Capability Set 2 call capabilities and supplementary services provided by the **Generic Functional (GF)** protocol ITU-T, 1996, but not referenced in the UNI. These include:

- Calling and Called Name Identification Presentation (CNIP/CONP),

- Call Transfer (CT) transferring a call from A to C and B to C to one between A and B,

- Call Diversion (DIV)/Call Forwarding (CF),

- Call Completion (CC) allowing a call to complete even if the destination is busy,

- Call Offer (CO) allowing a call to wait on a busy user,

- Call Intrusion (CI) allowing a call to break into a busy user,

- Call Do Not Disturb (DND) allowing a user to block all calls or those from certain groups of users,

- Path Replacement (PR) allowing call rerouting through the network,

- Call Interception (CINT) allowing uncompleted calls to be redirected to a predetermined location.

Note that many of these additional functions are in fact optional. A UNI 4.0-compliant switch must only suppot multipoint connections, LIJs and Anycasting, while all are optional for end-systems. We describe the signaling procedures and various capabilities of the UNI in the following sections.

3.2.4 UNI 3.x/4.x signaling procedures

Before signaling may actually proceed, an ATM end-system must know its complete ATM address as well as that of the switch. This is accomplished via the ILMI or through manual configuration. Although equipment at the private UNI must support this address registration mechanism, this feature is optional for equipment connected to a public UNI. In the case of the private network, the network side will supply the IDP and HO-DSP to the end-system, while in a public network the network side will supply the complete E.164 address when used. Capabilities of the ILMI include, in addition to address registration, the ability to restrict certain combinations of network and user addresses as well as the rejection of unacceptable values. Under dynamic addition and deletion, this list of valid combinations may change over time. For example, the network prefix advertised by an ATM switch to a connected system may change when shifting from one higher-order service provider to another.

If in a data environment, the end-system must also resolve the destination's Layer 3 address to an ATM address. This is the role of the ATMARP, NHRP, and MPOA. Finally, the user may initiate the signaling request in accordance with the ATM Forum UNI 3.1 or 4.0. These messages establish a bi-directional VCC, in reality two uni-directional VCCs. Several messages exist, including those used to setup or release connections along with an inquiry message. These messages are contained within 53-byte ATM cells, although a special protocol discriminator is used to identify to the switch that the cell is for control as opposed to data. The remainder of the cell contains an identifier as to the signaling attempt, the call reference value, the type of signaling message, its length, and then the message itself.

Under actual operation (Figure 3.24), an ATM end-system wishing to establish a point-to-point VCC will send a SETUP message to the ATM network identifying the requested destination. The network will forward this request hop-by-hop to the intended destination. This message also contains additional parameters as to the requested QoS for the call. The network, upon recipient of the SETUP, will return a CALL PROCEEDING message to the source containing the VPI/VCI of the VCC. This message will also be sent by the destination to the network upon receipt of the initial call request. The destination, if it accepts the call, will then respond with a CONNECT message which is then forwarded to the source. The last message exchanged as part of call setup is the CONNECT ACKNOWLEDGE, sent by the source to the network as well as by the network to the destination. The end-to-end connection is now

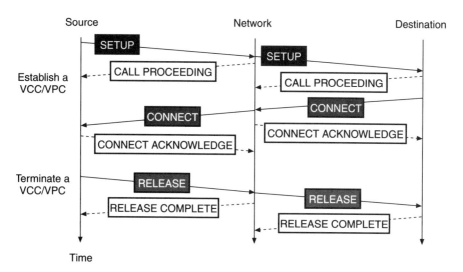

Figure 3.24 Point-to-point signaling sequence.

available for data transport. At the conclusion of the call, either party may initiate a RELEASE, triggering a RELEASE COMPLETE from the network to the source of the release as well as the same message from the destination to the network. Note that the network may also initiate the release if required, generating a RELEASE to both stations which then return a RELEASE COMPLETE. The last message type is the STATUS INQUIRY, sent by either the source or destination to request information regarding the connection. The device responding to the STATUS INQUIRY will send a STATUS message. This message may also be initiated by any system to report on network status.

The signaling sequence is somewhat more complex for point-to-multipoint connections, used for broadcast and multicast transactions. A **root** will originate the connection, which eventually terminates at two or more leaf nodes. The initial sequence of events is the same as above, the one difference being that the signaling request identifies the proposed connection as multicast. The root will signal to the ATM switch the address of the first leaf node, and will then add additional destinations via the ADD PARTY message (Figure 3.25). The next set of events varies depending upon whether the second destination is on the local switch or is distant. If local, the switch translates the ADD PARTY into a SETUP, which it then sends to the intented destination. Upon receipt, the destination responds with the CONNECT, which is translated by the switch into an ADD PARTY ACKNOWLEDGE. If on a distant switch, the local switch forwards the setup message to the switch serving the destination. The translation from ADD PARTY to SETUP and vice versa occurs only

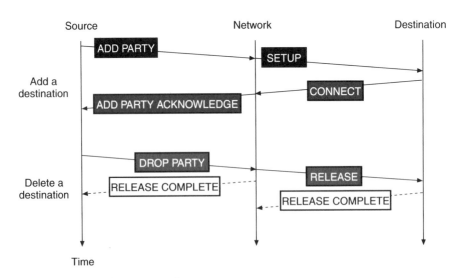

Figure 3.25 Multipoint signaling sequence.

Note   Assumes first destination has been signaled as above on the local switch. Just as a point-to-multipoint VCC is established sequentially, it may be torn down in the same way, with the DROP PARTY acknowledged with a RELEASE COMPLETE. A RELEASE in this instance will result in the termination of the entire point-to-multi-point VCC (Shelef, 1995).

3.2.5 Information elements and signaling for IP over ATM

Having introduced the basic signaling concepts, we now look at the actual **Information Elements (IEs)** which comprise a signaling message. To focus our discussion, we describe how they are used to signal an SVC supporting IP across ATM based on the Classical model. Note that two types of IE exist, some with end-to-end significance and others with meaning only to the ATM network itself. This first group includes the AAL parameters IE and the **Broadband Low-Level Information (B-LLI)** IE. The AAL parameters IE will contain the choice of AAL, along with the desired forward and backward MTU and an SSCS value. For IP over ATM, these parameters should be set to AAL5, a MTU (CPCS-SDU) with a default of 9188 and a maximum of 65,535 octets, and an SSCS of '0', signifying Null. The B-LLI IE specifies what Layer 2 and Layer 3 protocols will be using the SVC, and in effect identifies the use and type of the connection. In this case, we indicate LLC/SNAP. Other encapsulations not directly applicable to IP over ATM include VC-multi-plexing, Frame Relay, and HPR. Within ATM environments other than that defined under Classical IP, the LLC may terminate and therefore manage the call. In this case, no higher-layer identifiers will be required. But within the Classical model, a Layer 3 IP identifier will be included within the B-LLI. In the future, additional IEs for the **Broadband High Layer Information (B-HLI)** IE, **Network Layer Information (B-NLI)**, and application information between users (**B-UUI**) may be defined. RFC-1755 (Perez *et al*, 1995) references a method of encapsulat-ing IP directly over the ATM AAL by setting the Layer 3 IE to IP and omitting the Layer 2 IE. This method, though probably quite efficient for binding VCs to IP, has not yet been implemented.

The second type of IE, those with significance to the ATM network, include the Traffic Descriptor (known as the ATM User Cell Rate in UNI 3.0), the Broadband Bearer Capability, the QoS parameter, and ATM Addressing Information. The Traffic Descriptor will specify a **Peak Cell Rate (PCR), Sustainable Call Rate (SCR)**, and **Maximum Burst Size (MBS)** for an ATM PVC or SVC. This informa-tion is required by the ATM network to allocate resources within the switches and over the NNIs. Initial support of IP over ATM will be based on the **Best Effort (BE)** service, approximating the QoS provided by the Internet. Under this service, the IE will contain a PCR, SCR, and MBS combining both CLP=0 and CLP=1. One justification for specification of all three parameters (Flugstad, 1994) is end-system knowledge of the expected traffic profile. These parameters will then be used by the network in resource allocation. If the traffic profile is unknown, possible selection criteria for the three may include processor speed, operating system, kernel and hardware buffers available, and so on. Note that the calling party may also have some knowledge as to the capabilities of the called party via a central directory service. For VBR and CBR service, the Broadband Bearer Class is set to identify the connection, while CBR also specifies only the PCR (CLP=0+1).

Note that under BE service, the available throughput for a given VC may equal zero at any instant in time. If the ATM network is capable of supporting other QoSs, then the above parameters may be coded within the IE as well. Closely related to this IE is the Broadband Bearer Capability IE, used to specify the bearer class (A, C, or X) which is expected of the network. Types X (BCOB-X) and C (BCOB-C) are both acceptable for supporting multiprotocol data over ATM, and under Best Effort service, the Broadband Bearer Capability IE should be set to BCOC-X. We reserve BCOB-A for CBR. The QoS parameter IE provides support for both connection-oriented (Class 3) and connection-less (Class 4) data transfer over ATM. Initially, only the unspecified QoS class, Class 0, must be supported. This class is also the only one acceptable under BE service. Other implementations may specify Class 3 or Class 4.

The last IEs of significance contain ATM addressing information, and include the called party number, calling party number, called party subaddress, and calling party subaddress. Note that the calling party number will always be generated by an ATM end-system after auto-configuration. Looking at IP in greater detail, this end-system may support up to 256 different **Logical IP Subnets (LISs)** via the **Selector Field (SEL)** of the ATM NSAP format address. If this is the case, signaling messages will contain the ATM address corresponding to the IP entity requesting the call. In a public environment, multiple E.164 addresses should identify LISs. The above IEs will contain both the addressing plan in use (ISDN/E.164 or NSAP) and the actual ATM address.

Building upon the concepts described in RFC-1755, [Maher 96] extends this to cover Signaling 4.0. This document describes support for ABR and UBR+ (frame discard), Leaf Initiated Joins, Anycasting, and Switch Virtual Path (SVP) service. Additions to the SETUP message which must be provided for include: ABR Setup Parameters, ABR Additional Parameters, Connection Scope Selection, Extended QoS Parameters, and End-to-End Transit Delay.

As an alternative to the null SSCS and LLC encapsulation described above, the AAL5 UNI will also support **Frame Relay (FR)** service convergence based on RFC-1490 (NLPID) encapsulation. If this is the case, both the FR-SSCS and NLPID will be specified in the SETUP message. This SSCS acts as an intermediary between the upper layer protocol and the Common Part Convergence Sublayer, and is considered part of the ATM AAL. Therefore, it is carried as part of the AAL parameters IE. Note that negotiation between the FR-SSCS and the null SSCS is not possible. This may present problems for end-systems that wish to use FR over ATM and those which are incapable of this mode of operation. To preclude interoperability problems, the RFC sets out some guidelines for use in transiting from ATM to FR and vice versa.

Two terms are introduced:

- **Network interworking**, where an ATM-connected end-system is aware that the destination is a FR/ATM Interworking Unit (IWU) and thus will implement the FR-SSCS, and

- **Service interworking**, where the operation of the IWU is transparent to all end-systems.

In this latter case, the IWU will perform NLPID to LLC encapsulation translation. In the FR to ATM direction, the IWU will act on behalf of the FR system by placing a call to the ATM-connected system. Under network interworking, we specify the use of both RFC 1490 and the FR-SSCS as part of the signaling message. If this call fails, the IWU may retry the request if it is capable of service interworking. In the oppo-

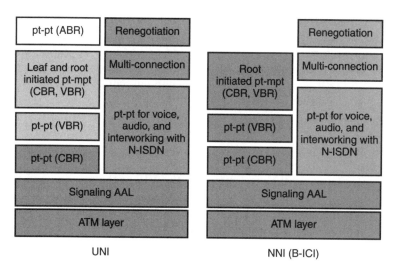

Figure 3.26 Comparisons between ATM Forum and ITU-T signaling. Source: ATM Forum.

ITU-T Recommendations adopted by ATM Forum

ITU-T Recommendations under study by ATM Forum

ATM Forum Specifications adopted by ITU-T

ATM Forum Specification under study by ITU-T

site direction, the ATM-connected system will always attempt to place a call using LLC encapsulation. If the IWU does not support service inter-working, it will reject the call specifying 'AAL parameters not supported'. This may result in a failed call if the originating station is then incapable of RFC 1490 encapsulation. Solutions to this problem include providing ATM-connected stations with knowledge of FR destinations and provid-ing FR-connected stations with knowledge of RFC 1490-capable ATM stations. The FR to ATM interworking function will be covered in greater detail in the next chapter.

In closing, it may be useful to compare signaling features as stan-dardized by both the ATM Forum and the ITU-T at the UNI and NNI. As is obvious in Figure 3.26, there is a great deal of convergence, and almost all open issues are under discussion within both bodies. With recent increased cooperation between the Forum and the ITU-T, the adoption by the latter body of specifications such as ABR should be quicker to appear. Areas for future work include transparent mapping between ATM Forum and ITU service classes.

3.2.6 Soft PVCs and SVC tunneling

Two signaling techniques used in both public and private ATM networks are worth noting since they are supported by a number of the ATM switch vendors. The first is known as **soft PVCs**, and allows PVC-capable end-systems to be easily supported across an SVC-capable ATM network. The network administrator need only configure the PVC across the first and last hops. The switches between each of these locations will create a VC dynamically, binding these two PVCs together. The second technique, **SVC tunneling**, is very useful across a wide-area ATM service which is incapable of supporting SVCs. Consider a user in two locations who wishes to run SVCs internally. The service provider will provision a VP between the two locations, and the signaling VC, norm-ally VPI=0, VCI=5, will be redirected to the VPI of the provisioned VP. A problem with this solution is the lack of support for multiple signaling channels per physical interface on most ATM switches. Thus, three switches connected together will require two physical interfaces, each supporting a VP and a signaling channel. Note that the capability of a single signaling channel to support multiple VPs will not suffice here, since a non-SVC capable cross-connect will not be capable of terminating this single channel and splitting it to the two destinations.

3.3 Trunking and routing

Though early emphasis within the ATM Forum was on the UNI, just as important is the interface connecting ATM switches. As all but the smallest of ATM networks will consist of two or more switches, we require an inter-switch protocol capable of transporting signaling and QoS information for use in establishing end-to-end connections. Since many ATM networks will include switches from multiple vendors, this protocol must be open as opposed to vendor-specific. The first ATM Forum standard capable of supporting SVCs between switches of multiple vendors is known as the **Interim Interswitch Signaling Protocol (IISP)**. This protocol, providing for some table-based rerouting but no topology discovery, is intended as an interim solution for small ATM networks until all switch vendors implement the PNNI. We detail this IISP in a later section. The PNNI is the first open ATM trunking protocol supporting topology discovery via the distribution of reachability information, hierarchical routing and addressing, and QoS, and is expected to be implemented on the majority of the switches in the future. If vendors have proprietary trunking implementations which satisfy user requirements, nothing precludes the continued use of these protocols. Also, some switches may be incapable of supporting the full PNNI due to design limitations. In either case, these vendor-specific domains may be gatewayed to PNNI at switches supporting both systems or via the IISP (Figure 3.27). The design of an ATM trunking protocol is complex, in that it must operate over all ATM switches regardless of processor performance and buffering. In addition, implementing the protocol should not require a great deal of additional configuration or prior knowledge of the structure of the ATM network distant from the local management domain. In 1994, the PNNI SWG of the ATMF set out to conquer these problems, leading to the completion of the PNNI Phase 1 at the beginning of 1996 (ATM Forum, 1996a).

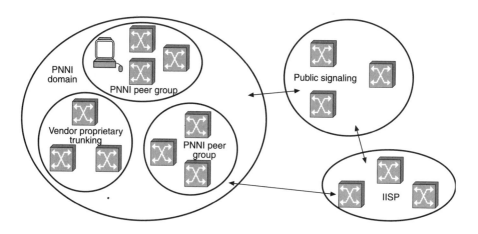

Figure 3.27 PNNI routing domains and peer groups.

3.3.1 PNNI Phase 1

The Private Network–Network Interface (PNNI), sometimes referred to as the Private Network-to-Network Interface since we may apply the protocol to interconnect both switches and networks, is a trunking, routing, and signaling protocol which applies to a network of ATM switches and in some cases, ATM-connected end-systems. This second point is important, since many consider the protocol to apply only between ATM switches. Consider an ATM host, router, or LAN switch requiring redundancy. If we dual-home this system, the PNNI may be used to select the proper interface. The protocol includes provisions to ensure that ATM traffic is not routed via this system. In order to be able to deploy ATM globally, or even corporate-wide, we require an ATM layer protocol with the same scalability features as those used within the Internet. In fact, this protocol is more complicated since ATM is connection-oriented and each VCC has an associated QoS. Therefore, the protocol must carry not only reachability information but data as to trunk capabilities as well. If we expect this network to scale on the order of thousands of switches or more, we must introduce hierarchy, whereby network details are summarized at each level. This is no different from the Internet, where a corporation does not advertise internal topology. The ATM routing protocol must therefore be capable of handling this hierarchy for topology and addressing. Finally, unlike traditional routing protocols which are divided into two classes, intra-domain or interior (that is, OSPF and IS-IS), and inter-domain or exterior (that is, BGP-4), the PNNI covers both instances.

From an economic standpoint, the amount of processing power and memory required must be acceptable to vendors deploying this protocol on all classes of ATM switches. During development of the PNNI, design goals included support of both UNI 3.0/3.1 and later, UNI 4.0 traffic classes. The developers knew that meeting all of these requirements would not be an easy task, but after over a year of very concerted effort, the PNNI Phase 1 became a reality. Future enhancements or revisions to the protocol including more sophisticated link metrics and security, a Phase 2, will be considered after we gain practical experience with the current implementation. In looking at the PNNI, we first look at the ATM network hierarchy, and examine the details of the protocol's operation, including its support of routing, addressing, and QoS.

Hierarchy

The first requirement relates to visibility of the network topology by the ATM switches. We must balance the desirability of providing each switch with full information as to network topology and link utilization, and the cost and overhead of distributing and maintaining this information. Consider a flat network of 30 or so switches, where each is required to maintain information for every physical link and reachability information for every node. At 30 nodes this would just work, at 300 nodes it may work, but only on the most powerful processors, but at 3000 nodes it clearly would not. Therefore, the PNNI supports address summarization and topology abstraction. It accomplishes this by providing switches with detailed information about their local topology and summarized information about more distant parts of the ATM network (see Swallow, 1994). As an example of this, consider the various levels of topology abstraction available on traditional roadmaps. A traveller crossing the United States requires a map showing interstate highways; he is not interested in details of towns along the way. But upon reaching the destination state, a more detailed map showing local roads will prove useful. Finally, a town map detailing each and every street will be required to find the ultimate destination. In the same way, the implementor of an ATM network will work with various levels of abstraction. We expect a single corporation to utilize anywhere from two to a maximum of ten levels of hierarchy (although the PNNI supports 105 levels). One possible rule of thumb here is that a network of size 'N' will require a hierachy equal to In(N).

Within the PNNI hierarchy, groups of nodes form smaller domains known as 'peer groups', analogous to OSPF areas. Nodes within a peer group share a peer group identifier, usually a prefix of the NSAP address space. They exchange reachability information, and therefore have an identical view of the group of which they are a member (Figure 3.27). At the lowest layer of the PNNI hierarchy, these nodes represent physical devices (Dykeman, 1995). Within a peer group, one switch is elected as the **Peer Group Leader (PGL)** based on the configured ATM address or under operator control. For example, a network manager may decide that a switch with more powerful processing capabilities or greater redundancy should be the leader regardless of its ATM address. This leader summarizes topology information within the peer group, akin to OSPF or IS-IS, as well as peers with members of the next higher-order peer group. It injects a summary of its local peer group information into this higher-order group, and acts as the forwarding point into the local peer group for summarized information about these higher-order groups. Thus, the entire peer group at one level appears as a single **Logical Group Node (LGN)** at the next higher level, and the peer group leader announces reachability to the peer group as opposed to individual nodes.

These logical nodes in turn form a peer group (via logical links) and exchange reachability information, a process repeated up the hierarchy. The formation of the complete PNNI hierarchy therefore occurs from the lowest peer groups upward. Summarized topology information will then be passed back down through the hierarchy (Figure 3.28). Note that the support of a peer group hierarchy results in a truly scalable protocol, unlike the flat (BGP) or two-layer (OSPF, IS-IS) protocols used within the Internet. Though the protocol is hierarchical, note that the size of a given peer group is still limited to the volume of PLSP traffic which the nodes are capable of processing.

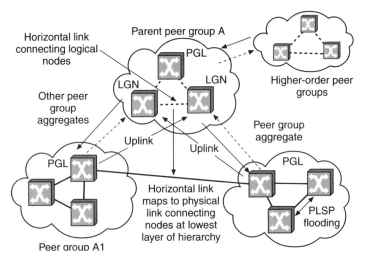

Horizontal link connecting logical nodes

Parent peer group A

PGL

LGN

LGN

Higher-order peer groups

Other peer group aggregates

Peer group aggregate

Uplink

Uplink

PGL

PGL

Horizontal link maps to physical link connecting nodes at lowest layer of hierarchy

PLSP flooding

Peer group A1

Figure 3.28 PNNI hierarchy. Source: Cisco Systems.

PGL   Peer Group Leader
LGN   Logical Group Node

During protocol initialization, ATM devices will exchange PNNI 'hello' packets to determine whether they should form a peer group based on the peer group identifier. If in the same group, based on associated ATM address prefixes (which may be modified by configuration), they will then exchange topology and routing information via 'inside links'. Since we base group membership on a variable length field, network administrators may create networking hierarchies using a smaller or larger number of ATM addresses at each level of the hierarchy. This is no different from adjusting an IP subnet mask, but in this case an address includes a node ID along with an identifier corresponding to the layer of the hierarchy. At the lowest layer of the hierarchy, this peer group ID is the 13 higher-order octets of the switch's NSAP address. By default, this peer group may therefore contain 256 switches at this level if we align to octet boundaries. At higher levels, a parent's peer group ID defaults to a shorter prefix of the lower level peer group ID. The switch's node ID is the same as the switch's ATM address at this lowest level; at higher levels, it consists of an indicator as to the level within the hierarchy along with the peer group ID.

In building the hierarchy, nodes will exchange reachability information via **PNNI Topology State Packets (PTSPs)** to all adjacent nodes at regular intervals or when triggered by some topology or capacity change within the network. These packets are used by the switcher for database synchronization. In doing this, switches at the boundaries of a peer group will realize that they are in contact with nodes belonging to a different peer group. Consider two nodes, A.1.2 and C.5.1. As the hierarchy is formed, A.1.2 will learn that it is a member of A.1 while C.5.1 will learn that it belongs to C.5. This information is now exchanged between the two nodes, leading to A.1.2 forming what is known as an uplink into C.5, while C.5.1 will do the reverse into A.1. Next, A.1.2 learns that it is in A, and C.5.1 learns that it is in C. Both repeat the uplink procedure. Finally, both learn that they are members of some higher-order address region. The horizontal link connecting the LGNs for A and C at the highest layer of the hierarchy is reflected in a horizontal link connecting A.1.2 and C.5.1 at the lowest layer (see Figure 3.28). This link is used by these border nodes to inject reachability information into their peer group.

If an existing proprietary ATM network is connected to the PNNI-based network, it may appear as a separate peer group within the hierarchy, with all internal topology information summarized at the domain boundary. In effect, it will appear as a single node. Alternatively, it may exist completely separate from the PNNI domain, connected via IISP or an equivalent.

Addressing and routing

The PNNI relies on NSAP address summarization to build the routing hierarchy. Think of a number of corporations using a single ATM service provider. Ideally, the service provider delegates portions of its address space to these users, who then further subdivide the space based on corporate structure. If this summarization did not exist, the protocol would be required to transport a great deal of additional addressing information. We may draw parallels to the Internet, where routing tables are large since summarization only exists in some places.

In Figure 3.29, all members of a given peer group share that peer group's address prefix, enabling effective summarization. For example, all end-system addresses A11x, A12x, and A13x may be summarized as A1. This summary information is passed up the hierarchy. The same applies

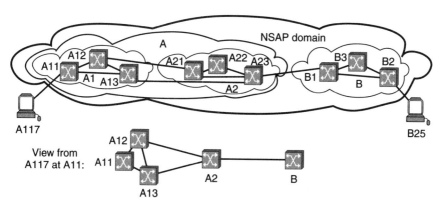

Figure 3.29 PNNI routing.

for end-systems within A2: A21x, A22x, and A23x. They are summarized as A2. The next order parent peer group, A, also summarizes A1 and A2 as just A. Addresses which allow this summarization are known as 'native', and contrast to 'foreign' addresses which adversely affect summarization. If peer group A1 were to contain an end-system with the foreign address C123, this could not be summarized and would be propagated as a separate entry up the hierarchy. Needless to say, it will be wise under PNNI operation to take advantage of summary addresses as far as possible in much the same way that Internet service providers attempt to preserve their CIDR blocks. Since some switch vendors are shipping systems with pre-configured NSAP addresses, if a user's PNNI address summarization is to be maintained, these addresses must be reconfigured. We look at these addressing issues in the next section.

Before we look at routing within the PNNI, a brief review of routing algorithms and metrics is in order. We consider two types of routing algorithm: source routing and hop-by-hop. In source routing, the forwarding path is calculated at the source and placed in the packet header. Tradeoffs in this approach balance the flexibility of being able to centrally specify the route against the need for full link routing information and higher packet overhead. Hop-by-hop routing forwards the packet at each point in the network based on its destination address, and in the case of the present-day Internet (although this is changing), without any QoS awareness. During times of congestion, this may lead to delays and possible packet drop. This unpredictability would not suffice for ATM's ABR class, much less for CBR or VBR. Thus, we require a QoS-aware protocol capable of relaying this information. A larger problem with hop-by-hop routing is its performance under transient conditions. For example, a failed link resulting in inconsistent routing tables (for a short time) may result in looping. Although datagram routing includes provisions to avoid a packet from looping indefinitely, when PNNI was under discussion this was not considered desirable since it would have complicated the signaling protocol. This is another justification for source routing.

Parallel to the selection of a routing method is the choice of a routing metric. This metric will determine the complexity of the path computation, and involves tradeoffs between comprehensive support of QoS requirements and efficiency of calculation. A solution may be to combine multiple metrics into a single value for use in routing calculations. For example, a metric based on delay and cost may not be used to request bandwidth or reliability. The parameters must also contain no redundant information and should not be inter-dependent. An important conclusion is that four common parameters – delay, loss probability, cost, and jitter – are interdependent. Thus, the only valid combination will be bandwidth and one of the above four, with delay the most viable. A great deal of effort has been expended to develop these routing metrics for use by both the PNNI and by proprietary ATM trunking protocols. Depending upon the vendor implementation, all or some of the PNNI metrics and attributes as described in the next section may be supported.

Ideally, a source would have accurate data as to whether nodes along the signaling path are capable of supporting the PCR and SCR of the connection request. As this is not the case, the PNNI replaces the **Connection Admission Control (CAC)** algorithm with a **Generic CAC (GCAC)**. This GCAC, actually divided into a simple and complex form, is a way of modeling general switch connection acceptance behavior without having knowledge of all switch parameters, such as trunk capacity and buffering. The Simple GCAC advertises an ACR at the switch, making use of calculation based on the PCR and SCR of the connection request to determine whether a link is suitable. For more precise control, the Complex GCAC includes the CRM and VF, two parameters decribed a bit later. Note that the GCAC applies to CBR and VBR connections; for UBR, we only determine if the node is capable of supporting the connection, and for ABR we amy use the advertised ACR to set the transmission rate of the source. Once we determine the set of acceptable paths, a shortest path calculation taking into account the **Administrative Weight** will result in a preferred route. Additive link metrics will now come into play, and the source may load balance across the remaining paths if it chooses to do so. However, it is unknown whether load balancing by traffic type (that is, routing a new ABR request to a trunk with few existing ABR connections in preference to a trunk with many existing connections) will have positive benefits. It now constructs a **Designated Transit List (DTL)** describing the route to the destination and will insert this into the signaling request. Each node along the path will perform its CAC on the request. If the request fails, the PNNI will 'crankback' the connection request to a previous node. This node, if capable of constructing a DTL, will then re-forward the request. If source routing were not used, the signaling request would be subjected to a full CAC at each and every node, resulting in a large number of crankbacks. Crankback helps to improve the call success rate, while also providing for immediate rerouting without waiting for the propogation of topology updates.

Alternatively, if a suitable path cannot be found, a technique known as 'fallback' may be used whereby specific attributes of the connection request (for example, delay, PCR), are relaxed and paths recalculated. Remember that the summarization which results in PNNI's scalability also results in the aggregation of QoS metrics within the hierarchy. This affects the accuracy of this information since it will only approximate the switch and link attributes available at a given level. To lessen this problem, a peer group may be modeled as a 'complex node' with an internal structure. The peer group is then associated with a radius approximating the metrics across the actual network. Note that this increasing accuracy results in additional data which must be carried by the PTSPs. The PNNI also supports 'soft' VPs as previously described. Finally, the protocol will support multicasting via point-to-multipoint connections. This will allow the operation of server-based or overlaid point-to-multipoint connection-based multicast groups. It does not provide for true multipoint-to-multipoint connections, leaf-initiated joins, or group addressing as defined in UNI 4.0. This support will probably be incorporated in a future PNNI Phase 2 or an update to the first release.

As an example of PNNI routing, consider the network topology depicted in Figure 3.29. We are at source A117, and wish to reach destination B25. Our signaling request is first forwarded to our local ATM switch, A11. Via the PNNI, this switch has detailed topology information for A1, and summary information for all other peer groups. Thus, it knows that B is reachable via A2, and A2 is reachable via A12 and A13. Depending upon the requirements of the signaling request, it may route the connection over either path. If we assume A12, the request's DTL will contain [A12][A2][B]. At the entry to A2, switch A21 knows that B is reachable via A23, also over two paths. Assuming we route the call via A22, the DTL is now [A22][A23][B]. This node has removed the DTL describing the peer group just crossed as well as the summary entry for A2, and will add the detailed DTL for A2. Assuming no crankback, the request now reaches B1, which knows that B25 is connected to switch B2. The new DTL will now contain only [B2]. Consider the map scenario again, but in this case, both highways and local roads are used to cross the country. A map showing only main roads will allow one to reach a given town, but to cross the town, we require a more detailed map. Upon leaving the town, the higher-order map may be used once again. An advantage of this transit list mechanism is apparent if a signaling request reaches a node where it cannot proceed (for example, due to insufficient resources). This is where crankback takes effect, where the request backtracks to the last node capable of generating a new segment (DTL) of the source route.

An important feature of the PNNI is the concept of a non-transit node, capable of participating in the PNNI protocol but configured to forward only some or no traffic. In the former case, it could be the first or last node in a DTL but never an intermediate node. Callon and Salkewicz, 1995, outline a number of cases where this behavior may be desirable, to include placing the PNNI PGL functions in a workstation as opposed to the switch based on processor and memory requirements, optimizing routing to a critical server attached to multiple ATM switches, or ensuring that only traffic from certain user groups may traverse an ATM layer firewall. Devices acting in this last way are known as restricted transit nodes. Alternatively, routers implementing Integrated PNNI or PNNI Augmented Routing (PAR) (described in a later chapter) must be configured as non-transit nodes when establishing ATM SVCs, as we would not want to attempt to signal a VCC across a router.

One of the last concerns in deploying the PNNI is how it will interact with public network ATM routing and signaling. It is doubtful if the public service providers will allow whatever ATM trunking protocol is used in the public domain to directly exchange reachability and QoS information with the PNNI (or with any vendor-specific trunking protocol, for that matter). Therefore, mapping between both of these parameters must occur at the boundary between the two domains. Needless to say, there is a lot of work to be done in this area, now receiving a great deal of attention in the ATM Forum.

QoS support

Once we understand PNNI routing, we may look at just what information the protocol uses to decide over what path to forward a signaling request. The information used in this decision-making is stored as a database, summarizing the capabilities of a horizontal link or uplink, and capturing the properties of a physical node or logical node representing a lower-layer peer group. In essence, this link state database contains information as to the capability of each link to support the QoS requirements of a new connection. In generating this information, tradeoffs occur, such as whether to exchange more detailed capacity and utilization information at the expense of overhead and processing. This is possibly one of the most fundamental points in deploying a routing protocol: greater visibility into the QoS support of a distant area is at the expense of protocol scalability, for there is a limit to the amount of information which the PNNI may exchange. These concerns are relevant in larger networks where multiple transit paths may exist between two local ATM environments. When determining whether or not the QoS requirements of a new connection may be supported by the network, we use two types of link parameter: non-additive link (topology) attributes applying to a single link, and additive link (topology) metrics applying to all links and nodes across the end-to-end path (Table 3.14).

Of all the parameters, the AvCR is the most dynamic and reflects the amount of bandwidth available at any given time although the PNNI advertises only significant changes to this attribute. The administrative weight is set by the network administrator and may be used to designate a link as desirable or undesirable. For example, a company may lease two connections at the same data rate, one having lower latency but costing more. Looking back at the GCAC, we have two mechanisms available: simple and complex. The simple GCAC relies only on a calculation involving the AvCR of the link and the PCR and SCR of the connection, while the optional complex GCAC includes the CRM and VF.

The PLSPs contain the above information, as well as data pertaining to individual nodes across the network. This latter feature is especially important if the node represents a lower-order peer group. At present, the QoS of a connection depends on those parameters requested at the time a VC is established. Though future versions of the UNI will support renegotiation, this capability has not yet been incorporated in the PNNI.

Table 3.14 PNNI link metrics and attributes.

Link or topology metrics	CBR	rt-VBR	nrt-VBR	ABR	UBR
Maximum Cell Transfer Delay (maxCTD) in μs per traffic class	Yes	Yes	Yes	NA	NA
Maximum Cell Delay Variation (ppCDV) in μs per traffic class	Yes	Yes	NA	NA	NA
Administrative weight $(1\text{-}(2^{32}-1))$	Yes	Yes	Yes	Yes	Yes
Link or topology attributes					
Maximum Cell Loss Ratio (maxCLR) in order of magnitude $(10^{-1}$–$10^{-15})$ for CLP$=0$ cells	Yes	Yes	Yes	Yes	NA
Maximum Cell Rate (maxCR) in cells/second per traffic class	Opt	Opt	Opt	Yes	Yes
Available Cell Rate (AvCR), the available bandwidth in cells per second, per traffic class; measures the MCR for ABR	Yes	Yes	Yes	Yes	NA
Cell Rate Margin (CRM), the difference between the bandwidth allocated for a given traffic class and the requested SCR of the new VC	Opt	Opt	Opt	NA	NA
Variance Factor (VF), a measure of the CRM normalized by the variance of the aggregate cell rate on the link	Opt	Opt	Opt	NA	NA

Note   Opt Optional

3.3.2 IISP

Although the UNI 3.0 was approved in 1993, no comparable NNI was defined at the time, presenting users with difficulties in deploying multi-vendor ATM networks. To enable this interoperability before the release of the PNNI in 1996, the Forum specified an interim ATM trunking protocol at the beginning of 1995 known as the **Interim Inter-switch Signaling Protocol (IISP)** (ATM Forum, 1994d). Originally known as the PNNI Phase 0, its name was changed to avoid any chance of confusion as to forward compatibility (none) with the PNNI Phase 1. It is a signaling protocol only, as opposed to the PNNI which supports signaling and routing. Routing between switching systems is supported via manual configuration of NSAP prefixes reachable over trunks. The protocol does support a limited degree of redundancy, though, by allowing the network administrator to configure a primary and backup trunk.

As the IISP maintains no topology data (that is, via the exchange of LSUs), the design of loop-free networks is based on configuration guidelines. Therefore, the protocol does not support dynamic routing between nodes, and relies on the ATM end-systems to recognize when a

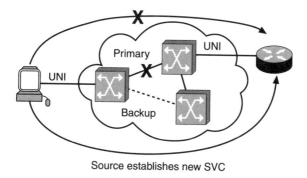

Source establishes new SVC

Figure 3.30 IISP.

trunk has failed and then to initiate a new signaling request as depicted in Figure 3.30. This will probably be due to a higher-layer timeout (that is, a Layer 3 routing protocol). Finally, the interim protocol, containing no QoS capabilities, was designed to support primarily UBR connections, with PNNI Phase 1 required for robust CBR, VBR and ABR support. This protocol, based on asymmetric signaling, also requires the network administrator to configure each end of a link differently (unlike the symmetric signaling used as part of the PNNI). The most important thing to remember about the IISP is that migration from this interim protocol to the PNNI Phase 1, or even interoperability for that matter, is not planned; the PNNI is a totally new protocol.

3.3.3 B-ICI

The **Broadband Inter Carrier Interface** (**B-ICI**) connects ATM networks of two ATM service providers. This connection may be via a transit ATM network or direct. For example, in the United States an ATM network operated by a **Local Exchange Carrier** (**LEC**) may interconnect with a transit network operated by an **Inter-Exchange Carrier** (**IEC**) and then back to a LEC network. Alternatively, two LEC or IEC networks may interconnect. In Europe, the same situation may result where a user connects to a metropolitan ATM network operated by a carrier with no wide-area connectivity. The terminology is different though the concepts remain the same. We depict these different possibilities in Figure 3.31. The B-ICI defines services and signaling between networks operated by different service providers. This includes service-specific (**Frame Relay Service** (**FRS**), **Cell Relay Service** (**CRS**), SMDS/CBDS, and CES) traffic management and performance parameters as well as procedures for managing ATM connections across the B-ICI. The ultimate goal is to provide for end-to-end national and international ATM services. These recommendations include service

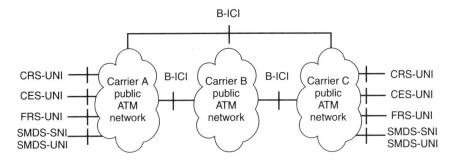

Figure 3.31 B-ICI reference configurations.

CRS	Cell Relay Service	CES	Circuit Emulation Service
FRS	Frame Relay Service	SMDS	Switched Multi-megabit Data Service
UNI	User–Network Interface	SNI	Subscriber Network Interface

definition, signaling, traffic management, operations and maintenance, and accounting.

The physical layer of the B-ICI is based on the ITU NNI with the addition of DS3 and E3, while re-using the ITU-T B-ISUP signaling protocol and the ITU-T MTP Level 3 routing protocol. Remember that the B-ISUP is a call and connection control signaling protocol, while MTP includes signaling message handling and signaling network management functions. Version 1.0 of the B-ICI (ATM Forum, 1993), released in August, 1993, supported PVC-based services and SMDS over multi-carrier networks. This specification includes two sections – common aspects and service aspects. The first section deals with physical and operational aspects, while the second defines methods of supporting FR-ATM interworking, SMDS, CES, and CRS. Efforts at the end of 1994 and into 1995 focused on two parallel paths. The first, Track 1, included enhancements of the PVC-based B-ICI 1.0 to include support of additional physical interfaces, usage metering, and operations. These features are included in the B-ICI 1.1. The second track focused on SVC support, and resulted in the B-ICI 2.0 released in 1995 (ATM Forum, 1995j). This revision of the B-ICI is based on the UNI 3.1 and the B-ISUP Release 1 with CS-2 extensions (described in Section 3.2), and includes support for: SVCs, VBR, congestion management, multipoint connections, symmetric and asymmetric connections, OAM, and ATM end-system addressing (partial support).

We expect future releases of the B-ICI to support the following capabilities:

- Capability to send requests and receive responses from databases;

- Separation of call and connection control to achieve flexibility and re-usability in support of multiparty, multi-connection, and multi-media calls;

- Capability to negotiate the traffic characteristics of an already established connection;

- Support of point-to-multipoint and multipoint-to-multipoint connections;

- Support of multi-party and multi-connection calls, to include connection negotiation, adding and removing parties from a multi-party call, simultaneous or sequential establishment of the call and associated connection(s) for single- and multi-connection calls, call establishment and clearing without bearer connections, support of the **Common Routing Connection Group (CRCG)**, and correlation of connections composing a multi-connection call;

- Support of additional resource capabilities by using look-ahead procedures as an example;

- The ability to establish associations between network elements which are not on the connection path, including separation of call control (edge-to-edge) and bearer control (link-by-link); for example, VPCs providing a particular QoS may only be available for special routes;

- Support services and interwork with intelligent networks and cellular networks.

As with the UNI, the B-ICI uses a protocol reference model containing user, control, and management planes. Briefly reviewing the three, the user plane provides for user information flow, the control plane performs call and connection control functions to include signaling, and the management plane, consisting of layer and plane management, is responsible for coordination between planes and management flows. These three vertical planes interact with the physical, ATM, adaption, and higher layers. Higher-layer functions include signaling in the control plane, network supervision in the management plane, and service-specific functions in the user plane.

Connections across the B-ICI may use either VPCs or VCCs depending upon the switch capabilities and services desired. An area of complexity is the mapping of the various VPCs and VCCs at the UNIs into unique values across the B-ICI for CRS and CES. For Frame Relay, the DLCIs may be carried end-to-end or translated into a VPI/VCI. In the case of SMDS, the L3_PDUs may be encapsulated in **Inter-Carrier Interface Protocol Connectionless Service (ICIP_CLS)** PDUs which we then map into ATM cells. Alternatively, SMDS L2_PDUs may be mapped to specific VPC or VCC values. Three types of SMDS exist across the B-ICI: exchange, exchange access, and inter-exchange. The first refers to end users in the same service area, the second refers to an access service provided by a LEC to an IEC in support of the IEC's inter-exchange service offering, while the third involves users in different exchange serving areas making use of an IEC SMDS offering.

3.4 Addressing

Just as traditional phone sets use E.164 (ISDN) addresses and computer systems use network layer addresses such as IP and IPX, ATM-connected devices will use an ATM layer end-system address in addition to a possible network layer address. While PCs and workstations will almost always include both ATM and network layer addressing, ATM-connected video CODECs often may dispense with the network address. In contrast to data systems, PABXs connected to an ATM switch will only have ATM addresses assigned. This ATM address will differ depending upon whether the end-system is connected to a private or public ATM network, and identifies this single end-system system within the ATM network.

For private networks, the ATM Forum has defined the use of **Network Service Access Point (NSAP)** format addresses for end-systems. Although this address conforms to the NSAP address structure, it is not a true NSAP address in that it does not terminate at the network layer. This NSAP format address may take multiple forms, as described in the next section, and although these addresses need not be globally unique, they should be. In the public domain, addresses are assigned by public service providers from within the globally unique E.164 address space. Within each of these address types, Anycast addresses are identified through the use of special address ranges. This last address type, Anycast, is an unfamiliar concept to some people, and is used by services on the network to advertise their presence. Although we have standardized ATM address formats, this does not preclude the use of non-standardized address schemes within private ATM networks.

Parallel to the definition of the various address types, work has proceeded on developing NSAP address strategies for nations and organizations. Though some confusion exists as to the best scheme, a great deal of progress has been made to date. Finally, questions arise as to the relationship of ATM and network layer addressing within the various ATM data models. We summarize current discussions and alternatives at the end of this section.

3.4.1 ATM End-System (AES): NSAP format

The ATM Forum has defined an AES address for use in private ATM networks based on the OSI NSAP address format. These 20-octet AESs consist of two parts: an **Initial Domain Part (IDP)** consisting of an

Address Format Identifier (AFI) and an **Initial Domain Identifier (IDI)**, and a **Domain-Specific Part (DSP)** encoding both the **High Order DSP (HO-DSP)** and a low-order part consisting of an **End-System Identifier (ESI)** and a **Selector (SEL)** where required. The AFI defines the overall format of the NSAP, and may contain an identifier as to the international organization responsible for the address space. This AFI is two decimal digits in length. The next field is the IDI, with a length and content dependent upon the AFI. The DSP is also based on the AFI, and may contain decimal or binary values. The lengths of the IDI and DSP are summarized in Table 3.15.

Data Country Code (DCC) format addresses, identified by AFI=39, use an IDI corresponding to a particular country (as identified in ISO 3166) and administered by the ISO National Member Body within each country. **International Code Designator (ICD)** format addresses, identified by AFI=47, are allocated by the British Standards Institute, and identify international organizations. For both DCC and ICD formats, a 1-octet field, the **Domain Format Identifier (DFI)**, identifies the address format used by the body responsible for assigning the **Address Authority (AA)** field. In most cases, this AA field contains an organizational identifier. These AAs may structure the remainder of the 10-octet HO-DSP based on divisions, buildings, or switches, to name a few possibilities. The ESI identifies an actual end-system, and must be unique within a particular IDP and HO-DSP. In almost all cases, this ESI will be based upon a globally unique 6-octet IEEE MAC address. Though the final field, SEL, is not used for routing, it may be used by ATM end-systems for multiplexing to identify subinterfaces. Finally, in the case of an encoded E.164 address (AFI=45), the IDI consists of the E.164 number usually corresponding to the public UNI of the private network (Figure 3.32). An organization requiring an NSAP format address will obtain it via the same channels as used to obtain traditional NSAP addresses. In fact, once this address is obtained it may also be used when running CLNP over ATM or even when migrating to IPv6. However, if a CLNP address was previously assigned, the reverse (that is, re-use of the CLNP for ATM) may not necessarily hold true. This has created some confusion when deploying NSAPs. In addition, although some corporations have obtained ICD's, this practice is frowned upon.

Note that, with the release of UNI 3.1, changes have been made to the structure of the higher-order part of the address with the release of

Table 3.15 ATM NSAP formats.

| Initial domain part | | | Domain-specific part | |
AFI (1 octet)	IDI	Length (octets)	(Format)	Length (octets)
39	DCC	2	Binary	17
47	ICD	2	Binary	17
45	E.164	8	Binary	11

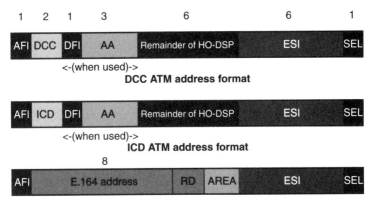

Figure 3.32 Private ATM address formats.

AFI	Address Format Indicator	AA	Address Authority
DCC	Data Country Code	RD	Routing Domain
ICD	International Code Designator	ESI	End-System Identifier
DFI	Domain Format Identifier	SEL	Selector

the UNI 3.1. Whereas UNI 3.0 specifies DFI, AA, RSRVD, RD, and AREA fields, UNI 3.1 does away with these distinctions and groups them together into the HO-DSP. However, the DFI and AA fields still have meaning if the NSAP address has been assigned by a central authority.

Questions also sometimes arise on how best to map existing network layer (IPv4 and IPv6) addresses into the NSAP structure. One advantage of an algorithmic mapping would be to preclude the requirement for an ATMARP. Dwight (1995) and Carpenter (1995) describe methods by which this may be accomplished. For this address format, the ICD would contain a value delegated to the IANA, and the four-octet IPv4 address would then be mapped into the four high-order octets of the HO-DSP. The remaining six octets would not be used. The remaining NSAP octets would contain the ESI and SEL. Laubach (1995) outlines an implementation method whereby an ATMARP server is aware of all IPv4 addresses which it services. If the target protocol address was within the appropriate range, the ATMARP server would automatically map the IPv4 address into an NSAP address. This mechanism differs from the proposal above, in that the IPv4 address would first be mapped into the 16-octet IPv6 address. The three high-order octets, however, remain as above. We depict this mapping in Table 3.16.

Table 3.16 Algorithmic mapping of IPv4 addresses into ATM NSAP addresses.

Octet	0	1	2	3 through 14	15	16	17	18	19
Description	AFI	ICD		Unused		IPv4 Address			SEL
Value	47	00	90	00	Octet 0	Octet 1	Octet 2	Octet 3	00

Table 3.17 E.164 format address.

U, M	Country Code			Area, City, Exchange, End-System											
1	2	3	4	5	6	7	8	9	10	11	12	13	14	15	16

3.4.2 E.164

In contrast to the multiple NSAP formats, only one E.164 address structure exists, based on the global ISDN numbering plan. When connecting a private ATM domain to a public network, only the UNIs connected directly to the public network will be assigned E.164 addresses. This is due both to management considerations, where a large corporation will want to have addresses from a single address space, as well as to the scarcity of public addresses. The E.164 address comprises 16 digits formed from 8 octets (Table 3.17). The highest order 4 bits designate the address as unicast or multicast, while the next 1 to 3 digits identify the country code. The remainder of the E.164 address is nationally assigned, containing in most cases a city or area code, an exchange code, and an end-system identifier. Referring once again to the NSAP form at addresses, one option encapsulates E.164 addresses into the NSAP structure.

3.4.3 Broadcast

An end-system wishing to send a packet, frame, or cell to all other end-systems within a network 'broadcasts' this data. This broadcasting is no problem over a shared media such as Ethernet or Token Ring. At the data link layer, an end-system will send the frame to a broadcast MAC address; it will be received by all stations on the LAN segment. Over a wide-area network such as X.25 or Frame Relay, an end-system wishing to broadcast a packet must replicate the packet over every virtual circuit. In this case, a circuit may be defined as 'broadcast capable' even though no data link broadcast address is in use. This is due to the lack of broadcast capabilities within the two WAN technologies. ATM's capabilities are actually in the middle of these two extremes. Although ATM is not inherently broadcast-capable, ATM switches are capable of establishing point-to-multipoint connections. Therefore, an ATM-connected end-system such as a router, PC, or workstation, capable of signaling a multipoint connection, will be capable of somewhat efficiently emulating a broadcast capability across the ATM backbone. This in fact is the mechanism used by the **Broadcast and Unknown Server (BUS)** within the ATM Forum LAN emulation standard. LAN emulation clients will send all broadcast and unknown packets to this BUS which will then be responsible for signaling a multipoint connection through the switch. Alternatively, under the Classical model we may use the MARS with or without an MCS for broadcasting. Though a broadcast MAC address triggers the sending of the packet to the BUS, and its replication to all end-systems via the switch, no broadcast format ATM address is in use. In fact, a multipoint connection starts out as a point-to-point connection with additional end-systems added one-by-one via the UNI signaling protocol. Alternatively, end-systems incapable of multipoint signaling may send broadcast packets across every VCC.

3.4.4 Multicast

Just as broadcasting involves sending the data to all end-systems connected to a network, multicasting is the act of sending the packet, frame, or cell to only a subset of the end-systems. This is very useful when a system wishes to advertise a service or transmit data to a group of systems on a network. Thus, in many cases multicast addressing is also known as group addressing (that is, E.164 group addresses), though this terminology is not always correct. Many network layer protocols such as IPX and DECnet in fact use data link layer multicasting for the advertisement of essential services. The mapping of Layer 3 multicasting such as PIM into ATM layer multicasting is almost simpler in that this mapping may be assisted via a multicast-address capable ATMARP server. This scenario will be covered in greater detail as part of the discussion on ATM multicasting alternatives. Although multicast format NSAP addresses are still being defined, and may reach standardization at the same time as mpt-mpt signaling, there are current methods of supporting multicasting across ATM based on MARS/ MCS architectures, described later. If we look at LAN emulation, the BUS, also responsible for multicasting, functions by establishing a pt-mpt VCC.

3.4.5 Anycasting

Signaling 4.0 defines a new ATM service known as Anycasting, based on group addressing. A group address is a well-known identifier which may be shared by multiple end-systems which belong to this group, and is used to identify a particular service across the ATM network. Consider address resolution, directory, and video servers deployed as part of a complete ATM service. For ATM-connected end-systems to take advantage of these servers, they must have an efficient way of identifying where on an ATM network these resources reside: thus the concept of ATM groups, a set of ATM end-systems sharing a common objective. This is no different than emergency phone numbers within the phone system or Novell Get-Nearest-Server requests. When a pt-pt call is made to a group address, it will be routed to the nearest end-system which has registered the associated service. If required, it may be routed to multiple group members via a pt-mpt call request. Operation is as follows. Nodes will use an extension of the ILMI to inform the network that they support a specific group address and how widely this information should be distributed. The network will map this scope into the ATM routing hierarchy. A node requesting a connection to this group address may establish a point-to-multipoint connection to all nodes which have registered. If a requesting node only specifies a point-to-point connection, it will be routed to the nearest registered node. The source will also specify one of a number of scopes for the connection request, capable of spanning anywhere from a local area to the globe.

Within the NSAP structure, a group address has the same format as a standard ATM address with one exception. The ISO has paired each individual address AFI with an equivalent group address. Examples for the three AFIs defined by the ATM Forum are given in Table 3.18.

As part of group addressing, a 'well-known' address will be used to identify an ATM group associated with a well-known service. For example, the ATM Forum's prefix is 0xC50079. Within this prefix, LAN emulation configuration servers and MPOA servers could all be assigned well-known addresses.

Group addressing relies on the concept of membership scope which specifies the routing hierarchy in which one's membership will be known, and applies to both an end-system making use of a resource as well as the system advertising the service. This scope should be specified during the ILMI registration procedure. The end effect is that calls made to a given group address by ATM end-systems within this routing range will reach the member, while those made by a system outside of the range will not. This range is based on an indirect mapping between a user's membership scope and the actual routing hierarchy. Levels of this hierarchy include: local (that is, segment), site (no inter-building or WAN links), intra-site (local location), organization, community, regional, and global. These levels closely approximate the levels of hierarchy typically found in an organization.

Table 3.18 Example AFIs.

AFI	Individual	Group
DCC	39	BD
ICD	47	C5
E.164	45	C3

3.4.6 Addressing plans

Probably the area of greatest debate is just how end users, large corporations, and national networks should implement NSAP addressing. This is a country-by-country decision which will have a major impact on the end user. Though some organizations have had some experience in the deployment of NSAP addressing, most notably through CLNS efforts, this experience is not universal, much needs to be changed and, in the United States, implementors are basically starting again from the beginning, despite GOSIP efforts. Within Europe, some countries, via public service providers and/or through national academic networks, have approached the creation of a logical NSAP addressing structure very effectively. Other countries have just begun their efforts.

Looking at the United States, an ATM Forum contribution (Wetzel, 1995) actually outlines some of the concerns and solutions in obtaining and implementing an address structure. Referring back to the DCC NSAP format, an organization will be identified via its official organization name. This is maintained by the ISO national body, in this case ANSI, and is actually identified under the ASN.1 tree: (joint-iso-ccitt(2) country(16) USA(840) organization(1)). Thus, a complete 'US' NSAP format address will then contain the following fields: AFI=39, IDI=840, DFI=128, and a three-octet organizational name. The **Domain Format Identifier (DFI)**, also assigned by ANSI, is always equal to 128. The remainder of the address contains the remainder of the HO-DSP (6 octets), the ESI, and the SEL. Note that this implies that organizations have only 6 octets for defining their PNNI hierarchy (assuming the use of hardware-based ESIs over which the network administrator will have no control). The actual procedure for obtaining the organizational name is described in Appendix C.

In the UK, in 1995, UKERNA, the organization overseeing the UK academic/research network, looked at addressing issues relating to the UK academic network, SuperJANET, and to ATM NSAP addressing applying to Europe as a whole (Howat, 1995). A major concern among those beginning to implement NSAP addressing concerned the perceived need to re-address at some point in the future if the original plan was not correctly chosen. The most fundamental conclusion was that a flat addressing scheme divorced from geography was not acceptable for the future. Some national networks (for example, Funet and SURFnet) have created address structures based upon either the ICD or DCC whereby the national network is divided into domains based on geography and organization. The SURFnet scheme is interesting in that it is unified for both CLNS and ATM; the two systems are identified via a SURFnet Format Identifier within the NSAP structure. Within UKERNA, a scheme based on the UK DCC (826) in combination with a provider code identifying the academic community has been proposed. The remainder of the HO-DSP would consist of a site and local identifier consisting of a zone, JANET site code, and a field for local use. Concerns surrounding the use of a unique provider code instead of that of a possible service provider are unanswered as of yet.

A recommendation for use by Audio visual Multimedia Services (AMS) implementations was one of the first to suggest the use of E.164-format NSAP addresses. This would provide the hierarchy required while overcoming the supply shortage for traditional E.164 addresses.

Probably the most important aspect of any chosen ATM addressing scheme will be its scalability and ease of aggregation. The proper functioning of the PNNI will require both of these points. In addition, the scheme should be easy to manage, facilitate interoperation between public and private ATM domains, and uniquely identify an ATM endpoint. One problem with many schemes is the possibility of sub-optimal routing or aggregation at the level above the organization or network. For example, two organizations located in the same city may be assigned totally different codes, preventing this level of address aggregation based on topology. Although an organization may initially be homed to a single ATM service provider, at some point in the future it may wish to switch providers. The unique organization code is one element of the NSAP structure which may not be shifted, and may present the problem outlined above. Countering this argument is the observation that a single organization may have multiple points of entry into the ATM network, and therefore does not wish to be locked into a single location. This limitation is partially solved by the E.164 NSAP format from the standpoint of the network, though some of the same problems which currently exist with large corporations reachable via multiple points on the phone network are left open. This could almost require the deployment of an 800-format number or routing internally from a single point of entry. One observation is that an organizationally-based address structure may not be optimal, leading to the deployment of provider-based prefixes. On a global scale, current ICD and DCC assignment practises may present real problems when peering. Where ICDs have been assigned by vendors, these should be used only as an interim solution until a user obtains an address within a DCC or under a service provider's address space.

As users will have little influence over the assignment of public addresses, which conform to the international ISDN numbering plan (<country<>city/region><exchange><subscriber>), the remainder of this section will consider ways of deploying the NSAP address and any guidelines which should be adhered to. Organizations beginning to deploy ATM on a wide basis are faced with the proper selection of an NSAP addressing structure. A proper one-time selection will eliminate the requirement to re-address at some point in the future (although views are mixed as to the complexity of readdressing within ATM due to autoconfiguration). Many European countries have an advantage in this

Table 3.19 NSAP addressing example: ICD format.

AFI	47 (ICD)	1 octet
IDI	0023 (NORDUnet)	2 octets
Version	00	1 octet
Network	000003 (Finland, Funet)	3 octets
Tele traffic area	xx	1 octet
Funet member identifier	xxxx	2 octets
Member access point	xx	1 octet
Area	xx	1 octet
Switch	xx	1 octet
MAC-address	xxxxxxxxxxxx	6 octets
N selector	xx	1 octet

regard, as they have deployed large CLNS networks based on NSAP addressing. Two examples are included below, the first based on the ICD and the second on the DCC. Funet, Finland's academic research network, has defined the fields shown in Table 3.19.

We now look at a corporate addressing structure, in this case using the DCC format. In the UK, the British Standards Institute administers the **UK Domain Part (UKDP)** based on procedures outlined in BS 7306 (British Standards Institution, 1995). Using AFI=39 as an example, we code the NSAP address with a maximum of 20 hexidecimal octets. Note that the standard also includes support for AFI=38 which uses a maximum of 40 decimal digits. Within AFI=39, the BSI will assign the UKDP, consisting of a **UK Format Identifier (UKFI)** and a **UK Domain Identifier (UKDI)**, with the remainder of the address known as the **UK Domain-Specific Part (UKDSP)**. The length of the UKDI will depend upon the size of the corporation as shown in Table 3.20.

Using a large corporation as an example (see Table 3.21), we assign UKFI=1 and UKDI=101. Thus, the complete NSAP address prefix (AFI+DCC+UKFI+UKDI) is: 39.826F.1101. The 'F' is the UK country code of 826 padded with '1111' to end on an octet boundary.

Here, we create the PNNI hierarchy (described later), first by assigning a unique network number and then by assigning switches 1000.0000.00 and 2000.0000.00 at the root of the tree. Switches at each

Table 3.20 UK NSAP structure.

UKFI	UKDI	Maximum UKDSP
1 (large corporation)	/aaa (Note 1)	15 octets
2 (medium corporation)	/aaaaa	14 octets
3 (small corporation)	/aaaaaaa	13 octets

Note 1 / denotes hexidecimal digits

Table 3.21 NSAP addressing example: DDC format.

AFI	39 (DCC)	1 octet
IDI	826F (UK)	2 octets
DFI/AA	1	1 nibble
UKDI (corporation)/AA	101	1 octet + 1 nibble
User group /AA	560	1 octet + 1 nibble
Network	150	1 octet + 1 nibble
Switch	xxxx xxxx xx	5 octets
MAC address	xxxx xxxx xxxx	6 octets
Selector	xx	1 octet

lower layer of the hierarchy, aligned on nibble boundaries, are then designated as 1100.0000.00, 1110.0000.00, and so on. A typical end-system address is then:39.826F.1101.560.150.1111.0000.00.0000.0C 13.8E2F.00.

3.4.7 Mapping E.164 to NSAP

In interworking between public and private ATM domains, each based on different address structures, four scenarios have been defined (Cole *et al*, 1996): private host to private host with and without intervening public networks, private host to public host, and public host to public host. The first possibility is the easiest to implement, in that the ARP must return only an NSAP formatted address. In the case of an intervening public network, the connection request from one host to another will transit one or more public networks. In this case, a routing decision must be made at this time as to which egress point from the public network must be used. This egress will be in the form of an E.164 address. Under this scenario, the ARP will return the NSAP address of the ultimate destination, then map into an E.164 address at the ingress to the public network. The third possibility, that of connecting a private host to a public host, is probably the most complex of all due to the need to provide for address resolution in both directions. Between the public and private nodes, the public node must resolve the NSAP format address of the private node, and with it the E.164 address of the best egress point from the network. Whether the ARP should return this E.164 address is a subject of some debate. In the opposite direction, the private network node will resolve the E.164 address of the public node. This address will be formatted as an NSAP making use of the E.164 private ATM address format, with RD, AREA, and ESI set to zero. Conversion between this NSAP format address and the native E.164 address will be trivial. The last scenario is also quite simple, in that all signaling requests will use native E.164 addresses.

3.4.8 Integrated ATM and network addressing

Separate from discussions on how best to interwork between different ATM address structures are efforts focused on how to best optimize routing across an ATM network. Unlike the current overlay model, where ATM layer addressing is decoupled from the network layer addressing, an integrated model may use the same NSAP format addressing for both layers.

3.5 Traffic management

Just as signaling and addressing are essential elements of a network architecture, so is an ability to control the amount of traffic entering the network with a view to maximizing efficiency and minimizing data loss. Although one may expect users to be 'good network citizens' and limit their traffic into the network, the network itself must have some way to control this traffic during times of heavy utilization. An analogy to this is the phone system: during times of heavy loading, the network may be incapable of completing a long-distance call if capacity does not exist. This in fact occurs quite rarely (for instance, on some of the more popular holidays) unless a network outage has occurred. The same applies within existing data networks, with some (X.25) relying on link-by-link flow control while others (Frame Relay) rely on the flow control provided by end-systems. ATM presents some interesting problems for upper-layer traffic due to its use of fixed length cells. As will be seen below, the effect of cell loss on throughput within an ATM network may be drastic. Therefore, an efficient and standardized mechanism must be implemented which will allow an ATM network to provide an acceptable QoS to all users under times of heavy loading.

A congestion avoidance system must guarantee both fairness and stability. In the absence of traffic management, the only method of ensuring that congestion does not get out of control is by dedicating bandwidth to each VCC. This would apply even to bursty sources, and in effect transforms ATM into nothing more than a TDM network. A critical element of ensuring the two properties above is providing the necessary buffering throughout the network. This relates to the amount of traffic in flow due to propagation delays. These concepts are all covered in the following sections.

For clarification, we may look at the whole continuum of congestion avoidance in terms of time. This process begins with proper network planning (that is, capacity planning and topology design), leading into network management. On a shorter timescale, control is based on **Connection Admission Control (CAC)**, call routing, and network resource allocation. Shorter still, once a connection is established, both end-to-end transport layer flow control, ATM layer congestion control, as

well as end-to-end and link-by-link ATM layer flow control are important. Though work within the ATM Forum concentrates on this latter
concern, focusing on explicit control, there is an awareness of the potential effects of ATM layer flow control on higher-layer protocols and
whether this ATM layer control is even necessary. This may be especially true for protocols such as TCP which cannot make full use of lower-
layer flow control indications, but which do include their own implicit
control mechanisms. An in-depth discussion of flow control should begin
with a look at the operation of TCP over high-speed networks, including
implementation experience. This will lead us into a description of the
various methods of flow control across ATM, finishing with the mechanisms chosen to be the ATM Forum standard along with a mention of
other voices within the networking industry.

3.5.1 Throughput

In contrast to the bandwidth of a physical link, throughput is the actual
rate at which data may be transmitted across this link. The throughput
is limited by the end-system protocols, buffering within end-systems and
intermediate systems, delay, and data loss across the link. This last
concern leads into data loss avoidance via flow control, discussed in the
next section. Assume that flow control is operating correctly and therefore no data is lost within the network itself. Performance is then limited
by the first two factors outlined above. When analyzing throughput,
discussion centers on TCP, the most common transport protocol. For a
relatively old protocol, TCP has held up remarkably well in the face of
bandwidths and requirements unanticipated at the time of its inception.
The goal of much research has been to increase the capabilities of TCP,
and to allow it to take advantage of the higher bandwidths available
under the new high-speed technologies of which ATM is only one. Since
the research outlined below relates to the performance of TCP over any
wide-area high-speed medium, lessons learned concerning window sizes
and buffer requirements are universal.

3.5.2 Theory and TCP

Multiple considerations drive the expected performance of a network in
the local and wide area. These include bandwidth, delay, a bandwidth-
delay product incorporating the two and very relevant in discussing wide
area connections, and the link utilization. Within the ATM environment,
an interesting consideration is the wide range of bandwidths deployed.
In contrast to LAN technologies where a bandwidth is associated with a
given technology, and in contrast to X.25 and Frame Relay where the
variation in line rate is two orders of magnitude at most (19 Kbps to 2
Mbps for X.25), ATM physical interfaces will normally be deployed at 2
Mbps to 155 Mbps, but will also exist at sub-rates of 2 Mbps ($n \times 64$k) and

at 622 Mbps and above in the future. This 3–4 order of magnitude difference has major implications on buffering and flow control. The second major concern is delay. This delay is the amount of time which a cell will take to traverse the network, and is a function of three factors. Delay due to distance will be minimal in the local area, but between cities and across oceans will be quite substantial due to the ultimate limiting factor in data transmission – the speed of light. In fact, the actual transmission speed will actually be less than this due to the physical limitations of the copper and fiber transmission media. Delay due to transmission is a function of the speed of the physical link and the length of the data packet or cell transmitted. For example, at a given data rate, a 53-byte cell will require a finite amount of time to transmit onto a connection. The last type of delay is that caused by the switching system itself. Once a cell has completely entered the switch, it will require a certain number of copy and queue operations. This delay is referred to as **cell times**, and may be minimized in a well-designed matrix but may be substantial in the face of extensive queues. To relate delay to actual implementations, two examples may be cited. For WAN traffic, and CBR in particular, the distance element will play the major part, while with ABR-based LAN traffic, queuing delay may predominate.

Though both bandwidth and delay influence network performance, consideration of a combination of the two – the **Delay Bandwidth Product** – is more critical in network design. This product will determine the number of bits in transit between a sender and receiver at any instant in time, and directly relates to the amount of interface buffering required. For example, the product may be quite minimal in the local area and at low data rates – 0.025 bytes will be in transit over a 1 km 64 Kbps connection. In contrast, 1.3 Mbytes will transit a continental (5000 km) OC-12 (622 Mbps) connection. Though 1.3 Mbytes may not sound excessive based on current memory prices, the peak bandwidth assigned to a group of ABR VCs will usually far exceed the physical interface speed. If many VCCs converge on a single outgoing interface, the memory requirements will prove excessive.

Recently, the performance of the most commonly used transport protocol, TCP, has been more deeply analyzed in its performance over high-bandwidth, long-delay links. As described above, the delay bandwidth (RTT*BW) product is a measure of the number of bits in transit between a sender and receiver. When data is lost due to network congestion, the sender will be unable to react to this data loss until RTT*BW bits have been transmitted. Though most studies to date have concentrated on the behavior of TCP over long-distance leased lines, the results are directly applicable to routers or workstations at the ingress of the ATM network.

TCP has not remained static in the face of new technologies; it has evolved since its original release in 1980 (see Postel, 1981). A fundamental change in the behavior of TCP resulted from the introduction of van

Jacobson's slow start and congestion avoidance algorithms in 1988 (see Braden and Jacobson, 1988). Slow start provides for an initial exponential growth in TCP window size. Once packet loss occurs, the window size will be halved and then only gradually increased. If timeout occurs, TCP repeats slow start, this time with a window size of one. The related fast retransmit and fast recovery algorithms control the detection of loss and then the retransmission of packets. In situations where single packets are dropped, close to the full bandwidth will be utilized and retransmits will be minimized. If fast retransmit does not detect a packet drop, the TCP timeout described above will very much reduce TCP's performance due to slow start. Additional changes to the operation of the TCP/IP stack included implementation of MTU discovery (see Mogul and Deering, 1990) which allows hosts to exceed the 512 byte MTU coded in most early TCP/IP implementations. Use of MTU discovery eliminates the chance of fragmentation while maximizing performance due to larger segment sizes. Changes to TCP described in Borman *et al* (1992) were the first to address the performance of the protocol over high-speed connections, for example, those connecting remote supercomputers. These included a provision for larger window sizes as well as fast transmit and recovery. When implementing RFC 1323 (Borman *et al*, 1992), hosts are no longer limited to a 64 Kbyte window size. This is most apparent when comparing performance over a 70 msec delay transcontinental link, where a 64 Kbyte window limits throughput to 7.3 Mbps. Windows exceeding this 64 Kbyte limitation may more closely model the $D*BW$ product for long links, and thus will be capable of making effective use of link bandwidth. Complications result from multiple TCP flows sharing the same link and whether a queue set for a long delay link is also applicable to shorter distances.

Practice will show that the $RTT*BW$ of each TCP flow, and thus the queuing required, is equal to the round trip time multiplied by the session's share of the physical bandwidth. Thus, the total queue may equal the $RTT*BW$ of the link. A critical point here is that the individual flows must remain unsynchronized, in that their predicated peaks will occur at different times. A factor causing synchronization is packet loss, resulting in the simultaneous queuing of bursts. A method of reducing this synchronization is through the implementation of the **Random Early Detection (RED)** algorithm. RED limits queue utilization, and thus prevents synchronization, by introducing feedback which will result in controlled packet drops. In an actual network environment, the introduction of RED resulted in marked improvement in performance under load. In an environment where buffer sizes may not correspond to the TCP window size, RED will avoid throughput collapse on shorter delay paths (20 ms) when the TCP window exceeds the output buffers on a router or workstation. On longer delay paths (68 ms), RED avoids suboptimal performance with buffer sizes less than $RTT*BW$. Collapse under RED will therefore only occur when the TCP window is much greater than both the RTT*BW and the queue size. An easy way to avoid this will be to ensure that the queue size exceeds the RTT*BW product.

These results point out the need for careful control of the TCP window size in the face of high-speed wide-area links. But there is a flip side of the problem in that a window set for optimal wide-area perfor-. mance may result in less than optimal local-area performance. This common problem is mostly eliminated with RED. A second side effect of the algorithm is avoiding TCP's tendency to favor flows with lower round-trip times in the face of congestion. Though the tests described above were conducted with the FDDI MTU, results may be extrapolated to smaller packet sizes with more serious implications. This is due to buffer utilization in the face of small packets which often require a full MTU buffer. Relating this to ATM, if buffers are set to the MTU of 9180 the situation will be exacerbated.

These results are applicable to the design of ATM networks in that though sufficient queuing at the ingress to the ATM network will improve throughput under load, additional optimizations will be required to guarantee throughput under load while allowing flexibility in setting the TCP window size. An analogy may be drawn between setting a too large window size and the implementation of buffers in excess of RTT*BW at the ingress to the ATM network. Both interfere with the proper operation of the windowing and retransmission algorithms within TCP, and in the absence of algorithms such as RED may result in ATM congestion collapse. (See Villamizar and Song, 1994.)

A final characteristic relates to link utilization. If an interswitch trunk experiences 90% loading, some congestion control techniques and design rules will cease to function correctly. This is analogous to the situation with other technologies, where performance degrades non-linearly with utilization. Queuing requirements are just one factor, in that queues will begin to fill when a link becomes congested, directly influencing delay.

Effect of cell loss

Theory is fine, but a more realistic idea of the impact of the bandwidth delay product on network performance may be gleaned by analyzing TCP throughput and relating this throughput to expected loss rates. For TCP, throughput will degrade based on the formula $1/(1+2PW)$ where P is the loss probability and W is the bandwidth-delay product. As packets are lost, TCP's window size will decrease and throughput will recover slowly based on the slow start algorithm. Note that retransmission of buffered data will only occur after the round trip timeout at a minimum. As an example, a 155 Mbps LAN (1 km outer diameter) experiencing a 0.1% loss will still pass upwards of 99% rated TCP throughput. In contrast, a wide-area (20 ms delay and above) 622 Mbps link experiencing an even lower loss probability – 0.001% – will suffer a 35% throughput degradation.

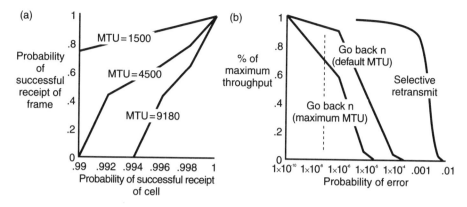

Figure 3.33 Probability of success. (a) Probability of successful receipt of frame/cell. (b) Percentage of maximum throughput/probability of error. Source: DEC, ATM Forum.

This degradation may be further exacerbated in the ATM environment since the loss of a single ATM cell implies loss of the entire higher-layer data frame. Some research into the effect of cell loss on throughput was conducted by Dunbeck (1993) showing the requirement for strict control over end-to-end cell loss. For example, a 9180-byte IP packet will be segmented into 192 ATM cells (48 bytes of data per cell). The loss of a single cell requires the retransmission of all 192. Percentage-wise, the loss of one percent requires retransmission of more than 75% of the packets. This effect is summarized in Figure 3.33(a).

As part of the work on wireless ATM, additional investigations have taken place comparing throughput at various error rates in the presence of different retransmission mechanisms. Looking at Figure 3.33(b), the throughput at the default MTU (192 cells) drops significantly at an error rate above 1×10^{-6} if the entire MTU must be retransmitted upon cell loss. Needless to say, results are even worse at the maximum MTU of 1366 cells. However, if we implement selective retransmission whereby only lost cells are re-sent, the throughput improves considerably in the presence of even very noisy links. The overhead with such a system is a one-byte sequence number and two-byte CRC, inserted after segmentation and removed before reassembly (Dellaverson, 1995). Over wireless links, where error rates of 1×10^{-2} occur, and possibly other connections where a low BER cannot be guaranteed, this is an acceptable overhead. Looking back to an earlier discussion of forward error correction, the amount of overhead required to be able to recreate lost cells, under an FEC scheme, would be prohibitive at this loss rate.

The situation is exacerbated by the retransmission of these corrupted packets. This effect is called throughput collapse, as most of

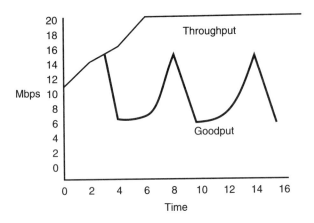

Figure 3.34 Congestive collapse. Source: Dunbeck (1993)

the new packets will be discarded. The phenomenon is most obvious when throughput is analyzed over time, as depicted in Figure 3.34.

Since the loss of a single cell will corrupt an entire upper-layer data frame, there should be some way to intelligently discard cells within a frame. Many current ATM deployments do not take this fact into account, and drop cells at random. A solution to this, suggested by Sun, and known as **early packet drop**, inspects the ATM cell headers and will drop all remaining cells from a data frame. This has important implications in that useless data is no longer propagated across the ATM network. The technique, now known as **Early Packet Discard (EPD)**, has been accepted by many of the ATM switch vendors for AAL5 traffic and is part of Signaling 4.0. Interfaces on the ATM switches track the AAL5 cell header for the PT, indicating the end of a higher-layer packet. If a cell must be discarded, the switch will proceed to discard all remaining cells until it reaches the cell with the PTI set. As will be seen later, some larger ATM switches with frame-based interfaces (for example, Frame Relay or FDDI) will also implement this mechanism, feeding back cell-side notifications to the frame side of the line interface.

As another example, throughput within NFS may suffer excessively if even a single cell is lost. This is due to both the standard NFS datagram size of 8 Kbytes and the lack of a windowing mechanism in UDP. If the aggregate traffic from multiple sources exceeds the bandwidth of an outgoing connection at a given instant, it must be buffered or lost. In a typical LAN switching environment, upwards of 50 workstations may be accessing a single ATM-connected NFS server. In this case, if all cells must be buffered for each session, the ATM switch must be capable of buffering 50 * 170 (cells per UDP datagram) or 8500 cells on the one interface. These non-ATM optimized protocols thus will have a major impact on switch buffer design. However, note that the 180 Kbyte buffer is still an order of magnitude lower than the buffer requirements described above for high-speed wide-area connections.

Practical experience

In testing conducted over commercial ATM networks during Fall 1994, some of the performance degradation problems with TCP alluded to above were verified in live networks. The configurations in question included speed mismatches between 100 Mbps local-area ATM and a 45 Mbps ATM WAN at the local-area to wide-area border switches, along with small buffers in these switches. This latter point is critical, in that switches equipped with a 256 cell buffer (not uncommon at the time), interconnected over a 40 ms delay W-ATM service, would only be capable of buffering two TCP segments during a burst condition from the local to wide area. Assuming 9180 byte segments, the ultimate bandwidth over the link would be limited to 3.7 Mbps. Bandwidth degradation to this extent was not uncommon.

Assuming that we provide adequate buffering in the switches, or that the bandwidth available to local- and wide-area links is about equal, performance of TCP will depend on the end-system implementation. Vendors that have already implemented RFC 1323 include SGI, DEC OSF, IBM AIX, SunOS, Solaris, and Cray. Note that the large window sizes still do not allow TCP to effectively utilize the entire bandwidth available over a wide-area link. For example, TCP will only support 5.9 Mbps per session over a New York to Los Angeles link at the default RFC-1323 settings. As an aside, even at this limited bandwidth one can predict just how quickly the currently planned Internet backbone links will be saturated. Instead of the hundreds of individual TCP sessions currently sharing a physical link, even at the default window size an OC3 link will only support 150 cross-country or 15–40 local sessions.

The above effects may be divided into three problem areas:

1. The ability of a large MTU to exceed switch buffers unless all links are equal and uncongested,

2. TCP's tendency to probe past available bandwidth, resulting in cell drop and triggering slow-start unless a complete window is buffered at the switch,

3. The inability of switches to drop all cells in an AAL5 frame if a single cell has been discarded.

Ultimately, the answer to the TCP throughput and loss problem is not too difficult. Remember that TCP will allow for outstanding data up to its window size, a value derived from the feedback loop equal to RTT*BW which determines how long the source will take to receive acknowledgment that the data has been received by the destination.

Over an end-to-end TCP connection, all systems must be provided with buffering at least equal to this value since the source may send up to this amount – data which may potentially be held at any point of congestion along the path. This requirement does not only apply to ATM switches at potential points of congestion along the path, but to all intermediate systems. Router and ATM networks are the same in this respect, although, as we have seen earlier, cell loss within an ATM network is many times worse than packet loss within a datagram network. Note that this requirement also infers that the TCP end-systems also have buffers equal to the BW*RTT. The third concern is addressed by switches which implement packet discard.

3.5.3 ATM Forum traffic management

Why the focus in the ATM Forum on traffic management? If all applications operated at a constant data rate, traffic flows across a network would be quite predictable and network design would be an easier task. Unfortunately (or fortunately, as the case may be), the vast majority of data, video, and even voice traffic is quite bursty, with wide ranges between traffic peaks and valleys. Admittedly, this burstiness is to the advantage of users and not network service providers at first glance, since the latter group must take this into account when sizing network resources. However, it does lead to efficiencies in terms of statistical multiplexing if the network is properly designed. In a landmark paper, Leland *et al* (1993) point out that the length of a burst is unpredictable; it may be short or long in duration: 'There is no natural length of a burst ... at every timescale from a few milliseconds to minutes and hours, similar looking traffic bursts are evident.' In addition, aggregation has no effect, in that bursts will still appear, and often intensify: '... aggregating streams of such traffic typically intensifies the self-similarity (burstiness) instead of smoothing it.' The goal of an ATM network planner is therefore to design a network to effectively handle these bursts, while maintaining a low probability of data loss. This loss is expressed as a **Cell Loss Ratio (CLR)**, where 1 in 10^9 will equate to leased lines and 1 in 10^5 may be acceptable for some data traffic. The former CLR should be the design goal for ATM networks.

Traffic management includes those functions designed to prevent and control congestion across an ATM network, required if user applications and services are to receive their required QoS. Building upon the previous paragraph, two sources of congestion include unpredictable fluctuations in traffic flows or faults within the network. Within ATM, we divide traffic management into two domains: traffic control, those actions taken by the network to avoid congestion from ever occurring, and congestion control, action taken to minimize the intensity, spread, and/or duration of a congestion condition.

Although we describe these two forms of traffic management in greater detail a bit later, we introduce them here. During the signaling phase, an ATM network will implement **Connection Admission Control (CAC)** as well as **PNNI's Generic CAC (GCAC)** to determine whether it should accept or reject a connection. Once a connection is established, the network implements feedback between the switches and traffic sources based on changing traffic conditions. This connection is also subject to **Usage Parameter Control (UPC)**, the network policing function which insures that the traffic generated by an ATM source is in conformance with its **traffic contract. Network Parameter Control (NPC)**, is included within UPC. Both the CAC and UPC rely on the Generic Cell Rate Algorithm (GCRA) as defined in I.371 to judge whether or not traffic is conformant. Two forms of the GCRA exist: virtual scheduling and the leaky bucket, with the latter algorithm providing the basis for most switch-based policing mechanisms. Later, we describe the much understood 'dual leaky bucket'. **Priority control** makes use of the CLP bit in allowing users to mark cells subject to discard and the network to discard these cells under times of congestion. An end-system will implement **traffic shaping**, while **Network Resource Management (NRM)** involves those actions taken by a central management system to allocate network resources. Finally, **frame discard** is quite useful as frames made corrupt by the discarding of one or more cells should have all remaining cell discarded (Sathaye, 1995).

Though congestion avoidance theory will help in the understanding of how the network functions under loading, a more important task is to associate a given application profile with an ATM service class by looking at the application's QoS requirements. As a baseline, we may group applications by whether they are conversational, messaging, distribution or retrieval. Within each of these groupings we find video, voice, imaging and data (Table 3.22).

Conversational or interactive applications imply that there are users on each end of the connection. Messaging implies user-to-machine communication, while retrieval is the opposite. Finally, a machine transmitting to multiple users or machines will use a distribution application. The last group of applications are strictly machine-to-machine. One application not included in the above list though very important to the successful functioning of the ATM network is signaling, which may be provided with a QoS equal to that of a remote procedure call or distributed file service.

A given application will adhere to a specific traffic profile and fall into two categories: elastic and real-time. Elastic applications, though adapting to changes in bandwidth, may still be sensitive to delay if interactive. This category also includes traffic insensitive to delay, such as bulk data transfer, which is no different from best-effort delivery (such as that over the Internet). Interactive applications also fall into this category, though they are more sensitive to delay. Recently, fractal modeling

Table 3.22 Application types.

Application type	Example
Interactive video	Videoconferencing
Interactive audio	Telephone
Interactive text	Banking transaction; credit card verification
Interactive image	Multimedia conferencing
Video messaging	Multimedia E-mail
Audio messaging	Voice mail
Text/data messaging	E-mail, telex, fax
Image messaging	
Video distribution	Television, distributed classrooms
Audio distribution	Radio, audio feed
Text distribution	News feed
Image distribution	Weather satellite pictures
Video retrieval	Video on Demand (VoD)
Audio retrieval	Audio library
Text/data retrieval	File transfer
Image retrieval	Library browsing
Aggregate LAN	LAN interconnection or emulation
Remote terminal	Telecommuting, Telnet
Remote procedure call	
Distributed file service	
Computer process swap	

has been shown to describe this traffic profile (see also the discussion on congestion control). Care must be taken in network planning to predict the interactions between the various types of elastic traffic. For example, the introduction of an FTP transfer to a physical link supporting an existing Telnet connection may result in unacceptable service for both parties. Real-time data usually requires the network to guarantee a throughput, though it may be willing to sacrifice throughput to maintain timeliness. This elastic category is divided into two traffic types as well: guaranteed and predictive. Under guaranteed service, an application will inform the network as to its QoS requirements; the network in turn will do its best to meet these requirements by reserving bandwidth and/or raising priority. Predictive service is based on a user-defined maximum delay. Any data not delivered within this delay bound will be dropped. The user is therefore willing to sacrifice some data (and throughput) in order to preserve timeliness. Since the throughput is more variable than with guaranteed service, the delay and jitter should be reduced. In the next chapter as part of our discussion of RSVP, we look at these service classes in greater detail.

A system implementing support for these traffic profiles will probably use a fair queuing mechanism, under which sources cooperating in traffic management will not be negatively affected by those that do not. If data flows sharing a physical interface are divided into two classes based

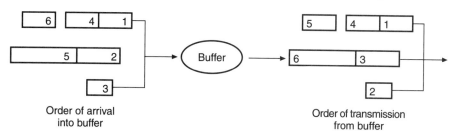

Figure 3.35 Weighted fair queuing. Source: Cisco Systems.

on bandwidth, then an algorithm may be implemented which provides the low-bandwidth connections with requested bandwidth and high-bandwidth connections with equal bandwidth (under times of congestion). The actual mechanism may be implemented in a number of ways, one promising method known as **bitwise round-robin fair queuing**. As data arrives at an interface, data on a given connection is considered in-transit until its last bit has arrived. This traffic will be scheduled into a queue and therefore transmitted based on the arrival time of this bit. The actual transmission is based on the assignment of a sequence number for each message based on the previous sequence number (for the same connection) and the message length. Since low-bandwidth connections receive lower sequence numbers, they are transmitted in a timely fashion compared to the potentially delayed high-bandwidth connections. This is depicted in Figure 3.35. Once fair queuing is implemented, we may predict delay as part of the QoS (Cisco Systems, 1995a). The use of WFQ does not infer that other queuing mechanisms such as FIFO will also be widely deployed within switching systems, however.

Once we understand applications, we may then identify the following QoS-related issues:

- Constant versus variable bit rate
- Degree of burstiness
- Suitability for statistical multiplexing
- Real-time delay constraints
- Delay tolerance for non-real-time applications
- Degree of interactiveness
- Loss tolerance
- Priority requirements
- Ability to use free bandwidth

- Coding

- Fairness.

Of these constraints, the most important may be the application's requirement for real-time response. Interactive traffic between two users places very high demands on the amount of jitter and acceptable packet or cell loss. For example, total delay for conferencing applications may not exceed a few hundred msec in most cases if it is to remain unnoticeable. In contrast, applications without these constraints are much more tolerant of variations in QoS.

As part of the original B-ISDN standard, the ITU defined a number of service classes (or bearer classes) in support of these application service requirements. Currently, these are defined as ATM transfer capabilities within I.371. Although some of the ATM service catagories align to this recommendation, others do not. For example, ATM Forum CBR is known as **Deterministic Bit Rate (DBR)** while VBR is standardized as **Statistical Bit Rate (SBR)**. Although the Forum has subdivided VBR into rt-VBR and nrt-VBR, the ITU leaves rt-SBR for further study. Another discrepancy is UBR which has no equivalent within the ITU. Finally, I.371 defines an **ATM Block Transfer (ABT)** mode which has no equivalent within the ATM Forum while ABR is still under study within the ITU. In any case, both ABT and ABR rely on network feedback for bandwidth allocation. For all practical purposes, the service classes as defined within the ATM Forum are being implemented by both the ATM LAN and WAN vendors, while the ITU terminology (that is, SBR and ABT) has found little acceptance. Therefore, the ATM Forum service catagories provide the basis for our discussions. These include:

- Constant Bit Rate (CBR)

- real-time and non-real-time Variable Bit Rate (rt-VBR, nrt-VBR)

- Unspecified Bit Rate (UBR)

- Available Bit Rate (ABR).

Though the first two, CBR and rt–VBR, are easier to model, and in fact closely relate to the original B-ISDN service classes, the latter two more closely reflect the majority of data transfers and LAN interconnection requirements. Associated with each class are intended application profiles and ATM attributes, including QoS parameters such as **peak-to-peak Cell Delay Variation (ppCDV)**, **Maximum Cell Transfer Delay (Max CTD)**, **Mean Cell Transfer Delay (Mean CTD)**, and **Cell Loss Ratio (CLR)**.

Although use of traffic profiles such as CBR and VBR is more widespread at present, many references still use the ATM bearer capabilities as defined by the ITU. This has caused some confusion when trying to equate the two terminologies. As part of the UNI 3.0, the Forum defined signaling capabilities for Classes A (CBR), C (nrt-VBR), and X (unspecified). Class C was redefined within UNI 3.1 to correspond with UBR, and included Class B for VBR. Class B, intended for VBR with synchronization, and Class D, for connectionless traffic, are now either undefined or not implemented. With the release of TM/Sig 4.0 and the PNNI, these ambiguities are mostly eliminated since the user signals a number of individual parameters, along with a QoS class for backward compatibility with UNI 3.1 and the ITU. For completeness, Table 3.23 includes both the ATM Forum service catagories and the ITU bearer classes and transfer capabilities.

In describing an ATM connection, we look at both the characteristics of the source and the services offered by the network. The source will conform to a traffic contract, made up of quantitative or qualitative traffic parameters describing the characteristics of the traffic source. These source traffic descriptors include the **Peak Cell Rate (PCR)**, and optionally, a **Sustainable Cell Rate (SCR)**, **Maximum Burst Size (MBS)**, and **Minimum Cell Rate (MCR)**. At the UNI, the characteristics of this connection are known as the **connection traffic descriptor**. This includes the source descriptor along with the CDVT (set by the network) and a traffic conformance definition. The conformance definition is based on the GCRA and relates to the policing of cells via UPC at the UNI. A network will offer a QoS, which includes the ppCDV,

Table 3.23 Bearer capability and AAL-centric service classifications.

Attribute	Class A, X, VP (Notes 1, 2)	C, X, VP, (B – Note 3)	C, X, VP	(D –Note 3)
Applications	Circuit emulation – CBR	Real-time VBR	CO data; user– network signaling messages; Non-real-time VBR	CL data Non-real-time
Adaptation	AAL1 (Note 4)	AAL5, AAL2	AAL5, AAL3/4	AAL5, AAL3/4
Traffic profile	CBR (DBR)	rt-VBR (SBR)	nrt-VBR (SBR); UBR, ABR (ABT)	ABR (ABT), UBR
Timing relation between source and destination	Related		Non-related	
Connection mode	Connection oriented			Connectionless

Note 1   Class X also proposed for user-identified constant or variable bit rate, timing, and whether connection oriented or connectionless; this is not UBR

Note 2   VP service is different from BCOB-X since we transport the VCI and PT field transparently across the network

Note 3   Undefined within the ATM Forum's TM and Signaling 4.0

Note 4   AAL1 is also used in some instances for VBR traffic, though this has not yet been standardized

Max CTD, Mean CTD, and CLR. Note that these parameters apply to each direction of the connection.

The PCR is the maximum instantaneous rate at which the user will be permitted to transmit. Note that this parameter is the inverse of the minimum intercell time. Over a longer interval, the average rate at which a source is permitted to send is known as the SCR. The **Burst Tolerance (BT)** makes use of the leaky bucket algorithm to limit the maximum burst size which may be transmitted at the PCR. All cells entering the network are placed in this bucket, which is drained at the SCR. The BT is the depth of this bucket, and is related to the number of back-to-back cells which may be sent at the PCR, known as the MBS, by the following formula: $BT = (MBS-1)(1/SCR-1/PCR)$. Finally, a more recently introduced QoS parameter relating to ABR support is the MCR. The QoS offered by the ATM network is judged by the CLR. Note that this parameter may be specified for both cells with $CLP=0$ and $CLP=1$. When transmitting real-time data, the **Cell Transfer Delay (CTD)**, sometimes called Max CTD which incorporates all delays along the path and the **Cell Delay Variation (CDV)**, and related to the network's **Cell Delay Variation Tolerance (CDVT)**, are also of importance.

A node requesting a connection across the ATM network will first inform its local switch via the UNI of the source traffic descriptor, service category, and optionally, the QoS. This is the traffic contract for the connection. The switch now performs a CAC based on this information to determine if resources exist, and optionally, whether local policy permits the connection. If accepted, the switch now uses the PNNI to identify a source route through the network and will forward the request. Each switch along the path in turn performs its own CAC. Upon reaching the destination, and assuming it is accepted, the network confirms the connection. During the connection lifetime, the switches may monitor the connection via UPC and policing to determine whether it complies to the traffic contract.

ATM service categories

We may arrange ATM service categories (sometimes called service classes) into two groups: those supporting real-time applications, and those which do not. Real-time service classes are CBR and rt-VBR. The non-real-time service classes, nrt-VBR, ABR, and UBR, each have their use depending upon the higher-layer application. The nrt-VBR class ensures Mean CTD and CLR based on the signaled traffic contract. Thus, cells which do not conform to the contract or those with a $CLP=1$ may be discarded. Connections which have exceeded their contract should not normally affect those which have not. VBR will normally rely on resource reservation as part of the signaling request to ensure a given QoS, and if the request cannot be met, the connection will not be accepted. VBR sources which have exceeded their traffic contracts and then reduce their transmission rate due to an indication from the network (for example, EFCI) will not be guaranteed a CLR unless they back off to a pre-determined traffic contract. ABR, though not providing a set CTD, does ensure a CLR at variable transmission rates if a given connection conforms to the ABR service definition. The entire operation of ABR is based on network feedback, and is described in detail later. Finally, UBR offers no guarantees at all though this does not imply that a large percentage of the data will be discarded. In addition, fairness between connections whereby each will receive a 'fair' share of available bandwidth may not be guaranteed either (Table 3.24 and Figure 3.36).

In designing an ATM system, planners implement various techniques and designs to properly support the applications (and associated traffic classes) described above. These include selection of appropriate queuing mechanisms (FIFO, round-robin, WFQ), priority support and enforcement (via control or buffering), feedback-based flow-control mechanisms (FECN/BECN, credits, rate enforcement via RM cells), and the overall switch design affecting delay, CDV, and loss. The reason the service class concept is important is that it is a method by which properties and requirements of applications may be summarized and then used to develop the switch architectures. This is preferable to attempting to

Table 3.24 ATM layer service categories.

| Attribute | ATM layer service category | | | | |
	CBR	rt-VBR	nrt-VBR	ABR	UBR
Guarantee	BW and delay	SCR, ppCDV	SCR, Mean CTD	CLR (not zero)	Nothing
Load predictability	100%	<100%		No	No
CAC/prior reservation	Yes	Yes, some		Yes, for MCR	No
UPC/policing	Yes	Yes		Optional	Optional
Flow control	No	Possible		Yes	No
Congestion control	No	Yes		Yes	Yes
PCR and CDVT	Yes (250 µsec)	Yes (250 µsec)		Yes	Optional
SCR and BT (MBS)	N/A	Yes		N/A	N/A
MCR	N/A	N/A		Optional	N/A
CDV/CTD	ppCDV, Max CTD (150 µsec)	ppCDV, Max CTD (150 µsec)	Mean CTD	No	No
CLR (CLP=0)	Yes (1.7×10⁻¹⁰)	Yes (10⁻⁷)		Yes	No
CLR (CLP=1)	Yes or No	Yes or No		Yes	No
Feedback control	Optional EFCI	Optional EFCI		EFCI, RR, ER	Optional EFCI

Note   Values for CLR, CTD, and CDV from Bellcore TA-1110

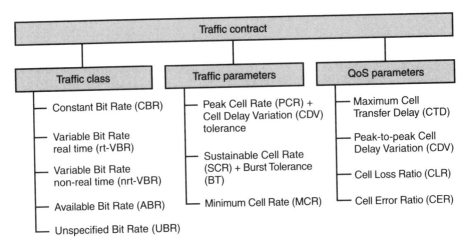

Figure 3.36 Service categories and attributes.

consider each and every application in terms of ATM traffic parameters (PCR, BT, CDV, and so on). In general, we support guaranteed services (CBR, rt-VBR, and nrt-VBR) via admission control, bandwidth reservation, UPC and policing, scheduling (that is, CBR), and for CBR and rt-VBR, minimizing buffer size. Best effort services (UBR, ABR) rely on buffer management, discard techniques (CLP, TPD, RED, and so on), feedback (that is, ABR), and slow start. These classes use large buffers to control cell loss.

Figure 3.37 provides an insight as to the operation of an ATM trunk under different service categories. We first allocate a portion of the bandwidth for the CBR VCCs. This bandwidth, specified by the sum of the CBR PCRs, is unavailable for any other forms of traffic. Next, the rt-VBR and nrt-VBR VCCs are characterized by their PCRs and SCRs. The SCR is the average BW which the VBR VCC requires. Now looking at the

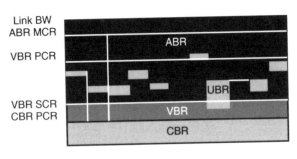

Figure 3.37 ATM trunk loading by service category.

trunk from the top, we subtract the ABR MCRs from the remaining bandwidth. Any bandwidth remaining is now free for use by the variable rate ABR sources. Depending upon the demands of the VBR and ABR VCCs along with the efficiency of the form of ABR used, there may be some remaining bandwidth for UBR traffic. The amount of this bandwidth and when it appears is not guaranteed, however.

The **Constant Bit Rate (CBR)** service class is most commonly associated with CES across ATM. For example, PABX and some video-conferencing applications require a predefined dedicated bandwidth. Other applications may include video messaging and distribution, though in these cases VBR or even ABR service should suffice. If a traffic source is found to generate a bit rate approximately equal to a constant bandwidth even after compression, it will justify CBR. This service may also be justified if a user's response and reliability requirements warrant use of a dedicated channel. The CBR service provides for end-to-end timing recovery, and the user data is provided with a QoS profile stating that a certain percentage of the traffic will arrive within a given delay interval. This is a requirement, as cells which arrive after an expected CTD will be of little use. Timing issues are discussed in greater detail as part of our earlier description of AAL1, the AAL for CBR traffic.

CBR service has been developed to service real-time applications which contain video and audio information. An end-to-end PCR is defined, and the originating application will be assumed to offer traffic at this rate. Note that this may result in less than optimal use of bandwidth if the application is more bursty than expected. For example, a video application may generate a signal with a peak to average ratio between 3 and 10. These values may justify statistical multiplexing. As part of CBR, an acceptable CLR, CDV, and maximum CTD are defined as well.

Applications which are bursty may benefit from the statistical multiplexing within VBR. As with CBR, the **real-time Variable Bit Rate (rt-VBR)** service class specifies an acceptable CLR and CTD as well as a CDV. In contrast to CBR, where a constant amount of bandwidth is pre-reserved, VBR sets an SCR and MBS. Therefore, a proper implementation will require knowledge of the traffic source and an appreciation of user expectations from such a service. Looking once more at our ATM trunk figure, VBR has used an average bandwidth equal to its SCR. As with CBR, cells arriving after the CTD are of less use to the destination application. Any audio or video application which can benefit from statistical multiplexing is a candidate for rt-VBR. Although AAL2 was originally designed to support VBR traffic, some vendors have implemented this profile across AAL1, possibly leading to standardization of VBR over AAL1 at some point in the future.

The **non-real-time Variable Bit Rate (nrt-VBR)** differs from rt-VBR by placing less stringent requirements on the network for CDV and CTD, with only an average CTD specified. This makes nrt-VBR more suitable for data services as opposed to voice or video transport. Possible applications include transaction processing and Frame Relay transport.

The **Unspecified Bit Rate (UBR)** is intended for non-real-time applications requiring no guarantees of bounded delay. In this case, the end-system applications are expected to handle any cell loss and delay, no different to the best-effort service provided by the Internet in most places. These lack of guarantees allow a higher degree of multiplexing between sources. Applications suitable for UBR service include those tolerant to delay or not requiring real-time response. Some examples are E-mail, fax transmission, file transfers, Telnet, and LAN interconnection. In all these examples, the source is also characterized as sending non-continuous bursts of cells. In effect, UBR models most data transmissions and is the type of service associated with the Internet. Though not having the real-time delay constraints, the applications outlined above may be sensitive to cell loss. At present, these applications use large buffering, minimizing loss at the expense of delay. The FIFO queuing used within the Internet is an example of this. No bandwidth is allocated on a per-VC basis, allowing a great deal of multiplexing to occur.

The downside of UBR service is that cell delivery is not guaranteed, with retransmission occurring at higher layers. However, a properly dimensioned ATM network implementing congestion control and traffic shaping at the source should not pose a problem in this respect. A network with intelligent cell discard mechanisms such as EPD or **tail packet discard** (described later) may in fact provide reasonable support for UBR (or UBR+, as many in the industry term this improved UBR service). These mechanisms prevent the transmission of cells across the network from packets which have already been destroyed due to cell loss. The only attributes specified as part of UBR are the PCR and the CDVT, with the PCR only providing an indication of a physical bandwidth limitation within a VC. Under UBR, no GCRA parameters are implemented. This implies that the applications cannot specify a cell delay, jitter, or loss rate. Basically, the QoS results from network design guidelines and end-system applications as opposed to anything operating within ATM. UBR uses AAL5 as the AAL, though AAL3/4 may be used as part of SMDS/CBDS across an ATM network.

A concern with UBR is its viability as a public service due to a lack of knowledge of peak bandwidth requirements. A service provider will need to allocate some bandwidth for multiple UBR VCCs without any knowledge of the actual service requirements. This is further complicated due to rerouting where available bandwidth may change at short notice. Ultimately, UBR in the WAN could become more complicated to deliver and more costly to implement than a more constrained service class such as nrt-VBR or ABR.

The **Available Bit Rate (ABR)** service is intended for sources which may vary their transmission rate but which require service guarantees. These guarantees relate to cell loss, as many end-system applications may tolerate delay but require low loss across a network if throughput is to be maintained. New feedback mechanisms are required to support this service class, which provides for maximum use of available bandwidth while guaranteeing a maximum cell loss if the source is compliant with the service class definition. For example, some applications are less tolerable to cell loss, while others, including NFS, require a bound on delay. In addition to the PCR specified as part of UBR, the ABR user also specifies a minimum usable bandwidth, known as the MCR. During data transmission, the bandwidth provided by the network should not drop to below this MCR. Under ABR, users are assumed to be 'well-behaved,' in that they will not transmit at a rate exceeding that which the network can support. A compliant source is guaranteed a certain CLR. We describe the operation of ABR and its various modes later. Two common concerns with ABR service are the fairness provided by the network to the various traffic sources and the guarantee that conforming users will not suffer undue cell loss. Thus, the feedback mechanism must scale with network size and transmission rate, no set of circuits may be favored or discriminated against, the network must function in the presence of non-compliant end-systems, and the control loop must converge to a steady state. Both require enforcement of ABR attributes as well as proper network sizing. To accomplish this, the ABR service definition addresses control in the context of a packet scheduling algorithm, a buffer allocation policy, and a dropping algorithm. Scheduling algorithms include FIFO and WFQ. Buffering algorithms include FIFO and one based on per-VC allocation. Finally, cell discard algorithms may be based on FIFO or RED. As with UBR, ABR is based on AAL5.

Many applications will benefit from the loss and fairness guarantees provided by ABR service. Though the flow control available within TCP provides some control over end-to-end performance, higher-layer protocols are ineffective and incapable of either allocating or monitoring network resources. In addition, due to the control loop, they cannot minimize congestion as effectively as a mechanism relying on feedback from congested nodes within a network. With this in mind, how will the ABR feedback-based flow control interact with TCP since ABR operates independently of the latter's windowing mechanism? We will require deployment experience to determine whether or not TCP performance improves and what design considerations are important at the non-ATM to ATM boundaries.

Finally, support within ABR for pt-mpt VCCs is worth considering, as these types of connection will be widely used within an ATM network (for example, LAN emulation, VoD). The interaction of the ABR feedback mechanism with the leaves and branch points of the pt-mpt tree is important, and a mechanism is needed to consolidate reverse direction **Resource Management (RM)** cells (described below) at these same branch points. Also, since an entire pt-mpt connection is typically signaled with a single QoS, congestion at one point in the network may adversely affect other leaves which could theoretically maintain their data rate if each leaf could be provided with a separate QoS. Initially, support for pt-mpt ABR VCCs is left to vendors for implementation, which may affect interoperability.

Congestion avoidance: background and requirements

The need for congestion control over ATM was recognized early in the development and adaptation of standards, and is related to end-systems which look upon a connection to an ATM network in the same way which they would look at an Ethernet connection: any and all available bandwidth is 'good.' These applications will use all 'available' bandwidth, and require the creation of ABR to guarantee the fair sharing of network resources in the presence of bursty sources. Any traffic management implementation must address the tradeoff between providing excess bandwidth for bursts and the simple fact that bandwidth is not an infinite resource, while at the same time ensuring fairness. Ideally, under congestion, the bandwidth available to each station should be predictable. The results of many investigations and experiences resulted in standards which apply to the UNI as well as to the PNNI. We must ensure that management of all traffic classes such as pre-allocation of bandwidth for CBR and EPD/TPD for UBR, do not adversely affect each other. Practical considerations playing a part in implementing a given congestion control mechanism include its ability to support a large number of VCs over high-latency (for instance, satellite) or high-speed (622 Mbps and above) links. This per-VC granularity is no small task, since typical end-systems must support hundreds of VCCs while ATM switches are rated in the thousands. As will become apparent in discussions on alternative congestion control schemes, the number of VCCs supported plays a role in whether or not a given alternative may be economically implemented.

In any computer network, congestion will occur when the sums of the various inputs exceed the capacity of the output. Schemes to minimize and/or avoid congestion operate at various layers of the reference model, and may be categorized as to their suitability in handling congestion of various durations. For example, network capacity planning must be conducted with an eye toward minimizing congestion in the first place. Over long time intervals, CAC within ATM will help to avoid congestion by rejecting new connections if network capacity is insufficient. As the time interval is shortened, congestion control must apply to already established connections. End-to-end and link-by-link feedback are examples of this. Finally, we apply buffering short bursts. Thus, a properly engineered network will contain elements of multiple congestion control schemes (Jain, 1995).

Any congestion control mechanism selected must meet the needs of a large, multivendor ATM network incorporating both private and public domains. Criteria include scalability, fairness in bandwidth allocation, robustness, and ease of implementation among different switch architectures and classes. Of these parameters, fairness is worth a closer look in that it will drive how effectively links are utilized. Basically, each traffic source is provided with an equal bandwidth on every link provided it can use it. The point of maximum contention will be the judge of how much bandwidth the system will provide to a given VC. Finally, any congestion control algorithm should be able to operate in the presence of persistent, staggered (starting and ending at different times with ramp-up/ramp-down), and bursty sources.

Congestion control and avoidance is required for implementing an effective multiswitch ATM network, by providing functionality which allows ATM UNIs and NNIs to be loaded to near capacity without the fear of cell loss. Cell loss is caused by buffer overflow within the ATM switches as well as by header corruption. This queue optimization is therefore one goal of traffic management. As an example, consider the two ATM switches connected by a 150 Mbps trunk in Figure 3.38. Sources A and B at switch 1 transmit at 75 Mbps each. The destination for A is E at switch 2, connected via a 150 Mbps UNI, while the destination for B is F connected at the same data rate. With no other sources transmitting, all data will be delivered. Now add 50 Mbps sources C and D at switch 2, both transmitting to E. The total destined for E is now 175 Mbps, a congestion situation. With each VC provided an equal share of the available bandwidth, 25 Mbps of source A's data will be dropped. If no network-wide congestion avoidance is implemented, 25 Mbps of the trunk's capacity is now filled by cells to be dropped, obviously less than optimal. With congestion avoidance, source A will throttle its input rate to 50 Mbps, and source B may now use 100 Mbps. The trunk is now fully utilized. Thus, traffic management is global in nature, requiring cooperation between the ATM switches and ATM-connected end-systems.

Without a flow control mechanism, the bursty nature of data traffic could and will load a given interface on an ATM switch to the extent that cells will be lost. A simplistic way to avoid this situation is to reserve bandwidth for each VC, in effect turning ATM into a cell-based TDM network. This is obviously not the most efficient use of bandwidth, as 100 VCs sharing a 155 Mbps physical interface would each be allocated only 1.5 Mbps each, less than the expected bandwidth of an Ethernet on a per-VC basis. Thus, we require some method of supporting a best effort QoS to avoid this clearly unacceptable behavior.

The actions taken by a network to avoid network congestion are known as **traffic and congestion control functions**, and will normally be sufficient to avoid congestion. Traffic control functions include:

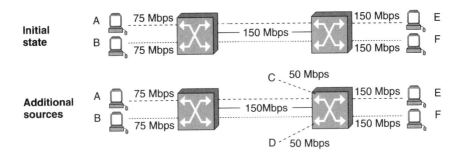

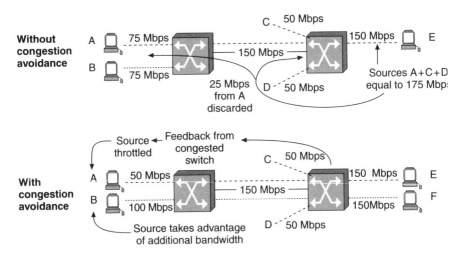

Figure 3.38 Traffic patterns.

- Network Resource Management (NRM)
- Connection Admission Control (CAC)
- Usage Parameter Control (UPC)
- Selective cell or packet discarding
- Traffic shaping and scheduling
- Explicit Forward Congestion Indication (EFCI)
- VP resource management
- The ABR mechanism.

Although traffic control functions are designed to avoid network congestion, a network may be placed under extreme stress due to unanticipated traffic fluctuations or failures within the network itself. In this case, the network will implement congestion control functions. In implementing both traffic and congestion control, the various mechanisms and procedures may be applied to individual VCs or to VPs consisting of multiple VCs. VPs may be useful in shielding the network from VC granularity while allowing for management of the aggregation of VCs; this is a function of NRM. We now look at each of these traffic control and congestion control capabilities in turn.

CAC consists of the actions taken by the network during signaling for SVCs or as part of PVC management to determine whether a VCC or VPC may be accepted. A new connection will be accepted only if resources are available end-to-end to support its source traffic descriptor and QoS while at the same time maintaining the QoS of existing connections.

UPC protects the network against sources exceeding their negotiated QoS, and applies to both VCCs and VPCs. Its use is optional at the private UNI, and required at the public UNI. Well-implemented UPC should provide quick response while at the same time not affecting or inappropriately policing compliant connections. This function should not negatively influence the CLR, Max CTD, Mean CTD, and CDV, though it may add to the CTD and CDV. UPC takes place at the first point of link termination within a network. For example, if the first switch connecting an end user operated on VPs only, UPC would take place on these VPs, while a VC switch further on in the network would operate on VCs. In either case, UPC will pass, tag, or discard cells. Tagging involves resetting the CLP=0 to CLP=1. Note that connection monitoring at the NNI is referred to as NPC.

Selective cell discard takes place when the network discards CLP=1 cells or cells which belong to a non-compliant connection. The intent is to still meet network performance objectives, however. Closely related to this function is selective packet discard (or Early Packet Discard, EPD), described below, which relies on feedback to the traffic source or the identification of packets within the ATM switch (that is, via the PT field under AAL5) to intelligently discard remaining cells belonging to a packet where one or more cells have already been lost. This prevents the forwarding of cells belonging to corrupt AAL5 frames through the ATM network, thereby conserving bandwidth. Since useless cells are not forwarded through the network, 'goodput' increases and the chances of congestive collapse due to end-system retransmissions are minimized. EPD is especially useful for UBR traffic.

Traffic shaping may be performed by both the end-system and the network. In the case of the latter, cells arriving on a VCC or VPC may have their inter-cell arrival time adjusted within the ATM switch to reduce the CBR or conform to a given MBS. This shaping mechanism is very useful when aggregating various service classes (CBR, VBR, ABR, and so on) at a trunk. A more sophisticated form of shaping is known as traffic scheduling, where cells are played out into a switch matrix at precise intervals. This is more useful for CBR where intercell times should be controlled with a goal of minimizing CDV. At a traffic source, a network planner with information as to the capabilities of the ATM network and application profiles may implement very sophisticated and effective traffic shaping. This is almost required in the absence of end-to-end congestion avoidance, such as that provided by the rate-based flow control scheme in support of ABR traffic.

EFCI is a mechanism by which a bit is set in the cell header if the network is experiencing congestion. The destination will use this information to lower its transmission rate. This mechanism is one way of implementing ABR in the absence of RM cells, and should be used with caution. We describe some observations concerning EFCI usage later.

If managing network resources through the use of VPs, the work required to establish individual VCCs is simplified. Although some control of per-VC QoS is lost, the advantages of VP management in being able to relate a group of VCCs to a given service category will often make up for this. Thus, end-systems and switches must implement traffic management for both VCC and VPCs. Note that VPCs may span user–user, user–network, or network–network. In the first case, the network has no knowledge of the service requirements of the VCCs contained within the VPC.

The above techniques fall into two domains: preventive and reactive. Preventive congestion control includes those actions taken to ensure that the traffic entering a network will comply with the design parameters of the network, and include traffic shaping (SCR, PCR, MBS), admission control (CAC), and traffic policing mechanisms (GCRA). Reactive mechanisms include the ATM Forum ABR standard (explicit, relative, and EFCI-based) along with many proprietary implementations. We summarize where these actions take place in Figure 3.39.

During the course of 1994, various vendors submitted to the ATM Forum variants of their proprietary congestion avoidance mechanisms along with many unimplemented proposals for consideration as a standard. It soon became clear that two fundamentally different approaches were being taken: one based on credits, and a second utilizing rate-based controls. Towards the end of the debate, an integrated approach was submitted by the credit supporters as the rate-based mechanism gained momentum due to perceived complexities with buffering under the credit scheme. A vote for one system or another would of course have a major impact on hardware and software developments for a given vendor, affecting time-to-market based on past investment as well as product differentiation. When finally voted upon, the rate-based mechanism was passed by an overwhelming majority (104 to 9). Although a mechanism based on rate control eventually won, ultimately, multiple methods will co-exist. This is evident by what is now known as the **Quantum Flow Control** specification, a variant of the credit-based scheme. In an opera-

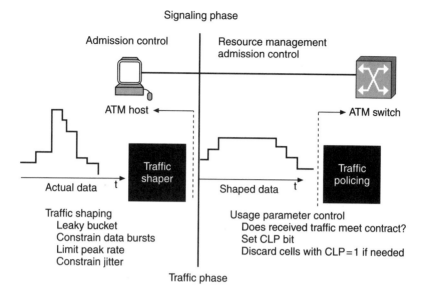

Figure 3.39 Locations for congestion control.

tional network, end-to-end congestion avoidance may therefore consist of a combination of standardized and non-ATM Forum preventive and reactive mechanisms, the latter including both rate- and credit-based schemes.

Preventive congestion control

One method of minimizing congestion at the entry to the ATM network is through the use of the leaky bucket algorithm, a form of the GCRA. We denote this as GCRA (I, L), where I is the amount by which the bucket is incremented upon cell arrival and L is the limit parameter. I+L equals the total depth of the bucket. This is a form of preventive congestion control, where the network attempts to control the amount of ATM traffic at the input of the network in the hope of preventing congestion from ever occurring. Remember that the QoS of a given VCC includes a PCR and an SCR. Thus, I will determine the maximum PCR or SCR, while L, the CDVT, determines the averaging interval and burst. Cells will arrive at the switch policing function at a rate somewhere between zero and the physical speed of the link. These cells enter the first bucket, whose depth is set to PCR (CLP=0 + CLP=1). Any cells not meeting this criteria are marked as non-conforming, while CLP=1 cells within the PCR are marked as conforming. Next, CLP=0 cells are sent to the second bucket, with a depth of SCR (CLP=0). Any cells meeting this criteria are forwarded as conforming, while cells not meeting the SCR are marked as

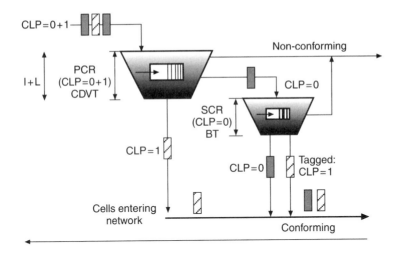

Figure 3.40 Dual leaky bucket. Source: Cisco Systems/ATM Forum.

non-conforming. CLP=0 cells may also be 'tagged' at this point, where their CLP is changed from 0 to 1. In this case, they are then marked as conforming. These two buckets relate to the GCRA as shown in Figure 3.40.

The first bucket's depth, PCR (CLP=0 + CLP=1), is in reality GCRA (1/PCR, CDVT), while the depth of the second bucket is equal to GCRA (1/SCR, BT+CDVT). These parameters, PCR, SCR, BT, and CDVT, are what actually determine the operation of the GCRA. For example, a GCRA of (1.5, 0.5) implies a bucket which will increment by 1.5 upon cell arrival. Over the next time interval 't', it will then empty by 1. As a cell is transmitted its total depth, (1.5+0.5) is therefore more suitable for constant traffic flows. In contrast, a GCRA of (4.5, 7) is more suitable for bursty traffic since the bucket depth in this case is 11.5. Note that one instance of the GCRA is required for the policed data rate, and a bucket will never overflow in reality since cells which would cause this to occur are marked as non-conforming.

The UNI also defines two methods of feedback-based flow control: **Generalized Flow Control (GFC)** and EFCI. The first, using four bits within the ATM cell header, has not been implemented. The second, one bit in the header which may be set by switches during periods of network congestion, is included as part of the ABR standard.

One way to look at traffic shaping and the way in which it may be implemented could be to first revisit the concept of the PCR, which is inversely related to the minimum intercell transmission rate, and the SCR, equal to the rate at which an application will generate the data over time. Since all applications are not ideal, with PCR=SCR, some form of traffic shaping should be implemented. Even with CBR traffic, cell separation may change across the network due to queuing and propagation delays. The receiver must therefore be capable of accepting data with variable inter-cell arrival times. This is known as a CDVT. Closely related to the CDVT is the MBS, the number of cells which may be transmitted at the PCR.

If sources are to comply with this MBS, they may shape their outputs, whereby cells are spaced out over the physical connection. Consider a 155 Mbps STM-1 connection. Unshaped cells may be transmitted at a maximum data rate of 149.75 Mbps. With some degree of traffic shaping, these same cells may be spaced, resulting for example in a peak rate of 37.44 Mbps. This lower peak will provide for better buffer and bandwidth management. However, one has to be careful not to space out the shaped cells beyond that tolerated by the source's CDVT. The GCRA as described above defines a relationship between the PCR and the CDVT. One possible way of implementing the GCRA is via a mechanism known as the **virtual scheduling algorithm**. This algorithm has the following properties. Cells arriving at the PCR will have an associated inter-cell gap 'I'. This value determines the **Theoretical Arrival Time (TAT)** for cells over the connection. If a cell arrives after this TAT, then the cell is conformant and the TAT is reset to the cell's actual arrival time + I. If the cell arrives earlier than the TAT, it will conform if it has arrived after TAT–CDVT. In this case, the next TAT is also the current TAT+I. Finally, if the cell arrives after the TAT but within the CDVT, it will also comply. However, if it arrives after the TAT+CDVT, it may be dropped.

Thus, the selection of the CDVT will go a long way in determining the cells that will non-conform and therefore be subject to discard when the source generates bursty traffic. If the CDVT=0, then there is no leeway if a cell arrives before or after its expected arrival time. Depending upon the amount of jitter expected by the source, the CDVT should be set accordingly. For example, a source generating 25,000 cells/second over an STM-1 link would need to transmit these cells at a constant rate to comply under CDVT=0. In comparison, a great deal of burstiness is acceptable if the CDVT is set to 100 μs. Alternatively, if the source were to transmit at the PCR for the physical link, even this CDVT would be quickly overrun. A quick calculation to determine the number (N) of back-to-back cells which may be transmitted is as follows:

$$N = 1 + (\text{Tolerance}/I - (\text{Transmission time of 1 cell}))$$

Consider a 155 Mbps connection and an SCR of 25,000 cells/second. In this case, $I = 39$ and the cell transmission time is equal to 2.83 μs. Various values of the tolerance could then be inserted into the formula to determine the number of cells which would be transmitted in a burst. For a CDVT of 1000 μs, this would equate to 28 cells (Byers, 1995). We summarize minimum cell arrival times at various links speeds in Table 3.25. This provides an idea of the length of a burst when

Table 3.25 Link cell rates and inter-cell arrival times.

Link type	Data rate (Mbps)	Actual data rate (Mbps)	Cell rates (cells/sec)	Cell time (μsec/cell)
OC-3c/STM-1	155.52	149.76	353,208	2.83
T3/PLCP	44.736	40.704	96,000	10.41
E3/G.832	34.368	33.73	79,551	12.57
E1	2.048	2.048	4830	207
DS1	1.544	1.544	3641	274
512 Kbps	0.512	0.512	1207	828

combined with the MTU. For example, an MTU of 9180 octets (equal to 192 cells) as defined in RFC 1626 will result in a burst of 543 μs at OC-3c/STM-1 rates. Therefore, care should be taken wehn working with CDVT in the presence of bursty sources.

A second method of minimizing congestion at the ingress of an ATM switch is based on selectively discarding cells belonging to AAL5 frames depending upon whether or not a user has violated its traffic contract or if buffers are in short supply due to network congestion (as opposed to making a decision based on the CLP). One form of packet discard is known as EPD, where the switch will drop all cells belonging to a single higher-layer AAL5 frame as opposed to dropping cells at random from multiple frames. In an ATM switch, buffer queue thresholds may trigger EPD. Alternatively, if a cell has been discarded from an AAL5 frame due to UPC, CLP selective discard, or buffer overflow, the switch may implement TPD (sometimes known as partial packet piscard) where all remaining cells belonging to the frame are discarded until we reach the UU-SDU identified within the header's PTI. This precludes the transmission of partial packets through the network. More sophisticated forms of EPD or TPD may result in increased network performance. For example, consider a TPD function which, upon recognizing that a cell from an AAL5 frame has been discarded, goes on to discard all following cells up to and including the EOF. This will result in a reassembly error at the destination for the next frame. Even if it does not discard the final cell of the frame, containing the EOF, the chances are that under congestion the network will have set this cell to CLP=1, making it more likely to be discarded further in the network. A better mechanism would be to set the CLP in this cell to 0, providing it with a better chance of making it to the destination. The following frame would therefore not experience a reassembly failure. Within the ATM Forum, many refer to the combination of UBR and EPD/TPD as UBR+. In Figure 3.41 we compare this scheme, known as intelligent tail packet discard with TPD and with no discard mechanism whatsoever.

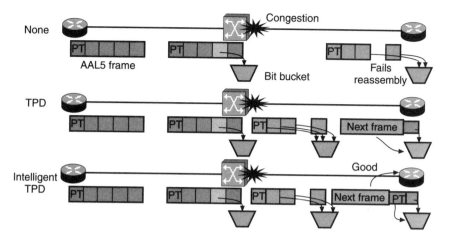

Figure 3.41 Intelligent tail packet discard. Source: Cisco Systems.

Reactive congestion control: rate based

Within an ATM switch, intelligence on output interfaces may monitor
current throughput and buffer utilization, generating status information
which may be propagated to the input modules or to other switches in
the network. This is known as reactive congestion control, and takes two
forms. The first is based on issuing credits to the sending stations, in
effect a windowing mechanism, while the second is based on regulating
the transmission rate of the source. Emphasis here is on the second, rate-
based scheme as it has been accepted within the ATM Forum.

Although the CBR and VBR service categories address applications requiring tight bounds on throughput and delay, and the UBR
service is intended to suffice for applications requiring no guarantees on
QoS, a large set of applications exist which require some minimal guarantee as to acceptable throughput and delay. This contrasts with most
LANs and the Internet which do not guarantee a minimum bandwidth at
present. For traffic prioritization in support of real-time transactions
and interaction with higher-layer protocols (for example, RSVP), the
support for a minimum throughput is desirable. In addition, support of a
minimum bandwidth will allow for the service to be used as a replacement for some leased-line networks where CBR or VBR is not required
due to extreme traffic fluctuations. The ABR category has been developed to provide for these applications, while at the same time guaranteeing an upper bound on expected cell loss to avoid loss of goodput due to
retransmissions. The network is capable of making such guarantees
since the end-system participates in the congestion avoidance mechanism by varying its transmission rate based on feedback from the
network (Bonomi and Fendick, 1995).

Rate-based congestion avoidance mechanisms first appeared within Frame Relay networks which defined the use of two congestion bits, **Forward Explicit Congestion Notification (FECN)** and **Backward Explicit Congestion Notification (BECN)**, in the header. An end-system, upon receipt of a frame indicating congestion within the network, would make a binary decision to either increase by a fixed amount or decrease by a proportional amount its sending window size. This algorithm is really a variant of that implemented earlier as part of DECnet. The control is end-to-end, in that the end-systems interpret the congestion notification information. Moving forward, the ATM cell header supports a binary scheme in the form of the EFCI bit, and its use is one method of supporting ABR. Use of this bit provided the basis for the first ATM rate-based proposal, relying on the destination to generate RM cells only if the EFCI was not set by the network. These RM cells would indicate to the source that it may increase its transmission rate by a fixed increment. If the source did not receive an RM cell, due either to the EFCI or because they were lost due to network congestion, it would decrease its rate proportionally. Within the ATM Forum, this scheme was adapted to support an initial cell rate and modifying the sending of RM cells to indicate congestion (that is, negative feedback). Note that this last modification reduced the robustness of the protocol while potentially reducing the number of RM cells transmitted.

In response to these proposals, the **Proportional Rate Control Algorithm (PRCA)** was submitted, once again modifying the feedback (to positive) but setting an upper bound on the number of RM cells to a fraction of the total ABR bandwidth. At the same time, a number of proposals were brought to the Forum providing the source with more flexibility as to its transmission rate. The various proposals were unified under the **Enhanced PRCA (EPRCA)**, which contained the binary elements of the PRCA along with the explicit rate features described above. Switches and end-systems would then have the option of implementing either method. This proposal provided the basis for the decision in favor of a rate-based mechanism made by the ATM Forum in 1994. Bonomi and Fendick (1995) document these various mechanisms in greater detail.

In leading to the decision within the ATM Forum to pursue rate-based flow control, Bellcore, Sandia Labs, the National Institute of Standards and Technology (NIST), and others conducted extensive research. These simulations included both TCP/IP traffic sources and stochastic modeling. The result of this research was a realization that the rate-based scheme would be preferable to credit-based mechanisms. 'Rate-based' implies that the network will adjust the sending rate of each VC. This contrasts to the credit-based approach where the network communicates to each source (VC) the amount of buffer space available for a given VC, the source sending only if it knows that the network can buffer the data. The rate-based approach is not hop-by-hop or end-to-end;

this depends upon implementation, though in most cases end-to-end will be chosen. Note that a hop-by-hop implementation will spread buffering across multiple switches within the network as opposed to end-to-end's tendency to concentrate buffering at the edges, possibly resulting in an increased likelihood of packet loss. Though the selected paradigm does not use buffering in the same way as the credit-based approach, buffering is still required, in this case a single buffer for all ABR VCs on a given link (as opposed to the per-VC buffering required under credit mechanisms). This single buffer may be quite large, though, especially over WAN connections due to propagation time for new configuration information to reach the source.

Two things to note regarding rate-based mechanisms include the effect of TCP slow-start on the network and the lack of 'burst accumulation'. During slow-start, data generated by an end-system may exceed the burst capacity of the network, in turn exceeding the rate mandated by the network. This situation may be avoided by proper traffic shaping and buffering within the end-device. Also, in contrast to credit-based flow control where an end-system may build up future transmission credits by sending at less than capacity, the rate-based scheme does not carry over this information. In actual implementation, some devices may combine elements of both schemes, with rate information translated into a credit value as long as the sender knows to only use these credits at a rate not exceeding the burst tolerance in the traffic contract (Dwight, 1994).

Of interest is the actual performance of both the binary and explicit mechanisms. Though the binary scheme is easier to implement, and may be the method of choice at very high data rates over the next year or two, it does have tradeoffs in regard to stability and fairness. The second concern, fairness, has been recently addressed by adding more intelligence to the setting of the EFCI bit. In simulations with multiple sources and destinations, crossing a variable number of hops, the intelligent marking of the EFCI bit leads to much better enforcement of maximum and minimum fairness. Switch vendors implementing binary control should implement this functionality. The first concern, dealing with stability of the system, is more difficult to solve under the EFCI scheme. Consider a multi-hop network with sources initiating transmission at random intervals. Results clearly show the advantage of explicit mechanisms in terms of stability, though whether the fluctuations visible under EFCI are noticeable at the application layer is subject to debate. If a large number of sources and switches are interacting, and if some of the results described in Leland *et al* (1993) hold, these fluctuations will be visible. Under actual operation, we expect the EFCI mechanism to allow trunks to run at 80% utilization, while trunks implementing the full rate control mechanism should approach 99% utilization.

The rate-based framework includes a number of devices which together participate in the closed-loop (also known as feedback-based) congestion control scheme. These include a source and destination (end-systems), one or more switches (intermediate systems) and, optionally, virtual sources and destinations. A key requirement of the source is that it must be capable of generating cells at a controlled rate. Switching systems are considered to be limited resources, and will implement cell scheduling mechanisms for bandwidth management and cell buffer management. The switch will also monitor congestion within the network and generate congestion indication messages to the end-systems when appropriate. As a minimum, a single control loop (feed-back loop) will exist between the source and destination. It may be desirable to segment this loop via virtual sources and destinations either to reduce the length, and thus delay, of the control loop or to create separate control domains based on management requirements. Both switches and end-systems may implement different forms of buffering, ranging from a single, shared FIFO buffer to implementations of WFQ and per-connection buffer management. Vendors are tending to implement the latter due to possible increases in performance in terms of throughput, fairness, delay, and delay variance. More sophisticated schemes also act to the advantage of higher-layer protocols such as TCP/IP.

The framework chosen by the ATM Forum provides for the coexistence of multiple rate-based schemes based on cost and complexity. Thus, systems implementing explicit schemes will interoperate with those capable of only binary control based on the EFCI. Also, a network may contain one control loop or may be segmented into multiple domains. This latitude of implementations is made possible by the specification of a number of requirements, to include the content and format of RM cells, a definition of source and destination behavior, and a definition of expected switch behavior.

ABR service

Under ABR, the available bandwidth provided by the network may and is expected to change during the duration of a connection. The user is then expected to adapt to this by varying the transmission rate (the **Explicit Rate**, or **ER**) in order to receive a fair share of the available bandwidth. The network, in response to this, will guarantee an acceptable QoS (CLR). At the time of connection establishment, the user specifies a PCR and MCR (which may be equal to zero). The PCR is the maximum rate at which the user is expected to transfer data into the network, while the MCR is the minimum acceptable bandwidth which the user will accept. Note that a guarantee of an MCR>0 will require some resource allocation within the network, and the availability of these resources will influence whether or not connections are accepted (CAC function). Thus, the following attributes are relevant to ABR service: PCR, CDVT, CLR, and MCR.

The underlying assumption of ABR is that network resources will be shared fairly by traffic sources. This fairness applies only to those sources participating in the mechanism; not those 'misbehaving' sources which do not participate in closed-loop rate control. Note that fairness does not imply equality. Within the traffic management specification, a number of criteria are listed relating to ABR. These include: timescale invariance, fairness, robustness, stability, implementability, and support of existing applications and protocols. Timescale invariance implies that the feedback mechanism should be independent of any timescale. This provides for scalability as to distance, link speeds, and number of nodes. Fairness states that no set group of connections should be provided with increased resources at the expense of any other group (Sathaye, 1995). What the fairness calculation says is that, basically, any available bandwidth will be divided among those users requiring additional bandwidth. A second important aspect of fairness is that any mechanism must not degrade the performance of CBR/VBR traffic. Looking once again at our ATM trunk figure, ABR VCCs will only receive those network resources left over once CBR and VBR sources are satisfied. To protect against sources which are non-compliant with the feedback mechanism (due to lack of or improper implementation) the system must be robust, providing for isolation of users, and capable of recovering from loss of control information. In any case, we must avoid congestive collapse under times of extreme stress. Stability implies convergence to a steady state over time, and implementability relates to the ease of deployment in terms of switch architectures, end-systems, and the type of control information passed. Finally, protocol support includes different network topologies, Layer 2 and Layer 3 protocols, and, from an efficiency standpoint, an ability to use as close to 100% of the available bandwidth as possible.

ABR: protocol operation

During protocol operation, a source initiates an ABR VCC as part of call setup. As part of this request, the source specifies a number of ABR-specific parameters, to include:

- PCR, negotiated between source and network;

- MCR, requested by the source and guaranteed by the network;

- **Initial Cell Rate (ICR)**, the initial transmission rate;

- **Rate Increase Factor (RIF)**, controlling the increase in cell transmission rate;

- **Rate Decrease Factor (RDF)**, controlling the decrease in cell transmission rate, and signaled as RDFF;

- **Transient Buffer Exposure (TBE)**, formerly called Cells in Flight or CIF, the number of cells transmitted by the source before receiving a returning RM cell;

- **Fixed Round Trip Time (FRTT)**, an estimate of the round trip time for sending an RM cell from the source to the destination and back.

Additional ABR parameters are set to default values, including the **Number of RM** cells (**Nrm**, specified by the network, the number of cells sent between RM cells). ATM Forum (1996b) details the other parameters while Table 3.26 summarizes the most relevant ABR parameters.

The source initiates transmission at the ICR, always greater than or equal to the MCR but never exceeding the PCR, while the **Acceptable Cell Rate (ACR)** will also be set to the ICR at a maximum. It will send an RM cell at intervals not to exceed 100 ms if data is transmitted. If the source is considered to be 'idle' before transmitting, a function to protect the network is implemented. Consider a source which was transmitting at a high ACR and then stopped. If it immediately began sending data at this ACR, it could cause network congestion due to network loading. Instead, while idle, it will reduce its ACR by the RDF for each RM interval until reaching ICR. The ACR has the same property as the ICR in that it will never drop below the source's MCR.

The source will also send an RM cell every Nrm−1 data cells, which will be used by the source to adjust its transmission rate upon their return. These RM cells contain the sources ACR, placed in the **Current Cell Rate (CCR)** field, and a desired rate (which may be the PCR), placed in the **Explicit Rate (ER)** field. As the RM cell traverses the network, switches along the path may either adjust the content of the ER field or set the **Congestion Indication (CI)** or **NoIncrease (NI)** bit to 1. A switch will average the ACRs on a given interface, compare this to the bandwidth actually available, and generate a rate equal to what may be realistically supported. The destination, upon receipt of the RM cell, will set the DIR, adjust the ER, CI or NI fields if required and also set the CI bit to 1 if the EFCI bit was set in the last data cell. Along the return path, switches may once again alter the ER field. Note that the destination may actually generate RM cells at a maximum rate of 10/second. (ATM Forum, 1996b).

Table 3.26 Source and destination ABR parameters.

Name and unit	Description
PCR (Peak Cell Rate in cells/second)	Policed by network
MCR (Minimum Cell Rate in cells/second)	Guaranteed
ICR (Initial Cell Rate in cells/second)	Start up rate after source is idle
RIF (Rate Increase Factor)	Permitted rate increase: RIFF = RIF*Nrm/PCR
Nrm (Number of cells/RM cell)	$2^N(Nrm-1)$ data cells between RM cells
RDF (Rate Decrease Factor)	Reduction: RDF = Nrm*RDFF
ACR (Allowed Cell Rate in cells/second)	Current permitted transmission rate.

Table 3.27 Relevant RM cell payload fields.

Field	Length	Description
Protocol ID	8	Describes the function of the RM cell
Direction (DIR)	1	Indicates whether or not the cell is traveling from the source to the destination (0) or the reverse (1) direction
BECN (BN)	1	Indicates that the RM cell has been generated by the switch; this field will be set by a switch which reverses the RM cell and sends it back to the source under times of heavy network congestion
Congestion Indication (CI)	1	Set by the switches or by the destination if the source should not increase its transmission rate.
No Increase (NI)	1	If set to 1, prevents source from increasing its ACR but does not cause a decrease
Explicit Cell Rate (ER)	16	Set by the switch or destination to the transmission rate which the sources should use
Current Cell Rate (CCR)	16	Contains the current transmission rate of the source; this field is used by the switch to calculate the new acceptable rate (ER)
Minimum Cell Rate (MCR)	16	Contains the minimum rate at which the source will send
CRC	10	Checksum for the RM cell payload

Upon receipt of an RM cell, the source will first look at the CI flag. If set, it will reduce its ACR by at least ACR*RDF to a minimum of CDR. If not set, it will increase its ACR by no more than RIF*PCR to a maximum of PCR. If NI=O, the source will not increase ACR. Now, the source looks at the ER field and adjusts its rate to the lower of the new ACR or the ER, but now below MCR. This RM cell is expected to be received by the source after the network round-trip time. If this has not occurred, it will decrease its sending rate (the ACR) by RDF at the RM generation interval until reaching its MCR. The RDF is a predefined reduction factor. If a returning RM cell is received but delayed, the source will still reduce its transmission rate. Other fields within the RM cell contain information as to direction and MCR. This is just a standard 53-byte ATM cell with the protocol type field in the header set to 110. We outline the relevant RM cell fields in Table 3.27, while I.371 contains additional information.

A switch may implement binary (EFCI), **Relative Rate (RR)** marking, or **Explicit Rate (ER)** marking based flow control and comply with the specification (Figure 3.42). This will allow both end-systems and switches to participate in the mechanism to some degree if they cannot be upgraded to generate or respond to RM cells. If EFCI-based (mandatory for ABR but optional for CBR, VBR, and UBR), the switch will set the EFCI bit in the forward data cells to indicate congestion. Note that the source under this scheme may be slow to react since the cell must pass to the destination and back. A switch implementing RR marking may set

Binary based on EFCI bit

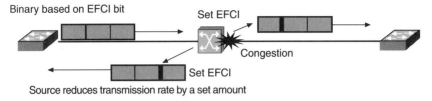

Source reduces transmission rate by a set amount

Relative Rate (RR) and Explicit Rate (ER) marking, based on RM Cells

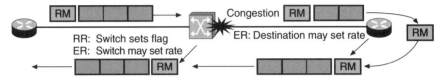

Source reduces/increases transmission rate by set amount if RR or by value in RM cell if ER

Figure 3.42 End-to-end ABR operation. Source: Cisco Systems.

the CI or NI in either the forward or reverse RM cells to indicate congestion, but will not set an actual rate. Finally, if implementing the full ER-based mechanism, a switch may set the ER field within the RM cell and in addition may also set the CI or NI fields. Alternatively, a switch receiving an RM cell with a CCR larger than that which may be supported may set the ER and forward the cell in both the forward and reverse directions. This new reversed RM cell will have BN=1 and either NI or CN set to 1.

Although we expect most ATM-connected data systems to eventually implement both the ER and RR modes of ABR, in the interim we may implement the EFCI ABR mode. Note that we do not expect to encounter situations where the end-system implement full ABR while the network supports only the binary (EFCI) mode, since ER and PR support is easier to implement in the ATM switches. Under EFCI, a source generating a data stream will periodically inject an RM cell on the VCC. A switch along the path experiencing congestion will now set the EFCI bit in the data cell headers. The destination, upon recipt of these tagged data cells, may then adjust it's transmission rate via some vendor-specific method of transferring the EFCI state into the upper layers. It will then set the CI bit in the RM cell transmitted back to the original source. Upon receipt of these RM cells, the source should lower its transmission rate if the CI bit is set or if no RM cell has been received. Alternatively, if the bit has not been set it may raise its rate. If RM cells are not used, a network element experiencing congestion may still set the EFCI in the cell header. This mode is optional for toher ATM service categories. (Figure 3.43). A problem with EFCI is that the mechanism by which end-systems are to determine whether they are congested or not is

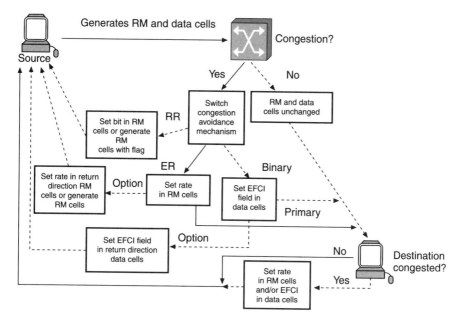

Figure 3.43 State diagram for EFCI, RR, and ER ABR modes.

────── Primary path if congestion experienced and switches implement explicit rate control.

undefined. If a system implements an EFCI scheme which does not accurately reflect the true status of the system and of the network, resulting oscillations in bandwidth may do more harm to throughput than good. Other potential problems with this binary scheme include slow response to changes in network congestion, made worse as the delay in the path increases. This is due to the end-to-end control loop of EFCI in contrast to ER and RR where the switch may provide immediate feedback to the source.

If an end-to-end connection is divided into virtual sources and destinations to shorten the control loop, each virtual source will act as a physical source and the same will hold true for each virtual destination. For example, a switch acting as a virtual source and destination will terminate RM cells on one port and regenerate them on another. A typical configuration may consist of a local area network based on workgroup switches implementing binary rate control connecting to an ATM WAN based on enterprise switches which implement explicit control (Sathaye, 1995).

ABR: implementation concerns

The traffic management mechanisms used by ATM end-systems and intermediate systems only provide half of the picture. Looking at ABR, a complete view is only possible if we have knowledge of issues surrounding implementation, including hardware/software complexity and the various ways of segmenting the congestion avoidance control loop. Complexity influences the cost of equipment and time-to-market, while the method by which ABR is implemented in the local and wide areas will influence its responsiveness. Both will ultimately affect user acceptance.

The generation of the RM cells will of course require the deployment of new SAR hardware if any degree of performance is desired. Consider a physical trunk interface with 1000 VCs. If an RM cell is generated every 32 cell times, over 10,000 cells per second must be processed by this single interface. This has implications in switch interface design. In addition, ABR will introduce a level of overhead into the cell stream (in addition to that dedicated to the exchange of trunking information). In a local area this overhead may be acceptable, but over a wide area with higher propagation delay a tunable value may be more efficient.

A congestion avoidance mechanism must prove useful over both local and wide areas. Since the ABR service relies on network feedback, which then relates to queue sizes, the wide area was automatically considered to be the driving force behind buffer sizing. In reality, the local area must be considered as well, since the buffering relates to the amount of data in transit and not to the absolute delay on the link. Thus, a very high-speed MAN connection (for instance, STM-16) may present the same sizing problems as a lower-speed WAN link (for example, E3/DS3). The next concern is just how the available bandwidth on a link will be calculated. This relates to fairness, with the bandwidth divided among the multiple VCs based on a number of methods.

In implementing a traffic management mechanism, it may be useful to benchmark the performance. The speed at which the switches within an ATM network can react to changes in congestion and then relay this information to the sources should be measured. This is almost analogous to measuring the convergence speed of a complex Layer 3 network (which unfortunately has not yet been widely done due to the current emphasis on PPS benchmarking). Looking back to the complexity of implementing any RM-based congestion avoidance scheme, some vendors are exploring performance tradeoffs between the RR and ER schemes. Remember that an end-system supporting the ER must implement the UNI 4.0 and switches the PNNI. Within a campus or workgroup, the RR mechanism may in fact lead to throughputs approaching that possible via ER. This is known as **ABR Lite**, and in fact switches and end-systems implementing this may approach within 5%–10% of ER throughput (noting that UBR with EPD/TPD will also approach these values).

One deficiency in the rate control mechanism is the response time over long, multi-hop links due to the round-trip time of the VCC.

Remember that the algorithm may be implemented end-to-end or hop-by-hop. Within a given VC, both methods are viable. A wise boundary may be within switches connecting the local area with the ATM WAN. In a local-area network, switches may be less sophisticated and therefore capable of less buffering. This may not be the case with switches deployed over a WAN. If the control loop is closed at this boundary, the workgroup ATM switches will not need to provide the buffering required by the algorithm. When deployed in this manner, intermediate points terminating the loop are known as virtual sources and destinations. An added advantage will be quicker response to change via the RM cells and more visibility over where congestion in a network may be occurring. In addition, if required, each of these segments may implement a different congestion avoidance system, resulting in advantages both to local- and wide-area ATM switches. The local switches no longer are required to implement buffering (with inherent costs) required over a wide area while the wide-area segment is isolated from local users which have not implemented congestion control. Working against the implementation of virtual sources and destinations is the requirement to implement per-VC queuing at these points.

As discussed above, a potential problem with the rate-based scheme is its reliance on a single buffer and flow control for the physical connection, as opposed to the per-VC control available within the credit-based system. This may present a problem if, for example, an end-system does not support RM cells, has been permitted to connect to the network, and continues to send data in the presence of congestion. The same situation occurs in Frame Relay networks, where one internetwork layer protocol (CLNS, for example) may respond to the FECN or BECN, and throttle back, while other protocols (IP) have limited knowledge of the notifications. In this case, the 'well-behaved' protocol is penalized at the expense of those less compliant protocols. From a cost perspective, rate-based systems will save buffering, though at the expense of some hardware complexity. The tradeoffs may include additional parameters to be set and, more importantly, a loss of precision in bandwidth allocation. This latter situation may result from ATM end-systems setting arbitrary bandwidths, which are then adjusted by the network via the RM cells. But this adjustment is not instantaneous. Thus, a given station may decide to begin transmission with a bandwidth which is either higher or lower than the network is capable of supporting, resulting in a loss of efficiency.

ABR end-systems will negotiate certain parameters as part of signaling, while others are preset to default values. Fang and Lin (1995a and 1995b) look at these defaults for binary-mode switches in the context of the 'parking lot' configuration, a classical network simulation configuration, and go on to recommend a number values for best performance. This analysis is quite important, as a number of 'ABR-compliant' ATM switches will only implement binary ABR during most of 1996.

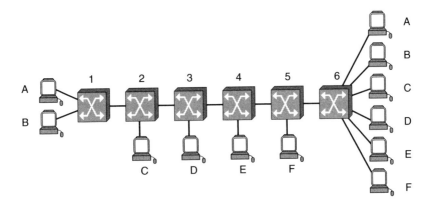

Figure 3.44 Parking lot configuration. Source: ATM Forum.

Figure 3.44 depicts this configuration, consisting of six switches and six sources/destinations.

Under operation, the link between switches 4 and 5 is subject to congestion. Thus, most analysis takes place at this point. Initial observations (Fang and Lin, 1995a) show that the use of the BECN will result in better fairness than the EFCI at both low and high ICR settings. More important are results derived from buffers with a maximum size of 1024 cells. Fairness suffers and TCP retransmissions increase under both EFCI and BECN. Fang and Lin (1995b) build upon these results by looking at performance in the presence of background and reverse direction traffic and over WAN distances. ABR is also compared with UBR and UBR with EPD at this point. The chief result from these analyses is that the improper choice of parameters may result in worse performance under ABR than UBR or UBR with EPD.

If we look at the performance of UBR and TPD in contrast to ABR, some simulations show that, within a LAN, binary mode ABR TCP performance is about equal to UBR+TPD for TCP. Over a wide area, its performance is in fact slightly worse than EPD and it suffers in throughput. One reason for this is ABR's burst performance due to slow start and the time required for the switch to inform the source that it may transmit at a higher rate. Hence the focus on end-system behavior within the Forum.

As is obvious, there is still work to be done in determining the best traffic management architecture for a given traffic class and application. Over the next year or two, we will gain experience in implementing the ABR modes, packet discard, and their interactions with each other as well as with higher-layer flow control mechanisms. Over the course of time, we will gain an understanding as to the proper mechanism to implement in a given instance, and will be able to deploy switch architectures capable of supporting these mechanisms at an acceptable cost. In a later chapter, we take a closer look at these switch architectures.

ABR: effect of mixed (ATM and non-ATM) architectures

Additional congestion control issues arise when we implement mixed ATM and non-ATM architectures. End-user applications running over traditional protocol stacks including TCP and UDP over IP have no knowledge at present of ATM-based ABR links. Because of this, the application control loop is unable to interact with any congestion control mechanisms implemented at the boundary of the ATM cloud. In looking at the effect on end-to-end protocol performance, we should analyze two types of application. The first is 'cooperative', which backs off its transmission rate under network stress. TP4 in DECnet and the TCP Slow Start are two examples of this. 'Disruptive' applications which continue to transmit at full rate fall into the second category. Any end-to-end congestion avoidance mechanism should apply to both of these traffic types. The ATM ABR section of the path is intended to be loss-free, with adaptive buffering possibly up to the BW*RTT product implemented. This buffering may result in a step-function based flow, with an increase in delay accompanied by a decrease in bandwidth. An end-system, having no knowledge of this increase in delay above and beyond that predicted by the original probing for RTT, may timeout because of this. This problem is exacerbated by the buffering, in that data assumed to be lost due to the timeout was in fact not lost at all; it was only queued. Thus, the ABR congestion avoidance mechanism is in effect interfering with the end-to-end congestion and bandwidth discovery scheme. In the case of TCP, bandwidth changes are normally recognized in one RTT but, when buffering, the time to discover a problem is increased. Yet another problem may occur as a result of routers attached to ATM networks, where the ATM connection is at a lower data rate than the router's non-ATM interfaces. The solution to these problems is to have the routers be ATM-aware; knowledgeable of the end-to-end bandwidth. IP entities on the end-systems must therefore interact with the ATM congestion control mechanism. This perceived mismatch between TCP and ABR is one reason why some user communities prefer more 'frame-oriented' mechanisms such as UBR with TPD.

Possible interactions between ABR and TCP flows are indicative of more general concerns within the networking community as to how QoS information may be exchanged between Layer 3 internetworking protocols and ATM. As we begin to deploy resource-aware applications and accompanying protocol support within the internetwork, we must provide for interworking between the different traffic profiles within the Internet, described in the next chapter, and ATM traffic classes. This includes support on both sides of the ATM boundary of not only best-effort applications requiring ABR and UBR, but those guaranteed service applications requiring CBR and VBR as well. If this is done properly, we will have achieved end-to-end quality of service support. If not, user applications will suffer. During the latter half of 1996, we should see the first attempts at this as vendors implement interworking between RSVP and ATM. Recently, the community has begun to investigate ways of propogating QoS information across the non-ATM (datagram) portion of the network. Remember that current Layer 3 routing protocols such as OPSF do not pass QoS data. Proposals include **PNNI Augmented Routing (PAR)** where ATM edge devices such as routers will be provided with some *a priori* information as to the current capabilities of the ATM network. They may then forward this data in some yet undetermined way into Layer 3. Looking a bit further afield, an internetwork supporting QoS-based applications on a wide scale should have some way to propogate QoS data. Two alternatives include QoS extensions to the traditional routing protocols or use of the I-PNNI (also described in the next chapter).

Switch buffering and traffic management

As introduced during the section on congestion avoidance, the amount of data in transmit over a physical connection, the bandwidth delay product, relates to the amount of buffering which must be provided at an interface. If this buffering is not available, a higher-layer protocol such as TCP, which expects buffering equal to the window size, will operate inefficiently. In the local area, where the delay is not as great, buffering still comes into play as it will allow switches to effectively handle sudden changes in traffic profiles, such as bursts during client–server exchanges.

An interesting way to look at buffering within an ATM switch is to associate the buffers with time as opposed to a strict cell count. Outgoing interfaces will then be provided with buffers equal to a certain delay, for example 100 ms, a value derived from maximum wide-area propagation times. Remember that this is due to the feedback delay for congestion control information across this link. In this configuration, we provide an OC-3 (STM-1) trunk with a 48K cell buffer (15 Mbits in transit over a 100 ms RTT link = 1.9375 Mbyte = 36,556 cells), while a DS3 would require 16K. Time-based buffering may be the proper way to quote buffer sizes as it more closely reflects the characteristics of a given link (delay) and may be used to quickly determine if a given switch is suitable for the wide area. Local-area ATM switches, though not affected by wide-area propagation delays, should also be provided with buffering adequate to effectively buffer the MTU of the data since this may be sent as a burst. The difficult part is to determine how many active connections each physical interface must service at this MTU. Consider an ATM swith with multiple incoming ports, all highly loaded with traffic destined to one outgoing port. Without buffer management schemes internal to the switch, the outgoing interface would need to buffer the expected bursts from the total of the incoming interfaces. In fact, if the cell buffering required due to a WAN link exceeds the expected MTU, we would need BW*RTT buffering at the single output for the total number of incoming interfaces. This is obviously unacceptable. If we implement some feedback, or backpressure mechanism within the switch, we can inform a buffer at an incoming interface whether or not buffering is available at the output. We are then able to manage traffic at this incoming interface by applying feedback to the source, discarding packets, or even dropping cells on a per-traffic class or per-VC basis. When we discuss switch architectures in Chapter 5, we will see that some buffering schemes are better suited to be able to handle bursty data than others.

A concern when deploying large buffers is their impact upon traffic requiring low delay or delay variance. Voice, videoconferencing, and video distribution fall into this category. A properly designed switch will prioritize this traffic in such a way that it may cut through the buffers totally (for example, CBR). Since bandwidth is pre-allocated for this traffic profile, the large buffers are not required.

Closely related to the size of an ATM switch's buffers is how they are allocated in implementing ATM Forum traffic management. Consider the five traffic classes described earlier: CBR, rt-VBR, nrt-VBR, ABR, and UBR. A switch must be able to guarantee resources for each of these classes. In Figure 3.45, we depict an example of an enterprise switch where incoming traffic is placed in dynamic buffers based on the QoS of the incoming VCC. This ensures that the VCCs, QoS may be maintained. While the data is divided by traffic class, real-time VCCs

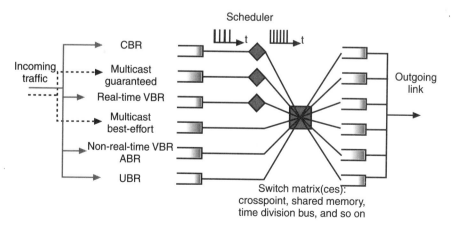

Figure 3.45 Switch traffic management.

(CBR and rt-VBR) may optionally be fed through a device known as a scheduler. A scheduler will smooth unequal cell spacing caused by CDV along a link.

Traffic management on a typical ATM end-system operates in much the same way. Remember that traffic shaping may conform to the I.371 continuous-state leaky bucket algorithm. In simplest terms, this mechanism attaches a bucket to each VC. To transmit a cell through a VC, the bucket must contain tokens. We remove one token after transmitting a cell, and we place tokens in the bucket periodically. Using the Cisco ATM Interface Processor as an example, consider the command `atm rate-queue 0 50`. This sets queue 0 (of a total of eight queues) to a peak (PCR) of 50 Mbps. Now we associate a VC with this rate queue via the command `atm pvc 1 1 1 50 25 100`. VPI=1, VCI=1 is now attached to queue 0 with an average rate (SCR) of 25 Mbps and a burst size of 3200 cells (100*32). When a cell arrives at the queue, the traffic shaping state machine checks if the bucket associated with this PVC contains a credit. If so, we send one cell to the physical layer and remove one credit from the bucket. The average rate determines how often a credit is put into the bucket, while the burst determines how many credits the bucket may contain. Therefore, if this PVC has a high traffic volume to send, it may start with the 50 Mbps peak until no credit remains, at which time it must back off to its average. Note the burst size above, 3200 cells. When connecting an end-system to an ATM switch, we must be aware of the buffers available at both ends of the connection. For example, some public ATM switches have very small buffers which would be quickly overrun by such a large burst.

Other – credit based

Credit-based congestion control is analogous to the windowing mechanisms used in X.25 and TCP. The mechanism operates as follows. An ATM end-system will have a number of VCs open at a given time. Each VC is provided with a buffer, along with a predetermined number of credits. When a cell is transmitted over the VC to an ATM switch, a credit will be returned to the end-system only if the cell was forwarded to the next switch towards the destination. If the cell was not forwarded, no credit will be issued, and the original end-system will stop sending. One feature of the credit-based algorithm is that it operates on a per-VC bases. Thus, a given VC may never monopolize the buffers on a switch at the expense of other users. Though this system ensures that data will never overrun an intermediate system, a question may arise as to what buffer size an end-system or switch must maintain for each VC. An often heard complaint is that a buffer must be maintained for each VC. Though this is correct, the cost of implementation should be less on end-systems. In reality, the cost of the credit-based system should be equal to the cost of implementing alternative schemes and, when viewed from a more global perspective, the cost of the actual switch and end-system hardware is only a small part of the total cost of ownership. One element of this total cost is management and, if the proponents of this system are correct, ease of configuration may be a plus. There are two parts to the credit-based puzzle – a static system for use in the local area, requiring no configuration, and an adaptive mechanism for the wide area. This latter system is interrelated to the link state database maintained by the PNNI protocol. Another consideration deals with the responsiveness of a given mechanism. In this case, the system operates on a link-by-link basis.

The credit-based approach was one of the two contending mechanisms hotly debated through the course of 1994. Though supported by a number of vendors and considered feasible (at least technically), it was dropped in favor of the rate-based scheme. An initial version of this mechanism, termed **Flow Control Virtual Circuit (FCVC)**, would have required a buffer to be maintained for every active VC equal to the bandwidth-delay product of the link. This was one problem with the original proposal. The second is due to the possibility of loss of the credits generated by the receiver. Both were addressed in an adaptive-FCVC which provided each VC with a fraction of the original buffer. This fraction is dependent upon the rate at which the VC uses the credit, and is therefore larger for the more active VCs. A problem with this approach, though, is the potential delay between the time a VC begins transmitting at its full link rate and when the credits have been allocated.

Not to be left behind by efforts within the ATM Forum, a number of vendors have banded together in favor of the credit-based scheme. This Flow Control Consortium has released a document titled *Quantum Flow Control (QFC)* outlining a per-VC, hop-by-hop protocol based on buffer levels. The shorter control loop addresses a fault which some people find with the rate-based scheme. Another advantage is the ability of ABR traffic to use any available bandwidth if it is not used by higher priority services. One item of note is that this mechanism is compatible with UNI 3.0/3.1 signaling. Information about this consortium is given in Appendix C.

Analysis

During mid-1996, there were actually four different flow control mechanisms undergoing standardization, each with supporters. The ITU in I.371 has defined an ABR mechanism that is more or less aligned with work within the ATM Forum. However, there are still differences, which should be resolved by feeding work from the Forum back into the ITU. This would also help to align the signaling specification, Q.2961.2, with the Forum. A second ABR-type service also exists within the ITU. This is the French ABT proposal, found within I.371. The fourth mechanism, described above, is **Quantum Flow Control (QFC)**. As is clear, ATM flow control may take some time to fully stabilize, resulting in a degree of uncertainty, confusion, and lack of interoperability in the short term. Ultimately, the situation will stabilize based on the ATM Forum's work, with products conforming to QFC interoperable at boundaries between the two systems. Even within the ATM Forum, alignment between Signaling 4.0, the PNNI Phase 1, and the traffic management specification (defining ABR).

Ideally, switches and end-systems will implement the Forum's rate-based congestion avoidance scheme based on the exchange of information between ATM switches and ATM-connected routers, LAN switches, PCs, and workstations. Here the choice is whether to implement the full ABR scheme with its associated complexity or just a subset providing simple feedback. Alternatively, vendor-specific algorithms can be suitable if they can be made to interwork with the standard. Implementations until summer 1996 use proprietary congestion avoidance schemes (either rate-based or credit-based), binary congestion avoidance based on the EFCI field, or none at all. It is only into the second half of 1996 that we expect to see wide deployment of the ABR mechanism. Large networks may include EFCI in the local area and proprietary schemes in the wide area, but whether these two mechanisms will interwork is vendor specific. As introduced earlier, there is some concern as to how well the EFCI mechanism will operate. Alternatively, an end-to-end network may consist of traffic shaping at the source and a proprietary scheme at the core. In no case is deployment of ATM on any scale without some mechanism recommended. This is especially true for wide-area ATM networks.

3.6 Management, security, and directory services

A sometimes overlooked element of building a successful network is management and though this may take many forms, underlying concepts are the same. The goal of any management architecture is to provide for the control of devices and services within an internetwork. Requirements fall into five major areas: fault, configuration, performance, accounting, and security. In the paragraphs below, we identify various devices and protocols to allow for this control.

Within a network, one or more management stations will act as focal points for many managed devices and services. Devices may be switches, routers, modems, and any other networking or computing device which is capable of communicating with a management system. Network services, overlaid on the physical network devices, support user applications. These services, as simple as LAN emulation or as complex as a public VPN offering, must be managed as well. The management station is responsible for issuing configuration commands and receiving status information from the managed devices (either by initiating the request for status or by receiving device-generated messages, or **traps**). Most importantly, the station must also be capable of relating the data and presenting it to the manager in a rational and understandable way. Comprehensive management platforms should also be capable of communication amongst themselves, providing for a level of redundancy and distribution of tasks. The entity on a managed device is called an agent, which in turn communicates with the management station via a network management protocol. This protocol may take a number of forms, either standardized (for example, SNMP, CMIP) or proprietary.

An example of a network management protocol in common use throughout the internetworking industry is the **Simple Network Management Protocol (SNMP)** (see Rose, 1993). Though this protocol was originally developed for the management of the old NSFnet in the US, it has been adopted by everyone from printer manufacturers to software developers and is even found in some central office phone switches. As part of the description of SNMP, we look at **Management Information Bases (MIBs)** and the **Interim Local Management Interface (ILMI)**, note that the concept of a MIB is not SNMP-specific. A successor to the original SNMP, now known as SNMPv1, is **SNMPv2**. We describe this protocol, currently under development and which should see wide deployment during 1996, later. Though SNMP is a good basis for network management, it is only a starting point when looking at end-to-end management of ATM networks. This includes not only device management, but management of the physical infrastructure (focusing on OAM), interworking with external management systems via ATM Forum defined interfaces, and service provisioning. These concerns, though many times thought of as applying only to public networks, also apply to private ATM networks. Looking forward, totally new approaches to management based on Web technologies are in the early phases of deployment by management software developers and networking vendors. A typical architecture will include a Netscape and Java enabled NMS drawing on a relational database and a server in each managed device. During the next year or two, this may totally change many NMS environments.

Related to network management is network security. Although the need for security within an ATM network has been recognized for quite a long time, only recently has the ATM Forum begun detailed work on the requirements for security and possible solutions. In developing these solutions, they are seeking guidance from the ITU and the IETF. Until their work is complete, security within an ATM network will rely on network and application layer security along with static configurations at the ATM layer and vendor proputary extensions.

Directory services allow users to identify resources within a network. This is an area in which the ATM Forum has recently begun work, looking at the needs of ATM users and the capabilities of existing systems.

3.6.1 Network management framework

A starting point for the management of ATM networks is the ATM Forum network management framework, based on the five functional areas (configuration, performance, fault, accounting, and security management) of the ISO management model which we introduced earlier. Both private and public network management are included within this model, which provides for management at the UNI via the ILMI and SNMP, end-to-end circuit management, and 'total' management of ATM networks and services. This management model is actually contained within a larger model known as the **Telecommunications Management Network (TMN)** (CCITT, 1992). The TMN is a parallel network to the network being managed, and consists of five layers: the **Element Layer (EL)**, **Element Management Layer (EML)**, **Network Management Layer (NML)**, **Service Management Layer (SML)**, and **Business Management Layer (BML)**. The first three are applicable to the management of a physical network, and may be mapped to the ATM Forum's management framework as shown in Figure 3.46. The NML provides the network manager with a unified view of the network under one management domain. This layer will operate

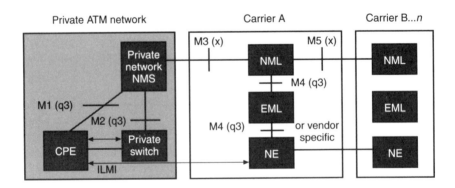

Figure 3.46 ATM Forum network management framework.

NML   Network Management Layer
EML   Element Management Layer
NE   Network Element

through the EML, which provides for the grouping of similar **Network Elements (NEs)**. Data generated by the NEs may also be filtered at this layer. The lowest management layer, EL, performs basic management of the ATM equipment.

Each interface, M1 to M5, has certain characteristics and provides for different management capabilities. As a start, the ATMF focused on the M3 and M4 interfaces, as standards and MIBs for M1 and M2 were developed external to the Forum. The M1 and M2 are interfaces between a private network management system and either CPE or the private ATM network. Interfaces between private and public networks are required for service activation, service assurance (that is, troubleshooting), and usage metering (for example, gathering of accounting data for billing). The most basic form of this interaction is over the ILMI, allowing devices at either end of the UNI to share basic configuration information.

Where more functionality is required, a **Customer Network Management (CNM)** system based on the M3 interface may be deployed. This private network to public carrier interface provides this functionality for inter-management system communications, and is divided into three capability classes:

- Class 1, an SNMP-based information exchange interface where the user may gather configuration and status information from the public network;

- Class 2, also based on SNMP, allows the user to add and delete logical/virtual connections if they are pre-authorized;

- A third class, not yet totally defined but capable of using SNMP or **Electronic Data Interchange (EDI)**, will allow a user to request new connections.

When extended to the public domain, the interface between the private management system and the CNM agent within the operator's environment is also known as the 'X' interface.

The next interface, M4, defines an SNMP or CMIP management connection to a public switching system. This interface may actually be subdivided into two sub-interfaces: one connecting the network element and the EML, and another connecting the EML with the NML. Finally, the M5 (also 'X') interface connects one TMN to another for carrier-to-carrier information exchange. Capabilities include circuit ordering and provisioning, configuration data verification, trouble administration, performance, and accounting. Often, a Q3 interface is also referenced. This interface is one connecting management systems (NML and EML for example) or connecting a management system with a managed entity (NMS and CPE or private ATM network) (see Fowler, 1995).

In attacking this model, the Forum has first focused on network element and network management by defining M4 requirements and a logical MIB which provide the basis for the M4 CMIP and SNMP MIBs. The requirements document, along with its M3 and M5 parallels, forms the basis for current work on service management. At present, business management is under the responsibility of the NM Forum. Looking at areas where the ATM Forum has generated documents, they have first focused on fault, configuration, and performance management, leaving accounting and security as major areas to be addressed.

To relate these black boxes and interfaces to reality, let us look at a typical ATM deployment consisting of a campus network connected into a public ATM service. Local ATM switches along with ATM-attached LAN switches, routers, PCs, and workstations, will be managed from the private network management platform via SNMP. These are the M1 and M2 interfaces outlined in Figure 3.46. In addition, end-systems connected to the private ATM switch will use the ILMI, described in a separate section. The network administrator of the private network may also want visibility into public ATM service performance. In this event, a CNM capability will be provided by the public service provider over what is known as the M3 interface. Looking once again at the public domain, the interface between the service provider's network management platform and switch is nominally the M4, but in reality current implementations differ very little from the M2 interface used in the private domain. M5 interfaces between service providers are still in the very early stages of implementation.

ATM layer management consists of those network management actions which take place at the ATM cell level and below. These actions, which allow network elements to obtain information about the end-to-end ATM connection, may be divided into three categories: alarm surveillance and connection performance monitoring via OAM, and management of valid/invalid VPIs/VCIs via the ATM cell header. We describe connection performance monitoring via OAM flows and their identification via the ATM cell header in a later section.

Related to ATM system management and to TMN in particular are efforts within the multivendor **Telecommunications Information Networking Architecture Consortium (TINA-C)** to developing a management application framework. TINA integrates telecommunications and computing technologies into existing management architectures, in effect an implementation of the TMN concepts providing for multicarrier and customer network management at the application layer (as opposed to the system layer exchange of management data or developing new MIBs). One concept of TINA is a **Telecommunications Service Agency (TSA)**, capable of brokering service requests among multiple national and international carriers. Interactions between this TSA and the carrier-based network management systems are based on **Computer Supported Cooperative Work (CSCW)** applications.

These systems are under development and are expected to be completed in 1997.

3.6.2 SNMP

SNMP is the most popular management protocol in contrast to the **Common Management Information Protocol (CMIP) and Services (CMIS)**, which has seen less support within the internetworking community due to complexity and a lack of interest. Nevertheless, with the deployment of public ATM networks, some vendors are having to re-evaluate their CMIP strategy. The IETF defines two versions of SNMP: SNMPv1 and SNMPv2. SNMPv1, widely implemented, defines a minimal set of commands for manipulating and querying a management agent residing on any manageable system, while SNMPv2 originally built upon this framework by providing additional functions such as security (MD5 and DES) as well as multiprotocol and manager-to-manager support. At the end of 1995, the future of SNMPv2 was in doubt due to debate concerning sections of the protocol's administrative framework, specifically public key encryption and remote security configuration. Due to complexities in deploying and administrating these two areas, a simpler version of the protocol termed SNMPv2t ('t' for trivial) was eventually adopted. In effect, the security provisions of what is now known as SNMPv2c ('c' for classic) were left for future work. Any security to be included within an SNMP network management framework will now be the task of the application developer or NMS vendor.

Commands within SNMP are known as SNMP-PDUs, and include a `get` to retrieve management information, a `get-next` used to retrieve information by traversing a MIB, and a `set` used to alter information. These three commands are issued by the management station. In addition, the agent on the managed platform may generate additional SNMP-PDUs: a `trap` to report critical events, a `get-response` used to reply to a `get`, `get-next`, or `set-request`. Every manageable system will include support for one or more MIBs as described earlier.

3.6.3 CMIP

Although virtually every piece of internetworking equipment and, in fact, some ATM central office switches, implement SNMP, the CMIP is worth some attention as it provides an example of scaling network management beyond the capabilities of SNMPv1. CMIP is based on the ITU-T X.700 series of recommendations, along with extensions for TMN via the M.3000 series and technology or interface specific standards such as ITU-T G.774 for SDH. The protocol does have some advantages in comparison to SNMP for building very large network management systems at the expense of additional complexity. These include assured transfer of management data as opposed to SNMP's use of UDP. CMIP includes automatic event notification, where the managed entity may generate traps based on set conditions. Only recently has the SNMP environment included this functionality via RMON extensions. Next, CMIP includes the concepts of containment and inheritance, whereby the status of a more global object is reflected in less global elements. For example, a non-operational switch will automatically cause its ports to assume the same status, requiring only a single trap. SNMP would require a trap for the switch and for each of its ports. Finally, CMIP includes event filtering by either the managed entity or management system. This increased functionality comes at additional expense in terms of software complexity and hardware requirements. Due to these requirements, a system must implement the full OSI protocol stack along with ACSE and ROSE on each CMIS/CMIP device. The protocol in the past has only been supported on larger systems where the invest-ment could be justified.

3.6.4 MIBs

Managed devices within an internetwork use what is known as an MIB to hold variables which may be retrieved or altered. The MIB is a tree-like data structure, where branches represent related functions or objects and end-points contain the actual information objects. Objects are defined in a language known as **Abstract Syntax Notation 1**

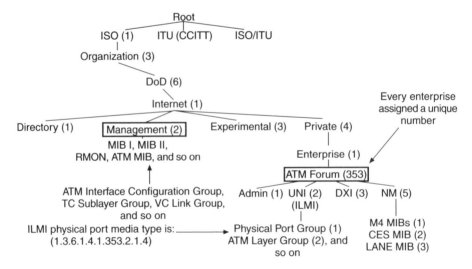

Figure 3.47 Abstract Syntax Notation 1 tree. Source: ATM Forum.

(ASN.1), a machine-readable (and semi-human-readable) method of describing the tree and its objects. The ASN.1 tree root splits into three branches: ISO, ITU, and ISO/ITU. We are concerned with the branches leading from the ISO branch as shown in Figure 3.47. Thus, Internet management MIBs fall under (1.3.6.1.2) while MIBs defined by the ATM Forum are identified by (1.3.6.1.4.1.353).

A single device will probably include multiple MIBs, some defined by the IETF, ITU, or ATM Forum, and others proprietary. Note that although MIBs are used within both SNMP and CMIP, the two forms are not interchangeable. In Table 3.28 we list the various MIBs defined by these organizations.

Table 3.28 MIBs relevant to ATM. Source: ATM Forum.

MIB	Purpose	Standard and part of NM model
ILMI	Configuration across a UNI	ATM Forum UNI 3.x and ILMI 4.0 (SNMP) [UNI (M2, M4)]
ATM MIB	Defines ATM-related objects for private networks and devices	IETF RFC-1695 (SNMP) [M1, M2 (M3)]
DXI MIB	Interface between a router and DSU	ATM Forum DXI 1.0 (SNMP) [M1]
M4 MIB – network element	ATM-related objects for carrier network elements	ATM Forum M4 (CMIP, SNMP) [M4]
G.ATM	ATM-related objects for carrier networks based on ATMF M4	ITU-G.ATM based on M3100 (CMIP) [M2, M4]
M4 MIB – network level	ATM-related objects for carrier networks	ATM Forum M4 NE [M4]
M3 MIB	ATM objects for customer's portion of public network	ATM Forum M3 (SNMP) [M3]
Transmission MIBs	Transmission media parameters for SDH/ SONET, and so on	IETF RFCs 1595, 1407, 1406 (SNMP) ITU G.704, G.774 (CMIP) [M1, M2, M3, M4]
LAN emulation MIB	ATM objects for LAN emulation	(SNMP); [M1, M2]
CES MIB	ATM objects for circuit emulation	(SNMP); [M2, M4]
Power management MIB	Reduce power when idle	(SNMP); [M1]
M5 network to network MIB	Interconnection of two carrier networks	ATM Forum M5; [M5]
ATM inverse multiplexer MIB	ATM over $N{\times}$T1/E1 physical links	(SNMP) [M2, M4]
Bellcore	Telco-specific extensions to M4 MIB	Bellcore GR-1114 Issue 2, Oct 95 [M4]
Network management	Service management	NM Forum [M4]

Other MIBs under development within the ATM Forum and the IETF.

The ATM MIB is the first ATM-specific MIB for use in the configuration of ATM networks, and provides for the configuration of VCs across an ATM network. This MIB defines some terminology which is useful in understanding the specifics of an end-to-end connection, although only some terms are used outside of network management. For example, the link between two ATM devices is referred to as a **Virtual Link (VL)**, and is identified by a **Virtual Channel Identifier (VCI)**. Intermediate systems cross-connect VLs to form segments of VCs. A VC in its entirety will traverse multiple segments. ATM hosts will terminate VCs by linking them to higher-layer protocols and applications. Though the MIB defines both **Virtual Path Connections (VPCs)** consisting of **Virtual Path Links (VPLs)** and **Virtual Channel Connections (VCCs)** consisting of **Virtual Channel Links (VCLs)**, both are treated in the same way. Finally, a given VC will be characterized by a traffic pattern, a QoS, and a topology (point-to-point, point-to-multipoint, or multipoint-to-multipoint). In defining connections via the ATM MIB, the user will first reserve the appropriate VLs, characterize the traffic on the VLs, and finally cross-connect the VLs in the intermediate systems and associate these newly-created VCs with user applications in the ATM end-systems. The complete definition process along with procedures for determining the configuration of a VC is described in Tesink and Brunner (1994). All ATM-connected systems, including routers, PCs/workstations, and LAN switches, should implement RFC 1695.

In a given ATM end-system, the ATM MIB will often operate in conjunction with MIB II and extensions outlined in RFC-1573 (McCloghrie and Kastenholz, 1994) for general system and performance management, the SMDS MIB (Brown and Tesink, 1994a), containing AAL3/4-specific along with SMDS over ATM variables, and the various transmission MIBs: SONET (Brown and Tesink, 1994b), DS3 (Cox and Tesink, 1993), DS1 (Baker and Watt, 1993), and so on. The ATM MIB's goal is to allow configuration and status reporting for the M1, M2, and M3 interfaces. An interesting MIB is that under definition for cable systems such as those supporting 802.14. This MIB includes traffic and signal quality monitoring, as well as address, service, and security management. Requirements critical to cable networks include remote access to devices, light weight access to end-systems in terms of CPU and memory, and secure management channels due to the shared medium (IEEE, 1995a). Implementing all of these MIBs allows for effective device management. Note that although a given MIB may allow one to set device parameters which may then be acted upon by the managed system, this action requires operator initiation via the network management system. MIBs in themselves do not manage a system. Parallel to MIBs defining physical entities, the Forum has also standardized on MIBs for use within the different ATM services such as the ILMI (described below) and the ATM-DXI. The ATM-DXI MIB assists with configuration and performance monitoring of non-ATM capable end-systems connect through an ATM-DSU.

Now looking at service management during 1995, a management framework was developed for the LAN emulation service, initially providing for configuration, performance, and fault management (ATM Forum, 1995k). These functions are critical in allowing a network manager to effectively configure and troubleshoot LAN emulation. Configuration management will include identifying, creating, and removing LECs, manually assigning an LEC to a specific VLAN, and identifying the various VCCs used within a VLAN. Initially, the specification applies only to the LEC and not to LECSs, LESs, or BUSs. Once the VLAN is operational, performance management allows identification and monitoring of both data and control traffic flows. This requires support from the LEC platform in terms of RMON, the AToM MIB, and so on. Finally, fault management allows monitoring of the physical status of LEC interfaces and their associated VCCs. This framework uses SNMP MIBs, and is based on SNMPv2 (although the use of SNMPv1 is acceptable).

Finally, the Forum has defined a protocol-independent MIB for the M4 interface able to interoperate with either CMIP or SNMP. From this basis, protocol-specific (CMIP and SNMP) MIBs are developed. These MIBs define objects along with their attributes required to perform management of an ATM network. Manageable entities include link terminations, cross-connects, connection terminations, UNIs, and the B-ICI. In the future, the MIB will be extended to support additional functions as outlined in Bellcore (1995). Though the use of SNMP is not addressed within TMN, its wide deployment and ease of implementation will make it a factor in public management networks.

3.6.5 ILMI

SNMP provides for communication between an NMS and a switch, router, or host to perform network management. In contrast, the ILMI, as shown below, is a peer-to-peer protocol existing solely between a private ATM switch and a host or router or between public and private ATM switches for the purpose of performing interface management. Though the ILMI uses the SNMP message syntax, both the switch and end-system issue requests. As additional ILMI MIB objects are defined, these systems will be able to exchange configuration and topology information with one another. This is in contrast to the pre-ILMI situation where the devices had to be configured separately. Each device participating in the ILMI implements the **ATM Management Entity (AME)**, as depicted in Figure 3.48.

The ILMI, as originally released at the time of the UNI 2.0, included in its MIB support for interface configuration, the maximum number of supported connections, speed, media type, whether the interface was

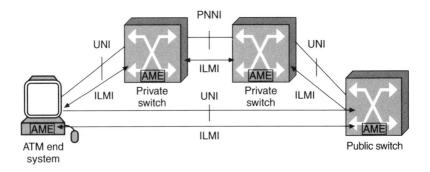

Figure 3.48 ILMI reference interfaces.

public or private, and the operational status and QoS for each PVC (both VPCs and VCCs). Parallel to the release of UNI 3.0, the devices could now register ATM addresses across the ILMI. This was very useful in that an ATM end-system could learn its NSAP network prefix from an ATM switch. The end-system first makes contact with the switch over VPI=0, VCI=16, the ILMI reserved VCC. It then uses this prefix information in combination with its local MAC address to form a complete NSAP address. With this system, no operator intervention is required for address configuration. As an analogy, consider the inverse ARP where a system, knowing its MAC address, queries for its network layer address. In this case, the protocol returns the network portion of the NSAP address (though remember that this is not a network address in the Layer 3 sense). Further changes at UNI 3.1 included provisions for multiple links between the same two devices as well as the support for ATM network topology discovery whereby the network-layer address of the device's management entity is coded as an MIB object. This address is then made available to the NMS via its neighbor over the ILMI. Ongoing additions to the ILMI include its use to exchange ATM addresses of services. For example, this may be used by a LANE client to identify the LANE configuration service. Other groups supported by the ILMI include physical port information, as well as ATM layer, virtual path, and virtual channel data.

Although the ILMI is based on SNMP, the ILMI MIB is not equivalent to the RFC 1695 (Ahmed and Tesink, 1994) ATM MIB. The address registration function across the ILMI, based on the network prefix and ATM address groups, does not exist within RFC 1695. Additional ILMI-only functions allow a host to obtain the address of the LECS and discover whether it is attached to a public or private UNI. Switches use the ILMI to discover how many bits a host uses for the VPI and VCI fields as well as to poll hosts regularly for the purpose of de-registering a host if the line is down. For network topology discovery, the ILMI works together with RFC 1695 in that a host uses the ILMI to obtain its neighbor's IP addresses which it then places in the RFC 1695 MIB.

The PNNI also uses the ILMI, to determine whether a given interface is a UNI or NNI. This is quite useful, in that switch interfaces may be configured for either mode of operation. Drawing on the ILMI, as described in the ATMF UNI 3.1, operation across the NNI will provide for automatic interface configuration, and an accompanying management MIB will provide ATM network devices with knowledge of PNNI status and configuration information.

3.6.6 RMON

Remote Monitoring, or **RMON**, is a method of gathering detailed statistics from a network segment (Figure 3.49). This allows for trouble-shooting and performance monitoring of the various networking devices connected to this segment. The MIB's (RFC 1757 for Ethernet and RFC 1513 for Token Ring) capabilities go beyond the data available as part of SNMP MIBs, and include nine types of information collected: segment statistics, historical statistics, host statistics, sorted host statistics,

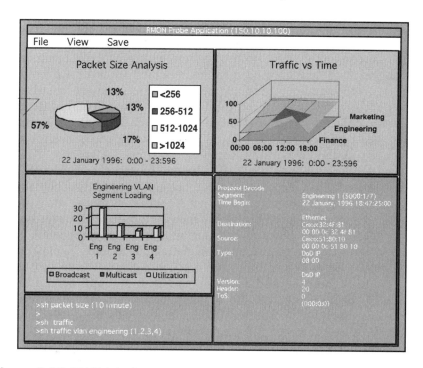

Figure 3.49 RMON display.

traffic matrix, alarms, events, filters, and packet capture. This level of detail requires a special RMON agent on the end-system, usually running on a companion processor. Though the first RMON-capable systems were standalone devices, there is a move within the industry to include this functionality on other networking devices such as LAN switches and routers. In fact, ATM switches in the future will include RMON support of alarm and event groups to allow the management platform to better monitor ATM MIB objects. RMON is valuable in that it may allow a network manager to proactively identify network problems before they occur. Some ways in which this is accomplished are monitoring traffic profiles, analyzing traffic flows and tracking segment utilization. Ultimately this should lead to increased network availability. Standard MIBs within SNMP do not provide this functionality, though some vendors have implemented many of these capabilities as part of proprietary MIBs.

3.6.7 OAM flows

Critical to the manageability of an ATM network are the **Operation, Administration, and Maintenance (OAM)** flows associated with the physical and ATM layers. As outlined in ITU-T (1995d), these flows perform the following functions: performance monitoring, defect and failure detection, system protection, forwarding of failure and performance information, and fault localization. They provide monitoring and troubleshooting of physical layer resources which SNMP is incapable of, and should lead to increased network availability. Within a network, these flows relate to the ATM and physical layers and are identified as F1 to F5 in Figure 3.50. For F4 and F5 they are carried within the ATM cell itself, while F1–F3 are part of the SONET/SDH overhead structure. The F5 and F4 flows relate to VC and VP monitoring respectively. Both of these exist at the ATM layer, and are identified via specific VCI and PT combinations in the ATM cell header. The specific OAM type and function is identified via a field within the cell payload. As their names suggest, both flows are terminated on ATM end-systems, with the F4 flow also terminating at ATM VC switches performing VPC termination. The purpose of both flows is to monitor channel or path availability, enabling rerouting on failure. Most, if not all, ATM end-systems implement monitoring of F5 and F4.

We designate F4 and F5 flows as either segment or end-to-end depending upon encoding within the cell header. An end-to-end flow is from one end-point to another, and is received only by the device actually terminating the ATM connection. In contrast, segment flows are from one connection point to another, a connection point where a VCI or VPI is assigned, reassigned, or terminated. Once we identify a cell as an OAM cell, we decode the payload to determine its function. Currently, the ATM

Forum UNI defines AIS, FERF (RDI), and loopback. For an F4 flow, the VCI field identifies the OAM as segment (VCI=3) or end-to-end (VCI=4). Note that the VPI in this case is equal to that of the user's data cells. Within the cell payload, the OAM function type identifies the cell as AIS (0000), FERF (0001), or loopback (1000). F5 flows operate in much the same way, with the VPI and VCI both set to that of the user's data flow. In this case, we use the PT to identify an OAM cell, with PT=100 signifying segment and PT=101 designating end-to-end. The function types are the same as with F4. In both cases (F4 and F5) the remainder of the OAM cell payload is function specific. AIS- and FERF-type cells include a failure type and location, while loopback cells include the source and loopback location IDs. These fields enable the 'ATM ping' implemented by some ATM switches.

F3, F2, and F1 relate to the transmission (physical) layer OAM, and draw on fields within the SDH/SONET frame for functionality (see Figure 3.50). Within a transmission system, the link from one ATM entity to another is known as a transmission path. This path may be further divided into digital sections and regenerator sections (or repeaters) depending upon the transmission equipment deployed. In any case, the SDH/SONET architecture provides for sophisticated monitoring of these physical layer intermediate systems. The F3 flow, actually

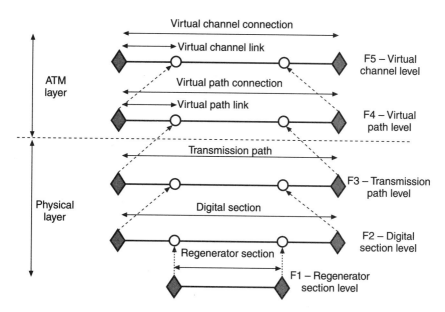

Figure 3.50 OAM hierarchy. Source: G.610.

◆ End-point of the corresponding level
○ Connectiong point of the corresponding levels

Table 3.29 OAM management flows.

Type	Description	Function	Location
F5	Virtual channel	Performance monitoring	ATM cell
F4	Virtual path	Performance monitoring	ATM cell
F3	Path termination	Performance monitoring – path error monitoring	POH: B3, G1 (1–4)
		Facility testing – path connectivity verification	J1
		Fault management – path AIS	H1, H2, H3
		Fault management – path RDI (Loss of cell delineation)	G1 (5)
Type	Description	Function	Location
F2	Line termination	Performance monitoring – line error monitoring	SOH: B2, Z2
		Fault management – line AIS, line RDI	K2 (6–8)
F1	Section termination	Performance monitoring – section error monitoring	SOH: B1

identified via the ATM cell header, is used for cell rate decoupling, cell delineation, **Customer Network (CN)** status monitoring, and **Administrative Unit (AU)** pointer operations. The net result of these functions allows for detection of loss of cell synchronization, whether or not CN is available, the loss of AU pointer, and the failure of insertion and suppression of idle cells. This monitoring is made possible by setting various fields within the SOH or POH of the SDH/SONET frame. F2 and F1 both provide for signal detection or frame alignment as well as section error monitoring. Loss of signal, loss of frame, or unacceptable error performance are all identified by fields within the SDH/SONET header.

We outline these five flows in Table 3.29. The location references a field identifier within the SONET/SDH section (SOH) or path (POH) overhead.

Within an ATM network, these F1–F5 OAM flows do not operate independently but in fact exchange information across the layers. For example, the loss of connectivity on the SONET/SDH section level (F1) will result in status passed to the line level (F2) and then up into the higher levels. This is only logical since loss of connectivity at any one layer will affect connectivity on all higher layers. Upon leaving the SDH physical layers, this information is passed to the ATM VP and VC level. Figure 3.51 depicts this layering.

When used for fault notification, an ATM network element detecting a fault will then notify other NEs in the connection of the fault. **Alarm Indication Signal (AIS)** cells are used to notify downstream NEs of the fault, while **Remote Defect Indication (RDI)** cells are sent by the distant NE in the reverse direction to notify the source. If the AIS and RDIs last for more than a few seconds, they become failures and the management system will be notified. As this occurs at each point on the

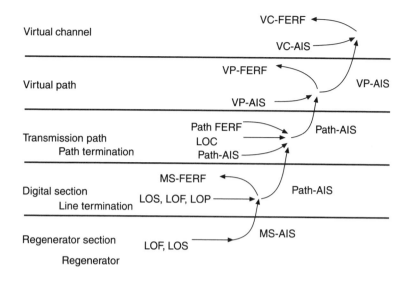

Figure 3.51 OAM flows.

AIS	Alarm Indication Signal	LOF	Loss of Frame
FERF	Far End Receive Failure	LOP	Loss of AU Pointer
LOC	Loss of Cell delineation	LOS	Loss of Signal
	(synchronization)	MS	Multiplex Section

VCC, no coordination between management systems over higher-layer interfaces is required.

Within the ATM Forum, three types of OAM cell have been defined: fault management, performance management, and activation/deactivation to initiate and terminate fault or performance monitoring. Two types of fault management cell include AIS and **Far End Reporting Failure (FERF)**. When an ATM switch fails, breaking the VCC, adjacent switches will generate an AIS, sending this to all downstream switches. This allows these other switches to attempt to re-establish the VCC across alternate paths. If only one side of the VCC is disrupted, a switch will generate an AIS and send it to the source of the traffic. This source then sends an FERF to the destination, at which point an alternate connection should be established.

For fault localization where the AIS or FERF is not helpful (for example, misconfigured VCCs), OAM loopback cells will be used to verify part of or the complete end-to-end connection. This cell includes instructions as to where it should be looped, and does not affect user data. Cells may be looped back within a local ATM network, across an intermediate network, or at a distant location. Loopbacks allow the administrator to verify connectivity, localize faults, and gather delay statistics. Three types of loopbacks are shown in Figure 3.52. Whatever functionality the

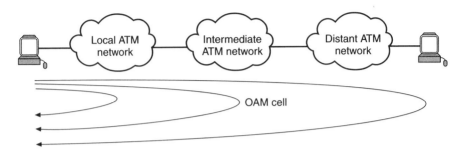

Figure 3.52 OAM loopbacks.

OAM cells may deliver, we still require some mechanism to deliver this information to the higher layer processes within the ATM devices or NMS. The ATM Ping described earlier is only one method, others will follow.

3.6.8 Public management and OSS

We now look at some management requirements specific to ATM as a public service. Although the network management model described earlier defines the various interfaces between public and private network management systems, it does not describe the actual management applications which will be required as part of a service offering. These applications include accounting, trouble ticketing, build control/inventory tracking, modeling and simulation tools, configuration tools, testing, and interfaces for **Customer Network Management (CNM)** and TMN. Note that these requirements are by no means ATM-specific. The public service providers have had a great deal of experience in implementing these management functions as part of their **Operations and Support System (OSS)**, most notably as part of both TDM and Frame Relay networks. Accounting is the ability to gather usage statistics on a per-port and, preferably, on a per-VCC basis. This data will then be transferred through a mediation system into a billing program for usage-based charging. An interesting point here is whether this usage-based billing is really required, and whether it is worth the effort in comparison to flat-rate accounting. The deployment of one tariff scheme or another will often depend upon the system used for other services and how the ATM service is positioned in comparison to these existing services. In many cases, a service provider may roll out an ATM service based on a flat-rate tariff and over time introduce time- and usage-based charging.

If faults are detected within the system, a method must be in place to track problem resolution and its affect on service availability, management applications exist to accomplish this. The ability to provide users with availability data is also related to accounting, in that contracts often specify a guaranteed network performance (for example, 99.98%). When changes to hardware or software are made, engineers must enter this data into a build control/inventory tracking system to enable quick isolation and resolution of either hardware or software failures. The assumption is that personnel given the task of correcting a fault may have never seen the system. In deploying a multi-user service, they require design tools able to effectively determine switch and transmission capacities. The service provider must be able to simulate traffic loads in order to pro-actively implement changes due to increased utilization or changes in traffic profiles. Although almost all network management platforms support device configuration, public operators require an efficient and intuitive way of provisioning circuits, since the switch vendor cannot assume that all personnel are network management experts. Testing is a separate requirement, and applies to the local area as well. In fact, both the ATM Forum and a new multivendor consortium are very active in this area. These developments are detailed in a following section. Finally, CNM is a separate and critical concern, providing users with visibility into a part of the public network for reconfiguration, if permitted, and monitoring. In most cases, the customer's domain is known as a **Virtual Private Network (VPN)**.

3.6.9 Testing

When implementing an ATM network, a sometimes overlooked though critical element of management is testing. The ability to troubleshoot network elements and perform traffic analysis during and after network deployment is critical in assuring proper operation. This includes deploying systems with integrated test capabilities or deploying stand-alone test sets where required. In the former category, LAN switches, routers, and even ATM switches are often capable of gathering various forms of traffic and system information via standardized or vendor-specific MIBs. Under traffic monitoring, the level of detail may be increased substantially if an RMON agent is deployed. For greater levels of detail, such as conducting frame or cell traces in real-time or decoding signaling messages, external test sets will be used. These may access the data stream in a number of ways, including connection to a dedicated monitoring port on an ATM-connected system, in-line connection across a UNI or NNI, or via establishing an in-band VC to an existing connection.

Within the ATM Forum, the SAA SWG has published a baseline document for testing, outlining conformance, performance, and interoperability testing as well as their relationship to each other (ATM Forum, 1994f). Conformance testing evaluates whether an implementation adheres to a specific protocol specification as outlined in a **Protocol**

Implementation Conformance Statement (PICS), Protocol Implementation eXtra Information for Testing (PIXIT), and abstract test suites. The Forum has prepared a number of these documents for interfaces and end-systems which vendors may use to document their conformation to a given specification. We summarize their use in Chapter 5. Performance testing includes measuring operational characteristics of an implementation to verify whether a device or facility is delivering the requisite QoS. Finally, interoperability testing will determine whether one implementation is interoperable with others, and the degree of this interoperability.

Parallel to Forum efforts, the **ATM Monitoring (Amon)** coalition consisting of ATM and test equipment manufacturers are developing a new MIB for VCC monitoring, standardizing the functionality which some vendors have developed. Under this standard, individual VCCs will be made available to an analyzer port. This circuit steering function is sometimes known as **port snooping**, and in the case of pt-pt connection, may be implemented by transforming this into a pt-mpt connection where one leaf is the snooping port. Adding a leaf to an existing pt-mpt connection will present no problem. The MIB enabling this function is known as the **ATM Circuit Steering (ACS)** MIB. This concept could eventually be expanded to include VPs as well. Since the creation of Amon, ACS work has also been taken up within the ATM Forum.

Many vendors have also implemented proprietary MIBs for their individual platforms. These additional MIBs allow a network manager to monitor the performance of the system with the goal of eliminating faults, along with providing ease of configuration. Examples of the information available through these MIBs include interface performance statistics, hardware environmental status, and processor utilization. More detailed traffic analysis and protocol troubleshooting will require the techniques outlined in the previous paragraph. If the managed system supports RMON, then this will be useful in gathering traffic data. But RMON is only so effective when one wishes to gather detailed packet or frame traces in real-time, and does not provide for cell-layer decodes. Also, RMON is in most cases only deployed on a small percentage of those systems likely to be found in an ATM network. In these cases, the network manager should use an external test set, optimized for the decodes required (layers, protocols). These standalone systems go by many names; one of the better known is the Sniffer by Network General, used for packet and frame decodes. In some instances, this device may be connected to a port on a LAN switch or router which has been configured for monitoring in that it will mirror the traffic found on any other port. More complex broadband analyzers are required to decode ATM-rate data, usually capable of storing a timeslice of the monitored cell stream due to the amount of data involved.

A brief aside to describe the types of test system available and their capabilities is in order due to the dramatic rise in the number of vendors offering ATM test equipment and their differing capabilities. Although until 1995, ATM test sets were confined to development laboratories due to cost and complexity, this has now changed, with equipment available to take its place alongside existing LAN test sets in the corporate network. Taylor (1995) provides a good overview of the types of ATM test set available and their capabilities. We may group these test sets into three classes depending upon their intended use: ATM-equipped protocol analyzers, physical layer testers, and full R&D analyzers. The first set of devices offer lower-entry cost, as they are additions to conventional LAN analyzers in many cases. This leads to an advantage, in that testing between LAN media and ATM is possible within the same system. One area where this is especially useful is when testing a single device such as a router which will have both non-ATM LAN, non-ATM WAN, and ATM interfaces. The disadvantage appears when one tries to conduct more advanced testing based on the generation of line-rate signaling or when STM-4/OC-12 is a requirement. Physical layer test sets are designed for physical layer decodes and, while generally less expensive than the other two types, they do not support LAN interfaces. Some are even incapable of any higher-layer decodes (for instance, RFC 1483) at all. The last class of analyzers provides traffic generation and analysis at rates up to 622 Mbps. Most of these systems are designed to remain in the laboratory, and are priced accordingly.

In selecting a test set, questions to ask include the amount of buffering available, filter capabilities, lower- and higher-layer decodes, and selection of LAN and WAN interfaces. Of course, many of these questions can only be answered with an application in mind. Typical tests available will include physical (LOS, RDI, path/line/section data, coding errors, and so on), ATM (HEC errors, cell rates, CTD, CDV, percentage utilization, and so on), and AAL (assembled frames, payload and overhead bandwidth, percentage utilization, and so on) analysis on a per-VCC basis between two external devices or where the test set emulates a device. However, this per-VCC analysis may become quite tedious if the user must enter each and every VPI/VCI combination in use. Some vendors, realizing that this manual configuration of VCCs may be close to impossible, have included a feature to automatically detect all VPIs/VCIs in use. Higher-layer decodes will include IP, and other network protcol, along with the various data encapsulations across ATM such as RFC 1483 (Heinanen, 1993), RFC 1490 (Bradley *et al*, 1993), RFC 1209 (Piscitello and Lawrence, 1991), and LAN emulation. Finally, if the test set emulates an ATM switch or host, it should be capable of generating user-defined traffic and injecting errors at each of the layers.

3.6.10 Network management platforms

Having introduced the concepts of ATM network management, including

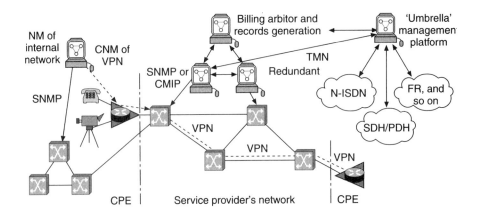

Figure 3.53 ATM system management.

the management model, the ILMI, SNMP, and RMON, the next question is how these various elements should be deployed in a useful way within an ATM network. In a typical network, one or more **Network Management Systems (NMSs)** running an open network management platform along with a set of management applications will be in contact with each of the devices within the network (Figure 3.53). The management platform should be based on an industry standard (HP OpenView, Sun Solstice Enterprise Manager, and IBM Netview/AIX for example) over which third-party application developers have designed device- or task-specific applications. Examples of applications include hub and router management, trouble ticket reporting, and security analysis. The NMS will in most cases communicate with the various switches, routers, and end-devices in the network via SNMP. As additional types of end-system are connected to ATM, including disk arrays, printers, and video coders/decoders, these too will be SNMP-manageable.

Additional lines of communication exist between ATM switches and ATM-connected end-devices over the ILMI. If PABXs and traditional video CODECs are deployed, it is possible that these will not be managed by the NMS. In this case, a separate management system (or a console interface) is required. Since all network management exchanges are in-band, the NMS may connect to the network at any point. The NMS may also support redundant operation, where the databases are duplicated at two or more points within the network. This may be useful in guaranteeing higher reliability of the management system in a large network, or providing for the handoff of management responsibilities at different times of the day. A simpler form of remote access to the NMS may be provided by placing remote terminals (X-terminals or PCs) with full or limited access where required. In addition, connections via an alternate path (for example, analog modem, Frame Relay) may be made to some network devices in the case of network failure. If provided with a modem connection, for example, these devices may still be remotely managed. As introduced earlier, over the next year we expect to see evolution in NMS architectures and paradigms with the introductions of Web technology.

3.6.11 Security

In comparison to application and internetwork layer security, ATM layer security is still in its infancy. In fact, it was not until the end of 1995 that a group within the ATM Forum was actually established to address this area. This is not to say, however, that parallel efforts are not underway within the ITU, ISO, ETSI, and IETF, though these groups are not necessarily concentrating on ATM. Requirements may be divided into a number of areas, including network-oriented secure signaling and management, as well as user-oriented services such as authentication, encryption, and closed user groups. These areas may be related to three types of interaction within the network: endpoint-to-endpoint, switch-to-switch, and endpoint-to-switch. For example, two end-devices expect authentication, may require confidentiality (via encryption), and require data integrity and security of signaling. This last requirement also applies to switch-to-switch interactions. Parallel to these requirements is an enabling infrastructure, such as key exchange and certification as well as the support of security-related parameters within signaling messages (ATM Forum, 1994g).

Authentication is the first step in establishing communictions between systems. Due to threats of spoofing, this is required before any other security mechanisms such as key exchange or encryption may be deployed. Current uses of authenticated exchanges include SNMP and OSPF. Methods of authentication include the use of symmetric algorithms such as DES, where the two parties must first share a secret key, or public key algorithms including RSA, where each node must only know the other's public key. This latter method is expected to become the default within ATM due to scalability, though it does not preclude the use of symmetric methods in some instances (for example, nodes which communicate frequently). Note that the maintenance of public keys leads into certification issues which have been well thought out, and are beginning to be implemented by some internetworking vendors. Schneier (1994) details many of these concepts and caveats. An important feature of any selected authentication framework will be its ability to support end-to-end security even if intermediate nodes do not provide these services.

Given two parties with verified identities, we may now provide confidentiality via encryption. Encryption may be implemented end-to-end or on a link-by-link basis. If end-to-end, encryption may still be supported even if every intermediate system does not support this service. Data integrity ensures that the information has not been altered in any way, either unwillingly or through malicious acts. This function may be provided by encryption. Looking at the network as a whole, a security framework will provide access control, whereby the users and the services which they may take advantage of are controlled. Any framework must prevent replays, whereby an intruder monitors transactions across the network (for instance, logins) and then uses the gathered information to impersonate a valid user. This may be avoided by strict controls on access (for example, one-time password generators) and encryption within the network.

When one looks at many current ATM deployments, an obvious security hole becomes apparent. Once an ATM connection is established, no intermediate systems take part in filtering higher-layer information. Thus, though access controls may be placed on which end-systems may accept which ATM sources (not taking into account ATM address spoofing) we have no methods to filter network layer data (for example, IP, IPX) along the link once it has been established. A VCC terminating on an end-system internal to a corporate network will bypass the organization's firewall. Firewall functionality on each and every end-system is of course not practical. One alternative method may be to include higher-layer protocol information via information elements in the connection signaling message. Intermediate systems (for instance, an ATM switch acting as a corporate firewall) could then filter on this information. Even though this information may be authenticated, this still does not guard against spoofing once the ATM connection is established. With this one-time filtering, a port, socket, and/or application may be bound to the ATM VCC in such a way as to cause any changes to destroy the connection. One problem with this architecture, however, is a less efficient use of a given VCC if bound to anything above the network layer. Another solution would be to terminate the ATM connection within the end-system at an application and not at the networking layer. This of course would preclude interconnection between the application and non-ATM users without the use of an application gateway.

Recently, vendors have proposed hybrid ATM switches capable of filtering without reassembly. All data traversing this switch would pass through a filter capable of identifying cell content and filtering on Layer 2 addresses or above. Though complex, this system is not beyond the reach of new high-performance hardware. A last solution, workable in the future though very rare at present, is to implement end-to-end user verification via PKE or some similar mechanism. We should see the first wide deployments of this mechanism in the coming years. At present, the most effective mechanism is to terminate the VCCs traversing the private and public ATM networks at a Layer 3 device capable of carrying out network layer (and above) filtering (Figure 3.54). Though this may seem a performance (bandwidth and latency) disadvantage at first, existing routers perform this function quite effectively at speeds of up to

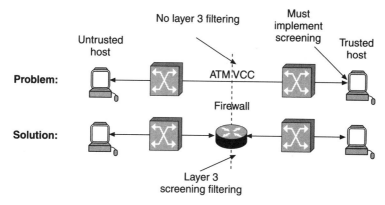

Figure 3.54 Possible security breach.

STM-1 (155 Mbps). All data SVCs (AAL5 and possibly AAL3/4) will terminate at this device, while CBR and VBR could be connected directly via pre-configured (and hopefully secure) PVCs.

This would allow network managers to pre-configure streams requiring better real-time support, such as voice and video, overcoming the major limitation of router architectures. These VCCs will probably terminate on dedicated devices. As outlined above, all data SVCs will terminate at the router for Layer 3 processing.

Shared media networks, such as those based on the cable TV infrastructure, are especially vulnerable from a security standpoint. Since all receivers on a cable segment will receive data sent downstream from the headend, closed user groups are required to protect data integrity. This mechanism in fact exists as part of IEEE's 802.1q and 802.14 efforts, and is described in Chapter 6.

A second very challenging area for security is wireless ATM. Consider mobile users within a public ATM network. Security requirements are not too different from existing cellular phone networks, and fall into four areas: unauthorized disclosure, denial of service, unauthorized manipulation of information, and unauthorized use. The first area counters attacks against user data, including content, location, and profile. If user data is intercepted, it may be manipulated. We must guard against service denial, caused by introduction of competing signals and blocking. Finally, service providers and users attempt to prohibit unauthorized use of the network or of network services (Dellaverson, 1995). Many of these challenges will be met by combining ATM security mechanisms as described above with those currently deployed as part of cellular networks, with GSM a particularly good example.

Finally, an ATM network requires security internal to both the internetworking devices and the network management architecture. The various switches, end-systems, and network management platforms require access security in the form of passwords, user permission levels, and physical security. Exchange of network management information between the various devices may range from minimal (for example, SNMPv1 community strings) to more complex forms of authentication and confidentiality. Securing the network management architecture is actually a complex problem, as was discovered during development of SNMPv2. Many of the security mechanisms which were to be part of this protocol have now been deferred.

Until the development of a complete ATM security architecture, users will depend upon network and application layer security for their needs. At the ATM layer, combinations of PVCs and static routing may be deployed when possible, though this of course reduces flexibility somewhat. As evidenced by the late formation of a Security SWG within the ATM Forum, this is an area where there is much work to be done.

3.6.12 Directory services

Within any internetwork, users require a means of identifying available services. If we look at the X.500 directory system or the Internet's Domain Naming System, we have a pretty good idea as to the type of services that ATM users will require. These include mapping from logical names to network and ATM layer addresses, identification of well-known services within the various data models, and possibly characteristics of end-systems for use in establishing VCCs with given QoSs. Some current ATM servers including the ATMARP, NHS, LECS, LES, and MARS are examples of systems which may be tied into a directory service. Tradeoffs in deploying a system include complexity versus functionality, and whether end-systems accessing the directory should be equipped with powerful browsers or simpler DNS-type interfaces. The ATM Forum, in evaluating these different alternatives, has chosen the Internet DNS as the basis for **ATM Name Services (ANS)** to be defined during the course of 1996. Note that this is only the first phase, and future revisions of the ANS may use the X.500 system with its richer support of redundancy and dynamic updates. Building on the DNS, the ANS defines both an ATM-specific resource record, TYPE A for CLASS ATM, along with an ATM.INT domain for reverse address mappings. This, of course, does not preclude the use of other domains for ATM hosts. ANS clients will resolve the address of the server via the ILMI or through use of a well-known address. An example of these mappings is as follows:

$ ORIGIN dat.tele.fi
salmon   ATM A 39.246f.000e70900031200010001.000012345678.00
char   ATM A 39.246f.000e7090031200010001. 000023456789.00
$ ORIGIN 1.0.0.0.1.0.0.0.2.1.3.0.0.9.0.7.e.0.0.246f.39.nsap.atm.int
00.001234567800 ATM PTR salmon.dat.tele.fi.
00.002345678900 ATM PTR char.dat.tele.fi.

4

Services

The network infrastructure which we have detailed so far is only a platform over which we may deploy different services. These services then support the various data, voice, and video applications for network users. Therefore, it is essential that we develop a set of standardized service models which different vendors may support in hardware and software. Parallel to efforts within the ITU and the ATM Forum to define the ATM infrastructure, these two organizations, along with other groups including the IETF and DAVIC are working to complete standardization of the ATM service architecture. Without these standardization efforts, there would only be chaos, leading to proprietary ATM services, hardware, and software.

Services offered across an ATM network may be roughly divided into two classes: those providing data interconnection and those providing support for stream-based information such as that generated by PABXs and video CODECs. The critical factor in both of these service classes is that they will use the same ATM infrastructure. Data services may be further categorized into those more suitable for the local area such as LAN emulation, and those intended for the WAN. Frame Relay and SMDS/CBDS fall into this latter category. The popular **Classical** data model, its extensions, and MPOA are intended for both local-area and wide-area deployment. Figure 4.1 depicts examples of the types of service one may expect to see over an ATM network, along with their related ATM Forum or IETF standards. We describe these various services in greater detail in the following sections.

Before we look at the ATM models in greater detail, a quick review of the network layer (Layer 3) is in order. The discussion of the models begins with a discussion of those standardized by the IETF, to include the Classical model and **Routing Over Large Clouds (ROLC)**, as well as those growing out of efforts within the ATM Forum such as **LAN Emulation (LANE)** and **Multiprotocol over ATM (MPOA)**. As both organizations are evaluating future ways of internetworking between

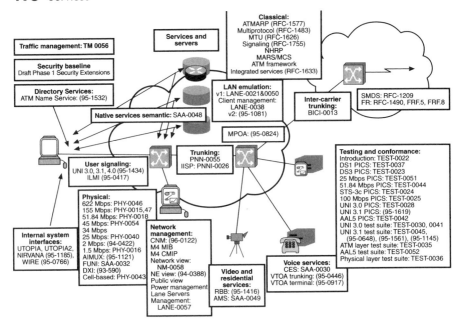

Figure 4.1 ATM services and standards.

the ATM and the network layers; we also look at some proposals in this area. Though the ATM data models have generated the most publicity, and form the basis for many early implementations, networks now include both voice and video over ATM. We describe the various techniques for transporting, encoding, and internetworking with these services.

4.1 ATM data models

ATM's first use was as a high-speed backbone for data traffic. Therefore, models had to be developed which would allow existing data networks, internetworking devices, and end-systems to connect to an ATM network. They allow LANs to use ATM as a campus backbone, emulate existing bridged environments, and provide for the transport of wide-area data services. These models may be summarized based on signaling and on the interaction between higher-layer protocols (for example, IP, TCP, and applications) and the ATM layer. End-to-end models include those based on the use of ATM as a subnetwork to the higher-layer protocols and those peering ATM with the network layer (Layer 3). By 'subnetwork' we mean that the existing Layer 3 protocols provide end-to-end connectivity while the ATM layer takes its place alongside other link layer technologies. Those models which treat ATM as a subnetwork in both the local and wide area, along with those supporting the transport of Frame Relay or SMDS across ATM, are sometimes known as **overlay models**. Support for these different WAN services is critical to the success of ATM because it allows service providers to use the technology as a single multiservice transport. By the same token, support for existing enterprise internetworks is critical to the end user since ATM is not intended as a standalone technology.

An end-to-end network may include multiple ATM and non-ATM segments, and current work within both the IETF and the ATM Forum focuses on optimizing deployment of this overlay model. This includes providing for Classical support of IP and other network layer protocols through the Classical model and ROLC extensions, as well as providing transparency across ATM for LAN environments via LANE. The term 'Classical' grew out of a need to make no changes in the internetworking paradigm when deploying ATM. A connectionless model, aligned with the Classical model but changing the nature by which end-systems (hosts) communicate with one another by placing control of circuit establishment with the end application, is also generating interest. A potential problem with all existing overlay models is that network layer routing is independent of ATM routing. This may and will result in the user being required to manage two disjoint routing hierarchies. The term **peer model** has been used in the past to loosely describe any model altering the relationship between the network and ATM layers in an attempt to avoid this problem. This single model has now been subdivided into solutions which peer ATM with the network layer and those which provide for integrated multilayer routing, known as the **integrated model** which includes I-PNNI. Vendors are beginning to investigate this integrated model. Finally, during the coming year MPOA should be standardized, combining some elements of both LANE and ROLC.

In looking at the various models, the following characteristics of IP over ATM networks as described in Cole *et al* (1996) are worth noting:

- The size of the IP over ATM internetwork (number of nodes);
- The size of ATM IP subnets (LIS) in the ATM internetwork;
- The geographic dispersion (and therefore delay);
- Single IP subnet versus multiple IP subnet ATM internetworks;
- Single or multiple administrative authority;
- Presence of routers providing transit to multihomed internets;
- The presence or absence of an IP routing protocol;
- The presence or absence of dynamic address resolution.

In addition to these characteristics, the underlying ATM service may or may not have the following qualities:

- Connection oriented versus Connectionless;

- QoS support (CBR, VBR, UBR, ABR, rate shaping, policing, and so on);

- PVC only or PVC and SVC capable;

- Broadcast capable (emulated or otherwise);

- Point-to-multipoint capable for supporting multicasting and Anycasting;

- The type of binding between the upper-layer protocols and ATM;

- The type of ATM administrative domains/networks, including addressing;

- Charging principles (investment cost, flat fee, distance and/or time based).

Although we sometimes use ISO terminology in describing the various devices forming an ATM network, to clarify matters, an intermediate system is nothing other than an ATM switch while an end-system may be a router, LAN switch, workstation, PC, or any other device which terminates the ATM network. Note that this classification has been the cause of some confusion, since routers, which are normally intermediate systems at the network layer, are usually considered to be end-systems within ATM. A subnet may be either broadcast capable in that it can send a single packet (a **Subnetwork Network Protocol Data Unit**, or **NPDU**) to multiple destinations at once or it may not be capable of performing this function. End-systems connected to this subnet share a common network address. If the subnet is incapable of forwarding broadcast and multicast packets without the deployment of additional servers, it is known as **Non-Broadcast Multiple Access (NBMA)**. The NBMA terminology, though referring to ATM in the current context, is also applicable to X.25 and Frame Relay networks. As outlined elsewhere in the book, intermediate systems deliver and receive data packets (NPDUs) from end-systems, and most importantly, relay these packets between both end-systems and other intermediate systems. Finally, an end-to-end path will consist of two end-systems communicating over an arbitrary number of intermediate systems and subnets.

Current vendor implementations focus on end-to-end overlay models. The first, referred to as Classical IP over ATM, treats the ATM technology as a link-layer media on a par with Ethernet in the LAN environment and leased lines in the wide area. This model's name is a little misleading, since it is capable of supporting multiple Layer 3 protocols. Though the treatment of ATM as a data link may seem to be a disadvantage at first glance, many applications will still gain by the transition to ATM. These gains include the support of greater data rates in comparison to most other technologies and the ability to define a QoS for a connection. Extensions to the Classical model to optimize routing, known as ROLC, have also been deployed, and form the basis for some work within MPOA as well. Closely related to the overlay model are encapsulation and internetworking schemes to support Frame Relay and SMDS/CBDS. Since the IETF drives these service models, they are only 'officially' defined for IP, though in reality they apply just as well to multiprotocol environments. Parallel to work by the IETF, the ATM Forum directly addresses the support of multiprotocol traffic over ATM within the MPOA group. Note that this emphasis is different from the stated goal of the IETF. Whereas the IETF is concerned with the support of IP over any underlying media, the ATMF is totally focused on ATM. Within the ATMF, the Multiprotocol over ATM SWG has taken the lead in defining the various data models, first addressing the subnet, or overlay model, and now, in cooperation with the PNNI group, beginning to look at various peering and integration possibilities. Still, initial efforts are based on the overlay model. The ATM Forum has also standardized upon a method of supporting a bridged environment over the connection-oriented ATM infrastructure, known as LAN Emulation (LANE).

In Figure 4.2, we depict how Layer 3 protocol addresses are resolved into ATM addresses within the overlay model. Edge device (a) with protocol address IP(a) resolves the protocol address IP(b) of the destination based on prior knowledge of ATM(b). At the ATM layer, the first switch knows that the destination ATM(b) is reachable via ATM(d). This is the task of the ATM layer routing protocols (IISP, PNNI, B-ICI).

In addition to the overlay, peer, and integrated models described above, two lightweight subnet models have been proposed, both of which seek to minimize the amount of IP header overhead transported across the ATM network once a binding has been established via signaling mechanisms. **TCP and UDP over Lightweight IP**, or **TULIP**, eliminates all but the IP protocol field since all else is determined at call

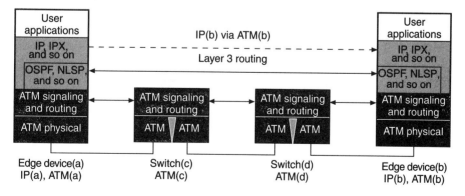

Figure 4.2 ATM overlay model. Source: Cisco Systems.

set-up time. AAL5 will ensure that packets are not fragmented or mis-ordered, and will also indicate the packet size. Since each end-system maintains its IP address, the basic routing over ATM paradigm is left unchanged. A feature of TULIP is that its use may be negotiated on a per-SVC or per-PVC basis. In contrast, with **TCP and UDP over a Non-existent IP Connection**, or **TUNIC**, no Layer 3 information is carried across the ATM network. Two applications will communicate via a dedicated VC utilizing TCP or UDP directly over AAL5. This binding of applications may require the use of well-known port numbers during call setup. Both TULIP and TUNIC are included for his-torical completeness, as they are not expected to play a major role in the future.

One reason why there is sometimes confusion regarding the various data models is a lack of understanding as to ATM's place in the OSI reference model. For example, the overlay model would lead one to believe that ATM is a data link protocol (Layer 2), on a par with Ethernet or Frame Relay. But this contradicts ATM's support for hierar-chical addressing and routing, characteristics of a Layer 3 protocol. In contrast to a link layer's flat address space (for example, the 48-bit MAC address), the 20-octet ATM NSAP format address provides for the deployment of scalable and stable networks based on hierarchical net-work design and routing. Most probably, the fault lies in the model itself, which does not effectively integrate the concept of an overlay network, where one network layer overlays another. The overlay concept is not new, for it is no different than that implemented for the transport of IP by X.25. To draw an anology, the telephone network is considered to be flat. This is incorrect, in that the global phone network is based on a hier-archical addressing mechanism of country codes, area/city codes, and local exchanges.

4.1.1 Internetworking

The different ATM data models rely on an understanding of internet-working, including the traditional roles of the network and link layers within the protocol stack. In the network model, the network (sometimes called internetwork) layer is responsible for end-to-end connectivity across different underlying link layer technologies. Whereas the network layer is based on logical and topological addressing, link layer address-es, though possibly unique (DECnet being an exception), are not under the control of the network planner and therefore may not be used in designing a network. There have been link layer technologies which have implemented structured addressing, most notably X.25, but except for a brief time during the 1980s, the idea of providing end-systems with X.121 addresses (the format used within X.25) never caught on. Within ATM, a possibility does exist to internetwork based on the ATM NSAP

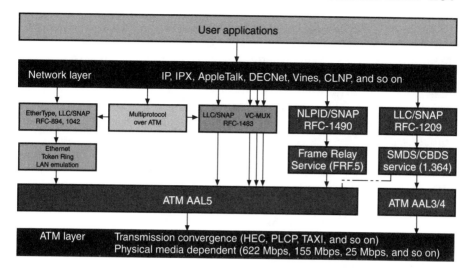

Figure 4.3 ATM data model protocol stacks. Source: Cisco Systems.

format address, but this will probably only apply to isolated workgroups for the foreseeable future. In Figure 4.3, we look at the internetworking stack for the more common ATM data models, LANE, MPOA, the Classical model, Frame Relay, and SMDS.

Addressing at Layer 3 is protocol dependent, with IP, IPX, AppleTalk and DECnet, all structuring their address spaces differently. The major difference between IP (and CLNS) and the other internetwork protocols is that IP addresses are theoretically unique based on an address request and assignment procedure. The same cannot be said of the other protocols. This uniqueness of addressing is at the basis of the global IP routing used at the core of the Internet. Routing is the exchange of topology data; fundamentally, which networks are reachable over a given interface. A routing protocol will propagate this topology data from one Layer 3 system, known as routers, to another. Some routing protocols, such as **Open Shortest Path First (OSPF)** and **Novell Link State Protocol (NLSP)**, are protocol specific, in this case IP and IPX respectively, while others including **Integrated Intermediate System to Intermediate System (Integrated IS-IS)** and **Enhanced Interior Gateway Resolution Protocol** (E-IGRP, a Cisco proprietary routing protocol), are suitable for two or more inter-network protocols. The trunking protocol implemented between ATM switches, PNNI, is in reality a routing protocol operating at the ATM layer. It may therefore share many of the characteristics of Layer 3 routing protocols, most notably the link-state topology discovery algorithm used within OSPF and IS-IS.

In contrast to the network layer, addressing on the link layer is based on addresses assigned to the physical interface. For most systems, this is a 48-bit Media Access Control (MAC) address coded into the interface by the vendor. The vendor derives the address from a section of the MAC address space as administered by the IEEE. Because of this, a user will have no control over the assignment of MAC addresses unless implementing an internetworking protocol such as DECnet which has the potential for reassigning these MAC addresses. This reassignment allowed DECnet network addresses to be calculated from the new MAC addresses. Jumping ahead to the section on ATM addressing, the NSAP-based private ATM addressing format includes the 48-bit MAC address. A common theme in currently-deployed ATM data models (Classical, ROLC, MPOA) is the requirement to resolve an end-system Layer 2 address if given a Layer 3 protocol address. This is a fairly easy procedure over most broadcast-capable LANs, and relies on the **Address Resolution Protocol (ARP)**. Across ATM, it is a little more difficult due to the lack of broadcast mechanisms within ATM. Thus the requirement for some of the address resolution servers outlined in the following sections.

4.1.2 IETF Classical model

The Classical model, though simple to implement in some respects, does not allow current internetworking protocols or current applications to take full advantage of ATM's capabilities. A major limitation often cited, the lack of QoS support, will not be much of an issue in the future as users deploy resource-aware applications. But Classical ATM does provide for the greatest degree of interoperability, as standards are outlined by both the ATM Forum in its UNI and by the IETF. Why the term 'Classical'?

As previously explained, this model requires no changes in routers or hosts, preserves the existing investment in deployed protocols, and is true to the IP host requirements as outlined in Braden (1989a and 1989b). The end result is that packets for a destination outside of the host's subnet address prefix are routed even if the destination is local to the host's NBMA network. In a later section, we present solutions to this limitation. The Classical model also conforms to the internetworking philosophy where end-systems use internetworking protocols such as IP or IPX to provide connectivity over multiple link layer media, and not only ATM. To clear up one misconception concerning the Classical model, though it is closely associated with routing, some implementations do support bridging. This bridging will not be widely implemented, however, due to LANE and then MPOA.

The most basic documents outlining the Classical model are the *Classical IP and ARP over ATM* RFC (Laubach, 1993) and its proposed update (Laubach, 1995a). These RFCs describe the interaction of ATM end-systems in an environment where user data is encapsulated for transport over the ATM network in accordance with the Multiprotocol Encapsulation over ATM AAL5 RFC (Heinanen, 1993). In addition, RFC 1577 (Laubach, 1993) describes IP address resolution entities within the ATM network which alleviate the need to manually configure network to ATM layer address lookup tables in ATM-connected end-systems. A companion RFC outlining the **Maximum Transmission Unit (MTU)** over ATM (Atkinson, 1994) is to be incorporated into the Classical model baseline document, while the original description of signaling over ATM (Perez *et al*, 1995), based on UNI 3.1, is being updated to include UNI 4.0 (Maher and Mankin, 1996).

In deploying the Classical model, consider a campus with a backbone based on Ethernet, Token Ring, or FDDI technology. In most cases, LAN segments in each building will be connected to this backbone via routers. In an IP environment, an IP subnet (a way of segmenting the IP address space) will be assigned to each of these physical LAN segments, while the backbone is assigned a subnet of its own. Over time, traffic load on the backbone increases to the point that the user requires a higher-speed core. This will occur in the nearer term for Ethernet or Token Ring, while FDDI may provide a bit more buffer space. In either case, after the backbone upgrade, one or more ATM switches will provide connectivity between the router-attached LAN segments. Note that no changes have been made in the backbone or LAN segment IP addressing.

Building upon the Classical model, we now have solutions for multicasting and broadcasting across an ATM network. Multicast and broadcast support has been a topic of great interest due to the need to integrate ATM within the end-to-end Internet multicasting paradigm. Finally, extensions to the model provide for optimal routing across ATM networks, essential for deploying scalable ATM services. This includes the deployment of the **Next Hop Resolution Protocol (NHRP)**, which we describe in some detail. We detail interworking with WAN services such as SMDS/CBDS and Frame Relay in a later section. Although they may share the same physical infrastructure as the Classical model, these services exist separately.

Classical IP and ARP over ATM

Classical IP and ARP over ATM (Laubach, 1993) and updates in Laubach (1995a) outline the functions of an ATM network acting as a replacement for existing Layer 2 media. In this configuration, the ATM cloud is treated as a single or as multiple **Logical IP Subnets (LISs)** in much the same way as IP treats Ethernet, FDDI, or Frame Relay. Requirements of the Classical model include the use of routers to connect members of different LISs, a single higher-layer frame size within the LIS limited to 9180 octets, LLC/SNAP encapsulation as outlined in Heinanen (1993), and no changes to the end-to-end routing architecture (in contrast to those changes envisioned by NHRP). A critical element of this model is address resolution over the ATM network, made possible by defining an ATMARP service.

As members of the same LIS, all hosts will share the same IP subnet address prefix, and will be directly connected to the ATM network. All communication between LISs sharing a common ATM infrastructure will take place via routers which are members of two or more LISs with non-ATM systems connected via routers as well. Note that although communication via a VCC may be possible between two hosts on different LISs connected to the ATM cloud, the Classical model does not support this mode of operation. Finally, the address resolution mechanism will function only across a single LIS, and all hosts must participate in this protocol. We depict the operation of the Classical model in Figure 4.4.

In Figure 4.5, we expand the deployment of the Classical model into the wide-area, where a service provider operates a core network (150.10 in this case). Users, each on separate IP networks, will interconnect via the service provider's network. In an enterprise network where ATM is replacing leased lines or X.25 services, users have two choices for addressing. Although campus addressing remains as is, two alternatives are available for the ATM WAN. The first scheme will model the WAN as a set of point-to-point connections, with a separate IP subnet assigned to each of these VCs. This closely models leased-line infrastructures. An alternative is to assign a single IP subnet to the WAN, approximating a packet or frame service as in Figure 4.5. These two alternatives will be discussed in greater detail in Chapter 5.

The Classical model relies on an address resolution mechanism known as the ATMARP, service is local to all hosts within a single LIS.

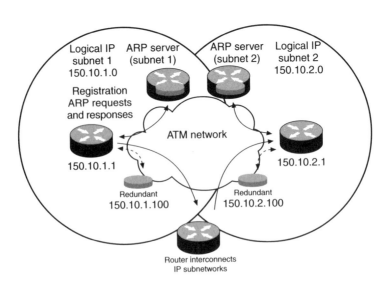

Figure 4.4 Classical IP and ARP over ATM.

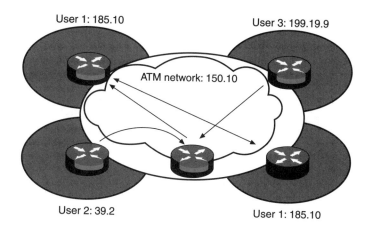

User 1: 185.10

User 3: 199.19.9

ATM network: 150.10

User 2: 39.2

User 1: 185.10

Figure 4.5 Classical IP and ARP WAN configuration.

IP routers provide connectivity to hosts outside of this LIS. In a later section on optimizing routing, we describe extensions to this architecture providing address resolution outside of the local LIS. Hosts use the ATMARP, an extension of the standard ARP protocol to include an ARP server, to resolve IP addresses to ATM addresses. In the reverse direction, they rely on an **Inverse ATM Address Resolution Protocol (InATMARP)** for both SVCs and PVCs. This InATMARP is closely aligned with the original Inverse-ARP. Inverse-ARP, as defined by Bradley and Brown (1992), is a method of resolving a destination's protocol address (for example, IP) given its hardware address. In this case, the ATM NSAP address functions as the hardware address. Under operation, the source will unicast the InARP request over a PVC to the destination. Upon receipt, the destination enters its protocol address in the InARP response and returns this to the source. Extending the Classical model, hosts may also support the NHRP for resolving addresses beyond the local LIS.

Under SVC operation, all hosts when 'joining' the LIS will initiate an ATMARP registration procedure by connecting to the ATMARP server(s). Server addresses are preconfigured within the hosts, though in the future may be made known accross the ILMI or advertised via Anycasting for redundancy. A server, seeing this VCC, will transmit an InATMARP request over this VCC to determine the IP address of the client, and will use the reply from this request to construct an ATMARP table cache. Entries in this cache will provide the basis for subsequent replies to ATMARP requests from other clients. A router is a special case, in that it will register with an ATMARP server for each LIS which it is a member of. If a router's ATM interface supports multiple subinterfaces, this may be easily accomplished by associating each of these subinterfaces with an LIS and assigning it a different SEL within the ESI belonging to the physical interface. Note that, in many cases, the router will also perform the ATMARP server functions for each of these LISs.

A host, wishing to resolve an address, will query the server(s) for the ATM NSAP or E.164 address corresponding to a destination's IP address. If the ATMARP server has an entry for this destination, it responds accordingly. If not, it will indicate this to the source, at which point the host may give up, query another ATMARP server, or begin to query the NHRP servers if it supports this protocol. Finally, to prevent the forwarding of obsolete or potentially invalid ARP entries, the server will age out its cache entries after an interval of 20 minutes.

Although RFC 1577 (Laubach, 1993) specifies single-server operation, users recognize that redundancy is essential in deploying mission-critical networks. (Laubach, 1995b) first addressed this, with (Luciani, 1996) outlining a likely deployment. This Server Cache Synchronization Protocol (SCSP) defines synchronization within a Server Group which may be aligned to a LIS (as an example). Detailing the protocol, the draft introduces the concept of a Local Server (LS), a Directly Connected Server (DCS) one hop from the LS, and a Remote Server (RS) greater than one hop from the LS. The synchronization protocol, very much like that used within OSPF, operates between the LS and its DCSs. Once servers are aligned, changes in membership (that is, addition or deletion of an NHRP entry) will cause update messages to be exchanged, much like a topology change triggering an update within a Layer 3 routing protocol. We hope that this single synchronization will be generalized for the other IETF servers (MARS, NHRP) as well as for LANEv2 and MPOA.

Server redundancy is only one element of network resilience. Consider the typical host homed to a single ATM switch. This switch, unless in the campus core or enterprise environment, will have minimum fault tolerance (that is, redundant processors, software images). Therefore, a single ATMARP server may not noticeably compromise the end-to-end reliability of the ATM network. Prior to the deployment of this server-to-server protocol, one suggestion made for reliability was to deploy parallel LISs covering the same end-systems but homed to separate ATMARP servers. If connectivity beyond the LISs is required, both LISs would be homed to a router. If the first ATMARP server fails, the end-systems could cut over to the second server. Where multiple routers are involved, each would join both LISs and would then establish the same set of BGP peers on each for connectivity into the wide area. The problem with this option is the necessity to designate an entire LIS as backup if address space is limited. It also does not address the additional management required for what is in effect a second network.

Laubach (1995b) also defines a 9180-octet IP MTU for use over ATM. Note that this MTU definition was originally part of a separate RFC (Atkinson, 1994), and is based on that defined for use over SMDS in

RFC-1209 (Piscitello and Lawrence, 1991). Using LLC/SNAP as an example, the AAL5 SDU will equal 9180 octets while the AAL5 PDU will grow to 9188 octets due to overhead. The MTU size, in contrast to those used within shared media, X.25, and Frame Relay, has advantages in that larger MTUs have been shown to provide better performance for TCP by eliminating fragmentation. With fragmentation reduced, applications such as NFS can take greater advantage of their large native MTUs. A large MTU will also result in higher host performance, since faster CPUs do not necessarily result in fast interrupt-intensive operations. Consider the five-fold decrease in interrupt handling between a 1.5K and a 9K MTU. In addition, routers will function more efficiently since throughput is usually measured in packets per second as opposed to bytes per second. The goal then is to minimize the number of packets processed.

The original MTU RFC includes references to both PVC-based ATM environments, where the MTU will default to 9180, and SVC-based networks. In the latter case, the MTU should be negotiated as part of the ATM signaling protocol. This negotiation will use two parts of the AAL parameters **Information Element (IE)** to exchange forward and backward MTU size information. Within an SVC environment, the MTU may actually be set to a maximum of 65535 octets. Though this is beyond the bounds of the current standard, ATM implementations based on 622 Mbps and above will probably prefer this value for efficiency reasons. On most systems, however, this size MTU is unrealistic due to the amount of buffering required (64 Kbps per active connection). An ATM calling party wishing to use either the default MTU or a negotiated value will set this within the AAL parameters IE of the setup message. As part of the connect message, the called party will either accept this value or attempt to renegotiate the maximum. Note that all stations implementing SVCs must support this field. In addition, all routers and hosts complying with the RFC are expected to implement the IP path MTU discovery mechanism as defined in RFC 1191 (Mogul and Deering, 1990). This will allow routers and end-stations to make the most efficient use of high-MTU networks along a path. The choice of the MTU has implications in mixed ATM networks, where routers, PCs, and workstations all connect to the same ATM cloud.

When implementing any internetwork, a problem sometimes experienced concerns IP fragmentation due to differences in MTUs across different networking technologies. For example, an ATM network may connect two user LANs, one being FDDI and the other Ethernet. If path discovery is not implemented on all end-systems or if the network administrators on each end do not take care to manually set the MTU, packets will probably undergo fragmentation upon leaving the ATM network at the Ethernet end. We try to avoid this fragmentation at all costs due to its performance implications on the router. MTU path discovery should therefore be implemented on all systems, precluding the need for manual configuration. Some systems currently supporting this RFC include Sun's Solaris, SGI, Windows NT, and the IBM RS-6000. Note that the same problem may exist between ATM-connected workstations and LAN-attached systems. The ATM systems must either implement the discovery RFC or set their MTU to that of the distant LAN. Problems due to MTU mismatches may be hard to detect, since under minimal network loading, problems due to IP fragmentation may not be apparent because of the ability of routers at the LAN boundaries to buffer and fragment. Real losses in performance will only become noticeable when the buffering can no longer pace the packets requiring fragmentation.

As an example, consider a workstation connected to an FDDI network, which is in turn connected across an ATM-connected router to two ATM-connected workstations. Over FDDI, the data link MTU (SDU) is 4470 bytes. This MTU should be therefore chosen on the router's ATM interface. If this ATM MTU were set greater, large frames entering the router from the ATM side would be dropped or fragmented. For completeness a second MTU, the protocol MTU, also exists. This is the commonly-quoted MTU of 4352 for FDDI and 9180 for ATM. The FDDI-connected workstation will have no problem in communicating with the ATM-connected workstation since it will have negotiated a proper IP-MTU. A problem only results when the two ATM workstations, in communicating among one another, negotiate an MTU of 9180 bytes. Though the data passes through the router (as the ATM and FDDI workstations are on different LISs), the lack of MTU path discovery support precludes the router being able to set a lower MTU (4470 bytes). Therefore, data sent from one of these workstations over the router to the FDDI will be dropped. With path discovery not implemented, the IP MTU on the router's ATM interface or either of the workstations' ATM interfaces should have been manually set to 4352 bytes.

Another concern when choosing the MTU is buffering on a router's ATM interface. Consider two of the above end-systems, one connected to an ATM switch and another to an FDDI on the router. Even though the MTU may be set to 4470 bytes, this may not be ideal as it will make less efficient use of the router's interface buffers than an Ethernet MTU, for example. If the traffic mix in terms of packet sizes is known ahead of time, this may be used to more effectively set different buffer sizes, but will, of course, introduce additional complexity.

The MTU of the data traffic will also affect the ultimate performance of a PC or workstation, as many systems are capable of saturating a 155 Mbps connection at an MTU of 8 Kbytes but not at 1500 Bytes due to interrupt handling. The negative side of this larger MTU is the amount of buffering required per active reassembly operation. Realistically, this should not be a problem, since current interfaces, though rated at up to 4096 VCCs, are in fact limited to 500 or so due to the speed of most current TCP implementations. In addition, since many packets will be below the MTU, dynamic buffering could help as well.

Multiprotocol encapsulation over ATM AAL5

The ATMARP mechanism as described above, along with the majority of VCCs in both the local and wide area, will utilize the LLC/SNAP encapsulation defined in *Multiprotocol Encapsulation over ATM Adaptation Layer 5* (Heinanen, 1993). This RFC actually defines two methods by which multiprotocol data may be transported over ATM AAL5. The first method, referred to as **LLC encapsulation**, is based on the LLC/SNAP technique, and is no different to that used for 802.2 and SMDS. An alternative method multiplexes Layer 3 protocols by separate VCCs, and is known as *VC-based multiplexing*. When the RFC was originally written, it was expected that VC-Mux would be more prevalent in the local area where SVCs were supported and the cost of VCCs was less of an issue. In contrast, LLC encapsulation would be more widely deployed in PVC environments where the goal would be to minimize the number of VCCs established. This would hold especially true for the wide area, where there might be a cost associated with each VCC. In reality, most implementations in both the local and wide areas use LLC/SNAP. Selection of the multiplexing method is either implicit in PVC networks and configured through network management or accomplished via signaling in SVC environments.

We encapsulate data PDUs within the payload field of the AAL5 CPCS-PDU, with a maximum length of 65535 octets. Note that this equates to the largest ATM-MTU possible under any circumstances, and is larger than that currently defined within RFC 1626 (Atkinson, 1994). Under LLC encapsulation, this payload field will contain an LLC header in compliance with IEEE 802.2 (IEEE, 1989). The header may identify an ISO PDU (0xFE FE 03), in which case the following byte will be a **Network Layer Protocol Identifier (NLPID)** (see Table 4.1). If the NLPID is set to (0x09) then the following four bytes will identify the packet's Layer 2 and 3 protocol IAW Q.933. If no Layer 2 protocol exists, then the first two bytes are set to (0x50 81). For example, IBM's HPR uses a Layer 3 code point of (0x70 85) while other values exist for Subarea SNA (FID4), Peripheral SNA (FID2), and APPN (FID2) (Dudley, 1995).

Alternatively, the header will indicate that an SNAP header follows (0xAA AA 03). In most cases, and always with IP, the SNAP header will be used to identify the protocol. This SNAP header takes the form of a three-octet **Organizationally Unique Identifier (OUI)** as well as

Table 4.1 PDU formats.

Format	LLC	NLPID	Layer 2 protocol	Layer 3 protocol	PDU length
Routed ISO PDUs	FE-FE-03	xx			$2^{16}-4$
ISO PDUs	FF-FE-03	09	xx-xx	xx-xx	$2^{16}-8$

a two-octet **Protocol Identifier (PID)**. Looking into the SNAP header, an OUI of 0x00 00 00 identifies the following PID as an Ethertype. The identification of the various internetwork protocols (IP, IPX, ARP) takes place at this level. This encapsulation also provides for the direct transport of bridged protocols by making use of the 802.1 organization code of 0x00 80 C2 and a PID identifying the medium in question. These PIDs are listed in Table 4.2.

Table 4.2 RFC 1483 LLC payload formats.

Format	LLC (Note 1)	SNAP OUI	SNAP PID	PAD/frame control	MAC Data dest. length (Note 2)		FCS	Trailer (Note 6)
AAL5 CPCS-PDU				**CPCS-PDU payload (2^{16}-1)**				(8)
Routed ISO PDU	FE-FE-03			**ISO PDU (2^{16}-4)**				(8)
Routed non-ISO PDUs	AA-AA-03	00-00-00		Ether-type (2)	**Non-ISO PDU (2^{16}-9)**			(8)
Routed IP PDUs	AA-AA-03	00-00-00	08-00		**IP PDU (2^{16}-9)**			(8)
Bridged 802.3	AA-AA-03	00-80-C2	00-01	00-00	(6)	(2^{16}-18)	Yes (1)	(8)
Bridged 802.3	AA-AA-03	00-80-C2	00-07	00-00	(6)	(2^{16}-17)	No	(8)
Bridged 802.4	AA-AA-03	00-80-C2	00-02	00-00-00/FC	(6)	(2^{16}-20) Note 3	Yes (1)	(8)
Bridged 802.4	AA-AA-03	00-80-C2	00-08	00-00-00/FC	(6)	(2^{16}-19)	No	(8)
Bridged 802.5	AA-AA-03	00-80-C2	00-03	00-00-XX/FC	(6)	(2^{16}-20) Note 4	Yes (1)	(8)
Bridged 802.5	AA-AA-03	00-80-C2	00-09	00-00-XX/FC	(6)	(2^{16}-19)	No	(8)
Bridged FDDI	AA-AA-03	00-80-C2	00-04	00-00-00/FC	(6)	(2^{16}-20)	Yes (1)	(8)
Bridged FDDI	AA-AA-03	00-80-C2	00-0A	00-00-00/FC	(6)	(2^{16}-19)	No	(8)
Bridged 802.6	AA-AA-03	00-80-C2	00-0B	Note 5	(6)	(2^{16}-21)	Note 5	(8)
Bridged PDU	AA-AA-03	00-80-C2	00-0E	BPDU as defined by 802.1(d) or 802.1(g) (length 2^{16}-9)				(8)

Note 1 The LLC header contains the following fields:
A 1-byte **Destination Service Access Point (DSAP)** field, set to AA for SNAP
A 1-byte **Source Service Access Point (SSAP)** field, set to AA for SNAP
A 1-byte control field, set to 03 for unnumbered information
The SNAP header contains the following fields:
A 3-byte OUI, set to 0 for Ethertype
A 2-byte information field, set to 08-00 for IP
Note 2 Data lengths are maximum
Note 3 The FC is a 1-octet frame control field
Note 4 XX: Any value; in the case of 802.5, this is the access control field which has no significance outside of 802.5
Note 5 These fields composing the common PDU header follow the 802.6 PID: Reserved (4 bit), BEtag (4 bit), BAsize (8 bit, specifying the length of the PDU). A common PDU trailer follows the MAC frame, and contains the CRC-32. The common PDU header and trailer is preserved to allow pipelining at the entry into an 802.6 subnetwork. The BAsize field allows the egress IWU to begin transmitting the 802.6 PDU before it has received the complete PDU.
Note 6 A 0–47 octet PAD field precedes the trailer for cell alignment. The 8-octet CPCS-PDU trailer includes: CPCS-UU (1 octet), CPI (1 octet), length of PDU (2 octets), and a CRC (4 octets).

Table 4.3 RFC 1483 VC mux payload formats.

Type/field	PAD	Destination	Data	FCS	Trailer
AAL5 CPCS-PDU		CPCS-PDU payload (2^{16}-1)			(8)
Routed PDUs		IP-PDU (2^{16}-1)			(8)
Bridged 802.3	00-00	MAC dest. (6)	MAC frame (2^{16}-9)	LAN FCS (VC dependent)	(8)
Bridged 802.4/5/ FDDI	00-00-00 or 00-00-XX	Frame control MAC dest. (6)	MAC frame (2^{16}-11)	LAN FCS (VC dependent)	(8)
Bridged 802.6	Common PDU header (2)	MAC dest. (6)	MAC frame (2^{16}-13)	Common PDU trailer (4)	(8)
Bridged PDU			MAC frame (2^{16}-1)		(8)

The second form of encapsulation, VC-based multiplexing, relies on an individual VC for each higher-layer protocol (Table 4.3). For this reason, the LLC/SNAP header is not required, resulting in less overhead and processing at the expense of additional VCs. For bridged protocols, we transport only those fields native to the bridged media in question (for example, frame control for 802.5 and FDDI) within the AAL5 PDU. The process of bridging over ATM is different to that over a shared medium, in that flooding will take place by sending a given PDU over VCCs to all appropriate destinations. Under initial implementations of bridging, scalability was somewhat limited since the source replicated the traffic over every open VCC. Newer techniques based on point-to-multipoint connections where replication takes place in the ATM switch have addressed this concern.

When deploying ATM for multiprotocol data, methods of encapsulation and address resolution play a part in the network design. Depending upon the encapsulation used (as specified in RFC 1483 (Heinanen, 1993)), multiple Layer 3 protocols may share a VCC between a source and destination or separate VCCs may be created for each. For example, LANEv1 relies on VC Muxing while IP over ATM as defined in RFC-1577 and MPOA are based on LLC/SNAP. Although the latter method may be desirable in most cases, when we introduce end-to-end QoS such as that supported by the Resource ReSerVation Protocol (RSVP), this may change. Depending upon the application's requirements and the QoS of existing VCCs, we may very well end up with multiple connections between a source and destination, even for a single

Table 4.4 RFC 1483 FR-SSCS payload formats.

Type/field	Header	Q.922 control	NLPID	Data	Trailer
AAL5 CPCS-PDU	Q.922 address (2-4)	Q.922 information (PDU payload)			(8)
Routed IP PDU	Q.922 address (2-4)	03	CC	(2^{16}-5)	(8)
Routed CLNP PDU	Q.922 address (2-4)	03	81 (Note 1)	(2^{16}-5)	(8)

Note 1 Other NLPIDs include: 80 (SNAP), 82 (ISO ES-IS), and 83 (ISO IS-IS)

Layer 3 protocol. Address resolution capabilities play a part in ease of management and configuration. For example, ATMARP (Laubach, 1993) supports automatic mapping for IP only, while other Layer 3 protocols require the nework manager to manually configure lookup tables. This limitation is overcome with MPOA which includes multiprotocol address resolution.

The proper operation of routing across an ATM network requires the creation of a mesh of VCCs over which the routing protocols will exchange their reachability information. This mesh will consist of PVCs established by the network administrator, or the routing protocol may trigger SVCs which will then remain open. If priorities are available, the level assigned to this routing mesh should be sufficiently high to preclude the loss of reachability information if the network is congested. Note that this requirement may conflict with other design parameters, as a source may use this same VCC for data transfer, data which potentially is assigned a lower priority. The only way around this would be to implement higher-layer filtering at the source (for example, by source address or by TCP port), where a separate mesh of VCCs would be used only for the exchange of routing (and possibly management) data.

The design of this routing mesh will depend upon the Layer 3 protocol or protocols in use. Consider an ATM network consisting of three switches (A, B, and C) surrounded by routers (A', B', and C'). Each switch is connected to a router (A-A', and so on), and we run IP and IPX across the ATM backbone. In the absence of subinterfaces on these routers, we run single PVCs from each router to the other two (A'-B', A'-C', B'-C'). If link A-B fails, traffic and routing information which originally flowed over the PVC from A' to B' must now follow PVCs A'-C' and C'-B'. Although the common IP routing protocols allow routing updates to flow in and out of the same physical interface (C'), other protocols such as IPX do not allow this. This is the split horizon issue. Thus, IP would continue to function while IPX would break. A solution is to implement subinterfaces on the routers, supported by most vendors. The single physical interface now appears as multiple logical interfaces to the routing protocol, and IPX will continue to function properly. In almost all cases, users should implement subinterfaces.

Multicasting and broadcasting

A valuable service offered across any internetwork is multicasting, where data is delivered to a group of users simultaneously. Though techniques for multicasting over shared media (for example, Ethernet) where the link layer natively supports this function have been developed and tested over the last few years, the integration of multicasting with ATM is just beginning. The intent of an ATM multicast service is to map existing network layer multicasting into ATM's support for point-to-multipoint VCCs. Efforts to define this service must reconcile differences between current network layer multicast services and those available within ATM, as summarized in Table 4.5.

One issue concerns the types of multicast group join permitted. Under existing network layer multicasting, membership in a multicast group is open to each and every end-system on a network. As part of this, a given sending station may have no knowledge of who is participating in a given group. There is actually no concept of even a sender, as any member of the group and even those who are not members of a given group may transmit data. In contrast, UNI 3.0/3.1-based multicasting functions via a point-to-multipoint VCC established from the originator of the transmission to all potential recipients before any cells may be transmitted. This sender, or root, must have prior knowledge of every recipient. Any new end-system wishing to connect to this group must notify the root via an external mechanism of its wish to participate. Some of these limitations disappear with UNI 4.0, where leaf-initiated joins allow potential end-systems to connect to an existing pt-mpt VCC. Still, some out-of-band security mechanism is still required whereby the root may determine whether a potential leaf is actually permitted to join the group, and potential multicast group members must still know what multicast sessions are available.

A second difference between the two technologies relates to group addressing. Whereas network layer protocols include the concept of groups (for example, IP Class D addressing), ATM under UNI 3.0/3.1 does not implement group addressing. We require methods of mapping a subset of a given network protocol's address space into a set of ATM unicast addresses and resolving addresses between the two layers. With the deployment of UNI 4.0 and ATM group addressing, this may change.

Yet a third difference relates to data distribution. Existing connectionless networks inherently support multicasting via a multipoint-to-multipoint capability within the datagram service. As noted above, ATM supports only pt-mpt unidirectional VCCs. Therefore, we require a method of simulating a bi-directional multipoint-to-multipoint VCC across the ATM fabric. At some point in the future, ATM is expected to support mpt-mpt VCCs.

Thus, using ATM as a basis for a network layer multicasting service is not trivial, and developing a workable solution has been the focus

Table 4.5 Differences between internetwork and ATM multicasting.

Internetwork multicasting	ATM multicasting
Bi-directional	Unidirectional
Multipoint-to-multipoint	Point-to-multipoint
Receiver-initiated join	Sender-initiated join (UNI 3.0/3.1)
	Leaf-initiated join (UNI 4.0)
Connectionless	Connection oriented
Open-group (non-members may send)	No multicast 'group' concept at present

of a great deal of effort within the IETF over the last two years. By the end of 1995, techniques for solving the problems described above had stabilized to the extent that code developers could begin implementation. Armitage (1996) describes this ATM multicasting environment, and though the document, a product of the IETF, focuses on IP-based solutions, the concepts and protocols are extensible for other network layer protocols. For example, the ATM Forum's MPOA group will use this work as a basis for their multicasting efforts. This rather extensive architecture document defines two new entities within an ATM network: a **Multicast Address Resolution Server (MARS)** providing address resolution, and an optional **Multicast Server (MCS)** used for mpt-mpt sessions. Future revisions (MARSv2) should include redundancy via general server synchronization as well. For the remainder of this discussion, we focus on IP multicasting.

Before we look at the two multicasting architectures in detail, we first must clarify some terminology. Remember the discussion of the Classical model and its use of a Logical IP Subnet (LIS). Since this is a very IP-centric term, and since a given group of multicast participants may span multiple LISs (described later), we require a new term. This is the **cluster**, a set of ATM end-points which are capable of establishing direct VCCs among themselves. Within IP, a cluster will often map to an LIS, with inter-cluster traffic passing through an inter-cluster device such as a multicast-capable IP router.

Multicasting at the network layer relies on Class D IPv4 addresses in the range from 224.0.0.0 to 239.255.255.255 (224.0.0.0/4) which identify the hosts that have joined a specific multicast group. An ATM end-point wishing to participate in multicasting will first issue a `JoinLocalGroup` to the address reserved for IGMP query messages, 224.0.0.1. At this point, it will begin to receive IGMP reports. Next, the host will issue a `JoinLocalGroup` to one or more specific multicast groups via their unique Class D addresses. In contrast to hosts, multicast routers must normally join all groups since they must relay the join requests upstream to the source of a given multicast group. Since this may present problems for routers in large multicast environments, the router may be restricted to a subset of the Class D address space. Remember that in RFC 1112 (Deering, 1989), hosts wishing to receive multicast traffic will generate an IGMP `Report` message and then multicast this to the other nodes in the given multicast group. A router will take note of this request and send multicast traffic to the node's subnet via a network layer multicast protocol (for example, DVMRP or PIM). If the router is not currently receiving the data for this group, it must send the request upstream to the nearest point where the data is available. A router also uses 224.0.0.1 to monitor the status of all groups it services, and will periodically generate an IGMP query for its groups. This query will be received by all nodes; those wishing to remain a member (or join the group in the first place) will respond with an IGMP `Report` message on one or more groups. One problem with most host IGMP implementations is that they do not yet support active departures from a group, a potential problem with video where a user may 'channel-surf' across many multicast groups. Too long a timeout will tend to tie up the local LAN segment. This limitation is expressed within IGMPv2 or v3.

Two approaches to establishing mpt-mpt connectivity exist, both relying on pt-mpt VCCs. The first relies on hosts or routers to maintain a multipoint VCC to each destination, using the MARS to resolve membership information, and is known as a VC mesh. The MARS, as introduced above, is an extension of the ATMARP server as defined in RFC 1577 (Laubach, 1993), but in contrast to the unicast (pt-pt) mappings maintained by the ATMARP server, the MARS maintains pt-mpt mappings. End-systems participating in this multicast environment use the MARS to register their joining and leaving of a multicast group, while at the same time querying the server for group membership information. In the second mpt-mpt approach, end-points establish a unicast VCC to the MCS which then reassembles and relays the data to all group members via a pt-mpt VCC. Note that the MARS is still required for address registration.

These two forwarding models have both advantages and disadvantages. Advantages of the VC mesh include potentially higher throughput and lower latency (due to the lack of the MCS reassembly). In addition, the VC mesh lacks the MCS's single point of congestion (though the MCS function may be distributed). Lastly, the VC mesh will tend to result in a more optimal pt-mpt VCC. In contrast, this model requires a larger number of VCCs, consuming resources in the end-systems. For example, each participating node must maintain an incoming VCC per group member in addition to its own pt-mpt if transmitting, while when using the MCS, each member maintains only two VCCs. Signaling load is also a concern, since when group membership changes within a VC mesh, each end-point is affected since every sender must add or delete the leaf in question. With the MCS, the only signaling actions are at the end-point in question and at the MCS. Finally, if the user is charged on a per-connection basis, the VC mesh is less financially viable. When running multiple multicast groups across ATM, the additional overhead incurred under the VC mesh model may be substantial. One solution here may be for transmitting stations to re-use connections to destinations which are members of multiple groups.

Mapping the above procedures to ATM is the function of the MARS. The MARS is a process which may exist in any ATM-connected router, PC, or workstation, and is an evolution of the ATMARP server. In real networks, these two functions are normally resident on the same platform. Just as a router may implement separate ATMARP server functions for each LIS it services, a router on the boundary of two or more multicast clusters may run multiple MARS processes. Cluster members will be configured with the ATM address of the primary MARS and possibly a backup as well. Communication between an ATM end-point and the MARS takes place over a pt-pt VCC which may be used for both ATMARP and MARS queries/replies. The MARS also maintains a pt-mpt VCC terminating at every cluster member, known as the ClusterControlVC. This connection is used to monitor group joins and leaves once we establish the pt-mpt VCC.

An ATM end-point will first establish a pt-pt VCC to the MARS, over which it will `JoinLocalGroup` to 224.0.0.1. The MARS will now add this client as a leaf on its ClusterControlVC, and will assign a unique **Cluster Member Identifier (CMI)**. The end-point is now an ATM multicast cluster member (Figure 4.6). Note that routers, acting as multicast forwarders for devices on attached LAN segments or via WAN interfaces, will almost always be cluster members. The client will now join one or more multicast groups. For each group, the MARS will pro-pogate the address of this client over the ClusterControlVC to all other nodes in the group and will add it to its ARP table for the Class D address in question. Other nodes will add the new member as a leaf on their pt-mpt VCCs. If the client wishes to transmit data to the group, it must also query the MARS for a list of group members, at which point it will establish a pt-mpt VCC for use in sending data. The reverse process via the `LeaveLocalGroup` request occurs when a node leaves a group.

Remember that a single instance of the MARS is responsible for IPmc traffic within a single LIS/cluster. Inter-LIS/cluster IPmc traffic will flow through an IPmc-capable router connected to two or more LISs/clusters as shown in Figure 4.7. Note that this router may also act as the MARS for these clusters.

In server mode, ATM end-points forward all multicast data to the **Multicast Server (MCS)**. This server reassembles the AAL5 frames and forwards them over a pt-mpt VCC to each destination within a given group. Under the MCS, each end-point will have only two data VCCs, one pt-pt to the MCS for sending data and one pt-mpt from the MCS on

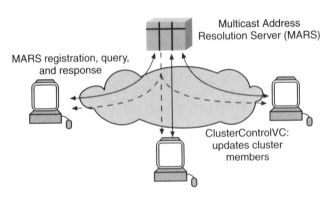

Figure 4.6 Multicast Address Resolution Server (MARS).

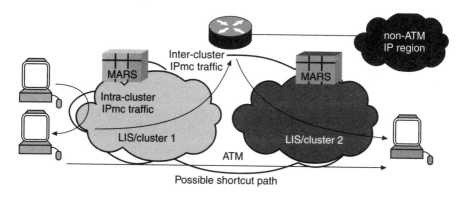

Figure 4.7 Inter-LIS/cluster IP multicast.

which it will receive data. This contrasts to the mesh of VCCs described above. The MCS cooperates with the MARS over a ServerControlVC to obtain the list of nodes in a particular multicast group. This MARS uses this connection as well, to obtain the list of active MCSs within a cluster. When implemented, a user wishing to send to a given multicast group will still query the MARS, but will now receive the MCS's address as opposed to those of the actual end-points since the MARS knows that this group is serviced by a MCS. The user then proceeds to send all data to the MCS over its existing pt-pt connection. As shown in Figure 4.8, a single LIS/cluster may be served by multiple MCSs for scalability and redundancy. One complication with MCS operation results from packet reflection, where data sent from a given host will be returned from the MCS. To avoid this, Armitage (1995) describes a new subset of LLC/SNAP encapsulation (also used within NHRP), whereby a source can identify via its CMI whether or not it should discard the data. There are, however, conflicting views on whether this new encapsulation type

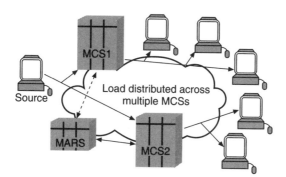

Figure 4.8 Redundant multicast servers.

is actually necessary or desirable, although today this seems to be a moot point. The discarding of reflected packets will now occur either at the ATM layer via this encapsulation or at the network layer. As the amount of processing may not be too different in either case and, as the latter protects the installed base, defining a new encapsulation for the MARS case alone may not have been a requirement. One element of the MARS (and other) protocol(s) worth mentioning is its use of **Type-Length-Value (TLV)** fields which allow additional functionality to be included within the protocol at a later date. Thus, the protocol as currently defined will be extensible for the future.

A potential problem within ATM multicasting is router IGMP behavior. On broadcast-capable networks, routers multicast IGMP queries to the group address 224.0.0.1. This is of course inefficient over an ATM network. The MARS implements a `grouplist` query and reply which will return the same information as that available under the IGMP query. If a given router does not service the complete Class D address space, this may make this known as part of the query. A second problem is the number of connections required under VC mesh operation. As described above, these connections require resources in the end-systems and may place a burden upon the switches due to the signaling required when the group changes. These two points will ultimately limit the number of members in a group or cluster. Looking at IP for example, a trend is to attempt to flatten the addressing scheme when deploying ATM. Though 2000 users could potentially share a common subnet, these 2000 users could not form a single multicast cluster. They would need to be split into smaller groups of 50–100 users via routers. Thus the need for multicasting will have a major impact on the addressing plan used within an ATM network. In looking at alternatives to the MARS/MC, other methods of implementing mpt-mpt functionality have been discussed, including associating a SVP connection with a group, although it is still undecided as to whether or not SVPs are to be used by end users in this way. Note that AAL3/4 accomplishes this in another way via the MID, though the future of this adaptation is in doubt. Alternatively, we could associate a multicast session with an ATM 'call', a concept originating from within the ITU to aggregate connections which has promise.

The model is extensible for multicast paths spanning traditional LAN segments and ATM LISs. For example, a router may receive multicast traffic on a LAN interface. This will then be transmitted onto the ATM network using the methods described above. A distant multicast-capable router operating in 'promiscuous' mode (that is, a member of all groups) will receive the packet and forward it out via its LAN interface. This method has advantages over simple multicast tunneling over ATM in that ATM-connected end-systems may participate in the multicast group. But as stated above, this may present a problem for the multicast routers (note that unicast tunneling routers suffer from the same problem in that they must open an individual VC for every destination). In this case, the methods described above whereby the router will only respond to certain blocks within the Class D address space must be implemented. For example, certain Class D addresses may be reserved for use by ATM-based multicast groups.

Alternatives to MARS

Farinacci (1995) outlines a different solution for solving the multicast across ATM problem, avoiding the need for MCS or MARS-like entities within the network. The solution draws on host IGMP caches to determine the leaves of a pt-mpt VCC. Under this proposal, hosts first establish pt-mpt connections to their eligible routers over which they send IGMP reports for the group address. Now, the router, upon receipt of an IGMP report for a specific multicast group from a host, will open a pt-mpt VCC to that host and to any others in the same group. One router, the **Designated Router (DR)** will periodically send an IGMP query down the pt-mpt connection. A host, upon reciept of this query, will reply with a report. The router now forwards these reports over its multipoint VCC to other hosts in the group, which will then use this information to add the new host as leaves on their pt-mpt connections. A VC mesh for the group results. Fault tolerance is provided by DR failover. Since an ATM host may not be capable of supporting a large number of connections, we may scale this solution by dividing the single large multicast group into separate groups of VC meshes, connected via multicast routers.

If full mpt-mpt connectivity is not required, a simpler solution relies on the end-systems to maintain multicast group information, whereby the MARS is not required. This is in effect a subset of the problem described in the previous paragraph. We focus on **Protocol Independent Multicasting (PIM)** as the network layer multicast protocol (although **Multicast OSPF (MOSPF)** and the **Distance Vector Multicast Routing Protocol (DVMRP)** would function in much the same way), with initial efforts directed towards mapping this into ATM. Consider the video distribution network in Figure 4.9 with a source and multiple clients, all directly attached to the ATM network via routers. Any sources or clients connected to non-ATM interfaces are external to this problem, since PIM will operate unchanged. For example, Ethernet-attached PCs connected to the client routers use IGMP to register their intent to receive a given channel via the ATM-connected client. IGMP is running as part of PIM between the source and all clients via a dedicated VCC. We assign each video channel originating at the source to a separate IPmc group and this group will map to an ATM pt-mpt VCC, terminating at each of the clients. Though this is a good first step, the client has no method of signaling to the source its desire to receive only a subset of the available channels. Thus, an out-of-band mechanism is

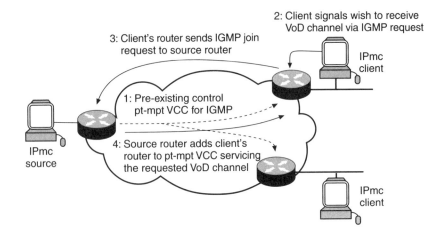

Figure 4.9 IP multicasting across ATM.

required whereby the client router will send a PIM join request to the source, who will then add it to the channel's pt-mpt VCC. Note that this mechanism does not require the deployment of an external MARS, and circumvents the lack of leaf-initiated-joins under the UNI 3.0/3.1 by relying on the root for all signaling.

If the root of the pt-mpt VCC is not the PIM **Rendezvous Point (RP)**, then the system still functions with only the initial data passed through this RP. Once the client learns of the true source, it will join the source-rooted pt-mpt VCC. This may occur when multiple sources rely on the same RP. We also envision video sources connected directly to the ATM network implementing a subset of PIM. RSVP, described in a later section, may interwork with many of the same mechanisms as outlined above. Finally, note that this pt-mpt based multicasting is much preferable to previous methods relying on router-based replication for forwarding over non-shared media which were obviously unscalable.

Extending the multicast group

Though the techniques described above are sufficient for users to begin to deploy multicasting across ATM, they do not really address problems with scaling these multicast groups. If we look at methods of optimizing routing across ATM (described in the next section), we would also like a way to extend multicast groups across multiple IP LISs in the same way while avoiding undesirable artifacts such as multicast routing loops. Why? Consider large multicast sessions which include multiple user communities. The ultimate examples of this are proposed large-scale virtual environments (for war-gaming, among other uses). Developers of simulations and applications within these environments predict requirements to support upwards of 100,000 simultaneous users. A step in this direction, parallel to efforts to define mpt-mpt connectivity, is inter-LIS multicasting (Rekhter and Farinacci, 1995). An ATM-attached router or host (assuming the host supports PIM) would use the NHRP mechanisms to resolve addresses to multicast sources or RPs. Looking at the PIM example described above, this technique would allow one (that is, a service provider) to deploy pt-mpt VCCs across LIS boundaries.

Solutions for broadcasting

Although we have described solutions for multicasting across ATM in some detail, there is an additional class of traffic for which we must also provide. Consider an end-system connected to a LAN which generates a broadcast packet to all IP hosts on a subnet or network. Examples include diskless workstations during bootup, file servers generating service advertisements, and end-systems which implement routing protocols. The PC or workstation accomplishes this broadcast by sending a packet to one of three broadcast addresses:

- 255.255.255.255 (the 'all ones' broadcast);

- x.y.z (a subnet directed broadcast, where x is the network number, y is the subnet number, and z is the remainder of the address, set to all ones);

- x.z (a network directed broadcast, where x is the network number and z is also the remainder, set to all ones).

Looking at the classical architecture, in all three cases, all members of the LIS will receive a copy of the packet. Now, if we consider broadcast to be a special case of multicasting, then all hosts may join the 255.255.255.255 group, with the MARS maintaining the registry of all group members, in this case all end-systems within the LIS. Although this mechanism requires no changes to the MARS, since all hosts will join this group, an obvious question of scalability arises. Looking back at the MCS, this broadcast group may be the first to use this entity since the volume of traffic is not expected to overwhelm this server (that is, we do not expect the broadcast group to be used for video distribution) (Smith and Armitage, 1995).

4.1.3 Optimizing routing

Building upon the Classical model are efforts to optimize network layer routing and data transport in general over ATM networks. Within the IETF, the ION (combined ROLC and IP-ATM) working group coordinates closely with the ATM Forum to define approaches aimed at reducing routing hops across **Non-Broadcast Multi-Access (NBMA)** networks which contain hosts, small and large routers, and route servers. A routing hop, or **extra-hop** occurs when IP datagrams leave and re-enter the same link-layer cloud as a result of an IP routing decision. In the case of ATM, this may be highly sub-optimal in terms of resource use or tariffing. NBMA networks share three characteristics. The first is that many user communities may share the same physical infrastructure. Therefore, X.25, Frame Relay, and SMDS as well as ATM are examples of NBMA networks. The second characteristic of an NBMA network is that the network is normally incapable of providing broadcast and multicast capability except via additional servers or the creation of multicast circuits. A last characteristic of an NBMA network is that nodes are normally not physically or administratively restricted from directly communicating with one another. Thus, a wide-area ATM deployment may in fact be viewed as a number of overlapping NBMA networks if it is subdivided into administrative domains (sometimes known as **Virtual Private Networks**, or **VPNs**).

Parallel to these efforts within ROLC, the IP over ATM group takes a larger view in an attempt to rationalize the way network layer protocols and applications interact with the ATM network. The peer model, where the ATM network peers with traditional network layer protocols at the periphery of the ATM cloud, originated in this group. We continue the discussion of the peer model within Section 4.1.5. More recent proposals aimed at optimizing this interaction include the conventional model and a proposal which redefines the concept of a LIS and how end-systems interact with routers which we call the connectionless model. This last proposal is quite promising and may in fact have major implications for how we deploy ATM.

Specific network topologies addressed by the ROLC group include: a small number of routers with many hosts behind each, many directly-connected hosts, many routers with small subnets behind each, and many routers with many hosts behind each. Within these topologies, any protocol must optimize routing when two end-stations connect directly to the ATM cloud or when one or both are located on a distant LAN segment. In the latter cases, the protocol must ensure optimal entry and exit points while avoiding looping. While addressing a protocol for these topologies, the group stated its intent that the support of complex models should not burden the implementation of simple solutions, adversely affecting time-to-market. Compatibility with existing networks and the ability to support QoS requirements in the future are also important. The ION group bases their models on the assumption that IP routing is not analogous to ATM routing, and is therefore aligned with the separated addressing (or overlay) model where the ATM network is a subnet to the network layer (in contrast to the peer addressing model). The goal of the ROLC group is not only to provide for routing between any two entities, but also to preserve filtering mechanisms and compatibility with existing routing protocols.

As outlined above, direct routing from one entity to another not necessarily in the same IP subnet will require relaxation of a rule that has governed internetworking since its inception. This rule states that we use routers when sending datagrams between subnets. One concern when relaxing this rule relates to firewall routers. We cannot subvert their role via the mechanism, and therefore any path which traverses a firewall as part of the normal routed path must continue to do so under shortcut routing.

Next Hop Resolution Protocol (NHRP)

The NBMA Next Hop Resolution Protocol (NHRP) (Katz *et al*, 1995) is intended to optimize routing across NBMA networks, and is an extension of both the Classical model and of the **NBMA Address Resolution Protocol (NARP)**, an earlier experimental protocol defined by Heinanen and Govindan (1994). Whereas the Classical model's ATMARP servers provide for only a single LIS, the NHRP follows a more general approach and takes into account end-systems not connected directly to the same link-layer cloud. In most cases, the NHRP server, known as a **Next Hop Server (NHS),** will reside in a router, though nothing precludes its deployment in workstations. In the future, the NHS may be deployed in LAN and ATM switches with Layer 3 modules. Note that NHRP is not a routing protocol; it is an inter-LIS address resolution mechanism which uses existing network layer routing to resolve a destination's address.

An IP source station will use NHRP to determine the best IP and link layer (NBMA) address to use to reach a destination station. This 'next hop' address returned may be that of the destination itself, the closest exit router to the destination, or an intermediate router, possibly due to Layer 3 policy restrictions. Note that the choice of paths in this instance is the role of the NHSs and not of the end-system. Thus, the protocol does not support the application-driven model as described in the next section (*Direct connections*). Under protocol operation, participating hosts will first register with their NHS (or NHSs if redundancy is available through group addressing or manual configuration). This NHS maintains tables of IP to ATM address mappings for all nodes utilizing the NHS or for IP networks reachable through routing nodes served by the NHS. In most cases, this set of nodes served by the NHS will share a common address prefix.

As an example of NHRP operation, consider a single NBMA domain where all hosts may communicate with one another. Katz *et al* (1995) refer to this as a **Logical NBMA Subnetwork**, or just **NBMA Subnetwork**. Within this subnetwork we have NHRP servers (NHSs) and NHRP clients. A NHS will respond to next hop resolution requests, and serve a set of destinations. In addition, it will probably participate in intra- and inter-domain routing and may support ATMARP functionality. This NHS maintains a next-hop resolution cache containing IP to NBMA address mappings gathered from monitoring queries or responses or via manual configuration. In a typical deployment, NHSs will exist along all routed paths between NHRP clients. We configure these NHRP clients with the address(es) of one or more NHSs. Some of this information may be learned from an NBMA configuration server, roughly analogous to the LECS, or the NHRP MIB. This will preclude the need for manual configuration. Note that NHSs are also capable of forwarding data along the normally routed path to the destination, avoiding delay while the shortcut path is resolved, and that routers which lie on the boundary between two NBMA domains will act as NHSs for each.

A source (S) will initiate the query/response sequence when it must resolve the NBMA address for a path to a destination (D) (assuming that it has not previously queued this information). S will first attempt to determine the next hop to D through normal routing processes. If this next hop is across the NBMA network, it will then generate a next hop resolution request containing D's IP address as the target destination, its own IP address as the source, and its NBMA address. While waiting for the reply from the NHS, S will probably forward the packet along the normally-routed path to D, though it may also queue the packet until the shortcut route is resolved. The NHS, upon receiving the request, checks as to whether or not it serves D, in which case it replies with D's NBMA to IP mapping. If not, it forwards the request to the next NHS along the routed path to D. This is repeated until the destination's NHS is reached, at which time a reply containing the NBMA link layer address of D will be forwarded back along the path to S or, if permitted, it may be sent directly to the source. This address will also be cached by NHSs on the return path for use in future lookups. S, upon receipt of this address mapping, may now open a direct connection to D (Figure 4.10). In this figure we also compare the NHRP solution with the number of connections required when using ATMARP.

NHRP supports a number of valuable features which will ease deployment and operation of NBMA networks. The protocol supports network layer policy restrictions which may not allow a connection to be

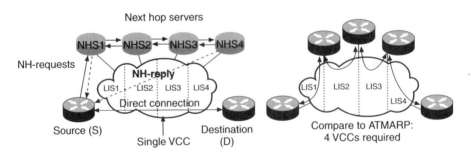

Figure 4.10 Next Hop Resolution Protocol (NHRP) and comparison with ATMARP.

established to a final destination. In this case, an NHS along the path will intercept NHRP requests and respond with their own address as a forwarding point. This allows NHSs to be deployed as firewalls between NBMA administrative domains. A desired QoS for the final path may also be included in NHRP requests. Full error indications as well as forward and reverse route recording are also supported by the protocol. This feature will allow hosts and NHSs to detect routing loops within the NBMA network. NHRP also includes support for address aggregation. As outlined above, the NHS may return an address/subnet pair as opposed to a single end-system IP address. Finally, a protocol ID field will allow the use of IPng and other network layer address formats in NHRP requests and replies.

Over the next year or so, as we move from ATMARP to a mix of ATMARP and NHRP and then finally to NHRP, we must ensure that any changes taking place within the server structure of the network do not adversely affect the end-systems. During this transition, the following sequence of events may take place. Beginning with an RFC 1577 (Laubach, 1993) environment, we phase-in NHRP servers. During this phase, hosts will continue to register with the ATM ARP server; these servers will in turn leak the registration information to NHRP servers. This will avoid NHRP-capable hosts having to register twice unless they wish to set NHRP-specific parameters. NHRP hosts will of course send all address resolution requests to the NHRP server and, as an alternative, may send ARP requests to the local ATMARP server if the NHRP server returns a negative acknowledgment (NAK) to a request and if the destination is in the same LIS. Finally, NHRP servers will completely replace ARP servers, and all hosts are NHRP-capable at this point. Note that this migration path, although providing for mixed environments, will not allow RFC 1577-based hosts to establish direct connections to NHRP-based hosts. A router will be required to interconnect these two domains.

One problem identified with NHRP is the possibility of routing loops between routers when deployed in an internetwork combining both NBMA and non-NBMA networks, due to the ability of the NHRP protocol to carry reachability information but not full path attribute or metric information, thus suppressing the existing hierarchical routing structure. We therefore require a method of determining if previously valid paths are invalid so a new one may be established. Consider a path from a source to a destination, both located off the NBMA network but crossing this network via multiple paths. When the path hits the ingress router, this router initiates an NHRP request which will eventually be resolved by the egress router. We will then have established a shortcut path across the NBMA network. As the network topology changes, this path may become invalid (for example, due to failure of a non-ATM link towards the destination), possibly resulting in a forwarding loop. Cole *et al* (1996) present an excellent example of this scenario. This loop would not form if the information from an external interdomain routing protocol such as BGP or IDRP were injected into the NBMA network. The ROLC group is investigating this approach, whereby a subset of the inter-domain routing protocol would establish a limited adjacency between two NHRP routers. This would be used to exchange information as to topological changes within networks external to the NBMA network. A simpler solution, also under consideration, would have the advertising NBMA router invalidate the routing advertisement for some time period after a routing change. An option based on special configuration of all NBMA border routers will not scale. Note that the situation described above cannot occur between end-systems and routers since these systems do not forward data.

Rekhter and Cole (1995) also propose solutions to this problem, by drawing on routing information from a subset of the routers along the original non-shortcut path across the NBMA network. The routers forming this subset are known as **border routers**, and translate or aggregate routing information. Now, instead of resolving a shortcut path directly from the ingress to egress routers, it will terminate at each of these border routers. This does result in more than a single hop across the NBMA network, though, and is therefore suboptimal. A better solution would be to have the border routers store state information concerning requesters and paths. Now, if they detect a change in the routed path, they could initiate a new NHRP request and/or generate a purge message to the original requester. This method avoids extra hops across the NBMA network at the expense of NHS complexity. A last alternative, not relying on the border router concept, would have all NHRP clients periodically revalidate routes by generating NHRP requests. The time interval of these requests could be based on traffic volume.

Extensions to NHRP allowing for greater scalability include the ability to handle autoconfiguration of end-systems and support for multicast/broadcast connections in addition to possible inter-domain extensions as described above. The ATM Forum's MPOA group is in fact using NHRP as the basis for inter-IASG routing in a multiprotocol environment. As a final note, at the end of 1995, ROLC and IP-ATMs MARS harmonized their packet formats which will simplify matters for those implementing the two protocols, and plan to use a common configuration service as well.

For completeness, we should describe an earlier proposal for optimizing routing known as the **NBMA Address Resolution Protocol (NARP)** (Heinanen and Govindan, 1994). This is a method by which an end-system connected to an NBMA network may determine the address (ATM in this case) of a destination terminal connected to the same link-layer cloud. A source, wishing to communicate with a destination across an NBMA network, will first determine whether or not this destination is in its same LIS. If so, it will resolve the address via ATMARP, for example, and open the SVC. If in a distant LIS, the source formulates a

NARP request which it sends to the **NBMA ARP Server (NAS)**. This NAS will resolve an address local to its logical NBMA network, which may be a subset of the greater physical NBMA network. If the local NAS cannot resolve the address, it may forward the request to one of its peers for resolution. In this aspect, it shares many characteristics with NHRP, with the NAS analogous to an NHS. The IETF has relegated NARP to that of an experimental protocol as NHRP is advanced on the standards track both within the IETF and the ATM Forum.

Although NHRP allows more efficient routing across an ATM network by breaking through the limitations of the LIS-based Classical model, it still does not address the question of whether or not a direct connection should actually be opened. These decisions are left to application-driven SVC management, described in the following section.

Direct connections

To introduce the concepts described by Rekhter and Kandlur (1995), a brief review of the Internet model (earlier called the Catenet) is in order. Within an internet, links (data link layer subnetworks), each with a unique address, are interconnected via routers, with end-systems on a given link will be assigned an address consisting of a link number and host number. An end-system wishing to send a packet to a destination will first determine whether the destination is connected to the same link (local) or not (remote). This decision is based on the source and destination addresses as well as the IP subnet mask. If local, the end-system will use ARP to resolve the destination's MAC address, and will then send the packet directly to the destination. If remote, the end-system will forward the packet to a router connected to the local link. This model conflicts with the concept of an NBMA network where multiple IP networks are connected via a common data link layer. Using the mechanisms outlined in RFC 1577 (Laubach, 1993), a host will always set up a connection to a destination within its own IP network (LIS), sending all packets to non-LIS destinations to the nearest destination. NHRP still requires connections in all cases, only now they may be established between LISs. In both routing models, end-systems establish VCCs between one another for the exchange of data. Between any two of these end-systems, all data may traverse a single connection, or a separate connection may be established for each flow. This is where some of the models have failed, in that they have not looked at the applications.

Rather than forcing these applications to use a connection setup and routing philosophy which may not be suited to NBMA environments, it may be better to look at the application profiles themselves and then implement a networking model based on these profiles. This is what Rekhter and Kandlur (1995) set out to do, by dividing applications into four classes: those with short duration and traffic volume (for example,

DNS, ping), those with short duration and large traffic volume (for example, FTP), those with long duration but low traffic volume (for instance, Telnet), and those with long duration and high traffic volume (for example, videoconferencing). A common problem with both the Classical model and NHRP is the requirement to establish SVCs for all four of these traffic classes. The latency incurred during this connection setup phase contrasts to the connectionless nature of the traditional Internet, and in a large deployment with complex topology, this setup procedure, which includes address resolution and signaling, may take some time. ATMARP and NHRP servers are limited in the number of requests they can process at a given time, while switches are limited to a certain number of signaling requests per second. Thus, it may not make sense to establish an end-to-end connection for every data transfer, especially when the transfer is limited to only a few data frames such as DNS or SNMP.

This model places SVC management under the control of the end application, utilizing direct ATM connections only when the QoS guarantees of ATM are required. If not, the data would be relayed through a router, even if in the same **Local Address Group (LAG)**. The LAG is a set of host and router addresses assigned from a single prefix. Routers within the group advertise routes to the prefix, and devices within the group may establish SVCs between each other. In assigning addresses to an LAG, care should be taken that they may be aggregated into a single prefix for route advertisements. Finally, all routers within an LAG will be one hop from any host. Although an LAG may seem identical to a traditional IP subnet, the behavior of the local/remote decision is completely changed. It is now under the control of the application, with hosts permitted to forward packets via a router for a 'local' destination. Note that this last element also changes the behavior of routers in that they would no longer generate redirects for hosts reachable in the same subnet or network. The router connection would of course be shared by multiple applications, and may also be used by applications which have tried to establish a direct SVC but could not for some reason (for example, lack of network resources for the QoS requested in the signaling packet). Network layer broadcasts across the LAG operate as expected when using directed broadcasts. The destination address of this LAG directed broadcast is the IP address prefix of the LAG. Comparing this model to NHRP, remember that, under next hop, only the local action is changed, allowing for cut-through paths. NHRP does not permit hosts within the same subnet address prefix to act as if they were remote. However, the NHRP address resolution mechanisms could be used with this model if the query/response included application QoS awareness.

Although full implementation of this architecture requires these QoS-aware applications, a partial implementation could be based on filtering at the router (for example, by TCP port) as to whether a direct SVC should be established or not. For example, high-bandwidth

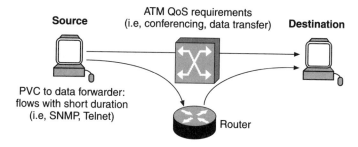

Figure 4.11 Connectionless model.

and long-lived flows would be sent via a signaled connection and low-bandwidth, short-lived flows would be forwarded via a router as in Figure 4.11. Examples of these latter flows would include SNMP and Telnet, as shown below. In a large ATM network, this could require the deployment of routers with frame-forwarding capacity a magnitude greater than that currently available. This is probably a requirement in any case, since traffic from an end-system in one administrative domain to one in another, though both on the same NBMA network, will be required to pass through a router. In an RFC 1577-based LIS, migration to this new model could be graceful, with routers configured not to generate ICMP redirects and hosts configured to ignore these messages if they do occur. Alternatively, in a smaller APR, every host could be configured to be on a separate subnet, with router interfaces configured for all subnets.

In effect, Rekhter and Kandlur (1995) redefine the LIS concept. Instead of implying a single IP network or subnet, the LAG would now describe those hosts and routers which could establish direct connections to one another. This router (or routers for redundancy) would also act as the last hop for hosts within the LAG. During a transition phase from an RFC 1577-based LIS, hosts may be configured to ignore ICMP redirects (sent by routers if the host is using the router to relay packets within a single subnet) and routers may be configured to accept multiple subnets on a single physical interface (that is, subinterfaces). Eventually, the router should be modified to suppress the generation of ICMP redirect messages. Within a host, all traffic except that generated by QoS-aware applications would be sent to the router. This in effect is no different than that deployed in the existing Internet. It is expected that those new applications requiring ATM's QoS capabilities will be made QoS aware. We summarize forwarding criteria in Table 4.6.

By Spring, 1996, hardware and software supporting this model was available. This system (Ipsilon, 1996) relies on a device known as an 'IP Switch', capable of supporting both routing of IP as well as ATM switching. Hosts, routers, or IP Switch Gateways connected to this

Table 4.6 VC establishment criteria.

Application	Connection oriented	Hybrid	Connectionless
Paradigm	Always signal a VC	Signal a VC if RSVP indicates that it is necessary	Always forward hop by hop. Use IP layer queuing to support RSVP QoS.
Short duration UDP (DNS)	Signal a VC. Teardown on timeout.	Forward hop by hop.	Forward hop by hop.
Short duration TCP (SMTP)	Signal a VC. Teardown on timeout or end of session	Forward hop by hop. RSVP may indicate the need for a signaled VC.	Forward hop by hop.
Elastic (TCP) bulk transfer	Signal a VC.	Forward hop by hop. RSVP may indicate the need for a signaled VC.	Forward hop by hop.
Real-time	Signal a VC based on QoS carried in RSVP	Forward hop by hop. RSVP may indicate the need for a signaled VC.	Forward hop by hop.

switch initially forward all traffic to the IP routing function across a default VCC. As longer-lived flows are identified based on TCP or UDP ports, the switch informs the upstream and downstream end-systems to establish an ATM Layer path over a separate VCC, bypassing the routing function. The switch is able to identify these flows via flow labeling as described (Newman, 1996). Once a flow has been identified, it is shifted from the default VCC (VPI=0, VCI=15) and LLC/SNAP encapsulation to a flow-specific virtual channel and is now labeled IAW (Newman, 1996a). VCC mappings within the switch are accomplished via the General Switch Management Protocol (Newman, 1996b), which also provides for switch monitoring and troubleshooting. The IP switch system is one way of addressing the requirements of high-speed connectivity across ATM while at the same time providing for routing where needed. In addition, it does not have a high degree of complexity in comparison to some of the other ATM data models. As an aside, remember the NHRP also optimizes forwarding paths across ATM but does not yet include support for the reverse where some flows within or between LISs would always be directed to a routing function.

In closing the discussion of IETF data models, we summarize data paths under the Classical, the NHRP, and what we will call the connectionless model in Figure 4.12.

Cole *et al* (1996) also define a transition model, in effect a combination of ATM networks and routers connecting end-systems using one or more data models. This is no different to Figure 4.12.

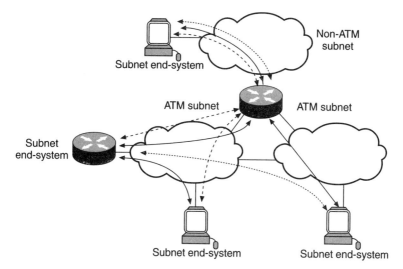

Figure 4.12 Classical, NHRP, and connectionless data paths.

Conventional model

Looking beyond methods to optimize routing, more radical architectures have been suggested. The first, known as the conventional model, retains the IP network layer (and thus the overlay architecture) but provides for multiple ATM subnets. A fundamental difference is that routers may relay IP packets cell-by-cell, and not only on a per-packet basis. In effect, an ATM switch now becomes a multilayer entity. These same concepts play a part in the requirements outlined in the I-PNNI and in the direct connect model described in the next section.

Analysis

Given a choice of the Classical model, NHRP, and the connectionless model described above, what may we expect as an ATM migration strategy? We assume wide implementation of the ATMARP server. As vendors make NHRP servers available, it will also see wide use based on its capability to optimize routing. Later, as end-systems evolve, we should see early implementations of application-based SVC management. The MARS and MCS or multicast alternatives will play a part in all of these models. Also driving future evolution of NHRP and the MARS will be their use within MPOA (described later). With these various servers

(ATMARP, NHS, MARS, MCS), a general ATM configuration server has been proposed to coordinate their operation and allow easier configuration for end-systems. This will build upon the configuration servers developed for LANE and MPOA.

4.1.4 ATM Forum LAN emulation

Although the Classical model and its extensions suffice for many forms of data traffic across ATM, a large group of users are looking towards ATM to provide support for existing LAN environments. This solution is known as LAN Emulation (LANE), and the easiest way to look at this service is to draw an analogy to existing Ethernet, Token Ring, and FDDI networks, sometimes referred to as 'traditional' or 'legacy' LANs. Under LANE, we simulate, or emulate, a traditional LAN. In effect, one emulated LAN is equivalent to one segment of coaxial cable or UTP-5, and provides the necessary connectionless service and multicasting across the ATM network which will allow applications on end-systems to interact as if they were attached to traditional LAN segments. When connecting traditional LAN segments across an emulated LAN, we refer to the end-to-end Layer 2 domain as a **Virtual LAN**, or **VLAN**.

Background

Development on LANE began when users saw a need for data transport over ATM without relying on the Classical model, which requires routing at the ingress and egress of the ATM network. In addition, these users were hoping to solve a management problem not related to ATM but commonly associated with large campus or high-rise networks, a problem of workgroup dynamics. Consider the typical organization structured along functional lines (for example, engineering, finance, and manufacturing). The majority of user data will remain internal to each of these workgroups. When deploying a campus network, the network architect will seek to couple these data patterns with a traditional campus networking infrastructure consisting of LAN segments connected via routers. Each of these LAN segments is assigned a network number. In the case of IP, this is an IP subnet.

Using IP as an example, if users in a workgroup are co-located, they will therefore all share the same IP subnet number; if distributed among multiple LAN segments, a single workgroup will consist of multiple subnets. This simple model may hold only for a short while, however, since users are constantly shifting location (the moves-adds-changes problem), fragmenting the workgroup. Thus, routing often takes place within even smaller workgroups. Although this routing scales for Ethernet, Token Ring, and even FDDI backbone speeds, the introduction of gigabit backbones may result in routing requirements solvable but often unacceptable in terms of cost. Moves-adds-changes also present an additional management burden since every end-system moved from one routed LAN segment to another must be re-addressed. In a large organization, this function may require a substantial amount of effort even in the presence of protocols such as the Dynamic Host Configuration Protocol (DHCP).

LANE allows one to connect traditional LAN segments across an ATM backbone in such a way that the LAN segments appear to be bridged or hubbed together into a single segment. Within a single LANE domain, multiple VLANs will co-exist, supported by edge devices. Consider one such device with ten Ethernet ports and one ATM port. In this example, three Ethernets may be assigned to the Engineering net, three others to Finance, and the remainder to Manufacturing. Another device connected to the same physical ATM network may have only Engineering and Finance segments, and a third may support two segments on Engineering, two on Manufacturing, and six on Sales. Taken together, the Engineering LAN segments form one VLAN, the Finance segments another VLAN, and so on. As each VLAN is a Layer 2 bridged domain, a routing function or MAC-based filtering will be required to transfer a packet from one VLAN to another. We describe these options later. Parallel to ATM-based VLANs are proposed standards for shared media VLANs including those based on IEEE 802.1g. This VLAN technique and its place in enabling end-to-end multi-technology VLANs is described in a later chapter.

A quick review of LAN protocols

To aid in an understanding of the reasoning behind LANE and the functions which we must emulate across an ATM network, we first look at the operation of Ethernet. This widely-deployed LAN technology actually consists of two standards: 802.2 and 802.3. The 802.2 standard specifies the **Logical Link Control (LLC)**, accessed by higher-layer protocols via **Service Access Points (SAPs)**. Multiple data flows are multiplexed at this sublayer and identified by unique **Source-SAP (SSAP)** and **Destination-SAP (DSAP)** values. The sublayer below this LLC is the 802.3 standard associated with Ethernet in most references, and specifies a method of accessing the physical media based on **Carrier Sense Multiple Access/Collision Detection (CSMA/CD)** at 10 Mbps. Within a LAN-connected PC or workstation, higher-layer applications may ride above the network layer (for example, IP, IPX). This network layer accesses the MAC services via standardized MAC drivers, including the **Network Driver Interface Specification (NDIS)**, the **Open Data-Link Interface (ODLI)** or, in the UNIX environment, the **Data Link Provider Interface (DLPI)** as shown in Figure 4.13.

Token Ring, specified in 802.5, also uses 802.2 though it relies on a totally different method of physical media access. Both Ethernet and

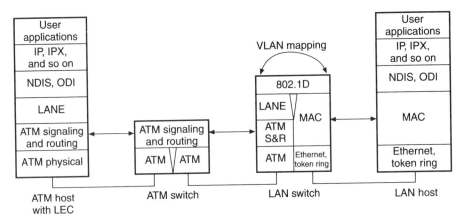

Figure 4.13 LAN emulation. Source: Cisco Systems.

Token Ring use 48-bit MAC addresses, normally globally unique physical interface addresses administered by the IEEE. If the address supplied with the interface hardware is not locally overwritten, it is considered to be a **Universally Administered Address (UAA)**; if overwritten due to local management considerations or requirements of Layer 3 protocols, it is a **Locally Administered Address (LAA)**. Both protocols (802.3 and 802.5) are inherently broadcast-capable and thus include support for multicast and broadcast address types. If all 48 bits of the MAC address are set to '1', it will be broadcast to all systems within the bridged domain. Multicast addresses, identified by a '1' in the highest-order bit, will also be sent to all destinations but only those end-systems within the multicast group will further process the frame. On a given LAN segment, both routable and non-routable protocols will co-exist. Routable protocols, including TCP/IP, IPX, and AppleTalk, use the network layer to interconnect Layer 2 domains, while non-routable protocols such as DEC LAT and NETBIOS will be bridged across multiple LAN segments. Support for these non-routable protocols was one of the goals in developing LANE.

Though most network designers deploy routers to interconnect LANs supporting routable protocols, some users still prefer to bridge between segments in a limited geographical area. By the same token, non-routable protocols must always be bridged. Bridging is a method of interconnecting LAN segments at Layer 2 (LLC/MAC). A bridge acts on the MAC address within a frame, comparing this address against a forwarding table to decide whether to forward it to a remote segment. A frame from a source to a destination not contained within the forwarding table will be sent on all the bridge's interfaces, a process known as **flooding**. Since a bridge operates at Layer 2, its functions are transparent to higher-layer protocols, leading to the term **transparent bridging**. As bridges may be interconnected to form multiple paths between

LAN segments, which would adversely affect the flooding algorithm, the protocol must include a method of preventing data loops. This method is known as the **spanning tree**. Under the spanning tree algorithm, if two bridges connect LAN segments, one will be placed in stand-by. Bridges exchange this control information with one another via bridge-PDUs.

A different form of bridging is that found within the IBM environment. **Source Route (SR)** bridges rely on the end-system to specify a route across the network. Each frame contains a header known as the **Routing Information Field (RIF)** identifying the route. These RIFs consist of segment identifier, bridge identifier pairs. A bridge receiving an SR frame will look at the RIF to determine whether its bridge identifier is present. If so, it will forward the frame on the appropriate port, equal to a physical segment. If not, it will discard the frame. An end-system will generate the RIF by transmitting a **single-route explorer** frame to the intended destination. This frame will be replicated by each bridge until the frame is received by the destination. Upon receipt, the destination will return an **all routes explorer** to the source. Bridges along the return path will add the segment and bridge pair to this frame and broadcast it on all other ports. As the source will eventually receive multiple frames each with one possible route, it will now select the frame with the optimal path. Based on the above description, it is obvious that any ATM-based emulated LAN will be required to support not only transparent bridging and the spanning tree algorithm but source route bridging as well (UIA, 1994).

Since the Classical model does not directly solve the mobility and management problem as described earlier (though it does have other advantages as described in a previous section), LANE was introduced as a way of aligning the ATM network with workgroup dynamics by providing Layer 2 connectivity across the ATM backbone. The first LANE proposals were submitted to the ATM Forum in February 1993 by IBM and, at the time, the proposal contained suggestions for FDDI, as well as higher-layer emulated LANs (TCP/IP, OSI, and APPN) in addition to the Ethernet and Token Ring eventually standardized (IBM, 1993a). At the end of 1994, the LANE specification based on separate Ethernet and Token Ring encapsulations across ATM was finalized, final approval took place in February, 1995, and compliant devices have been available since Fall 1995. Just as a historical note, during standardization, the working group evaluated an alternative, canonical format for encapsulating LANs as part of LANE. This was abandoned in favor of implementing separate encapsulations for each LAN type.

The LAN emulation service

The LANE service emulates a number of critical features which exist in traditional LANs, to include connectionless service, multicast services, and the support of MAC driver interfaces in ATM end-systems (ATM Forum 1995c). A benefit of ATM is that we may create multiple emulated LANs over the same physical network, as well as gaining in efficiency by only sending data to intended recipients. Finally, we must connect these emulated LANs to existing LANs.

A single ELAN is one of two types: Ethernet (802.3) or Token Ring (802.5), with FDDI and fast Ethernet supported via translational bridging at the edge of the ELAN. An ELAN consists of multiple **LAN Emulation Clients (LECs)** and a single **LAN Emulation Service (LE Service)**. Each LEC is an entity within an ATM end-system, acting on its own behalf and on the behalf of traditional LAN users identified by MAC addresses. This LEC is a software process running on any ATM-connected LAN switch, router, PC, or workstation. Since the LEC is a Layer 2 process, LAN switches are expected to comprise the bulk of LECs due to their lower cost per LAN port in comparison to routers. The LE Service may also be implemented within any ATM end-system (router, PC, or workstation) or within an ATM switch, though the scalability of the underlying hardware and software in this case will be a deciding factor. The Service includes a **LAN Emulation Configuration Server (LECS)**, a **LAN Emulation Server (LES)**, and a **Broadcast and Unknown Server (BUS)**. Once we emulate broadcast services via the LE Service, it becomes possible to forward such traffic only to certain end-systems by selectively establishing connections and filtering. Although the first version of the standard takes a simpler approach by forwarding this broadcast and mutlicast traffic to all stations, requiring the end-system to filter any undesired traffic as is the case with existing LANs, this will change with the introduction of LANE v2. Though traditional LAN users will connect to the LE Service via LANE-capable bridges, native ATM end-systems may also wish to connect to the service and utilize existing LAN applications. This is possible via the introduction of a MAC device driver (for example, NDIS or ODI) over the ATM interface driver as depicted in Figure 4.13. Thus, we have end-to-end transparency through the use of these MAC drivers.

The service supports the interconnection of existing LANs and ATM networks via existing bridging methods (traditional level 2 bridges, ATM-connected LAN switches, and LANE-capable routers). Thus, the LE Service fills an important gap in allowing existing LAN applications to run in an ATM environment. Though different types of emulation may be defined (for example, network via MPOA layer emulation), the standard defines a method based on the MAC layer. Finally, as opposed to creating a single emulation service capable of supporting any traditional LAN standard via translation, the Forum standard as defined specifies an emulation mechanism for only the two most common LAN types – Ethernet and Token Ring.

As shown in Figure 4.14, the interface between the LEC and the LE Service is known as the **LAN Emulation User to Network**

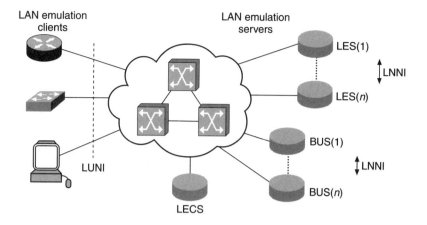

Figure 4.14 LAN emulation interfaces – LUNI and LNNI. Source: Cisco Systems.

Interface (LUNI). The LANE protocol operating over this interface includes facilities for initialization, registration, address resolution, and data transfer. The initialization phase includes obtaining the ATM address(es) of the LE Services and joining or leaving a given ELAN. Registration is the next step and consists of the LEC informing the LE Service of the non-ATM end-systems that the LEC represents via a list of MAC addresses and, if in a Token Ring environment, a list of source route descriptors that the LEC represents for source route bridging. An alternative to sending an explicit list of addresses is for the LEC to indicate its willingness to act as a proxy, in which case it will participate in the LE ARP protocol to resolve the addresses for non-LES-registered LAN-connected hosts. Next, a source LEC must obtain the ATM address of the distant client through which a given MAC address (singlecast, broadcast or segment/bridge pair) is reachable. Once this is accomplished, the LEC may signal an SVC to the destination (unless PVCs are used), encapsulate the data, and forward it on its way. Under the first release of LANE, each LEC is in contact with one LES and one BUS, with a single LECS providing configuration services for the multi-ELAN domain. Under the second revision of the service, a server-to-server interface known as the **LAN Emulation Network–Network Interface (LNNI)** allows inter-LES and inter-BUS communication. This will allow an LEC to contact multiple LECs and BUSs for redundancy or load sharing. We describe this LNNI in greater detail later.

LANE defines a number of connections between the LEC and the LECS, LES, BUS, and other LECs. Connections are also defined between the LES and the BUS. These connections may be permanent or transient, and fall into two domains: those for control, such as transmitting

LE ARP requests, and those for data. Note that a given VCC will carry traffic for only one ELAN. Thus, an end-system supporting multiple ELANs (and therefore multiple LECs) will use multiple VCCs when transmitting data to a distant system also supporting multiple ELANs even though a single VCC might be more efficient. The first type of control connection, known as a Configuration Direct VCC (Figure 4.15), is used to obtain the address of the LES. This particular connection may be torn down once configuration is complete. A Control Direct VCC is a bi-directional connection from the LEC to the LES to send and possibly receive control traffic. Finally, a Control Distribute VCC is an optional point-to-point or point-to-multipoint connection established between the LES and the LEC(s) for the purpose of distributing control traffic.

Data VCCs are established between LECs and between LECs and BUSs. The first type, a Data Direct VCC, is a point-to-point connection between LECs for the exchange of almost all unicast ELAN traffic. In most cases, the same VCC will be used for all traffic between two LECs within a single VLAN. This precludes the need to establish new connections for each MAC address pair. Note that this does not, however, eliminate the need for a separate VCC for each Layer 3 protocol in use since the VCCs are based on VC-muxing (see the discussion on RFC 1483, under *Multiprotocol encapsulation over ATM AAL5*, earlier in this chapter). An interesting feature of LANE concerns what actions should be taken if a given LEC cannot (due to resource restrictions or inability to resolve an address) establish a Data Direct VCC to a destination. In this event, the LEC will not continue to send data to the BUS, and must either attempt the connection at a later time or tear down an existing Data Direct VCC to another LEC. Multicast connections consist of a point-to-point Multicast Send VCC for sending multicast data to the BUS, as well as for sending the first few unicast frames to a destination until its address is resolved, and a point-to-point or point-to-multipoint

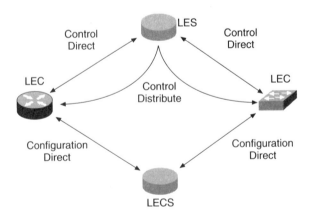

Figure 4.15 LAN emulation control connections – LECS and LES.

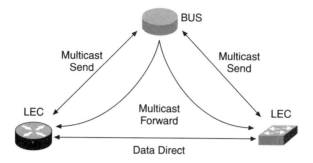

Figure 4.16: LAN emulation data connections – bus and direct.

Multicast Forward VCC used by the BUS to distribute data (Figure 4.16). Both of these connection types are unidirectional. Since LANE does not provide QoS guarantees, data direct connections will be UBR or possibly ABR.

Note that all of the above connections assume the use of SVCs even though the standard allows a PVC-based ELAN. Though possible in theory, PVCs are not feasible in reality. Consider a five-LEC ELAN. The following PVCs are required:

● Five PVCs between LECs and LECS

● One PVC between LES and LECS

● Five Control Direct PVCs between LECs and LES

● One point-to-multipoint Control Distribute PVCs from LES to LECs

● Five Multicast Send PVCs between LECs and BUS

● One point-to-multipoint Multicast Forward PVCs from BUS to LECs

● Ten Data Directs between all pairs of clients

This is clearly unmanageable without the assistance of some ELAN-oriented PVC tool. The problem is compounded with each additional LEC and if multiple ELANs share the ATM network. What may be possible, however, is the use of PVCs to connect the LECs with the LECS if required.

Procedures

As introduced above, the functioning of the LE Service includes distinct phases for initialization, registration, address resolution, and connection management. Initialization includes those actions which a LEC must perform to become a member of an ELAN. Before any initialization occurs, the LECs and the LES will have *a priori* knowledge of certain parameters. Some of these include the LEC's ATM address and LAN type to be emulated, the maximum data frame size (1516, 4544, 9234, or 18190 octets), and any route descriptors if the LEC also functions as an IEEE 802.5 source route bridge. The client will also indicate whether it is capable of and willing to perform proxy functions for LAN-connected end-stations. This function will allow the LEC to respond to LE-ARP requests for stations which it has not registered with the LES. Note that in responding to these LE-ARP requests, the LEC will set a flag indicating that the LAN-attached end-system is a 'remote address.' If proxy is not set, then the LEC will not attempt to resolve LE-ARP requests for non-registered stations. A last important parameter is the LAN name, formatted as an SNMPv2 display string with a maximum length of 32 octets.

The LEC now establishes a Configuration Direct VCC to the LECS to be used in determining the identity of the ELAN to join. The LEC will know the ATM address of this LECS via either the ILMI or may contact it via its well-known NSAP address (47.0079.0000.0000.0000.0000.0000.00A0.3E00.0001.00). If an SVC may not be established, the LECS should also be reachable via VPI = 0 and VCI = 17. Configuration parameters obtained from the LECS include the ATM address of the LES, the type of LAN emulated, and the maximum PDU size of the ELAN. In some cases, the configuration parameters described above may be pre-configured at the LEC, in which case contact between the LEC and the LECS will be unnecessary. The LEC is now ready to initiate an ELAN join, whereby it will establish the required control connection(s) to the LES. If this join is successful, the LEC will be assigned a unique LECID as well as receiving information as to the ELAN's maximum frame size and LAN type. Rejection may be caused by a LAN type or frame size incompatibility, or more importantly, by a security violation. Next, the LEC may register a number of MAC addresses and/or route descriptors with the LES if it has registered as a 'proxy' node. This is in addition to the LEC's MAC address registered as part of the join phase. In this case, it will also obtain LE ARPs as part of LANE operation. Finally, the LEC will establish a connection to the BUS whose address is learned via an LE ARP. The LEC may now transfer data to other clients within the VLAN or to a Layer 3 device for forwarding to other VLANs.

During the registration phase, the LEC will provide address information to the LES. This information consists of LAN-based destinations identified by either MAC addresses or Token Ring route descriptors, and may include all local LAN destinations or an indication that the LEC is acting as a proxy for unregistered end-systems. These registrations are not permanent, in that they may change over time as LAN stations are connected or disconnected. Consider a LAN switch with multiple Ethernet segments. If a new user connects to one of these segments and joins a VLAN which is active (that is, the LAN switch is established as an LEC), then the joining is simpler than a new user joining a VLAN on which the LAN switch is not an LEC. In this latter case, the LEC must carry out the actions described in the previous paragraph.

Next, when the LEC has data to send, it will attempt to associate a distant LAN destination with either the ATM address of another LEC or, in some cases, that of the BUS. This address resolution function is necessary if LECs are to signal for Data Direct VCCs. When an LEC receives a frame with an unknown destination (or one which it has not yet cached) it will attempt to resolve this address by sending an LE-ARP request over its control VCC to the LES. If the LES has prior knowledge of the destination address, it will issue an LE-ARP reply. If not, it may forward this request via either the Control Distribute VCC or one or more Control Direct VCCs. The LE-ARP reply from the proper LEC will be forwarded by the LES to the original requesting LEC. It may also help to forward the response to other LECs so that they can cache this information. Within the LEC, an ARP table containing all LE-ARP replies is maintained. This table is aged over time based on values listed in IEEE 802.1d, with a minimum of 10 seconds, and a default and maximum of 300 seconds.

Data forwarding, also known as connection management, consists of establishing connections between LECs, LESs, and BUSs via UNI signaling. For signaling, LANE uses AAL5 and a null SSCS. In contrast to some ATM implementations, a client will specify the maximum frame size (CPCS-SDU) as part of the setup message, a function of the Ethernet or Token Ring emulated LAN. As part of connection setup, a peak cell rate usually equal to the line rate will also be specified, the broadband bearer capability will normally be set to service type X (BCOB-X), and we specify Class 0 as the QoS parameter. Though the contents of the above fields are much the same as those defined for Classical IP and ARP over ATM, differences appear within the **Broadband Low Layer Information (B-LLI)** field which is used to convey signaling information regarding protocol type and purpose. Within the B-LLI, we set the SNAP field to that of the ATM Forum OUI (00 A0 3E), and the PID to one of five values:

- 0001 for an LE Configuration Direct VCC, Control Direct VCC, or Control Distribute VCC;

- 0002 for an Ethernet Data Direct VCC;

- 0003 for a Token Ring Data Direct VCC;

- 0004 for an Ethernet Multicast Send VCC or Multicast Forward VC;

- 0005 for a Token Ring Multicast Send VCC or Multicast Forward VCC.

The LEC uses this information in combination with the ATM address (including the SEL field) to identify the purpose and VLAN identity of each connection. Once the LEC has established the VCC, it will encapsulate incoming data with the LANE header for Ethernet or Token Ring. This header is just the traditional LAN header with the addition of a two-octet LECID.

Remember that an LEC will forward all frames to the BUS until the destination address has been resolved and a Data Direct VCC is established. During this time, the BUS floods these frames to all LECs. The justification for this is as follows. If the destination MAC address has not yet been registered with the LES, the BUS must forward the frame to all LE proxy clients. An 802.1D transparent bridge connected to the ELAN may not know the identity of all LAN-connected destinations. In this case, the frame must be forwarded to all bridge ports via the BUS and a direct VCC will not be established. Also, some protocols may be intolerant to the potential for data loss or excess latency while waiting for the direct VCC to be established. For this reason, an LEC must be capable of forwarding unicast traffic to the BUS. An LEC will always forward multicast traffic to the BUS. A question sometimes arises as to how an LEC, upon receipt of a data frame from the BUS, will be able to identify whether or not it has originated the frame and thus should ignore it. This is accomplished via the LECID field within the data frame, which the BUS must preserve. Thus, a given LEC may filter based upon this field. Another concern deals with proper frame ordering over an ELAN. This is due to the possible existence of multiple connections between a source and destination LEC, one via the BUS and another via a Data Direct VCC. During the transition from a BUS path to a data direct path, frames may arrive at a destination out of order. A flush protocol has been implemented to ensure the proper order of delivery. This protocol makes use of a control cell sent down the BUS transmission path following the last packet. Upon acknowledgment of this cell, the direct VCC may be used to send packets. If end-systems do not use this flush protocol, they may wait until address resolution completes before sending data. Figure 4.17 outlines the processes described in the above paragraphs.

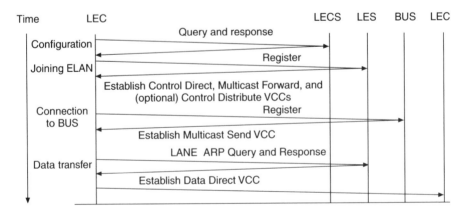

Figure 4.17 LAN emulation operation.

If LANs are interconnected via the LANE protocol and via external bridges, the IEEE spanning tree protocol becomes critical. In this case, LECs within LAN switches will exchange spanning tree bridge PDUs by multicasting these through the BUS. If a loop is detected, a port will be deactivated, and since the spanning tree protocol weighs ports by bandwidth, the ATM connection will be preserved. Faster spanning tree convergence in an LANE environment is made possible through the support of LE-Topology-Request messages. These are sent upon detection of any topology change, and result in a quicker ageing of cached ARP information. This results in the generation of up-to-date reachability information. A final message type, the LE-NARP, may be used by LECs to inform an LES that an address thought to be remote from a given LEC is now reachable locally.

An aspect of LANE which caused (and continues to cause) some debate is that of an intelligent BUS. This BUS, instead of flooding packets, would be able to resolve destinations (via contact with the LES or by participating in LE-ARP) and forward them across the Multicast Send VCC connection to LECs. The BUS in effect becomes a connectionless server (CLS), allowing the deployment of LECs with minimal intelligence and capability (for example, in PCs). Though the BUS may become a bottleneck, some have supported this approach. To preclude use of the BUS as a high-performance CLS, the LANE specification states that LECs are required to open Data Direct VCCs and that any traffic sent to the BUS is limited to 10 frames/second. Nevertheless, it will still be possible for vendors to deploy BUSs avoiding this limitation.

Data forwarding between VLANs

When looking at the actual operation of LANE, it is useful to look at the functions performed by the LAN switches and routers participating in LANE. Consider a user deploying multiple VLANs over a single ATM infrastructure. The operation of LANE consisting of multiple Layer 2 ATM-connected LAN switches (LECs) and a router as LES will be as follows. A given LAN switch, operating separate LECs for multiple emulated LANs (assuming multiple workgroups are connected), will treat these as totally different Layer 2 entities. Assume two ELANs, 'A' and 'C', each with an associated IP subnet. The router at the center of the LANE environment is a member of both ELANs, and is capable of routing between the two subnets.

If a server on subnet A (ELAN A) wishes to send data to a workstation on subnet C (ELAN C), then the server will first mask the destination IP address with its local IP address, at which time it will determine that it is on a remote subnet. This server will then forward the packet to the default router on ELAN A by first generating an ARP request for the default router's MAC address given its IP address. Upon receipt of this address, the source will send a packet to the LEC with the default router's MAC address. The LEC forwards this packet over the ATM interface to the default router located on the ATM network by mapping the router's MAC address to its NSAP address. Once the router receives this packet, it will perform normal IP layer processing to determine the output port by which ELAN C is reachable. Note that a router supporting subinterfaces on a single ATM physical interface will in fact forward this packet over the same physical interface. After the router initiates an IP layer ARP for the MAC address of station C on ELAN C, and receives a response, it will forward the packet to the destination's LEC via LANE. It relies on the LANE protocol to resolve the MAC address of C against its NSAP address.

A brief word on NSAP addressing, covered in greater detail as part of the LANE examples within Chapter 5, follows. As currently defined, LANE uses NSAP addresses with either the DCC or ICD formats. Within LANE, the SEL field is also considered part of the address, and is used by some systems as a way to identify subinterfaces as part of a physical interface. An LEC will always have an ATM address, which it may share with no other systems. The same applies to the LECS, though multiple LECSs may share this address if it is 'well known.' LESs and BUSs must have at least one ATM address, may have more than one, and may share this address.

Source route bridging concerns

Source routing, used in Token Ring (802.5) environments, presents some complications when supported over LANE. Since an end-station may use a combination of both source-routed and non-source-routed frames, an LEC must support source routing and transparent bridging. A source-routed frame will contain a **Routing Information (RI)** field in addition to destination (DA) and source addresses (SA). This RI field contains a list of **Route Descriptors (RDs)** indicating the path the frame should traverse through the network. In essence, it is an ordered list of which SR bridges will be crossed, and will be used by the LEC to determine whether a frame should be forwarded to an SR bridge or to a station directly connected to the ELAN. If the frame should be sent to an SR bridge, the destination will be the next route descriptor. If not, it will be sent to the destination address. In either case, the frames will be sent over a Data Direct VCC established upon completion of the LE ARP process. Note that an LEC supporting Token Ring must support the address resolution of RDs in addition to MAC addresses. Frames are either **Non-Source Routed (NSR)**, **All Routes Explorer (ARE)**, **Spanning Tree Explorer (STE)**, or **Specifically-Routed Frame (SRF)**. Each of these frame types must be supported in a specific way.

An LEC will send an NSR frame, an SRF frame with an RI less than six, or an SRF with a last hop on the local ELAN on the Data Direct VCC for the frame's DA. In all three cases, if the VCC is unknown, then the LEC generates an LE_ARP request for the DA and the frame may be sent to the BUS. Multicast, ARE, and STE frames are sent to the BUS. The LE client, if not part of a bridge, will assume that, if the RI field of an SRF frame has a length of six or more, then the local SEGMENT ID is the first RD in the list and the 'next RD' is the SEGMENT ID of the second RD in the list (order depending on the RI direction bit) and the bridge number located between those two SEGMENT IDs. The last hop is therefore not on the local ELAN. In this case, the LEC will send the frame on a direct VCC to the next_RD. As above, if this destination is unknown then the LEC will generate an LE_ARP request and may send the frame to the BUS. Finally, if the RI field is invalid, has an odd length, or an SRF frame has an RI field which does not contain an RD which matches the ELAN's SEG_ID, the frame may be discarded by the LEC. These actions are summarized in Table 4.7.

The LANE standard also supports multiple maximum data frame sizes based on an MTU negotiated as part of the Data Direct VCC establishment. Though this MTU may be different to that found on the traditional LAN segments of a given VLAN, within the ELAN, all LECs must use the same AAL5 SDU size for connections to the BUS and for connections to each other. This SDU size is based on the number of octets in a traditional LAN, and must be set to one of four values as listed in Table 4.8.

An interesting situation arises as to the support of frame sizes larger than 1516 octets over an Ethernet ELAN. For example, an ELAN supporting only native ATM hosts or connecting FDDI networks may use a larger MTU than that corresponding to the traditional Ethernet MTU. As traditional Ethernet LANs are limited to this value, a problem may arise with the type/length fields within the various Ethernet frame formats. This is solved by setting the type/length field to X'0000' on IEEE 802.3 packets greater than 1536 octets, in which case the actual length

Table 4.7 Token Ring destinations for LAN emulation. Source: ATM Forum, 1995c.

LAN destination of Token Ring frames		
Frame type	Unicast	Multicast
Non-source-routed (NSR)	VCC (DA)	BUS
Explorer (ARE or STE)	BUS	BUS
Specifically-routed (SRF)	See below	BUS
LAN destination for unicast SRF Token Ring frames		
Routing information	Destination	
No hops	VCC (DA)	
Last hop	VCC (DA)	
Not last hop	VCC (next_RD)	

Table 4.8 LANE maximum data frame sizes. Source: ATM Forum, 1995c.

AAL5 SDU maximum octets	AAL5 PDU maximum octets	Basis for SDU
1516	1536 (32 cells)	IEEE 802.3/Ethernet – 1500-octet information field
4544	4560 (95 cells)	IEEE 802.5 Token Ring 4 Mbps – 9.1 msec THT
9234	9264 (193 cells)	RFC 1626
18190	18240 (380 cells)	IEEE 802.5 Token Ring 16 Mbps – 9.1 msec THT

is indicated by the AAL5 SDU length field. For Ethernet packets exceeding this length, the type/length field will be used to indicate the protocol type.

VLAN mappings and mobility

Once we understand the mechanisms by which LANE operates, we can look into the ways of mapping one or more workgroups into VLANs across the ATM network. Some additional terminology which may be useful includes the type of port one will find on a LAN switch. These include **static** and **dynamic ports**, capable of supporting only a single VLAN, **trunk ports**, where traffic from more than one VLAN is explicitly tagged (that is, LANE), and **multi-VLAN** ports. This last port type supports more than one VLAN but is not a trunk, relying on filtering to identify traffic belonging to different workgroups.

The simplest VLAN example, keeping to the LANE standard, connects two workgroups via LAN switches acting as LECs. In Figure 4.18,

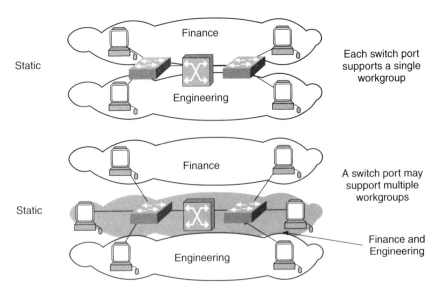

Figure 4.18 Static VLAN mappings.

Finance and Engineering each map to physical ports on the LAN switches. A more sophisticated form of mapping allows a single switch port to support multiple workgroups. This multi-VLAN mapping is useful where a single server must be shared by two or more workgroups, Finance and Engineering, for example. A tradeoff in placing a single device on two or more workgroups, however, is the additional background load to which this device will be subjected. In addition, some protocols such as DECnet will not operate in this environment since all interfaces of a DECnet host may have the same MAC address. Note that in both of these environments, routing does not yet come into play, as we have not spoken of inter-VLAN connectivity.

A second example provides for what is known as port mobility. Consider the same two workgroups, Finance and Engineering, as in the example above. Now, LAN switch ports may dynamically take on the identity of either of these workgroups (Figure 4.19). A user moving from one location on a campus, for example, may attach to an unassigned port at a new location. Depending upon the level of security required, this port will automatically take on the identity of the user's workgroup based on a MAC or network layer address. Alternatively, the port may be configured to only accept connections by certain MAC addresses or into certain workgroups. The most sophisticated form of control will rely on one or more configuration servers which will authorize connection to a given port. Towards the end of this book, we look at how such a server may be used not only within LANE but across all VLAN types. This mobility is one of the goals in deploying LANE, although the previous example provides for greater security unless the above access control systems are deployed.

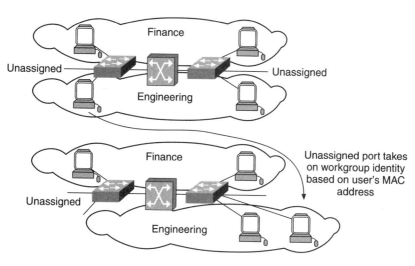

Figure 4.19 MAC mobility.

Next, we assign VLANs based on network layer addresses in addition to the MAC layer. In Figure 4.20, users within Finance and Engineering are each assigned to VLANs. Within each of these workgroups, some use IP as a network layer protocol, while others use IPX. The VLAN management system allows the IP or IPX file servers to be shared by users from both VLANs. Alternatively, the management system may automatically assign users to a given VLAN based on their Layer 3 protocol and network layer address, in which case the file servers will be assigned to separate workgroups. A user in this scenario may actually be a member of multiple VLANs as well. Note that this automatic VLAN assignment, sometimes known as 'subnet-centric,' works only for routable protocols. Port and MAC-based VLANs are still required for non-routable protocols.

A totally different type of VLAN assignment is based on filter offsets within the data frame. Consider a LAN switch capable of filtering on source or destination addresses, the LLC field, or even a pattern within the network layer header. In theory, this has a great deal of appeal but can quickly become unmanageable if implementing multiple filters. The problem of connectivity between VLANs is still not solved with filters, since Layer 3 filtering can only establish which groups of users are able to communicate with each other. The actual communication must take place via routers unless each and every end-system is capable of acting as a default router.

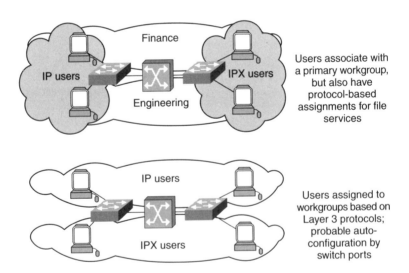

Figure 4.20 Complex VLAN mappings.

Management

A common concern with LANE is its security provisions. These concerns are closely related to network management, where mobility within a VLAN and connectivity between VLANs are defined. For example, within a VLAN, three levels of user mobility may be defined. The first will associate a given user with a given emulated LAN at any point within the network. Each physical LAN port on every LEC will automatically associate itself with the user's VLAN. This allows for the greatest leeway in moves-adds-changes, but may also open the network to possible security violations if the LECs cannot be physically secured. A second level of security is possible if the LAN ports on the LECs are preassigned to given VLANs. This provides for a higher level of physical security, but still allows mobility. The highest level of VLAN security is provided if the VLAN is preconfigured with MAC address to physical port relationships. In this case, any physical moves must be registered via network management. Note that this option eliminates many of the mobility advantages of LANE, but still allows users to take advantage of the overall functionality of LANE.

A separate aspect of LANE management concerns the administration of the VLANs, including visibility by the management system to all layers of an emulated LAN environment: Layers 1, 2, and 3. No longer is it adequate to provide only Layer 3 views of routers and interfaces, or Layer 1 views of hubs. An effective VLAN management system must provide for effective control of the security relationships described above. This management environment becomes more complex when multiple VLANs co-exist over a single ATM infrastructure. Management will then take the form of MAC-layer configuration and filtering within a workgroup (if required, noting that the definition of a workgroup usually infers unlimited connectivity) and also network-layer configuration and filtering between workgroups. This network-layer filtering must be created for each Layer 3 protocol in use.

An additional feature of VLAN management is the ability to conduct on-line analysis of traffic flows. This may be accomplished in a number of ways. The first involves physically attaching to a port on an ATM switch, LAN switch, or router for data capture. Devices which are capable of redirecting traffic from any port to a monitoring port facilitate this. A second method is to attach to an existing VCC. Though this may be difficult for a point-to-point VCC unless provisions are included within the ATM switch to allow this, it should be quite simple for point-to-multipoint VCCs. The point-to-point problem may be solved if the VCC is re-established as a point-to-multipoint circuit when monitoring is desired. Other aspects of network management were addressed in a more global perspective in the previous chapter.

Scaling LAN emulation: applicability of multilayer switching to Classical ATM and LANE

Though LANE addresses bridging over ATM, and with this the support of VLANs, it does not extend the concept to provide for more than a single VLAN over the same ATM infrastructure. The first generation of edge devices, primarily LAN switches, will operate at Layer 2 only. They are effectively fast bridges, and a single-bridged VLAN domain will eventually suffer the same problems limiting traditional bridged networks. Large organizations must deploy multiple VLANs, connected via a router or equivalent internetworking device, due to an upper bound on the number of systems which may share a single VLAN.

In the VLAN configurations described above, the ultimate size of a single Layer 2 domain will depend upon the protocol(s) in use and the ability of end-systems to handle the background broadcast and multicast traffic. Remember that a given end-system must at a minimum process all multicast traffic addressed to the multicast address of the vendor code for its NIC. As the number of end-systems grow, the percentage of the network bandwidth on the LAN segments occupied by this background traffic increases. Even with ATM in the background, we are still limited to 10 or 16 Mbps on LAN segments. A rule of thumb is that a Layer 2 IP domain should be limited to 1000 stations, IPX to 500, and AppleTalk to 200. In a mixed environment, the VLAN should contain no more than 500 stations. These values may be increased a bit if broadcast and multicast throttling is invoked at the LAN switches. Looking back at the VLAN mapping options, port-based VLANs may not encounter this limitation. However, consider MAC-based VLANs where a single end-station may be assigned to multiple VLANs. The user will receive broadcast and multicast traffic for each VLAN, and if the end-station is connected to three or more VLANs, it may encounter overload. Thus, a more logical architecture would be to limit each end-system to a single VLAN while placing central servers on two or more VLANs. This is easily accomplished, and will be described in Chapter 5.

Where routers are used to interconnect VLANs, an often-voiced concern is scalability. Even assuming 'well-behaved' workgroups, a certain percentage of the traffic will cross workgroup boundaries. Therefore, routers do not just disappear in a large VLAN deployment. Though more traffic now remains within single Layer 2 domains in comparison to a classical architecture, most VLANs will not be well behaved, with large servers connected to multiple VLANs solving just part of the problem. As much of the traffic is client–client, and since users cannot have membership in every VLAN, routers still play a critical role in this environment. The number of routers in comparison to the Classical model will depend on the inter-workgroup flows and the total bandwidth requirement of the network. In fact, as many users transfer to this architecture, the total routing capacity required may actually increase due to the increased bandwidth in use, resulting in a higher packets-per-second requirement. As is obvious, designs which suddenly eliminate all routers but one will not scale or even properly function in a production environment.

We usually assume that all workgroups will initially be connected via a single router. In fact, there is nothing precluding the deployment of multiple routers, each responsible for a subset of the VLANs. The routers will then be interconnected via VCCs, either through subinterfaces on the main ATM interface or via second ATM interfaces used only for inter-router and, therefore, inter-VLAN traffic. This first generation architecture, with Layer 2 VLAN edge devices forwarding all inter-VLAN traffic to a central router(s) for forwarding is not infinitely scalable, due to the potential for bottlenecks and the additional assembly and resegmentation required. A LAN switch which includes this Layer 3 functionality, sometimes called a multilayer switch, is one method of scaling LANE. In effect, the LAN switch becomes a workgroup router, as it performs both route table calculation and Layer 3 forwarding. It is therefore not bound to a single data model, and will function both within LANE and Classical domains. In Section 4.1.5, we revisit this multilayer switch and the role it plays within the MPOA environment. In Chapter 5, we provide guidelines as to the placement of routers and the amount of routing required within a switched internetwork.

Analysis

Is LANE for every environment, or will the Classical model suffice? Some users are quick to point out that the Classical model is more in keeping with existing networking paradigms, but that LANE has some definite advantages in providing for mobility. Other users will implement a mixed network, with LANE in the local environment and the Classical model or MPOA in the wide area. As with any new networking architecture, LANE presents some questions to which only partial answers are available. A given hardware platform may provide LES functionality for multiple VLANs, while at the same time allowing Layer 3 connectivity between these VLANs. At the same time, this platform may also act as the VLANs' BUS. The number of VLANs supported will be a factor of VLAN LECs, the ATM switching matrix interface speed, and the capability of the actual hardware. Some implementation guidelines are included in Chapter 5. Another question concerns how many LECs should share a VLAN, and at what point it may be wiser to split a workgroup. As described above, a VLAN may support many more users than a standard bridged LAN due to the fact that most traffic will be point-to-point as opposed to broadcast. Still, there will be an underlying broadcast and multicast traffic flow which is unavoidable. The acceptable volume of this traffic on the lowest bandwidth connection will determine the number of LECs which the VLAN may support. However, long before this limit is reached, the VLAN will probably be split due to security and management considerations.

A definite advantage of LANE is its ability to break through the distance limitation of conventional LANs. In fact, as described later, some service providers may implement LANE as a public service. In contrast to its advantage, possible problems with LANE result from its very purpose in hiding the ATM network from the end-station. Because of this, a given user will not have visibility into ATM's QoS capabilities, all traffic is either UBR or ABR. This is one disadvantage not seen under the Classical model. Of course, if a user is content with the service levels of LANE and does not want to be concerned with some of the complexities of ATM configuration, then LANE is a very viable solution. More technical issues surround the MTU transported by LANE in comparison to the MTU defined within the Classical model. The frame size on VLAN will equal the frame size of the source LAN. When emulating an Ethernet, for example, this will be 1516 bytes. An ATM network is capable of supporting a much larger MTU without difficulty. Another concern involving the LAN frame relates to the basic function of LANE, where a bridged environment over ATM is created at the expense of segmenting and reassembling a LAN frame. Though this may not result in noticeable delays, the process does result in an encapsulation overhead and must be compared to transparent bridging over ATM or even LANE over media which preserve the original frame MTU (FDDI or Fast Ethernet, for example).

LANE is proposed as a solution to the problem of providing for the support of existing applications over ATM. In addition, it is also positioned as the method of choice to respond to constant change within a corporation (accounting for 10% of operating expenses). Nevertheless, some real concerns are voiced as to its true scalability and manageability. Some of these failings of early VLAN releases were addressed by vendors during the first half of 1996 through the introduction of optimized and standardized ATM edge systems along with usable graphical tools for virtual workgroup management. Still, some concerns raised in a 1994 commentary (Lippis, 1994) should be noted as they are still relevant. In addition, the compatibility of LANE and another commonly deployed protocol in the IP environment, the **Dynamic Host Configuration Protocol (DHCP)**, is questionable.

Management of VLANs is a major issue since network managers must currently manage different types of networking device from multiple vendors. Benefits of LANE must more than outweigh the drawbacks of introducing yet another management system. This is only possible if graphical tools are provided, as opposed to requiring manual configuration of each VLAN at the MAC address layer. These tools must also be capable of mapping the logical (VLAN) network in addition to the traditional physical network. An additional aspect of network management relates to troubleshooting, in that the broadcast domain is now segmented across VLANs. Network managers must therefore implement a new strategy for the use of protocol analysis devices.

How will VLANs support multiple networking technologies? At present, LANE defines a method for emulating an Ethernet or Token Ring VLAN. Interworking between these two technologies and with FDDI or fast Ethernet must occur at the boundary of the LANE domain, either within a router or LAN switch. Depending upon the requirement, this interworking may occur at Layer 2 or Layer 3. Consider a user wishing to establish Layer 2 connectivity among users on both Ethernet and Token Ring. Under LANE, these users may not share a single VLAN, but nothing prevents translational bridging between these two technologies. This same translational bridging will support interworking between either of these technologies and other link layer media. This last case, with a single VLAN spanning both shared media and ATM, assumes the existence of a management application where the network manager may configure a single VLAN across multiple technologies. This in fact is now possible, where the user has the ability to create VLANs spanning both ATM via LANE, FDDI via 802.10, or Fast Ethernet via 802.1g (described towards the end of this book). In the case of FDDI, existing networks or hosts may be interconnected via LANE without the need for fragmentation since the standard supports large MTUs. When converting from FDDI to an Ethernet ELAN, the LECs implement translational bridging IAW IEEE 802.1h and IEE 802.1i, while Token Ring ELANs are supported by 802.1x. Therefore, we do not require a separate FDDI ELAN type (ATM Forum, 1995). When connecting devices to this ELAN which use different MTUs, an LEC may convert between the two sizes if hosts are incapable of MTU negotiation.

The suitability of LANE v1 for multicast applications may also create a problem. Consider multicasting under the Classical model, where end-systems may initiate point-to-multipoint SVCs in support of multicast meshes. Within LANE, LECs have no capability to signal these connections, and must send all multicast traffic to the BUS. This use of the BUS as a multicast server is in fact one of the alternatives for multicasting across ATM in general, but at present no MARS is included within the LANE architecture. Thus, multicast traffic, though intended to be limited in scope, must be flooded to all LECs within a VLAN. This has obvious implications for scalability even if the BUS is optimized for multicasting or if this function is distributed. A solution will be to allow the LEC, presented with a multicast destination, to resolve a multicast address via an extension of the LES. It could then signal a pt-mpt SVC. Alternatively, the BUS could signal a pt-mpt VCC to only those active members of a given multicast group. As part of the discussion of the next iteration of LANE (v2), we describe ways in which procedures may be modified to effectively support multicasting.

Parallel to the theorizing and debating (heated at times) regarding the suitability of LANE for various application environments as well as its overall manageability is the question of just where to place each LANE element. This includes the LECS, LES, BUS, and which end-systems are most suitable for use as LECs. It may sometimes seem as if each and every vendor has a different opinion regarding this issue depending upon their area of expertise. Discussion focuses on the LES and BUS, and whether to place these server functions on an ATM switch, a router, or a workstation. Most early implementations focused upon a given vendor's forte: router vendors implemented on a router, while workstation vendors implemented on the latter platform. In 1996, as vendors seek to optimize their implementations, they have taken a step back in identifying the optimal location within an ATM network for each of these functions. First consider the LECS, accessed by all subsystems within LANE but not playing an active part in data forwarding. Given proper management and reliability, vendors may deploy this on almost any physical device. Preferred solutions include workstations and routers. At the opposite end of the spectrum, the LEC is the client system, suitable for deployment on LAN switches, routers, PCs, workstations, and almost every other type of ATM-connected device. The choice of hardware architecture will depend upon application, connectivity required, performance, and budget. This is not an area for debate, leaving the LES and BUS.

The LES is used for registration and address resolution, but is not in the data forwarding path. Thus it too may be deployed on any platform given manageability and reliability (solved in this case via the LNNI). The LES will function adequately whether it is a process in a router, a module within an ATM switch, or a program in a workstation. Note that the LES function is decoupled from another critical function in scaling LANE, the routing between VLANs. The last subsystem is the BUS, used for forwarding of data before creation of a pt-pt VCC between LECs or for forwarding of data where the destination is unknown or is a broadcast or multicast address. Thus, the BUS plays an active part in the data forwarding path, warranting its optimization. BUSs at central points within a network only scale so far, as data must often follow non-optimal paths once replicated. Including the BUS function in one ATM switch only solves a small part of the problem, as the data must still pass from the switch matrix to a co-located BUS. Savings here are due to the elimination of an external device and its physical link. Ultimately, the BUS may be located in each ATM switch if possible, allowing attached LECs to pass broadcast and multicast data over a single link, at which point it will be replicated. This is akin to co-locating a BUS with each LEC, also a possibility. In either case, data forwarding and link utilization across the ATM network is now optimized.

Although we have concentrated on the deployment of LANE within local ATM networks, interest has been shown by the service providers in offering such a service over a metropolitan area or greater. This of course introduces security requirements beyond those faced by individual corporations implementing LANE. It may be useful at this point to review the fact that an individual user (single management and security domain) implementing LANE over an ATMWAN will still have control over all LESs, LECs, and routers providing interworking between VLANs. The ATM in this case will only provide an SVC-based transport for the user's extended workgroup. This of course is not the case when LANE is offered as a public service. A service provider must maintain multiple VLANs for each user. For example, consider a metropolitan area with four users connected to a VLAN service. Assuming each user defines three workgroups (a very low number), each associated with a single VLAN, the provider must maintain 12 instances of the LES. In addition, the provider must not only ensure that security is maintained between VLANs, but between users as well. To simplify matters, note that the maintenance of security between users will occur at the network layer (Layer 3) and is therefore no different to that provided by LAN interconnect services.

The question is then whether LESs from multiple users should be implemented on one platform – cost savings at the expense of management complexity – or multiple platforms offering the reverse. Note that this problem is more or less equivalent to that raised in offering client–server services over a public network. Should two or more users share the same physical data server? A consideration in offering this service concerns the VLAN identifier. Within a single platform, VLAN identifiers should be unique unless this platform is reachable over unique ATM addresses. If unique, the service provider may wish to implement a standard naming mechanism, possibly based on a substring of the user's DNS entry or a substring of the NSAP concatenated with a workgroup identifier. In any case, the support of multiple LANE users on a single hardware platform should be feasible.

The LNNI and LANE Version 2

Although Version 1 of the LANE specification is a good starting point for implementation, it does not allow true scalability due to a lack of redundant servers within a VLAN. In addition, since the ATM network is in effect invisible to the end-systems, they have no method for requesting QoS (or ABR service class, for example) from the ATM backbone. Next, traditional Layer 3 multicasting (for example, PIM or DVMRP) maps very poorly to the LANE mechanisms. Finally, at times LANE may make less than optimal use of connections across an ATM network due to its use of VC multiplexing. Thus the need for a second iteration of the protocol, detailed by Keene (1995) for the LUNI. At the end of 1995, LANE was chosen by the ATM Forum MPOA SWG as the default Layer 2 forwarding mechanism. As part of this integration, the MPOA group stated that the features outlined above must be included in the next LANE specification.

The first requirement, redundancy, is met by the creation of a server-to-server interface, the **LAN Emulation Network–Network Interface (LNNI)** (ATM Forum 1996c). Remember that a VLAN requires the LECS for configuration, the LES for registration and address resolution, and the BUS for default forwarding. If any of these two latter servers failed, no changes to the VLAN would be possible (though existing SVCs or PVCs would continue to operate). The failure of the LECS is less critical since most of its functionality may be provided by manual configuration of the LES, BUS, and LEC. This LNNI defines an inter-server protocol over which they can exchange management information. The synchronization model to be used for the LNNI is known as the 'peer tree', where nodes, consisting of LES-BUS pairs, form a tree but may also peer with each other. These nodes are either single entities or 'complex', consisting of fully meshed servers. If a forwarding path along the tree fails, a peer link, normally non-forwarding, will take over. This results in a very robust architecture.

By Spring 1996, it had become apparent that two separate server synchronization protocols, one for the LANE LNNI and the other for IETF servers, would add a degree of undesirable complexity in networks already running a Layer 3 routing protocol, the PNNI ATMARP, and so on. Proposals (Smith, 1996) were therefore put forward to combine the two mechanisms, whereby the LNNI would use the server synchronization protocol developed for the IEFT (Luciani 96), while the latter group would reference LNNI mechanisms for building and maintaining the server topology. This joining of efforts would reduce both complexity and time-to-market.

Looking back to multicasting within the Classical model, efficient use of ATM resources requires us to know which end-systems or routers wish to participate in a given multicast session, and thus which should receive the data. This is the basis for the MARS or equivalent mechanisms. Under LANE v1, LECs forward all multicast traffic to the BUS for default forwarding to all LECs within a VLAN. This is hardly an efficient use of resources unless we know ahead of time that we have a group member on every LAN switch or router. Now that MPOA will use LANE to provide intra-IASG multicasting, we must ensure that this capability exists. Depending upon how many changes are to be made to LEC and LES behavior, two mechanisms are available as a solution to this problem. Under the first, we provide each LEC with the capability of opening a pt-mpt VCC across the VLAN. It would use a LANE analogy of the MARS to identify the leaves of this multipoint connection and to monitor changes. The disadvantage of this scheme is complexity. Allowing LECs to open pt-mpt VCCs and including the necessary control between the LEC and the LANE-MARS will require changes and/or extensions to both the LANE data and control connections.

The second method is analogous to the MCS, also described within classical multicasting. LECs would now forward all multicast traffic to this server, which would also use a lookup mechanism as above to resolve addresses. Unlike the VC mesh, under this architecture only the MCS would be required to resolve group membership and establish multipoint connections; LECs would send all multicast data over a pt-pt connection to this server. This MCS could (and most probably would) be co-located with the BUS, either in standalone systems or ATM switches, but would be intended for production data multicasting (whereas the BUS is only intended for forwarding of broadcasts and packets until the destination is resolved) (Arora and Civanlan, 1995). Co-locating this server (or BUS(s) for that matter) with ATM switches may result in better for-warding paths as traffic must pass only once across a given link. Note that under this scheme we create additional complexity through the introduction of the MCS as well as at the LES itself (which must man-age the MCS). Still, since we have fewer LESs within LANE and we expect them to be more tightly managed, this may not present a problem. The only requirement, then, is the availability of high-performance multi-cast servers.

QoS support may be the most difficult feature to include within LANE due to one of its original intentions of shielding end-systems. Under LANE, if SVCs are to be created with a certain QoS, either the LEC must be pre-configured with this information based on destination addresses (or more complex multilayer filters), for example, or the end-systems must support some form of resource reservation mechanism (for instance, RSVP) which would allow them to convey their requirements to the LEC.

The last area of concern deals with some of the more protocol-oriented issues, specifically the type of VCC encapsulation to use and when. Consider a LAN switch or router serving multiple VLANs. Under LANE v1, for LEC, it must open separate data and control VCCs to the servers and to any destination LECs. If large numbers of VLANs are in use, this may present scalability problems. Finn (1995) introduces a solu-tion to this problem based on LLC/SNAP encapsulation with the addition of a global ELAN ID field, with the proposed LANE v2 packet format as follows:

[LLC][ATMF OUI][2-octet packet identifier for control or data frames][6-octet identifier for administration domain][2-octet ELAN selector within domain][remainder is identical to LANE v1 packet]

Note that this could change as the IEEE 802.1 committee defines a method of identifying VLANs via tagging. This VCC conservation comes, however, at significant changes to the LANE protocol and addi-tional per-frame computation costs on the edge device due to this new header. For security, LECs may filter on the identifier field to avoid spoofing attacks. In addition, we could implement a mechanism at the LES whereby a LEC could determine which VLANs may share a common VCC. When accepting new connections, this 'paranoid' client could hold all incoming data until it verifies proper VLAN membership across its control connections (the same procedure as with LANE v1). Looking at compatibility with LANE v1, a LEC may identify (via B-LLI values) which VCCs belong to distant v1 and v2 clients. This does require some support at the LECS, LES, and BUS however, for supporting dual-mode LECs and relaying requests.

An often asked question concerns the real need for multiple VLANs per LAN switch port, a subject of much debate within the industry. One reason given is the need to share common resources such as servers between VLANs. This infers a single non-ATM interface on the server assigned to two or more VLANs as opposed to solving the problem via routed connectivity, direct ATM connection, or multiple physical interfaces. This also infers a lack of port-based firewalling as provided by routers. A direct ATM connection may in fact be the best solution as opposed to placing the servers on 10 Mbps Ethernet. For 100 Mbps Ethernet, 802.1g (described towards the end of the book) is a possibility. The solution is not so clear if downstream shared hubs are connected to the LAN switch ports. In this case, users may request per-MAC address VLAN assignment. Disadvantages of this implementation are the requirement to manage VLAN membership on a MAC address basis, resulting in complex filters and administration, and the lack of any control over the propagation of broadcast packets. For example, how does one map a destination to a given VLAN if the destination is the broadcast address? This is not as great a problem with source-based filtering. Therefore, filtering and broadcast packets have an obvious effect on network scalability. Also, remember that filtering requires examination of every packet, a consideration with hardware design. An extension of this Layer 2 filtering model is port-based Layer 3 VLANs. The problem with this approach is not as much the concept as the implementation: the complexity of developing Layer 3 code. The viability of these architectures for multiprotocol data is in question.

Another interesting problem, possibly resulting from end-systems on multiple VLANs, is known as **transitivity**. Consider a system on 'A' able to communicate with one on 'B' and a system on 'B' communicating with a third user on 'C'. Under this scenario, 'A' assumes that it is able to communicate with 'C'. With complex VLAN mappings, this may not be the case. Negative effects on one protocol, AppleTalk, are obvious. Since AppleTalk clients choose their names dynamically, they rely on a 'name defense' mechanism whereby a new client issues a broadcast packet announcing the choice of a name. Any existing client may then respond if the name is in use. However, if two clients are capable of hearing the broadcast frames sent by the server but are incapable of communicating with each other, they may choose duplicate names. In the case of multiple IP routers on a subnet, if a given host is using the first router but this router determines that the second is better, it will send an ICMP redirect informing the host to use the second router. The first router assumes that the host can reach this second router.

VLAN Architectures

Concepts introduced in the paragraphs above, including multilayer switching and VLAN management, form the basis for the virtual workgroup architectures proposed by a number of router, hub, and even wide-area ATM switch vendors. These VLAN systems, sometimes marketed under quite esoteric names, usually include ATM switching, LAN switching, integrated management, and some method of inter-VLAN connectivity based either on routing or multilayer filtering. Their complexity and lofty goals has caused some in the industry to label them 'Marketectures' (Saunders, 1995), just as announced but undelivered software is known as 'Vaporware.' Essential to all offerings is a management system allowing the network administrator to configure groups of users into a VLAN and then control connectivity between different VLANs. If router based, inter-VLAN traffic will pass from Layer 2 LAN switches or hubs to one or more central routers. An extension of this architecture allows this router to redistribute routing tables to the LAN switches at the periphery of the ATM cloud. These switches then act as multilayer switches, forwarding inter-VLAN traffic locally. These methods of scaling LANE are summarized in Table 4.9.

Note the use of the term 'multilayer switch' in both distributed routing and route distribution in Table 4.9. A common misconception is that route distribution allows the multilayer requirement to be dispensed with. This is the opposite of the truth, as these edge devices, making use of the downloaded routing information, will still be required to carry out Layer 3 forwarding. Variations on these options include deployment of a connection management system which controls the setup of VCCs between end-systems. Other architectures dispense with routing

Table 4.9 Scaling LAN emulation – options.

Option	Advantages	Disadvantages	Availability
Central router(s) to connect VLANs	Simple to deploy Current technology	Inter-VLAN connections limited to interface speed of routers, although routing hierarchy possible Latency	Mid-1995
Multilayer LAN switches incorporate full Layer 3 capability in hardware or software	Totally distributes routing Inter-VLAN connections scale	Cost of deployment versus performance – LAN switches become routers	1H96
Route distribution from central route servers to multilayer LAN switches	RobustCost of deployment – LAN switch costs do not increase Inter-VLAN connections scale	New protocol Redundancy of route servers	1H96 (proprietary) 2H96+ (MPOA)

Table 4.10 Representative VLAN architectures.

Vendor (Note 1)	Architecture (Note 2)	Features
3Com	Transcend	LANE and routing between VLANs
		Packet filtering between VLANs
Agile	Relational Network	Network layer relational LANs (TCP/IP only)
	Architecture	LANE (proprietary)
Alcatel	Avanza	ATM Forum LANE
Bay	BaySIS	ATM Forum LANE and routing between
VLANs		
Cabletron	Synthesis	LANE and proprietary routing between
	Virtual	VLANs (IP only)
	Networking Service	Multilayer switching
Cisco	CiscoFusion	ATM Forum LANE and routing between
		VLANs
		Multilayer switching
		MPOA planned
Crosscom	Clearpath	LANE and routing between VLANs
Digital	EnVISN – Enterprise	ATM Forum LANE and routing between
	Virtual Intelligent	VLANs
	Switched Networks	
Fore	ForeView	ATM Forum LANE MPOA planned
IBM	SVN – Switched	ATM Forum LANE and routing between
	Virtual Networking	VLANs
Newbridge	VIVID	LANE (proprietary)
		pre-MPOA
UB Networks	GeoView	ATM Forum LANE
Xylan	ATMman	Packet filtering between VLANs
		LANE (proprietary)

Note 1   Includes acquisitions – Fore/Alantec, Cabletron/SMC, Bay/Centillion, 3COM/Chipcom

Note 2   Architecture refers to strategy name where available or management system

in defining VLANs and rely on Layer 2 and/or Layer 3 filtering. The scalability of this filtering in terms of manageability and security, even if controlled by a sophisticated network management system, is still unknown. When selecting an architecture, the decision will depend upon the installed base, expected network growth, and budget. Ultimately, the optimal method of routing between VLANs may be based on MPOA. In any case, each vendor's offering, based on one of the above architectures, seeks to differentiate itself in some way. We summarize announced and/or delivered offerings from a number of the larger vendors in Table 4.10.

4.1.5 ATM Forum Multiprotocol over ATM (MPOA)

Whereas the Classical model and extensions within ROLC attempt to solve the problems of IP over any underlying technology, with ATM just one of the alternatives, work within the ATM Forum's **Multiprotocol**

over ATM (MPOA) SWG focuses on the support of any Layer 3 protocol over only ATM. This group has been given the task of developing an ATM networking architecture which will support all Layer 3 protocols while at the same time allowing these protocols to take advantage of ATM's QoS capabilities. Thus, MPOA is an evolution of LANE as well as Classical ATM. MPOA will use LANE for Layer 2 forwarding within a single Layer 3 subnet (to use IP terminology). We cannot compare MPOA with LANE, though, since there are fundamental differences. Whereas LANE is limited to a single subnet and hides ATM (and QoS) from end-systems, MPOA is just the opposite. Thus, we can consider it as an evolution of LANE, now including Layer 3 routing as well as LANE's Layer 2 bridging. It provides the benefits of a fully routed environment across ATM, while taking maximum advantage of ATM's bandwidth and service classes. By separating routing and switching functions, it also evolves the internetworking architecture overall. Finally, as introduced above, it is the first method of providing a unified approach to Layer 3 across ATM.

To allow direct connectivity between hosts in different subnets, MPOA will adapt the NHRP protocol from the IETF for address resolution. This, along with use of RFC 1483/RFC 1577 (see Heinanen, 1993, and Laubach, 1993) encapsulations and re-use of the MARS/MCS for multicast forwarding, results in a great deal of basic compatibility between work taking place within the IETF and within the ATM Forum. In fact, the desire for such an approach was communicated to the Forum's Multiprotocol BOF (as MPOA was known at the time) and later released as an informational RFC. Building upon both LANE and NHRP, MPOA also includes route distribution and emulation of Layer 3 broadcasts. Other requirements include integration with LANE, support for firewalling and protocol filtering, and auto-configuration of ATM-attached hosts. We will discuss these services in greater detail.

An MPOA domain will contain a number of devices acting as MPOA servers and clients, as shown in Figure 4.21. This basic concept is no different to LANE (the, LECS, LES, BUS, and LEC) or the Classical model (the ATMARP server, NHS, MARS/MCS, and clients). Servers are those devices providing Layer 3 coordination, address resolution, route distribution, and broadcast/multicast forwarding. Clients are users of the MPOA service, and will include routers, LAN switches, PCs, workstations, and any other devices implementing the MPOA protocol. Working together, these devices enable multiprotocol data forwarding across an ATM network. A key component of MPOA, and a new device within internetworking, is the **route server**, described in greater detail below. This server calculates reachability information and forwards this to clients capable of forwarding at both Layer 2 and 3. Thus, for the first time, we have decoupled the Layer 3 route calculation and data forwarding functions.

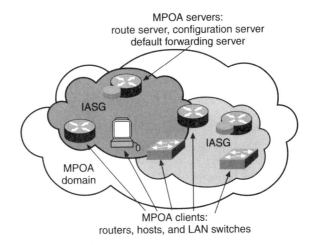

MPOA servers:
route server, configuration server
default forwarding server

IASG

IASG

MPOA
domain

MPOA clients:
routers, hosts, and LAN switches

Figure 4.21 MPOA system architecture.

Architecture

The basic unit of organization within MPOA is the **Internet Address Sub-Group (IASG)**, equivalent to a non-overlapping range of internetwork layer addresses summarized by a Layer 3 routing protocol. In the case of IP, this will equate to a subnet. Note that an IASG defines both a Layer 3 protocol and an associated address space. If a host or router is running more than one protocol stack, it will join multiple IASGs. The set of MPOA server functions and their clients servicing an IASG is known as an **MPOA service area**, with multiple IASGs forming an MPOA domain (Figure 4.21). In looking at the various data models one last time, MPOA is an example of the separated addressing model, often known as the overlay model. This model requires an address resolution function between the ATM and Layer 3, and currently uses a layered routing model where internetwork layer routing (for example, OSPF) operates on top of and separately from ATM routing (PNNI). These models contrast with the peer addressing model and integrated routing, also under discussion within both the IETF and the ATM Forum.

Be aware that as this book was going to print in Spring 1996, the MPOA specification more than any other was still in a state of flux, with final approval not expected until Winter 1997. Thus, as we delve further into MPOA components, information flows, and protocol operation, some information is subject to change. This is to be expected if past changes in MPOA architecture are any indication of the future. The same applies to the implementation example later in this book. Terms and architecture are current as of the MPOA R6 draft.

Within MPOA, the logical component performing a set of functions is known as a **functional group**. Note that we leave the physical entity (or entities) forming this 'black box' undefined. For example, MPOA clients will include MPOA-aware routers, LAN switches, and hosts. In the former two cases, the components form an **Edge Device Functional Group (EDFG)**. These act as Layer 3 edge devices and are capable of forwarding data between legacy LANs/WANs and the ATM network, with routers implementing routing protocols while LAN switches will use MPOA route distribution. In the latter case, the components form an **ATM-attached Host Functional Group (AHFG)**. These directly connected MPOA hosts, also acting as clients, will have no attached LAN or WAN segments.

Servers within an MPOA IASG include an **IASG Coordination Function Group (ICFG)** which coordinates the distribution of an IASG across multiple traditional LAN ports and/or ATM-connected hosts. The **Default Forwarder Functional Group (DFFG)** forwards traffic within an IASG if no direct client–client connection exists, and also performs the MCS functions within MPOA. This entity may also forward traffic to a destination outside of the IASG if the source is unable to open a direct connection to a forwarding server. The **Route Server Functional Group (RSFG)** runs Layer 3 routing protocols, provides inter-IASG address resolution and, optionally, forwards routing information to caches in EDFGs, while the **Remote Forwarder Functional Group (RFFG)** is responsible for forwarding traffic between IASGs or between an MPOA client in one IASG and a second IASG. The ICFG and DFFG will be co-resident. In addition, if the same platform implements the

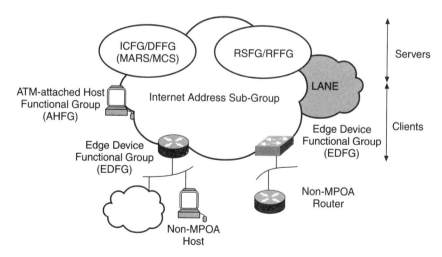

Figure 4.22 MPOA functional groups.

IASG	Internetwork Address Sub-Group	LANE	LAN Emulation
AHFG	ATM-attached Host Functional Group	EDFG	Edge Device Functional Group
ICFG	IASG Coordination Functional Group	DFFG	Default Forwarder Functional Group
RSFG	Route Server Functional Group	RFFG	Remote Forwarder Functional Group

RSFG and RFFG, these functional groups will be co-resident as well. MPOA servers maintain knowledge of the MAC and Layer 3 topologies for their IASG (Brown, 1996), and may be replicated for redundancy and scalability. Thus, a single IASG may be served by a distributed ICFG, RSFG, RFFG, and DFFG. We depict a typical MPOA topology in Figure 4.22.

Connections within MPOA include client–server and server–server, and are all based on SVCs with LLC/SNAP encapsulation. EDFGs and AHFGs will establish control connections to each of the servers within MPOA, including the RSFG, the RFFG, the ICFG/MARS, and the DFFG/MCS+. In addition, since we use LANE for Layer 3 forwarding within MPOA, EDFGs, the MPOA servers and, optionally, AHFGs if they support LANE, will also maintain the necessary connections into the LE Service. Server–server connections within MPOA include those used for redundancy as well as connections between functional groups located in different IASGs.

Looking more closely at how the various components within MPOA communciate, remember that EDFGs use LANE for Layer 2 (intra-LASG) forwarding while AHFGs may use the DFFG (Figure 4.23) for routable and LANE (or some future equivalent) for non-routable protocols. In both cases, the RFFG provides the inter-IASG forwarding. Also remember that while connections from the AHFG to the ICEG/MARS and DFFC/MCS+ are required, those to the RFFG and RSFG are optional. If we look at an AHFG with data to transmit, it will first make an NHRP query to the ICFG, which is then passed amongst the RSFGs.

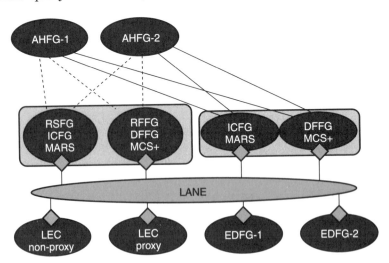

Figure 4.23 MPOA control connections.

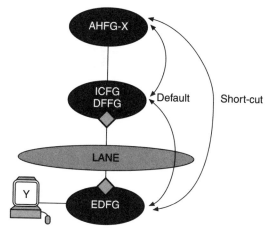

Figure 4.24 MPOA short-cut paths.

The destination's RSFG/ICFG will send the eventual reply, providing the AHFG with the information it needs to open a direct VCC.

We now look at the difference between default and short-cut paths across MPOA. Consider station x, an AHFG, wishing to communicate with y, attached to an EDFG (Figure 4.24). When using the DFFG for forwarding, the DFFG IP-ARPs adds a MAC header, and transmits the packet from x. In the opposite direction, y will first IP-ARP for x. The DFFG responds with the MAC address and, upon receipt of the packet from y, will strip the MAC header and forward the packet to x. Though forwarding all traffic through the DFFG may be acceptable, we wish to establish short-cut paths between x and y. A 'simple' EDFG will not initiate the set of events leading to a short-cut path. On the contrary, the ICFG will notice that a lot of traffic flows from the EDFG to x. It will send a cache entry to the EDFG, which then uses this to signal a direct VCC to x. A more sophisticated EDFG will notice on its own that a short cut path is better. It will send an NHRP request to the ICFG for x, and will then signal the direct VCC. Finally, the AHFG may request the short cut path. Here, the AHFG will notice that a direct path may be better. It NHRPs to the ICFG and, based on the response, now opens a direct VCC to y.

Operation

In looking at MPOA operation, we first need to understand the information flows within an MPOA domain as well as which functions apply within an IASG and which operate between IASGs. Information flows between the various MPOA functional groups include: configuration flows for the retrieval of configuration information, data transfer flows, client–server control flows used by clients to inform and query the various MPOA servers, and server–server flows to distribute functions between multiple servers for redundancy and scalability.

Connections between MPOA clients and the ICFG and DFFG/MCS+ serve the same functions as those within LANE but at Layer 3. In addition, MPOA adds a new set of control connections between the RSFG and RFFG and the client. These connections include: an RSFG Control VCC used to obtain address and routing information for inter-IASG data transfer, an ICFG Control VCC for intra-IASG address resolution and the registration of LAN-connected devices, connections to and from the DFFG for sending and forwarding frames within an IASG in the absence of a direct connection (and also for broadcast and multicast traffic), and connections to and from the RFFG for sending frames between IASGs in the absence of direct client connections. Server-to-server flows include VCCs between RSFGs within an IASG to forward destination resolution queries, and between ICFGs within an IASG to distribute topology information. Note that all inter-IASG data flows are not part of the MPOA standard.

Devices within an MPOA domain will first enter into a configuration phase, then registration and discovery, next destination resolution, and finally data transfer. The configuration phase consists of all functional groups contacting a configuration server to obtain required information including a list of servers as well as the identity, extent, protocol, and MTU within the IASG. Given this information, the functional groups may then proceed to establish the necessary control connections. EDFGs will register with each ICFG/DFFG and RSFG/RFFG reporting LAN-attached devices to the ICFG to ensure that the MPOA servers have accurate knowledge of the IASG at both the MAC and internetwork layers. Note that an EDFG will perform this operation for each IASG it supports. The same applies to AHFGs except for the reporting of LAN-attached devices. RSFGs will also register with the ICFG, indicating which IASGs they support. Next, ICFGs will register with peer ICFGs. With all of these registration processes complete, the MPOA service is now operational. Note that MPOA clients and servers implementing LANE will follow a parallel path for LANE configuration and initialization.

When an AHFG wishes to send data, either within the IASG or to an external destination, it must first resolve the destination's ATM address. The ICFG will query the ICFG for this information. EDFGs operate a bit differently since they may receive address resolution requests from connected LAN segments. For destinations within an IASG, the AHFG may respond with a cached entry containing the MAC address of the target AHFG. Note that this function is equivalent to LANE, though a QoS requirement may also be included.

Now consider the EDFG receiving a packet to be bridged or routed from a connected LAN segment into MPOA (Figure 4.25). Remember that all clients have registered their address with the ICFG

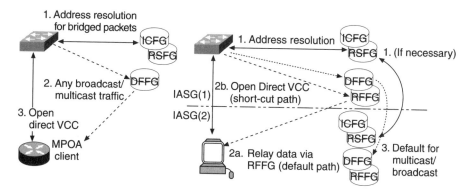

Figure 4.25 MPOA Operation.

responsible for the local IASG. We first must determine whether the packet should remain within the IASG or whether its destination is on another IASG. This decision is based on whether the packet contains the MAC address of a router within the IASG, and draws on routing information either internally generated or downloaded from an RSFG. This routing information may contain 'cut-through' routes to a distant IASG. Assuming that the EDFG knows the MAC address, and that it is to remain within the IASG, it will forward the packet using LANE. This forwarding path is also similar if the destination is within the EDFG itself.

If the MAC address is not known to the EDFG, the packet will be forwarded to the ICFG for either forwarding based on a cached MAC entry or passed to the DFFG for forwarding. For routed packets, the EDFG either forwards the data if it knows the internetwork address or queries the RSFG if it does not. Upon receipt of the destination address, the client will open a direct connection either within the IASG, to a distant IASG, or directly to a client in a distant IASG. In the two latter cases, the flow is known as **short-cut unicast data transfer**, and NHRP-like mechanisms come into play. Note that a router connected to MPOA may implement multiple server functions, and in fact may also act as an EDFG for local segments. Alternatively, the EDFG may send the packet to the RFFG for forwarding, known as **default unicast data transfer**. In the opposite direction (MPOA to LAN) the reverse of the above applies. AHFGs operate in much the same way when presented with inter-IASG traffic. However, both EDFGs and AHFGs could at some point use RFFG-like default data forwarders for instances where a direct VCC is not warranted based on QoS requirements. This relates to the connectionless model previously discussed.

Multicasting across MPOA is based on the mechanisms defined within the IETF for IP over ATM. Remember that the basic MARS and MCS concepts are protocol independent. MPOA only extends the two server functions into a multiprotocol environment. We would expect to see MARS functionality within the ICFG and multicast client capability as part of both the EDFG and and AHFG. The MCS equivalent should reside within the DFFG as depicted earlier.

Mapping MPOA to physical systems

Looking more closely at the physical devices within MPOA, we need to look at the proper hardware platforms for both MPOA servers and clients. Depending upon vendor implementation, the various functional groups (ICFG/DFFG and RSFG/RFFG) may be contained within traditional routers, high-performance PCs or workstations, modules within ATM switches or devices known as multilayer LAN switches (described below). Selection criteria will include cost, network scaling, and requirements for redundancy. In most configurations, the RSFG/ RFFG will probably be part of a high-performance router platform. In contrast, since the ICFG does not participate in actual data forwarding, it may be placed on a PC or workstation if required. We anticipate that vendors implementing MPOA will attempt to limit the number of actual physical devices within a domain, combining as many functions as possible onto a single platform. Drawing an analogy with LANE, a single physical device may provide MPOA services to multiple IASGs.

A device known as a multilayer LAN switch will commonly act as the hardware platform for an EDFG. This component, described by a number of vendors (even within LANE architectures), differs from conventional LAN switches in that it may perform Layer 3 forwarding, but only carries out a subset of those functions traditionally associated with routers. Whereas routers perform both route determination (the processing of routing protocols to determine reachability leading to the creation of next hop or link state routing tables) and packet forwarding (the actual transfer of a packet from one interface to another), multilayer switches may dispense with calculating the routing table and instead rely on cached entries from a central route server (RSFG). This does not, however, preclude a multilayer switch from running an intra-domain routing protocol, since in most cases the overhead of Layer 3 forwarding far outweighs that of route table calculation. The price per port of these devices should be lower than that of routers due to reliance on optimized, ASIC-based switching hardware.

This price optimization depends, however, on the ability to carry out Layer 3 functions in these ASICs. Since the routing table download is only part of the problem, and ATM edge devices optimized for Layer 2 switching and filtering will not be capable of high-performance Layer 3 forwarding without the addition of hardware. Note the emphasis on high performance. A number of vendors have announced or delivered software-based Layer 3 capabilities for their LAN switches. Without dedicated routing hardware, this is limited to around 50,000 pps, a far cry from the 200,000+ pps Layer 3 forwarding required by high-performance modular LAN switches. A network designer deploying such a software solution must be very careful in assigning VLANs. Ultimately, we expect the price-per-port of these multilayer switches to decrease though not to that of Layer 2-only devices. Note that traditional routers implementing the MPOA protocol may also function as EDFGs and, in fact, this deployment may be common as vendors develop their multilayer LAN switches. In Chapter 5, we describe a possible MPOA network based on the current state of the specification (Winter 1996) as well as on some of the above hardware assumptions.

4.1.6 Frame Relay and ATM

Although we focus on ATM, another critical networking technology, at least in the WAN, is **Frame Relay (FR)**. Due to the high cost of ATM connectivity, and its questionable use at sub-DS1/E1 rates, many users will deploy hybrid networks consisting of both ATM and Frame Relay: ATM to the larger sites and Frame Relay to the branches. Thus, we require an efficient mechanism within the network to interwork these two technologies. We describe two forms of interworking, network and service interworking, below. Separate from the interworking problem is the use of ATM to provide additional bandwidth in the Frame Relay backbone. As the service grows in popularity, some carriers see ATM trunking as the only way to interconnect their Frame Relay switches. This option also fits well with the goal of using ATM as a universal service platform. Frame Relay Forum (1994) outlines both of these solutions, summarized in Figures 4.26 and 4.27. In the first figure, ATM-

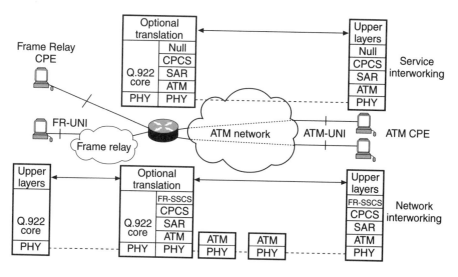

Figure 4.26 Frame Relay to ATM interworking.

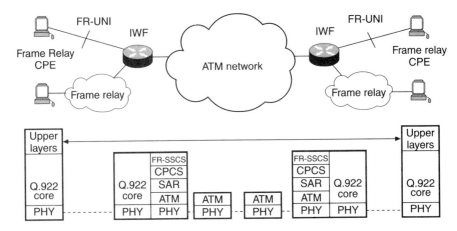

Figure 4.27 ATM as Frame Relay transport.

connected users communicate with FR-connected users, while in the second figure the ATM network provides a transparent backbone to the FR users.

ATM as a Frame Relay transport

This scenario uses the added bandwidth provided by ATM as a backbone networking infrastructure. A locally deployed Frame Relay service, in a metropolitan area, for example, will use the ATM infrastructure for trunking, sharing this new backbone with other WAN services and thus avoiding duplication of core switching and transmission hardware. At the interface between the Frame Relay and ATM network, an inter-working function provides the necessary remapping and encapsulation to preserve the Frame Relay service parameters over ATM. We accomplish this by remapping the Frame Relay protocol stack into an ATM stack at the ingress of the network for segmentation and transport over AAL5. This process is reversed at the egress where reassembly occurs. When Frame Relay is deployed in this way, the use of ATM will not be visible to end users.

Frame Relay CPE to ATM CPE interworking

When interworking between ATM UNI-based Frame Relay and a Frame Relay CPE, the specifics of the ATM network will be invisible to the Frame Relay-aware upper-layer protocols. However, depending upon the type of interworking deployed, the ATM-connected end-system may or may not be required to support the Frame Relay SSCS and RFC 1490. In one scenario, the **Interworking Function (IWF)** not only remaps the Frame Relay service parameters but changes the data encapsulation as well. This is known as **service interworking**, outlined in Frame Relay Forum (1995). A simpler form of interworking which presents the ATM user with Frame Relay data encapsulation is defined in Frame Relay Forum (1994).

IWF

The services provided by the Frame Relay to ATM IWF include PDU formatting and delimiting, error detection, connection multiplexing, loss priority and congestion indication, and PVC status management. This first function is remapping from the variable length FR PDU to ATM AAL5 and then into a number of ATM cells. The PDU header at the IWF, consisting of the Q.922 core with the exception of the CRC-16 and flags, will consist of two, three, or four bytes depending upon the length of the DLCI field. Only the two-byte variant is implemented at present. This header, as shown in Figure 4.28, includes the connection identifier (DLCI), indications for network congestion (FECN, BECN), and whether a frame is more likely to be discarded in the presence of network congestion via the DE bit. The CRC-16 found in the native FR PDU is not mapped to ATM due to the use of the AAL5 CRC-32 to provide data integrity.

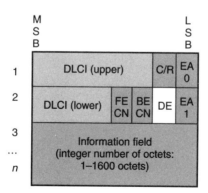

Figure 4.28 Frame Relay header.

DLCI	Data Link Connection Identifier
C/R	Command/Response
EA	Address Extension bit
FECN	Forward Explicit Congestion Notification
BECN	Backward Explicit Congestion Notification
DE	Discard Eligibility

Data encapsulation remapping depends upon whether we implement service or network interworking. Remember that we encapsulate FR user data in RFC 1490 (described below), while ATM AAL5 traffic is commonly carried in RFC 1483 (Heinanen, 1993). These two data encapsulations are incompatible. If implementing service interworking, the IWF will convert between these two encapsulations, remapping the RFC 1490 NLPID (also known as FRF.3 (Frame Relay Forum, 1993)) to RFC 1483 LLC/SNAP (and only LLC/SNAP – VC mux is not supported). An IWF performing these conversions is operating in **translation mode**. The ATM end-system protocol stack is therefore unaware that the destination is located on a Frame Relay network. IWFs used for network interworking do not remap data encapsulations, and rely on the ATM end-system to support the FR-SSCS, including RFC 1483 and NLPID. One area which we do not look at in detail, though supported, is the interworking of non-data protocols such as voice. In this case, the IWF operates in **transparent mode**, performing no remapping or fragmentation/reassembly.

Within the IWU, we must also provide a means of mapping between FR DLCIs and ATM VPIs/VCIs in a deterministic way. One alternative maps multiple FR logical connections into a single ATM VC, and we preserve end-to-end DLCI identity via the FR-SSCS. This is used within network interworking. The second method allows one-to-one mapping between DLCIs and individual VPIs/VCIs. (For the two-byte header, the DLCI should be chosen in the range from 16–991; the default is 1022.) Note that this method is the same scheme used when converting from the ATM-DXI to the ATM-UNI via an ATM DSU in Mode 1. Although every IWU must support one-to-one multiplexing, one-to-many is optional.

How do we map the FR DE bit to the ATM CLP when converting from FR to ATM and vice versa within networking interworking? Two ways are possible when mapping FR to ATM. The first calls for copying the DE bit in the native FR cell header into the FR-SSCS PDU header while at the same time setting the CLP in all ATM cells, and the second also copies the DE bit but sets all CLPs to either 0 or 1, a value set at the onset of the ATM connection. Two methods are also available in the ATM to FR direction. One option is to set the DE bit of the native FR header if either the FR-SSCS DE bit is set or if one or more ATM cells have the CLP set. An alternative is to copy the FR-SSCS DE bit into the native FR DE field without taking the status of the CLP into account. Just as with the DE bit, we map both forward and backward congestion indication fields in the two directions (Figure 4.29). Service interworking follows the same technique in the FR-ATM direction with the exception of the FR-SSCS PDU header which does not exist on the ATM side of the IWU. In mapping from ATM to FR, the IWU will either set the DE field if one or more cells have their CLP field set, or we set the DE field to a constant value (0 or 1) at service subscription.

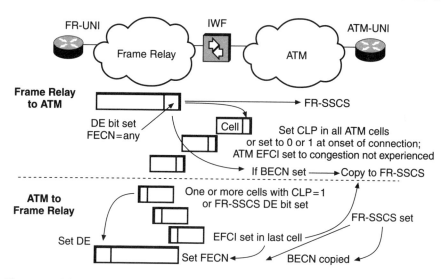

Figure 4.29 ATM to Frame Relay network interworking.

Now looking at congestion indication under network interworking, in crossing from FR to ATM, we copy the FR FECN field into the FR-SSCS, and the ATM cell EFCI is set to 'congestion not experienced.' In the reverse direction, the native FR FECN will be set if either the FR-SSCS field indicates congestion or if the EFCI field of the last ATM cell of the original FR PDU is set. The inverse of the above applies for the BECN field. In mapping from ATM to FR, we copy the BECN from the FR-SSCS to the native FR header, while in the reverse direction, the field will be set if indicated in the native FR header or if the EFCI was set in the last ATM cell crossing the boundary in the opposite direction. This signifies that the network is experiencing congestion. In addition, we may implement a timer to exit this congestion state after a defined interval if no new congestion information is received. Under service interworking from FR to ATM, we may map the FECN field of the Q.922 frame to the ATM EFCI in every cell. Alternatively, if we do not need to map this field, the EFCI is set to 'congestion not experienced' in all cells. In the opposite direction, if the EFCI field is set then the FECN is set to 'congestion experienced.' For BECN, we ignore this field in the FR to ATM direction, while setting the BECN field of the Q.922 frame to 0 in the reverse direction.

We must also map traffic parameters must also be mapped between the two technologies. For example, ATM PCR, CDV, SCR, and MBS should be associated with Frame Relay throughput and burst characteristics (CIR, committed burst, excess burst, access rate). The ATM Forum's B-ICI specification outlines the required conversions and provides some guidelines. Though protocol encapsulation and service convergence provide for interworking, the IWU should also support interworking between management on the Frame Relay side of the IWU based on Q.933 Annex A and those on the ATM side which rely on the ATM UNI or B-ICI including OAM and ILMI. Finally, if compression IAW (Frame Relay Forum, 1996) is implemented on the Frame Relay side of the IWF, a second IWF on the ATM side or the ATM end system is itself responsible for decompression. We identify the use of compression via NLPIS=×BØ.

RFC1490

Bradley *et al* (1993) and FRF.3 (Frame Relay Forum, 1993) define the means by which we encapsulate multiprotocol across a Frame Relay network. This encapsulation is of course used at native Frame Relay CPE, but is also found at the ATM UNI as part of network interworking. Data is encapsulated within a Q.922 Annex A frame, which contains addressing information, the Q.922 control field, a **Network Layer Protocol Identifier (NLPID)**, the user data, and a frame check sequence. In Table 4.11 we outline the various ways of transporting routed and bridged data within these frames. This NLPID is a method of identifying the higher-layer protocol carried within the frame. In most cases, the NLPID will point to an SNAP header containing an OID and protocol identifier. An NLPID indicating an SNAP header (0×80) may be used for any Layer 3 protocol. These are identified by the appropriate PID. For example, IPX has a PID=0×8137. The remainder of the frame will then contain the IPX packet.

The RFC also addresses Frame Relay parameter negotiation, though this function is not supported by most end-systems at present. Fragmentation may take place at the edge of the Frame Relay network, though this should not be required since the network itself is usually capable of supporting all LAN frame sizes with the exception of the largest Token Ring frames. In interworking from ATM to Frame Relay, a frame with the maximum AAL5 MTU (9180 octets) will require fragmentation. A special PID (0×00-0D) in combination with a sequence number is used for this fragmentation. Finally, Frame Relay supports ARP using an SNAP header with a PID=0×0806. This is important if we wish to support SVCs on one or both sides of the IWF, remapping the FR ARP (Plummer, 1982) and inverse ARP (Bradley and Brown, 1992) requests to the ATMARP (Laubach, 1993) and vice versa. One method of accomplishing this for PVCs is to equip IWF with a map of Frame Relay port numbers and DLCIs to their ATM equivalents. SVCs may be supported by also including Frame Relay E.164 and ATM NSAP or E.164 addresses. FRF.8 (Frame Relay Forum, 1995) describes this process in greater detail.

Table 4.11 RFC1490 encapsulations.

Format		Ctrl	PAD	NLPID	OUI (Note 1)	PID	PAD/frame ctrl	MAC dest. addr.		LAN FCS (Note 3)
Routed with Ethertype PID	Q.	03	00	80	00-00-00	Ether-type		Datagram		
Routed IP PDUs	9	03	N/A	CC		IP datagram				
Bridged 802.3	2	03	00	80	00-80-C2	00-01	N/A	(6)		Yes (1)
Bridged 802.3	2	03	00	80	00-80-C2	00-07	N/A	(6)		No
Bridged 802.4		03	00	80	00-80-C2	00-02	00/FC	(6)	D	Yes (1)
Bridged 802.4	A	03	00	80	00-80-C2	00-08	00/FC	(6)	a	No
Bridged 802.5	d	03	00	80	00-80-C2	00-03	00/FC	(6)	t	Yes (1)
Bridged 802.5	d	03	00	80	00-80-C2	00-09	00/FC	(6)	a	No
Bridged FDDI	r	03	00	80	00-80-C2	00-04	00/FC	(6)		Yes (1)
Bridged FDDI	e	03	00	80	00-80-C2	00-0A	00/FC	(6)		No
Bridged 802.6	s	03	00	80	00-80-C2	00-0B	Note 2	(6)		No
Bridged PDU	s	03	00	80	BPDU IAW 802.1(d) or 802.1(g)					

Note 1 00-80-C2 is the OUI for 802.1
Note 2 802.6 fields include: Reserved, BEtag, BAsize, and common PDU trailer after data
Note 3 All encapsulations include a one-octet frame FCS; thus, some bridged formats include two FCSs

Analysis

Frame Relay will succeed both as an access method for ATM and as a service offered over ATM. In the former case, the large installed base will create a demand for service interworking, whereby a user connected to a native ATM service is provided with transparent interworking with locations connected to Frame Relay. As a service offered over ATM, the service providers will realize economies of scale by deploying Frame Relay as one of many services across an ATM backbone. Of all the data services, Frame Relay is expected to be the most important in comple-menting ATM, as evidenced by projected 1996 service revenues of $1.6 billion and equipment sales of $1.2 billion. This is by far the fastest uptake of any networking service to date (Broadband Networking News, 1995).

4.1.7 SMDS/CBDS and ATM

LANE is only one method of supporting connectionless service across an ATM network. An alternative, conforming to the **Switched Multimegabit Data Service (SMDS)** and **Connectionless**

Broadband Data Service (**CBDS**, or sometimes, **Broadband Connectionless Data Bearer Service, B-CDBS**) profiles, is based on ATM end-systems supporting AAL3/4 (or more recently, AAL5) communicating with a **Connectionless Server Function (CLSF)** located within the domain of the ATM service provider. Thus, SMDS/CBDS is found within the public domain as opposed to LANE which is more suited to private ATM networks. In reality, there are two methods to support LAN interconnection across the wide area. The first method is based on a full mesh of VCs connecting each and every LAN. This approach therefore has scalability limits. The preferred approach relies on the CLSF, whereby the ATM network will transparently support LAN connectivity without the requirement for a full or partial mesh of PVCs or SVCs. LAN segments connect via routers or bridges (termed **Interworking Units**, or **IWU**) to one or more connectionless servers. These devices resequence the user data while at the same time broadcasting or multicasting the data as required. Thus, the ATM network is capable of supporting the same connectionless service currently provided by DQDB-based networks.

ATM as an SMDS/CBDS transport

A typical environment will consist of a customer LAN connected to the SMDS/CBDS service via an ATM-equipped router. This router will adapt the user data in conformance with the **Connectionless Network Access Protocol (CLNAP)** as defined in ITU-T I.364 (ITU-T, 1993b). This data will then be segmented based on AAL3/4 and transmitted over the ATM-UNI at any suitable physical line speed. First public implementations supported 140 Mbps (E4) based on ITU-T I.432 (ITU-T, 1993a), 34 Mbps (E3) based on ETSI ETS-300337, and 155 Mbps (STM-1) based on ETSI ETS-300300. Note that although the physical line speed may be 34 or 155 Mbps, the SMDS/CBDS service will implement access class enforcement, limiting the throughput of the SMDS/CBDS VC to 2, 4, 10, or 25 Mbps. At the ATM switch, the cell stream will be forwarded to a CLSF based on destination. An additional protocol, the **Connectionless Network Interface Protocol (CLNIP)**, has been defined for CLS-CLS interaction. Whether this protocol will be implemented or whether the end-system will direct its data to the proper CLS is under discussion.

CLSF

A CLSF is a device within the core of a public ATM network emulating the SMDS/CBDS service. A CLSF will resequence and reassemble the ATM cells into the original data packets which will then be sent on appropriate VCCs to the intended destination(s). A resequencing function is essential, as cells from multiple packets, identified by a MID, may be interleaved over the VC. The same functionality applies to broadcast and multicast traffic which will be forwarded across all VCCs. In most cases, a public CLSF will be integrated into a telecommunication management network environment via the Q3 interface, supporting GDMO, CMIS/CMIP, X.730 series, and so on. A service provider may operate both a national and international server as part of an SMDS/CBDS over ATM service offering.

The first CLSFs were placed into commercial service in France at the end of 1994. These devices, supporting the ATM-based LAN interconnect service, were provided by Thompson-CSF. Total throughput at the time was limited to 300 Mbps, upgradable over time. Coincidental with the introduction of this service, an ATM internetwork consisting of both CBDS and IP over AAL5 users was demonstrated at Interop '94 in Paris. This demonstration consisted of an FDDI LAN connected through a Cisco AGS+ router and then over an HSSI to an ATM-DSU. This DSU, generating AAL3/4 cells, then connected to the Thomflex 3010-S CLSF via 34 Mbps. This CLSF in combination with a Thomflex 5010-L ATM switch formed the core of the network. This ATM switch provided connectivity to two users. The first user made use of the CBDS via a Cisco 7000 router equipped with an ATM-UNI supporting AAL3/4, while a workstation was connected directly to the switch via AAL5. End-to-end connectivity was provided by implementing both AAL3/4 and AAL5 at the router, with the 7000 acting as an interworking unit between the two ATM adaptations. Thus, FDDI users were able to communicate with the ATM-equipped workstation across a multiservice (CBDS and IP over AAL5) ATM network. Note that the Thompson system made use of an external CLS. Though this allows the CLS architecture to be decoupled from the switch architecture, and thus makes it more easily upgradable, it does introduce some latency by requiring all cells to enter and leave the CLS.

The CLS may operate in either cell-based or frame-based modes. If cell-based, the CLS or IWU will send cells immediately upon receipt. This implies that cells from different sources may be interleaved on a single VC pointed to the destination, and therefore AAL3/4 with its MID capability is required. Alternatively, frame-based forwarding may be used whereby the entire data frame is reassembled before being forwarded. Current interest in the support of AAL5 for SMDS/CBDS over ATM focuses on this mode of operation. Note that there are tradeoffs in both approaches. Cell-based forwarding introduces less latency but requires more sophisticated switching equipment. The opposite holds for frame forwarding, where the latency is equal to one or more frames awaiting transmission at a given line speed.

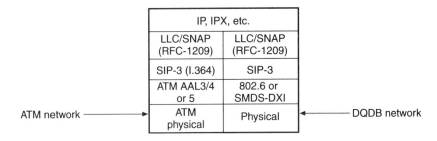

Figure 4.30 SMDS interworking.

IWF

Interworking between SMDS/CBDS based on ATM and that based on DQDB may occur at either the service or internetworking layer. In the former case, the cells used in both technologies are preserved; only the header information is remapped. Though this has been tested, most current interworking takes place at Layer 3 due to the higher performance of existing internetworking devices. Since SMDS is not optimized for the transport of voice, maintaining the cell structure from SMDS to ATM is not critical in this case. Deployment of this IWF may be based on a router connected into an SMDS network via the SMDS-DXI on one side and then into ATM via an AAL3/4- and 5-capable UNI as in Figure 4.30. Although SMDS over ATM is based on AAL3/4, some service providers may not wish to offer this, and instead convert directly to AAL5-based VCCs. This eliminates the additional overhead associated with AAL3/4 while providing interoperability with a greater range of end-systems since AAL5 is more widely implemented. Note that this IWF is separate from the IWU defined above. The IWF connects two dissimilar networks supporting SMDS/CBDS, while an IWU connects a conventional LAN to the ATM network.

RFC 1209

This RFC (Piscitello and Lawrence, 1991) defines a method of encapsulating IP and ARP packets for transmission across an SMDS network. Unlike RFC 1490, which does much the same thing for Frame Relay, RFC-1209 is not inherently multiprotocol. Nevertheless, most vendors have based their multiprotocol transport on the concepts outlined in this document. The interface between the CPE and the SMDS network is known as the **Subscriber Network Interface (SNI)**, over which the **SMDS Interface Protocol (SIP)** based on the DQDB protocol as standardized in IEEE 802.6 (IEEE, 1990) operates. This SIP encapsulates the IP packet in LLC/SNAP (thus its multiprotocol support) and then through what is known as SIP Level 3 (MAC) and SIP Levels 1 and 2

Table 4.12 SMDS SIP encapsulation for IP packets.

SIP					LLC/SNAP					IP
SIP...	HLPI	...	DSAP	SSAP	Ctrl	Organization code			Ethertype	
SIP...	01	...	AA	AA	03	00	00	00	08	00	IP...

(DQDB). Across this SIP, the maximum MTU is 9180 octets for IP end-systems. Table 4.12 depicts the necessary encapsulation for an IP packet.

Routers, instead of implementing SIP, connect to SMDS networks via SMDS-DSUs which implement the complete stack. The interface between the router and the DSU is known as the SMDS-DXI.

SMDS networks were the first place where the **Logical IP Subnet (LIS)** concept came into use. Since SMDS is a public service offering, multiple customers share the same physical network. Each of these customers configures its hosts to be part of an LIS, with inter-LIS connectivity via routers. This router is a member of two or more LISs. Though NHRP is applicable to SMDS, and would optimize connectivity, this has not yet been deployed. An important feature of SMDS is the concept of group addressing, where all members of an LIS share a common group address used for broadcast and multicast traffic; thus the connectionless support offered by SMDS, including support for ARP. Though SMDS defines a group address, no broadcast address format exists. Therefore, one group address must be configured to contain all members of the LIS. SMDS, envisioned as a public service, also includes powerful address screening whereby a group of SMDS (E.164) addresses will be associated with a user group, and thus an LIS. Security between LISs is then maintained via manipulation of these address tables.

Scalability

The scalability of SMDS/CBDS over ATM is a function of CLS capacity and interconnection. As stated above, in initial deployments and smaller deployments, end-systems could be directed to the CLS serving the intended destination. Of course, this implies that these systems must be capable of maintaining multiple VCCs to the CLSs. Alternatively, intelligence could be introduced into the network whereby broadcast and unknown traffic is originally sent to the CLS while unicast traffic will be sent via a direct VCC. As may be obvious, this approach closely parallels LANE. If implementing a true CLS-based service, the individual servers could be connected in a tree topology based on the hierarchical E.164 address structure (used for SMDS). If overloading the CLSs at the root of the tree is a concern, CLSs at each level of the hierarchy could be interconnected. This is known as a **partitioned tree topology**. Yet another

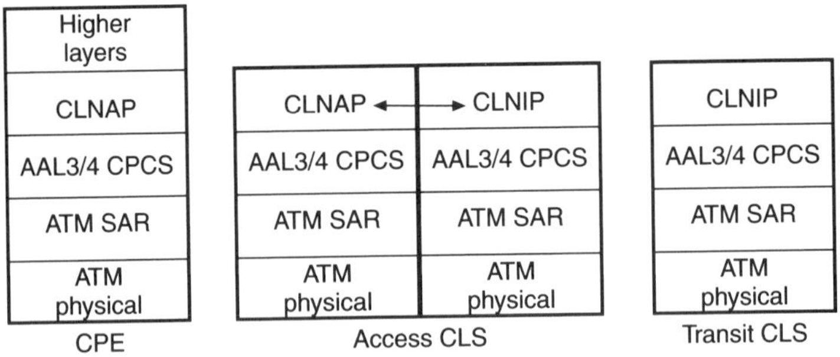

Figure 4.31 Scaling SMIDS/CBDS over ATM.

CLNAP   Connectionless Network Access Protocol
CLNIP   Connectionless Network Interface Protocol
CLS   Connectionless Server

approach suggested, though unlikely to be implemented, would be to connect the CLSs in a ring, duplicating the DQDB topology. Address resolution if not based on a server mechanism relies on the CLS flooding the ARP request to all IWUs belonging to a closed user group. As this method has scalability limitations, the server method is preferable (UIA, 1994). The CLNIP, introduced above, allows interconnection of multiple CLSs into an end-to-end network as shown in Figure 4.31.

Analysis

Although most current SMDS networks are deployed using the DQDB technology as developed by QPSX and based on the IEEE 802.6 **Metropolitan Area Network (MAN)**, the future of this service will rely on close integration with ATM. SMDS will then become one of a number of public offerings across an ATM WAN, in parallel with connection-oriented LAN interconnect (SVC- or PVC-based), Frame Relay, CES, VoD, and so on. The reasons for this migration from DQDB to ATM are based on limitations of the current generation of DQDB switching equipment and network management systems which support only SMDS. This contrasts with an ATM infrastructure capable of supporting multiple service offerings. Savings in terms of equipment, trunking, sparing, and training are obvious. This migration has given SMDS, a service which some analysts (especially in the US) considered past its prime, a new basis for the future. It is expected that the DQDB-based networks in many European countries will migrate to this architecture. PTTs and Telcos will migrate current SMDS customers to the new architecture, while new customers will be attracted by the ease of using SMDS over the WAN for LAN interconnection as well as the security guarantees offered by the SMDS model. Though many ATM-based services will compete with SMDS, we expect this service to remain a strong element of a service provider's portfolio, at least in Europe.

4.1.8 Other data service interworkings

Although current implementations focus on those interworking scenarios for which standards have been developed, nothing precludes ATM interworking with other wide-area services such as data over ISDN (as opposed to ATM to N-ISDN voice interworking described below) and X.25. A user on either of these two services would be provided with seamless connectivity at the service layer to a user located on ATM. Currently, interworking with both of these services exists via routers.

ISDN data

For ISDN data users, an IWF could be deployed within the network which would convert from PPP over ISDN, probably to RFC 1483. The function would be much like the service interworking which exists from Frame Relay to ATM at present. This IWF would be responsible for encapsulation conversion, and just as important, conversion of addressing spaces. This latter issue is solveable since either native E.164 addresses or NSAP addresses capable of transporting E.164 are used within ATM. A second, more complex form of interworking would define a new encapsulation over ATM compatible with PPP. This would not only streamline the operation of the IWF but would allow the ATM-connected user to use some of PPP's facilities. The host or router supporting this function would of course be more complex. Of interest is the IWF's ability to support the QoS requirements of the ATM user. Depending upon the bandwidth required, $N{\times}64$ Kbps will be made available for the connection and, once established, the ISDN portion of the end-to-end connection is very predictable. One may question the viability of interworking between ISDN's traditionally low data rates with ATM. These rates are no different, however, to those in use over Frame Relay.

X.25

Support of X.25 interworking within ATM is more complicated due to the X.25 protocol itself. Unlike Frame Relay, X.25 contains what is in effect a network layer, with end-to-end addressing based on X.121. Two solutions exist to this problem. At an IWF, X.25 would be mapped to an ATM VCC, with the X.121 address translated to the ATM E.164 or NSAP. Thus, an address resolution mechanism would be required if static tables were not to be used. This would also allow the use of existing ATM encapsulations such as RFC 1483. Alternatively, a new encapsulation may be defined which preserves the X.121 addressing. In both cases, operation of the ATM portion of the end-to-end connection will be unique since the VCC must first be extablished at the ATM layer and then at X.25. If true support of X.25 across ATM is not critical, an alternative would be to use the Frame Relay encapsulation across ATM, feeding into a Frame Relay to X.25 IWF beyond the edge of the ATM network. Looking at the problem from a different perspective, service providers will at some point in the future wish to offer X.25 service across an ATM backbone. In this environment, X.25 IWFs providing connectivity to the customer may surround an ATM core network.

4.1.9 Frame-based interfaces

Frame-based interfaces into ATM have been deployed for two reasons. The first deployed, and in fact the first available interface of any type for internetworking into ATM, is known as the **ATM Data Exchange Interface (ATM-DXI)**. This provides for interoperation with non-UNI capable end-systems. A newer interface, the **Frame UNI (FUNI)** was developed with an understanding that the ATM method of segmenting frames into 53-byte cells introduces unacceptable overhead over low speed ATM interfaces (those under 2 or 1.544 Mbps) if used for data transport only. This was not a design goal of the ATM-DXI. In addition, the FUNI is capable of providing for signaling, QoS, and OAM support. A third method of accessing an ATM network over a frame interface is via the **SMDS-DXI**. This is in reality a variation of the ATM-DXI, making use of a different encapsulation over the DXI (RFC 1209 as opposed to 1483 or 1490) and, normally, AAL3/4 at the UNI between the ATM-DSU and the ATM network. Of these three possibilities, only the FUNI will play a large role in future deployments.

ATM-DXI

Though most current ATM implementations focus on the ATM-UNI, the interface connecting end-systems supporting native ATM interfaces with ATM switches, an alternative method exists to allow non-ATM-capable devices to connect to an ATM network. This method is based on the ATM-DXI, a distributed solution combining an end-system such as a router acting as a DTE and an **ATM Data Service Unit (ATM-DSU)** acting as a DCE (Figure 4.32). This second device converts the HDLC formatted data from the end-system into the ATM cell stream. The ATM-DXI, defined within the ATM Forum, describes the data link protocols and physical interface between this non-ATM end-system and the ATM-DSU. To aid in management of the ATM-DXI, a **Local Management Interface (LMI)** is defined as well. The interface is capable of supporting both AALs 3/4 and 5 making use of any currently-defined service-

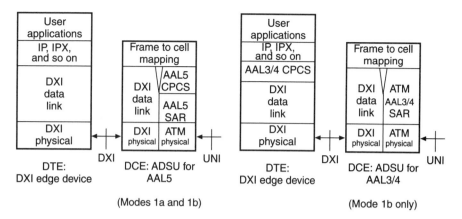

Figure 4.32 ATM-DXI protocol architecture.

specific convergence sublayer. For AAL5, this is currently RFC 1483 or RFC 1490, while AAL3/4 relies on RFC 1209 in support of SMDS/CBDS over ATM. Though many original DXI implementations made use of RFC 1490 NLPID encapsulation, RFC 1483, based on LLC/SNAP, is more useful in that it provides for interoperability with the majority of ATM endsystems (workstations, routers). One reason for the early deployment of RFC 1490 was due to the ease in mapping the Frame Relay header DLCI fields into the ATM VPI/VCI. Under RFC 1483 this DLCI-like field is preserved; only the encapsulation mechanism has shifted to LLC/SNAP from the NLPID. Thus, there are no problems combining ATM-DXI- and ATM-UNI-based devices on the same network. The two encapsulations are summarized in Figure 4.32. The DXI interface is not capable of transporting AAL1 commonly used for CBR traffic.

The ATM Forum's DXI specification (Version 1.0) defines three modes of operation: modes 1a, 1b, and 2. Modes 1a and 1b are designed to use AAL5, while mode 2 based on AAL3/4 supports of SMDS/CBDS over ATM. These three modes are summarized in Figure 4.33 and Table 4.13. Two encapsulations are possible, RFC 1483 (LLC/SNAP) and RFC 1490 (NLPID). We have summarized IP frame formats for these two encapsulations during discussion of the Classical model and of Frame Relay interworking.

Physical connectivity between the end-system and the ATM-DSU relies on any supported physical interface, including V.35, EIA/TIA 449/530, and, where E3/DS3 data rates are required, EIA/TIA 612/613 (HSSI). A DTE first creates the DTE-SDU, the information field to be used by a given AAL. This SDU is then encapsulated into a DXI frame containing addressing information and the FCS. Under AAL5, the DSU, upon receipt of the DXI frame, strips off the DXI header and trailer and then encapsulates the SDU in an AAL5 CPCS-PDU. This PDU is finally

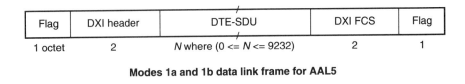

Modes 1a and 1b data link frame for AAL5

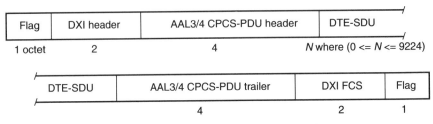

Modes 1a and 1b data link frame for AAL3/4

Figure 4.33 ATM-DXI header.

segmented into AAL5 SAR-PDUs before being passed to the UNI. This protocol stack is shown in Figure 4.32. This changes for AAL3/4, where the DTE has the responsibility of performing the AAL3/4 CPCS encapsulation before adding the DXI header and trailer. Referencing Table 4.13, this DTE is only required to support a single AAL3/4 VC under mode 1b. Mode 2 operation is different in that all VCs are AAL3/4-encapsulated at the DTE. It is then the responsibility of the DCE to strip off this AAL3/4 CPCS header and trailer if the given VC is designated as AAL5.

The addressing across the DXI is known as the **DXI Frame Address (DFA)**. This DFA, a part of the DXI frame header, allows the DTE to pass VPI/VCI addressing information to the DCE. Under modes 1a and 1b the DFA is 10 bits, while under mode 2 it is 24. The mapping between the DFA and the VPI/VCI is not straightforward. Under modes 1a and 1b, and referencing the DXI header, we depict the mapping in Figure 4.33 and 4.34.

All non-defined bits are set to zero in the direction DTE-DCE and ignored in the opposite direction. Note that this support of only 4 VPI

Table 4.13 ATM-DXI modes, maximum VCs, and MTUs.

Mode	Maximum VCs	AAL(s)	Maximum SDU	FCS
1a	1023	5 only	9232 octets	16 bit
1b	1023	3/4 for at least 1 VC	9224 octets	16 bit
		5 for all other VC	9232 octets	16 bit
2	16,777,215	3/4 and 5	65,535 octets	32 bit

Bit: 8	7	6	5	4	3	2	1	Octet:

	8	7	6	5	4	3	2	1	
Flag	0	1	1	1	1	1	1	0	0
DXI	DFA						RSVD	0	1
Header	DFA				CN	RSVD	CLP	1	2
Data	Maximum 9232 octets for AAL5 or 9224 octets for AAL3/4								
DXI	2^8	2^9	2^10	2^11	2^12	2^13	2^14	2^15	*n*-1
Trailer	2^0	2^1	2^2	2^3	2^4	2^5	2^6	2^7	*n*
Flag	0	1	1	1	1	1	1	0	*n*+1

Figure 4.34 ATM-DXI modes 1a and 1b data link frame.

RSVD   Reserved: these bits are set to 0

DFA

DFA		VPI		DFA		VCI	
Octet	Bit	Octet	Bit	Octet	Bit	Octet	Bit
1	6	2	8	1	8	3	2
1	5	2	7	1	7	3	1
1	4	2	6	2	8	4	8
1	3	2	5	2	7	4	7
				2	6	4	6
				2	5	4	5

FCS   16-bit frame check sequence based on CCITT Q.921 CRC-16.

CN   If PTI = × 01 in the last ATM cell composing the DXI frame, then DCE sets CN (Congestion Notification) equal to one for that DXI frame; otherwise, the DCE sets CN equal to zero. The DTE always sets the CN to zero.

CLP   The DCE copies the CLP bit sent from the DTE into the ATM cell header CLP bit. The CLP bit from the DCE to the DTE is always set to zero.

and 6 VCI bits leads to the 1023 VC limitation of these two modes. The DXI also provides for two additional fields within the header; a **Congestion Notification (CN)** and a **Cell Loss Priority (CLP)**. The CN is set in the direction of the DTE if the PTI=01 in the last ATM cell composing the DXI frame, while the CLP is copied in the direction of the ATM network from the CLP set by the DTE.

An LMI defined between the DTE and the DCE provides for the exchange of DXI-, AAL-, and UNI-specific information. Though the LMI relies on SNMP, objects defined are confined to the LMI alone via the DXI LMI MIB. Within a live network, an ATM switch could send an LMI request to the DTE via the DCE. The ATM-DXI supports ATM-DSU-based SNMP in addition to the LMI. The LMI operates over VPI/VCI 0/16 and provides access to MIB-II and RFC 1695 (Ahmed and Tesink,

1994) objects. The ATM-DSU alternative would be to access ATM and physical layer statistics directly from the DSU's agent.

Some early ATM deployments were based on routers connected to ATM-DSUs over the SMDS-DXI. These DSUs were in effect modified SMDS-DSUs due to similarities in the SMDS SNI 802.6 cell structure and the ATM cell. Thus, minimal modifications were required. Due to the use of the SMDS-DXI, connectivity to the ATM network was via AAL3/4. But instead of providing SMDS service across ATM via a CLS, these networks made use of AAL3/4 PVCs. Only later did AAL5-capable DSUs appear.

FUNI

The Frame UNI (FUNI) was developed to provide an efficient means of transporting data traffic into an ATM network at speeds up to and including DS1/E1 where the cell overhead may be unacceptable. Consider the typical 10% cell overhead in contrast to the 1% frame overhead. For a high-speed link, this is acceptable, but at speeds below T1/E1, and especially at 56/64 Kbps, it is not desirable. The basic FUNI reference model is shown in Figure 4.35, where mapping between the frame-based interface and ATM cells takes place at an FUNI interface performing the conversion. Though the FUNI precludes the transport of CBR traffic (for example, PABX), in many cases a service multiplexer will be deployed between the customer and the service provider. This multiplexer will combine FUNI traffic with other data and voice traffic, breaking it out again at the central office for distribution to respective ATM and N-ISDN switching systems. Under both DS1 and E1, the FUNI is carried over a payload of $N\times64$ Kbps forming a concatenated payload. E1 operation may use either structured (required), or unstructured

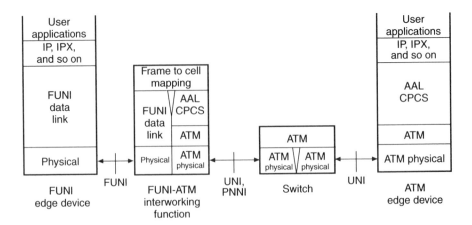

Figure 4.35 Frame UNI.

(optional) framing modes. Finally, the FUNI relies on the DS1/E1 MIB for management, and actually supports the transport of OAM cells.

Goals of the FUNI are to provide low-speed ATM access, along with supporting interoperability with ATM signaling, traffic management, and OAM functions. The specification (see ATM Forum, 1995m), completed in mid-1995, describes the interworking unit which converts FUNI frames into ATM cells, and includes two modes of operation, as shown in Table 4.14.

Note that both the maximum number of VCCs and the maximum SDU of the FUNI is different to those of the **ATM-DXI (ADXI)**, which are 1023 and 9232 respectively. Since the FUNI supports signaling, the lower half of the VCI range (0–31) and VPI = 0 are reserved. In reality, the FUNI could therefore support $15*32$ VCCs, or 480 VCCs, in contrast to the DXI's 1023, although most implementations will support 256. Mode 1a is required, while mode 1b is optional. A FUNI frame will consist of a two-byte header, a two-byte FCS, and two flag bytes. These are identical to the structure outlined for the DXI by replacing the DXI header and trailer with the FUNI equivalents and noting that the maximum SDU is normally 4096 octets. Within the FUNI header, the DXI DFA is known as the **Frame Address (FA)**, although the bitwise mapping within each octet is identical. The 1% overhead outlined above is based on a frame of 1024 bytes or greater. Most importantly, and in contrast to the DXI, the FUNI frames are converted to ATM UNI cells at the IWU in such a way as to preserve signaling, traffic management, and network management (to include an ILMI). We show this interworking function in Figure 4.35. Frame headers also include congestion notification and CLP flags. FUNI signaling makes use of the same protocol as the ATM-UNI, allowing code in end-systems to be re-used. Finally, the FUNI is backward compatible with the DXI, allowing end- systems only capable of supporting the DXI to connect to switch FUNI interfaces (Reeves, 1995).

Table 4.14 FUNI modes of operation.

Mode	Maximum VPs	Maximum VCs	AAL(s)	Maximum SDU	FCS
1a	15	256 (Note 1)	5	4096 (Note 2)	16 bit (32 bit optional)
1b	15	256 (Note 1)	3/4, 5	4096 (Note 2)	16 bit (32 bit optional)

Note 1 May support greater than 256 connections
Note 2 Maximum of 64K optional

Analysis

Frame-based interfaces provide an ideal way to access an ATM network where a native UNI is infeasible due to equipment or undesirable due to cost and/or data rates. The first frame interface was the ATM-DXI, used to interconnect non-ATM capable routers and end-systems with early ATM service offerings. This has been superseded by the FUNI, providing QoS and signaling support. Though the FUNI has only been recently standardized, we expect it to be supported by the majority of end-systems and switches. It will be the preferred method of access for ATM at rates below DS1/E1 when users require direct connection to an ATM service. Other methods of connection at these bandwidths include Frame Relay, SMDS (via the DXI), and ISDN.

4.1.10 Integrated PNNI (I-PNNI)

The I-PNNI, as proposed to the ATM Forum, is an attempt to solve the duplication of effort problem; the need for complete routing at both the ATM and internetworking layers. Thus, it is orthogonal to the overlay versus peer model debate, and in fact may be implemented as part of either. If part of the overlay model, Layer 3 reachability information would be carried transparently through the ATM network by the routing protocol; if implemented in conjunction with the peer model, Layer 3 addresses for each network protocol would be mapped into NSAP addresses. A basic premis of the I-PNNI is ubiquity; it was originally proposed to run on all switches, hosts, and routers (as opposed to only those connected to ATM). Since many users have only recently deployed OSPF and E-IGRP, this would have resulted in a great deal of potential disruption. The present proposal backs off from this somewhat and only proposes that the I-PNNI be implemented on those systems connected to an ATM network. Although this could result in a better use of resources (CPU, bandwidth) within the network, in effect, systems will still run two sets of routing (one for each layer) so this may not turn out to be so much of an advantage. The I-PNNI would also play an integral part in the exchange of Layer 3 reachability information under the peer model, although problems identified with this proposal are some of the same as those identified under the peer model.

Some problems in implementing the I-PNNI include address summarization, which may be poor if the multiprotocol ATM address space is not carefully planned. Also, the ATM addressing hierarchy and that of the Layer 3 protocol(s) need to closely align if efficient summarization is to be possible. Control would also need to be included to preclude the use of non-ATM links for calls requiring an ATM QoS, though this is solved both within the PNNI and through the use of ATM layer access lists. Finally, if implemented in conjunction with the overlay model, we must still implement a routing optimization function (for example, NHRP).

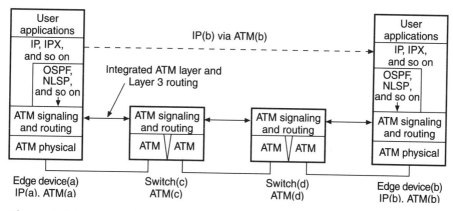

Figure 4.36 Integrated PNNI. Source: Cisco Systems.

Whether the I-PNNI solves some of the potential routing problems identified with NHRP is unknown. In any case, despite the problems identified with the I-PNNI, we expect so see some implementations capable of solving the basic goal, that of providing integrated routing, within the next year or so once implementation experience from both the PNNI and ROLC is available. Extending the I-PNNI concept into the non-ATM domain, the PNNI could be use for routing across other media types as well. This is known as **integrated routing**, and must take into account the interaction of PNNI and existing routing protocols as well as its operation across broadcast media. A last interesting point about the I-PNNI is that it requires all ATM edge devices to implement full router functionality, actually a step back from the multilayer forwarders proposed within MPOA.

In Figure 4.36, we show the mapping from a Layer 3 routing protocol into the PNNI at the boundary of the ATM network. This requires route redistribution from the non-ATM routing protocol (for example, OSPF, Integrated IS-IS, E-IGRP) into the PNNI unless a modified form of the PNNI is implemented across the non-ATM network. As we have based this figure on the overlay model, the I-PNNI carries the Layer 3 protocol address unmodified.

4.1.11 Peer model for data and the integrated network

Though present efforts focus on the Classical model, LANE, and MPOA, a totally different way of looking at the relationship between ATM and network layer protocols has received serious consideration. End-to-end data transmission is normally the responsibility of the network layer; Layer 3. For example, IP provides connectivity over any physical media:

Ethernet, FDDI, and even wireless. This is the commonly accepted view of internetworking: a clean division between the network layer and the underlying networking technology, often referred to as the link layer (though as was shown earlier, this analogy runs into some difficulty when we consider ATM). Questioning this assumption is ATM, one of the few lower-layer technologies capable of supporting end-to-end services in addressing and routing. This has led some to propose ATM as a 'peer' to existing network layer technologies in much the same way that earlier X.25 implementations sometimes peered with IP (though never widely implemented).

Under this scenario, IP or any other Layer 3 protocol would terminate at the ATM boundary, replaced by ATM routing and addressing. This is shown in the right side of Figure 4.37, where IP maps to ATM addressing within the end-system, possibly based on an algorithmic scheme. At the last switch in the connection capable of peering, the IP address structure would once again be recreated. The network would provide this interworking and mapping function, capable of converting addressing, routing, and QoS parameters. Under the peer model, some end-stations would be true ATM clients without an intervening network layer (although ATM would be considered the network layer in this context). The ultimate extension of this peering, eliminates the traditional network layer protocol in its entirety, allowing applications to map directly into ATM. However, this architecture does not recognize the current realities of internetworking, including both the heterogeneity of existing networks and the current generation of applications, along with the potential complexity of supporting this peering in intermediate systems. For this reason, it has been laid aside for the foreseeable future within both the ATM Forum (since MPOA is based on the overlay model) and the IETF, although active work continues within the research community.

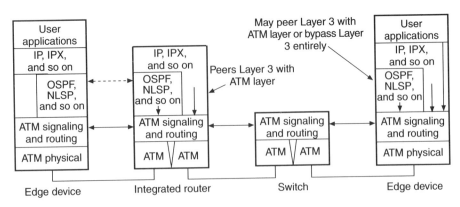

Figure 4.37 Peer model. Source: Cisco Systems.

One example of a peer model implementation is the xbind project (see xbind). In fact, this project goes beyond simple data models by looking at ATM signaling in general, with a goal of developing interoperable signaling software. Thus, a vendor could offer platform-independent signaling code which would spur the development of new services. The project description draws an analogy to PCs, where software and hardware are uncoupled, resulting in no end to new applications. A precedent for this architecture lies within distributed systems, and xbind draws on the same platform (binding architecture), CORBA, for its work. As of the beginning of 1996, xbind had been implemented on at least two ATM switches and a number of operating systems.

Though the peer model seems simple to implement and capable of solving problems identified with the Classical model and ROLC, upon closer examination some shortcomings are apparent. The model implies that a host will require an ATM address for each Layer 3 protocol peered in addition to an original ATM address. This may result in both manageability problems and the defeat of effective address summarization. Because of these independent addresses, protocol multiplexing as in RFC 1483 is not possible, affecting manageability and costs if charged on a per-VC basis. Next, all systems participating in the peer environment, to include ATM switches at the edge of the network, must understand Layer 3 addresses unless all hosts implement the mapping. This requirement in effect requires these systems to implement router functionality, where they would be required to support address tables incorporating both ATM NSAP addresses as well as other network layer addressing schemes. When integrated into a topology incorporating both ATM and non-ATM domains, scalability comes into question. The peer model is often proposed in conjunction with IPv6 on hosts, where IPv6's flow ID could be mapped to a VCC's QoS and the 16-octet address would be embedded within the ATM NSAP format address. Due to these similarities, when and if IPv6 is widely deployed, the peer model will once again receive serious consideration.

For completeness, we look at two proposals for peering ATM with the network layer. In 1992, one vendor drew a distinction between ATM as an end-to-end network layer technology and existing link layer technologies such as Ethernet. These shared media networks require source and destination addresses for each data frame, while ATM, based on point-to-point connections, does not. This is analogous to the X.121 address used by X.25 applications before the addition of IP and the E.164 addresses used within the public network. Next, the ATM address is hierarchical and thus is capable of being used for routing. This is another differentiating factor between an ATM E.164 or NSAP address and the NIC MAC address used in LAN environments. The real problem arises with the conversion from existing end-system protocol addresses, IP and AppleTalk for example, to E.164 or NSAP addresses. This same concern relegated X.121 addressing to a pseudo-link layer.

A suggestion was to include multiprotocol capability in each ATM switch, to include topology discovery and connection establishment. In reality, the proposal suggested the use of the existing network layer addresses for routing within the ATM network, with no new ATM layer address (E.164 or NSAP) implemented. This is almost a reversal of what eventually came to pass, and might have been very interesting. A second element of this proposal was the creation of a **multi-protocol packet overlay**, capable of connectionless service over ATM. Note that this is very similar to SMDS. In the case of IP, an IP routing entity would be included within each ATM switch. End-systems wishing to send an IP datagram would forward this on a dedicated VC to the IP overlay process, which would then forward the cells to an IP router. The datagram would then be forwarded over a VC to its next hop. We can probably draw analogies between this and the conventional model and, in fact, the architecture is not altogether different to what we would expect in an integrated ATM switch/router. The proposal stated that efficiency would be gained by re-using the same mechanism for the overlay routing as is used for connection setup. Transport of multiple address types across the public network was provided for via address translation functions at the public-to-private boundary. Two questions were addressed: carrying the protocol addresses across the public network and interoperation with 'native' E.164 devices. For protocol addresses, information would be transported within the sub-address field of the call setup message.

Finally, the proposal dealt with problems inherent with the 48-bit ATM address under discussion at the time, drawing an analogy between LANs and internetworks. The goal was to facilitate ATM internetworks and not only ATM LANs. Thus, the 48-bit address space would be totally inadequate. Still, the 48-bit address is very useful in differentiating hosts within one addressing domain, and in fact was the original Xerox definition of the address in its use as a station ID and not as a MAC address. This address is required in that it forms a part of some protocol (OSI, XNS) network layer addresses while at the same time being used as a starting point in dynamic host configuration.

Switch-to-switch interfaces would support protocols for routing and topology discovery based on industry standards (OSPF, IS-IS). Since these protocols do not support the level of granularity required for scalability, the proposal predicted that multiple small switches would be connected via some proprietary mechanism, with only the aggregate under the control of an open routing protocol. In a final analysis, cost savings were presented as the justification for the elimination of an additional addressing structure: cost savings during both implementation and administration. In addition, the connectionless architecture suggested would more closely follow that of existing internetworks. The use of a single routing protocol and paradigm for end-to-end connectivity was inferred to be able to support better selection and control of QoS parameters among multiple, ATM and non-ATM technologies (Lyon *et al*, 1992).

A second, related proposal is known as the **Integrated Network (IN)** (Perkins and Liaw, 1994), which attempts to eliminate the duplication of functionality and the perceived suboptimal use of resources by routing at both the IP and ATM layers. In this contribution, the authors contrast the capabilities of ATM with X.25 and Frame Relay, addressing the question as to why these two technologies do not successfully peer with the internetwork layer. One important reason lies in differences in transmission speed, in that a transparent end-to-end link including LAN and WAN segments should support LAN applications. Both X.25 and, to a lesser extent, Frame Relay, are incapable of this support, in contrast to ATM. Thus, ATM is the first technology capable of successfully peering with network layer protocols in both the LAN and WAN.

An IN will support hosts using traditional network layer protocols along with those running applications directly over ATM. At the boundary between these two domains, an **integrated router** (one possible name) will convert ATM encapsulations and signaling to Internet protocols and vice versa, while algorithmically mapping IP addresses to ATM addresses. The peering of routers and ATM switches in this environment is in contrast to the routing and address resolution mechanisms outlined in Braden *et al* (1994). These mechanisms (hop-by-hop redirect, extended routing, extended proxy ARP, and routing query) all have drawbacks in that they do not use ATM routing policy information. The need for external servers to emulate these functions within the various ATM data models is cited as a major impact on network management and as additional sources of network failure.

Building upon both the Integrated Services Internet and ATM QoS, the architecture supports both unicast and multicast data delivery, end-to-end QoS, and separation of individual user flows. However, note the absence of a defined transport layer on the ATM side. This function, which provides error-free or ordered delivery, must somehow be emulated by the ATM end-systems. If we were to use TCP over ATM, an API in the end-system would translate TCP's requirements into ATM. Crowcroft (1995) speculates as to the structure and capabilities of this new ATM transport, an ATCP. First, we evaluate what ATM provides and may therefore be eliminated from the transport header. ATM multiplexes, so port numbers are no longer required. If the AAL provides a checksum, this may also be eliminated. Q.2931 signaling provides the handshake, so we are left with a sequence and ack number. In total, the transport header is compressed to 12 bytes. With an MTU of 48 bytes, this could be further compressed since the sequence number and ack would just number the individual cell. All of this of course assumes end-to-end ATM, with interworking at protocol converters (a more difficult task than standard routing).

Stated advantages of the IN model include coherent routing across technologies, greater security, ease of management, elimination of external address servers, and better resource utilization due to the use of a single routing protocol. Additional design goals of INs include the implementation of high-speed filtering mechanisms, better support of end-to-end QoS due to integration of resource and topology data, and the re-use of existing protocols. End-system complexity is reduced by the need for only one end-system address, either ATM or the network protocol address.

Looking once again at Figure 4.37, a host may connect to an integrated router which is capable of mapping the network layer protocol into ATM. These integrated routers interconnecting the two domains will use the PNNI on the ATM side and a Layer 3 routing protocol (OSPF, IS-IS, E-IGRP, and so on) on the user side, thus supporting both the PNNI and the UNI. The ATM-connected system at the right of the figure will use Q.2931 signaling for connection setup, which is then translated to Internet resource reservation commands (for instance, RSVP) by the integrated router.

Note that the implementation of INs within ATM preclude end-to-end transparency at the service layer within existing network models. For example, interworking between IN and LANE, Classical IP over ATM, non-IN-capable ATM switches, and even public ATM networks will in most cases require the use of routers since we must insert the network layer protocol at some point in the network. Note that this may result in a less than optimal segmentation of a physical ATM infrastructure. A second alternative would be to deploy IP to ATM protocol converters, though these devices in the past have had less than stellar performance. Consider what to do with the TCP checksum which includes the IP pseudo header. When interworking with NHRP domains, an integrated NHRP server may be implemented at the domain boundary, capable of responding with either an IP address or an IN NSAP format address. In this case, a connection may be opened to an IN destination. In contrast, Classical ATMARP-based subnets will require routers for interconnectivity. Finally, although some of the IN mechanisms have been worked out in some detail for IP, support for other Layer 3 protocols (IPX, AT, CLNP, and so on) is not fully defined. Therefore, multiprotocol hosts must implement the LLC/SNAP or VC mux encapsulations defined in RFC 1483.

4.1.12 Application QoS and resource reservation

Probably one of the least understood and most complex areas of data networking across ATM is the end-to-end support of application QoS requirements. This means different things to different people, and includes such topics as application resource reservation, 'native' ATM applications without an intervening internetwork protocol, and the mapping of IPv6 into ATM. In this section, we first look at the concept of resource reservation and QoS in general, including a discussion of the Integrated Services Internet. This leads us into an analysis of the various ways for end-systems to request resources from the network, with a focus on the **Resource ReSerVation Protocol (RSVP)**. Implementing the RSVP will require end-system networking stacks which are 'resource-aware.' Finally, we touch on IPv6 and its potential future impact on QoS guarantees. One area which we look at only briefly includes end-systems which do not implement a traditional networking layer, instead relying on the application to signal ATM QoS directly. This is related to the peer model, introduced earlier. Though a small proportion of end-systems may implement such functionality, we do not believe that they will form the majority anytime soon. Thus, we focus on the much larger internetworking community. Consider these ATM-only end-systems to be a subset of the larger problem, using an API to map application QoS requests into ATM signaling instead of into the networking layer.

Although the Classical IP and LANE models enable early implementation of ATM, they do not provide for automatic mapping between higher applications and the QoS capabilities of the ATM network. For the most part, ATM is still 'hidden' from applications running over both of these models, precluding the use of many of ATM's QoS capabilities. As an example, a given conferencing application requiring a set bandwidth and latency on a switched Ethernet segment, or even when directly connected to an ATM LAN, should be capable of establishing a VCC with these QoS characteristics across the ATM network. Ways by which this may be accomplished include the mapping of TCP ports directly into ATM VCCs through the use of resource-aware protocol stacks. A short-term fix whereby network administrators must manually configure applications on a per-port basis to individual ATM VCCs is not universally supported by the NIC vendors. To see just how we may support QoS, it may be useful to step back from ATM for a moment and discuss the concept of resource reservation and flow control over any arbitrary medium. With the understanding of resource reservation and the various protocols allowing this to take place we can better appreciate how to provide end-to-end QoS across both ATM and non-ATM segments of an internetwork.

Resource reservation and flow control rely on end-systems which are capable of requesting a QoS from the network. Until recently, due to lack of support within host stacks and routers or LAN switches, this was not the case. As real-time applications have become more common across both local- and wide-area networks, the Internet architecture has evolved to be able to support integrated services. Requirements of this new architecture include the support of greater bandwidth, provided by ATM and LAN switching, efficient multicasting over both ATM and non-ATM, and the support for both real- and non-real-time applications. A common element involves host internetworking stacks capable of mapping application QoS requirements into network resource requests. Branden *et al* (1994) provide a good description of these requirements.

The Integrated Services (IS) Internet

As applications evolved, a fundamental weakness in the existing Internet architecture had become apparent: a lack of proper support for real-time exchanges due to variable queuing delays and congestion losses caused by best-effort data delivery. The traditional service provided by the Internet (and router-based enterprise internetworks in general) may be generalized as **Best Effort (BE)**, offering a single class of point-to-point traffic. For conferencing and visualization to operate properly, this infrastructure must support real-time QoS with control over end-to-end delay. In addition, support for multicasting should be an inherent part of this new service model, as well as the ability to assign percentages of a physical link's bandwidth to different traffic classes. This new model is known as the **Integrated Services (IS) Internet**, and provides for different QoSs under a common infrastructure and using a unified protocol stack. The IS Internet supports **Real-Time (RT)** service in addition to the traditional BE service. Most importantly, it guarantees fair sharing of links among users.

In defining a new model, we make two basic assumptions. The first is that bandwidth must be managed via resource reservation and admission control. This is in contrast to some views concluding that bandwidth in the future will be infinite, that a simple prioritization scheme will suffice, or that applications will always adapt to network quality. Two rebuttals to these views are that bandwidth will not be infinite everywhere, and even if videoconferencing applications adapt to end-to-end delays on the order of seconds, for example, they will be all but useless for real-time interaction. Thus, we define **flows**, whereby sessions are assigned QoSs based on requests and network capabilities. This implies the implementation of flow mechanisms at not only the end-systems but also on intermediate systems.

The new service model supports different classes of application by providing a commitment as to the maximum and minimum packet delay across a network. Note the absence of a guarantee on bandwidth. If the network meets an application's latency and delay variation guarantees, we assume that it is providing guarantees at any bandwidth the application requires. This view results from the Internet model, where bandwidth is less of a factor in charging than on public ATM networks, for example (thus the emphasis on bandwidth within ATM). Traffic classes include real-time and elastic applications as shown in Figure 4.38. Real-time applications are based on packetization of a source signal, transmission of this signal across the network, and then depacketization at

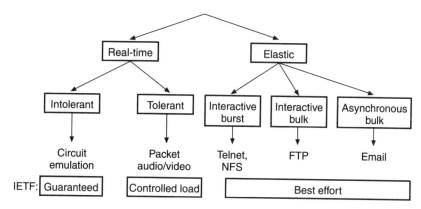

Figure 4.38 Application taxonomy.

the distant end. The delay across the network influences the 'playback point,' and, taking buffering into account, any data arriving before this playback point may be used to reconstruct the original signal, while any data after this point will be useless. These real-time applications should have some knowledge of expected network delay, either from a service contract or by observing actual packet delay across the network.

We may further characterize applications by latency and fidelity. For example, two-way communication is sensitive to latency, while unidirectional traffic is not. Fidelity is a little harder to characterize, as most applications will tolerate some data loss. The two factors are interrelated, in that the latency, determined by delay, may result in packets arriving outside of the playback interval described above. Thus, fidelity will suffer. If an application can tolerate this loss, it may be considered adaptive, and may use 'controlled load' or 'controlled delay' service. This service supplies a generally reliable bound on packet delay. Where applications are intolerant to loss in fidelity, the service must place an upper bound on the maximum delay for each packet. This service is called 'guaranteed service.' A justification for these two service classes in contrast to a single guaranteed class is that, in the former case, network utilization may be increased resulting in a lower service cost. We describe the traffic control necessary for the support of these services below.

Elastic applications will wait for incoming data and then use it immediately without buffering. As opposed to the maximum delay driving real-time applications, the performance of this class will be a function of the average delay. Included in elastic applications are several categories, including interactive burst (Telnet, NFS), interactive bulk transfer (FTP), and asynchronous bulk transfer (E-mail). The service model as applied to these applications will provide for best effort, and may include several classes of delay based on the categories described above.

Though support for real-time applications, primarily voice and video, is an important goal of ATM, interestingly enough, many applications which people consider to be real-time are just the opposite (Villamizar, 1994). For example, a supercomputer simulation may either take much longer than real-time to complete (climate simulations, genetic modeling) or may generate results faster than real-time. In both cases, the resulting data set is downloaded and rendered locally. The researcher in this case is free to examine the result at leisure.

A contribution to the ATM Forum (Kwok, 1995), though focusing on broadband residential services, provides a good analysis of application classes and includes some interesting observations. We speak of real-time and non-real-time applications but, as outlined above, a second side of the equation is the delivery requirement; whether the information content is time-based or not. For example, applications such as video-conferencing and image browsing may be considered real-time applications, although the latter uses non-time-based information. Image browsing is still real-time, however, since a maximum response time is required. In contrast, the transmission of video clips and E-mail are examples of non-real-time applications, though the former contains time-based information. The burden of preserving this time base is at the destination.

Integrated service specifications include Guaranteed Delay, Guaranteed Load, Predictive and Controlled Load. The first guarantees bounds on the maximum end-to-end packet delay by reserving a rate at each node. Controlled Delay service allows applications to request three service levels, all better than best effort but not guaranteed. Within this class, a node will only make an estimate as to the delay. Predictive Service provides a maximum bound on delay, but differs from Guaranteed in that the link is not loss-free. The last class, Controlled Load, allows an application to recieve a QoS approximately equal to that which it would receive across an uncongested network.

Within intermediate systems, the support of different QoSs for real-time applications, termed 'traffic control,' is implemented by three mechanisms – a packet scheduler, a classifier, and admission control. The packet scheduler, also implemented on end-systems, determines which packets will be transferred to the physical medium and in what order. It should be implemented in such a way as to allocate a proportion of the bandwidth to each flow (**Weighted Fair Queuing**, or **WFQ**) as opposed to strict ordering by priority. On ATM or other media capable of bandwidth allocation, this scheduler will have knowledge of the VCCs. An extension to the scheduler is the estimator as described by Jacobson. This algorithm may be used to develop traffic profiles, such as average and peak bandwidth requirements, as well as burstiness by measuring the outgoing packet stream. Note that this algorithm may have important implications in determining what type of ATM SVCs should be established. Any mechanism used to determine which packets should be discarded under buffer congestion should also coordinate with the scheduling function.

The classifier maps incoming packets into a given class for equal treatment by the packet scheduler. For example, a class may contain all video flows or may correspond to a single session. Two options exist for the operation of this classifier. The first, relying on the establishment of IP VCs, is equivalent to the architecture of ATM. An approach more in keeping with the connectionless aspect of existing IP would rely on fields within the packet header for classification. For example, a video stream with a well-known UDP port will be treated differently to a Telnet TCP session. An option under this approach would be to include a 'flow-id' as part of the header which could be cached by intermediate systems resulting in better performance.

Finally, admission control determines whether or not a new flow may be established without affecting existing sessions. This mechanism is implemented at each node; thus, a request for a new flow may be accepted or rejected at any point along the path. Two approaches based on calculating past requests or measuring actual usage by existing packet flows exist (Jamin *et al*, 1992). This latter technique, though subject to greater overload, may provide better link utilization.

Between systems, some mechanism should be put in place to provide for the sharing of aggregate bandwidth among different entities. Various models govern this, including sharing by organizations, by protocols, and by services. In the first case, the parties involved may wish to guarantee a portion of the bandwidth to each under normal load, while allowing for use of idle bandwidth by any. Where multiple protocols share a link, each may be provided with a reserved bandwidth, while any spare capacity is available to all. Service sharing, based on TCP ports for example, is accomplished in the same way. The admission control mechanism as described above in conjunction with a WFQ algorithm will support this sharing.

Another element of support for real-time traffic is the ability to mark some packets as eligible for discard under network congestion. This may be extended by defining a class of packets even more subject to discard but on the other hand not subject to admission control. Both of these considerations will affect network capacity planning and thus service cost.

When IS BE service is compared with ATM ABR, some differences are obvious. Fundamentally, ATM starts with CBR capability, with other services such as ABR based on relaxing ATM's BW and timing guarantees. In contrast, the Internet starts with BE and builds upon this to provide for constrained delay and guarantees on throughput. ATM ABR provides for a MCR and multiple CLPs. These make up for its single service level in comparison to the three available under IS-BE. In both cases, no definitive guarantees are made on QoS, and both provide for guaranteed fairness across a link, robustness, and stability. In summary, the limitations of IS-BE are more than made up for by its media independence.

Although it may seem easy to predict an application's resource requirements, mapping this to an operational network is much more difficult. Consider high-speed LANs connected via an ATM connection. If many users share this single connection, each reserving a QoS for an application, bandwidth sharing may be sub-optimal. The problem is compounded by ATM-attached systems which may be requesting resources from servers which may or may not be connected to ATM. In this case, what parameters should this first system use in its signaling request? We describe a solution in the next section.

Resource ReSerVation Protocol (RSVP)

Although the concept of the IS Internet holds a great deal of promise, how do we translate this into reality? How do we actually guarantee to an application an end-to-end QoS? This is the function of the **Resource ReSerVation Protocol (RSVP)** (see Zhang et al, 1993a and 1993b), a resource reservation setup protocol which has progressed from being relatively unknown to an area of major discussion, over the past year. In looking at RSVP, we first review some general concepts regarding QoS reservations, then look at RSVP's operation in detail, and finally map RSVP into ATM in support of end-to-end QoS guarantees. This last task, taking place at the periphery of the ATM network, is an area of great interest within both the IETF and the ATM Forum, both of which have commenced work on the integration issue. Without this piece of the puzzle, ATM will be unable to fulfill its promise as an integral part of future QoS-driven internetworks.

RSVP defines host and network behavior in providing QoS guarantees. At a host, an application will specify a desired **flowspec**, while the types of packets to receive these resources are determined via a filter specification, or **filter spec**. The flowspec, consisting of the application's QoS requirements including bandwidth and delay, is used by the router's admission control and packet scheduling mechanisms, while the filter specification determines to which packets this flowspec will apply. The combined flow descriptor, consisting of the flowspec and filter spec, form the RSVP reservation.

The protocol operates in simplex mode, allowing separate reservations to be established in both directions. Note that this maps quite well into ATM, where we may assign a separate QoS to each direction of a VCC. A reason for unidirectional flows is the profile of many QoS-driven applications such as video or data distribution. RSVP builds on IP, IP routing protocols, and multicast routing (PIM, for example), but does not in itself transport any data; it control the transmission of data by reserving bandwidth and advising the network as to queue management and discard policy. Current platform and application support for RSVP include Intel, SGI, Sun, IBM, Starlight, NetManage, InSoft, and Precept, with many more expected to follow.

In an RSVP-enabled network, sources will characterize their flows by generating PATH (TSPEC) messages, transmitted downstream (source to receivers) along the data packet route as determined by the unicast or multicast routing protocol. These messages, containing a description of the data stream, cause path states to be established in the downstream nodes. A receiver, taking note of these PATH messages belonging to a given flow, will now generate an RESV (RSPEC) message. These are sent hop-by-hop upstream to the unicast address of the previous RSVP hop, and follow the reverse of the downstream data packet route. The RESV message is used by the sender to set first hop traffic parameters.

A node, upon receiving a reservation request, will make a reservation based on the flowspec and filterspec if resources are available and if the request does not conflict with policy. If admission control succeeds, the node will use the flowspec to set up the packet schedules for the desired QoS and the filter spec to set up the packet classifier. It now forwards the request upstream based on the 'scope' of the request. Note that the forwarded request may be different than that which was received. Consider a node aggregating flows from different downstream branches. In this case, the node will forward the request with the maximum flowspec upstream. It propagates up the tree to a point where an existing reservation request is equal or greater than that being requested. These resources reservations are 'soft-state', meaning that no end-to-end paths are maintained by the routers. This approach has advantages in that refresh messages will automatically install a new state along a new route after a topology change. Contrast this to 'hard-state' where we must rebuild the reservation at each node after a change within the network. One element of RSVP not initially implemented is the AdSpec, used in guaranteeing delay across the network. Vendors are still determining the best way to support this parameter.

A separate issue is the current lack of QoS-based routing within the datagram Internet. As we scale RSVP, it will be useful to have a network-wide awareness of bandwidth and delay capabilities as opposed to learning this information on a node-by-node basis. Two alternatives include implementing extensions to traditional IP routing protocols such as OSPF or alternatively, deployment of the I-PNNI. Finally, current resource reservation efforts focus on IP, though the concepts contained within RSVP are extensible to other network layer protocols as well, and will find use within MPOA.

With an understanding of RSVP, we can now approach the most interesting questions of all: how best to integrate this with ATM given the differences in the two networking environments. An outline of some of the issues with this integration and a proposal for a logical approach to solving them is given in Borden (Borden, 1996). Some of the major issues include the criteria for establishing a VC across the ATM network, mapping of IntServ models to ATM and receiving feedback as to the mapping, and how to most effectively merge the connectionless world of IP with the connection-oriented ATM.

If we look more closely at mapping RSVP control and data flows into ATM, we may divide the problem into four areas: reservation setup for both unicast and multicast flows under UNI 3.x and under Sig 4.0. For unicast traffic, RSVP Path messages crossing an ATM network in the downstream direction follow the routed path. If the network consists of multiple LISs, the message breaks out of ATM at the routers connecting each LIS. Path messages flowing upstream follow the same procedure. Remember that the RSVP control message flow across best-effort VCs, while the actual data packets are associated with a given QoS. Under UNI 3.x, we may establish these QoS VCCs with the CBR, VBR, and UBR service categories. Release 4.0 also includes finer granularity of QoS by allowing one to choose individual traffic parameters along with introducing the ABR and rt-VBR traffic classes.

Multicast flows are a bit more difficult to map due to differences between RSVP and ATM as well as differences between versions of the UNI. The UNI 3.x does support multipoint signaling, whereby we may map IP multicasting and RSVP (IGMP JOIN/LEAVE and RSVP RESV/RESV TEAR) to ATM's add and drop party functions. As mentioned earlier, a single pt-mpt connection supports a single QoS. Once destination addresses for multicast group members have been resolved, via the MARS for example, RSVP Path messages travel along the best effort pt-mpt connection to all group members. Resv messages follow the reverse path, with each router upstream (once again assuming multiple LISs) opening a pt-mpt connection with the required QoS. We now extend this architecture to provide for shortcut paths. Under the UNI 3.x, Resv messages in the upstream direction will carry sufficient information for the ingress router to open a direct connection across the multiple LISs. Note that under this scheme, Path messages will continue to flow over the routed path but Resv messages are now suppressed. Once the network migrates to Sig 4.0, a user may initiate a join to an existing multipoint connection via the LIJ facility. Path messages are now modified to include a 'global connection identifier', used to identify a unique pt-mpt connection. A router at the egress of the ATM network will therefore have sufficient information for generating a LIJ based on receipt of an Resv message flowing in the upstream direction. This Resv message may now be forwarded along the routed upstream path for use by routers further upstream from the ingress router (Birman95). A concern when interworking RSVP with both UNI versions across pt-mpt connections are the reverse direction messages which will converge on the root of the multipoint tree.

Two proposals to optimize these data flows include modifying

RSVP to establish the shortcut or relying on NHRP for address resolution. Under the first method, either the ingress (closest to the upstream sender) or egress (closest to the downstream receiver) router to the ATM network may take responsibility for setting up the optimized path. In the nearer term, we may optimize the flow of data across multiple LISs by establishing shortcut paths in both directions through the use of NHRP. A possible solution for a PIM environment is outlined in Rekhter (Rekhter, 1996). Another way in which RSVP could scale better across ATM would be to map multiple RSVP flows to a single VCC capable of supporting the aggregate QoS or using VPs to manage multiple flows. Neither of these changes require fundamental changes to either RSVP or ATM, and ultimately, a deciding factor in which methods to deploy will be their compatibility with multicasting and with Sig 4.0.

We now look at one way of actually mapping the Tspec and Rspec into ATM by applying a few general rules. If the Tspec peak rate is equal to approximately the token generation rate, then we should use CBR service. If not, we may use VBR, UBR, or ABR depending upon the requirements of the receiver. RSVP best-effort service may be mapped into ATM taking advantage of the CLP and EPD. One example of mapping, where r is the token generation rate, **b** the bucket depth, and **P** the minimum of the incoming link and the actual peak rate of the flow, is as follows: SCR-r/48, MBS=b/48, and PCR=P/48. Note that this does not take into account segmentation overhead (Onvural, 1996). If this overhead is to be applied, we must modify the formulas as follows: SCR-ar, MBS=ab, and PCR=aP, where $a=(1+(p/48))/p$ and **p** is a minimum AAL5 packet size in bytes. This is a conservative estimate for small values of p, and is refined in (Birman, 1995).

Finally, we outline a deployable method of mapping RSVP's control mechanisms into ATM for the purpose of establishing end-to-end QoS. Consider a receiver (r) connected to router (R) at ATM address (b) wishing to receive a video multicast on a known multicast group (G). The source (s) connected to router (S) at ATM address (a) originates this transmission. The receiver will first join G associated with the application. This request is propagated by R to all other routers within the network, including S. At the same time, R sends a join to the MARS (G, b) or the root of the multicast tree will take note of the new receiver depending upon whether or not the MARS has been implemented. The source is transmitting RSVP PATH messages into the multicast group, with S possibly resolving (G,b) via the MARS. The PATH message contains the flowspec (TSPEC) which includes the session bandwidth requirement. All routers and destinations within the LIS participating in G receive this PATH message via a best-effort pt-mpt VCC. R now opens a pt-pt best-effort VCC to S, over which it will send an RSVP reservation message (RSPEC) originating at r outlining its desire to receive the video feed at the given bandwidth. S takes note of this, opens a QoS-based pt-mpt VCC across the ATM network in the direction of R, and propagates the request to s. Later, a second receiver (r') may join G via its local router (R'). R' propagates to join via multicast routing and will inform the MARS of the new receiver. S now uses this information to add r' to its pt-mpt VCC. (Berson, 1995). One important point is that RSVP PATH messages must follow the same IP path as data, implying that the ingress and egress points of the ATM network must be the same in both directions for both control and data.

RSVP versus Q.2931 signaling: disconnects and possible solutions

Looking at the procedure described in the previous paragraph, the flow of events required to establish a connection across an ATM network when initiated by RSVP may seem a bit convoluted. This is outlined in Table 4.15

Note a disconnect which may occur when a new user wishes to join an existing pt-mpt connection at a higher or lower QoS. In the absence of signaling which would allow a single pt-mpt VCC to support multiple QoSs, the new receiver would either be locked out of the application or would force the source to recreate the entire tree at a lower QoS. However, this new connection, combining the resources of the existing connection and the new request, may fail due to the allocation of resources for the existing connection. Both of these are sub-optimal solutions. One less than ideal workaround would be to establish multiple VCCs, each with a different QoS. This is one of the justifications for QoS modification, not yet available within the ATM

Table 4.15 Comparison of ATM, RSVP, and ST-II signaling models. Source: Delgrossi and Berger, 1995.

Category	ATM	RSVP	ST-II
Orientation	Sender-based (receiver-based in UNI 4.0 via LIJ)	Receiver-based	Sender-based (receiver-based optional)
State	Hard state (explicit delete)	Soft state (refresh/timeout)	Hard state (explicit disconnect)
QoS setup time	Concurrent with route establishment	Separate from route establishment	Concurrent with stream setup
QoS changes	Static QoS	Dynamic	Dynamic
Directionality	Bi-directional allocation for unicast Unidirectional for multicast	Unidirectional resource allocation	Unidirectional resource allocation
Heterogeneity	Uniform QoS to all receivers	Receiver heterogeneity	Receiver heterogeneity

Forum's UNI 3.1 or 4.0, though defined by the ITU in Q.2964.

However, recent debate focuses on whether this support is necessary or even desirable since receivers within a group may support approximately the same flowspecs.

How may we optimize the internetworking procedure as outlined in the previous section with a view to reducing latency and optimizing the flow of control information? One alternative in discussion would be to use a hierarchical **Resource Reservation Server (RRS)** analogous to the MARS used for multicasting. Senders and receivers (not limited to the Classical model, but including the peer and integrated models as well) would register their capabilities at this server, and new receivers would only need to query it to determine what flows were available. We could extend this server architecture to include ATM signaling, with capabilities beyond that of simple address/QoS registration and lookup. This would be one way of implementing the QoS-driven connection model described earlier. When we begin to scale the service to this extent, we will require some form of RSVP hierarchy due to the expected volume of RSVP requests in comparison to MARS transactions as well as RSVP's tree structure (aligned with IP multicasting). In fact, the functions and control VCCs of the MARS and this RSVP server could be combined into a single entity, using the combined packet format chosen for MARS, NHRP, and so on (Crowcroft, 1996a).

Ultimately, we must better integrate RSVP with Q.2931. This will take many forms, including possible support of QoS renegotiation (planned but not yet available), adding the concept of soft states to ATM signaling, and adding native mpt-mpt support, probably the most difficult to achieve. One element of this may be to allow end-systems to map RSVP requests directly into ATM signaling as opposed to using the various out-of-band mechanisms described above. This leads into a discussion of what is known as **lightweight ATM signaling**, where we attempt to optimize the ATM signaling protocol to more closely align with RSVP (or other resource reservation techniques). A basis for this is a feeling within some parts of the internetworking community that the Q.2931 signaling mechanisms are too complex and unnecessary for some traffic profiles. In addition, as outlined above, Q.2931 was not originally designed to adapt dynamically to changes in traffic flows (thus the work on ABR and QoS renegotiation). One suggestion would be to allow the presence or absence of traffic to invoke a connection without the use of a separate signaling channel. This infers a network with adequate resources for these types of call, however.

The Internet Streams Protocol: ST-II

Though we assume the use of protocols such as IP over both ATM and non-ATM networks to carry real-time data, there is some debate as to whether a more suitable network layer protocol may be deployed and as to which resource reservation style is most appropriate (Borden *et al*, 1995). If we look at goals once again, they include supporting both ATM and non-ATM-connected hosts as well as mapping the IS Internet service classes into the ATM classes. One alternative to IP and RSVP is the Internet Streams Protocol v2 (ST-II) (Topolcic, 1990, and Delgrossi and Berger, 1995). If we compare the ST-II signaling with ATM, it aligns closer with Q.2931 in its use of hard states, sender-initiated joins (which the hosts and routers must track), and the simultaneous setup of the stream with a given QoS. Looking again at Table 4.15, we compare ST-II's characteristics with those of RSVP.

Although ST-II may at first glance seem to have advantages over RSVP, this is only half of the implementation question. As opposed to RSVP, which operates over the traditional IP, ST-II in effect replaces IP with a new network layer known as IP Version 5 (though it does re-use the IP address format). Thus, end-systems must implement changes in both the network stacks as well as the API between the application and this stack. For interoperability, hosts would be required to implement two stacks: ST-II and IP. Also, ST-II suffers the same problems as RSVP with regards to dynamic QoS changes and the use of unidirectional flows. Thus, we require some of the same workarounds with ST-II as with RSVP. Whether ST-II will see wide support within the commercial sector (its current supporters mostly lie within the government) is unknown.

Other possibilities

As described earlier, a number of methods have been proposed for running applications or transport protocols directly over ATM. Approaches outlined in RFC-1932 to minimize the network layer include **TCP and UDP over Lightweight IP (TULIP)** and **TCP and UDP over Nonexistent IP (TUNIP)**. One reason for these proposals was the belief that the existing TCP/IP stack could not be made to scale effectively over networks operating at ATM's bandwidth. A reason why this approach is incorrect is that it is IP that is usually the subject of attempts at minimization. In reality, performance degradation is due to the operation of the transport protocol, in this case TCP. With the release of optimized TCP implementations (see Section 3.5.2), ATM data rates may be maintained across a local and wide area if supported by the network. With TCP performance no longer an issue, the negative aspects of these minimal stack proposals – that they only allow interoperation to other users implementing the approach as opposed to the greater Internet community – become apparent. Users of network layer protocols rely upon them to provide universal connectivity without the use of an application gateway. The proposals outlined above do not allow this.

Deploying QoS and the ATM Programming Interface (API)

Given the IS Internet as previously defined, the next question is how we allow applications running on ATM-connected systems to reserve resources across the ATM network. In effect, an RSVP-like mechanism operates internal to the host's networking stack, mapping application QoS requirements to ATM VCC parameters. Figure 4.39 shows this 'middleware' layer of a host supporting RSVP, mapped to ATM. To accomplish this mapping, the application will require a standard interface over which it may have access to these ATM parameters. This is the job of the **ATM Programming Interface (API)**. Since ATM offers support for different traffic types, this API is important in comparison to other technologies such as X.25 and Ethernet.

Within the ATM Forum, work has focused on defining the requirements for a native ATM interface as opposed to actually generating an API specification. Although this was not the original goal of the group, they have in effect left the final step to the industry bodies, including WinSock for Microsoft and X/Open for UNIX and Apple. The advantage of this approach is a possible quicker time-to-market, while the disadvantage is that no single open API for ATM will exist. We describe the efforts of these various fora in the next section. A semantic specification (Callaghan, 1995) outlines a set of characteristics which this interface should offer to a higher-layer application. This contrasts with a 'syntax' API, which is now left to industry. It offers what are known as **native ATM services**, and includes the procedures for data transfer, setting up SVCs and PVCs, offering various traffic types and QoSs, the distribution of connections to the proper application, and network management via OAM and the ILMI. Though many developers focus on an API as a real-

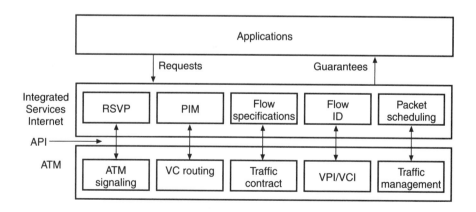

Figure 4.39 Application Programming Interface (API). Source: Cisco Systems.

ization of this interface, the concept is extensible to any software or hardware which uses these native services, to include operating system kernel interfaces, as well as PABX and ATM switch internal interfaces. As part of continuing work, the Forum's API group will work with WinSock and X/Open to finalize their respective APIs, WinSock 2.0 and the **X/Open Transport Interface (XTI)** (Sweeney, 1995b).

Within the API, applications may use three types of **Service Access Point (SAP)** within ATM. The first, Type 1, will be used to address entities which reside at Layer 2 of the protocol stack, such as those on Ethernet or Token Ring. The application therefore places itself logically at the data link layer, and may use a single ATM VCC to send and receive data from multiple Layer 3 protocols. LANE clients and servers are examples of entities that will use Type 1. Type 2 concatenates a Layer 3 address with an ATM address. Because of this, a VCC will be capable of carrying data from only a single Layer 3 protocol. Classical IP users are an example of Type 2 entities. Finally, Type 3 SAPs rely on only the ATM address. This type therefore applies to native ATM applications (Ross, 1995).

Looking beyond these current efforts by the application developers, IPv6 also holds promise for future QoS support. In concluding our discussion of APIs, we will look at compatibilities between IPv6 and ATM.

UNIX

Due to the penetration of UNIX in research communities, these platforms have supported the earliest of QoS application requirements by ATM. For example, by the end of 1995 implementations were available for both Sun and SGI. Implementations include reference code from ISI (ftp.isi.edu/rsvp/release/) and for Solaris (playground.sun. com/pub/rsvp/solaris-rsvp-latest.tar.Z). We expect some future API work to center around X/Open's XTI.

WinSock 2

The concept of an IS Internet, though holding a lot of promise, remains just theory without application support, while the ATM Forum, as opposed to initially defining an actual API, has only defined a set of requirements which the API should meet. Thus, we require a final link in the chain, at present addressed in the PC environment with the release of WinSock 2 (Intel, 1995a), a network programming and service interface for the Windows environment. A feature of the WinSock environment is that it is independent of a specific Layer 3 protocol or any Layer 2 network. Though we concentrate on IP, it applies equally well to

IPX and NetBEUI. The **Service Provider Interface (SPI)** (Intel, 1995b) is accessible by networking stacks, and acts as the intermediary between the application and the network. The WinSock supports QoS, allows applications to utilize both pt-pt and pt-mpt VCCs, and uses ATM addressing.

QoS support within WinSock 2 is based on the flow specification defined by Partridge (1992) which characterizes a unidirectional flow across the network. An application will associate this flow with a socket at the time of the connection request. A flow specification includes a source traffic description, latency, a level of service guarantee, the cost, and a method of extending the flowspec with additional parameters. An important feature is the network's ability to provide feedback as to resources available, which an application may then use to adjust its QoS requirements. The service guarantee will be set to guaranteed, predictive, or best effort. Though guaranteed and predictive QoS may result in the same performance, the latter may make better use of available network resources. Under WinSock 2, a service provider offering guaranteed service will implement a queuing algorithm which will attempt to isolate the flow in question from other classes of service. Because of this, it guarantees the average transmission rate (known as the **token rate**) and the latency. The one difference with predictive service is that it will not guarantee a latency. Finally, under best effort service, the service provider attempts to comply with the flowspec but makes no guarantees as to bandwidth or latency.

The source traffic descriptor uses a **token bucket size** and **token rate** concept. This rate is specified in bytes per second, while the bucket maps to bytes. In a process analogous to the leaky bucket used at ATM switches, the bucket, with a size equal to the token bucket size, will fill at the token rate. If the bucket contains credit, the application may send data while the bucket decreases the number of available credits. If none are available, the application must discard data. This is how bursts are handled: an application sending a rate below the token rate will build up credits which may be used by a burst. These values relate to the peak bandwidth, which is the maximum rate at which an application may send data. For bursty applications, the token rate and the peak will be quite different, while CBR service may result in a peak equal to the token rate. **Latency**, the time elapsed between a bit sent by the sender and arrival at the destination, is calculated in microseconds, while **delay variation** is the difference between the minimum and maximum latency. This determines the amount of buffering required. The **cost of call parameter** is as yet undefined, while the **network availability** field is set by the network to indicate whether an outgoing connection exists. An interesting feature of the specification is the ability to register applications with a default QoS. These may be registered through the WinSock 2 Clearing House.

Novell

Although we have focused thus far on IP to an extent, there exist other internetworking protocol suites. We look at Novell NetWare as an example, where solutions have been proposed based on the Classical model, LANE, and direct support of ATM services. The use of the Classical model and RFC 1483 allows Novell servers and clients to participate in a routed ATM environment, though an automatic ARP mechanism such as that which exists for IP under RFC 1577 does not yet exist. Looking at the protocol stack, the WAA module supports RFC 1483-based encapsulation, while the **Topology-Specific Module (TSM)** provides virtual connection management. Finally, the **Hardware-Specific Module (HSM)** supports the network adapter (Figure 4.40). Alternatively, a user may wish to deploy LANE services across both servers and clients. These services should be interoperable with those of other vendors. For example, a NetWare LES/BUS would support third-party LECs. Both models rely on the TSM and HSM, together comprising Novell's ATM **Open Device Interface (ODI)**. Application and service developers interface to the ATM layer via this module. Ultimately, this interface should also provide QoS support to higher-layer applications.

IBM APPN and HPR

Though we seem to focus on multimedia applications when speaking of QoS awareness, a totally different application enironment is poised to use ATM's QoS guarantees. These are the mainframe transaction-oriented applications. The protocol stack best positioned to accomplish

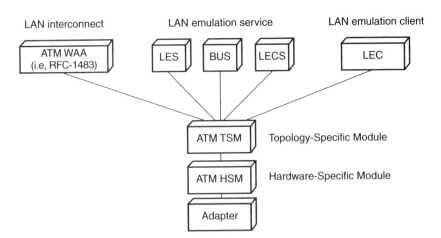

Figure 4.40 NovellL ATM support. Source: Novell.

this is IBM's **Advanced Peer-to-Peer Networking (APPN)** in combination with **High Performance Routing (HPR)**. HPR provides class-of-service and dynamic routing, easily mapped into ATM, with implementation specifics described by Dudley (1995). Note that this implies migration to APPN (or in some cases LANE) for **Systems Network Architecture (SNA)** users if they are to take full advantage of ATM. By mid-1996 the first routers, hubs, and end-systems supported this combination. Elements of the proposed specification will allow APPN's route security, transmission priority, and bandwidth reservations to be mapped from an HPR-based network into ATM VCCs. The one caveat in this deployment is that users must widely deploy HPR, which is not a certainty. Therefore, users will probably also deploy interworking between non-HPR APPN and ATM based on vendor-proprietary techniques, IPv6, or MPOA.

When interworking between APPN/HPR and ATM, three methods are available: LANE, Frame Relay transport, and the deployment of a native ATM **Data Link Control (DLC)**. Dudley (1995) details this third possibility in providing ATM QoS support to users. A reason for deploying HPR is its support for the **Rapid Transport Protocol (RTP)**. If cells are lost across the ATM network, resulting in packet loss, RTP allows for selective retransmission. This contrasts with the go-back-N error recovery found within IEEE 802.2 type 2 and used for LANE. Under ATM DLC, the **Logical Data Link Control (LDLC)** provides reliable delivery for some APPN flows (for example, XID), while most data including CP-CP and LU-LU is delivered by RTP. Data from both transport protocols is encapsulated in accordance with RFC 1483, and then segmented based on AAL5 with a null SSCS. AAL5 was chosen since the multiplexing within AAL3/4 is performed by APPN/HPR at a higher layer, RFC 1483 requires AAL5, and hosts supporting SAAL, Frame Relay, and LANE will also use AAL5. This allows multiprotocol systems combining APPN and IP to be easily deployed. Although LDLC and RTP provide reliable transport, this is only half the story. To use ATM's services, an interface between the higher-layer protocols and the network adapter driver is required. IBM has proposed a **low-level ATM interface** as an API which describes the necessary interface semantics.

APPN across ATM uses what is known as the **connection network model**. Under this model, the ATM network appears as a **Virtual Routing Node (VRN)** to the APPN nodes, with each node establishing one or more **Transmission Groups (TGs)** to the VRN. The unpalatable alternative to this would be to require each APPN node to create a TG to all other nodes. Addressing information to allow nodes to establish these links is returned as part of directory services and requires CP-CP sessions between APPN nodes. The connection network is further split into two types: demand and non-demand. Within a demand network, a single session will activate a new SVC, providing for close control over QoS.

Alternatively, sessions belonging to a TG within a non-demand network share a single SVC. Therefore, the QoS will apply to the entire SVC. This is what is implemented at present. Looking more closely at QoS, APPN generally requires the following ATM performance characteristics:

- Cell error rate $= 10^{-8}$

- Severely errored cell block ratio $= 10^{-8}$

- CLR $= 10^{-8}$.

- Cell misinsertion rate $= 10^{-8}$

- CTD $= 30$ msec

- CDV $= 10$ msec.

In setting priorities within APPN, the goal is to prevent large transfers of batch traffic from affecting interactive traffic while preventing lower-priority traffic from being completely blocked. When mapping an APPN session with its associated **Class of Service (COS)** and transmission priority to ATM, APPN **Topology and Routing Services (TRS)** will choose a TG across the ATM network most suitable for the COS in question. If a TG does not exist with these characteristics, the TRS function will create a new one, based on profiles defined by Dudley (1995). Depending upon session type, it will map to either a best-effort or reserved TG, each with an associated bandwidth, cost, and delay. The general rules are that batch traffic will favor higher bandwidth while ignoring delay, while interactive traffic will favor less delay and higher bandwidth. Both classes attempt to avoid expensive TGs. An additional feature to help reduce expense is the ability to deactivate sessions or entire TGs if inactive. These **TGs** are known as **limited resource**. Although current APPN applications are not capable of specifying throughput requirements, it is expected that this will change in the future. This will require use of the demand connection network where the application requests a certain bandwidth as part of call setup, resulting in a dedicated SVC.

Finally, HPR supports an adaptive rate-based congestion control (ABR) function which allows it to dynamically adjust its transmission rate based on the available bandwidth of the connection. HPR will first establish a connection across ATM with a bandwidth based on the TG profiles described above. This bandwidth is used by HPR to ensure fair sharing among different users. In the future, the ATM Forum's ABR mechanism will allow HPR to dynamically adjust its transmission rate.

IPv6

The currently deployed IP protocol is known as IPv4 (IP Version 4). Although this version of IP has sufficed for many years, limitations are apparent. This has led to the specification and limited deployment of a 'next generation' IP, officially standardized as IPv6 but sometimes also referred to as IPng, for IP Next Generation. IPv6, an evolutionary step up from the existing IPv4 designed to provide additional functionality and scalability, is of importance to ATM due to the protocol's native support for hierarchical addressing and flow specifications. Major features of IPv6 include an expanded, hierarchical address space allowing for more efficient routing, a simplification of the header, improved option support, authentication and encryption capabilities, and, most important for ATM interworking, an inherent support for QoS. Note that this last capability, the support for real-time applications, has recently been incorporated within IPv4 with the deployment of QoS-aware applications and RSVP-capable routers). These capabilities were covered in greater detail earlier in this chapter.

At first glance, the most obvious difference between IPv4 and IPv6 is the length of the address field. IPv4 provides for a 4-octet (32-bit) address space which results in the common a.b.c.d address format, while IPv6 extends this to 128 bits which provides for both hierarchical addressing and the ability to include auto-configuration of end-systems based on 48-bit MAC addresses. Looking at current address assignment efficiencies, this will allow anywhere from 8×10^{17} to 2×10^{33} end-system addresses, or a minimum of 1,564 addresses for every meter^2 of the Earth (Huitema, 1994). Address types within IPv6 include unicast, cluster, and multicast. Cluster addresses are new, allowing a packet to be sent to the 'nearest' member of a group of nodes sharing a common prefix. This is much like Anycast addressing at the ATM layer. Under IPv6, intermediate systems no longer need to process options, as these are now included in a separate header located between the IP header and the transport-layer header. Most options are transported transparently across the network from one end-system to another, and are not limited to IPv4's total option length of 40 bytes. Since routers along the path will not be required to process these option fields (as they were required to do under IPv4), performance gains will result. Important options include the ability to specify source routes along with the ability to guarantee authentication, data integrity, and confidentiality. Application QoS support is based on a flow label within the header which will make it easier for end applications to specify their requirements, while the source routing option will allow users to specify service providers as well as supporting host mobility. An IPv6 **authentication header** will normally use MD5 to verify sources while the IPv6 **encapsulating security header** will normally rely on DES (Hinden, 1995). We depict the header structure of IPv6 in Figure 4.41.

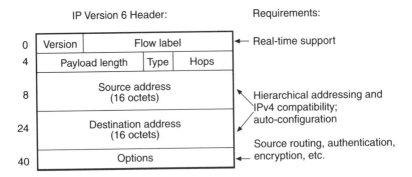

Figure 4.41 IPv6 header.

The flow label warrants further discussion, as it will be used by an intermediate system such as a router to map end-system application QoS requirements to ATM service profiles. The label includes a traffic class field which may contain values mapped to both flow-controlled and non-flow-controlled traffic. Though not very intuitive, flow-controlled traffic includes (in order of increasing priority), news, E-mail, FTP, Telnet, and control (for instance, routing and SNMP). Real-time traffic is non-flow-controlled, and includes both video and audio. One area of debate is the use of this identifier. Proposed uses include signifying a PNNI-like router and therefore a set of flows, or a single flow. This point will be resolved in the near future.

In deploying IPv6, one area which should receive some attention is address mapping between the 128-bit IPv6 address and the ATM NSAP if peering the two or when implementing the I-PNNI. This mapping may be accomplished in a number of ways, and depends upon whether one maps in the IPv6 to ATM direction or vice versa. In the former case, the 16-octet IPv6 address may be mapped quite easily into ATM, while in the latter case we may require some pre-planning. Within the IPv6 address space, the segment beginning with '0000001' (1/128th of the total IPv6 space) has been allocated for mapping of NSAP addresses. Bound (1995) describes a method of effectively mapping existing NSAP addresses into the shorter IPv6 address space. Note that this requires planning when assigning ATM addresses since this only allows six octets of routing hierarchy (the remainder is used for the AFI, IDI, and end-station identifier). A second option when remapping would be to carry the full NSAP address as an IPv6 destination option. In the opposite direction, mapping is a bit easier, with an AFI=47, and ICD=0090, the 16-octet IPv6 address, and a one-octet selector field (of no use to Ipv6). A concern when attempting to map between IPv6 and ATM is whether the addressing (and therefore routing) hierarchies will really align. The gain in efficiency upon which integrated routing (that is PNNI) is predicated will only occur if this is the case.

Within a local area, IPv6 hosts are expected to generate a unique 8-octet link-local address. Groups of hosts attached to the same 'link' can communicate with each other without the aid of a router. Thus, this **logical link group** (Armitage, 1995) is roughly analogous to an IPv4 subnet, and would be equal to the LIS or MARS cluster in ATM. If mapping from an NSAP address, the 7-byte ESI+SEL fields will form this local address. The left-most octet in this case is set to zero. Looking at the complete IPv6 address, the highest order bits are set to '1111111010', designating a link-local address and the remaining 54 high-order bits are set to zero. Note that these addresses are not forwarded beyond the local link. For completeness, yet another form of Ipv6 addressing which we may need to map into ATM is the [registry][provider][subscriber] format beginning with the prefix [010]. This format in fact may be used by a large majority of IPv6 users.

Other concerns when running Ipv6 across ATM include the encapsulations for unicast and multicast data. Using RFC 1483 as a guide, Armitage (1995) outlines the necessary formats for both data types. Unicast data will take the form: [LLC=0xAA-AA-03][OUI=0x00-00-00][IPv6 PID=0x86-DD][IPv6 packet] while multicast data will be carried as: [LLC=0xAA-AA-03][OUI=0x00-00-5E][PID=0x00-01][CMI][0x86-DD][IPv6 packet]. In both cases 0x86-DD is the Ethertype for IPv6.

Note that routing within IPv6 is almost identical to that under Ipv4 with the exception of the address length. Thus, existing routing protocols (OSPF, IS-IS, E-IGRP) will function with only slight alterations. Other major enhancements include provider selection based on policy, cost, and so on, host mobility, and auto-readdressing. IPv6 end-systems may take advantage of autoconfiguration much like that which exists within ATM across the ILMI. An IPv6 host will know its local MAC address and will receive its address prefix from the local router. Since the flow label and priority fields within the Ipv6 header may be used to identify packets requiring different QoS, remapping to IPv4 RSVP and ATM QoS should be straightforward. Finally, IPv6 includes powerful authentication and confidentiality provisions, though these capabilities are also beginning to appear within Ipv4.

4.1.13 Evolution of routers

Before moving onto ATM as a multiservice offering, we take one last look at routers and how they fit into current (and future) ATM deployments. This discussion is quite useful since there has been a great deal of misunderstanding regarding the role of ATM switches, LAN switches, and routers in both the LAN and WAN. One common misconception is that with the deployment of a high-bandwidth switched infrastructure, the requirement of the Layer 3 intelligence provided by routing magically disappears. This is the opposite from reality, as many a network designer have learned. The internetwork has not been abandoned; we have only deployed a more efficient link-layer infrastructure. The same workgroups exist, though they may be interconnected at different points within the network. Finally, although a greater proportion of traffic within a workgroup may remain at the switching layer due to this more efficient infrastructure (i.e., via the deployment of VLANs), this is more than made up for by a massive increase in total bandwidth across the network. Campus cores which may have been based on a combined bandwidth of 100 Mbps now interconnect workgroups at multiples of 155 Mbps. Ultimately, the Layer 3 processing within the network is bound to increase. The question, then, is how the router will envolve to meet this requirement.

At present, routers fulfill a number of function within an ATM network in addition to traditional routing and Layer 3 internetwork core functions (i.e., DNS caches, NTP, Firewalls). These new functions include acting as ATM servies: ATMARP, NHRP, Multicast, LAN Emulation, and MPOA. Within the QoS-based (connectionless) models, they act as default data forwarders for many types of traffic. Finally, they will provide interworking between traditional Layer 3 routing protocols and the I-PNNI. Looking forward, we expect to see routers playing an integral part of any MPOA-based route distribution protocol. In this case, we introduce a clear separation of the Layer 3 route calculation function and the frame forwarding (switching) function. Currently, these two processes take place on a single hardware platform, but as part of MPOA, they are expected to be distributed between the RSFG and the EDFG platforms. This division of effort leads us to next generation platforms based on Layer 3 routing processes surrounding an arbitrary core hardware technology, either frame or cell. In effect, this once again collapses the functionality which we distribute within MPOA, and paves the way for truly scalable multigigabit router. We describe this convergence of routing and switching in the next chapter.

4.2 Circuit Emulation Service (CES) and Voice and Telephony over ATM (VTOA)

An important element in fulfilling ATM's role as a multiservice platform is its support of time-delay sensitive traffic (both CBR and VBR), the circuit-oriented traffic traditionally carried over leased lines and TDMs. Though the data-oriented ATM models were the first to be implemented, and for some users may be the only service of interest, true end-user cost savings across the wide area and as part of tariffed services will result from being able to combine the data traffic with voice and possible CODEC-based video over a single physical connection. This idea is not new at all, for many large corporations operate private TDM networks which already combine traffic types. ATM, by replacing these TDMs, offers the promise of more efficient bandwidth utilization and better integration of end-systems. However, concerns in deploying CBR traffic across ATM include timing recovery, delay, and jitter across the network. ATM's support for CBR is known as **Circuit Emulation Service (CES)**, and may be deployed in two ways, both based on ATM AAL1. The first presents a clear channel (T1 or E1, for example) to an existing end-system via an entity known as an **Interworking Function (IWF)**, commonly part of an ATM switch or service multiplexer. Conversion to AAL1 in this case takes place within the switching system. The second method is based on the deployment of soon to be available 'native' AAL1 voice and video systems. We focus on the first alternative, the basis for current implementations. Later, we look at packet-based (AAL5) voice across ATM and interworking with AAL1.

The basic concepts behind a CES are outlined in ITU-T I.363 and ANSI T1.630, which define the AAL for use by CES, AAL1, along with clock recovery and indications of lost or errored data. Drawing on these documents, the ATM Forum has standardized on two types of CES, defining bit rates, OAM procedures, network management, and some signaling procedures. The first, termed **unstructured service**, and sometimes known as circuit emulation, approximates as closely as possible a wireline. The second, **structured**, or $N\times64$ service, capable of decoding DS1/E1 framing, is further divided into two types: DS1/E1 and logical, each with or without signaling. This signaling takes two forms, **Channel Associated Signaling (CAS)** and **Common Channel Signaling (CCS)**. The ATM Forum *Circuit Emulation Service Interoperability Specification* (ATM Forum, 1995b) and the **Voice and Telephony over ATM (VTOA)** specifications (Kumar, 1995) describe these services. These documents are quite complete in their coverage of services, signaling, and management. In Figure 4.42, we chart the various CES alternatives.

Each service provides an increasing level of sophistication, allowing an ATM network to perform many of the functions of existing TDM

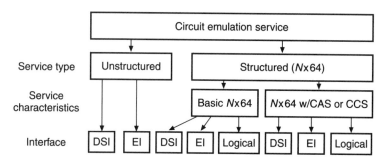

Figure 4.42 CES taxonomy. Source: ATM Forum, 1995b.

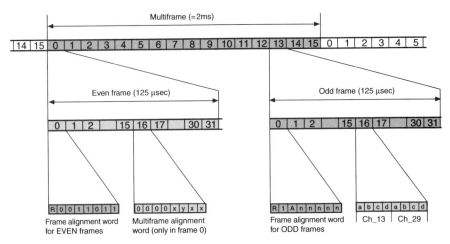

Figure 4.43 E1 framing. Source: Cisco Systems.

R	reserved for international use (if not used = 1)
A	remote alarm indication (alarm present = 1)
x,n	reserved for national use
y	multiframe synchronization alarm
a,b,c,d	channel associated signaling bits

and cross-connect systems. In doing this, the network must in effect emulate DS1 and E1 leased lines, standards for which are outlined in ANSI T1.403, along with ITU-T G.703, G.823, and G.824. The CES document, though not detailing the mechanisms required to provide on-demand CBR connections, does support this mode of operation. It is expected that ATM switches capable of supporting CES will also include support for signaled CBR when required. For the remainder of this section, we consider DS1/E1 and DS3/E3 CES as equals. DS3/E3 CES is described by Stodola (1995) and is expected to be standardized as part of a Phase 2 CES for unstructured service. There will be no structured DS3/E3 service. The CES based on either PDH or SDH will be capable of interpreting the transmission system's alarm signals and then passing them to the ATM layer and above. This will prove useful for circuit and service management. Other CES data rates, including J2/E2 and SONET/SDH are expected to be standardized in the future.

4.2.1 Service types

In looking at CES, we should first briefly review DS1/E1 framing. Within both the North American (DS1, OS3) and European (E1, E3) hierarchies, the basic unit of transport is known as a **timeslot**, equal to 64 Kbps. A 125 μs frame consists of multiple timeslots, 24 for DS1, and 32 for E1. Thus, each frame (and the timeslots within the frame) repeats 8000 times/second. This is the origin of 64 Kbps voice: 8-bit (256 levels) res-

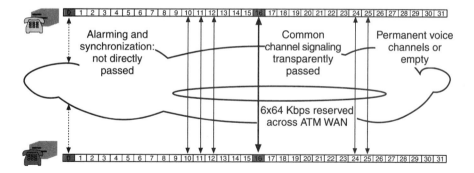

Figure 4.44 CES fractional.

olution at 8000 samples per second. Each hierarchy uses different methods for frame delineation. Under DS1, we 'rob' a bit from within the sample, while E1 uses timeslot 0 for this purpose. We group frames together into a 2 ms 'multiframe', important when we look at signaling. Whereas DS1 builds a multiframe from 12 (D4/Superframe (SF)) or 24 (Extended Superframe (ESF)) frames, E1 consists of 16. Signaling is another important concept, and will determine the sophistication of the services between PABXs and across the ATM network. CAS relates the signaling information to each 64 Kbps timeslot. Under DS1, this CAS is carried as part of the timeslots in the same way as frame delineation. Thus, only 56 Kbps is available for data transport, the origin of the 56 Kbps ISDN service in the US. In contrast, E1 conveys this signaling information within timeslot 16, leaving the full 64 Kbps for user data. As an E1 multiframe is transmitted, each timeslot 16 contains CAS information for two of the timeslots. Thus, by the end of the multiframe, all CAS data will have been conveyed (Figure 4.43). CCS always uses a separate timeslot, leading to 23B+D or 30B+D ISDN service. This CCS offers more sophistication than CAS since it operates as a protocol across the signaling channel. As part of our discussion on CES, we look at both of these signaling techniques in greater detail.

The unstructured service provides for point-to-point circuit emulation over PVCs, and uses AAL1 unstructured mode. As this is a pure circuit emulation service, any DS1/E1 or DS3/E3 signal will be transported independent of underlying framing. This service, though simple in conception, does have one shortcoming in that we dedicate the entire bandwidth which makes it unavailable to any other ATM users. Consider two PABXs connected via an E1 CBR circuit. In a given configuration, only a fraction of the voice channels available may actually be in use. As this CES has no knowledge of internal framing, the unused channels will still be transmitted, wasting ATM backbone bandwidth. In addition, due to ATM overhead, E1 CES may not be transported within an E1 ATM trunk. This may be a major limitation in deploying private ATM back-bones. Thus the justification for fractional circuit emulation, also point-to-point but now including support for D4, ESF, and G.704 framing. We depict this fractional CES in Figure 4.44, where only the predefined channels (in addition to timeslot 16) must be allocated across the ATM network. In the following three figures we base our examples on E1; T1 is similar but uses timeslots 0 to 23 with timeslot 12 reserved for signaling. Note that the physical interface between the PABX and the CES IWU at the ATM switch is still E1. We have only reserved a part of the available timeslots. This service does have some limitations since we do not interpret the signaling. Thus, we must pass timeslot 16 unchanged between any pair of locations. For example, if we wanted a connection to multiple destinations from a headquarters site, we would require multiple E1 interfaces at the headquarters PABX. Finally, since we interpret framing, we must implement synchronous network timing, described below.

Under $N\times64$ cross-connect service, we only reserve those channels actually required, though this reservation process is still the job of the network manager. An advantage of this service includes the ability to route different timeslots or groups of timeslots to different locations. Thus, a single DS1/E1 physical interface may terminate CBR links from multiple points, which more than makes up for the need to pre-assign which timeslots are routed to which destinations. We depict this functional emulation of a DS1/DS0 or E1/DS0 cross-connect in Figure 4.45. At the CES IWF, we forward the CAS information in timeslot 16 (or all timeslots in the case of DS1) to the IWF serving the destination. Looking back at the CES taxonomy, this is known as basic service (without CAS). This cross-connect service is not intended for use with CCS since we can-

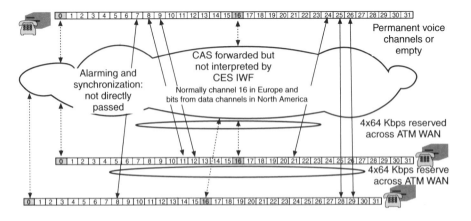

Figure 4.45 CES cross-connect.

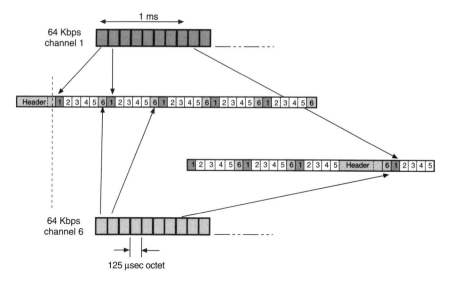

Figure 4.46 Mapping 64 Kbps channels into AAL1. Source: ATM Forum (Duault and Caves, 1995).

not split the CCS protocol without actually interpreting the signaling information. This signaling support for both CAS and CCS will need to wait for the dynamic service described below. As with fractional service, we must implement synchronous network timing.

When implementing AAL1 structured mode for this $N\times64$ basic service, we send the octets in sequence from each of the timeslots. Coding is a little more complicated where CAS is used. This involves splitting the AAL1 block into two sections, the first for the $N\times64$ payload and the second for signaling. The AAL1 pointer (see section 3.1.7) is required for all structured service since the payload part of the structure is $N\times24$ octets in length for DS1 and $N\times16$ for E1, whether or not CAS is used. Multiple AAL1 cells are therefore required in most cases. Note that there is no correlation between the AAL1 structure boundary and the ATM cell boundary.

We should be aware of one concern with running CBR circuits at E1 and lower trunk speeds: delay. For example, the segmentation delay for a 64 Kbps voice circuit is 6 ms, the amount of time required to build the 53-byte ATM cell. This is due to the 125 µs octet time at 64 Kbps. With only one 64 Kbps circuit, we must wait for all bytes within the ATM cell to be filled. Therefore, under VTOA, we recommend a minimum of six channels allocated, reducing the segmentation delay to 1 ms. Various methods have been proposed to reduce this delay, including sending out partially filled cells at the expense of throughput. We discuss this concept later as part voice compression. As a rule, we should not exceed 30–50 ms of total of switching and propagation round-trip delay over a

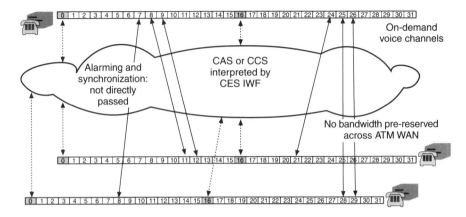

Figure 4.47 CES dynamic allocation.

VC if we are to avoid echo cancellation. Thus, network planners must adhere to a rather strict delay budget, and any opportunity to reduce this delay within a network will help. Finally, if we combine voice and data over the same ATM trunk, a well-engineered ATM switch should be capable of injecting the voice cells into the physical stream at predictable intervals if the CES is to comply with the jitter and wander values outlined in G.824, G.823, and ANSI T1.403. Figure 4.46 illustrates mapping 64 Kbps channels into AAL1.

The most complex form of voice support is where we interpret the signaling information transported by CAS or CCS. In the case of CAS, the CES IWF must create SVCs on-demand based on the contents of timeslot 16 (or all timeslots in the case of DS1). CCS is probably the most complicated to implement, since the IWF must support the complete signaling protocol such as Q.SIG or other ISDN variants implemented by the PABX. In Figure 4.47 we depict this signaled CES. Note that we no longer need to reserve any bandwidth across the ATM network, making the most efficient use of the ATM trunks.

4.2.2 Timing

With an awareness of delay over low-speed links, a second area of concern with CBR services is generation and recovery of timing. If clocking was not provided, circuits would lose synchronization, an event known as a **frame slip**. This slippage would of course result in a loss of data or a noticeable degradation in voice quality. Thus, ATM end-systems transmitting or receiving cell streams must include some method of timing recovery, and the ATM Forum, sometimes drawing on existing standards, has specified methods for accomplishing this as part of the CES. Consider an ATM network with timing injected from an external source at one or more points. This synchronization with other non-ATM domains is critical in allowing end-to-end circuits to be established providing a QoS (for example, bit error rate and delay) equal to that obtainable across traditional links. Timing sources are known as **Stratum-x**, with 'x' referring to the level of accuracy. A public network will rely on a Stratum-1 source as its master clock, while a private network may use a timing function internal to ATM switches.

The three methods of clock recovery across ATM are known as **synchronous clock recovery, adaptive clock recovery**, and **synchronous Residual Timestamp (SRTS)** (Figure 4.48). Synchronous timing supports network-based timing distribution, whereby the sources and destinations are timed to the same central timing source. Here, we propagate timing data across the network through the switches and finally to CPE such as PABXs. Therefore, the ATM switches must be capable of receiving and propagating this information. Also, the switches must have knowledge of a secondary source in case the primary fails, and be capable of re-establishing a non-looped timing path within the network. The next two methods are known as **asynchronous clocking**, in that all clocking is supplied by the end equipment and carried through the ATM network. adaptive clock recovery relies on IWFs to recover timing, with the destination under Adaptive timing expected to adjust its cell reassembly rate. One method of accomplishing this is through the use of a buffer which varies in depth depending upon whether the timing of the incoming data is fast or slow in comparison to the destination.

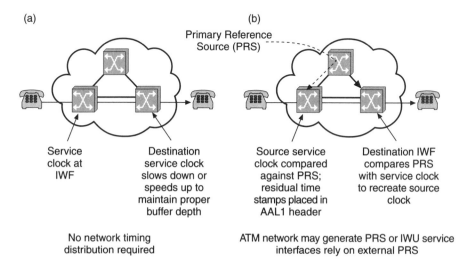

(a)

(b)

Primary Reference
Source (PRS)

| Service clock at IWF | Destination service clock slows down or speeds up to maintain proper buffer depth | Source service clock compared against PRS; residual time stamps placed in AAL1 header | Destination IWF compares PRS with service clock to recreate source clock |

No network timing
distribution required

ATM network may generate PRS or IWU service
interfaces rely on external PRS

Figure 4.48 CBR timing options. (a) Adaptive. (b) Synchronous Residual Time Stamp (SRTS).

This queue length will then drive the output clock frequency and thus reassembly. Though easy to implement, the CDV inherent in multiple hop networks may cause this method to fail Telco timing standards unless we implement variable depth buffering based on the CDV to minimize delay. In contrast to adaptive recovery, SRTS relies on network clocking, but only uses this information to synchronize both source and destination. At the source, the local clock is compared to this reference clock, with the difference transmitted across the network in the form of a **Residual Timestamp (RTS)**. This RTS is contained in special AAL1 cell header bits, formed by counting the number of reference clock periods which pass during the generation of eight cells. At the destination, the RTS is combined with the network clock to regenerate the input clock frequency (Fedorkow, 1994).

4.3 Voice interworking

If we are to successfully deploy voice services across an ATM network, we must also provide for interworking with non-ATM users in the LAN and WAN since ATM will provide voice services to only a subset of users. In addition, even ATM users are faced with two options for voice: AAL1 and AAL5 (Figure 4.49). This interworking operates at multiple layers, including conversion between different physical media (for example, ATM and 64 Kbps ISDN), ATM AALs (1 and 5), and the insertion or removal of the network layer. Additional aspects of this interworking include support for signaling, compression, different encoding rates, and silence suppression. As is obvious, this is a very complex area, subject to a great deal of effort and debate within the ATM Forum and the internetworking community as a whole. The business case for this integration of voice and data in the WAN, the elimination of redundant links between sites or between a user and service provider, was discussed earlier. We first look at interworking in the campus environment, and then extend this to the WAN.

4.3.1 ATM to non-ATM

In the campus, and with the deployment of high-performance PCs with multimedia capabilities, many users will begin to deploy desktop conferencing. Though useful in isolation, if the PC is ever to become the single desktop interface, then we must provide interworking with traditional voice systems. Looking at Figure 4.48 once again, this is the job of the voice server or interworking unit, which recognizes voice sessions which are intended for non-PC users. A PC user wishing to communicate with a CES subscriber must first resolve the destination address via some form of directory system. At this point, a connection may be established to the voice server which will perform the actual signaling to the destination. This two-step signaling process does not preclude the deployment of software at the user's end capable of directly calling the destination via the server. All signaling and format conversion is carried out within this device, including the removal of the networking layer which almost all desktop conferencing systems will use. In addition, if the call destination is non-local, the IWU will compress the signal as appropriate for transport across the WAN. This compression phase may be critical, as we expect campus voice at bandwidths in excess of 64 Kbps. (Looking ahead to Figure 4.53, the BTE is in effect the ATM side of the IWF.)

4.3.2 AAL1 to AAL5

Users connected directly to ATM will use one of two AALs for voice. The first, AAL1, is the stream-oriented encapsulation over which CES is based. Conventional PABXs use AAL1. AAL5 will also see wide deployment, since it is more suitable for packet voice and internetworking protocols. In the campus, AAL5 therefore provides simpler interworking to non-ATM voice. Although VTOA has selected AAL1 as the adaptation of choice for ATM voice terminals, we expect many users to deploy AAL5 due to the reasons outlined above. This will require interworking in the same way as described above, and outlined in Figure 4.49. Once a user establishes a connection to the IWF, AAL5 voice traffic generated at the source will be reassembled at the server and then resegmented into AAL1, this time without the network layer protocol. Note that AAL5

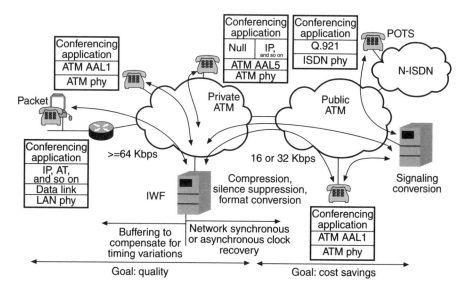

Figure 4.49 Voice interworking.

does not preclude the use of conferencing without the networking layer, and in fact the terminals described in the section *Video interworking*, later in this chapter, perform this function. However, we expect AAL5 with a full networking stack to be more common in the near- and mid-term. Once native ATM applications have been deployed, and voice is one area where they may be justified, the server may implement a function to convert between the two AALs at the ATM layer.

4.3.3 ATM to 64 Kbps ISDN

Expanding upon the transport of CBR traffic across ATM via the CES, the next step is to provide interworking between 64 Kbps ISDN and ATM. This takes two forms, the first where ATM acts as a transport for N-ISDN trunks, and the second enabling interworking between N-ISDN and ATM subscribers. Parallel to these interworking scenarios is the support of more sophisticated voice-related features across ATM such as compression. Within the ATM Forum, the VTOA group has taken the lead in this area, publishing a baseline document (Duault and Caves, 1995) which outlines these features.

The ITU has been addressing interworking between ATM and 64 Kbps ISDN for some time, outlined in ITU-T Recommendation I.580. The recommendation describes five scenarios (B-ISDN used in place of ATM) as depicted in Figure 4.50.

The initial service to be offered under VTOA is based on scenario

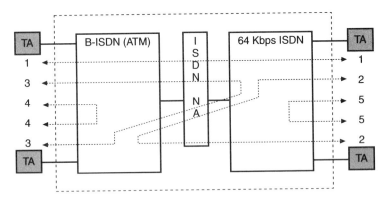

Figure 4.50 Voice interworking options.

1. Interconnection of B-ISDN and 64 Kbps ISDN with one user interface in each domain
2. Both user interfaces in 64 Kbps ISDN, using B-ISDN as a carrier
3. Both user interfaces in B-ISDN, using 64 Kbps ISDN as a carrier
4. Both user interfaces in B-ISDN, emulating 64 Kbps ISDN
5. Both user interfaces in 64 Kbps ISDN

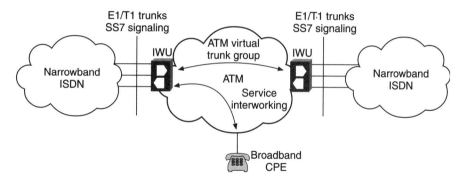

Figure 4.51 64 Kbps ISDN to ATM virtual trunk groups and service interworking. Source: ATM Forum (Duault and Caves, 1995).

2, whereby ATM acts as the transport for 64 Kbps ISDN trunks. This transport is known as an ATM **Virtual Trunk Group (VTG),** and is an ATM VCC which serves $N\times64$ Kbps ISDN trunks (Figure 4.51). At the IWU, the ISDN trunk is split into two components, with the user data converted to AAL1 CBR while the signaling component is forwarded over the SAAL (AAL5). As described in an earlier section on AAL1 structured mode, a minimum of 6×64 Kbps channels per cell will be used to minimize delay due to cell assembly. The choice of six channels limits a single cell to voice samples from a maximum of 8×125 μs frames. This results in a 1 ms maximum delay for the reassembly. In contrast, with two channels per cell, yielding 24 octets per channel, reassembly delay would equal 3 ms. This is possibly unacceptable IWU overhead at a single. At the other end of the spectrum, reassembly drops to 125 μs worst case for 47 voice channels or more.

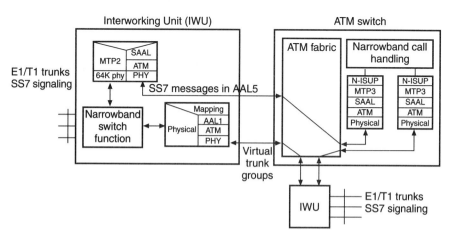

Figure 4.52 64 Kbps ISDN to ATM IWU operation. Source: ATM Forum (Duault and Caves, 1995).

In the VTG scenario, the interworking unit performs the adaptation as described above and forwards the VTGs and signaling information to the ATM switch. A narrowband call-handling function within the switch handles switching of the VTGs to the intended output ports (Figure 4.52). Note that 64 Kbps ISDN (N-ISUP) to ATM (B-ISUP) signaling conversion is not required for VTG transport.

The next step is to provide interworking between N-ISDN and ATM subscribers based on scenario 1 of I.580 derived from ITU-T Q.2931 Annex E. For this type of interworking, we convert the N-ISDN (both public and private) and B-ISDN signaling as depicted in Figure 4.53.

This **Network Adapter (NA)** will terminate all ATM-specific layers, including the user plane AAL. Conversion from the N-ISDN Q.921 (LAPD) datalink to the B-ISDN SAAL also takes place at this point. Signaling protocols on the N-ISDN side – Q.931 and ISO 11572 (Q.SIG) – are converted to the ATMF UNI or to Q.2931. We also remap the CS 1 supplementary services (DDI, MSN, and so on), introduced in Section 3.2, between DSS1 and DSS2. These are supported across the ATM network. Another type of interworking also depicted in the figure allows us to interconnect a private BTE to one on the public network (Kumar, 1995).

As part of optimizing bandwidth, users often require voice compression over the ATM WAN. Although VTOA has begun work in this area, current implementations are proprietary. Thus, there is a need for an interoperable standard which will also address voice interworking

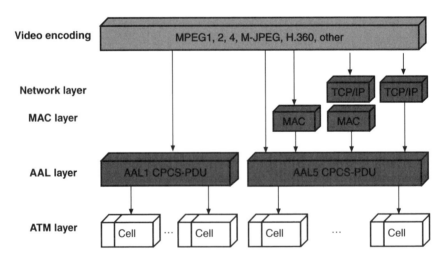

Figure 4.53 64 Kbps ISDN to ATM signaling.

Note   Q.293 DSS2
        Q.931 DSS1
        Q.SIG PSS1

Table 4.16 Voice compression algorithms for ATM. Source: Noah, 1995.

Data rate	Coding technique	Standard
64 Kbps	Pulse Code Modulation (PCM)	ITU G.711 for A-law and Mu-law
32 Kbps	Adaptive Differential PCM	ITU G.726/G.727
(16, 24, 40 Kbps)	(ADPCM)	
16 Kbps	Low Delay Code Excited Linear	ITU G.728 (2 ms coding blocks;
	Predication (LD-CELP)	to be extended to 9.6 and 12.8 Kbps)
8 Kbps	Algebraic CELP (ACELP)	ITU G.729 (10 ms coding delay)
Note	ADPCM provides for embedded coding whereby the least significant portions of the sample may be dropped to reduce the data rate	

between ATM and Frame Relay as outlined in FRF.9. One challenge in deploying low bit rate voice is the delay introduced when filling the ATM cell. For example, whereas a 64 Kbps stream requires 6 ms to fill a 48-byte payload, this increases to 12 ms at 32 Kbps and 24 ms at 16 Kbps. This last value is at the edge of what may be tolerated without additional echo cancellation. In reality, the delay will be reduced by using an algorithm which allows for partial cell fill at the lower data rates. A second alternative is to multiplex two or more voice channels into a single ATM cell. When interworking with voice over Frame Relay, additional concerns arise. In one scenario, the Frame Relay voice packet should be set no larger than an ATM cell. Alternatively, a longer Frame Relay frame may be segmented at the IWF, with the Frame Relay header converted to an ATM header.

When standards-based voice compression is implemented, a number of schemes will co-exist. An ATM or Frame Relay access device should support all or a subset of the compression algorithms as listed in Table 4.16 (Noah, 1995).

The 32 Kbps ADPCM is proposed as the standard for an ATM access device. All coding techniques described above are sample-by-sample, allowing for partial cell fill. Since the ACELP coding technique is not suitable for the access device, VTOA and ANSI are investigating alternatives at data rates between 4 and 13 Kbps. The standard algorithms listed here do not preclude the use of vendor-specific coding techniques, identified during call setup.

4.4 Video coding, conferencing, and distribution

ATM, with its possibilities for high bandwidth and bounded delay, is ideally suited as a technology capable of supporting video services both in the local and wide area. In theory, and from the point of view of some ATM users, an end-to-end ATM world would be ideal. Reality, as usual, is a little more complex. Various organizations are providing input as to the best way of providing video, voice, and data services to the home. These bodies include the Forum, as mentioned above, along with the DAVIC and the ITU. We find video over ATM in the workgroup, the Enterprise backbone, within the media industry, and in the residential environment. These different applications required differing protocol stacks, encoding standards, and as with voice, internetworking. We discuss each of these issues in turn.

4.4.1 Encoding standards

Over the last year or two, there has been somewhat of a transition from H.261, an ITU coding standard which was considered to be the front-runner for videoconferencing, to MPEG-2, more recently standardized by the ITU as H.262. MPEG-2 is also the coding standard of choice within the ATM Forum and within DAVIC. This is therefore our primary focus, although we expect ATM-connected videoconferencing systems to also support H.261 in the future as detailed later. Other video coding standards of note include Intel's Indeo, Apple's Quicktime, M-JPEG, introduced above, and proprietary techniques. Focusing on MPEG-2, the first and foremost reason for its popularity is its capability to support broadcast quality video at a reasonable data rate. The bandwidth requirements of the various encoding standards are summarized in Table 4.17.

The next question to be asked is how the chosen video encoding standard will be transported across the ATM network. There are multiple ways of accomplishing this, depending upon whether CBR, VBR, or ABR service is chosen. Figure 4.54 outlines these possibilities. Any of the standards may use direct AAL1 encapsulation for CBR or, more recent-

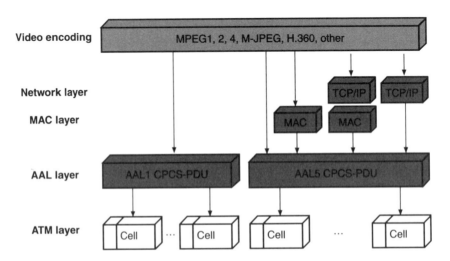

Figure 4.54 Video protocol stacks.

Table 4.17 Common video encoding standards. Source: Cisco Systems.

Encoding technique	Bit rate	Resolution	Broadcast standard
H.261	64 Kbps–2 Mbps	176×144	QCIF (conference)
		352×288	CIF (VHS quality)
(M-JPEG)	3–8 Mbps	352×288	CIF (VHS quality)
	15–25 Mbps	720×486	CCIR601 (PAL)
	60–100 Mbps	1920×1080	HDTV
MPEG-1	1.2–3 Mbps	352×288	CIF (VHS quality)
	5–10 Mbps	720×486	CCIR601 (PAL)
	20–40 Mbps	1920×1080	HDTV
MPEG-2 (H.262)	1–2 Mbps	352×288	CIF (VHS quality)
	4–5 Mbps	720×486	CCIR601 (PAL)
	8–10 Mbps	960×576	EDTV
	20–30 Mbps	1920×1080	HDTV

Note MPEG-2 encoding rates are not exhaustive: see DVB profiles below

ly, VBR service. This will be most commonly seen in the wide area or large campus, where an enterprise ATM switch capable of supporting CES has been installed. More widespread will be video encapsulated in AAL5, either making use of a network stack such as IP or transported directly over the AAL. Note that the IP and/or MAC will facilitate interoperability with PC- or workstation-based users, while direct encapsulation may be more suitable for VoD. Both the ATM Forum and the DAVIC have chosen AAL5 transport as the AAL of choice for both conferencing and video distribution. During the discussion of MPEG-2, we will see why this was a wise choice.

MPEG

Whereas H.261 is only suitable for the quality of videoconferencing or video distribution expected from 64 Kbps-ISDN, and in fact is based on multiples of the 64-Kbps B channel, MPEG-2 is intended for deployment in an environment capable of supporting higher bandwidths. A major difference between the two standards is that H.261 will suffer loss of quality if the image moves suddenly while MPEG-2 will not. Other standards listed above include JPEG, a picture-by-picture encoding mechanism, and MPEG-1, more suitable for lower bandwidths due to encoding mechanisms, although it has been deployed at broadcast quality. MPEG-1 is primarily used over ATM to distribute VHS-quality video to desktops from corporate VoD servers. Other uses include CD-ROM-based videos, becoming popular for home PCs. To complete the standards picture, a further refinement of MPEG, MPEG-4, is designed for 64 Kbps-based audio/video conferencing. This last standard may or may not be relevant to ATM in the future. In summary, the early deployment of higher bandwidths along with the availability of MPEG hardware will be at the expense of wider H.261 deployment.

MPEG is also able to make better use of the variable bandwidth provided by ATM as opposed to H.261 which is more or less tied to a given bandwidth within the ISDN structure. H.261 is commonly deployed at a video rate of 68.8 Kbps or 108.8 Kbps when using two B (BRI) channels, 326.4 Kbps when using six (H0), and 1798.4 Kbps when using 30 (H12 or PRI). This contrasts with the typical MPEG coder which may use any available bandwidth depending upon the loss factor (and resulting picture quality upon decoding) desired. Within ATM, a hybrid coder may be deployed capable of supporting both standards. The H.261 coder will generate cells tagged with high priority (CLP=0) due to H.261's sensitivity to cell loss, and a second MPEG coder will generate supplementary data to improve resolution. This, however, requires the CLP value to be preserved by the network, which may not be guaranteed. If interworking with H.261 is not required, this technique may still be applied to MPEG exclusively with the basic image data encoded with a higher priority. Another feature of MPEG coding over alternatives, and a reason for its reduction in bandwidth requirements, is its bi-directional motion prediction mechanism.

Within MPEG, motion at time 'x' in the future is fed back into buffered intermediate frames. This reduces the amount of coding required, and contrasts with the lack of any prediction mechanism under JPEG or the unidirectional forward prediction within H.261 (Hoffmann *et al*, 1993). In contrast to the frame-by-frame JPEG encoding (the basis for a number of currently deployed video compression systems), MPEG makes used of three frame types: I, P, and B. The Intermediate (I) frame contains full information (equivalent to a JPEG frame). Predicted (P) frames are generated from I frames or from other P frames, while Bi-directional (B) frames are interpolated from I and/or P frames. During operation, an encoder will first generate an I frame. A P frame will be

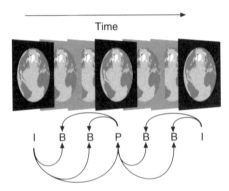

Figure 4.55 MPEG-2 framing. Source: Cisco Systems.

sent a fixed interval later (set by configuration, but typically 90–100 ms). B frames at about 30 ms intervals are interpolated from these two. Thus, a possible sequence may be: IBBPBBPI. We depict this flow in Figure 4.55. Typically, I frames are generated every 400 ms and are separated by 10–12 P and/or B frames. This generation interval would of course be reduced if MPEG-2 is used for videoconferencing where this level of buffering is unacceptable. The tradeoff between these frame types is as follows: B frames will produce smoother playback, but require greater buffering in the decoder. In implementing MPEG-2, care should be taken to ensure the delivery of I frames; under severe congestion, P and B frames may be dropped.

We now look at MPEG over AAL5's timestamp capability. This **Program Clock Reference (PCR)**, used for the ordering of I, B, and P frames does not depend upon the ATM layer for timing, and therefore MPEG does not require the timing capabilities of AAL1. This results in lower overhead. In the local area, ABR will be the ATM service type of choice, while in the wide area, VBR over AAL5 will also be deployed. Alternatively, rt-VBR and CBR may be used over AAL1 or a future AAL2-like adaptation in the wide area. This will require the regeneration of timing via adaptive clock recovery, the SRTS mechanism, or via some universal external system (for example, GPS).

Another deployment issue is whether to encapsulate MPEG directly over the AAL or via a traditional networking stack. For desktop conferencing, MPEG will usually be encapsulated over IP or some other networking protocol for interoperability with non-ATM systems, while VoD will use direct transport many times, for reasons of ease of deployment and lower overhead. These two different encapsulation schemes do not preclude interoperability, as a video interworking unit may convert between the two. Alternatively, a video server may operate in 'dual mode' depending upon destination.

MPEG-2 transmissions are based on a transport stream consisting of video and audio, and constructed as a **Single Program Transport Stream (SPTS)**. Two SPTSs, each 188 octets in length, are then mapped into a single ATM VCC using AAL5. This number may be decreased to a single SPTS via signaling or network provisioning. Additionally, if the AAL5 payload contains a **Transport Packet (TP)** which contains a **Program Clock Reference (PCR)**, this TP must be the last TP in the AAL5 payload. Since an SPTS will contain only a single video program, users wishing to select one program or another will do so by selecting an individual VCC, each delivered over a single SPTS.

Looking back at Table 4.17, one major advantage of MPEG-2 is its versatility in encoding rates and sophistication. DVB in fact defines a total of 11 bit rate and profile combinations known as **comformance points**. These bit rates for compressed signals span from 4 Mbps for $352 \times 240 \times 30$ ($352 \times 288 \times 25$ in Europe) to 80 Mbps for $1920 \times 1080 \times 30$ ($1920 \times 1080 \times 25$ in Europe). Note the difference between these data rates and our earlier chart. DVB assumes maximum encoding quality, while making a number of observations such as BT.601 studio quality requiring 9 Mbps and PAL/SECAM requiring only 5–6 Mbps. The bit rates are defined as **Low Level (LL)** which is 1/4 of BT.601, **Main Level (ML)** equivalent to BT.601, **High-1440 (H14L)** with 1440 samples/frame, and **High Level (HL)** with 1920 samples/frame. Possible aspect ratios are 4:3, 16:9 (shadow box), and 20:9. Profiles include a **Simple Profile (SP)**, a **Main Profile (MP)** with bi-directional prediction, **SNR Scalable Profile (SNRP)** and **Spatially-Scalable Profiles (SSPs)** offering increased signal-to-noise ratios and resolution, and a final **High Profile (HP)** allowing for encoding line-simultaneous color-difference signals (capable of 4:2:2, equivalent to the D1 format). The various conformance points are referenced by DVB as SP@ML, MP@HL, and so on (DVB Project Office, 1995), with SP@ML or MP@ML, both at $720 \times 480 \times 30$ ($720 \times 576 \times 25$ in Europe) requiring 15 Mbps expected for initial broadcasts. Later deployments based on either H14L ($1440 \times 1080 \times 30$) requiring 60 Mbps or HL ($1920 \times 1080 \times 30$) requiring 80 Mbps are expected as technology progresses. Note that these higher data rates outlined by DVB do place some constraints on the types of physical architecture which we have previously described, and we expect the higher profiles to see use initially only within the broadcast industry.

Although these higher resolutions exceed what we may expect at the home cinema in the near future, they only begin to touch on the bandwidths required within the media industry. Consider two production houses exchanging uncompressed digital video at $1920 \times 1080 \times 30$ fps with a color depth of 30 bits. Why uncompressed? In the production environment, the images must be manipulated unaltered, and not subjected to any compression/decompression process. Where time is of the essence, the cost of this process, even if loss-free, may not be justified. This resolution requires a bandwidth of 1.8 Gbps, unobtainable by any end-system. This is also the minimum bandwidth we may expect for digital cinemas, bypassing the use of film. Over the next year or so, as the use of ATM becomes even more critical to these industries, we may expect to see ATM networks providing this bandwidth to end-systems at multiples of 622 Mbps.

CLR and latency

The network transporting this MPEG-2 stream should guarantee a CLR of less than 1.7×10^{-9}, a CTD across the network of 4 ms (limited to 150 µs per switch), and an end-to-end CDV of under 500 µs. The CTD, or latency across the network, is sometimes debated, and is really a factor of the quality of traffic. For example, whereas a low-end, 64 Kbps videoconference may tolerate 300 ms CTD, a high-end conference at 1.5 Mbps will tolerate only 5 ms. This is the justification for the 4 ms limitation. In some instances, even this may be unacceptable. Consider remote surgery based on HDTV-quality video. At this data rate, an end-to-end delay of under 1 ms must be guaranteed. Parallel to acceptable delay for video is the acceptable delay for the voice component. This is primarily a factor at lower data rates, where 300 ms may be acceptable for 64 Kbps video, but the delay for voice (and therefore for the entire conference stream) should be limited to 100 ms. Research shows that somewhere between a 100 and 250 ms delay, two-way interaction becomes annoying. Note that these values apply to two-way conferencing only. For video distribution, any reasonable delay is acceptable, and jitter may be compensated for by larger buffers in the end-systems. The objective here is to minimize the cell loss, which is not difficult since the bounds on delay are less stringent.

Compression loss

When working with video compression protocols, the compression algorithm selected may result in a 'lossless' or 'lossy' signal. If lossless, the original video stream may be recreated at the destination with no loss of signal quality (that is, resolution, color). In contrast, a lossy algorithm will result in a recreated signal as close as practical to the original program. The fidelity of the recreated signal will be based upon the amount of acceptable loss. Depending upon the choice of compression standard (for example, MPEG, M-JPEG, H.261), different degrees of compression are possible. This is the reason that one standard may be capable of transporting a broadcast quality signal at 4–5 Mbps (MPEG-2) while another may require 15–25 Mbps (M-JPEG). Under MPEG, the compression ratio is known as the Q factor, where a higher Q results in greater possible compression at the expense of fidelity.

4.4.2 Video distribution

Having defined a set of services (AMS, LANE, MPOA, VTOA, native ATM services) and a video encoding technique (MPEG-2), the next question concerns the type of transmission architecture to deploy to support these requirements over ATM to the residence. This is an area of multiple paths within the ATM Forum, other standards organizations such as DAVIC and the IEEE, and especially industry, where the use of end-to-end ATM is not a foregone conclusion. The many alternatives are due to differences in installed base, planned service offerings, the regulatory environment, and vendor capabilities. Transmission systems under consideration for the RBB market include the **Asymmetric Digital Subscriber Line (ADSL)**, **Hybrid Fiber-Coax (HFC)**, **Fiber-to-the-Home (FTTH)**, **Fiber-to-the-Curb (FTTC)**, and the **Very high-speed**

Digitial Subscriber Line (VDSL). We have already described these various technologies. Probably the most important fact underlying all these architectures is their compatibility with ATM.

Looking back at the section on physical interface standards, including HFC, FTTL, FTTH, and ASDL, and comparing this with the above example, it is clear that the service providers and competitive service providers, are undecided as to their ultimate strategy. The discontinuity lies in the installed base of the two types of service provider. Focusing on Telcos and cable providers, the former offer a switch-based star architecture suited to two-way communications but without the necessary bandwidth. In contrast, the cable providers offer the bandwidth but, due to a traditional bus architecture, can only offer it on an asymetrical basis. The best of both worlds is required: the topology of the Telcos and the bandwidth of the cable providers. Currently, the debate concerns the cost of connecting each user, with the architectures most capable of fulfilling the two requirements above, such as FTTH, which are not under consideration due to a higher initial cost. An often-heard argument concerns the perceived asymmetrical data requirement of the typical household, with high bandwidth downstream for delivery of content, and much lower upstream bandwidth for voice and some data. In fact, with the emergence of telecommuting and more home businesses, this may no longer be the case. Symmetric bandwidth requirements can quickly lead to the overload of bus-based architectures such as HFC. Possibly, the service providers should take a step back and look at the total market requirements, not only over the next year or two but further into the future. Only then will they be capable of determining the most appropriate delivery technology.

4.4.3 Video interworking

Just as voice interworking between different AALs will play a part in determining the success of ATM, the same functionality will be required for video in both the local and wide areas. Consider the diversity of video encoding standards, and the possibility within a single standard such as MPEG-2 for totally incompatible systems. A PC user with MPEG-2 over the network layer would not be capable of making use of a VoD server where MPEG-2 was implemented directly over ATM. Therefore, some form of interworking capability will be required in most ATM networks. A second justification for this capability is destination-based encoding, where a user in the local area may wish to encode at a higher data rate, and therefore better picture quality, since line- and possibly usage-based charges are not an issue. This video server would be capable of converting between multiple encoding formats and accepting end users' requests for encoding based on destinations, as depicted in Figure 4.56. In the case of MPEG-2, the capability should exist to insert or remove the network layer without re-encoding/decoding the basic video stream.

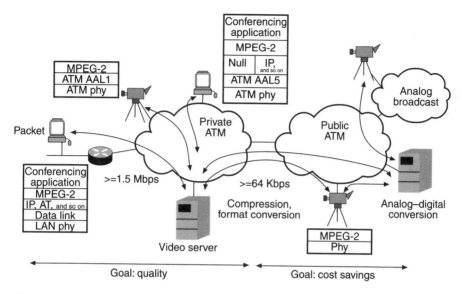

Figure 4.56 Video interworking.

Towards the end of 1995, one vendor had in fact announced a device with these characteristics. Its capabilities included transcoding of voice and video as well as acting as a multimedia PABX, allowing users to place voice and video calls within a local area or onto a WAN.

Alternative approaches to video interworking place the responsibility for format support with the end-systems. Most work in this area is within the ITU, and focuses on methods of interworking between the various H.32x-type terminals. Consider a user connected to ISDN and using an H.320 terminal. This device supports H.261 video and G.711/G.722/G.728 for audio over the H.221 mux/demux function. Likewise, a PSTN user terminal conforming to H.324 supports H.261/H.263 video and G.723.1 audio over H.223. We therefore require an interworking function to allow communication between these two systems. Looking at the ATM domain, we have two alternatives. The first is H.321, which uses the same video and audio coding as ISDN but over AAL1. Two newer profiles, H.310 RAST-P and H.310 RAST-C include MPEG1 audio support. RAST-P supports both H.261 video coding over H.221 and then AAL1, as well as H.262 video coding over the MPEG-2 transmission stream and AAL1 or AAL5. Nothing precludes the use of H.261 and H.221 over AAL5, however, and this is one way in which we may deploy these devices in the near term. This is due to the later availablily of H.262 CODECs which operate at studio broadcast quality (NTSC – profile SP@ML or PAL–profile MP@ML) requiring about 15 Mbps. The RAST-C profile only allows both video coding techniques but only over MPEG-2 and AAL5. We expect most ATM desktops to implement one of these two options. In either case, we require only physical layer format conversion for interworking between ATM and ISDN. Interworking is also possible to LAN-based systems based on the H.322 or H.323 profile and mobile systems using H.32P/M (Kobayashi, 1995).

4.5 Residential and small office services

Although most of our discussion thus far has focused on the business applications of ATM, another world is opened if we can extend the service offerings enabled by ATM into the home and small office. When we look at these environments, a number of ATM-delivered services are seen as commercially viable, including communications, entertainment, education, commerce, and control. We see entertainment evolving from simple VoD into forms of distributed gaming, while, in the **Small-Office-Home-Office (SOHO)** environment, communications will include telecommunicating. Control, where utility companies are able to remotely read meters, or where security monitoring is streamlined, is an often forgotten service. Within the ATM Forum, both the Residential Broadband (RBB) services group and the Audio Visual Multimedia Services (AMS) group focus on this environment. AMS concentrates on the service definitions as opposed to the underlying technology. Thus, work by AMS is applicable to any architecture, and in fact is not limited to the residence. We have previously looked at the home delivery technologies and standards under consideration by the ATM Forum's Residential Broadband (RBB) Services group.

ATM is the technology of choice to deliver these services due to its versatility in terms of bandwidth scalability, low delay, redundancy, and manageability. It is probably the only networking technology capable of supporting all services as envisioned in a commercially viable way.

4.5.1 Audio Visual Multimedia Service (AMS)

The ATM Forum in its Audio Visual Multimedia Services (AMS) document defines a number of services to be supported over the home network. Phase 1 (Wright, 1995a) describes an MPEG-2-based VoD service, while proposals for a second phase (Wright, 1995b) define additional applications including multimedia desktops, video- conferencing, interactive distance learning, and post-production editing.

Video on Demand (VoD) is a service whereby the end user controls the material to be viewed as well as the playback time. This requires signaling to the source, usually out-of-band from the distribution channel. Ideally, the user is provided with functions equivalent to those available on a standard VCR. A variant of VoD is based on timed delivery of programs (for example, every 30 minutes), and is known as

Near Video on Demand (NVoD). This will allow for efficiencies through the use of pt-mpt connections as opposed to the pt-pt connections found as part of the basic service offering since multiple users share the connection, and may be applied quite well to the more popular programs.

A multimedia desktop service provides for the transfer of voice, video, and data between two locations. This service is independent of underlying video and audio compression standards. Closely aligned with the multimedia desktop is video conferencing, providing pt-pt or mpt-mpt video and voice conferencing. This is more of a business rather than residential service. Note that the support of mpt-mpt conferencing within the network requires the deployment of what is known as a **Multipoint Control Unit (MCU)**, described as a **Multicast Server (MCS)** within the discussion of the Classical model.

The next service, **Interactive Distance Learning (IDL)**, allows a teaching environment to be extended beyond a single physical location. This service has great promise in many parts of the world where educational resources are limited in comparison to the ability to deploy a networking infrastructure. In other locations, IDL may be used to provide specialized education to select audiences.

Finally, post-production editing draws on the bandwidth of ATM to connect multiple locations. Traditionally, the transfer of this data required physical media, with its associated cost and delay. If the editing houses are connected via an ATM network, this intermediate step may be avoided.

4.5.2 IEEE 802.14 and TIA multimedia services

IEEE 802.14, introduced earlier as a delivery mechanism for HFC, defines a number of services which may be delivered to the business or residence. These include symmetric and asymmetric data (file sharing, LAN interconnect, game downloads), interactive video (VoD), messaging (E-mail, voice mail), bi-directional or un-idirectional multimedia (video conferencing, interactive games, image retrieval), and telephony (POTS, ISDN). These services fall under all currently defined ATM traffic classes – CBR, VBR, ABR, and UBR – and are summarized in Table 4.18.

It may be more interesting if we look at some of these services in greater detail. IEEE 802.14 (IEEE, 1995a) also provides insight into the demands placed on the network infrastructure when offering some of the more well-known services such as voice, videoconferencing, VoD, and data. We summarize this information as it relates to HFC networks in Table 4.19.

Table 4.18 Home and small business services. Source: IEEE, 1995a.

Service	Characteristic	Example
Symmetric data	Asynchronous ABR	File sharing, LAN interconnect
Asymmetric data	Asynchronous, ABR	Game downloading
Interactive video	Store and forward, CBR, VBR	Video on Demand (VoD)
Messaging	Store and forward, ABR	E-mail, voice mail, billing
Bi-directional multimedia	Real-time, VBR, CBR	Videoconferencing, document conferencing, interactive games
Unidirectional multimedia	Store and forward, ABR	Image retrieval
Telephony	Real-time, CBR	POTS, ISDN

Table 4.19 Home and small business service characteristics. Source: IEEE, 1995a.

	Voice	Video-conferencing	VoD	Data
Penetration	125%	10%	80%	80%
Calls/busy hour	3	1	0.4	0.8
Call holding time	3 minutes	9 minutes	120 minutes	10–120 minutes
Forward bandwidth	64 Kbps	384 Kbps	1.5-20 Mbps	64 Kbps–10 Mbps
Reverse bandwidth	64 Kbps	384 Kbps	30 PDUs/call	10 Mbps peak

Note   Calls/busy hour relates to network dimensioning. The network must be dimensioned to accept this number of call attempts per connected subscriber per hour. Voice prenetration infers that the average user subscribes to 1.25 voice lines

Parallel to efforts within the ATM Forum and the IEEE, the Telecommunications Industry Association (TIA) is also working to define home services, summarized in the Multimedia Premises Reference Architecture (Telecommunications Industry Association, 1995) document. The TIA envisions an architecture where the home connects to multiple service providers, both ATM and non-ATM. All devices, including home monitoring and appliances, connect to a **home network controller**, which then connects to the one or more NIUs at the periphery of the residence. The palette of services available borrows heavily from other documents, including the DAVIC 1.0 specification (Digital Audio Visual Council, 1995), and includes: delayed broadcast, network and interactive gaming, data services (including Internet), interactive television (including teleshopping, VoD, and Pay-Per-View), movies on demand (emulating a VCR), Intelligent Near-VoD (pausing and restarting a staggercasted movie), POTS, telemedicine, videoconferencing, and telecommuting. Although any of the access network technologies described earlier may be used to deliver these services, HFC and FTTC are noted as being furthest ahead in terms of deployment. The document also references other widely-deployed technologies including direct broadcast satellite, multichannel multipoint distribution service, and the local multipoint distribution service, though these are not relevant to our discussion due to limited upstream bandwidth.

5

Implementing ATM

How do we now deploy the various standards and services described in the previous chapters? We need to map what we have learned into implementation examples, focusing on the various issues faced when deciding upon a given technology. In this case, our technology basis is ATM. We first analyse requirements, looking at problems to be solved and available solutions. Once this preliminary (and necessary) planning is complete, we are ready to proceed with detailed network design. This chapter presented an in-depth look at the various design alternatives, looking at the various ATM multiservice models in both the local- and wide-areas, and drawing an standardized, multivendor solutions. Common to all implementation examples are some additional concerns, including: redundancy, management, security, evolution, and cost.

5.1 Requirements

The three initial implementation phases include service and model selection, data gathering, and finally vendor and technology selection. A case may be made that the selection of which ATM services and what model to implement may only be made once available offerings are known. This may be true, but the network designer should first match requirements to the best possible solution and only later back off to an alternative. This analysis must then be interrelated with organizational dynamics (that is, moves, adds, and changes) and the existing systems that must be supported within the new networking environment. Where multiple services and models will serve an application profile equally well, this should be noted first. For example, data, voice, and video alternatives exist in both the local and wide area. After evaluating these various models, an implementor will then produce a document outlining requirements and goals which will be distributed to potential vendors. The ATM Forum has published a widely-used 'mock RFI' which provides an excel-

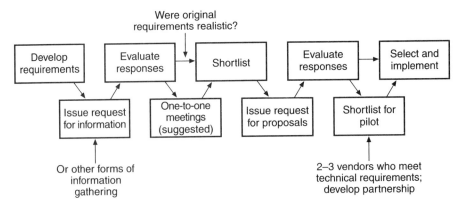

Figure 5.1 Project planning and implementation.

lent baseline for gathering vendor data. In fact, many vendors have prepared generic (project independent) responses to this document which are updated regularly. Vendors also complete an additional standards-oriented set of documents known as **Protocol Implementation Conformance Statements (PICS)**, although these documents do not provide as great an insight into overall capabilities and strategies as the RFI. However, one must be careful with placing too narrow an emphasis on standards, as far too many network planning groups omit the initial analysis phase and merely send out a long questionnaire to all prospective equipment suppliers. These 'shopping lists' often contain lists of every ITU recommendation, ATM Forum specification, and IETF RFC with no regard to what has actually been implemented or, for that matter, what has been found to actually work.

Based on responses to the RFI and vendor consultations, and depending upon project size, a short list of vendors may be compiled for pilot purposes or a vendor(s) may be selected for project implementation. This phase includes issuing a more detailed and binding **Request for Proposal (RFP)**. This selection involves matching vendor capabilities to the equipment and services required. As part of this, an honest effort must be made to determine which hardware capabilities and standards are required, desired, or non-applicable. The user should initiate detailed network design only after determining vendor capabilities and product information. We summarize these steps in Figure 5.1.

5.1.1 Service selection

Possibly the most important decision made is determining what services are required to support existing and planned applications. This requires a detailed analysis of data, voice, and video needs in both the local and wide area. Looking at data requirements in the local area as an example of the type of analysis required, users evaluating the deployment of ATM to solve network congestion and latency problems face a decision as to which model to implement based on currently available standards and equipment – the Classical model, LANE, or MPOA. In addition to the demands listed above, corporations are looking to preserve their existing investment in internetworking devices while solving these problems, and often in addition seek to preserve their current logical infrastructure. Other users, while still wishing to preserve investment, are more open to implementing a new logical structure if it will provide them with ease of management and support of 'moves, adds, and changes' within the work-group environment. The Classical model supports the first migration strategy, while LANE will support the latter. Implementation may actu-ally include both models sharing the same physical infrastructure, each serving a subset of users.

When evaluating the two models, a number of factors should be considered. These include: currently installed internetworking equip-ment (if any), existing network layer addressing schemes (if any), intra-workgroup, inter-workgroup, and external security requirements, and manageability. In most cases, users who have an installed base of hubs, routers, and, more recently, LAN switches, will be looking for incremen-tal change. Others, implementing a totally new workgroup architecture, will have more flexibility in the choice of models and associated address-ing schemes and management systems.

One category of users will probably be implementing ATM as a way to boost performance over an existing or planned high-rise, campus, or wide-area backbone. For example, a university may have a campus core comprising Ethernet or FDDI or a corporation may have installed a WAN based on leased lines. In both cases, routers provide the intercon-nection between LAN segments or remote sites and the backbone. These routers segment the enterprise network into logical units based on geographically-assigned network addresses (IP networks or subnets, IPX networks, and so on). For these pre-existing networks, the implementa-tion of the Classical model as a high-speed backbone replacement will require no re-addressing and the introduction of no new management paradigms. The user gains in bandwidth and may use ATM's QoS sup-port. Functionality to be implemented within the ATM infrastructure will initially include RFC 1577-based ATMARP servers and possibly the deployment of **Next Hop Resolution Protocol (NHRP)** servers for optimal routing over the ATM cloud.

The second category of users seek to solve problems of mobility, workgroup connectivity, and support for existing bridged applications (NetBIOS, DEC LAT) over a high-bandwidth infrastructure. Support for mobility draws on the fact that most organizations are in a constant state of flux – realignments, employee reassignments and relocations. The goal here is to provide each and every user with the capability to connect to his or her workgroup at any network access point. Present schemes based on topologically-assigned addresses make this all but impossible except for short periods of time (for example, IP mobility) or in small networks via DHCP. Thus, we require a new workgroup networking paradigm supporting workgroup-based addressing. This new paradigm will also solve the second problem, that of efficient workgroup connectivity. Under the Classical model, even if mobile hosts participate in dynamic configuration (increasingly common), connectivity to workgroup servers will be less than optimal after relocation due to the Layer 3 routing required. This is especially true for workgroup-oriented protocols such as IPX. By providing for logical address assignment, LANE will in effect flatten the workgroup network. All intra-workgroup communications now occur at Layer 2, providing for more efficient client–server interaction, while supporting bridging as well. Thus, the third requirement, that of support for non-routable protocols over ATM, is also met. Nevertheless, a case may be made for the continued segmentation of workgroups based on topologically-assigned subnets. If this works well at present, why not in the future? Corporations redeploy servers to 'server farms' for reliability and manageability. Under the Classical model, these servers would be located on a separate IP subnet or IPX network, with intra-workgroup client–server traffic always traversing one or more routers. On Ethernet or FDDI, shared media technologies, this may not present a problem, as routers can easily deal with these bandwidths. At ATM bandwidths, users must evaluate whether routing between clients and servers in the same workgroup is desirable.

If LANE solves so many problems, why may it not find universal acceptance, at least in the local area? For one reason, many network administrators are reluctant to change philosophies; this is especially true if their IP internetwork has been operating efficiently for only a short time. Also, not every corporation will redeploy servers; many will remain co-located with users. Finally, the Classical model requires less effort to conceptualize and implement in contrast to LANE. Nevertheless, LANE is expected to comprise a significant proportion of local-area ATM installations in the future.

Extending this evaluation into the wide area, two additional data services are available: Frame Relay and SMDS/CBDS. Consider a user with the requirement to communicate with sites at locations where native ATM services (cell relay, classical LAN interconnect, LAN emulation) do not exist. If Frame Relay is offered at these sites, the user will take advantage of ATM-to-Frame Relay interworking offered by the service provider. The same applies to SMDS/CBDS, where in a number of countries (in Europe especially), interworking with native SMDS subscribers is a requirement. SMDS/CBDS is also a viable service across ATM in enabling LAN interconnection. Although LANE is often put forward as a solution to this requirement, the security and service class capabilities of SMDS/CBDS will in many instances position it better in a multi-customer environment than LANE. Finally, a user requiring Internet connectivity to other organizations may also subscribe to this service. As part of the Internet offering, the service provider may make available value-added features across features.

Though data transport is an important service offered by ATM, the ultimate success of this technology will be based on the support of voice and video traffic as well. CES is used to interconnect PABXs across an ATM network. Depending upon the sophistication of this service offering, CES will range from simple clear channel support of PABX trunks to providing cross-connect capability allowing $N \times 64$ Kbps connectivity. The most sophisticated offerings include support for PABX signaling. A user taking advantage of this service will deploy as CPE an ATM service multiplexer connected to both the PABX and a pre-existing router, a service multiplexer with integrated LAN and Layer 3 support, or an ATM switch with CBR interface. Video across ATM is an entirely different issue. Consider the possibilities outlined earlier in the book, where video may be transported directly across ATM or may utilize the TCP/IP stack. For both of these scenarios, the architectures for multipoint videoconferencing and VoD are different. Where video traffic is encapsulated without an intermediate network layer, it will look much like CBR data and, in fact, the same CBR interfaces will support this service. Multipoint conferencing in this environment will use a conferencing bridge no different to that currently deployed in conventional conferencing networks. In contrast, if the video traffic uses TCP/IP (or some other network layer Protocol), it may be generated at a traditional CODEC or on a PC or workstation. In both cases, the multipoint conferencing architecture includes elements of the ATM and the network layers, while VoD will make heavy use of Layer 3 multicasting techniques. A user requiring support for video must look at all these alternatives. Decision criteria include whether multipoint conferencing is required, whether interworking with LAN-based video sources and destinations is a part of the architecture, and whether 'legacy' videoconferencing equipment must be supported. We summarize the various data, voice, and video service offerings across an ATM infrastructure in Table 5.1.

Table 5.1 ATM data, voice, and video service offerings.

Service	Characteristics	Infrastructure
Cell relay	Most basic ATM service, providing the direct ATM cells to the user for data, voice, or video.	ATM service multiplexers and/or CPE ATM switches connected to core ATM switches.
LAN interconnect – Layer 3	ATM supporting high-speed LAN interconnection. Data only.	ATM-capable edge devices (routers, PCs, workstations) or ATM service multiplexers with routing capability connected to core ATM switches.
LANE	ATM supporting LANE service. Data only.	ATM-capable edge devices (routers, PCs, workstations, LAN switches) supporting LEC. LES/BUS deployed in core of network.

(continued)

Service	Characteristics	Infrastructure
Frame Relay transport or internetworking	ATM as high bandwidth Frame Relay backbone. Interworking with external native Frame Relay network. Data only.	ATM switches provide backbone and implement internetworking with native Frame Relay.
SMDS/CBDS	SMDS/CBDS across ATM network. Optional interworking with external DQDB-based SMDS network. Data only.	ATM-capable edge devices supporting SMDS/CBDS encapsulation at the ATM UNI. Switches at core provide interworking with SMDS and attach to **Connectionless Server (CLS)**.
Internet access	Much like LAN interconnect but includes value-added Internet-specific applications. Data only.	ATM-capable edge devices supporting Layer 3. Internet servers (E-mail, WWW, DNS, and so on) at core of ATM network. Service provider connection to Internet.
CES	Interconnection of PABXs across ATM network. May include clear channel, cross-connect, and optional signaling support.	ATM service multiplexer. This may also include LAN interfaces and Layer 3 capability. Alternatively, CBR interface at ATM switch.
Videoconferencing (CBR/VBR)	Interconnection of video CODECs across ATM network. Service provider may define multiple QoSs.	ATM service multiplexer. This may also include LAN interfaces and Layer 3 capability. Alternatively, CBR interface at ATM switch. Multi-cast server required for mpt-mpt.
Videoconferencing (ABR/UBR) RSVP ATM mapping	Interconnection of packet-based video CODECs across ATM network. QoS supported by	ATM-capable edge devices with RSVP mapping from non-ATM systems. Multicast address resolution server and optional multicast server required for mpt-mpt conferences.
VoD (CBR/VBR)	Multicasting of video feeds across ATM network to residences/business.	Video server connected to ATM switch. CPE consists of video decoders (set-top boxes). Video is directly over ATM.
VoD (ABR/UBR)	Multicasting of video feeds across ATM network to residences business.	Video server connected to ATM switch. CPE consists of ATM-capable edge devices supporting Layer 3 multicasting and, optionally, RSVP. Video encapsulated in Layer 3.

5.1.2 Vendor capabilities

To aid in the preparation of ATM Requests for Information (RFI), the Enterprise Network Roundtable of the ATMF has prepared a document titled *Mock ATM RFI White Paper* (ATM Forum, 1994h). The objectives of this paper, created by end users within the ATMF, are twofold. The first is to create a template for use by users and vendors which would accurately reflect the trend towards interoperable and flexible network architectures. And the second is to place in writing a list of questions regarding ATM features and functionality which may be used as a basis for data collection in support of an ATM implementation. The core of the document is structured along the lines of an actual RFI, to include the description of a fictional corporation and its global internetworking requirements. Specific areas covered by the mock RFI include:

- The respondent's company profile, including revenue, R&D, part-nerships and alliances, affiliation with ATM consortia, and whether or not the vendor is capable of offering an end-to-end solution.

- Hardware capabilities including switch functions and architec-tures, buffering, interfaces, redundancy, and scalability. Hardware also includes end-systems, focusing on ATM adapters, interoper-ability testing, host requirements, signaling and encapsulation support, and management.

- Software capabilities including network management accounting capabilities, platform support, and service contract definition. Signaling and connection management are also software consider-ations, with the latter including the integration of new services, SVC interoperability testing, the scalability of the connection management entity or system, and redundancy.

- Routing and traffic handling including actions taken upon link failures, load sharing, NNI implementations, multicasting and broadcasting, congestion control, clocking, and interoperability.

- Support and training, an important, although often overlooked area, including preventive maintenance schedules and support, coverage of this support, technical assistance staffing, and train-ing.

- Pricing and distribution including distribution channels and pric-ing for product vendors as well as service costs and pricing models for service providers.

- Differentiating features, offering the respondent a chance to build a competitive business case based on a comparison with other sup-pliers while at the same time addressing ATM's ability to reduce customer costs and provide greater value in contrast to potential competing technologies.

The areas described above may prove most useful not only in developing an RFI, but will also encourage potential respondents to act proactively in gathering and properly summarizing the data. It is hoped that the RFI will encourage organizations planning to deploy ATM to take a realistic view when contacting potential vendors by concentrating more on overall capabilities as opposed to responding to verbatim check-lists of ATMF and ITU standards which unfortunately was the case with many early RFIs/RFPs.

5.1.3 Detailed requirements

Building upon the above document, the following more detailed standards and strategy-related questions may be used in vendor selection (Table 5.2). Note that some questions will apply only to certain platforms, while others may apply to both end-systems and switches. End-systems in this context include ATM-connected routers, LAN switches,

Table 5.2 Vendor capabilities.

ATM physical interface support for switches and ATM-connected end-systems	
Data rates and standards:	Physical media support:
25 Mbps (Desktop ATM25)	Singlemode, multimode, and plastic fiber
51, 155, 622 Mbps SONET/SDH	Coaxial cable
100 Mbps TAXI	Twisted pair (for example, UTP-5, UTP-3, STP)
1.544 or 45 Mbps North American PDH	Other (for example, wireless)
2.048 or 34 Mbps PDH; E2 or J2 PDH	Connector type (for example, ST, SC, MIC, BNC)
Other physical interface support for some switches and ATM-connected end-systems	
Data rates and standards:	Physical media support:
10 Mbps Ethernet (half/full duplex)	Singlemode fiber
4/16 Mbps Token Ring (half/full duplex)	Multimode fiber
100 Mbps fast Ethernet	Twisted pair (for example, UTP-5, UTP-3, STP)
(half/full duplex) (or 1 Gbps in future)	
100 Mbps VG-AnyLAN	Coaxial cable
(or higher speeds in future)	
FDDI (half/full duplex)	Other (for example, wireless)
ISDN BRI, PRI	Connector type (for example, ST, SC, MIC, BNC)
	Plastic fiber
G.703/704 (channelized)	
Video (for example, MPEG-2, M-JPEG, H.261)	
Circuit emulation (for example, T1, E1, E2, J2, T3, E3)	
SMDS-SNI or SMDS-DXI	
Frame Relay, FUNI	
AIMUX (ATM Inverse Mux)	
Other (for example, fiber channel, HIPPI, IBM ESCON)	
Residential access (for example, ADSL, VDSL, FTTC)	
Conformance to the ATM Forum UNI for switches and ATM-connected end-systems	
ATMF UNI 3.0 (Q.93B) signaling and/or UNI 3.1/4.0 (Q.2931) signaling	
Signaling messages implemented (all or a subset)	
Setup messages implemented (mandatory elements and optional elements)	
Q.SAAL SSCOP and/or Q.2110 SSCOP	
ILMI	
Support for pt-pt, pt-mpt, and mpt-mpt (future) SVCs, SVPs, PVCs, PVPs	
SVC tunneling, soft PVCs	

(continued)

Conformance to the ATM Forum NNI for switches
ATM Forum PNNI Phase 1, IISP
Vendor proprietary topology management and route computation algorithm
B-ICI
Traffic and congestion control for switches and ATM-connected end-systems
UPC support and leaky bucket, I.371
Traffic shaping and cell spacing
Granularity of shaping and policing
Rate-based flow control mechanisms (FECN, BECN, ATM Forum ABR EFCI, RR and ER.)
Early packet discard for AAL5
Service category support for switches and ATM-connected end-systems
CBR, rt-VBR, nrt-VBR, ABR, UBR
Network management for all systems
Global network management strategy across product line – private and/or public
Management platform and capabilities – operating system support and release strategy – single or multiple platforms?
Service management and circuit provisioning
Physical and logical management of systems and services
SNMPv1 and v2 if applicable
MIBS: MIB II (full/partial/planned), ATM MIB (RFC 1695), physical interface MIBs, ILMI MIB, LANE client MIB, vendor-specific MIBs and capabilities, Amon MIB and circuit-steering capabilities
Physical layer management (F1, F2, F3) and ATM OAM flows (F4, F5)
Non-SNMP-based management tools and capabilities
Conformance to IETF standards for some switches and ATM-connected end-systems
RFC 1577 and follow-on (architecture for the support of Classical IP and ARP over ATM) and updates
RFC 1483 (defines multiprotocol encapsulation over ATM AAL5) LLC/SNAP (bridged and routed protocols), VC mux (bridged and routed protocols)
RFC 1626 (defines a default IP MTU for use over ATM AAL5)
RFC 1755 and follow-on (defines UNI 3.1 signaling in support of RFC 1577) and updates describing UNI 4.0
RFC 1209 (defines IP encapsulation over SMDS)
RFC 1490 (defines multiprotocol encapsulation over Frame Relay)
Other (for example, NHRP, multicasting, RSVP)
LANE and MPOA for switches and ATM-connected end-systems
pt-mpt SVCs and ILMI
LANE server (scalability, where implemented)
LANE client (where implemented)
Broadcast and unknown server (where implemented)
Support for multiple VLANs – how and what protocols
Route redistribution – vendor proprietary or ATM Forum (for example, MPOA)
ATM Forum MPOA – implementation timeframe
Other services for switches and ATM-connected end-systems
Frame Relay service and/or network interworking: compliance with FRF.5 and FRF.8
SMDS/CBDS CLSF: integrated connectionless server, interworking with DQDB-based SMDS networks
Video encoding, distribution, and interworking: videoconferencing, multipoint video bridging, video servers, multicasting and broadcasting for video, distance learning, video compression techniques and interfaces to dynamically optimize bandwidth
ATM Forum CES and VTOA; voice interworking; N-ISDN to ATM signaling: DS1/E1 digital voice interface, ISDN PRI and/or BRI, analog voice interface, fax/modem detection and bypass, echo-cancellation, voice compression (for instance, ADPCM, GSM), CAS and/or CCS signaling support, CBR support over ATM UNI (not CES)
Other services and interworking functions TBD

hosts, service multiplexers, and any other potential devices such as cameras and set-top boxes. Responses may consist of yes, no, or clarifications. In using a list of capabilities, one should not develop a 'shopping list' outlook, as it is very difficult to convey a vendor's potential added-value by responding to a pre-selected set of questions. These are only guidelines.

5.1.4 PICS and conformance testing

Two aids in verifying vendor compliance with standards are the PICS and Conformance Testing Suites as published by the ATM Forum. The first set of documents, Protocol Implementation Conformance Statements, are tables to be completed by vendors identifying compliance (or lack of support) for each item of a referenced specification. For example, the 100 Mbps Multimode Fiber PICS references the ATM Forum UNI, while the DS1 PICS references the supplementary DS1 specification (ATM Forum, 1994a). All vendors should complete the PICS, and users should gather these completed documents as part of the planning process. PICS released by mid-1996 are listed in Appendix A, and additional documents are expected based on new interfaces and services.

The second set of documents, the Conformance Test Suites, detail test plans for verifying a system's compliance with the standards. These draw on the testing concepts outlined in ISO/IEC 9646, *Information Technology – Open Systems Interconnection – Conformance testing technology and framework*. For example, the suite for end-systems (ATM Forum, 1995m) includes tests for ATM cell structure, ATM layer functions, and management. In testing an end-system, a test system will be inserted in place of the ATM switch (intermediate system). We summarize test suites released as of mid-1996 in Appendix A.

Parallel to conformance testing is performance benchmarking of ATM switches. The goal here is to determine how well a given switch will support the ATM traffic classes and higher-layer applications. Performance metrics include: throughput, frame loss rate, back-to-back burst size, latency, and call establishment time. The throughput is the rate at which the switch can pass cells without loss. Closely related to this is the frame loss rate at a given load. If we generate a burst of frames by an application, we can determine the maximum back-to-back burst size by increasing this value until cells are lost. The latency is a function of the last bit in to the first bit out, while the call establishment time is the amount of time needed to establish a new VC. Another metric is how well the switch reaches steady state when new VCs are established (Jain and Nagendra, 1995). These various metrics are used to determine how well a given switch design lives up to its specifications and whether it is suitable for a given deployment. Over the coming years, we should see a number of very detailed switch comparisons, not only focusing on support of standards as in the past but detailing performance as well.

5.1.5 Project planning

Worth mentioning, though possibly more suited to a book on project management, are some of the issues which go into implementing an ATM internetwork once vendor and technology selection is completed. In a typical RFP, a given vendor will be asked to address these very points. These issues include, but are not limited to:

- Assessing the risks associated with implementing the new technology/architecture

- Timing, including equipment deployment, training, cutover, and so on

- Migration strategies for hardware, software, and operating procedures

- Problem escalation and resolution

- Test and acceptance plans and procedures

- Management system integration

- Documentation and training

- Change control and upgrade procedures; change management

- Installation and build processes

- Site surveys

- Standards compliance

- Safety and EMI compliance

- Project management staff

5.2 Infrastructure

An ATM network as deployed will consist of an underlying physical infrastructure, ATM switches, routers and LAN switches connecting existing LAN segments, and possibly directly connected PCs and workstations. The user will deploy combinations of these various devices depending upon the extent of the network and connectivity required. To begin, the Layer 1 physical infrastructure will normally consist of fiber as a local-area, backbone, or wide-area transmission media, twisted pair in the local area, and various combinations of optical and electrical patch panels. Other less common media types such as coaxial cable and wireless technologies may be employed where required. Depending upon the ATM data model in use, LANs will connect to the ATM core via either LAN switches or routers. For example, the LANE standard makes heavy use of LAN switching, while the Classical model/MPOA is more dependent upon routers. Routers will provide connectivity between the different ATM domains and between ATM and external networks. Last and certainly not least, the choice of an ATM switch, be it workgroup, enterprise, or central office, will depend upon the extent of the network, services required, and budget.

5.2.1 Role of networking equipment

As an introduction to the physical infrastructure of an ATM internetwork, it is useful to first look at the functions of the devices introduced above, to include their purpose and their function as part of an end-to-end network. The ATM switch is probably the most visible element in any ATM network and, though the primary role of the switch is to forward cells from one physical interface to another – the data or foreground path – this same switch is also performing a number of background functions. Cell forwarding will be accomplished through the use of highly-optimized hardware (for example, custom ASICs or specialized hardware), while a more general-purpose processor (for example, RISC or CISC) will generate the topology database, and accept signaling requests and process SNMP queries and responses, to name a few functions. The software within the switch controlling ABR, generating the PNNI tables, and controlling QoS, will operate both in the foreground and the background. Thus, the switch must have some level of sophistication, not only within hardware, but within its software as well.

A router is somewhat analogous to an ATM switch in that it will perform foreground and background functions as well, with the foreground processing operating on a higher layer than that of the ATM switch. Layer 3 packet forwarding through the router is the task of optimized interface and switching hardware, much like that found on the ATM switch but now operating on a packet basis, while generation of the routing table is carried out in the background by the general-purpose route processor. In this case, as opposed to operating on the ATM layer, this processor relies on Layer 3 routing protocols, IS-IS, OSPF, and E-IGRP as examples, to generate its topology database and thus the list of networks reachable over each interface. A router may participate in ATM layer routing as well.

LAN switches connect existing LANs to the ATM backbone at Layer 2. In effect, they are intelligent multiport bridges with ATM interfaces, and are the basic edge devices used as part of LANE. If LAN switches are provided with Layer 3 functionality, they may participate in

Layer 3 routing. Since a LAN switch operates at Layer 2, it will normally forward all traffic between workgroups to a central router. As opposed to forwarding this inter-workgroup traffic to a router, efficiency will increase if this LAN switch is provided with the capability to internally forward packets from one workgroup to another. The objective is to provide LAN switches with the additional capability at only incremental cost; hence the concept of **multilayer switching**, where a LAN switch will not only forward packets based on Layer 2, but will also be capable of making use of cached Layer 3 reachability information. This cached data is generated by one or more central route processors, located preferably on traditional routers, though an ATM switch or even a workstation may be provided with this route generation capability. Note that in the case of the ATM switch, it is in effect turned into a router, and in the case of the workstation, no stable multiprotocol routing software (that is, capable of IP, IPX, AppleTalk, Banyan Vines and DECnet) has yet been deployed.

Finally, PCs and workstations connect to an ATM network via **Network Interface Cards (NICs)**. These NICs include the necessary hardware to adapt and segment data packets for transmission over the physical interface. The NIC will also include the necessary encapsulation software, depending upon the data model, along with drivers which will interface to the higher-layer application programs. As opposed to routers or LAN switches, which may be capable of participating in a Layer 3 routing protocol, a PC or workstation will normally default to its nearest router. Therefore, these end-systems will not participate in ATM layer routing (for example, PNNI).

When looking at ATM as an end-to-end technology and infrastructure, a question arises as to the role of routers and routing. This question should really be rephrased in the context of the above discussion into one of processes – foreground packet or cell switching functions and background topology calculation and management functions. Each of these functions may then be related to the layers of the protocol stack – the ATM layer, the MAC layer, and the network layer. The question is then clear: will ATM layer switching ever replace MAC and network layer switching? If so, will ATM layer topology calculation ever totally replace network layer calculations? Some have drawn an analogy between ATM and the phone system, a globally transparent system which includes diverse end-systems and methods of maintaining reachability based on a universal addressing scheme. At some point in the distant future, a ubiquitous ATM network may in fact take the place of both the global phone system and all LANs. The ATM layer would provide end-to-end connectivity, with reachability information (ATM layer routing) exchanged via private and public NNI protocols. For the foreseeable future this will not be the case, and existing LANs and the various WAN technologies are not capable of transparently exchanging reachability information between one another. For example, the Frame Relay NNI will not interact with the ATM NNI. Thus, reachability information must be exchanged on some higher layer – Layer 3. This is the function of the route processor within the router and of existing Layer 3 routing protocols. Though the physical appearance of the router will surely change, with functions distributed between traditional integrated routers, switches, and workstations, Layer 3 will still provide the end-to-end global connectivity.

5.2.2 Redundancy

When planning an internetwork for a production environment, the question of redundancy invariably arises. Redundancy can take many forms, but within the networking community it usually refers to attempts made to ensure that traffic will continue to flow across a LAN or WAN when intermediate systems or their interconnects fail. ATM presents an interesting problem, in that it is not redundant in its most basic configuration: if an ATM switch fails, all users single-homed to that switch will loose connectivity. This is in contrast to FDDI, commonly used for campus backbones. FDDI provides for redundancy via two identical rings, a primary (A), and a secondary (B), while at the same time allowing for dual-homing of end-systems. In the wide area, redundancy is usually achieved by providing for an alternative path between sites. For example, a leased line user will often install an ISDN or analog dial-up connection in case of primary link failure. Neither of these options may be viable in the ATM environment, since the degree of redundancy provided by a 64K ISDN connection backing up a 64K leased line may not be appropriate for ATM speeds. However, ATM networks do provide redundancy internally based on rerouting of trunks via the PNNI or IISP. In addition, the underlying transmission infrastructure may provide rerouting. For example, SDH/SONET may be deployed in this configuration. In both the local and wide areas, a degree of redundancy may be provided via dual homing from an end-system to one or more ATM switches. Connectivity to two switches is suggested for the following reason. Though a switch may be marketed as fully redundant, and, in fact, it may be provided with multiple power supplies, 1:1 interfaces, and even multiple processors, there is always the possibility that failure will be caused by not hardware but software. In addition, the switch may be put of action from an event affecting its physical surroundings. Thus, as with all networking and computing devices, total reliability may only be achieved by physical diversity of systems. This dual-homing recommendation, though logical for local-area ATM (and using the PNNI), may not be feasible in the wide area due to tariffing considerations. For example, a campus may utilize a 34 Mbps access into the public ATM service. It is doubtful that funds will be available to provide for a second link. Two alternatives in this case would be to use primary rate (E1 or DS1) ISDN service or an intermediate-bandwidth (E1 or DS1) Frame Relay or leased service. With either of these alternatives, compression increasing available bandwidth by a factor of 2+ may also be implemented. Of course, neither will replace the bandwidth lost upon ATM link failure – they will only provide for the continued delivery of mission-critical data (for example, pre-defined via prioritization and queuing) until the ATM connection is re-established.

5.2.3 Physical media

The choice of cabling will depend in part on the extent of the network, the capabilities of the interfaces on attached routers, switches, and end-systems, and, possibly most important, on the investment in the existing cable infrastructure. Looking from the workgroup outward, many users have deployed structured cabling systems based on UTP or STP to the desktop. The majority of PCs and workstations will therefore connect in this way. Servers, if located on the floor, will also connect via copper, but many will be located closer to the ATM switch where fiber may be employed. The campus backbone and the riser in large buildings is usually fiber. This provides the backbone for interconnecting ATM switches, and will also be the medium of choice for connecting routers and LAN switches to the ATM backbone. Though campus fiber is multimode in the vast majority of installations, singlemode fiber is also deployed in places. Finally, connectivity to the wide area will be via singlemode fiber or copper (both twisted pair and coaxial) depending upon data rates and distance. In some environments where fixed cabling is not desirable, wireless technologies including radio, microwave, and laser may also be employed.

Fiber

The fiber infrastructure will include a mix of **multimode (MM)** and **singlemode (SM)** fiber optic cable. Major differences in the fiber types include bandwidth supported, allowable distance, and cost of installation. Whereas SM is more expensive to terminate, it can easily support 622 Mbps at distances of 30 km and above. In fact, some SM reaches have been tested at 75 km+ without the need for repeaters. In contrast, MM fiber may be terminated with LEDs, and is therefore less expensive, but is limited to lower data rates and distances. A great deal of MM exists on campus due to the deployment of extended distance Ethernets, Token Rings, and of course FDDI. For those making the transition to ATM by replacing existing LAN extenders or FDDI concentrators with ATM switches and end-system interfaces, the preservation of investment in the existing cabling plant is of importance. In most campus and high-rise environments, MM will prove sufficient for the planned distances and bandwidth. This may not be the case in large industrial campuses such as those found in the auto or chemical industries, nor to 'metropolitan' campuses (ports, military bases). In these environments, SM may be the only option. SM may also be required when bandwidth requirements are expected to exceed those possible with MM. For example, a user may plan ATM trunks at 622 Mbps and above. In installing a new cable plant, we suggest both types of fiber if funds permit. This cost may be justified if the cost of the actual cable is compared to the installation cost. The SM need not be terminated until such a time as it will be placed in use.

We summarize the distance limitation for the various fiber types in Table 5.3.

Though singlemode connectors on ATM equipment are often listed as being compliant with the intermediate or long range classifications, in many cases light budgets may vary. For actual deployment, the anticipated link distance should be used in conjunction with the light loss over the fiber and splices to calculate the sensitivity required. This may then be compared against the specifications of the interface. For example, a singlemode fiber run should have a loss from 0–12 dB (ANSI T1E1.2/93-020R3). If the fiber complies with EIA Class IVa, then its loss should be a maximum of 0.3 dB/km (measured with an optical TDR). Allocating 0.5 dB per splice, a single run of 30 km with 4 splices would therefore have a loss of 11 dB. Assuming an ATM interface rated at a 19 dB worst case power budget, the margin would be 8 dB, acceptable in this case. Stretching the calculation, a high power interface with a 32 dB power budget would allow a link of over 75 km while staying within acceptable

Table 5.3 Fibre optic cable characteristics.

Fiber type	Classification	Distance	Cable	Bandwidth	Light budget
POF (Note 1)	Home/office	50 m	1 mm	50/155 Mbps	17 dB
Multimode	None	2 km	62.5/50 μm	155 Mbps	10 dB
Multimode	None	100 m	62.5/50 μm	622 Mbps	9 dB
Singlemode	Local reach	2 km	8.5 μm	155 Mbps+	9 dB (Note 2)
Singlemode	Intermediate reach	15 km+	8.5 μm	155 Mbps+	19 dB
Singlemode	Long reach	40 km+	8.5 μm	155 Mbps+	32 dB

Note 1 Proposed **Plastic Optical Fiber (POF)** for in-home or office use. Typical transmit minimum power of −8 dB with a maximum of −2 dB; receive minimum of −25 dB and maximum of −2 dB.

Note 2 From UNI 3.1, MM transmit minimum of −20 dB and maximum of −14 dB. Receive minimum of −29 dB and maximum of −14 dB. Worst cast is therefore 9 dB. SM interfaces typically deployed have worst case of 19 dB for intermediate reach and 32 dB for long reach. Another parameter is the dynamic range, the difference in power between the highest transmit signal and the lowest receive signal. For example, an MM fiber with −20/−14 transmit and −30/−14 receive will have a light budget of 10 dB and a dynamic range of 16 dB.

margins. This same calculation may be applied to multimode fiber which complies with the FDDI specification (ISO/IEC 9314-3). Based on a 500 Mhz/km capability, loss per km should not exceed 1.5 dB. Allowing an attenuation across the path of 0–9 dB, the maximum length of the fiber run should not exceed 2 km. This is based on an attenuation of 3 dB (2×1.5 dB/Km) and 6 dB loss from less-than-optimal splices. While direct fiber runs and precision splices may allow a 4 km link to satisfy the light budget, the constraint here will be the dispersion of the fiber, which will still tend to limit the ultimate distance to 2 km.

In many cases, a user must also contend with the differences in commonly deployed fiber plants between North America and Europe. In the former, where most ATM equipment is sourced, 62.5/125 μm is common, while in Europe, both 50/125 and 62.5/125 μm are the norm. Though 62.5 interfaces may be connected to a 50 μm cable plant, some loss in power will result. As an example, the loss from 62.5 to 50 micron fiber will be $10\log 10((62.5/50)^{\wedge 2})=1.9$ dB. This is about four times that of a typical optical patch (0.3 dB loss actual; 0.5 dB loss for planning purposes), and is acceptable if no alternative is available. The 1.9 dB loss will affect the maximum distance of the fiber runs as calculated in the previous paragraph. Many manufacturers will publish minimum transmit power values for both 62.5 and 50 μm and these values should be used in link design. Though connection to 50 μm fiber is acceptable, another workaround, this time connecting multimode directly to singlemode fiber, clearly is not. The loss when converting from 50 micron multimode fiber to 10 micron singlemode is 14 dB, and from 62.5 to 10 is 16 dB. Thus, a conversion from either type of multimode fiber to singlemode is not recommended, and the use must deploy the proper physical interface or an external converter.

Also of concern is the wide variety of fiber connectors in use: FSD, ST, SC, and FC. The **Fixed Shroud Duplex system (FSD)**, also known as MIC, was specified originally for FDDI interfaces. This was carried over into ATM since the 100 Mbps TAXI specification is derived from FDDI. ST is a round, bayonet or twist-lock coupling connector, while SC to is a push/pull coupling connector similar to ST, but square instead of round. Finally, an FC connector is round and threaded. Confusion exists as to public SDH/SONET deployment, primarily for singlemode fiber. Though the ATM Forum has standardized on SC (used more in the local area) as an alternative to FC (used by the Telcos/PTTs), equipment exists with ST and FCPC as well. Thus, conversion cables are frequently required.

An interesting side note relates to the choice of wavelengths for use over fiber. Although 1300 nm is the norm for ATM installations, local deployments of fiber include 850 nm while 1550 nm appears within public transmission equipment. These wavelengths relate to the attenuation curve of fiber. Below 1300 nm, the attenuation grows, though cheaper termination equipment may be deployed. At about 1400 nm, attenuation spikes due to water absorbtion, while 1550 nm provides low attenuation but is more expensive to terminate.

Twisted pair

Twisted pair cabling includes the commonly installed **Unshielded Twisted Pair Type 3 (UTP-3)**, **Type 5 (UTP-5)**, as well as a future **Unshielded Twisted Type 6 (UTP-6)** and **Shielded Twisted Pair (STP)**. Each of these cable types has associated transmission rate limitations. Twisted pair is installed between end-systems and a wiring closet, usually located on a floor of a building. Connections to a workgroup ATM switch are usually made at this point, along with links to the building or campus fiber backbone.

The various types of UTP cable available in order of increasing quality included Cat 3 (UTP-3), Cat 4 (UTP-4) and Cat 5 (UTP-5). A future Cat 6, capable of 300 and 600 Mhz response, will support higher bandwidth connections in comparison to Cat 5's 100 Mhz limitation. Note that the transmission rate of the data (25 Mbps, 100 Mbps, 155 Mbps, and so on) is not the coding rate at which the information is carried over the wire. For example, the MLT-3 coding used for FDDI over UTP-5 is a three-level coding resulting in a maximum frequency of 30 MHz. Other coding techniques include QPR-IV which reduces the frequency to 15 MHz for 100 Mbps bandwidth and CSMA/CD (two level). This use of multilevel coding is no different to that found within modems, where 14.4 and 28.8 Kbps modems code the data in such a way as to fit into the 3 KHz analog voice spectrum over phone lines. Another important consideration in the transport of high data rates over twisted pair is the resulting electromagnetic emanation. For example, in Europe, emission levels may not exceed the values within EN55022. The quality of a given cable is dependent upon a number of factors, to include impedance, attenuation, **Near End Crosstalk (NEXT)**, and **Far End Crosstalk (FEXT)**. A single value coming into use summarizing the total quality of the cable is the **Attenuation Crosstalk Ratio (ACR)**, a relation of the NEXT to the attenuation. This in effect is analogous to the cable's **Signal-to-Noise Ratio (SNR)**.

STP is the 150 ohm cable used for most Token Ring networks. It consists of Types 1 and 2, both of which are capable of 100 meter runs. An additional STP, Type 6, is suitable for use as patch cabling. In installing UTP and STP, care should be taken to not exceed 90 meters between patch panel and wall connector. This will leave 10 meters for connections within the patch and between the wall plate and the user. Installed cable will consist of two- or four-pair 100 or 120 ohm in the case of UTP, or two-pair 150 ohm STP. In Table 5.4 we summarize the various local media types along with some observations as to cost and probable acceptance.

Table 5.4 Local-area ATM summary.

Standard	Media	Bandwidth	Distance	Cost	Acceptance
STM-4 (+)	SM fiber	622 Mbps (+)	15 km+	High	1996+
STM-4	MM fiber	622 Mbps	100 meters	Moderate	1996+
STM-1	SM fiber	155 Mbps	15 km+	High	Wide
STM-1	MM fiber	155 Mbps	2 km	Moderate	Wide
STM-1	UTP-5	155 Mbps	100 meters	Low	Wide
STM-1	UTP-3	155 Mbps	100 meters	Low	1996+
TAXI	MM fiber	100 Mbps	2 km	Moderate	Decreasing
STS-1	UTP-3	51 Mbps	100 meters	Moderate	Little
Desktop ATM25	UTP-3/5/STP	25.6 Mbps	100 meters	Low	1996+
STM-1	Plastic fiber	155 Mbps	50 meters	Very low	1996+
STS-1	Plastic fiber	51 Mbps	50 meters	Very low	1996+

Wide-area connectivity

In connecting a local area ATM network with a public ATM network, the physical interface will depend upon the transmission service and bandwidth offered. For example, a PDH E3 (34 Mbps) local loop will normally terminate in G.703-compliant coaxial cable. The same holds true for the somewhat limited E4 (140 Mbps) deployment. In contrast, STM-1 at 155 Mbps may be provided either optically or electrically. If optical, SM fiber is the norm. Refer to Table 3.2 in Section 3.1 for the various wide-area physical interfaces, data rates, cable types, and connectors.

Wireless

In some environments, alternatives to fiber and copper may be deployed. Consider a large manufacturing campus divided into two or more regions by a public right-of-way. If user-owned cable runs do not exist, transmission based on microwave or laser technologies may be more cost-effective to deploy than either leasing Telco-owned fiber with its associated tariff or installing fiber runs if permitted. Wireless alternatives may also be justified on a large campus if network nodes are widely separated, resulting in high cable installation costs. Four considerations are important in deciding whether to deploy wireless technology. The first is the bandwidth required; ATM data rates fall at the upper end of most microwave technologies. Related to bandwidth is distance: the extent of the campus, and whether multiple hops are acceptable. Two interference-related considerations include weather, in that some technologies are very susceptible to rain, fog, and so on, and radio interference. This latter consideration will play a role in technology selection, as microwave and other radio technologies may be unacceptable in some environments. The three contenders in the local area are radio, microwave, and laser. Of the three, the last may be the most viable for short- to mid-range due to bandwidth and resilience to interference from weather and RF. Once the distance limitations of laser systems are exceeded, digital microwave may be considered. Note that we speak of the campus and metropolitan area here; of course microwave and satellite systems are of course suitable for the wide area.

Laser systems are suitable for high bandwidth wireless transmission over a limited area (2–5 km). One currently deployed system is capable of transmitting at a data rate equivalent to the SDH-based ATM at 155 Mbps. As introduced above, an advantage of laser-based systems is their immunity to electromagnetic radiation. Because of this, multipath distortion does not influence the signal and the technology may be used in interference-prone environments including airports and nuclear power plants. In looking at 'non-traditional' technologies for building wide-area ATM networks, satellite systems have often been relegated to the sidelines due to their high latencies and limited transponder bandwidth. If the switches within the network are able to work with the latency by providing adequate buffering and/or directing traffic by application profile, then one part of the problem is solved. The bandwidth limitation has been overcome by a CODEC announced through the International Telecommunications Satellite Organization (INTELSAT). This device, developed by the Australian Space Center for Signal Processing, is capable of transmitting at 155 Mbps over the standard 72 MHz satellite transponders in use by INTELSAT satellites. Digital radio and microwave systems are also capable of supporting ATM, though not normally at STM-1 rates.

A concern with all wireless systems is the BER, which may be translated into an expected ATM cell loss. This is usually caused by aberrations in the atmosphere: dust, water, and heat. Using the effect of rainfall on the laser system as an example, the design goal was to preserve an acceptable error rate over 1 km during a rainfall of 20 to 30 mm per hour. This measurement is derived by directly correlating the optical attenuation in dB and the expected error rate. At a bit rate of 125 Mbps, the BER increases from 10^{-9} at 28 dB attenuation to 10^{-5} at 30 dB and greater than 10^{-4} at 32 dB. These final two BER figures are greater than that tolerated by ATM due to cell loss.

5.2.4 Intermediate systems: ATM switching

The choice of an ATM switch is not as simple as it may seem at first glance. Selection criteria will include the geographical extent of the network, the number of users and their bandwidth requirements, and whether multiple services such as voice are projected. A large ATM network is hierarchical, with different types of ATM switch optimized to perform different functions. This is analogous to the phone system switching infrastructure, where various sizes of PABXs connect to **Central Office (CO)** switches, which in turn connect to tandem switches, responsible for wide-area trunking and international connectivity, and to large router-based internetworks consisting of core, distribution, and access routers. In the same way, a fully deployed ATM network will include workgroup switches, supporting small groups of users, in turn connected to larger, multiservice campus switches. These devices will then connect to either CO access switches or directly to larger CO nodes if the end user makes use of a public service. Alternatively, if constructing a private ATM WAN, these switches may be trunked with one another over the wide area. Each type of switch is optimized to perform certain functions in terms of feature set (interfaces, services), and will differ in terms of redundancy, management, and cost. In some cases, a single switching platform may be positioned at more than one layer of the hierarchy. This is especially true with the campus switch, often suitable for both CO access and corporate core networks. We summarize classes of ATM switch in Table 5.5.

An ATM switch, be it workgroup, campus, CO access, or CO, will consist of a number of basic elements, to include input and output ports, a switch fabric, and a management and control processor. The input and output ports are in turn managed by controllers which are responsible for buffering, cell duplication, cell processing, virtual channel translation, traffic multiplexing/demultiplexing, and establishing path reservations through the switch fabric where required.

The switch fabric is responsible for establishing paths between input and output ports as well as implementing a mechanism which will avoid or minimize internal blocking. This fabric will of course support multiple simultaneous connections within the switch. Switch fabric designs include shared memory and shared medium, both time division architectures, as well as single and multiple path space division switches. Time division architectures multiplex memory or a bus among the inputs, and are common in workgroup switches. The shared memory design is cost effective in that, for N ports, the architecture requires multiport memory with $2N$ ports, requiring a growth in complexity (and cost) of the memory only proportional to N.

Table 5.5 ATM switch classes.

Switch class	Interfaces	Throughput	Criteria	Cost
Workgroup/ campus	ATM	2.5–10 Gbps	Cost	<$1000/port
Enterprise/ large campus	ATM, circuit, frame, (LAN)	2.5–10 Gbps	Services, reliability	<$10,000/port
Central office edge (or access)	ATM, circuit, frame	10+ Gbps	Services, reliability, management	<$10,000/port
Central office core	ATM	40+ Gbps	Throughput, reliability, management	<$10,000/port

Note   Throughput assumes switch architectures common in the 1997 timeframe

Space division architectures support multiple connections based on non-conflicting paths within the switch, and may provide a single path or multiple paths between input and output ports. Two methods of routing within such a switch include self-routing and label routing. The first relies on the interconnection of the switching elements within the switching fabric, while the second makes use of the VCI field in the cell header for routing decisions. For both, arbitrary paths through the switch may be used on a cell-by-cell basis. In describing switch architectures, vendors speak of 'blocking' or 'non-blocking' switch fabrics (Figure 5.2). One of the most basic elements in good buffer design is avoiding the **Head-Of-Line (HOL)** blocking problems associated with **First-In-First-Out (FIFO)** buffers. This is a situation where cells destined to multiple outputs may be held up by a cell destined to a congested port. A method of avoiding this is through the establishment of a windowing mechanism where cells behind the first in line are examined for destination. Consider five cells on an input all destined for the same output link. The problem is exacerbated if a high-speed input link is a feeding combination of low- and high-speed outputs. Congestion at the low-speed output may lead to buffer starvation at the input, affecting the other high-speed outputs in turn. The Banyan and Delta architectures, both space division switches, suffer from this limitation. As a solution, most implementations of these architectures employ internal speedup mechanisms to minimize contention.

As an example, a switch implementing a single 10×10 matrix is subject to a 36% blocking probability if input and output line rates are equal. This blocking percentage results in a 64% switch efficiency, with

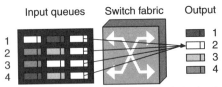

Cells for port 2 block transit of cells further back in queue.
Switch is only 25% utilized at one switch clock cycle.
HOL blocking limits switch utilization to approximately 58%.

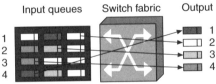

Tagging at switch input or intelligent queue management eliminates HOL blocking problem.

Figure 5.2 Avoiding head-of-line blocking.

cells blocked within the switch fabric having to be reinserted by the input cell buffers. Since this efficiency is clearly unacceptable, vendors have implemented ways to lower the blocking percentage. Once method is by doubling the rates of the output ports within the switch matrix. This reduces the probability of blocking to 8%, resulting in a 92% switch efficiency. This contention problem may also be avoided by sorting cells according to their destination before placing them into the switch fabric. One well-known sorter network is the Batcher (thus the term 'Batcher-Banyan' when referring to some switch designs). Further complicating matters, blocking within a switch may be further compounded by cascading switch matrices. In contrast to the efficiency derived from the single 10×10 matrix, a switch constructed of cascaded 4×4 or 2×2 matrices will be subject to a degradation in performance equal to the multiplier of the blocking probability at each stage.

A concern with any of the above switch fabrics is scalability, important in determining how suitable a given architecture is for growth. For example, a vendor may wish to deploy 16 port workgroup or 64 port campus switches based on the same architecture. Whereas the complexity of a simple matrix switch rises with the square of the number of interfaces, with obvious implications on scalability, Banyan and Batcher-Banyan fabrics require only $n*(\log n)$ or $n*(\log m)^{\wedge 2}$ respectively. This is further reduced by time division architectures which scale linearly with the number of ports. In the final analysis, viable workgroup and campus switches may implement a combination of time- and space-division multiplexing. Also, the scalability of the matrix design may not be that much of an issue since, with a sufficiently fast matrix, lower speed ports may be multiplexed at input. Consider a 10×10 matrix with internal 800 Mbps channel. Though a single port is capable of supporting only a single 622 Mbps link, it may support 4×155 Mbps or an even greater number of DS3 or E3 connections. The same holds true for most other switch designs.

Time-division fabrics are viable due to the linear behavior exhibited when increasing the number of ports, the support of multicast connections with little additional complexity due to the broadcast nature of shared mediums, and the ability to support ports with higher data rates by configuring a higher transmission priority or by utilizing additional internal timeslots. Supporters of space-division fabrics concentrate on suitability for implementation in VLSI logic and scalability. One proposed solution implements time-division technologies at the interfaces with space-division matrices within the core of the switch; the first supporting expandability and variability of interfaces rates, and the latter providing for multiple paths and speed (Rooholamini, 1994).

Looking back at shared memory architectures, these in fact may be the most viable due to the ease in providing high throughput (5 Gbps and above) and buffering efficiency. As opposed to almost all other architectures, the shared memory matrix allows all input and outputs to share a common buffer pool. Thus, interfaces experiencing congestion may take advantage of any buffers available at a given instant. If we compare the amount of buffering required between 32 port shared memory designs and output-buffering while keeping a CLR at 10^{-10} for typical traffic profiles, the former architecture will use up to 800K cells of buffering while share memory requires under 40K. This 20-fold average gain in efficiency of course results in cost savings. In addition, multicast traffic may be efficiently handled since we only need to store a single copy of the data in the shared memory fabric at any given point in time. The next generations of workgroup, campus, and even core switches are beginning to implement this architecture due to cost advantages and traffic management capabilities.

One question yet to be answered for all switch classes concerns signaling support. Consider the beginning of a workday at a typical enterprise. During the night, many of the SVCs may have timed out, resulting in a signaling crunch as users re-establish contact with servers. The switch or switches at the center of a major campus should be capable of handling this load. Next, consider the numerous data transactions such as network management or name-server queries which will generate a constant signaling load. Looking back to the discussion on ATM data models and services, one way to avoid this unnecessary burden on the switch will be to create default forwarding VCCs for sessions of short duration. These VCCs would terminate at routers within the network. Since a given ATM switch will handle anywhere from 10 to 10,000 signaling requests per second, the above concerns must be taken into account as part of network design.

Switches at the low end, suitable for the workgroup and small campus, will implement signaling on a central control processor. In comparison, each interface module on large enterprise and CO access switches may handle SVC call setup. These two architectures have obvious tradeoffs in terms of cost, with the workgroup switch deployable at a much lower cost-per-port than the second class of switches. In fact, we have yet a third architecture based on central call servers, more closely aligned to that which exists within the public phone system. Redundant workstations implementing the signaling protocol will connect to one or more ATM switches. One advantage of this architecture is that decoupling signaling hardware from the switch allows one to increase performance as workstations evolve. When deploying an ATM network, this cost versus functionality will be one of the decision criteria in switch selection. Parallel to the discussion of a switch's ability to process signaling requests is its ability to maintain the VCCs. Different classes of ATM switches (for example, workgroup, enterprise, and CO) will of course have different capabilities.

Each VCC requires around 500 bytes of state information. Therefore, a switch is ultimately limited by memory in the number of VCCs it may service at one time. This state information also applies to

Table 5.6 ATM switch processes. Source: Cisco Systems.

Microseconds	10s Microseconds	Milliseconds
Hardware	Hardware/firmware	Software
Cell switching	Header recognition and reformatting	Configuration and discovery
	Adaptation to external service	Establishing virtual circuits
	Cell relay switching	Network management
	Rate control	Topology management
	Data forwarding based on type	Congestion management
	of service	Statistics collection
		Fault detection and recovery
Switch matrix	Line interface modules	Switch control processor

each leaf of a pt-mpt connection, resulting in additional memory require-ments. Consider a 32-port switch with a pt-mpt VCC directed to 20 output ports. This connection alone will require 10 Kbytes of state infor-mation within the switch. Now consider the number of pt-mpt connec-tions used within LANE or multicasting. On average, if a 40-port (STM-1) switch is to support in the order of 4K VCCs per port, it will require 80 MB of VCC state information. Parallel to the number of VCCs supported is a requirement for a high rate of call setup. Some insight as to the number of connection requests per second is given by Kwok (1995). Visible to the user is the connection setup time, which should be in the order of 100 ms. The contribution goes on to state that, in a residential environment, this should be closer to 10 ms. Looking at current switch designs, this will equate to 300 calls per second per OC3/STM-1 port, or up to 12,000 calls per second for a typical 40-port STM-1 switch. Using parallel architectures, support for this number of VCCs and setups per second is not beyond current technology. In the CO environment, the use of VPCs will provide some relief to the number of requests required since many SVCs will be aggregated within a VPC.

A typical ATM switch will distribute its functions between a control processor running management software, the hardware and microcode on the line interface units, and the switch matrix itself. This division of effort is a function of the speed at which the various control functions must be performed. Some of the various processes taking place within an ATM switch are listed in Table 5.6.

Workgroup

A workgroup (WG) ATM switch will provide connectivity for ATM-equipped workstations or PCs, routers, and LAN switches in a local envi-ronment. Interfaces will normally be ATM only, as price per port is the major design and purchasing criteria. These interfaces will usually be 155 Mbps (UTP-5, MM, and even SM), though 25, 622, and possibly 51 Mbps will also be deployed. If a WAN connection is required, the switch may be equipped with E3/DS3 interfaces as well. One or more of these 16–64 port switches will serve the needs of workgroup and campus ATM users. Although the workgroup and campus switch may support direct voice and video connectivity, this may contradict the first point of minimizing the per-port cost. Thus, in most installations, video encoding and voice adaptation will take place within an external device. Note that where video is supported in the workgroup, the majority will be generated at the desktop as opposed to by standalone constant bit-rate video CODECs. The WG switch need not be fully redundant, since most redundancy, where required, will be provided by dual-homing ATM end-systems. If appropriate, the switch may also be equipped to support server functionality, though possibly at additional cost. This relates to the different ATM data models which require varying degrees of intelligence within the ATM network. For example, the Classical model uses ATMARP and NHRP for address resolution, while LANE and MPOA rely on their own set of servers. In all three cases, most if not all of this server functionality may be incorporated within the architecture of the switch. Finally, the switch will of course support ATM traffic management, signaling, and trunking protocols.

The number of ports listed above, 16 to 64, addresses a commonly asked question concerning the deployment of workgroup switches, that of scale. At one end of the spectrum, a high number of small switches may be deployed, but these may not be cost effective due to the cost of the interfaces which account for up to half the cost of a typical switch (Anderson *et al*, 1992). This higher number of interfaces is due to the fact that a greater number of interconnects between switches will be required. In addition, each switch requires a minimal amount of processing to correctly support ATM signaling and traffic management (for example, ABR). At the opposite extreme, a very large switch with its high initial cost will often prove inappropriate for small workgroups. Incrementing capacity is also more expensive with larger switches, due to this initial cost and the rather large step function when installing additional switches. In the final analysis, 16 to 64 port switches are seen as suitable for workgroups.

We summarize the above results in Table 5.7, looking at desirable characteristics when selecting a workgroup or campus ATM switch.

Table 5.7 Workgroup and campus ATM switch desired characteristics.

Requirement	Description	Range
Trunking	Ability to support high-bandwidth trunks at the core of the network	Supports STM-4/OC-12
Capacity	Ability to support large numbers of high-speed interfaces	5 Gbps minimum supporting $32\times$STM-1 or $8\times$STM-4; modular
Capacity	Ability to support a large number of VCCs at any given moment	4096x number of STM-1 interfaces

(continued)

Requirement	Description	Range
Standards support	Compliance with user and network interface standards	UNI 3.x/4.x, PNNI, IISP, SVC tunneling
Buffering	Ability to buffer large amounts on incoming and outgoing interfaces during times of congestion	1000 cells per STM-1 interface
Bandwidth management	Ability to make optimal use of available bandwidth on trunks	ATM Forum traffic management; ABR, EPD/TPD
Congestion avoidance	Ability to control incoming connections based on network congestion	ATM Forum CAC and UPC
Performance	Ability to guarantee support for the different ATM traffic profiles in support of different services (for example, Frame Relay, SNA, LAN data, voice and video)	CBR, rt-VBR, nrt-VBR, ABR, UBR, separate buffering for multicasting
Availability	Redundancy balanced against cost	Redundant power supplies and OIR; possible switch matrix redundancy; most redundancy via network design
Management	Scalability of management for large networks	256 node minimum, scalable via hierarchical network management; circuit steering
Security	Support of CUGs based on ATM addressing	ATM address access lists

Enterprise

The next class of ATM switch is known as an enterprise switch, though it will also see exposure in the campus. These switches will be deployed at the core of large manufacturing campuses within office buildings, and will often form the backbone of private corporate ATM WANs. A campus switch, with some changes, may also be deployed as a CO access switch, described in the following section. A campus or enterprise switch is more versatile than a workgroup switch in that it supports multiple functions in addition to simple ATM switching and signaling. It must aggregate the ATM traffic from multiple WG switches and non-ATM traffic from traditional sources for connection to an ATM WAN at various data rates. In contrast to the workgroup switch where bandwidth costs do not usually enter into network design, this class of switch must implement sophisticated bandwidth optimization and congestion avoidance to make the most of expensive WAN links. Thus, the switch must support multiple traffic types at a wide variety of interface speeds and, in addition, it includes physical redundancy, with, at a minimum, dual switch matrices, control processors, and power supplies. Looking back at the workgroup switch, it may be more logical to deploy two switches, dual-homing the end-stations (remembering that campus bandwidth costs do not figure in the calculation), as opposed to paying for redundancy within the box. ATM WAN users do not have this luxury. If a greater degree of redundancy is required, interfaces may be replicated through the use of passive appliques connected to two switch line modules, whereby an incoming link will be switched to one of two line cards.

Modular interfaces will include SM and MM fiber, at speeds appropriate for both local- and wide-area connectivity. A reason that UTP is not expected to be supported is due to the higher price-per-port of this switch class. We do not expect to see a large number of end-systems connected, and where they are (for example, central file servers), fiber may be deployed to the end-system. For the same reason, low-speed ATM ports (for example, 25 and 51 Mbps) for ATM workgroups are also not expected due to the per-slot cost of these large switches. ATM connections to downstream WG switches, to servers and a few end users, and to inter-switch trunks will be available at 155 and 622 Mbps, while connectivity into the WAN will include data rates of DS1/E1, DS3/E3, STS-3c/STM-1, and STS-12c/STM-4. In addition, ATM-equipped PABXs may be connected via DS1/E1 ATM interfaces. This switch must also support non-ATM connections in both the local and wide area. Non-ATM systems may include PABXs and video CODECs connected via G.703 CBR interfaces, Frame Relay subscribers or devices connected through frame interfaces, and, in some instances, traditional LANs connected via FDDI or Ethernet. Note that every additional interface type adds cost and complexity to the switch in terms of hardware and software. In this way, the enterprise switch will perform the functions of both an ATM switching system and service multiplexer, eliminating the need to deploy additional platforms. As with the WG switch, the software should support private and public signaling, trunking protocols, and traffic management. Management, just as with the WG switch, will be based on SNMP and will include the various fault, performance, and configuration applications. If the switch is on the customer's premises, but is managed by the public service provider, it may be called a **premisys switch**.

Central office edge

An edge switch will provide a point-of-service aggregation for an ATM service provider. Thus, it offloads service adaptation from the core cross-connect. Its function in many ways is close to that of the enterprise switch, though we require higher density, greater fault tolerance, and different management architectures within the public service provider's environment. Interfaces will include frame and CBR adaptation in addition to ATM, while some service providers may also include LAN interfaces which will be extended to the customer's site. Important are the various service interworking functions, such as those between Frame Relay or SMDS and ATM. In many locations, this device must also be engineered in such a way as to comply with service provider physical device requirements. For example, in the US these are known as **Network Equipment Building Standards (NEBSs)**, referenced in Appendix A under Bellcore standards. Finally, the switch must integrate with the service provider's management system, interacting with the various circuit provisioning, billing, and fault reporting systems. In this environment we first see the use of public network management standards including CMIP, TMN, and the ATM Forum's M4 and M5 interfaces internetworking with the carrier's OSS. We described these various standards in Section 3.6.

When looking at these access switches, the regulatory environment in each country plays a major role. In some countries, and in the majority of locations where the PTT is government owned, this switch may actually be placed on the customer's premises. It will be delivered as part of an ATM service offering, and will be managed by the service provider.

We summarize some basic requirements for both enterprise and CO edge switches in Table 5.8.

Table 5.8 CO edge and enterprise ATM switch desired characteristics.

Requirement	Description	Range
Trunking	Ability to support high bandwidth trunks at the core of the network	Supports STM-4/OC-12; later STM-16/OC-48
Capacity	Ability to support large numbers of high-speed interfaces	8 Gbps offering 40×STM-1 or 10×STM-4
Capacity	Ability to support a large number of VCCs at any given moment	4096x number of STM-1 interfaces
Standards support	Compliance with user and network interface standards	UNI 3.x/4.x, PNNI, later B-ICI
Signaling	Ability to support a large number of signaling requests per second	300x number of STM-1 modules; distributed call processing
Buffering	Ability to buffer large amounts on incoming and outgoing interfaces during times of congestion	100 ms of round trip delay (100,000 cells at STM-1)
Bandwidth management	Ability to make optimal use of available bandwidth on trunks	ATM Forum and possible vendor-specific closed-loop congestion avoidance mechanism
Congestion avoidance UPC	Ability to control incoming connections based on network congestion	ATM Forum and possible vendor-specific CAC and
Performance	Ability to guarantee support for the different ATM traffic profiles in support of different services (for example, Frame Relay, SNA, LAN data, voice and video)	CBR, rt-VBR, nrt-VBR, ABR, and UBR
Availability	Redundancy providing for near non-stop operation	Redundant switch and control processors; non service affecting upgrades; 1:1 or 1+1 interface redundancy (50–100 cutover
Management	Scalability of management for large networks	No maximum via scalable network management hierarchy; statistics gathered in interfaces

Realizing that the number of physical ports on an edge switch is not limitless, how do we aggregate large numbers of lower-speed subscribers? The concept of an access shelf is often included while discussing edge switches. The core of this device may be cell or frame depending on the deployment, since its purpose is to aggregate hundreds or even thousands of low-speed (primarily 64 Kbps) frame-based subscribers and then uplink them to an ATM edge switch. Service interfaces will include Frame Relay, the SMDS-DXI, the FUNI, and even LAN where required. This device may also integrate routing, allowing it to act as a multiservice Internet point-of-presence. Total throughput of such a system is in the range of 1–2 Gbps, with ATM uplinks of 34, 45, 155, and 622 Mbps. An additional advantage of this access device is that it may be located closer to a large customer base, then uplinked to a more centrally-located ATM switch.

Central office

The final level of the switching hierarchy includes those switches developed and sized for use in Central Offices (COs). Just as a CO phone switch is a very specialized and complex device, a CO ATM switch must provide the same functionality in the broadband environment. High reliability is a major criteria of design, and the device must be scalable to support a very large user community. Availability, though sometimes grouped with reliability, is actually a different requirement. Whereas reliability deals with unplanned outages, the availability of a switch is dependent upon planned changes to the system: whether a card or interface may be replaced without deactivating the switch, or whether the software may be upgraded without requiring downtime. As with the Edge Switch, this platform must interface with the SP/CSPs existing OSS. The CO switch will interface to other CO switches, to CO access switches, and even to campus and WG switches. Though the device may support multiple service interfaces, it will be optimized for ATM access only, with FR and SMDS service support offloaded onto the CO access switch or shelf described above.

Originally, service providers envisioned ATM deployment centered around these large switches, with broadband subscribers all directly connected. With the advent of hierarchical switching, WG, campus, and CO access, this is no longer the case. Because of this, it is unknown just how relevant the massively scalable CO switch architectures will be in actual ATM deployments if the majority of users are connected via access devices. In addition, the PTTs may find it more efficient and cost effective to deploy a larger number of smaller ATM switches closer to the subscribers. This may be due to attempts to minimize the length of the local loop, to advances in distributed management, and to the sheer overhead in deploying a multistage switch fabric. In this scenario, the majority of

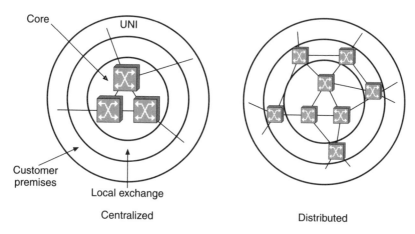

Core
UNI
Customer premises
Local exchange
Centralized

Distributed

Figure 5.3 Switch deployment options.

users will be connected to access switches at varying line speeds. These switches in turn may be connected to CO switches, but will also probably be trunked with one another directly, bypassing the CO switch for most traffic. The reverse side of this argument are the potential pitfalls from moving away from a centralized architecture, and include the suitability of premises, power requirements, maintenance response time, and security. Ultimately, the most viable architecture may consist of placing an ATM switch in each of the local exchanges. We summarize the two options in Figure 5.3.

5.2.5 End-systems: the office and home

With a physical infrastructure in place and the ATM switches deployed, selection turns to the various ATM end-systems. Note that the term 'end-system' draws on ISO terminology, just as an ATM switch may be considered an intermediate system. Standalone routers (as opposed to those imbedded in ATM switches) in this context are also considered to be end-systems to the ATM network, though they will probably function as intermediate systems in the internetwork as a whole. We first describe ATM-connected LAN switches operating on Layer 2, the router primarily operating on Layer 3, and then a recent concept known as **multilayer switching**, where the LAN switch is capable of performing Layer 2 and 3 functions. Next, we introduce the interface cards that connect PCs and workstations to an ATM network. These interfaces warrant a more detailed discussion as to architecture, performance, and features. The multiservice environment includes ATM service multiplexers and residential set-top units.

LAN switching

LAN switches, functioning at Layer 2 (the MAC layer), provide a cost-effective means for connecting existing LANs to ATM where Layer 3 (routing) capability is not required. Since LAN switches dispense with the route processor, a LAN switch may be offered at a 3–5x price reduction in the price-per-port when compared with a traditional router. A pre-configured or modular ATM-capable LAN switch will include any or all of the following interfaces: 10BaseT and 10BaseFL Ethernet, 100BaseTX, 100BaseFX, 100VG-AnyLAN, Token Ring, and FDDI. In many cases, the Ethernet and Token Ring interfaces will support full duplex operation, while the same Ethernet interfaces will be 10/100 Mbps selectable. The ATM interface will support AAL5 at a physical interface rate of 155 Mbps (SONET/SDH), 100 Mbps (TAXI), 34/45 Mbps (E3/DS3), and, for high-end LAN switches, 622 Mbps (SONET/SDH). Though some LAN switches may be equipped with an ATM backplane, in most cases packet backplanes (based either on a bus architecture or matrix) will be employed. Since a large proportion of the LAN switch traffic will remain local to the switch, a frame backplane will in most cases avoid the additional segmentation/assembly phase and associated buffering/congestion control requirements. Note that if LAN switching is implemented on a platform also positioned for wide-area use, this may not be the case. Most ATM-connected LAN switches will be deployed in the support of LANE. These LAN switches will act as LECs (and possibly LESs/BUSs for individual ELANs). Though a LAN switch may be deployed for non-LANE bridging, this early use of ATM LAN switching was very minimal. Note that, as of the end of 1995, any FDDI or 100VG-AnyLAN users connected to the LAN switch will be translationally bridged to LANE since the ATM Forum specification supports only Ethernet and Token Ring. In any case, an Ethernet ELAN may be used to transport these two traffic types across the ATM network, noting that the LANE MTU for Ethernet will support the FDDI MTU without resorting to fragmentation.

Routers

Routers are the devices found at the core of almost every internetwork, and combine a foreground packet switching function with a background topology discovery and routing table calculation function. The foreground function is equal to that performed by LAN switches but, in the case of routers, may be applied to both Layer 2 and 3. In high-end routers, the two functions are distributed among one or more switch processors based on optimized cell, frame, or packet forwarding hardware and one or more route processors based on CISC or RISC technology. Routers will exchange information as to which networks are reachable over which local interfaces via a Layer 3 routing protocol.

Examples of these protocols include OSPF for IP, NLSP for IPX, and E-IGRP for multiple protocols. Based on reachability data received via the routing protocol, the route processor will then generate a routing table. The switch processor may then cache part of this routing table for use in forwarding packets from an incoming to an outgoing interface.

Though most routers are standalone, and utilize specially designed hardware and software, a suitably programmed ATM switch, PC, or workstation may also function as a router. Note the limitations of these alternatives. The SAR function into an ATM switch's control processor will normally not support line-speed routing, while PC and workstation hardware and software is not optimized for route processing and packet forwarding. In addition to the interfaces described under LAN switching, routers are also equipped with serial interfaces providing for connection to non-ATM wide-area services (X.25, Frame Relay, SMDS, leased lines) at data rates from sub-64 Kbps to 34/45 Mbps (E3/DS3). Interfaces on routers to ATM will include 100 Mbps TAXI for use in the local area, 155/622 Mbps SDH for use in the local and wide area, and E3/DS3 for use in the wide area. Some routers may also be connected to ATM at E1/DS1. Software on the router, in addition to providing basic routing functionality, will also support multiple services over the ATM interface. These services, introduced in Chapter 4, are detailed in the next section. As a router includes both a switch and a route processor, its cost-per-port will of course be greater than that of a LAN switch.

When deploying routers within an ATM network, two important design criteria are the amount of routing required and the actual placement of the routers. This has been an area of some confusion with the deployment of VLANs. With the introduction of switched cores, the Layer 3 functions performed by routers shift from the center of the network to the periphery. We may refer to these devices as workgroup routers, performing all Layer 3 functions but not including WAN interfaces (at least initially). The multilayer switch deployed as part of MPOA is in essence a workgroup router. Connectivity to the enterprise internetwork will be via a WAN router, including LAN interfaces as well as ISDN and Frame Relay.

Upon introduction of ATM and LAN switching, if inter-VLAN bandwidth requirements are minimal (for example, 90% of the data remains within the source VLAN), a single high-performance router may suffice. This of course requires proper selection of VLAN membership, quite a challenge in many organizations. With non-optimized workgroups the question is then just how much routing is required, a function of the bandwidth required and the performance of the router.

We may calculate the required bandwidth by looking at the number of LAN segments serviced, the average loading on these segments, and the network architecture. Consider an ATM-connected LAN switch with 48 10 Mbps Ethernet segments, connected via ATM to a router at 155 Mbps. With 200 byte packets, the maximum theoretical load over the

Ethernet segments is 300,000 pps. If we assume a 20% average LAN utilization, and 25% inter-VLAN traffic, the router must forward 15,000 pps. With routers capable of allocating between 30 and 150 Kpps for inter-VLAN forwarding, we require one device for every 2–10 LAN switches configured as above. Remember that the router at the same time is providing value-added functions including: address summarization, route discovery and advertisement, policy-based traffic and access control, and broadcast supression (Cisco Systems, 1995b). Since traffic profiles and Layer 3 protocols in use will ultimately limit the size of a single VLAN, a larger proportion of the traffic may cross VLAN boundaries. This places additional requirements on the routers. For example, if 50% of the traffic is from one VLAN to another, in a typical network the number of routers required will double.

Multilayer switching

Multilayer switches are devices which combine Layer 2 LAN switching functionality with some Layer 3 capabilities and are the physical implementation of the MPOA EDFG. These devices function much like LAN switches when forwarding LAN traffic to ATM or between local LAN interfaces. In addition, extra software and hardware is included to enable the switch to carry out Layer 3 forwarding decisions. This is extremely useful in providing for efficient and scalable workgroup networks. For example, users belonging to multiple workgroups may be connected to a single LAN switch. Now assume that each workgroup is provided with an IP subnet number. Traffic within a workgroup will of course be bridged, but traffic from one workgroup to another will be routed. If the LAN switch is capable of Layer 3 forwarding, inter-workgroup traffic would not need to be segmented for transport over ATM, forwarded to a central router, reassembled, and then the reverse. More efficient traffic flow will be possible since routing now occurs at the periphery of the network in the LAN switch. Operation of LANE is also more efficient between the LAN switches, since traffic from one workgroup to another will no longer need to pass through a central router. This was the justification for multilayer switching, a device making use of a centrally-generated routing table, distributed by a route server, and then cached locally. The cost of this multilayer switch will lie somewhere between that of a Layer 2 LAN switch and that of a traditional router; since it still must include some local routing functionality. Whether it will in fact rely on central route servers or alternatively, calculate most forwarding information locally is a subject of some debate. As with traditional Layer 2 LAN switch a multilayer switch may be pre-configured or modular. If modular, it will support the multiple media types described under LAN switching. In adding this extra piece of hardware, we have come full circle to standalone routing.

PCs and workstations

Initially, ATM-equipped PCs and workstations will represent only a small percentage of the total number of devices connecting to ATM. To be more specific, for every computer directly connected to ATM, a LAN switch or router will provide connectivity to the ATM network for 10 or even 100 users. This is due to the capabilities of switched LAN and alternative (FDDI, 100 Mbps Ethernet) high-bandwidth technologies to support most applications, as well as to a desire by users to preserve existing investments in network interface hardware and software.

A computer connected to an ATM network will include an ATM **Network Interface Card (NIC)** with associated driver and encapsulation software. Since these NICs are physical media as well as hardware bus specific, and since driver software will be specific to an individual operating system, a great many combinations are possible. These various alternatives are summarized in Table 5.9, where one can, in principle, select an entry from each column.

As is obvious, a vendor's NIC offerings and support requirements may be quite extensive. No single vendor will of course support every combination of physical interface, system architecture, and operating system release. In many cases, an NIC designed for a given system bus may be fitted with different **Physical Layer Interface Modules (PLIMs)** and will also be capable of multiple OS support. This is the case with many PCI and EISA adapters.

An ATM NIC should support RFCs 1483 and 1577 (ATMARP), as well as the UNI 3.0/3.1/4.0 and LANE. For LANE, LEC functionality must be included as a minimum. As an added value it may also implement, the LECS, LES, and BUS, but only if the end-system has sufficient spare processor cycles. Note that this LES support will require considerable sophistication in the end-system if it is to support multiple VLANs and if routing between these VLANs is supported by the platform. Registration of the PC with the switch will take place via the ILMI, which should also be a requirement. Just as on routers, individual VLANs may be identified via the SEL field of the ATM NSAP format

Table 5.9 ATM NIC permutations.

Physical interface rate	Physical media type	System bus	Operating system
25 Mbps Desktop 25	SM fiber	PCI	Solaris
51 Mbps SONET	MM fiber	EISA	SunOS
100 Mbps TAXI	UTP-5	GIO	Windows/Windows NT
155 Mbps SDH	UTP-3	S-Bus	Novell NetWare
622 Mbps SDH	STP	VESA	IRIX (SGI)
1.544/2 Mbps PDH	Coaxial cable	VME	HP-UX
34/45 Mbps PDH	Wireless	ISA	DOS, OS-2
		MC	UNIX
		Turbo	Ultrix, AIX

address. Next, the **Segmentation and Reassembly (SAR)** function must be included on the NIC as opposed to drawing on the system processor, and support for a minimum of 1024 VCs is desirable (for large workgroups or multicast sessions), as well as the ability to traffic shape these VCCs. Many NICs implement DMA capability resulting in higher performance as well. Congestion control may be provided by including functions to dynamically adjust the **Peak Cell Rate (PCR)** of a VCC, looking to the time when NICs support ABR. This may be user-initiated, for example when increasing bandwidth over an existing SVC, or network-initiated in response to congestion. Finally, an NIC and networking stack should include network management capabilities via SNMP, the ATM MIB, and OAM cell support. Please refer to Section 3.6 for additional detail on these topics. Where required, a configuration tool should be included to assist in the creation of PVCs as well as providing some performance monitoring and error reporting capabilities.

When connecting a high-performance server to ATM, one area to watch out for is how many TCP connections this system can efficiently maintain. Although the ATM interface may be able to support upwards of 1000 VCCs due to SAR chip design and buffering, the internetworking stack may be more limited. For example, Berkeley-derived TCP/IP stacks can only support in the order of 500 active connections due to the actions required for each incoming packet. We suspect that most PC-based TCP stacks are capable of much less.

Service multiplexers

Although LAN switches, routers, and NICs provide connectivity into ATM, they all suffer from one limitation: the lack of voice and video CODEC support. In contrast to PC-based packet videoconferencing, some users only see ATM as a viable service offering if it can transport PABX voice and CODEC-based videoconferencing traffic. Consider a branch office which can justify only a DS1/E1 connection into ATM. At this data rate, deploying an enterprise switching platform is unnecessary and not cost effective. Still, they wish to combine a number of voice channels (trunked to a central PABX) with data. Enter the ATM service multiplexer (or concentrator), a standalone device capable of adapting one or more data and CBR streams into ATM. Though this multiplexer may be provided with native LAN capability as well, and possibly routing, these functions are not requirements, as many users will have an existing router which may connect into the service multiplexer. Still, a single box solution is a goal, and we expect to see integrated devices with these capabilities during the course of 1996. Depending upon the trunk bandwidth, normally DS1/E1 or DS3/E3 in some instances, the local side of the device will include ATM, $N \times 64$ Kbps CBR, and possibly integrated video coding and compression capabilities.

Video-on-demand and set-top

The last area of ATM deployment, and one generating a great deal of debate, is delivery of integrated services to the home and small business. In this environment more than any other, the cost of the end-system will determine whether ATM will take its place as a viable medium for delivery of services. In describing ATM switching and routing, we have already more or less addressed the core of such delivery networks. We now look at what types of device one will find in the home and operating in tandem with the internetworking equipment at the headend.

Co-located with ATM switching and some routing at the service provider's premises, we find video servers, acting as an intermediary between digitized content and the delivery system. These servers are manufactured by a number of different vendors, but most consist of high-performance workstations or PCs, a standard operating system such as UNIX or Windows, a large disk array, and a database application. The scalability of different approaches is still unknown, with current testing within pilot systems expected to produce guidelines for future rollouts. These servers are connected to the distribution network either directly via ATM or through an intermediate technology such as FDDI. In addition, video coders provide real-time compression.

Even with the availability of this hardware, the debate continues as to whether ATM is the most appropriate technology for delivery of services to the home or for use within the **Home Area Network (HAN)**. Truthfully, there are very few homes in the world with a large installed base of ATM hardware.

The role of the PC in future deployments is worth mentioning, since it would seem natural for many people to base future services on this platform. In fact, the average household does not have a PC with the capabilities to provide the necessary hardware (for example, MPEG-2 decoding) and software support for the proposed services, and will not even in the year 2000. One survey conducted in 1994 placed the number of 486+ PCs at only 4–5%. More importantly, PCs have, until quite recently, been considered as a 'work' item, in contrast to the TV's role for entertainment. Thus, TVs are found in the family room, with PCs located almost anywhere else. A factor changing this, however, is the growth in Internet services and the Web, where the fine line between work and entertainment begins to blur. Still, the Telcos and cable companies cannot target only those Internet-literate households with high-performance multimedia computers.

In the business environment, a different device known as the **cable router** will grow in importance. This device is a combination of the router located at many businesses with the cable modem, deployed as part of some early data over cable services. Instead of two discrete boxes, a single unit will provide Layer 3 functions including routing and firewalling with physical media interface capabilities, in this case coaxial or fiber cable. Though we assume the use of ATM over this infrastructure, in reality ATM will be one of many technologies. As we will see, ATM may operate at the core of such a network, with end-user delivery based on other technologies.

Desktop area networks

Possibly one of the most novel uses of ATM, and an area just recently receiving wide attention, is the use of the technology to interconnect computer subsystems. In looking at the limitations of current bus designs, this is not as strange an idea as it may at first seem. Consider the increases in processor performance, network bandwidth, and disk or memory capacity in comparison to advances in bus designs (Multibus-II, NuBus, PCI) and disk I/O (SCSI). Clearly, developments in buses and I/O lag behind the former areas. As opposed to carrying traditional bus-oriented designs into the future, the workstation may be completely re-engineered. What results is a **Desktop Area Network (DAN)** connecting the various subsystems (processor, memory, disk, network, video). ATM is the most viable technology to fulfill this role, sharing many properties with the requirements of intersystem communication. For example, PVCs may be used for synchronization while PVCs or SVCs may be used for data exchange (depending upon time requirements). The ATM cell structure also works to its advantage, as the majority of intersystem communications today are packet based. This makes for an effective use of AAL5. Where this is not the case, AAL1 may be used for stream data. The next question is just how well ATM compares with

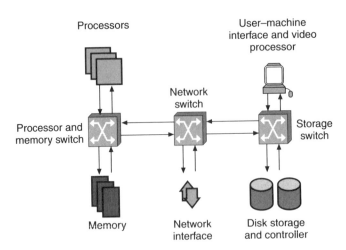

Figure 5.4 ATM-based workstation. Source: Rooholamini and Cherkassky, 1995.

existing bus designs in terms of latency. Rooholamini and Cherkassky (1995) compare ATM to the Multibus-II (a packet bus) and NuBus (based on bursts). After combining ATM's cell processing and transmission time with bus bandwidth and arbitration time, ATM at 622 Mbps has a lower maximum latency (1.364 µs) than the Multibus-II (3 µs) and a much lower latency than the NuBus (204 µs). The last question then concerns the type of ATM architecture that is most suitable in this environment. Based on simulations, a multiswitch design with or without hierarchy is most appropriate in terms of redundancy, scalability, and support of different traffic patterns. Figure 5.4 depicts a possible multiswitch workstation architecture.

5.2.6 Future cores: the convergence of ATM switching and routing

Having looked at the various types of ATM switch and router, the question we now address is if and when these two technologies will converge during the next few years. For business drivers, we only need to look at the near exponential growth of the Internet. In 1985, the core of the Internet consisted of 56 Kbps links. Only 10 years later, this had grown to multiples of 45 and 155 Mbps. At major nodes, the aggregation of bandwidth strains even the best high-performance router architectures. If there is an upper bound to frame architectures, the question then is how best to integrate the routing function with the throughput offered by ATM switching. Initially, this consists of tightly coupling high-end routers with existing ATM switches. In fact, this architecture was deployed as part of one Internet service by a service provider in the US during 1995. In the near future, we expect to see hybrid ATM switches with integrated routing capabilities. On a user-by-user or flow-by-flow basis, the system will determine whether to operate in connectionless mode, paralleling the existing Internet, or connection-oriented, akin to existing ATM networks. Note the close fit between this capability and the connectionless data model previously introduced. Probably all data, both connectionless and connection-oriented, will be segmented into equal length ATM cells for transit through the switch, though this is not a foregone conclusion. One equipment vendor has in fact delivered high-speed switching hardware capable of working with variable length cells (or packets). This would allow connectionless traffic to pass through the switch unfragmented, possibly resulting in increased efficiency at the cost of greater complexity. In any case, both architectures scale, and we expect these hybrid switches to operate in the 10+ Gbps range in the near future, with 100+ Gbps possible towards the end of the decade. This may just keep pace with Internet traffic growth.

If we look at the design of very high-performance routers, we usually have two processing modes. The first is highly optimized while the second requires additional processing. Although almost all packets will traverse the first path, an ARP cache miss will push the incoming packet into the much slower forwarding path. Over time, once the ARP cache has been populated, this should be not much of a problem. Ways to reduce this effect upon network startup would be for the router to ARP for all IP addresses within the LIS, possibly using an ATMARP server. One estimate places this load at 131K packets for an /16 address space, though it is still not known whether or not the ATMARP server will actually be capable of supporting this load. An alternative would be for the router to actually implement a server-to-server protocol which it could use to download the ATMARP server's database. This solution has an additional advantage in that the server can control the rate of transmission based on its capabilities (that is, not locking out other queries). Therefore, address resolution dynamics must play a part in future high-end router design.

Though this discussion focuses on hybrid switching, it raises the question as to just how fast we can route. This analysis is valid for devices based on either cell or frame architectures. Consider the differences in processing an IP header or conducting a VCI/VPI lookup. In the former case, the introduction of CIDR has introduced routing hierarchy which results in more efficient route lookups. Total forwarding time for a large MTU packet will be equal to that of a segmented packet since under ATM we still have the E.164 or NSAP lookup when establishing a connection. In addition, under ATM we require a VCI/VPI lookup for each cell. Extending the IP lookup from a simple FIFO to QoS-based routing, performance is roughly equivalent. We now classify the packet, based possibly on source and destination ports in addition to the IP source and destination, yielding an additional lookup for the QoS. Questions as to queuing delay may be addressed by cut-through architectures just as exist for Layer 2 LAN switching. If a queue does exist, it will be due to a burst of traffic from a source. The resulting delay variation will be no different to that which would be found within a pure ATM environment (Crowcroft, 1996a). These results bode well for the deployment of high-performance routing, either as part of a hybrid ATM switch or in parallel with ATM switching as part of a QoS-based data-forwarding model.

5.3 Applications

With an appreciation of the technologies and devices used in deploying ATM networks, we are now at a point where we may consider detailed implementation examples. First, a short digression is in order, as we look at some of the applications which these ATM networks are attempting to address. Remember that the needs of these applications in terms of QoS may be met by a number of different ATM service models: there is no one set way of solving a given problem, just as there is no single WAN technology optimized for all requirements.

5.3.1 Classical

'Classical' applications are those which have been deployed over the years by end users within corporations and across the Internet. They are classical in the sense that ATM will allow them to function more efficiently, and may allow for enhancements, but they are still capable of operating quite well over traditional LAN and WAN technologies. Examples of these applications include remote terminal access (Telnet, X-Remote), file transfer (FTP), locator systems and resolvers (DNS, Whois), multicasting (NV, VAT, shared whiteboard), and information retrieval (Mosaic, Netscape).

Terminal access

Terminal access programs include the universally deployed Telnet, DEC's LAT, and remote access to windowed environments such as X-Remote. As the first two applications are text-based, higher bandwidth will only have an effect on the latter. But this effect may be quite substantial if a user is manipulating a combination of text, still images, and video in multiple windows. As opposed to considering the terminal program as the application, it may be better to analyze bandwidth requirements based on the applications within each of the windows. Two major categories are multicasting and information retrieval, described later.

File transfer

File transfer programs include the File Transfer Protocol (FTP), FTAM within the OSI environment, and various vendor-specific offerings. Where large volumes of data must be transferred between systems, these programs will benefit considerably. In fact, a major intent of one of the first commercial ATMWAN installations was to transfer bulk data between mainframes. For example, the user may require backup of a 2 Gbyte file system every night. This transfer will require approximately two minutes over ATM compared with three hours using T1/E1 leased lines. Though the additional cost of the higher-speed connection may not seem justified by the time difference, especially if the transfer may be completed at night, remember that a large proportion of the host's resources are dedicated during the file transfer. Therefore, transfer time is critical.

Locators and resolvers

Within the Internet, the traditional **Domain Name Server (DNS)** systems for resolving host names against IP addresses, and the various locator systems for Internet users (for instance, Whois, X.500), are relatively static and use text only. Still, their performance may be improved if updates are propagated sooner, resulting in fewer misdirections. Also, as mobility increases in importance, information contained within the DNS and Whois will grow increasingly dynamic. In addition, as Whois evolves into a global directory, demands on the servers will be that much greater.

Multicasting

In contrast to most of the applications outlined above, multicasting over the Internet first appeared in the 1990s as part of the multicast backbone, or **M-Bone**. End-systems packetize voice, images, and video, broadcasting this information to multiple recipients. Images may consist of digitized photos, presentation files synchronized with voice and video, or electronic whiteboards. These workstations and PCs support a multicasting protocol which works in conjunction with IP. Within the Internet, routers also support these protocols, which include DVMRP, MOSPF, and, more recently, PIM. The scope of a particular multicast (for example, workgroup, campus, metropolitan, global) is limited by the protocol. As a multicasting end-system may generate upwards of 500 Kbps, multiple sessions may quickly overload even the best-engineered campus and wide-area networks. Within the local area, a campus or headquarters building backbone must be able to support around 10–20 high-quality (NTSC/PAL) video sessions in addition to user-generated conferencing. These broadcast sessions alone require 1.5–4 Mbps each, 60 Mbps total on average. ATM, offering vast improvements in both bandwidth and latency, is therefore the ideal technology to support multicasting. In the coming years, as a number of the various networks which comprise the Internet shift to ATM as a backbone technology, and as corporations deploy private ATM networks or use public ATM services, the number of wide-area multicast sessions supported will increase by orders of magnitude. Though an improvement to what currently exists, this first leap in capabilities delivered by ATM does not address the longer-term problem of effectively scaling corporate networks for multicast data.

Information retrieval

Parallel to the growth in multicasting is the exponential growth in data distribution based on the wide deployment of Web servers accessed by graphical front-ends such as Netscape or Spyglass/Mosaic. This Web phenomenon is recent, but has reached the point that business transactions may be conducted via these interfaces and schools are setting up **home pages**. The term 'home page' is used to describe the first screen seen by remote users when accessing a Web site; this screen is linked to additional screens, databases, image repositories, other sites, and even incoming video. This last type of information, live or stored video, is in reality a new form of multicasting. At some point, remote access to video must be integrated with multicasting so as to avoid waste of bandwidth and host resources. Possibly, a multicast session could be established when a user accesses this information; additional users would join this session. Alternatively, a given site could constantly or at timed intervals multicast this data. These both have real implications for bandwidth requirements. Yet another, and very promising solution, is to deploy caching servers. The data from a popular Web site would therefore be cached at multiple points throughout the Internet. User browsers are be configured to accept redirects to these servers. As remote users move from retrieval of text files to digitized images and video, server-server bandwidth requirements increase substantially. In both the local and wide areas, the network must be resourced appropriately to support queries from multiple users to multiple Web sites. This will be one of the primary design considerations in offering Internet services and will encourage the deployment of ATM.

5.3.2 ATM-enabled

In the preceding section, we discussed those applications which may benefit from the deployment of ATM. The latter two applications, multicasting and Web based data distribution, may be considered Classical or ATM-enabled due to the lack of scalability within currently-deployed networks to support them. An entirely new class of applications is made possible by ATM, though: applications which require the vast increase in bandwidth available within this technology, sometimes coupled with parallel developments in the computing and video fields. Those currently deployed include remote file storage and backup, collaborative research, and home services.

Server farms

In a reversal of the trend towards deploying file servers within the workgroup, many corporations are redeploying these NFS, NetWare, and Windows servers to central facilities for reasons of maintenance, data integrity, and security. The ultimate extension of this is redeployment to outsource file services with the devices now located on the service provider's premises. In either case, one in the local area and the other in the wide area, high-speed connectivity between end users and the file servers is required. ATM is capable of meeting these requirements, with latency characteristics capable of supporting LAN traffic. An interesting question is how successful service-provider file services will be, taking into account the importance of bridging in the workgroup. Will LANE be required in this case, will users choose to route, or will the service be offered in conjunction with SMDS/CBDS over ATM? Parallel to the redeployment of file servers is the growing realization that the duplication of data is critical. Backup servers may either be controlled by the corporation at some remote location, or may be offered as part of a public disaster recovery service. In either case, the bandwidths provided via ATM will make this backup process that much more efficient. Referring back to the discussion on classical file transfers, some users may be unwilling to pay the costs of wide-area ATM services for backup, especially if the backups are required only periodically. This may be fine in retailing, but for those service industries requiring 100% on-line access, finance and airlines to name two examples, data must always be available. ATM is the ideal technology in this case.

Collaboration

Collaboration really falls into two areas: connection of computer systems and access to generated data. As some computational problems are beyond the capabilities of even the largest parallel processors, a trend is to connect multiple systems over a campus or wide area, with a given problem worked in parallel. Due to the quantities of data exchanged in real time, high-speed technologies are critical; in fact, some of the earliest non-ATM high-speed links (DS3) were for this very purpose. At the time of writing, supercomputer connections have been tested at multiples of STM-1 via parallel I/O ports. One such system, the Cray Research Super Server, is rated at an aggregate of over 6 Gbps supporting up to 62 ATM connections. It is envisioned that future, previously 'unsolvable' problems (the 'Grand Challenges') will be tackled by hundreds or more supercomputers operating in parallel over a wide area. Clustering workstations for codebreaking is only one example. The deployment of national ATM networks connecting major research laboratories will open up an entirely new class of problems to solution. Access to the generated data is just as important as parallel computation. Though the concept of real-time response is not as critical here, since many visual sequences are downloaded to a user, stored, and then redisplayed, the time for this download may be decreased substantially with the deployment of ATM. In some environments, real-time access to generated imagery (for example, simulations manipulated on-line by the user) is critical. ATM is the only technology widely deployed capable of meeting this requirement.

Residential

In contrast to the commercial applications outlined above, residential applications are driven by different factors. The typical home has a requirement for all services commonly associated with ATM: voice, video, and data. If these three services could be delivered over a single link to the outside world, and at an equal or lower cost than separate services while at the same time offering greater convenience, the average consumer will be satisfied. With both the telephone and cable companies competing for business in some markets, the actual technology to be delivered to the home is not yet decided. In any case, ATM will provide the backbone infrastructure between phone exchanges, carrying unidirectional video distribution from ATM-connected servers, bi-directional voice, and mostly unidirectional data from provider-operated databases and Internet gateways.

The ATM Forum's RBB WG has developed a number of application profiles which will provide the basis for residential ATM services. These include: video-on-demand, interactive games, videotelephony, health care, home-based business, telecommuting, 'infotainment' (information-on-demand), distance learning, data delivery, telecenter, video arraignment, wireless/PCs with ATM, small business/multimedia on desktop, and security/surveillance. In developing more complete application profiles, the ATM Forum in the United States continues to liaise with the Multimedia Communications Forum (MMCF), the National ISDN User Forum (NIUF), and the Residential Broadband Network group.

5.4 Implementation examples

We now apply our knowledge of ATM standards, services, and technologies to actual migration scenarios. In this section, we look at ways in which we may deploy ATM in solving actual networking problems such as the need for increased bandwidth, mobility via VLANs, application QoS support, and internetworking with WAN services. In solving these problems, we introduce the Classical model, LANE, MPOA, Frame Relay and SMDS/CBDS, and video distribution among others. The examples are intended to reflect the challenges which network planners face on a daily basis, and are presented in such a way that they should be easily incorporated into actual network designs. In Table 5.10, we list the networking problems to be solved along with the solutions.

Towards the end of this section, we look at some actual customer implementations. Although less detailed than the examples outlined above, they provide some good guidance as to how ATM may be deployed in combination with some of the other workgroup and WAN technologies. We summarize these implementations in Table 5.11.

We also consider public ATM service offerings as implementations.

Table 5.10 Implementation examples.

Example	Problem	Solution	Techniques
Classical 1	Current multiprotocol FDDI backbone overloaded	Deploy ATM as new switched backbone to interconnect routers supporting IP, IPX, and AppleTalk	PVCs
Classical 2	Current IP backbone overloaded	Deploy ATM as new switched backbone to interconnect routers	SVCs; redundant IETF ATMARP servers
Classical 3	Corporation is split amongst multiple locations, interconnected by public PVC-only ATM service	Deploy ATM at each location using SVC techniques from Classical 2; tunnels signaling requests across ATM WAN	SVC tunneling
Classical 4	Need to connect non-ATM-capable routers to new backbone	Preserve investment in non-ATM-capable routers by deploying frame-based interfaces to ATM	ATM Forum ATM-DXI; FUNI
Classical 5	Sub-optimal routing across LIS boundaries for Classical 2	Deploy short-cut routing across ATM network	IETF NHRP
Classical 6	Efficient multicasting of training videos across corporate campus	Deploy ATM as high-speed backbone supporting IP-layer multicasting	IETF PIM; ATM pt-mpt VCCs
Classical 7	QoS to ATM non-ATM users	Deploy PSVP and internetworking with ATM QoS	RSVP
Classical 8	Parallel networks for multiprotocol traffic and APPN	Integrate IP and APPN traffic across single ATM backbone	APPN CoS support by ATM
LANE 1	OAM costs due to movements within small organization; no requirement for separate VLANs	Deploy single VLAN across ATM based on ATM Forum LANE	LANE deployed on a per-port basis
LANE 2	Small number of users require VLAN capabilities	Deploy VLANs across ATM based on ATM Forum LANE	MAC-based filtering to subdivide single Layer 2 VLAN
LANE 3	OAM costs due to movements within organization; requirement to support existing end-user protocols and applications		LANE deployed on a per-port basis; routing between VLANs

(continued)

Example	Problem	Solution	Techniques
LANE 4	Some servers require access from multiple VLANs	Build upon LANE 2 by attaching central servers to multiple VLANs	LANE-capable NICs; multiple VLANs on some LAN switch ports
LANE 5	Requirement to interconnect LAN in workgroup to Classical ATM WAN	Deploy devices capable of interconnecting the two domains	Router to interconnect LANE with Classical domain
MPOA	Requirement for multiple protocol across ATM backbone	Deploy MPOA	ATM switches, MPDA, edge devices, and routers
Frame Relay 1	Some corporate sites connect to Frame Relay, others to ATM; need transparent end-to-end connectivity	Deploy interworking between ATM and Frame Relay	ATM/Frame Relay service interworking
Frame Relay 2	Current Frame Relay backbone overloaded; require new, high-speed backbone to interconnect Frame Relay nodes	Deploy ATM as a new backbone inter-connecting existing Frame Relay switches	ATM Frame Relay Transport
SMDS 1	Current SMDS based on single-service equipment resulting in higher costs; bandwidth limited due to DQDB architecture	Replace DQDB-based SMDS service with ATM service	Transport of SMDS over ATM; CLSF
SMDS 2	Some corporate sites connect to existing SMDS service, others to ATM-based SMDS; need transparent end-to-end connectivity	Deploy interworking between ATM-based SMDS and DQDB-based SMDS	Gatewaying between ATM and DQDB-based SMDS
CES	Requirement to combine voice traffic over ATM WAN to reduce costs	Deploy ATM backbone with switches capable of servicing data, voice, and video	ATM Forum CES connecting PABXs and video CODECS
VoD	Requirement to deliver enhanced services to residential subscribers	Deploy ATM as multiservice backbone to the home	VoD with direct encapsulation of MPEG-2 over AAL5
Cable data overlay	Requirement to provide data services across existing cable infrastructure	Deploy ATM at headend of network and Ethernet services to the users	Modulation of data across existing cable plant

They are, but are more positioned as infrastructures over which users or the providers themselves may offer a wide array of ATM services. These service offerings are also in a state of great flux, as the ATM Forum and

Table 5.11 Customer scenarios.

Customer	Problem	Solution
Medical	Timely exchange of data; ability to collaborate	Campus ATM core connecting routers; some LAN switching to desktop
Brokerage	Response times to desktop	ATM core with LAN switching to desktop
Commercial banking	Lack of bandwidth in core; weary about ATM	Switched FDDI core based on ATM platforms
Automobile	Multiple WAN services; maintain internal network	Enterprise ATM WAN combining data, voice, and video services
Insurance	Multiple WAN services; high reliability necessary	ATM WAN service via service multiplexers; ISDN backup
Broadcast	Need to deploy digital VoD/NVoD and value-added services	ATM core with FTTC and SDV to the home
Service provider	Integrate WAN services over single backbone	ATM WAN with interworking to existing services

ITU finalize standards and as the vendors implement these standards, and what may not be offered one season may be a lucrative service the next. During the remainder of the decade, we expect the traditional Telcos/PTTs, cable providers, and other alternative service providers to evolve their ATM portfolio in terms of richness of offerings, geographical extent, and interworking with other WAN and LAN technologies. We list a number of these offerings in Appendix B.

5.4.1 Classical ATM: PVCs, SVCs, the ATM-DXI, and the FUNI

In this first set of examples we look at ATM campus and WAN deployments based on the Classical model and its extensions. The ATM network in effect replaces an existing LAN, campus, or WAN backbone. We first look at a PVC-based multiprotocol backbone, and then introduce SVCs while limiting the backbone to IP only. This SVC-based backbone is extended across a PVC ATM WAN using a technique known as SVC tunneling, and we also connect frame-based users via the FUNI. With a goal of optimizing routing, we introduce NHRP, and then describe one service well suited to an ATM backbone – multicasting. Finally, we integrate mainframe traffic into the IP backbone.

Classical 1: campus multiprotocol backbone

Problem
An existing campus backbone is overloaded due to one or more of the following factors: a growth in users, the deployment of new applications,

or new, more powerful end-systems. Thus, the FDDI, Ethernet, or Token Ring is no longer adequate to serve the bandwidth needs of the campus. Any solution must continue to support the existing multiprotocol applications, while maintaining as much investment as possible in the existing networking hardware.

Solution

We deploy an ATM backbone interconnecting the various routers. In this example, the ATM network is based on the Classical model using RFC 1483 and LLC/SNAP encapsulation for multiprotocol transport. In a later example, we propose an alternative based on LANE. Remember that the Classical model and ATMARP only provide for automatic address resolution for IP. Since the existing networking environment includes multiple Layer 3 protocols, we must create ATM to Layer 3 address maps in the routers for IPX and AppleTalk, the other two protocols in use. As the use of SVCs does not provide much added value in this meshed router configuration, we limit the implementation to PVCs. Note that the number of PVCs is not excessive since almost all users connect to LAN ports on the routers. We also include bridging to support nonroutable protocols. This **classical bridging** is worth a quick review. As opposed to LANE, here we use RFC 1483 encapsulation where the router (or other ATM end-system capable of bridging) initiates a pt-pt broadcast-capable VCC or a pt-mpt VCC over which the bridged traffic is sent. This is no different in philosophy to bridging over WAN services. Not described in any detail is the network management system. The switches and routers support SNMP for management, while we implement the ILMI between the switches and the ATM-connected routers and workstations. Finally, connectivity to the corporate WAN is via a serial interface on one of these routers.

Procedure

1. Deploy the ATM switches, routers, and PC ATM interfaces and verify physical connectivity. For this and all future examples, verification includes checking the cable infrastructure, the connectors, and the patch panels. If any of these tests fail, we may employ physical layer troubleshooting. In this environment, the routers and switches will be connected via SM or MM fiber, while the PCs are connected via UTP-5.

2. In Table 5.12, we identify the address ranges for the Layer 3 protocols used across the network. For this and following examples, we depict IP addresses as classless, while in the box below we provide some guidance as to IPX address assignment.

Table 5.12 Protocol addresses for Classical example 1.

Protocol	Network/mask
IP	150.10.1/24, 150.10.2/24
	150.10.3/24, 150.10.10/24
	150.10.20/24, 192.100.50/24
IPX	960A0100, 960A0200
	960A0300, 960A0A00
	960A1400 (see box)
AppleTalk	10, 11, 12, 150

A quick note about IP and IPX addressing
One simple method of generating IPX addresses in an IP and IPX environment is to re-use the existing IP network addresses by converting them to hex. Thus, IP network 10.0.0.0 will convert to 0A000000. We have used this technique in all examples. As an aside, Internet domain names may be mapped into Novell in such a way as they will appear in proper order as part of the service advertisements. Consider the DNS entry: harriers.heidelberg.de. We would just reverse the order to create the SAP entry: DE-HEIDELBERG-HARRIERS. The format of depicting IP addresses may also be unfamiliar to some. In a classless IP environment, the network number must always be associated with a mask. The standard method of depicting this mask as hex entries (for example, 255.255.255.0) is cumbersome if the mask is always contiguous. A simpler way is to sum the number of '1' bits in the mask. Thus, network 150.10.1.0 255.255.255.0 is easily rewritten as 150.10.1/24. They both mean the same.

---

3. We provide a sample addressing scheme in Figure 5.5, whereby two IP subnets cross the ATM network: 150.10.10 and 150.10.20. These two subnets join at router 'Sales.' We implement this second subnet to secure users within the Sales group from the remainder of the network. The ATM backbone could of course be based on a single subnet, or on more than two subnets. Note the use of two addresses on the ATM interface of the Sales router. Most ATM end-system interfaces are capable of supporting subinterfaces, sometimes known as virtual interfaces. This is a way of subdividing the physical interface into multiple logical interfaces, each with the characteristic of a physical interface. Due to this characteristic, we many configure each subinterface with an individual IP address, forming multiple subnets across the ATM backbone. Incidentally, this is an effective way of defeating the 'split horizon' problem. This occurs when we attempt to use a single interface (without subinterfaces) to accept and then retransmit routing

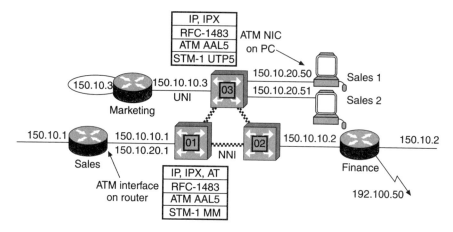

Figure 5.5 Classical 1 – PVCs

updates within a partial-mesh, remembering that in a full-mesh we send updates between all systems participating in the routing protocol. Although we may disable split horizon for IP, allowing these partial-meshes, we cannot do so for IPX or AppleTalk. Since a full mesh will become unmanageable and uneconomic in all but the smallest of networks, we use these subinterfaces to emulate multiple physical interfaces, and we can then deploy a partial routing mesh. In this example, we implement a full-mesh. This figure (Figure 5.5) does not include the IPX and AppleTalk addressing outlined in Table 5.12. Table 5.13 details the configuration information for Figure 5.5.

Table 5.13 Configuration details for Classical example 1.

Router	Interface	IP address/ mask	IPX (Note 1)	AppleTalk Zone	Addr.	Cable
Sales	ATM	150.10.10.1	960A0A00.00000C002F98	ATM	150.1	150–150
		150.10.20.1	960A1400.00000C002F98			
	Ether 1	150.10.1.1	960A0100.00000C0AD62C	SALES	10.1	10–10
Marketing	ATM	150.10.10.3	960A0A00.00000C00279D	ATM	150.3	150–150
	FDDI 1	150.10.3.1	960A0300.00000C05F941	MKTG	12.1	12–12
Finance	ATM	150.10.10.2	960A0A00.00000C002884	ATM	150.2	150–150
	Ether 1	150.10.2.1	960A0200.00000C00F32A	FINANCE	14.1	14–14
	Serial 1	192.100.50.5	na		na	
Workstation						
Sales 1	ATM	150.10.20.50	960A1400.000057D12F29	na		
Sales 2	ATM	150.10.20.51	960A1400.000057D73A22	na		

Note   We have assigned the MAC addresses for the ATM interfaces. If not assigned, many systems will use the MAC address from the first available LAN interface. For IPX these identical host IDs will not present a problem, however, since the network IDs are different for each interface (or subinterface).

4. Activate and configure the ATM interfaces on the routers and workstations by assigning IP addresses, QoS parameters for use by the PVCs, and routing parameters. Note that we do not require NSAP addresses since only PVCs are used.

    (a) Each router ATM interface must be set with an IP address and mask. These should correspond with the values listed in Table 5.13.

    (b) Assign a QoS to each PVC. For the three PVCs to be established between each of the routers, a PCR=8 Mbps, ACR=40 Mbps and BT=96 cells are all set via router configuration. These QoS parameters are set in both the forward and reverse directions, with the PCR, ACR, and BT applying to both CLP=0 and CLP=1. Note that the PCR pre-assigned for a router PVC may be different to that assigned to one on a PC due to differing capabilities and expected throughput. This does require some knowledge of end-system capabilities and application profiles. In the future, resource reservation protocols such as RSVP on end-systems attached to the router LAN segments or within the applications running on the ATM-attached PC will be capable of dynamically requesting a QoS which will then be used as part of the SVC setup. Table 5.14 summarizes the relevant PVC parameters, using a Cisco router ATM Interface Processor as an example. Although the router is capable of supporting rate queues in addition to the traffic shaping above, we do not use these in this example. These rate queues enforce an absolute maximum on the peak data rate. If more than one rate queue is in use, the different queues may be prioritized, though the problem here is that, depending upon design, lower priority traffic may be starved at the expense of traffic placed in the higher rate queue.

Table 5.14 Relevant PVC parameters for Classical example 1.

Cell Loss Priority (CLP)	0 (high priority) or 1 (low priority)
Peak Cell Rate (PCR)	Value in Kbps
Average Cell Rate (ACR) (sustainable cell rate)	Value in Kbps; should not exceed $\frac{1}{2}$ that of the PCR
Burst Tolerance (BT) (maximum burst size)	In multiples of 32 cells
Adaptation (AAL)	5 (all end-systems); 3/4 (some routers – for SMDS/CBDS only)
Encapsulation	LLC/SNAP (RFC 1483), MUX (RFC 1483), NLPID (RFC 1490), QSAAL (signaling), SMDS (RFC 1209)
MTU	9188 octets maximum

(c) Properly configure parameters for routing protocols if they are to operate across ATM. Using OSPF as an example, the OSPF hello interval is set to five seconds and the ATM subnet 10 is set as the backbone area. In addition, the mode of operation for OSPF should be set to 'broadcast' and we will configure neighbors across the network. This does not preclude the addition of other networks to the OSPF backbone. For example, a campus backbone may consist of both an ATM and an FDDI domain. In this case, the subnets used for each of these clouds will jointly form the OSPF backbone. Other possibilities for subnet-capable routing protocols include Integrated IS-IS, E-IGRP, and RIP-2. Note that RIP and IGRP would work in this simple example since we are using a full-mesh and every router is a member of the same major network (150.10.0.0). Thus, either would send reachability information for each LAN subnet (150.10.1, 150.10.2, and so on) across the ATM backbone. Here, we use a subnet-capable protocol for future growth. Routing updates will traverse the data PVCs. In Table 5.15 we summarize these data PVCs, both between the routers and between the routers and the workstations.

(d) Configure the NICs on the two Sales PCs for subnet 20. Assuming that these NICs support traffic shaping, set the PCR, ACR, and BT for each of these VCCs.

(e) Configure the above PVCs on each of the switches via a console connection or, preferably, through an SNMP-based management tool. We create the following PVCs at each of the switches for the routing VCCs and for those connecting the two Sales PCs to the Sales router (Table 5.16). Note that even for a small network of three switches and five end-systems, 20 interface descriptors must be configured. This is one of the fundamental problems of relying on PVCs when connecting many end-stations or when building large networks. Table 5.16 defines PVCs in the 'forward' direction, from the switch's router interface to the switch's backbone interface. In reality, these PVCs exist in both the forward and 'reverse' directions, although we must only define them once.

Table 5.15 End-system PVCs configured for Classical example 1.

Source	Destination	VCC number	VPI	VCI	AAL	ENCAP	PCR	ACR	BT
Sales	Marketing	1	0	60	5	LLC/SNAP	80000	40000	3
Sales	Finance	2	0	61	5	LLC/SNAP	80000	40000	3
Marketing	Finance	3	0	62	5	LLC/SNAP	80000	40000	3
Sales 1	Sales	4	0	80	5	LLC/SNAP	40000	20000	3
Sales 2	Sales	5	0	81	5	LLC/SNAP	40000	20000	3

Note   All values are for CLP=0

Table 5.16 Switch PVCs configured for Classical example 1.

Switch	Port	VPI	VCI	Port	VPI	VCI	Description	VCC
Sales	1	0	60	3	0	60	R-Sales - R-Mktg	1
	1	0	61	2	0	61	R-Sales - R-Fin	2
	1	0	80	3	0	80	R-Sales - Sales 1	4
	1	0	81	3	0	81	R-Sales - Sales 2	5
Finance	1	0	60	2	0	60	R-Fin - R-Sales	2
	1	0	64	3	0	64	R-Fin - R-Mktg	3
Marketing	1	0	61	2	0	61	R-Mktg - R-Sales	1
	1	0	62	3	0	62	R-Mktg - R-Fin	3
	4	0	80	2	0	80	Sales 1 - R-Sales	4
	5	0	81	2	0	81	Sales 2 - R-Sales	5

5. Verify connectivity between all systems on the network. As a second step, implement access lists on the Sales router and verify network partitioning. Also verify connectivity between the ATM network and external LANs/WANs connected to the routers if relevant. In the following example, we show Ethernets and an FDDI connected to the routers with the same IP network address (different subnets) and a WAN interface connected to a separate network.

```
!Example of PVCs across ATM with IP OSPF, IPX NLSP,
and AppleTalk E-IGRP routing.
!
!Global:
!
!(only ATM-related entries for routing)
!
!px routing 0000.0c0a.0b2c
ip internal-network 1
ipx router nlsp area1
area-address 0 0
appletalk routing eigrp 100
appletalk eigrp active-time disabled
appletalk route-redistribution
router ospf 100
network 150.10.10.0.0.0.0.255 area 0
!
map-list alpha
ip 150.10.10.3 atm-vc 1 broadcast
ip 150.10.10.2 atm-vc 2 broadcast
ipx 960A0A00.0000.0C00.279D atm-vc 1 broadcast
ipx 960A0A00.0000.0C00.2884 atm-vc 2 broadcast
appletalk 150.3 atm-vc 1 broadcast
appletalk 150.2 atm-vc 2 broadcast
map-list beta
```

```
ip 150.10.20.50 atm-vc 4 broadcast
ip 150.10.20.51 atm-vc 5 broadcast
!
!ATM Interface:
!
interface ATM 2/0
!
mtu 1500
ip route-cache cbus
atm rate-queue 1 155
!
!ATM Subinterfaces:
!
interface ATM2/0:1 multipoint
!
ip address 150.10.10.1 255.255.255.0
ipx network 960A0A00
ipx nlsp areal enable
appletalk cable-range 150-150 150.1
appletalk zone ATM
appletalk protocol eigrp
atm pvc 1 0 100 aa15snap 80000 40000 3
atm pvc 2 0 101 aa15snap 80000 40000 3
map-group alpha
!
interface ATM2/0:2 multipoint
!
ip address 150.10.20.1 255.255.255.0
atm pvc 4 0 200 aa15snap 40000 20000 3
atm pvc 5 0 201 aa15snap 40000 20000 3
map-group beta
```

Classical 2: campus IP backbone

Problem

An existing campus backbone is overloaded due to one or more of the following factors: a growth in users, the deployment of new applications, or new, more powerful end-systems. Since the backbone is IP-only, we may easily deploy SVCs.

Solution

We deploy an ATM backbone based on the Classical model. Redundant ATMARP servers provide address resolution between IP and ATM addresses, allowing the use of SVCs without the use of pre-configured address maps. Note that although this example is based on SVCs, we optionally create PVCs within the network for routing updates (unless

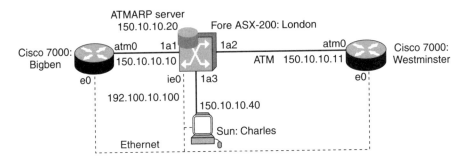

Figure 5.6 Classical 2 – SVCs and ATMARP.

we implement default or static routes or rely on the updates to trigger the SVCs). Next, we configure PVCs for, signaling and the ILMI. A question arises concerning whether the routing PVCs should be based on a full mesh of VCCs between the routers or whether an internal hierarchy is useful. Since the network in this case consists of a single IP network, and since the number of systems is limited, we maintain a full mesh. All PVCs and SVCs in this example are based on LLC/SNAP encapsulation. Finally, the MTU is set to 9180 octets throughout the network. Table 5.17 lists the network numbers in use throughout this workgroup, while Figure 5.7 shows the complete network.

In this example, we look at an ATM network based on some of the more popular devices currently installed, Cisco 7xxx routers connected via a Fore ASX-200 switch. We also include Sun workstations to complete this example of a workgroup or campus network. The example is adapted from NOAA, 1996.

Procedure

1. Verify that all equipment supports the UNI 3.0 or 3.1/4.0 with ILMI.

2. Verify that one or more devices on the network support the ATMARP server, and that all edge devices support the ATMARP client. In this example, we implement the ATMARP server on the ATM switch, although this server may also be deployed on a PC, workstation, or within a router.

Table 5.17 Protocol addresses for Classical example 2.

Protocol	Network/mask
IP	150.10.1/24, 150.10.2/24
	150.10.10/24
	192.100.10/24

Table 5.18 NSAP addressing plan for Classical example 2.

Field	Value	Length	Note
AFI	39	2 digits	
IDI	840	3 digits	ANSI
DFI	128	3 digits	ANSI
Organization AA	12F130	6 digits	'Global corporation'
Location	1200	4 digits	Office location (London)
Building	0010	4 digits	Building within location
Group	10	2 digits	Functional group
Switch	01	2 digits	Switch within group
ESI	xxxx xxxx xxxx	12 digits	Unique to end-system
SEL	xx	2 digits	Subinterfaces on end-system
End-system	**ATM NSAP address**		
Router Bigben	39 8401 28 12F130 1200 0010 1001 0000 0000 0001 00		
Router Westminster	39 8401 28 12F130 1200 0010 1001 0000 0000 0002 00		
WS Charles	39 8401 28 12F130 1200 0010 1001 0200 4806 0539 00		
Switch ATMARP Server	39 8401 28 12F130 1200 0010 1001 0200 481A 0268 00		

3. Deploy the ATM switches and router ATM interfaces and verify physical connectivity. As with the first example, the routers and switches will be connected via SM or MM fiber.

4. Assign an NSAP address to each ATM interface. These addresses are 20 octets long, equivalent to 40 hexadecimal (0-F) digits. For the purpose of this example, we have created an addressing plan (Table 5.18). The completed addressing plan is organizationally based, with an HO-DSP hierarchy consisting of a location, building, group, and switch number. For the remainder of this example, we are most concerned with this switch number. Though the NSAP addresses may seem a burden to configure due to their length creating the potential for error, in reality the network administrator will only configure parts of the address on each system. ATM-connected end-systems such as routers and computers will have the local part of the NSAP address pre-configured as a 48-bit MAC format entry. In contrast, switch configuration will include only the network portion. As part of the ILMI, the switches and end-systems will exchange this information, allowing them to build the complete NSAP address. This process for our example configuration is outlined below. Note that if the ILMI is not implemented between the end-system and switch, the network administrator must in most cases enter the entire 40 digits.

5. Properly configure parameters for routing protocols if they are to operate across ATM. Using OSPF as an example, the OSPF hello interval is set to five seconds and the ATM subnet 10 is set as the backbone area. In addition, the mode of operation for OSPF should

be set to 'broadcast' and we will configure neighbors across the network. This does not preclude the addition of other networks to the backbone. For example, a campus backbone may consist of both an ATM and an FDDI domain. In this case, the subnets used for each of these clouds will jointly form the OSPF backbone.

We first set the address and mask for the Fore switch via the console (note the similarities to UNIX for obvious reasons):

```
localhost::configuration ip>
address ie0 192.100.10.100
mask ie0 255.255.255.0
admin ie0 up
```

Now that the interface is up, we may not go to the workstation and Telnet into the Fore switch. This will make future configuration a little easier. Later still, when the network is operational, we may contact the switch in-band across ATM. The version command will show the current SW release:

```
localhost::operation> version
Current software version is FT342.1
```

Next, set the operator password and switch name:

```
localhost::operation> thames
localhost::configuration switch> name london
```

Optionally, cancel the auto-logout time and direct syslog (logging) to the workstation:

```
localhost::configuration system> timeout 0
syslog set 150.10.10.40
```

On the workstation, be sure to direct this logging to the proper subdirectory via /etc/syslog.conf. Now set the SNMP data on the switch:

```
localhost::configuration snmp> community read
                               richmond
                               community write
                               richmond
```

We now set the necessary parameters for Classical IP and the ATMARP server (RFC 1577):

```
localhost::configuration ip>   address qaa0 150.10.
                               10.20
                               mask qaa0 255.255.0.
                               0 admin qaa0 up
```

We first need to get the stored NSAP address for the switch:

```
localhost::configuration atmarp> getnsap
qaa0 NSAP address:
47000580ffe1000000f21a02680020481a026800
```

Note that this should be changed depending upon the local NSAP hierarchy in use. Based on this, we can set the configuration for the ATMARP server:

```
localhost::configuration atmarp arpserver>
set 39 8401 28 12F130 1200 0010 1001 0020481a026800
qaa0
```

The switch is now configured for SVCs and for ATMARP. Note that the ILMI is on by default under UNI signaling. We now set a default route for network management:

```
(localhost::configuration ip route> new default
150.10.10.10 3)
```

7. We now configure the Cisco router for SVCs and ATMARP. This configuration is not much different to those included as part of our earlier examples.

First Telnet into the router to verify the IOS version:

```
bigben>sh version
IOS (tm) GS Software (GS7-K-M), Version 11.0(2),
RELEASE SOFTWARE (fc1)
```

Now enter enabled mode to alter the system configuration:

```
bigben>en
Password: your password
bigben#conf t
Enter configuration commands, one per line. End with
CNTL/Z.
bigben(config)#
```

We now specify the ATM interface in use, and set its IP address and mask:

```
bigben(config)# interface ATM0/0
bigben(config-if)# ip address 150.10.10.10
255.255.0.0
```

Now set the PVCs for signaling and for the ILMI, all within the interface configuration:

```
atm pvc 1 0 16 ilmi
atm pvc 2 0 5 qsaal
```

A little later, we look at establishing an additional PVC connecting the two routers for routing traffic. Next set the end-system identifier. This is in effect the MAC address of the ATM interface (and subinterface):

```
atm esi-address 000000000001.00
```

We now tell the router that the Fore switch will be used as the ATMARP server. Note that the Cisco router may also be used as the server:

```
atm arp-server nsap 39 8401 28 12F130 1200 0010
1001 0020481a026800
```

If the only devices connected to the network are workstations, the MTU could be raised to 9180, the maximum specified in RFC 1626. This is not recommended if devices on the router's LAN interfaces will communicate with systems on the ATM backbone. In this case, we leave the router's MTU at the 4470 octet default.

Now leave configuration mode and save the new configuration:

```
bigben(config-if)#^Z
bigben#write
```

Repeat the above procedure on the second router, with the following changes:

```
westminster(config)# interface ATM0/0
westminster(config-if)# ip address 150.10.10.11
255.255.0.0
atm esi-address 000000000002.00
```

8. Now we configure the ATM interface on the Sun workstation. This example is based on a Fore NIC, although configuration for those from other vendors should follow the same principles. First display some general NIC information:

```
charles> adinfo fa0
FORE Systems Release: ForeThought_3.0.3 (1.5)
fa0: sba-200e media=oc3 hw=0.2.0 fw=3.0.0 seri-
al=1337 oc3rev=48 slot=1
```

If the NIC has been properly installed, the rc.local file will include the necessary commands to download the NIC firmware during system bootup. As part of the startup script (for example, /usr/etc/fore/rc.sba200), the ATMARP server will be specified:

```
/usr/etc/fore/atmarp -p
39 8401 28 12F130 1200 0010 1001 0020481a026800
qaa0
```

The end of the rc.local script should also have been modified to activate the fore snmp daemon. This allows the NIC to participate in the ILMI. Additional commands in rc.local should set the ATM NIC's address and netmask. SPANs may also have to be turned off.

```
ifconfig qaa0 150.10.10.40 netmask 255.255.0.0 up
/usr/local/fore/etc/atmconfig -s off fa0
```

Once the network is fully operational, we may write the router configurations to the tftp server. Repeat this for both 'bigben' and 'westminster'. Note that we could have also deployed an Ethernet to connect the switch control port, the workstation, and router interfaces for management. Although this would suffice in a workgroup ATM network, we cannot assume the existence of a parallel Ethernet network in an extended ATM network. Thus, all management takes place in-band across the ATM network.

```
bigben#writ net
Remote host []? 150.10.10.40
Name of configuration file to write [bigben-confg]?
Write file bigben-confg on host
150.10.10.40? [confirm]
Writing bigben-confg !! [OK]
```

We do the same at the switch, backing up the current switch configuration to a tftp server:

```
localhost::operation cdb> backup
150.10.10.40:london
CDB backup was successful
```

Since we are using the standard UNI and not SPANs for signaling, one suggestion is to remove all SPANs references in ForeView. We may accomplish this via the front-panel tool by selecting all ports and then configuring signaling.

We now verify the configuration, and thus network operation. Back on the switch, we should see the NSAP addresses of the attached routers and workstations:

```
localhost::> conf nsap ilmi show
```

The switch responds with:

```
Port NsapAddress
1A1 39 8401 28 12F130 1200 0010 1001 00000000000100
1A2 39 8401 28 12F130 1200 0010 1001 00000000000200
1A3 39 8401 28 12F130 1200 0010 1001 00204806053900
```

On the router, verify completion of the full NSAP (via the ILMI):

```
bigben>sh int atm0/0
ATM0/0 is up, line protocol is up
Internet address is 150.10.10.10 255.255.0.0
NSAP address: 39 8401 28 12F130 1200 0010
1001.000000000002.00
```

Finally, on the workstation we may verify the same:

```
charles> atmarp -z qaa0
NSAP addr for qaa0 is
39 8401 28 12F130 1200 0010 1001.002048060539.00
```

For added verification, we may check the ATMARP exchanges between both the router and the workstation to the ATMARP server:

```
bigben>sh atm map
Map list ATM0/0_ATM_ARP : DYNAMIC
arp maps to NSAP 39 8401 28 12F130 1200 0010
1001.0020481A0268.00
connection up, VC 23, ATM0/0
charles> atmarp -a
Outgoing connections:
qaa0: ? (150.10.10.20): NSAP 0x39 8401 28 12F130
1200 0010 1001.0020481a0268.00
vpi.vci=0.45 aal=5
flags=(Classical IP) peak rate=(unlimited)
```

Next, we may check that all router and workstation IP addresses have been registered by the ATMARP server:

```
localhost::> conf atmarp show
IPaddress  If NSAP Address
150.10.10.10   qaa0
0x39 8401 28 12F130 1200 0010 1001.000000000002.00
150.10.10.11   qaa0
0x39 8401 28 12F130 1200 0010 1001.000000000003.00
150.10.10.40   qaa0
0x39 8401 28 12F130 1200 0010 1001.002048060539.00
```

We are now ready to test the network by 'pinging' from one station to another. In this case, we ping the router 'bigben' from the workstation:

```
charles> ping -s 150.10.10.10 56 5
PING 192.168.1.2: 56 data bytes
64 bytes from 150.10.10.10: icmp_seq=1. time=2. ms
64 bytes from 150.10.10.10: icmp_seq=2. time=2. ms
64 bytes from 150.10.10.10: icmp_seq=3. time=2. ms
64 bytes from 150.10.10.10: icmp_seq=4. time=2. ms
—150.10.10.10 PING Statistics—
```

```
5 packets transmitted, 4 packets received, 20%
packet loss
round-trip (ms) min/avg/max = 2/2/2
```

The first ping is lost due to the ATMARP. The workstation and router will now show the newly created SVC:

```
charles> atmarp -a
qaa0:(150.10.10.10): NSAP
0x39 8401 28 12F130 1200 0010 1001.000000000002.00
vpi.vci=0.46 (vpi.vci=0.47) aal=5
flags=(Classical IP) peak rate=(unlimited)
bigben#sh atm map
ip 150.10.10.40 maps to NSAP
39 8401 28 12F130 1200 0010 1001.002048060539.00
broadcast, connection up, VC 34, ATM0/0
```

10. Although routing between the two routers will trigger an SVC, we may optionally create a PVC with a given QoS for this purpose. The additional configuration required on the switch is as follows:

```
localhost::) config vcc new 1a1 0 40 1a2 0 40
localhost::) config vcc new 1a2 0 40 1a1 0 40
```

The format of the above command is config vcc new *(input port) (input VPI) (input VCI) (output port) (output VPI) (output VCI)*. In this case, port adapter 'a' contains four interfaces: 1a1, 1a2, 1a3, and 1a4. The two routers are connected to ports 1a1 and 1a2. Likewise, as we saw earlier in the example, the workstation 'charles' is connected to port 1a3.

On 'bigben', we add the following configuration:

```
interface atm 0/0
atm pvc 1 0 40 aal5snap
map-group PVC
map-list PVC
ip 150.10.10.11 atm-vc 1 broadcast
```

On 'westminster,' we make the following additions:

```
interface atm 0/0
atm pvc 1 0 40 aal5snap
map-group PVC
map-list PVC
ip 150.10.10.10 atm-vc 1 broadcast
```

Quick review of the ILMI procedure
Initial state

- Router is configured with 48-bit local portion of NSAP

- ATM switch is configured with network portion of NSAP

ILMI

- Router initiates ILMI exchange with switch

- Router informs switch of local portion of NSAP

- Switch builds complete NSAP address for the interface connected to the router

- Switch returns network portion of NSAP

- Router builds complete NSAP for interface connected to switch

Registration

- Router registers its NSAP address and associated IP address with ATM-ARP server

Classical 3: SVC tunneling in an ATM WAN

Problem
A corporation expands, and implements SVC-based ATM backbones at a total of three sites. Bandwidth requirements dictate that the sites be interconnected via an ATM WAN. Although the service provider offers ATM, it is PVC-based. Thus, we must implement a way to tunnel the SVC signaling information across the ATM WAN.

Solution
A service provider offers an SVC tunneling service across the ATM WAN. As part of the ATM service, we provide the customer with CPE ATM switches which are capable of VP switching. The ATM switches within the core of the network (depicted with larger icons in Figure 5.7) are capable of VP switching as well. We configure the necessary VPCs between the CPE switches across the ATM backbone, remapping signaling requests, normally carried on VPI=0, VCI=5, to VPs other than 0. Within a given VPC, the signaling channel establishes VCCs on-demand. As Figure 5.7 shows, the circuit from Stuttgart to Heidelberg is remapped from VPI=2 to VPI=8 between the two locations, while preserving the signaling VCI. The solution provides for end-to-end SVCs even though the intervening ATM WAN service supports only PVCs. Note that the Figure 5.7 assumes that we support multiple signaling

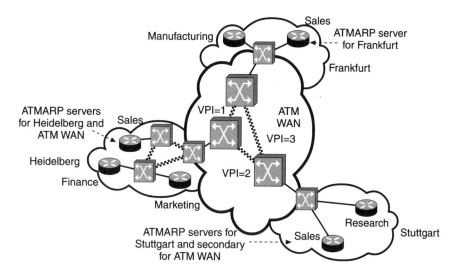

Figure 5.7 Classical 3 – SVC tunneling.

channels over a physical interface. If this is not the case, each CPE switch would require two physical interfaces into the ATM WAN.

Procedure

1. Configure the router ATM interfaces, signaling and ILMI PVCs, and network layer addresses as in the second example.

2. In this example, the user will not require knowledge of switch configuration since the CPE ATM switches are operated by the service provider. This provider will associate the necessary VPs to the outgoing interfaces. We remap the original VPI=0 into VPs between each pair of switches as shown in Table 5.19.

3. We deploy a new IP network, 150.10.100, for the ATM WAN. This is parallel to the backbone addressing used at each location. The completed address plan is as shown in Table 5.20.

4. Configure routing update PVCs across the ATM WAN as in the previous example. This will allow end-to-end dynamic routing between all locations.

Table 5.19 VP mappings for Classical example 3.

Source switch	Destination switch	VPI
Heidelberg	Stuttgart	2
Heidelberg	Frankfurt	1
Stuttgart	Frankfurt	3

Table 5.20 Classical 3 WAN addressing plan.

Location	Router	ATM interface IP address
Heidelberg	Sales	150.10.10.1 (Campus)
		150.10.100.1 (WAN)
Heidelberg	Marketing	150.10.10.3 (Campus)
Heidelberg	Finance	150.10.10.2 (Campus)
Stuttgart	Sales	150.10.80.1 (Campus)
		150.10.100.2 (WAN)
Stuttgart	Research	150.10.80.2 (Campus)
Frankfurt	Sales	150.10.70.1 (Campus)
		150.10.100.3 (WAN)
Frankfurt	Manufacturing	150.10.70.2 (Campus)

5. In implementing an ATM WAN, deploy ATMARP servers at Stuttgart and Frankfurt to service the local backbone IP LISs. Redundant ATMARP servers at Heidelberg and Stuttgart service the ATM WAN IP network.

6. Note that the user's ATM switches connect directly to the service provider's switches. Since the ATM WAN is PVC-based, it functions as a VPN. Thus, security is ensured. If the WAN supported SVCs, we would need to implement additional security such as ATM-layer access lists, filtering at the switch, or Layer 3 firewalling. These options are all described in Section 3.6.11.

7. As in the previous examples, verify SVC connectivity between the three sites.

Classical 4: frame-based connectivity to ATM

Problem
The user now wishes to connect a fourth site to the ATM WAN, but it does not warrant use of a high-speed ATM connection. Since the ATM cell overhead may be uneconomical at sub-E1/DS1 data rates, we implement a frame-based interface into the network. A variant of this requirement may exist in the local area, where a router incapable of supporting the cell-based ATM UNI must connect to the network.

Solution
This solution relies on a frame-based ATM interface. The first such interface, the ATM-DXI, was defined in 1993, while a newer, more sophisticated Frame-based UNI (FUNI) appeared in 1995. We focus on the FUNI since it is expected to replace most if not all ATM-DXI installations during the course of 1996 as vendors support the standard. For both the ATM-DXI and the FUNI, an ATM-DSU function provides the necessary

cell SAR for connection to the ATM switch. This function may exist in a standalone device or may be integrated into the ATM switch interface. Remember that the major differences between the ATM- DXI and the FUNI relate to signaling and traffic shaping. The FUNI is capable of supporting these functions, while the ATM-DXI is not.

Procedure

1. We build upon the previous example, Classical 3, adding a router, 'Munich,' to the ATM WAN as shown in Figure 5.8. Since this router connects to an ATM WAN service at 2 Mbps, we use a standard serial interface, in this case X.21. In a campus where higher speeds are required, the HSSI would be a viable alternative.

2. At Munich, configure the IP address to the router interface. Since the router connects directly to the ATM WAN it is given a WAN backbone address: 150.10.100.4.

3. Set the encapsulation to FUNI, configuring PVCs with RFC 1483 SNAP. Each of these PVCs will be mapped within the Munich router to the IP address of the destination router. For example, VCC=7 will map to IP address 150.10.100.1. We summarize the three PVCs configured in Table 5.21.

4. Configure the distant ends for each of these PVCs at the original three routers. Even if the other connections throughout the network rely on SVCs, these must still be defined as PVCs. The encapsulations used at each end of the VCC must be identical. For example, a PVC defined as LLC/SNAP at one router must be identical at the destination.

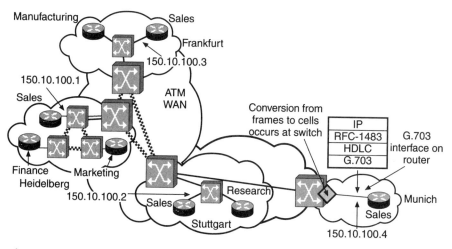

Figure 5.8 Classical 4 – frame-based connectivity.

Table 5.21 PVCs configured for Classical example 4.

Source	Destination	VCC VPI number		VCI	AAL	ENCAP	PCR	ACR	BT
Munich	Heidelberg Sales	7	1	70	5	LLC/SNAP	2000	1000	3
Munich	Stuttgart Sales	8	1	71	5	LLC/SNAP	2000	1000	3
Munich	Frankfurt Sales	9	1	72	5	LLC/SNAP	2000	1000	3

5. As in the first example, configure the new PVCs at each of the ATM switches.

6. Verify connectiviy between the new router and each of the original routers as well as with any other end-systems connected to the network.

7. Although we have implemented the FUNI, which supports SVCs, due to the need for dynamic routing, which would require a PVC in any case, we do not implement SVCs. With static routing, or if the network grew to encompass many more nodes, the use of SVCs would be desirable. We would then configure the required parameters across this interface, including the signaling and ILMI PVCs, QoS parameters, and the NSAP address of the ATMARP servers. This section of the procedure maps very closely to the second example, where we create maps for the SVCs based on the same QoS parameters as those used for the PVCs in Table 5.21.

Classical 5: NHRP in an ATM WAN

Goal

The goal is to optimize routing across an ATM WAN where sites do not share common network addresses. Multiple corporations or a single organization with multiple addresses may be connected to an ATM network. In either case, direct connectivity across the ATM network is preferable to jumping through routers due to addressing. Whereas the ATMARP as introduced in the second example is limited to a single network, as the Classical model forces an exit from the ATM cloud when connecting from one IP network to another, the NHRP provides for address resolution across multiple IP networks as well as enabling short-cut routing. This allows two end-systems on separate IP networks to establish direct VCCs across the ATM network. Remember the gains in efficiency which this allows when compared to ATMARP (see Chapter 4). In this example, we introduce a mesh of NHRP servers within the network which will provide for address resolution. As NHRP is limited to IP-only, we limit this example to the IP protocol. Also, we assume that the various sites within an NHRP environment are geographically separated. Since the switches must implement congestion avoidance and buffering mechanisms adequate to support application traffic across the wide area, enterprise or CO access/CO class switches will probably interconnect the four sites.

Procedure

1. Verify physical layer compatibility and connectivity between all systems. Be careful to set the end-systems to be compliant with the ATM switches and transmission systems. For example, a router connected to a public ATM switch in North America will be set to SONET framing, while one in Europe will be set to SDH. In Europe, two variants exist for E3 connections: PLCP and G.832. Interfaces on both the ATM end-systems and the switches must comply with the framing in use.

2. Configure each of the routers as in the first example, substituting the new IP addresses and eliminating references to the ATMARP server. We summarize the addresses used and the location of the NHRP Server (NHS) in Figure 5.9.

3. Configure the Sales routers at each location as NHSs. This includes enabling NHRP by assigning a number to the NBMA domain. Using Cisco IOS as an example, the only additional command is: (ip nhrp network-id 1)
   All NHSs will participate in this single NHRP domain, which includes networks 150.10.10, 150.10.70, 150.10.80, and 150.10.100.

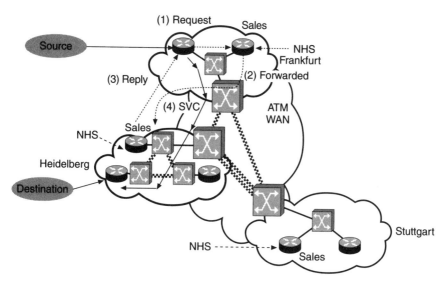

Figure 5.9 Classical 5 – Next Hop Resolution Protocol.

Table 5.22 NHRP configuration for Classical example 5.

Router	Local ATM	WAN ATM	Notes
Frankfurt Sales	150.10.70.1	150.10.100.3	NHS for 150.10.100, 150.10.70
Frankfurt Mfg	150.10.70.2		NHRP client
Heidelberg Sales	150.10.10.1	150.10.100.1	NHS for 150.10.100, 150.10.10
Heidelberg Finance	150.10.10.2		NHRP client
Heidelberg Mktg	150.10.10.3		NHRP client
Stuttgart Sales	150.10.80.1	150.10.100.2	NHS for 150.10.100, 150.10.80
Stuttgart Research	150.10.80.2		NHRP client

Quick review of NHRP operation

NHRP allows end-systems connected to an NBMA network to forward data directly between each other even if they are located on different Layer 3 networks. This is accomplished by Next Hop Servers (NHSs) which carry out address resolution. Under NHRP, we introduce the concept of a logical NBMA network, consisting of a number of LISs and served by a number of cooperating NHSs. This is an important concept relating to security, as a network provider may segment a large NBMA network into a series of logical networks. Traffic within a logical network remains at the ATM layer after address resolution, while traffic between logical networks must traverse a router.

In this example, we configure the Sales routers at Frankfurt, Heidelberg, and Stuttgart as NHSs. These routers are members of both the ATM WAN IP network (150.10.100) and the local IP network (150.10.10, 70, or 80). In Figure 5.9, a source local to Frankfurt but not located on the Sales router will query the NHS for the destination IP<-> ATM address. Since the Frankfurt NHS only has knowledge of 150.10.100 and 150.10.70, it will forward the request to the other NHSs. The Heidelberg NHS has knowledge of the destination mapping, and with forward its response to the source's router in Frankfurt. Supplied with this information, the source router may establish a direct SVC to the destination.

As part of NHRP, routers (or other NHRP-aware systems) must be capable of forwarding IP packets directly to an off-net destination without sending this data to the traditional default router for the LIS. This will require minor changes in most systems. If a PC or workstation were to participate in NHRP the procedures described above would not change, although this end-system would need to act as an NHRP client.

Table 5.23 VCCs configured for Classical model 5.

Source	Destination	PCR	ACR	BT
Frankfurt	Heidelberg	220000	110000	3
Frankfurt	Stuttgart	30000	15000	3
Heidelberg	Stuttgart	30000	15000	3

Note All parameters are for CLP=0

4. Configure all non-NHS routers to participate in NHRP by entering the NSAP and IP address of their NHSs (Table 5.22). Note that this NSAP address may in the future be the group address for NHSs. Options usually available as part of NHRP include access lists to decide which IP packets will trigger an NHRP request, route recording, and responder requests. These are not covered as part of this example.

5. Map each of the SVCs to a QoS. This is much more important in the local area, where all connections may be 155 Mbps in which case the available bandwidth may be equally divided between the VCCs. In the wide area, different backbone speeds are to be expected. For example, Frankfurt and Heidelberg may be connected at 155 Mbps, while the other two sites are only provided with 34 Mbps. This will require care when selecting average and peak cell rates. Also, the amount of buffering available on the switch will determine to what degree the trunks may be loaded, as previously discussed. Assuming the use of LLC/SNAP for best-effort data traffic across the WAN, we may summarize these VCCs in Table 5.23.

6. Verify connectivity between all end-systems and proper operation of the NHS.

Classical 6: video multicasting application

Problem
A user requires a more efficient way to disseminate new product information and training across a manufacturing campus. Any new system should use the ATM network deployed as part of the earlier Classical examples.

Solution
Deploy IP multicasting across the ATM backbone using network layer multicasting techniques and ATM pt-mpt VCCs. Note that this solution, deployed within a campus in this example, is also suitable for the metropolitan area or WAN where multiple video channels could be delivered

to subscribers. This is not true for Video on Demand (VoD), which we look at in a later example, since multicasting infers that a number of users wish to receive a given video feed at any instant as opposed to allowing each and every user to view an individual program. In an earlier chapter, we described the complexities in mapping IPmc to ATMmc within the Classical model. In this example we present a solution, with one source generating multiple channels. Clients of the service attach to routers, while PIM manages the network layer multicasting. For additional background as to why this example falls under the Classical model as opposed to LANE, refer to the discussion on LANE in Section 4.1.4.

Procedure

1. Verify physical connectivity between the routers and the ATM switches, as well as between the routers and the VoD server and clients on the LAN segments. Ensure that the routers and ATM switches support pt-mpt signaling and the interworking between this signaling and PIM (described below).

2. Configure the router ATM interfaces as in the first example, now adding multipoint signaling and multicast support.

   (a) Each of the router interfaces should be configured to accept and generate pt-mpt signaling requests. Note that this also requires pt-mpt support on the ATM switches, a separate issue. Although we could use static entries to create a pt-mpt connection to intended destinations, in this example we use PIM to identify those destination routers which should be added as leaves to a given pt-mpt VCC (which in turn is associated with a single multicast group, equating to a VoD channel).

   (b) Enable multicast routing and PIM sparse mode on all routers. Although this example focuses on PIM-capable routers, it does not preclude the use of PIM-capable end-systems (for example, VoD servers). Configure the RP for use by PIM. In this example, the RP should be at the router co-located with the VoD server. Additional control over multicasting is provided by access lists and TTL configuration. We do not include these parameters as part of this example.

3. Configure a control pt-mpt VCC for IGMP, over which the client routers will learn which multicast groups are available. This VCC may be a PVC since it does not change over time. Each channel at the source is mapped to a separate IPmc group. A client router wishing to receive a given channel will relay this expectation to the source router via IGMP. Finally, the source will add the client to the channel's pt-mpt VCC (Figure 5.10).

Quick review of PIM
PIM is a protocol which allows multicasting over an IP network. End-systems use the **Internet Group Management Protocol (IGMP)** to inform their nearest router of which multicast groups they wish to be members. The routers within a network implement PIM in two modes: dense and sparse. Dense mode is used when most end-systems (and therefore most routers) within a network wish to receive a multicast session. A source router will forward a multicast packet to all destinations, then pruning back those routers that do not wish to receive the session. This mode is most suitable for campus environments. In sparse mode, a source router assumes that other routers do not wish to forward the multicast packets. It will wait for the other routers to explicitly join a given group via a Rendezvous Point (RP). Sparse mode is more suitable for WANs, and forms the basis of our example.

4. Verify that the client routers are receiving the IGMP messages from the attached LAN segments and are relaying this information to the server router. Then verify that this server router at the root of a given pt-mpt VCC is using this data to add the client in question as a leaf to a group's pt-mpt VCC.

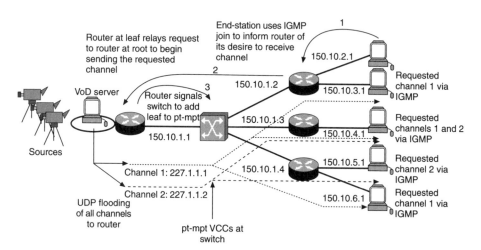

Figure 5.10 Classical 6 – video multicasting application.

Quick review of PIM operation across ATM
In this example, a VoD server connects to the source router via FDDI. This source router and three client routers connect to a single ATM switch. Finally, the intended recipients of the transmission connect to Ethernet ports on the client routers and understand IGMP. A given PC will listen to IGMP to determine which channels are available. If it now wants to receive channel 1, for example, it will issue a join request to the router (1) for the multicast group representing this channel. In this case, it joins group 227.1.1.1. The router will be a member of the pt-mpt VCC representing this group if another PC has previously requested to join. If not, it will send a join to the root of the multicast tree via PIM mechanisms (2). The root will then proceed to add this router as a leaf on the pt-mpt VCC for this group. This automatic operation is preferable to a static configuration whereby all client routers receive all multicast groups. Static operation, though feasible and scalable, is less bandwidth efficient. Using PIM and pt-mpt VCCs, packet duplication occurs at the furthest point downstream and only if required. This system, though potentially supporting a mesh of pt-mpt VCCs, does not allow for mpt-mpt connectivity within a single multicast group, and is therefore more useful for video distribution. True mpt-mpt connectivity will require the MARS with or without the MCS or alternatives outlined earlier in this book.

Note that we use ATM's ability to signal pt-mpt VCCs to support multicasting. The source router therefore only sends one copy of the packet for each multicast group. An alternative method of operation, whereby the router sends one copy to each destination over pt-pt VCCs is not recommended. This is known as NBMA-mode, and is only useful if the ATM network does not support pt-mpt signaling. Its scalability is dependent upon how many replications the source router is capable of performing.

Classical 7: RSVP and ATM

Problem
A user wishes to guarantee QoS for multimedia traffic across an internetwork consisting of both ATM and non-ATM segments.

Solution
Deploy RSVP on end-systems and routers within the network. Routers at the periphery of the ATM cloud will remap from integrated services QoS to ATM QoS. In this case, we have two sets of end-systems connected to the network. The first set implements RSVP within the networking stack, while the second, though incapable of generating and responding

to RSVP requests, is able to use static RSVP parameters as configured in the routers along the path. This will demonstrate the versatility of RSVP. This network is shown in Figure 5.11.

Procedure

The flow of events in setting up a reservation between source A and destination B across the network is as follows. We assume a multicast flow, using an audio video application as an example.

Receiver B first uses SD to determine which multicast group to join, and then uses IGMP to join this group. It now receives the data on this group at a best-effort QoS. This data includes the PATH (Tspec) messages from the sender.

In this case, the multicast session is sourced at station A (150.10.10.1). The video application requires a guaranteed BW across the network, which it sends as part of its Tspec. These PATH messages are sent to the multicast group or unicast destination of a flow. The destination for the PATH message is that of the receiver for a unicast flow or a session multicast address for a multicast flow. In the latter case, the receiver must join the session via IGMP to receive these messages. If a router is not configured for RSVP, it will forward the PATH message as a normal IP datagram. RSVP-capable routers will intercept the message and possibly modify it. This message is always updated with the previous hop, used by the receiver when generating the RESV message. If we were to look at this mapping in the first hop router, this would appear as: session IP=224.200.0.1, sender IP=150.10.10.1, protocol=UDP, destination port=1652, source port=1652, previous hop IP=150.10.10.1, previous hop interface=Ethernet1. The final two fields relate to the source of the Tspec. This information is sent across the network within the multicast session belonging to the video application, in this case 224.200.0.1.

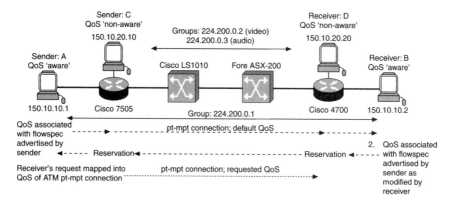

Figure 5.11 Classical 7 – RSVP and ATM.

Table 5.24 Possible mapping from a given Rspec into an ATM signaling request.

Integrated service	Attributes (Tspec/Rspec)	ATM service category	Attribute traffic descriptor
Guaranteed bandwidth	Tspec = {TB(r,b), p, m, M} Rspec = r	CBR rt-VBR	GCRA (PCR, CDVT)
Controlled load	Tspec = {TB(r,b), m, M}	rt-VBR	GCRA(SCR, BT), PCR = line_rate
Best effort		UBR or ABR	

TB(r,b) Token Bucket,   r bucket rate (bytes/second)
b bucket size (bytes)
m minimum policed unit (bytes)
M maximum packet size (bytes)
p peak rate (bytes/second)

The receiver, upon receiving this Tspec, turns this around and creates an Rspec which explicitly requests the type of service along with the bandwidth. Receivers derive these RESV messages from PATH messages, now including the BW and delay which they need. A router upstream from the receiver, upon receipt of the Rspec, would enter an entry as follows: session IP = 224.200.0.1, sender IP = 150.10.10.1, protocol = UDP, destination port = 1652, source port = 1652, previous hop = 150.10.10.2, previous hop interface = Ethernet 1, filter type = FF, QoS = Rate, bandwidth = 1000, burst size = 200. In this case, the previous hop and interface are in the direction of the receiver. FF stands for Fixed Filter. Other filters which could appear include shared explicit and wild card filter. Reservation types include load for controlled load and D 0 (or some other number, each higher number equal to a lower precedence) for controlled delay. Note that the future of controlled delay as well as predictive is in doubt, as the integrated services group may drop them. A router receiving this RESV message will determine if it has the resources on the interface in the direction of the receiver to support the requested QoS. If so, it will make the reservation; if not, it generates an error message. If multiple receivers request reservations through the same router, this router will compare these requests and generate the minimal reservation capable of supporting all.

We propagate this Rspec towards A, with each router along the path making the proper reservation. When this request reaches the router on A's side of the ATM network (via the best-effort multicast connection across the ATM cloud), this router must now either create a new connection with the required QoS across the ATM network or add B as a leaf to an existing connection. Possible mappings from a given Rspec into an ATM signaling request are given in Table 5.24.

Since this is a reservation for guaranteed bandwidth, we map the QoS request to ATM's CBR service, using the mapping of the Tspec and Rspec components as described above. We map the 1000 Kbps BW in the Rspec to the PCR of the ATM connection, while using a preconfigured value of 10ms for delay. The Rspec is now propagated to A via routers on the sender's side of the ATM network, and we have an end-to-end reservation.

If end-systems are incapable of participating in RSVP, we still may guarantee QoS across the network. Consider sender C and receiver D connected to routers at the periphery of the ATM network. Although the networking stacks in these two systems have no knowledge of application QoS requirements, the network administrator is aware of the expected QoS requirements. We know that C's conferencing application requires a bounded delay but does not require a set bandwidth. Thus, we will use controlled load as our service class. At C's, router, we enter a static RSVP mapping in the following way:

```
ip rsvp sender 224.200.0.2 150.10.20.10 UDP 1652
1652 150.10.20.10 Ethernet1.
ip rsvp sender 224.200.0.3 150.10.20.10 UDP 1651
1651 150.10.20.10 Ethernet1.
```

In this example, 224.200.0.2 and 224.200.0.3 are the multicast groups while 150.10.20.10 is C's IP address. The two reservations are required for the video and audio traffic. In effect, we emulate the transmission of Tspec messages by C on the router. At the router closest to the intended receiver(s), we make the following entries:

```
ip rsvp res 224.200.0.2 150.10.20.20 UDP 1652 1652
150.10.20.20 Ethernet 1 FF Load 500 60
ip rsvp res 224.200.0.3 150.10.20.20 UDP 1651
1651 150.10.20.20 Ethernet 1 WF Load 50 20
```

This emulated Rspec includes the traffic class ('load' for controlled load), along with a requested bandwidth and burst size. FF stands for Fixed Filter. Note that choosing which routers to configure requires some knowledge of what receivers are likely on the network. We have not used a wild card filter in this case since we associate the audio traffic with a single video stream.

If this network did not include ATM at the core, we would only have made the static RSVP entries within the routers closest to the sources and receivers. These routers would then emulate end-system behavior within the cloud. However, since we have introduced ATM into the network, we must map the RSVP parameters into ATM QoS. At the ATM boundary router on C's side of the ATM network, we map this reservation request into two VCCs. Due to the variability of bandwidth for both the video and audio, we make a guess on what PCR to use for the rt-VBR connections. For the first VCC, we set PCR=500 and SCR=250, while the audio VCC is set to PCR=50 and SCR=25 (all values in Kbps).

Reviewing end-system behavior

On the end-system, we map the application QoS requirements to RSVP through the WinSock2 SPI. Remember that this SPI is based on the concepts described by Partridge (1992), defining a flowspec as something which describes the QoS characteristics of a unidirectional flow across a network. Here, we associate a pair of flowspecs with sockets. We divide the flowspec into a Source Traffic Description, based on the token bucket traffic model and consisting of a rate, token bucket size, and peak bandwidth. We also include a latency, a level of service guarantee (for example, guaranteed versus best effort), a cost (not yet totally defined), and possible provider-specific parameters also undefined within the specification. The application will attempt to specify these parameters via the SPI and, if successfully completed, it may use the socket for data exchange. One element of this system is the ability to inform the client of changes in network conditions, information which the client may use to request future QoS guarantees from the network. Changes in the network may also occur during the course of an existing flow, in which case a source may renegotiate its QoS requirements.

Initially, WinSock supports the best effort, predictive, and guaranteed service types. If we compare this to Table 5.24 and mapping into ATM, we currently have the capability of mapping from either best effort or guaranteed. Based upon the level of guarantee, we may include the token rate (bytes/second), the token bucket size (bytes), peak bandwidth (bytes/second), latency (microseconds), delay variation (microseconds), cost (future), and whether the network is available or not (Intel, 1995a). It includes the source and destination addresses as well as the protocol (for example, TCP or UDP) and the source and destination ports. Note that in the future, predictive service may be exchanged for controlled load, which will more closely align to mappings into ATM.

We look at the three service types in turn. From Intel (1995a), when we specify guaranteed service, we implement a queuing mechanism which effectively isolates the one flow from all others, guaranteeing BW equal to the token rate for the duration of the session. However, if the sender exceeds the token rate, the network may delay or discard the excess data. Guaranteed service also places a bound on latency. This contrasts to predictive service which also places a guarantee on bandwidth but not on latency. Predictive service is more suited for video applications which may tolerate variation in quality. Finally, best effort service uses the flowspec as a guideline and, though attempting to maintain the QoS, does not make any guarantees.

We have described the concept of the token bucket earlier, but as a quick review, it is a bucket with a maximum volume (the token size) which fills at a constant rate (the token rate) and which is drained as an application sends data. If no 'credits' are available, the application must wait. An application sending at a lower rate than the token rate for some period of time will be able to send a burst until the accumulated tokens are expended. Using video as an example, we set the token rate to the average bit rate and the bucket size to the largest typical frame size. In contrast, for CBR applications we set the rate to the peak bandwidth and the bucket size to a small number capable of adapting to small changes in transmission rate while minimizing latency. The peak bandwidth is of course the rate at which an application may send packets back-to-back. Latency is the maximum acceptable time between transmission of a bit by the sender and its receipt by the receiver, while the delay variation is the difference between the maximum and minimum delay experienced by this bit. It is invaluable in determining the amount of buffering required at the receiver. The network availability field is interesting in that a single end-system with multiple outgoing links could use this field to determine whether a preferred media was available (for example, wireline) or whether it should use an alternative (for example, wireless) with necessary adjustments in QoS expectations. Finally, we may set a default flowspec available for use by applications where we do not specify the various QoS parameters. A step up from this default is the concept of a QoS template, usable by applications to retrieve a preset group of parameters from a registry.

Classical 8: SNA integration and APPN

Problem
A user currently has parallel networks for mainframe traffic and IP. To reduce costs, these two networks must be combined, while preserving the class of service for the transaction-oriented mainframe traffic.

Solution
Deploy an ATM network providing a high-speed backbone for the interconnection of IBM mainframes for use in disk mirroring. The APPN data will be carried across the ATM in native format (that is, not IP encapsulated). This AAPN transport as well as direct IBM channel interconnect, takes place at routers acting as network nodes (thus the classification of this example within the Classical model). IBM's High Performance Routing (HPR) allows us to support APPN session transmission priority and **Class of Service (CoS)** and then map this to ATM QoS. Note that this architecture does not support SNA. These users would upgrade to APPN or implement either LANE or IP encapsulation.

Table 5.25 TG parameters for Classical example 7. Source: Dudley, 1995.

Cost per connect time	128
Cost per byte	0
Security	0×20 (minimal)
Propagation delay	0×71 (terrestrial)
Effective capacity	0×91 (45 Mbps)

Procedure

1. Verify physical connectivity as in the previous examples. We introduce a new interface as part of this ATM WAN example, enabling the interconnection of mainframes and routers. Verify this interconnect as well.

2. Identify the APPN trunk group for transport across ATM. This will be mapped onto an ATM SVC as a switched connection (that is, either end may activate the link). Since this is a dedicated ATM WAN connection, we select a TG profile appropriate to this topology (Table 5.25). If the connection were best-effort as opposed to reserved, we would select different values. The connect time is given a cost since we assume that the SVC will only be held for the duration of the backup.

3. Verify end-to-end connectivity and session integrity. We depict this network in Figure 5.12. At the host, control traffic is encapsulated within the **Logical Data Link Control (LDLC)**, while session data uses the **Rapid Transport Protocol (RTP)**. Both provide for reliable delivery, while the LDLC also includes error control. LDLC and RTP pass through the **Network Control Layer (NCL)**, either into the ESCON physical interface or into RFC

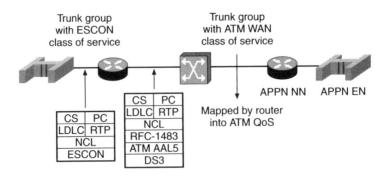

Figure 5.12 Classical 8 – APPN transport across ATM WAN.

CS	Configuration Services	RTP	Rapid Transport Protocol
LDLC	Logical Data Link Control	NCL	Network Control Layer

1483 for transport across ATM. Within RFC 1483, the NLPID encapsulation identifies the Layer 2 and Layer 3 protocols used.

5.4.2 LAN emulation

In this set of examples we look at various methods of implementing VLANs based on the ATM Forum LANE standard (AF-LANE-0021). LANE in effect virtualizes the workgroup while allowing ATM to emulate a traditional Ethernet or Token Ring LAN. Our examples include small deployments based on single VLANs or MAC-based filtering, and larger installations where we route between the VLANs. The last example proposes a solution to interconnect a LANE domain with the Classical installations in the previous section. We describe VLAN operation in Section 4.1.4.

LANE 1: single port-based ATM Forum virtual LAN

Problem
A user requires additional bandwidth to users and in the backbone due to the deployment of new applications. This is coupled with a requirement to contain network administrative costs due to staff movements – the moves, adds, changes problem.

Solution
We deploy ATM in the backbone and LAN switching to the existing hubs and to some end-systems. We virtualize the workgroup through LANE, allowing for greater mobility. Since this is a relatively small network, and the user requires no security between end-systems, we implement a single VLAN. We limit this example to port-based VLANs, where a single LAN port on a LAN switch or router is associated with a single VLAN. As we have implemented a single VLAN, a routing function is not required in this configuration, although a router is required for connectivity to an external network. Finally, we limit this example to an Ethernet ELAN, though the concepts will remain the same for Token Ring.

Configuration is relatively simple, with all ports on all LECs members of the same VLAN. Therefore, each LAN switch must implement only one LEC process. This single LEC points to a single LECS, LES, and BUS located on a router. Since support for the ILMI is assumed for systems participating in LANE, the LECs will learn their network prefix from the ATM switch. Also, the network administrator must only configure the NSAP address of the LECS, as the addresses for the LES and the BUS will be learned from this LECS.

Procedure

1. Verify physical connectivity between the routers and LAN switches in Figure 5.13. These devices will connect to the ATM switches via SM or MM fiber.

2. Verify that the routers, LAN switches, and ATM switches support at least UNI 3.0 and the ILMI, along with pt-mpt signaling. SVCs and pt-mpt signaling are required, while the ILMI will ease configuration and management. Note that there are four methods by which a LEC may learn the address of the LECS' preconfigured, via the ILMI, the well-known address, and the LECS PVC (VCI=17). Be aware of these differences and maintain consistency when deploying multivendor ELANs.

3. Configure the NSAP prefix on the ATM switches. This is the 26-digit high-order part of the NSAP not including the ESI or the SEL. These last two fields are a function of the end-system.

4. As in the first Classical example, configure the signaling and ILMI PVCs on each of the ATM interfaces (both router and LAN switch).

5. Configure the LES and BUS for the ELAN on the first router. Select a subinterface for the LES and BUS along with the name of the ELAN. Optionally, a LEC may also be configured. In this case, a Layer 3 protocol address for each protocol in use will also be configured. Note that although we configure these server functions on a router, vendors do support this same capability on external workstations or within LAN or ATM switches. The general configuration will remain the same, with subinterfaces used if the system is capable of supporting more than one VLAN. A sample configuration based on the Cisco AIP is as follows:

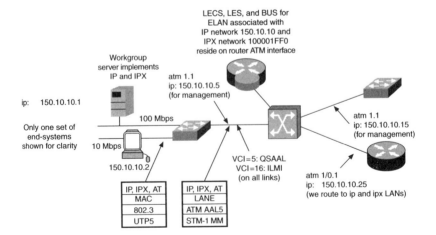

Figure 5.13 LAN emulation 1 – Single VLAN.

```
interface ATMI/0
    mtv 1500
    no ip address
    atm pvc 1 0 5 gsaal
    atm pvc 2 0 16 ilmi
    lane config atm1
    lane auto-config-atm-address
interface ATM1/0.1 multipoint
    ip address
    150.10.10.10.255.255.255.0
    ipx network 10001FF0
    lane client ethernet engineering
    lane server-bus ethernet engineering
```

6. Configure LECs on the second router and on both of the LAN switches. LECs may also be assigned to subinterfaces, and will include the ELAN name as well as one or more Layer 3 addresses.

7. Configure the LECS on the first router. Choose an LECS database name which will be global to the LANE domain. If more than one ELAN were defined, they would all use this database. Next, the ELAN's name should be bound to its LES. The LECS will also have the name of the ELAN entered. For example: lanedatabase atm 1 home engineering service-atm-address 47.0091.00.000000. 0000.0000.0000.0000 0021F123.01 default-name engineering. If more security is desired, individual LECs may be bound to ELANs by their ATM addresses within the LECS database. These are known as **Restricted Membership LANs**, and may be configured via network management. Note that this is not an issue for a single ELAN.

8. Enter the address of the LECS in the ATM switches. The LECs use this address to automatically determine the LECS address.

9. Note the use of network layer addressing in this example. LAN switches and routers operating as LECs perform their functions at Layer 2. Thus, they have IP addresses assigned for management only. In this example, router 150.10.10.25 services traditional LAN segments. It routes these into the LANE domain.

10. Verify connectivity between the LECs and then between end-systems connected to these LECs.

LANE 2: filtering

Problem

As in the first LANE example, the user requires greater bandwidth at the workgroup core while supporting existing applications. There is a need to partition the network, but the user does not want to introduce routing at this phase.

Solution
Deploy a LANE domain servicing multiple VLANs based on filtering. We may use this filtering at both the MAC (Layer 2) and network (Layer 3) layers to define membership within a VLAN. This filtering is used in conjunction with routing between VLANs, as we are maintaining the internetwork model. Note that if the entire domain is at Layer 2, and the user is confident of filter-based access control, this routing is not required. In this case, the total LANE domain is equivalent to a bridged network (with its associated advantages and drawbacks). For simplicity, we limit this example to a single Layer 2 domain servicing multiple VLANs. Only one ELAN is defined. A word of caution: the complexities of MAC layer address management will become obvious.

Procedure

1. Verify connectivity and signaling support as in the previous examples.

2. The LANE domain consists of two LAN switches. One switch acts as the LECS, LES, and BUS for the ELAN. Each LAN switch is configured with two or three Ethernet ports, each port servicing one or more users. Table 5.26 lists the MAC addresses in use. In developing the connectivity matrix, a clear view of access and security requirements is essential. For this example, the following rules apply:

   (a) All users have access to Server 1 (SV1).

   (b) Finance users have access to Server 2 (SV2).

   (c) Engineering users only have access to Server 1.

   (d) Finance users 1–3 have access to Finance users 4–5.

   (e) Finance users 4–5 also have access to HR users.

   Table 5.27 depicts a filter matrix for this connectivity.

Table 5.26 MAC addresses for LAN emulation example 2.

LAN switch 1 (LEC 1)			LAN switch 2 (LEC 2)		
Port	User	User MAC address	Port	User	User MAC address
1	Eng1	0040.0B00.000A	1	HR1	0800.0AA0.7612
1	Eng2	0800.0020.0125	1	HR2	0800.0810.100E
1	SV1	0800.0F57.1289	1	HR3	0040.A0FD.981A
2	Fin1	000A.1257.0001	2	Fin4	00C7.0030.DD1F
2	Fin2	000A.169B.0325	2	Fin5	0800.98C1.61FF
2	Fin3	0800.2000.000B	3	SV2	0800.5F11.7AC5

Table 5.27 MAC filter matrix for LAN emulation example 2.

	Eng1	Eng2	SV1	Fin1	Fin2	Fin3	HR1	HR2	HR3	Fin4	Fin5	SV2
Eng1	*	*	*									
Eng2	*	*	*									
SV1	*	*	*	*	*	*	*	*	*	*	*	
Fin1		*	*	*	*					*	*	*
Fin2		*	*	*	*					*	*	*
Fin3		*	*	*	*					*	*	*
HR1		*					*	*	*	*	*	
HR2		*					*	*	*	*	*	
HR3		*					*	*	*	*	*	
Fin4		*	*	*	*	*	*	*	*	*	*	*
Fin5		*	*	*	*	*	*	*	*	*	*	*
SV2			*	*	*					*	*	*

Note   * = may communicate

3. This matrix infers both incoming and outgoing MAC address filtering, configured on the LAN switches, hopefully with the assistance of a network management tool. An example of this filtering on the LAN switches is listed in Table 5.28. Note the one security hole in this filtering architecture: consider one of the engineering users spoofing as Server 1. This user will then have unlimited access to end-systems throughout the network. In this case, it would have been better to place the server on a separate LAN switch port, as is done with Server 2. If Server 1 was application specific (for example, E-mail), then higher-layer filters could be implemented to permit only those ports applicable to E-mail. This would ease security concerns. Though we have implemented relatively straightforward filtering based on the MAC address, more complicated filtering could be based on vendor-ID, protocol field, and offsets into the MAC frame. In addition, these fields may be compared through the use of complex expressions. For example, some switches support combinations of the following comparisons: Logical AND, Logical OR, Equality, Inequality, Greater than, Greater than or equal, Less than, Less than or equal, bitwise AND.

Table 5.28 LAN switch filtering for LAN emulation example 2.

Switch/port	Outgoing	Incoming
1/1	Permit SV1 (traffic from server)	Permit all (no filter)
1/2	Permit all (no filter)	Permit SV1, Fin4, Fin5, SV2
2/1	Permit all (no filter)	Permit SV1, Fin4, Fin5
2/2	Permit all (no filter)	Permit SV1, HR1, HR2, HR3, Fin4, Fin5, SV2
2/3	Permit all (no filter)	Permit Fin1, Fin2, Fin3, Fin4, Fin5

4. Verify connectivity (or lack thereof) between end-systems. Note that this Layer 2 filter-based architecture is already quite complex

with only 12 users. In a larger network, maintaining proper filtering may become quite a challenge.

LANE 3: multiple port-based ATM Forum virtual LANs

Problem

The organization has grown to the extent that a single VLAN will no longer suffice due to LAN scaling and security reasons. We must therefore subdivide the original workgroup into multiple VLANs based on function.

Solution

Configure a LANE domain containing multiple ELANs connected via a router. For each ELAN, we require an LES, a BUS, and one or more LECs. A single LECS will suffice for the entire LANE domain. In addition, we introduce the concept of port mobility at the LECs, whereby a single port may be assigned to multiple ELANs. This allows a file server, for example, to be connected to a single physical port on a LAN switch while serving multiple VLANs. The same applies to high-performance workstations connected directly to the ATM switch and implementing LEC software. Although a single port on a LAN switch now supports multiple Layer 3 addresses, it still functions as a Layer 2 device and therefore does not route between them. All routing between the different ELANs takes place at the ATM-connected router. Note that traffic which remains within a single ELAN will not traverse the router, as the LEC will be capable of establishing a point-to-point VCC. LECs in this example include LAN switches, a router, and an ATM-connected workstation. The LECS, LESs, and BUSs reside on a router which also interconnects the two ELANs. Remember that each ELAN is associated with a unique Layer 3 network. In this case, we implement IP and IPX. To generalize this example, a router will implement one instance of the LES and BUS for each ELAN supported, while a LAN switch, router, or other end-system will implement one instance of the LEC for each ELAN. Finally, remember that traffic within an ELAN will never be routed. The router is used only when traffic must cross from one ELAN to another.

Procedure

1. Repeat steps 1 to 4 from the first LANE example.

2. Using the previous example for guidance, configure the first router as the LECS and as an LES/BUS for two ELANS, Red and Blue. The Red ELAN is Ethernet, white Blue is Token Ring. The LES and BUS for Red and Blue should be assigned to different subinterfaces, each assigned to a different IP subnet and IPX network. This first router also acts as an LEC for both ELANs. One way of assigning MAC addresses is to provide a MAC address pool to the ATM interface, whereby an offset is added to the MAC address

depending upon whether the function is an LECS, LES, BUS, or LEC. Each instance of these servers may be identified within the NSAP address via the SEL field.

3. Configure the second router and the LAN switches as members of both ELANs. As with the first router, each LEC is assigned to a separate subinterface. Note that on all LECs, the interface will retain a single MAC address but the NSAP is derived from the subinterface of the LEC (using a Cisco router ATM Interface Processor as an example). In this example, we assign the following ATM, IP, and IPX addresses to the various devices as shown in Figure 5.14 and Table 5.29. The following pages summarize the various control connections created between the LECS, the LESs, the BUSs, and the LECs. These connection types are summarized in Figure 5.15. In Figure 5.15, we have not depicted any Data

Table 5.29 Protocol and NSAP addresses for LAN emulation example 3.

Device	Function	Intf.	ATM (ESI+SEL)	IP	IPX
Router 1	LECS	4/0	0000.0C03.505E.00	na	na
Router 1	LES Red	4/0.1	0000.0C03.505C.01	150.10.1.10	100.0000.0C03.505C
Router 1	BUS Red	4/0.1	0000.0C03.505D.01	150.10.1.10	100.0000.0C03.505C
Router 1	LEC Red	4/0.1	0000.0C03.505B.01	150.10.1.10	100.0000.0C03.505C
Router 1	LES Blue	4/0.2	0000.0C03.505C.02	150.10.2.10	101.0000.0C03.505C
Router 1	BUS Blue	4/0.2	0000.0C03.505D.02	150.10.2.10	101.0000.0C03.505C
Router 1	LEC Blue	4/0.2	0000.0C03.505B.02	150.10.2.20	101.0000.0C03.505C
Router 2	LEC Red	0/1.1	0000.0C30.41FD.01	150.10.1.2	100.0000.0C30.41FD
Router 2	LEC Blue	0/1.2	0000.0C30.41FD.02	150.10.2.2	101.0000.0C30.41FD
LAN switch	LEC Red	0.1	0040.0B50.A020.01	na	na
LAN switch	LEC Blue	0.2	0040.0B50.A020.02	na	na
Work-station	LEC Red	1.1	0000.0666.1234.01	150.10.1.50	100.0000.0666.1234
Work-station	LEC Blue	1.2	0000.0666.1234.02	150.10.2.50	101.0000.0666.1234

Note   The MAC address for each device is the ATM ESI without the SEL field
The IPX address is derived from the MAC address of the system

```
Device: Router 1
LE Config Server ATM4/0config table: testState: operational
ATM Address: 47.250F0100000000000000000.00000C03505E.00 (auto)
vcd    rxFrames txFrames callingParty
723    1        1        47.250F0100000000000000000.00000C03505C.01
726    1        1        47.250F0100000000000000000.00000C03505C.02
735    1        1        47.250F0100000000000000000.00000C03505B.01
736    1        1        47.250F0100000000000000000.00000C03505B.02
737    1        1        47.250F0100000000000000000.00000C3041FD.01
738    1        1        47.250F0100000000000000000.00000C3041FD.02
739    1        1        47.250F0100000000000000000.00400B50A020.01
740    1        1        47.250F0100000000000000000.00400B50A020.02
741    1        1        47.250F0100000000000000000.000006661234.01
742    1        1        47.250F0100000000000000000.000006661234.02
```

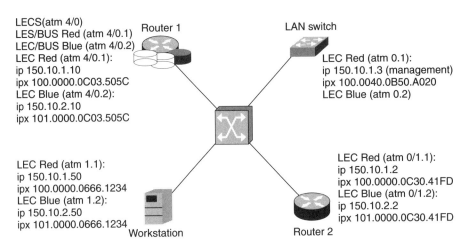

Figure 5.14 LAN emulation 3 – multiple port-based VLANs.

Direct VCCs between two LECs. These are created on-demand by the LECs. During the LANE domain configuration phase, the LECS will have VCCs open to each of the LESs and LECs. These VCCs may timeout over the course of LANE operation, and are summarized in the following examples.

The LANE domain is 'Test', and the first VCC listed, 723, connects to the LES for the Red VLAN. Note the use of the SEL field in the NSAP address – it identifies the subinterface (if any) of the LES or BUS. A LECS should always apply to the main interface and not to a subinterface. We now look at the first LES, for the Red VLAN:

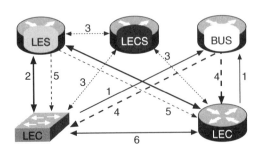

Figure 5.15 LAN emulation control and data connections.

| Multicast Send (1) | Configure Direct (3) | Control Distribute (5) |
| Control Direct (2) | Multicast Forward (4) | Data Direct (6) |

```
Device: Router 1
LE Server ATM4/0.1 ELAN name: red State: operational
type: ethernet Max Frame Size: 1516
ATM address: 47.250F0100000000000000000000.00000C03505C.01
Config Server ATM addr:
47.250F0100000000000000000000.00000C03505E.00 vcd: 724
control distribute: vcd 709, 4 members, 4 packets
```

VCC 724 points to the LECS as described above, while 709 is the Control Distribute VCC for this VLAN. The Red LES is on subinterface 1, identified by the SEL field. Red is an Ethernet ELAN with a standard frame size. The four LECs currently connected to Red are as follows:

```
control direct:
lecid vcd pkts MAC ATM Address
1 699 2 0000.0c03.505b
47.250F0100000000000000000000.00000C03505B.01
2 701 2 0000.0c30.41fd
47.250F0100000000000000000000.00000C3041FD.01
3 722 2 0040.0b50.a020
47.250F0100000000000000000000.00400B50A020.01
4 727 2 0000.0666.1234
47.250F0100000000000000000000.000006661234.01
```

The BUS for Red is also homed off the first subinterface, although with a different NSAP address as based on the MAC offset:

```
Device: Router 1
LE BUS ATM4/0.1 ELAN name: red State: operational
type: ethernet Max Frame Size: 1516
ATM address: 47.250F0100000000000000000000.00000C03505D.01
mcast forward: vcd 718, 4 members, 14 packets
```

Remember that the BUS uses a Data Forward VCC for distribution, in this case VCC 718. The four LECs connected to the Red BUS are:

```
mcast send:
lecid vcdpkts ATM  Address
1    711    12   47.250F0100000000000000000000.00000C03505B.01
2    715    2    47.250F0100000000000000000000.00000C3041FD.01
3    725    0    47.250F0100000000000000000000.00400B50A020.01
4    728    0    47.250F0100000000000000000000.000006661234.01
```

The first LEC for Red is also located on this router. A router acting as an LECS, LES, and BUS is not precluded from functioning as a LEC for the same VLAN. The VCCs between the LEC and the LES and BUS will not remain within the router, however; they will traverse the first ATM switch. Note the VCCs in use between this client and the various control functions for the VLAN:

```
Device: Router 1
LE Client ATM4/0.1 ELAN name: red State: operational
Client ID: 1
```

```
HW Address: 0000.0c03.505b Type: ethernetMax Frame Size: 1516
ATM Address: 47.250F0100000000000000000000.00000C03505B.01
VCD  Type            ATM Address
0    configure       47.250F0100000000000000000000.00000C03505E.00
702  control direct 47.250F0100000000000000000000.00000C03505C.01
707  control distrib
47.250F0100000000000000000000.00000C03505C.01
713  mcast send      47.250F0100000000000000000000.00000C03505D.01
716  mcast forward  47.250F0100000000000000000000.00000C03505D.01
```

We now look at the LES and BUS for the Blue VLAN, assigned to subinterface 2 of the router:

```
Device: Router 1
LE Server ATM4/0.2 ELAN name: blue State: operational
type: token ring    Max Frame Size: 4544 segment ID:001
ATM address: 47.250F0100000000000000000000.00000C03505C.02
control distribute: vcd 712, 4 members, 8 packets
control direct:
lecid vcd pkts MAC/RD ATM Address
1    700 2 0000.0c03.505b
47.250F0100000000000000000000.00000C03505B.02
2    729 2 0000.0c30.41fd
47.250F0100000000000000000000.00000C3041FD.02
3    730 2 0040.0b50.a020
47.250F0100000000000000000000.00400B50A020.02
4    731 2 0000.0666.1234
47.250F0100000000000000000000.000006661234.02

LE BUS ATM4/0.2 ELAN name: blue State: operational
type: token ring    Max Frame Size: 4544 segment ID:001
ATM address: 47.250F0100000000000000000000.00000C03505D.02
mcast forward: vcd 720, 4 members, 12 packets
mcast send:
lecid vcd   pkts  ATM Address
1     714   3     47.250F0100000000000000000000.00000C03505B.02
2     732   3     47.250F0100000000000000000000.00000C3041FD.02
3     733   3     47.250F0100000000000000000000.00400B50A020.02
4     734   3     47.250F0100000000000000000000.000006661234.02
```

The first Blue LEC is also on the first router, assigned to sub-interface 2 (noted in the SEL field). The following VCCs are in use:

```
Device: Router 1
LE Client ATM4/0.2 ELAN name: blue State: operational
Client ID: 1
HW Address: 0000.0c03.505b Type: ethernetMax Frame Size: 1516
ATM Address: 47.250F0100000000000000000000.00000C03505B.02
VCD  TypeATM Address
0    configure       47.250F0100000000000000000000.00000C03505E.00
703  control direct 47.250F0100000000000000000000.00000C03505C.02
710  control distrib47.250F0100000000000000000000.00000C03505C.02
717  mcast send      47.250F0100000000000000000000.00000C03505D.02
719  mcast forward  47.250F0100000000000000000000.00000C03505D.02
```

The three other physical devices connected to this LANE domain are a router, a LAN switch (Layer 2), and a workstation. These are all assigned as LECs on both the Red and Blue ELANs. We only show the entries for the Red LECs, as the only differences between Red and Blue are the value of the SEL field (it will change from 01 to 02), and of the ATM subinterface (which will also change from 0.1 to 0.2).

```
Device: Router 2
LE Client ATM0/1.1 ELAN name: red State: operational
Client ID: 2
HW Address: 0000.0c30.41fd Type: ethernetMax Frame Size: 1516
ATM Address: 47.250F0100000000000000000000.00000C3041FD.01
VCD  Type          ATM Address
0    configure     47.250F0100000000000000000000.00000C03505E.00
100  control direct47.250F0100000000000000000000.00000C03505C.01
101  control distrib
47.250F0100000000000000000000.00000C03505C.01
102  mcast send    47.250F0100000000000000000000.00000C03505D.01
103  `mcast forward47.250F0100000000000000000000.00000C03505D.01

Device: LAN Switch
LE Client ATM0.1 ELAN name: red State: operational
Client ID: 3
HW Address: 0040.0b50.a020  Type: ethernetMax Frame Size: 1516
ATM Address: 47.250F0100000000000000000000.00400B50A020.01
VCD  Type          ATM Address
0    configure     47.250F0100000000000000000000.00000C03505E.00
4    control direct47.250F0100000000000000000000.00000C03505C.01
5    control distrib
47.250F0100000000000000000000.00000C03505C.01
6    mcast send    47.250F0100000000000000000000.00000C03505D.01
7    mcast forward 47.250F0100000000000000000000.00000C03505D.01

Device: Workstation
LE Client ATM1.1 ELAN name: red State: operational
Client ID: 4
HW Address: 0000.0666.1234  Type: ethernetMax Frame Size: 1516
ATM Address: 47.250F0100000000000000000000.000006661234.01
VCD  Type          ATM Address
1    configure     47.250F0100000000000000000000.00000C03505E.00
2    control direct47.250F0100000000000000000000.00000C03505C.01
3    control distrib
47.250F0100000000000000000000.00000C03505C.01
4    mcast send    47.250F0100000000000000000000.00000C03505D.01
5    mcast forward 47.250F0100000000000000000000.00000C03505D.01
```

If we look at the control VCCs terminating at the first router for this small LANE domain, the need for SVCs becomes apparent (Table 5.30).

4. Configure the ATM-connected server as an LEC for each of the ELANs. This multiple ELAN support also relies on subinterfaces in the same way as the router. The same router which implements the LECs and BUSs routes between the two VLANs. Note that this file server, though theoretically capable of routing between VLANs, has not been configured for routing. This is not to say that this platform could not provide this functionality in smaller networks or if its physical interface and code have been optimized for multiprotocol routing.

Table 5.30 Router VCCs for LAN emulation example 3.

Interface	VCD	Type	AAL/Encaps	Description
ATM4/0	1	PVC	AAL5-SAAL	Signaling PVC
ATM4/0	10	PVC	AAL5-ILMI	ILMI PVC
ATM4/0	723	SVC	LANE-LECS	Configure Direct from LECS to Red LES
ATM4/0	726	SVC	LANE-LECS	Configure Direct from LECS to Blue LES
ATM4/0	735	SVC	LANE-LECS	Configure Direct from LECS to Red R1 LEC
ATM4/0	736	SVC	LANE-LECS	Configure Direct from LECS to Blue R1 LEC
ATM4/0	737	SVC	LANE-LECS	Configure Direct from LECS to Red R2 LEC
ATM4/0	738	SVC	LANE-LECS	Configure Direct from LECS to Blue R2 LEC
ATM4/0	739	SVC	LANE-LECS	Configure Direct from LECS to Red LS LEC
ATM4/0	740	SVC	LANE-LECS	Configure Direct from LECS to Blue LS LEC
ATM4/0	741	SVC	LANE-LECS	Configure Direct from LECS to Red WS LEC
ATM4/0	742	SVC	LANE-LECS	Configure Direct from LECS to Blue WS LEC
ATM4/0.1	709	SVC	LANE-LES	Control Distribute Red from LES to LECs
ATM4/0.1	699	SVC	LANE-LES	Control Direct Red from R1 LEC to LES
ATM4/0.1	701	SVC	LANE-LES	Control Direct Red from R2 LEC to LES
ATM4/0.1	722	SVC	LANE-LES	Control Direct Red from LS LEC to LES
ATM4/0.1	727	SVC	LANE-LES	Control Direct Red from WS LEC to LES
ATM4/0.2	712	SVC	LANE-LES	Control Distribute Blue from LES to LECs
ATM4/0.2	700	SVC	LANE-LES	Control Direct Blue from R1 LEC to LES
ATM4/0.2	729	SVC	LANE-LES	Control Direct Blue from R2 LEC to LES
ATM4/0.2	730	SVC	LANE-LES	Control Direct Blue from LS LEC to LES
ATM4/0.2	731	SVC	LANE-LES	Control Direct Blue from WS LEC to LES
ATM4/0.1	718	SVC	LANE-BUS	Multicast Forward Red from BUS to LECs
ATM4/0.1	711	SVC	LANE-BUS	Multicast Send Red from R1 LEC to BUS
ATM4/0.1	715	SVC	LANE-BUS	Multicast Send Red from R2 LEC to BUS
ATM4/0.1	725	SVC	LANE-BUS	Multicast Send Red from LS LEC to BUS
ATM4/0.1	728	SVC	LANE-BUS	Multicast Send Red from WS LEC to BUS
ATM4/0.2	720	SVC	LANE-BUS	Multicast Forward Blue from BUS to LECs
ATM4/0.2	714	SVC	LANE-BUS	Multicast Send Blue from R1 LEC to BUS
ATM4/0.2	732	SVC	LANE-BUS	Multicast Send Blue from R2 LEC to BUS
ATM4/0.2	733	SVC	LANE-BUS	Multicast Send Blue from LS LEC to BUS
ATM4/0.2	734	SVC	LANE-BUS	Multicast Send Blue from WS LEC to BUS

5. Verify that all control VCCs have been created and are capable of passing data. Then verify connectivity between LECs on the same ELAN and on different ELANs. At this point we assign local LAN segments belonging to the LAN switch and router to the different VLANs via network management. We may then verify connectivity between Ethernet-connected end-systems on each of the VLANs.

LANE 4: multiple virtual LANs per port

Problem

As the network grows, some systems must serve multiple workgroups. This may include central mail and Web servers, along with other resources, such as those within marketing, commonly shared throughout an organization. We must ensure that all workgroups have adequate access to these resources.

Solution

In the previous example, we included an ATM-connected server whose interface supported multiple VLANs. This is no different to a router or LAN switch ATM interface which assigns VLANs to subinterfaces. Here we expand the solution set to include those servers which must connect to a LAN switch Ethernet (10 or 100 Mbps) or Token Ring interface. One way of connecting a server to multiple VLANs in this instance is by installing a LAN interface for each VLAN. A problem with this option is that not every server will support this configuration. A second solution requires placing the server on its own VLAN, with all traffic routed to this system. Given high-performance routing, this will work for a small number of servers. This configuration is shown in Figure 5.16.

A totally different option allows a single LAN switch Ethernet or Token Ring interface to service multiple VLANs. If this scheme is to be efficient, we will require some form of filtering, however. Consider traffic originating at the server destined for the Finance VLAN. If we do not filter on the destination address, the data will be forwarded to all destinations. In the opposite direction, the LAN switch will forward all incoming traffic from the relevant VLANs to the server, which is not a problem. Note that this is not equivalent to the single Layer 2 domain described in the second LANE example, where we partition the single VLAN by MAC address filtering. Here, we may filter on Layer 3 addresses since each VLAN is assigned a different network number. The one concern with this architecture is the ability of the server to handle the background traffic generated by two or more VLANs, along with its ability to properly support multiple network layer addresses (common in IP but a problem with most other protocols). Given high-performance NICs and networking stacks, this should not be a problem just as it is not a problem with ATM-connected systems servicing multiple VLANs. Figure 5.17 outlines this configuration.

In the procedure below, we describe this second alternative, since the first relies on routing between VLANs, covered in the previous example.

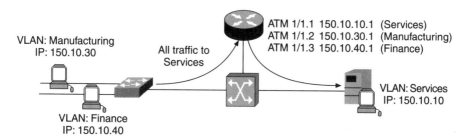

Figure 5.16 LAN emulation 4 – routing to central servers.

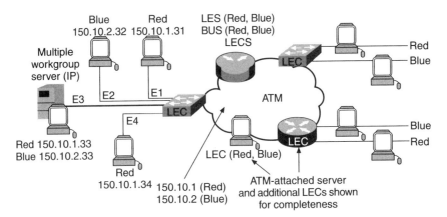

Figure 5.17 LAN emulation 4 – multiple VLANs per LAN switch port.

Procedure

1. Verify physical connectivity as in the examples above.

2. Building upon the third LANE example, we now detail the assignment of the switch ports to each of the VLANs in Figure 5.31. Note the mapping of Ethernet 3 to both VLANs, Red and Blue. Incoming traffic from the server on this LAN segment will be mapped to the appropriate LEC based on its destination IP address. For performance reasons, this is a function carried out by the LAN switch hardware. Note that all filtering is at the network layer; we do not need to manipulate the randomly-assigned MAC addresses.

3. Configure the various server functions as in the previous example and verify end-to-end connectivity.

Table 5.31 VLAN assignments.

LAN switch port	VLAN
ATM 0.1	Red
ATM 0.2	Blue
Ethernet 1	Red
Ethernet 2	Blue
Ethernet 3	Red
	Blue
Ethernet 4	Red

LANE 5: LAN emulation to Classical model interworking

Problem

A user deploys LANE throughout a campus, and now wishes to extend
ATM across the metropolitan area or into the WAN. Although LANE
may be offered as a service at some point in the future in these domains,
the only existing service is based on the Classical model.

Solution

Deploy interworking between the LANE and Classical domains. All
traffic leaving the campus will pass through a router connected to both
the campus ATM backbone and the ATM WAN. Remember that we
require routing for both inter-VLAN connectivity as well as for interworking to other data services.

Procedure

1. Verify physical layer connectivity between the devices on the net-
    work. In this example, we focus on two routers and a LAN switch
    connected to the ATM cloud.

2. Configure the first router in accordance with the Classical model
    as outlined in the second Classical example. Figure 5.18 depicts
    only the IP addresses, though any Layer 3 protocol addresses may
    be used as long as the router interconnecting the two models is
    capable of routing between these protocols.

3. Configure the LAN switch as LECs, where the router intercon-
    necting the two models is a member of all VLANs and will also act
    as the default router for traffic leaving each VLAN. The locations
    and configurations of the LECS, LES, and BUS are out of the focus

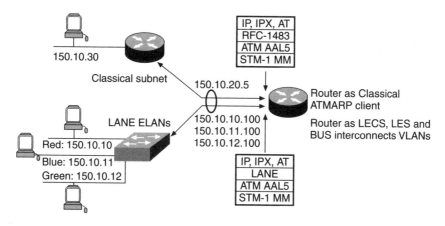

Figure 5.18 LAN emulation 5 – interworking between LAN emulation and
Classical.

of this example, although they may be processes on this same router. Refer to the first and second LANE examples for more detailed information.

4. The ATM interface on the router connecting the two domains will have one or more subinterfaces assigned to LANE and one or more assigned to the Classical model. In the example below, we outline one possible configuration based on a Cisco router with the ATM Interface Processor. Once data enters the router over one of these subinterfaces, it will be passed up to the routing processes for further action. Thus, other LAN and WAN interfaces may of course be connected to this router.

5. Verify connectivity between LANE and Classical model users.

```
! LAN Emulation Configuration
!
!
lane database test
name red server-atm-address
39.000001000001000000000001.00000c5123f9.02
name blue server-atm-address
39.000001000001000000000001.00000c5123f9.03
name green server-atm-address
39.000001000001000000000001.00000c5123f9.04
default-name red
!
! Note: router could also route/bridge to
! Ethernet, Token Ring, etc.
! We do not list these interfaces in this example
!
! ATM Interface Configuration
!
interface Atm2/0
mtu 1500
! Required for LAN Emulation
no ip address
no ip directed-broadcast
ip route-cache cbus
atm pvc 1 0 5 qsaal
atm pvc 2 0 16 ilmi
! Signaling and ILMI PVCs
!
! LECS Configuration
!
lane config test
lane auto-config-atm-address
!
```

```
! Classical IP Sub-interface
! This router is an ARP client for this LIS
!
interface Atm2/0.1 multipoint
description Classical IP ATM backbone
ip address 150.10.20.5 255.255.255.0
ip mask-reply
no ip directed-broadcast
no ip proxy-arp
atm esi-address 000000000005.01
atm arp-server nsap
39.000001000001000000000001.000000000001.01
!
! LANE Sub-interfaces
! This router is the LES/BUS and default router
! for each ELAN
!
interface Atm2/0.2 multipoint
description red ELAN
ip address 150.10.10.100 255.255.255.0
ip mask-reply
no ip directed-broadcast
no ip proxy-arp
lane auto-config-atm-address
lane client ethernet red
lane server-bus ethernet red
!
interface Atm2/0.3 multipoint
description blue ELAN
ip address 150.10.11.100 255.255.255.0
ip mask-reply
no ip directed-broadcast
no ip proxy-arp
lane auto-config-atm-address
lane client ethernet blue
lane server-bus ethernet blue
!
interface Atm2/0.4 multipoint
description green ELAN
ip address 150.10.12.100 255.255.255.0
ip mask-reply
no ip directed-broadcast
no ip proxy-arp
lane auto-config-atm-address
lane client ethernet green
lane server-bus ethernet green
```

5.4.3 MPOA and route distribution

In this example, we look at the latest method of data transport across an ATM network, Multiprotocol over ATM (MPOA). This standard, still under development within the ATM Forum at the time of writing, provides for multiprotocol internetworking across ATM while at the same time incorporating VLANs.

Earlier, we described the various MPOA client and server functions. Here we associate these various functions with actual physical systems. Of note are the interactions between devices known as multilayer LAN switches and MPOA route servers. If we look back to the third VLAN example, we interconnected multiple VLANs via a centrally-located router. MPOA permits us to distribute this routing function by incorporating some Layer 3 functionality in the LAN switches. This helps in deploying scalable VLANs.

Note that our choice of physical devices and information flows is based on the state of the draft standard as of Spring 1996. Since we do not expect the final MPOA document before Winter 1997, some of this may be subject to change.

Problem

Users require multiprotocol transport across ATM and interworking with LANE. Protocols in use include IP, IPX, and DECnet. Although we could deploy the Classical model, with ATMARP for IP and manually configured address maps for IPX and DECnet, the perceived administrative overhead in comparison to MPOA is unacceptable to this user.

Solution

Deploy MPOA across the ATM network. We connect existing LAN segments to this network via LAN switches acting as **Edge Device Functional Groups (EDFGs)**, and hosts acting as **ATM-attached Host Functional Groups (AHFGs)**. In addition, we connect an existing LANE domain into the same backbone, integrating it into the MPOA environment. As part of MPOA, we deploy a route distribution service between the **Route Server Functional Group (RSFG)** and the EDFGs/AHFGs.

Procedure

1. Deploy all hardware and verify network connectivity.

2. In our example, and using IP as an example, our MPOA domain is based on two **Internet Address Sub-Groups (IASGs)**, 150.10.100 and 150.10.120. (see Figure 5.19) MPOA clients (EDFGs and AHFGs) are members of one or both of these groups. The same will apply to IPX and DECnet, which we do not describe in any detail. Borrowing LANE terminology, we will associate each of these IASGs with a VLAN.

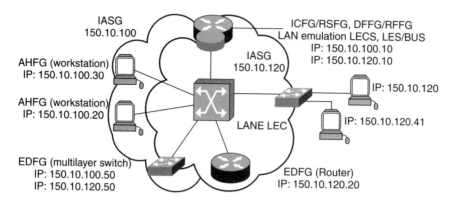

Figure 5.19 MPOA route distribution.

3. A router provides the necessary MPOA server functions, including: **IASG Coordination Functional Group (ICFG), Default Forwarder Functional Group (DFFG), Route Server Functional Group (RSFG),** and **Remote Forwarder Functional Group (RFFG).** In this example we do not include redundancy, although the protocol of course supports this. Since MPOA relies on LANE for default Layer 2 forwarding within a single IASG, we place the necessary LANE server functions, LECS, LES, and BUS, on this same platform. Note that we require one instance of each of these servers per IASG. Thus, the router is running two sets of server processes.

4. MPOA clients include a multilayer LAN switch, a router implementing MPOA EDFG code, and two hosts. An additional LAN switch supporting only an LEC participates in one of the IASGs (150.10.120).

5. Verify that the proper control connections have been established between the MPOA clients and servers after the configuration and initialization phase. These include connections from each of the EDFGs and AHFGs to the ICFG, RSFG, DFFG, and RFFG for each IASG. Note that some of these connections may be combined based on vendor implementation. In this example, and in keeping with the specification, we combine the ICFG and RSFG as well as the DFFG and RFFG. Since we operate two IASGs, we also require control configurations between the MPOA servers in each. In addition to these MPOA connections, we establish control connections between the EDFGs and the LEC to the respective LANE services.

6. Now verify that the data forwarding paths operate properly. These include the default and shortcut paths both within and between IASGs.

(a) Within an IASG, verify the LANE VCC between EDFGs as well as the MPOA connection between AHFGs and EDFGs. Also, verify forwarding through the DFFG for both configurations.

(b) Between IASGs, verify the MPOA default path between EDFGs via the RFFG. Next, verify the short-cut path between end-systems in each IASG.

(c) Verify use of the MARS/MCS for multicast traffic between groups of MPOA clients within an IASG.

5.4.4 Frame Relay transport and interworking

One way in which we will realize ATM's promise as a multiservice offering is by internetworking native ATM users with those connected to a **Frame Relay (FR)** network. As described earlier, the Frame Relay Forum working with the ATM Forum has defined an interworking framework by which users connected via an FR-UNI on a Frame Relay or ATM switch may interwork with users connected via the ATM-UNI. This interworking may take two forms. The first, known as **network interworking**, segments the FR frame at a device known as an **Interworking Function (IWF)** but preserves the native FR encapsulation based on RFC 1490. The IWF, though often depicted as a separate entity, will usually exist as part of the FR interface on an ATM switch or as part of an ATM interface on an FR switch. For this type of interworking, the ATM-UNI must also implement the FR encapsulation across one or more VCCs. This is supported by the FR-SSCS, and requires that the ATM system knows that the destination is reachable only across an FR network, and therefore uses NLPID for any VCCs directed to the IWF.

Service interworking requires encapsulation conversion at the IWF from RFC 1490 to RFC 1483. The ATM user now does not care if the destination is reachable directly over ATM or via Frame Relay. When considering Frame Relay in conjunction with ATM, we often also look at a third function, that of using the ATM network to provide for Frame Relay transport. We first look at the simpler service interworking, and then introduce ATM as an FR transport.

Frame Relay service interworking

Problem

A large corporation uses Frame Relay to connect branch offices to a central site, and now wishes to take advantage of the new ATM service to interconnect some locations. Users connected to the ATM service require interworking with sites connected via Frame Relay over the same ATM connection.

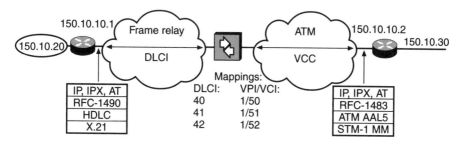

Figure 5.20 Frame Relay service interworking.

Solution

We deploy service interworking between the ATM and Frame Relay networks as shown in Figure 5.20. IWF converts between the DLCIs used across FR and the ATM VPI/VCI fields. To simplify the example, we describe the interworking where neither the Frame Relay nor the ATM user experiences congestion. Also, as almost every Frame Relay offering is based on PVCs at present, this example will use PVCs both at the FR-UNI as well as the ATM-UNI. At present, SVCs may be supported across the ATM network by looking at the Layer 3 destination address of packets arriving at the Frame Relay side of the IWF. This would require a router function and the ATMARP. In the future, with the release of Frame Relay SVC services, we should be able to map Frame Relay NSAP addresses to ATM NSAP addresses at the IWF.

In this example, the IWF maps between the three defined DLCIs – 40, 41, and 42 – and the three ATM PVCs. At the same time, in the ATM direction, it segments the data frames into cells and re-encapsulates the data from RFC 1490 (NLPID) to RFC 1483 (LLC/SNAP). Note that the network side addresses on both the Frame Relay and ATM routers are part of the same subnet. Additional functions performed by the IWF relating to congestion and QoS are detailed in Section 4.1.6. Under service interworking, the two clouds are connected by a service layer (link layer) entity. Therefore, no Layer 3 remapping takes place. Alternatively, a router could be inserted between the two networks in which case two distinct subnets would be used (unless the data was bridged).

ATM as Frame Relay transport

Problem

A service provider has evolved a public Frame Relay service over time to the extent that the existing core switches can no longer handle the traffic load. The network engineers require a solution which preserves the existing switch investment while providing long-term scalability in the

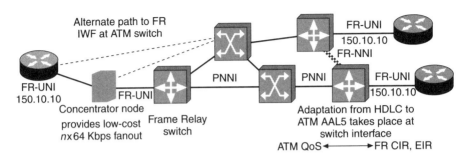

Figure 5.21 ATM as Frame Relay transport.

core. Options include installing higher-performance Frame Relay switches or deploying an ATM core.

Solution
We redeploy the existing Frame Relay backbone to the periphery of the network, inserting a new, higher bandwidth, ATM core. Most users will still connect to the existing Frame Relay switches or concentration nodes, though those requiring DS1/E1 and above may rehome to the ATM core using the FR-UNI, if the switch supports this, or Frame Relay encapsulation across ATM (Figure 5.21). This is a form of network interworking.

5.4.5 SMDS/CBDS transport and interworking

The **Switched Multimegabit Data Service (SMDS)**, also known in Europe as the **Connectionless Broadband Data Service (CBDS)** was the first commercial broadband service deployed in some countries. Since some service providers have a substantial investment in SMDS/CBDS hardware, expertise, and marketing, we require a method to evolve the service through the deployment of higher core bandwidth while also allowing for interworking between this new, ATM-delivered SMDS and exsiting DQDB-based SMDS subscribers. Note that we describe the operation of DQDB (802.6) in greater detail in Chapter 6.

SMDS 1: SMDS across the ATM-UNI

Problem
A service provider wishes to rationalize data services, delivering as many as possible over a common ATM infrastructure. This will allow for the decommissioning of the existing DQDB service-specific hardware and network management.

Solution

Deploy the SMDS/CBDS service across an ATM infrastructure. This service relies on a **Connectionless Server Function (CLSF)**, a device which is usually a hardware module part of an ATM switch, to maintain an address table and forward data to the intended destination. The CLSF multicasts or broadcast data where required although the service across ATM is often known as **Connectionless Broadband Data Service (CBDS)**, the two terms, SMDS and CBDS, are interchangeable. For the remainder of these examples, we use SMDS to refer to both. CPE may also connect to an SMDS concentrator node, which then will connect to the ATM network. This option is much like the Frame Relay example above. SMDS over ATM makes use of AAL3/4 as the ATM adaptation of choice for the service, though the use of AAL5 is also possible and is expected to replace AAL3/4 in the future. Note that all SMDS addressing is based on E.164 addresses in contrast to the NSAP format addresses used for all previous examples. In this example, the SMDS forms a single Layer 3 network, with all routers connected to the same PVC star terminating at the CLSF sharing an IP subnet. This does not preclude the support of multiple Layer 3 networks by terminating more than one AAL3/4 VCC at the end-systems. For example, some routers support this on each subinterface of the physical ATM interface. This will allow traffic intended for one set of destinations to be sent to one CLSF and traffic to other destinations sent to another.

Procedure

1. Verify physical connectivity across the ATM network between the routers and the ATM switches. Refer to the Classical WAN examples for concerns when connecting to public ATM switches.

2. Configure the router ATM interfaces in the same way as the first Classical example, eliminating references to the ATMARP server. If only SMDS based on AAL3/4 is configured, the signaling SVC does not need to be configured. Remember that a single ATM interface will support both AAL3/4 and AAL5, although on separate subinterfaces.

3. Establish a PVC to the CLSF using AAL3/4. In almost all cases, this PVC will be created by the service provider, who will supply a VPI and VCI pair to use. The service provider will also assign an E.164 format SMDS address and multicast address. Possible values for these addresses are given in Figure 5.22. Remember that this PVC defaults to RFC 1209 encapsulation in contrast to RFC 1483 used within the Classical model.

4. Configure the ATM interface for each Layer 3 protocol in use. In this example, we depict only IP. If required, bridging may also be configured across the network.

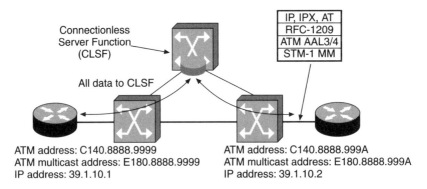

Figure 5.22 SMDS across ATM.

5. Verify connectivity between end-systems connected to the ATM network.

SMDS 2: interworking between ATM and DQDB-based SMDS

Problem

A user has subscribed to existing DQDB-based SMDS. New installations are based on SMDS over ATM. Thus, we require seamless interworking between the two networking technologies.

Solution

Enable interworking between users connected to an ATM-based SMDS and a pre-existing SMDS network based on DQDB (802.6) technology. This will provide for transparent interconnectivity between users on both networks. As far as the ATM user is concerned, the existence of the IWF between the two networks will play no part in end-system configurations. If an ATM-based CLSF is used, this device will forward cells as required to the ATM-DQDB IWF. Alternatively, the service provider may deploy a single CLSF/IWF, with all traffic from ATM users forwarded to this device which exists at the edge of the ATM network. This in fact was the method used for the earliest demonstrations of SMDS support across ATM.

Procedure

1. Configure the SMDS-attached router as above, with the AAL3/4 PVC pointing to the CLSF. Alternatively, it may point to IWU.

2. Routers connected to the DQDB-based network are configured for

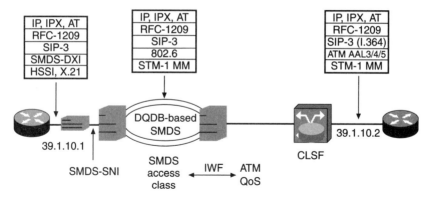

Figure 5.23 Interworking between ATM and DQDB-based SMDS/CBDS.

standard SMDS operation and rely on an SMDS-DSU to connect to the DQDB network. All users may still share the same IP subnet, as the IWU operates at the service layer and not at Layer 3 (Figure 5.23).

3. The network operator will implement ATM QoS to SMDS access class mapping at the IWU. The equivalent of these access classes on the ATM network may be provided by traffic shaping at the router or, more effectively, through the use of rate queues if supported.

4. Verify connectivity between users on the DQDB network and users connected to ATM.

5.4.6 Circuit Emulation Service (CES)

The CES provides for the transport of traditional voice and video traffic (AAL1) across an ATM infrastructure. This same ATM network will support data traffic (AAL3/4 or AAL5) as well. We describe a way in which the ATM network may replace existing dedicated lines or TDMs. Although we focus on a corporate user deploying a private ATM backbone, the solution principles also apply to any service provider offering CES. In the following example, we look at supporting **Common Channel Signaling (CCS)** across the ATM backbone. Note that the support of **Channel Associated Signaling (CAS)** is roughly parallel to this CCS support, with software differences only at the IWF. These services, along with VTOA, are summarized in Section 4.2.

Problem

A user wishes to replace an existing TDM network with ATM, combining

WAN data, voice, and video traffic across the same network. Due to more efficient use of bandwidth by ATM, since we may allocate and tear down VCCs on demand, this will result in cost savings compared to TDM.

Solution

Deploy ATM CES across the enterprise network, initially interconnecting three PABXs. The switches within the network support CCS for ISDN signaling when interconnecting these PABXs. Remember that we have two methods of allocating ATM bandwidth on demand for voice transport: CAS and CCS. We describe both of these signaling methods in Section 4.2. This is our first example where the network layer is not used, since CES relies on direct mapping of the voice stream into AAL1. Note that this example builds upon simpler CES services where we use the entire DS1/E1 ATM trunk to interconnect PABXs. A problem with this non-dynamic allocation of bandwidth is that the channels, when idle, are unavailable for any other traffic. In this example, we rely on the CBR service class, where bandwidth, when signaled, is reserved across the ATM trunks. This does not preclude the use, however, of rt-VBR to fulfill the same purpose. Unlike the other ATM service classes (rt-VBR, nrt-VBR, UBR, and ABR), CBR reserved bandwidth is not available for any other traffic.

The example below makes an assumption that the ATM switch has a pre-configured set of parameters in support of CBR service. These parameters include prioritization within the switch for the CBR service class. In this case, one trunk is E3 (34 Mbps) and a second is E1 (2 Mbps) (Figure 5.24). This 2 Mbps trunk effectively limits the number of voice connections which we may transport. In practice, we recommend a max-

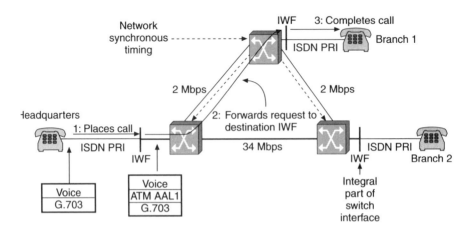

Figure 5.24 Circuit Emulation Service (CES) – common channel signaling.

Note: Timeslot 0 – E1 overhead
Timeslot 16 (only to IWF) – CCS

imum of half the trunk bandwidth for CBR or rt-VBR traffic due to QoS guarantees. Each of these physical interfaces will include timeslot 16 for signaling and N additional timeslots (provided on demand) for the voice service. Finally, clock recovery is based on network timing distribution, where we clock the PABXs off the ATM CBR IWFs. This provides for more accurate clock recovery than early implementations based on adaptive timing.

Procedure

1. Verify physical connectivity between the ATM switches and between the switches and PABXs. Refer to the earlier WAN examples regarding concerns when connecting to an ATM WAN.

2. Verify the support of ISDN signaling on the IWFs at each of the ATM switches. This includes the support of network timing within the ATM network. The PABXs will be timed off this central source.

3. Verify connectivity between all sites.

5.4.7 Residential services

This last set of examples outlines a number of methods of delivering video and data services to users over the existing residential infrastructure. We first outline a VoD network, concentrating on protocols, then describe a metropolitan data overlay. Although these two networks are based on HFC as the access architecture, the concepts apply equally well to the other access networks proposed by the ATM Forum's RBB SWG.

Residential 1: Video on Demand (Vod)

Problem

A public service provider must implement a Video-on-Demand (VoD) (or Near-VoD – staggercasting) service across the existing PSTN or cable infrastructure. Users of the service should be able to select pre-encoded or live video feeds. In the future, a voice service may be offered as well. Thus, the infrastructure must support this eventuality.

Solution

Use ATM as an infrastructure for the delivery of VoD. The physical delivery possibilities include FTTC, FTTH, ASDL, VDSL, and HFC. However, this example is independent of any of these delivery mechanisms since they all support ATM. In contrast to the video multicasting example based on the Classical data model, the delivery system in this example relies on direct mapping of MPEG-2 into AAL5, forgoing the network layer. Although our example is based on AAL5, the concepts apply equally well to AAL1 CBR or VBR. At the video source, commonly known as the 'headend,' the incoming NTSC/PAL/SECAM video stream is digitized in real-time by an MPEG-2 encoder. Alternatively, previously digitized and compressed content is stored on a video server. A number of server architectures exist which are capable of delivering large numbers of simultaneous VoD and NVoD streams. For example, 500 available movies would only require around 2 terabytes of disk storage using existing compression technology. These devices then encapsulate the resultant MPEG-2 transport stream into AAL5, where it is distributed to subscribers over pt-mpt VCCs in the case of NVoD or pt-pt for true VoD. Note that under UNI 4.0, a subscriber wishing to view an individual channel would only need to generate an add-leaf request to an existing pt-mpt VCC for NVoD. The selected channel would then be delivered to the subscriber. Each channel is a separate pt-mpt VCC at about 4 Mbps (equivalent to S-VHS) including 384 Kbps for audio. The subscriber, wishing to view an individual channel, only needs to select the proper VCC (Figure 5.25) via a pt-pt control VCC which also connects the set-top box with the server. An additional on-demand pt-pt VCC used for data services will also connect each subscriber to Internet servers as well as into routers for external connectivity. At the headend, in deploying this network, the upstream bandwidth available per subscriber is in most instances more constrained than the downstream bandwidth. Depending upon the type of access network implemented, this may present a problem if large numbers of customers require dedicated upstream bandwidth (for example, home offices, Web sites).

Between the ATM switch and the set-top box, we modulate the ATM VCCs for transport over the residential access network. The modulation technique is closely tied in with the delivery mechanism, along with the way in which we combine existing analog TV channels. At the subscriber's end, the set-top box demodulates the signal and splits off the

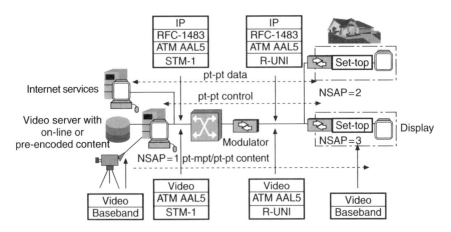

Figure 5.25 Video on Demand (VoD).

analog video. This device then decompresses the digital video and audio signals. If we were to include voice services, we would carry them across the network as separate AAL1 VCCs between a CES IWF located at the headend and the user's set-top unit. Adams (1994) describes many of these concepts in the context of an operational network, the Time-Warner Full Service Network located in Orlando, Florida, USA.

Procedure

1. Verify physical connectivity between the ATM switch at the core (that is, headend) of the network and the subscriber devices (that is, set-top boxes). The physical infrastructure may consist of a fiber-only network for businesses or a combination of fiber for distribution and ADSL or coaxial cable for local access. In the residential environment, the former is likely to be deployed by the telephone providers while the latter is expected to see wide deployment by the cable providers. A single network may of course combine multiple physical architectures.

2. Deploy a VoD server(s) at one or more central sites. These servers will include real-time MPEG-2 encoders and large file stores for pre-encoded content. The MPEG-2 data will be encapsulated in ATM AAL5 at the server or at an intermediate service multiplexer. The server will also implement a full network stack for the transmission/reception of control information. The subscriber units will also be capable of accepting the same encapsulations: MPEG-2 over AAL5 and control data over a network stack (for example, IP).

3. Verify connectivity between the VoD server and the subscribers. Verify proper operation of the control and data flows.

Residential 2: data overlay

Problem

A cable provider wishes to offer a data overlay service for Internet connectivity. This service must integrate with the existing cable infrastructure while providing necessary bi-directional bandwidth to all users.

Solution

Deploy a metropolitan data overlay network using the existing HFC infrastructure. The deployment of multiple distribution hubs introduces scalability, whereby the network is capable of supporting 200,000 or more subscribers. The number of subscribers served by a single fiber termination point will depend upon the installed fiber and coax cable plant along with the bandwidth expectations of the end users. In the diagram below, the 27 Mbps upstream and downstream bandwidth is shared by 500 subscribers, though some HFC installations reduce this to 100 subscribers, increasing the bandwidth per user (Figure 5.26).

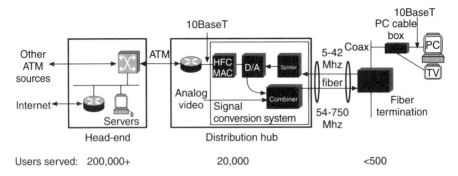

Users served: 200,000+   20,000   <500

Figure 5.26 Metropolitan data overlay.

5.4.8 Customer case studies

In this next set of examples we look at customer migration scenarios as opposed to detailing the protocols and addresses for each ATM service and data model. Drawing on these various voice, video, and data service models, we look at how they may be deployed in typical environments. In each case, we look at an existing network and then show how it may be evolved through the addition of ATM technology.

Medical school

Before

Data flows over an existing fiber-based Ethernet backbone, connecting the various buildings with the campus computer center. Users share LAN segments, while servers are on shared or dedicated segments. These segments are connected via routers to the Ethernet backbone. As the volume of data transfer increases due to new applications and greater use of networking, the backbone becomes congested and all users suffer. Some servers require higher-speed interfaces than that provided by even dedicated Ethernet.

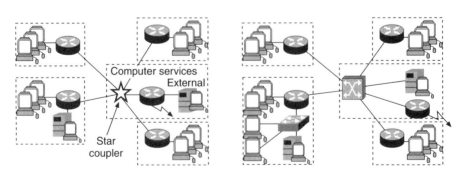

Figure 5.27 Medical school migration.

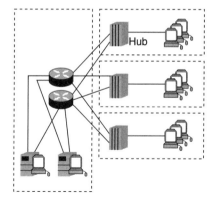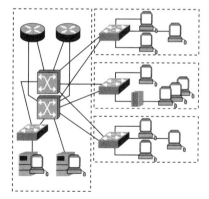

Figure 5.28 Brokerage house migration.

After
Ethernet backbone is replaced with ATM, interconnecting existing routers (Figure 5.27). Some servers are now connected directly to ATM, while some users are provided with dedicated Ethernet via LAN switching. These three steps introduce the necessary bandwidth where needed while requiring no changes in networking paradigms.

Brokerage house
Before
Dealers connect via hubs to redundant routers located in the building. Servers are connected directly to routers. The introduction of new applications and hardware requires a greater bandwidth than that provided by hubs and exceeds the throughput of central routers. Network managers also require greater control over workgroups and membership.

After
LANE is deployed via an ATM backbone, along with LAN switching to most users. Hubs are preserved where user bandwidth does not justify dedicated Ethernet (Figure 5.28). Switches are connected to redundant ATM core. Routers interconnect VLANs and provide LANE services. Some servers are connected directly to the ATM backbone.

Commercial bank

Before
Ethernet and Token Ring LANs are connected via routers to an FDDI backbone. Central servers are also connected to the FDDI ring. New applications and increasing use of the network results in congestion on

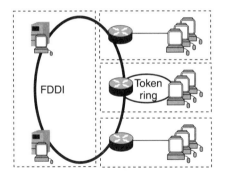
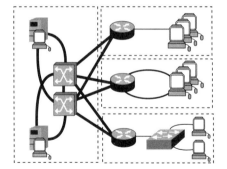

Figure 5.29 Commercial bank migration.

the backbone and sub-optimal access to servers. The user is not ready to migrate fully to ATM, and is comfortable with FDDI as a technology.

After
FDDI switching is deployed at the core, interconnecting existing routers (Figure 5.29). Servers also connect to these redundant FDDI switches. Switches use ATM internally, but only FDDI is visible to the user. This solves the current networking problem while providing a path for future ATM deployment.

Automobile manufacturer
Before
A global car manufacturer operates a TDM network interconnecting major sites. Voice traffic and multiprotocol data flows over this network. The user realizes that ATM may result in more efficient use of bandwidth while providing more controllable QoS for data.

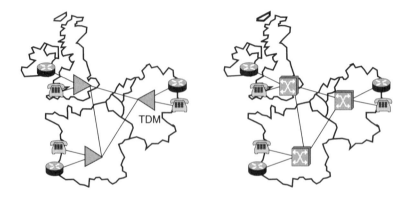

Figure 5.30 Automobile manufacturer migration.

After

The TDM network is replaced with an ATM backbone (Figure 5.30). ATM supports CBR service for voice and some videoconferencing, along with ABR and UBR for data. The bandwidth on trunks is dynamically allocated between traffic classes.

Insurance company

Before

Separate voice and data networks interconnect sites. As data volume grows, networking charges become excessive. Users wish to rationalize networking charges by connecting to the new ATM offering, but require high WAN reliability.

After

Voice and data services are provided by a nationwide ATM multiservice offering (Figure 5.31). CPE is a hybrid service multiplexer/router, with backup provided via ISDN for both voice and data traffic. Networking charges are reduced by combining access over a single service.

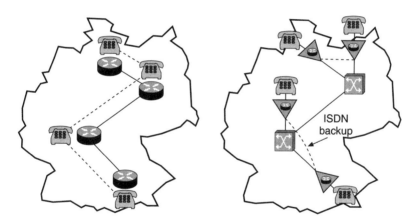

Figure 5.31 Insurance company migration.

Cable provider

Before

A cable provider is limited to a traditional video offering due to hardware and infrastructure limitations. Users rely on PTT/Telco for voice and data services. The cable provider wishes to provide both voice and data services across the infrastructure.

After

The cable provider deploys ATM-capable set-top boxes, integrating all services over a single infrastructure (Figure 5.32). An ATM switch at the headend combines video, voice, and data services.

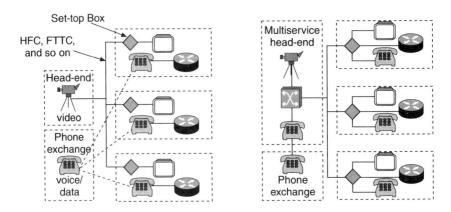

Figure 5.32 Cable operator integrated services.

PTT/Telco

Before

A public service provider maintains separate data networks for leased lines, Frame Relay, and possibly SMDS. This requires separate switching systems, trunks, management systems, and user interfaces. The provider wishes to rationalize the service offering while allowing interworking between the various services.

After

An ATM backbone integrates multiple services (Figure 5.33). Dedicated circuits, Frame Relay, and SMDS now share a single hardware platform and backbone, resulting in cost savings. Some sites not justifying ATM are still provided with Frame Relay. The backbone is also capable of integrating voice services, as seen in the insurance company example.

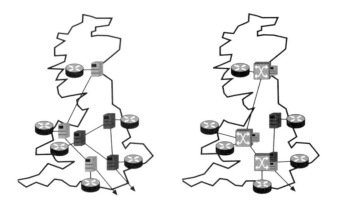

Figure 5.33 Telco/PTT integrated services.

6

ATM and other technologies

Though we have focused on ATM, alternative technologies exist in both the local and wide areas; alternatives which sometimes satisfy many of the technology and business drivers justifying the deployment of ATM. In the campus and high-rise backbone, high-speed Ethernet variants are receiving a great deal of interest as the newcomers, while FDDI switching has generated new interest in this mature technology. Either of these technologies coupled with QoS (RSVP) and VLAN (802.1q) support are viable alternatives to ATM for many applications. At the desktop, where lower bandwidths are often acceptable, Ethernet and Token Ring switching may suffice. Parallel to these mainstream technologies, niche technologies such as the Fiber Channel or HIPPI are available but will not see wide deployment. Alternatives to ATM also exist in the wide area and, depending upon the application and bandwidth requirement, ISDN, Frame Relay, or even direct mapping into SONET/SDH may be suitable. An additional high-speed WAN technology, the **Distributed Queue Dual Bus (DQDB)**, is also worth mentioning since it forms the basis for many SMDS networks.

Local-area alternatives have been the most widely debated, with vendors and analysts focusing on the relative merits of ATM to the desktop in comparison to other technologies. One such debate took place at the Fall 1994 Paris Interop, contrasting the relative merits of ATM and 100 VG-AnyLAN. Though one could say that VG-AnyLAN has not seen deployment to the extent of other technologies, many of the arguments used in favor of the VG-AnyLAN technology are also applicable to other non-ATM alternatives. Arguments used in favor of LAN switching, to include lower deployment costs, were quickly countered by claims of ATM's scalability and suitability for real-time applications due to the fixed length cell structure. A convincing argument in favor of ATM was the need to look at the total cost of ownership in contrast to initial installation costs, driven by the longevity of standards, the direction of the Telcos and computing industry, the ATM deployed base in contrast to

Table 6.1 802 series standards.

Group	Description	IEEE standard	ITU standard (latest)
802.1	Higher Level Interfaces	802.1 in 1990	ISO 8802-1 in 1994
802.2	Logical Link Control	802.2 in 1993	ISO 8802-2 in 1994
802.3	Carrier Sense Multiple Access with Collision Detection (Ethernet)	802.3 in 1992	ISO 8802-3 in 1993
	100Base-T	802.3u 1995	
802.4	Token Bus (ARCNET)	802.4 in 1990	ISO 8802-4 in 1990
802.5	Token Ring	802.5 in 1995	ISO 8802-5 in 1995
802.6	Metropolitan Area Networks (DQDB)	802.6 in 1994	ISO 8802-6 in 1994
802.7	Broadband Recommended Practices	802.7 in 1989	ISO 8802-7 in 1991
802.8	Fiber Optic Recommended Practices	802.8 in 1992	
802.9	Integrated Services LAN	802.9 in 1994	ISO 8802-9 in 1995
	IsoLAN	802.9a in 1995	
802.10	Standard Interoperable LAN Security	802.10 in 1992	
802.11	Wireless LAN	802.11 in 1991	
802.12	Demand Priority (VG-AnyLAN)	802.12 in 1995	
802.13	Not assigned		
802.14	HFC MAC over cable	In progress	

VG, and the number of vendors offering products, leading to competitive-driven pricing. Ultimately, both parties agreed to disagree, with the VG-AnyLAN supporters accepting ATM as a backbone technology while the ATM supporters accepted LAN switching, but not at 100 Mbps.

The IEEE standardizes many LAN and MAN technologies, with further standardization occurring through the ITU, as summarized in Table 6.1. Note that FDDI does not fall under the jurisdiction of the IEEE 802 committee, as it has been standardized within the ANSI. Please refer to Appendix A for additional standards and descriptions.

6.1 Local area

In the local area, alternatives to ATM include FDDI (along with its copper variant, sometimes known as CDDI), 100 Mbps Ethernet technologies, Ethernet and Token Ring switching, and a number of lesser-known alternatives which have either not received a great deal of vendor support or are on the edge of obsolescence due to newer technologies. When choosing a technology for use within a campus, high-rise, or in a small office, network planners look should look at the suitability of the solution for solving application-related problems. If more than one technology is deemed suitable, the alternatives may then be judged based on cost, stability of standards, ease of management, distance requirements, whether a shared or dedicated architecture is most suitable, and scalability. Looking back to the business drivers, surveys show no less than three high-speed technologies, ATM, FDDI, and 100 Mbps Ethernet, comfortably co-existing in the backbone over the coming years. Thus, network planners should not be concerned with obsolescence if choosing one of these three technologies. Existing Ethernet and Token Ring technologies will of course also experience healthy growth or even exceptional growth if deployed as LAN switching. The decision for ATM in the local area, either as a workgroup technology or even as an access medium to high-speed servers and processors, is therefore not a foregone conclusion. What are the selection criteria then, and why use an alternative technology in the local area if ATM will be the architecture of choice in the wide area?

Users looking for maturity in a technology will often select FDDI for the campus or workgroup backbone. At the desktop, either FDDI or CDDI may be deployed, although this is less widespread with the deployment of LAN switching. Nevertheless, those users with existing FDDI networks continue to expand their installations. Ultimately, limiting factors in FDDI are its perceived lack of scalability and unsuitability for voice. Though the second consideration is taken into account during decision making, and was the driving force behind the now defunct FDDI-II (described below), in fact most users are quite satisfied with existing parallel voice networks in the local area. Lack of scalability is another factor entirely, and though FDDI switching is available and becoming more popular, it is expected to remain a niche deployment in comparison to other technologies.

Moving to the two 100 Mbps alternatives, the first, 100Base-T, receives support from those looking to increase bandwidth where required while maintaining compatibility with existing 10 Mbps Ethernet installations. Unknown to many, 100Base-T may also be used as a campus backbone technology when deployed over fiber and, like ATM, it also supports VLANs. Since this fast Ethernet technology and ATM are more or less at the same point of maturity, the compatibility advantages of 100Base-T work in its favor. Working against this, however, are ultimate limitations on scalability and lack of support for non-packetized voice. Therefore, the technology may have its greatest success in the workgroup as opposed to being used as a campus backbone technology. The same holds true for 100 VG-AnyLAN, only this technology is better suited for real-time traffic at the expense of compatibility with existing Ethernet. Where multiservice support is a decision criterion, many users may opt for ATM. The long-term prospects for VG-AnyLAN are therefore less certain than those for 100Base-T. Recently, extensions to both of these technologies to allow operation in the Gbps range have been proposed. It is still too early to judge what effect these proposals will have on their future prospects as backbone technologies.

In the face of these high-speed LAN alternatives, what does the future hold for 10 or 20 (full duplex) Mbps Ethernet and 16 or 32 (full duplex) Mbps Token Ring? Though there was a perception that these technologies had lost momentum, this has changed dramatically with the wide deployment of LAN switching. With LAN switching, the con-

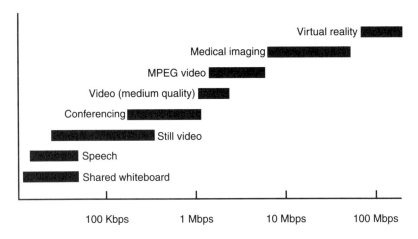

Figure 6.1 Application bandwidth requirements.

tention for bandwidth is no longer the limiting factor within the workgroup. The viability of these two technologies in the workgroup only comes into question during discussions on support for real-time applications, a concern countered by RSVP. Note the emphasis on the word 'workgroup.' Neither of these technologies is suitable for deployment in the campus or high-rise backbone, and will almost always be installed in conjunction with ATM, FDDI or Fast Ethernet. The increasing demand for LAN switching will probably have a detrimental effect on the deployment of FDDI to the workgroup, relegating this technology to the backbone. In relying on a shared-media backbone to support LAN switching, scalability and integrated service support becomes a question. Ultimately, the majority of LAN environments will consist of LAN switching to the desktop, ATM and Fast Ethernet where needed to servers and shared computing resources, and ATM in the backbone. As shown in Figure 6.1, the bandwidth provided by LAN switching will be more than sufficient for the majority of applications. The one 'killer application' often mentioned, videoconferencing, in fact does not use anywhere near the capacity of a switched Ethernet or Token Ring segment. The real killers are the overall increase in graphical peer-to-peer traffic and the use of high-performance file servers.

6.1.1 Whither FDDI?

Standardized by ANSI in 1993 (although deployed earlier), FDDI is still considered by some to be the most viable of the backbone technologies due to maturity of hardware and software, a wide installed base, inherent redundancy, and LAN characteristics (connectionless, native multicast/broadcast capability). With all of the coverage given to ATM, many network planners will no longer even consider FDDI and/or CDDI for a backbone as a workgroup technology. This attitude is self-defeating, in that FDDI is still suitable for many application profiles. This may be especially true where the redundancy inherent in the FDDI architecture is desired or in some bridged environments. In both cases, redundancy within ATM comes at a high additional cost, and the scalability of LANE is still in question. It may also be possible that a campus cable plant has been installed over time which is not suited to a star topology or end-systems have been installed which may not be capable of supporting ATM. If a cabling plant is configurable as a star, and if non-ATM-UNI capable routers interconnect LANs, an effective path forward may be to implement FDDI switching. Using one or more nodes, bandwidth may be scaled into the Gbps range with throughputs exceeding 1 million frames/second.

Two variants of FDDI exist. The first and most familiar is based on multimode or singlemode fiber. Multimode fiber is more common in the office and campus environment, while singlemode fiber has been used to build FDDI rings spanning entire metropolitan areas. If this is the case, why do we consider FDDI as a LAN as opposed to a WAN technology? From the point of view of a network design engineer, FDDI comes into consideration as a wide-area backbone technology very infrequently. A variant of FDDI is based on twisted pair and, though this is officially known as the TP-PMD, most refer to the technology as CDDI. From a cost-per-port standpoint, copper technology is more cost effective than fiber when deployed to end-systems within a workgroup, though it is unsuitable for use as a backbone technology due to its 100 meter distance limitation.

FDDI is based on fiber optic cabling, and the standard specifies that 100 Mbps of user data will be transmitted at a signaling rate of 125 Mbps, the additional 25 Mbps providing for overhead functions. Two rings are installed: an A ring as primary and a B ring as backup. The maximum extent of the fiber FDDI system is 200 km, with stations connected to both rings separated by a maximum distance of 2 km. At less than maximum distance, 500 stations may share the ring. FDDI frames have a maximum length of 4500 bytes, with the header containing the physical address of the destination FDDI station. The protocol, though sometimes compared to Token Ring, differs from this latter technology in two major ways: FDDI is based on timers as opposed to being driven by events, and in contrast to the single active monitor within Token Ring, the FDDI ring monitor function is performed cooperatively, so that each station does not need to perform ring monitor functions. An important aspect of FDDI design is which stations should single attach and which should connect to both rings. In most configurations, a station that is always operational (for example, a router or file server) is a **Dual Attached Station (DAS)**, while single-user end-systems are **Single**

Attached Stations (SAS). When connecting to a concentrator, stations will single attach. Access to the ring is via a token frame, only one existing on the ring at any given time. However, multiple data frames may exist on the ring at any given time due to latency.

As stated above, encoding over FDDI is at 125 Mbps. This provides for control, line state, data, and invalid patterns. The encoding on the fiber is NRZI, while the PMD provides for the optical link parameters, cables and connectors, and bypass switching. If copper, MLT-3 coding replaces NRZI. The physical layer is responsible for access from the MAC layer to the FDDI ring, clocking synchronization and buffering, code conversion, and ring continuity. Finally, the FDDI MAC layer includes the tokens and timers to determine the next sending station, maintains the timers, and generates and verifies the FCS. An important element in FDDI is **Station Management (SMT)**, responsible for ring management and token monitoring to ensure a valid token is always rotating. The SMT also handles connection management to establish and maintain physical connections and logical topology, and operational management to monitor the timers and protocols which includes connection to an external network management entity. In contrast to Token Ring, FDDI has a longer latency due to the transmission delay. This latency may be managed to an extent via the **Token Holding Time (THT)** para-meter (set via the **Target Token Rotation Time (TTRT)** parameter), which also determines throughput. The tradeoff is between a short THT resulting in a small amount of data transmitted by each station and long THT resulting in a longer wait by each station wishing to send. As may be clear, a short THT is more suitable for real-time data. In most cases, a value of 8 ms is recommended.

A common question concerns how the maximum FDDI frame length is determined. Within FDDI, an elasticity buffer of 10 bits is implemented in each station to account for timing mismatches from transmitter to receiver. As the specification calls for a clock speed of ± 0.005% at 125 Mhz, transmit and receive speeds may differ by a maximum of 0.01%. This will result in an average of 4.5 bit times requiring smoothing if the clock at the destination is at the maximum variance. This difference determines the maximum frame size (4.5 bits/ 0.01%)=45000 bits=9000 symbols=4500 bytes. The elasticity buffer is emptied at the end of each frame with a 16-bit idle pattern.

6.1.2 Ethernet and Token Ring switching

Ethernet switching is probably the ultimate extension of a protocol, first conceived of as part of the Aloha project in 1973, officially released as the DIX (Ethernet Version 1.0) in 1980, and finally internationally standardized as the ISO 8802-3 specification in 1990. The development path for Token Ring parallels this somewhat, but at a later date. First conceived of in 1980, Token Ring products were released by 1988 and the ISO completed standardization in 1992 as 8802-5. Still, until the 1990s, neither of these two technologies were considered suitable for high-speed networking due to their shared nature. This was especially true for Ethernet, which was subject to delay caused by collisions when loaded. In addition, Ethernet suffered from a maximum utilization percentage somewhat lower than 10 Mbps due to its frame size coupled with the physical segment length. Because of this, Token Ring was considered a more suitable technology for time-deterministic traffic such as transaction processing. Note that CSMA/CD's maximum throughput$=1/(1+6.44p)$ where p$=$end-to-end delay/transmission time. For example, on an 802.3 LAN at 10 Mbps, with a block length of 1000 bits (100 μs transmit time) and a length of 2 km (10.4 μsec) maximum utilization$=58\%$. At 100 Mbps the maximum is 13%. 100 Mbps is therefore useful where distances are short (<200 meters) and the block size is 1000 bytes and above as with images.

The introduction of LAN switching changed the paradigm completely, for users could now be provided with the complete bandwidth available offered by each technology: 10 Mbps for Ethernet and 16 Mbps for Token Ring. Under full duplex, these figures are doubled. This guarantee of bandwidth is probably more important for Ethernet, as collisions no longer exist. With the wide deployment of Ethernet switching beginning in 1993 and Token Ring switching in 1995, these two technologies could now support the bandwidth requirements of high-performance servers and multimedia conferencing. LAN switching therefore plays a major part in pushing the requirement for ATM in the backbone, and is an integral part of a network based on ATM Forum LANE.

As an example of the continued viability of 10 and 16 Mbps technologies, consider the actual bandwidth requirement of most forms of multimedia as depicted in Figure 6.1. Using optimized compression techniques, shared whiteboards require less than 100 Kbps, while teleconferencing and video distribution require between 650 Kbps and 1.5 Mbps depending on quality. If multiple video sources are made available to an end user by a video server, bandwidth utilization on the switched LAN segment may be optimized by higher-layer protocols such as PIM working in conjunction with the LAN switches. As with any packet-oriented technology, the challenge under LAN switching will be to minimize latency and control jitter through the deployment of resource reservation protocols such as RSVP.

By the beginning of 1996, what had originally been a single concept, LAN switching, had segmented into different market segments just as routing and ATM switching had coalesced into different domains based on requirements. We now divide LAN switching into three layers based on requirements and capabilities: desktop, distribution, and backbone. The desktop LAN switch will service one or a few users per port, and will be provided with one or two high-speed uplinks into the campus or building backbone. A desktop LAN switch is cost optimized, and will therefore not usually be capable of servicing a large number of discrete MAC addresses per port (for example, found when connecting hubs) and will not implement sophisticated multilayer switching functions. Moving to the center of the network, a distribution switch will aggregate desktop switches and provide connectivity to hubs. Sometimes, the same hardware deployed at the backbone is appropriate for the distribution layer. At this layer, we begin to see the need to implement some Layer 3 functionality for inter-VLAN routing and firewalling. The core of the LAN switching network will consist of one or more backbone LAN switches, offering multilayer switching and sophisticated multiple-media capabilities. Needless to say, the throughput of such devices will be expected to be in the 1 Gbps+ range. These backbone switches may be deployed in combination with ATM switching or as a self-contained core. This latter configuration is perfectly valid for many network requirements. Layer 3 capabilities will be provided via one or more attached routers or integrated into the LAN switch. The amount of routing required will depend upon the size of the network, the amount of inter-VLAN traffic, and requirements for external connectivity.

The discussion of LAN switching would not be complete without a mention of two technology questions surrounding products from different vendors. This first concerns the differences and relative tradeoffs between cut-through and store-and-forward technologies, while the second centers around the switch backplane (Figure 6.2). LAN switches may implement two types of forwarding scheme on their interfaces. Under

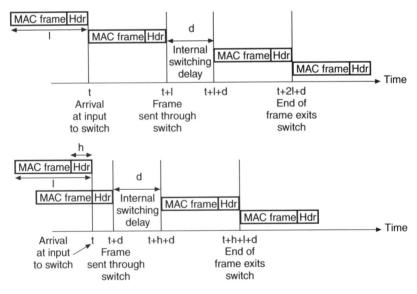

Figure 6.2 Comparison of cut-through and store-and-forward switching.

cut-through switching, only the MAC header is evaluated before the frame is forwarded through the switch matrix and to the output interface. Though this has some advantages for single-frame latency, (the time between the last bit in and the first bit out for store-and-forward; equals transit delay for cut-through) differences are not that great when looking at packet bursts since in either case the MAC frames will require a certain amount of time to physically arrive at the input to the switch. A disadvantage of cut-through switching is its tendency to propagate corrupt frames. For this reason, these devices have traditionally been deployed towards the periphery of the switched workgroup. In contrast, store-and-forward switches buffer the entire frame. They are therefore capable of carrying out filtering of corrupt data and, possibly more importantly, translational bridging. This is a requirement when interworking between the different Ethernet frame types or when switching to a high-speed backbone interface. For this reason, switches aggregating switched LAN ports to an ATM or FDDI backbone will implement store-and-forward. A newer hybrid architecture combines both techniques at the input, with frames following the cut-through path unless errors have been recognized or translation is required. In this event, the switch will redirect the frames into the store-and-forward path.

A LAN switch may be based on either a frame or a cell backplane. At first glance, the idea of a cell backplane may seem alien to a device which should be optimized to switch frames. In fact, very low latency FDDI and Ethernet switches based on ATM switch matrices are available, some with performance exceeding that of any available frame-based designs. One reason for this is that an ATM matrix is inherently more scalable than a frame backplane. The breakpoint is at about 2 Gbps, after which frame designs become difficult to deploy. In addition, a LAN switch based on an ATM fabric provides an upgrade path which has appeal if native ATM interfaces are also available. ATM-based designs have found greatest success as FDDI switches, though their applicability to fast Ethernet switching is obvious as well. However, a trade off exists when most traffic remains local to the switch or when combinations of ATM and Fast Ethernet are deployed. In this case, the additional SAR overhead may be undesirable.

6.1.3 High-speed Ethernet alternatives

Drawing on the existing Ethernet standard, the goal of any high-speed alternative should be to preserve the existing MAC logic, utilize UTP, and, most importantly, minimize cost. Two 100 Mbps alternatives vie for acceptance in the marketplace. Fast Ethernet (100Base-T), standardized as 802.3u, is derived from 10 Mbps Ethernet, preserves the CSMA/CD mechanism, and is able to operate over two cable pairs. 100 VG-AnyLAN, standardized as 802.12, eliminates the 802.3 mechanisms while providing better support for real-time data in shared environments.

Fast Ethernet: 100Base-T

Fast Ethernet breaks through the 10 Mbps Ethernet barrier by scaling the CSMA/CD protocol to 100 Mbps. Since both the MAC protocol and frame formats remain the same (64 to 1508 byte packet lengths and transmission in 'little endian' order), dual-rate interfaces may be deployed on hubs and LAN switches. The 100 Mbps data rate is supported over a number of physical media alternatives, to include twisted pair and fiber optic cabling (Table 6.2). 100Base-TX is for use with Cat 5 UTP or 150 ohm STP, and uses the same PMD as that developed for FDDI on STP (MLT-3). During operation, transmission is over one pair, while reception is over a second, the crossover from transmit to receive taking place at the repeater or the LAN switch. TX is limited to a distance of 100 meters and uses the same RJ-45 pinouts as 10Base-T. The second alternative, 100Base-T4, transmits over 4 Cat 3 UTP cable pairs (though it is also supported over Cat 5). The need for four pairs is a bit more involved. Two pairs are bi-directional, in that either end of a link may transmit on the pair. The other two pairs are unidirectional, with one pair used in each direction. A station recognizes collisions by monitoring the pair which it does not use for transmitting. The final fast Ethernet physical layer uses 1300 nm optical cable equivalent to that used under multimode FDDI. Supporting 2 km, one fiber is used for transmission while a second is used for reception of data. As with the above schemes, crossover occurs at the repeater or switch. The fiber interface allows 100Base-FX to be used as a backbone technology.

The repeaters mentioned above are a bit more complicated than those used in 10Base-T. Two types of repeater may be deployed: Class 1 and Class 2. A Class 1 repeater may connect dissimilar physical media (for example, 100Base-TX and 100Base-T4) with the limitation that only one such repeater may be deployed. Two Class 2 repeaters capable of supporting only a single PMD may be deployed. Due to the speed of the technology, the total network diameter is limited to 205 meters. The TX and FX PMDs may be deployed in full duplex mode (200 Mbps), in which case repeaters are always replaced by bridges or switches. All links are now point-to-point, and the workgroup may now be extended to 2 km using fiber optic cabling. Devices implementing the FX PMD will often connect to the fiber via a **Media Independent Interface (MII)**. To enable the operation of both 10 and 100 Mbps stations over the same bridges or LAN switches, a signaling protocol (NWAY) has been introduced which will allow end-systems to negotiate whether they wish to operate at 10 or 100 Mbps and in either half- or full-duplex modes. Note that the T4 physical media will not support 100 Mbps FD due to the four-pair limitation. This four-pair requirement has possibly hampered the acceptance of T4, as many structured cabling systems rely on one cable pair for voice traffic. Because of this, it may be relegated to the sidelines as users install TX when seeking to preserve cable pairs or 100VG-AnyLAN (described below) where pairs are available.

An implementation of Fast Ethernet known as **Priority Access Control Enabled (PACE)**, supports multiple priority levels for both 100 Mbps and 10 Mbps Ethernet. These priority levels address latency and jitter, two deficiencies commonly associated with Ethernet in the multimedia environment. Multiple vendors have announced support for PACE, and have formed an alliance to promote the technology. If different applications could register their resource demands with an intelligent PACE Ethernet driver, then this technology could be quite viable. Note that the IETF is standardizing RSVP which will allow applications to request these same QoS parameters from the network. Whereas RSVP is positioned between routers with PACE envisioned as operating at the LAN switch.

Demand priority: 100VG-AnyLAN

100VG-AnyLAN, also known as 100Base-VG, was originally proposed by Hewlett-Packard as a high-speed alternative to Fast Ethernet. Now the protocol is standardized by the IEEE as 802.12 demand priority. Originally supporting only Ethernet frames over Cat 3 UTP, support for 802.5 was included by IBM. Though the network supports both of these frame types, only one format may be configured at a given time. PMDs supported include 4-pair Cat 3 and 5 UTP, 2-pair Cat 5, and 500 meters of 850 nm or 2 km of 1300 nm fiber (Table 6.2). Over Cat 3 UTP, the protocol splits the MAC data stream into four parts, first scrambling each part, then coding it via 5B/6B NRZ code, and finally transmitting it using a two-level encoding scheme. During transmission or reception, all four pairs will be in use, while control and signaling use two pairs in each direction. As 802.12 makes use of a new MAC protocol, it is incompatible with existing Ethernet or Token Ring implementations.

Unlike 802.3, the maximum extent of the network is undefined and, clearing up one misconception, multiple stations may share a single segment (that is, LAN switching is not a requirement). A centrally-located hub will grant access to the network via a signaling mechanism, under which a station will signal a request to transmit to the local hub if the link is idle. This hub will constantly scan its ports, servicing them in order. When a request arrives, the hub will grant the station the right to transmit one packet. Upon completion, the hub will then wait for a specified interval to allow new requests to be signaled. If hubs are daisy-chained, the hub at the top of the 'tree' will control the transmission order, with requests propagated to this root hub. When implementing an 802.5 service over VG-AnyLAN, operation, in contrast to traditional Token Ring implementations, is actually improved upon. First, packets now take the shortest path between two nodes as opposed to circling the network; second, a requesting node may be granted immediate access by the hub as opposed to having to wait for the token rotation. The protocol is known as **demand priority** due to its support of two priority levels, normal and high. As expected, normal priority requests will not be serviced until all high priority requests are completed. Blocking is avoided by bumping the priority of normal requests to high if pending more than 300 ms.

Gigabit Ethernet

Looking more closely at gigabit Ethernet proposals, both the 100VG and the 100Base-T groups have submitted proposals to the IEEE. As of Spring, 1996, the VG group had officially begun work within the 802.12 working group, with a standard expected by Summer, 1997. The Base-T camp is a bit earlier in its work, with standardization expected sometime in 1998. Both gigabit standards will reuse the MAC proctocols of their 100 mbps variants, as well as the Fiber Channel PHY layer. This will allow reuse of Fiber Channel hardware, allowing for earlier delivery and lower costs (Roberts, 1996). Although distances are limited when using copper, and especially across UTP, this may not be as much of a problem since the primary use of gigabit Ethernet will be in the backbone. Current debates surrounding this technology include relative costs in comparison to 622 Mbps ATM as well as its ability of efficiently transport real-time data.

6.1.4 Fiber channel

The fiber channel is a high-speed networking architecture to interconnect both traditional networking devices such as PCs and workstations as well as hardware traditionally connected to system busses. This provides an alternative to the **Desktop Area Network (DAN)** described in Chapter 5 for interconnecting processors, disk drives, and other peripherals, and is based on hubs, loops, or circuit switching. In contrast to ATM, fiber channel is intended as a data-only architecture, which of course does not preclude it from transporting packet-based voice and video, especially in combination with higher-layer resource reservation and prioritization mechanisms. Standardization, which began in 1988 and now takes place within ANSI's X3T11 technical committee, currently defines data rates at 133, 266, and 531 Mbps, as well as 1.06, 2.134 and 4.25 Gbps. We summarize these data rates along with distance limitations in Table 6.2.

The standard includes five layers, FC-0 to FC-4. FC-0 is the physical layer, defining the electrical and mechanical specifications for any of the data rates. FC-1 is the transmission protocol layer, including the 8B10B coding. FC-2, the singaling protcol layer, defines the data framing, class of service, and a congestion control mechnanism. The frame

Table 6.2 High-speed LAN alternatives.

High-speed Ethernet		Bandwidth	Media	Cable pairs	Distance
100Base-TX	(802.3u)	100 Mbps	Cat 5 UTP	2 pair	100 meters
			Type 1 STP	2 pair	100 meters
	Full duplex (802.3x)	200 Mbps	Cat 5 UTP	2 pair	100 meters
100Base-T4	(802.3u)	100 Mbps	Cat 3 UTP	4 pair	100 meters
			Cat 4 UTP	4 pair	100 meters
			Cat 5 UTP	4 pair	100 meters
100Base-FX	(802.3u)	100 Mbps	62.5/125 fiber	1 pair	400 meters
	Full duplex (802.3x)	200 Mbps	62.5/125 fiber	1 pair	2 km
100Base-T2	(802.3y)	100 Mbps	Cat 3 UTP	2 pair	100 meters
			Cat 4 UTP	2 pair	100 meters
			Cat 5 UTP	2 pair	100 meters
VG-AnyLAN					
100Base-VG-AnyLAN (802.12)		100 Mbps	Cat 3/4/5 UTP	4 pair	100 meters
(400 Mbps, 960 Mbps, and 4 Gbps			Cat 5 UTP/STP	2 pair	150 meters
under discussion)			62.5/125 fiber	1 pair	2 km
FDDI		100 Mbps	62.5/125 fiber	1 pair	2 km
			9 μm fiber	1 pair	200 km
			Cat 5 UTP	2 pair	100 meters
Fiber channel					
FC-PH Rev 4.3, X.3.23 and		200 Mbps	SM fiber	1 pair	10 km
FC-PH-2,Working Draft Rev 6.5		(quarter	MM fiber (laser)	1 pair	2 km
		speed)	MM fiber (LED)	1 pair	1.5 km
			Coaxial	1 pair	75 m
			Mini-coaxial	1 pair	25 m
		400 Mbps	SM fiber	1 pair	10 km
		(half	MM fiber (laser)	1 pair	1 km
		speed)	MM fiber (LED)	1 pair	1 km
			Coaxial	1 pair	50 m
			Mini-coaxial	1 pair	15 m
(1.6 and 3.2 Gbps under		800 Mbps	SM fiber	1 pair	10 km
discussion)		(full speed)	MM fiber (laser)	1 pair	50 m
			MM fiber (LED)	1 pair	500 m
			Coaxial	1 pair	25 m
			Mini-coaxial	1 pair	10 m

consists of a 4-byte frame marker, a 24-byte header containing addressing information, and a data field with a maximum length of 2112 bytes. This field is followed by a 4-byte CRC and a 4-byte EOF marker. Due to this framing overhead, we actually have a user throughput of 200 Mbps for the 266 Mbps data rate. Likewise, 531 Mbps yields 400 Mbps while 1.06 Gbps yields 800 Mbps. At the same layer as the frame, we have **ordered sets**. These 10 bit messages provide link control and congestion management. One or more related data frames going in a single direction form a **sequence**. Finally, we form an **exchange** from a set of sequences in one or both directions. We map commands and data into separate sequences, then send them as a single exchange. Class of service support includes Class 1, a dedicated connection suitable for applications requiring high throughput and long duration. Class 2 provides for bandwidth sharing, and is better used for network protocols that guarantee delivery such as TCP or SPX. Finally, Class 3 does not guarantee delivery, requiring buffers on each end of the connection. This service class may be used for videoconferencing or shared whiteboard.

The next layer, FC-3, includes support for services such as multicasting and hunt groups. Finally, FC-4 is responsible for the **Upper Layer Protocols (ULPs)**. These ULPs may be either channel-based (SCSI and HIPPI) or network transports such as Ethernet or IP. In fact, AAL5 may also be carried within FC-4. Though some vendors propose the fiber channel as a general networking solution, its greatest use will be in the desktop arena to interconnect peripherals or high-performance devices in workgroups. It will probably not extend beyond the limited workgroup in any major way. Gigabit Ethernet will use the Fiber Channel physical layer. This should result in lower component costs.

Although originally positioned as a replacement to technologies such as IBM's block mux channel and the SCSI bus for device interconnect, the use of fiber optic cabling allows one to substantially increase the range of a fiber channel network. In addition, since data frames include addressing information, we are not limited to point-to-point configurations. A fiber channel fabric (or switch) allows nodes to interconnect. A simpler configuration based on an arbitrated loop technology is supported directly by the fiber channel hardware in end devices.

6.1.5 Others

Other high-speed LAN architectures have been proposed, standardized, and even deployed in some user communities. In any case, due to either the complexity of the standard, lack of vendor support, or the earlier than expected availability of ATM to the workgroup, their future success in the marketplace is in question. Well-known alternatives include the **Integrated Services LAN (ISLAN)**, Isochronous Ethernet, FDDI-II, and the FDDI Follow-On. An additional class of high-speed local connect architectures do enjoy success but are limited in scope due to their intent of connecting supercomputers and associated devices over a limited area (HIPPI) or are based on a proprietary architecture (IBM ESCON). In both of these cases, the protocols are optimized for the transmission of high-speed data only and are limited in the number of end-systems supported.

Integrated Services LAN (ISLAN)

ISLAN is a mix between 802 technologies and ISDN. Though standardized by the IEEE as 802.9, its future is in doubt due to the early adoption of local area ATM. It supports both asynchronous and synchronous traffic by multiplexing MAC and TDM between end users and an access unit (interconnections based on 802.9b). ISLAN supports bandwidths from 4.096 to 20.48 Mbps dependent upon distance. The ISLAN is subdivided into multiple channel types, very similar to those proposed in original B-ISDN implementations. A P channel supports 802 MAC data (equivalent to Iso-Ethernet 802.9a), while the TDM channels are further divided into the B and D channels found in N-ISDN and C channels providing service at multiples of 64 Kbps. For example, the C30 supports 1.920 Mbps. Structurally, the ISLAN combines LLC, isochronous, and LAPD data link layer traffic above a common hybrid multiplexing sublayer. These services are managed via a layer management entity, defined as part of the 802.9 standard (802.9c). Interestingly, MAC frames are segmented into 63-byte payloads in much the same way as with ATM. The main difference is that synchronous traffic in the form of B and D channels is carried in a separate region of the ISLAN frame.

Isochronous Ethernet

Closely related to ISLAN is the Isochronous Ethernet, standardized under 802.9a as a multimedia workstation. As with ISLAN, this technology relies on a star topology, with all stations homed to a central hub. 4B/5B provides for encoding of data at 16.384 Mbps, but the channelization structure is a bit different to that found in ISLAN. The 16.384 Mbps is divided into two channels – one at 10 Mbps connecting to the hub in a bus topology, and a second at 6.144 providing synchronous support. This latter channel is composed of 96×64 Kbps (ISDN B) dedicated circuits, and is equivalent to the wideband channel found in FDDI-II. Two additional channels provide for call setup (64 Kbps ISDN D) and physical layer maintenance (M-channel). Unlike FDDI-II, which is limited to a total of 16 of these wideband channels, Isochronous Ethernet is limited only by the number of hub connections. A major fault with this standard is that it does not provide for switching of MAC data traffic (at least, no devices have been delivered with this capability).

Extensions to FDDI

FDDI-II is an extension to the original FDDI permitting the simultaneous transmission of voice and isochronous data. This is accomplished through the addition of an isochronous MAC and a TDM sublayer above the physical media access layer, much like ISLAN. FDDI data is passed unchanged, transported in one channel of the TDM frame. Isochronous traffic is transported in 6.144 Mbps wideband channels each capable of 96 64 Kbps circuits. A total of 16 of these wideband channels may be defined, each dedicated to packet or isochronous traffic. Finally, a dedicated packet group provides for a minimum of 768 Kbps packet data even if every wideband channel is dedicated to isochronous traffic. A potential problem with FDDI-II concerns intermixing FDDI and FDDI-II stations. If FDDI stations are placed on the ring, it will not be capable of supporting isochronous services.

The FFOL, also standardized within ANSI, seeks to solve the problem of implementing a backbone connecting multiple FDDI networks, while providing interconnection to wide-area networks and ATM. FFOL would operate at SDH-based data rates of 600 Mbps and above, and be supported over existing multimode and singlemode FDDI cabling.

With the apparent lack of support for FDDI-II and FFOL, ANSI has begun standardization of yet another FDDI variant, this one known as FDDI-III and capable of data rates up to 1 Gbps. In contrast to FFOL, which was intended for multiple service types (and thus ended up competing with ATM), FDDI-III is a high-speed data network. It could be based on 800 Mbps fiber channel technology, and may use existing FDDI MAC and SMT software. Initial goals include preserving investment, risk, and minimizing time-to-market. Whether FDDI-III could compete against ATM or Gigabit Ethernet for high-speed computer interconnection is in serious doubt.

Wireless

A discussion of the various alternatives to ATM in the local area would not be complete without a mention of on-going work in the wireless area regarding LAN and WAN standards. This is different from the use of wireless technology as a transmission media for ATM, described earlier, or as a basis for Ethernet or FDDI. Within the IEEE, the 802.11 committee is attempting to develop a MAC standard for wireless transmission at data rates from 1–20 Mbps. Wireless also of course includes point-to-point links (for example, via microwave and laser) as well as WAN systems (for example, GSM-based or low-speed commerical services based on alternative technologies). Whether 802.11 will see success in comparison to any of the other LAN technologies over wireless remains to be seen.

6.1.6 Analysis

In the final analysis, we expect multiple high-speed technologies to co-exist with ATM. In most instances, end-systems will connect to the backbone via LAN switches or routers, with a proportion of these systems provided with direct ATM, FDDI, and 100 Mbps Ethernet connections. The backbone, initially based on switched FDDI or Fast Ethernet, will migrate to ATM over time. Some technologies such as Fiber Channel will survive, but possibly only in niche markets. Where multiservice support enters the equation, ATM will be deployed earlier due to latency considerations and interoperability with wide-area services. Over time, the trend will be toward greater deployment of ATM to end-systems, but it is only towards the end of the decade that LAN switching may begin to be replaced by large user ATM desktop communities.

6.1.7 Virtual LAN interoperability

Though the focus of this book is ATM, many customers will be faced with a scenario where they will need to interconnect ATM-based VLANs based on LANE and non-ATM VLANs. These shared-media VLANs may rely on early deployment of the 802.10 security mechanism or alternatively, they may be vendor proprietary or may rely on the evolving IEEE 802.1q standard. Since these technologies must interwork, any management system deployed must enable the configuration of VLANs across both ATM and shared media. This requires a management overlay which allows each LAN switch and router to know which VLANs are active and over which trunks they are reachable. Configuration information for these VLANs will be stored in what is a generalization of the LECS, only this time applicable to any VLAN architecture. Members will register and deregister with this server, and will be permitted to access a given VLAN on a per port, per MAC address, or per protocol address basis.

Under 802.1q, initially, a one layer tagging scheme based on a new ethertype and two bytes of a VLAN ID field is specified. In the future, a second layer containing a source and destination MAC address may be specified (Figure 6.3). In essence, frames are tagged by LAN switches, routers, or hosts as they enter the VLAN fabric, allowing for identification of different VLANs. Given proper management, this may allow shortcut paths to be setup from one Layer 3 network to another across LAN switches. Thus, the technique is much like that used for MPOA but is not dependent upon ATM. As a takeoff on MPOA, this architecture is coming to be known as Multiprotocol over LANs (MPOL).

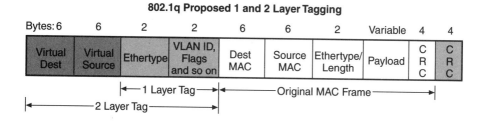

Figure 6.3 802.1q encapsulation.

ICV Integrity Check Value   SAID Security Association Identifier
SDE Secure Data Exchange   MDF Management Defined Field (optional)

6.2 Wide area

As in the local area, many alternative technologies and services exist. But in contrast to the local area, ATM will eventually be the technology of choice for users requiring moderate to high bandwidths and integrated services. This deployment may not be ubiquitous, however, as the typical WAN is not flat. If we look into the structure of a corporate network, an access layer, distribution layer, and core are evident. The access layer services branches, the distribution layer services larger sites and aggregates the branches, while the core provides the high-bandwidth secure backbone for the enterprise. ATM will first see deployment in the core, where bandwidth requirements are often first identified. At the access and distribution layers, Frame Relay and ISDN will often be used even into the future.

Decision factors in the wide area include corporate structure, application traffic and bandwidth requirements, maturity of standards, scalability over time, and, most importantly, the availability of a given service and whether it is tariffed appropriately. During the 1980s, the technologies of choice for building corporate backbones were somewhat limited. Most core networks were built using leased lines, initially 64 Kbps, and later 1.544 or 2 Mbps and above. In some countries X.25 was also used as a core technology but at reduced speeds. Access to the core network was either via low-speed leased lines (9600 bps−64 Kbps) or via dial-in (1200 bps−14.4 Kbps). During the first half of the 1990s, options have expanded considerably. Leased lines (often in conjunction with TDM equipment to provide for voice traffic) until just recently were still the most viable for high-speed cores from the standpoint of security and cost. Where lower speeds are adequate, and especially in the access environment, the wide deployment of Frame Relay and ISDN place these technologies into the forefront. By 1995, many corporations had installed private Frame Relay networks, and public services were available in many parts of the globe with access rates up to 2 Mbps. Organizations would sometimes build Frame Relay cores or would combine Frame Relay with leased lines.

Just as important in enabling high-speed access to every branch location is the widespread deployment of ISDN. Initially used as an access technology providing 144 Kbps (BRI=2B+D) and above, some users are now basing a large part of their network on ISDN or on a combination of ISDN and leased lines due to the wide availability of PRI (24B+D or 30B+D) service. If traffic on the core fluctuates widely, the ability to activate and deactivate individual 64 Kbps channels on demand results in cost savings. An additional WAN service, SMDS, is offered by a number of carriers as a precursor to future broadband offerings. Although early deployment of this service was based on DQDB technology, the service is now offered over ATM. Where available, SMDS is a viable alternative for both access networks and corporate cores. A strength of SMDS is its scalability, with access classes from 64 Kbps to 25 Mbps. Working against SMDS until recently, though, has been a customer (and PTT) perception that it is an interim service. In addition, international connectivity in Europe and inter-RBOC connectivity in the US is relatively new.

Also worth noting are techniques for mapping higher-layer data (and voice) directly onto the underlying transmission frame structure minus the ATM convergence, adaptation, and cell overhead. Replacing PDH, SDH is a viable transmission platform for voice, multiplexed data, and ATM. In contrast to public perception that ATM will be the universal technology, carriers may look at SDH/SONET as this ubiquitous underlying technology, with ATM just one of many services running over SDH/SONET. Voice transport adds another element to the discussion. At what point will N-ISDN exchanges begin to migrate into ATM switching? In public networks, SDH will provide the underlying transmission infrastructure for all deployment alternatives.

6.2.1 64 Kbps ISDN

ISDN may be considered as an alternative to ATM since it provides for both voice and data. When discussed in conjunction with ATM, the technology is often referred to as 64 Kbps ISDN (or N-ISDN) to eliminate ambiguity, just as ATM is also known as B-ISDN. The basic information channel within 64 Kbps ISDN is the 64 Kbps B channel, a clear transmission path suitable for digitized voice, data, and any other service. This B channel is signaled via an out-of-band 16 Kbps D channel. Of note is the capability to transmit both X.25 and Frame Relay traffic over this D channel (deployed and tariffed in some countries). The basic small business and residential user interface is known as the **Basic Rate Interface (BRI)**, consisting of $2\times B$ and $1\times D$ channels. For data transmission, these two B channels may be signaled to two different destinations or may be aggregated to a single destination. The service is therefore quite versatile in this respect. Though a user may subscribe to multiple BRIs, use of a **Primary Rate Interface (PRI)** where available becomes advantageous after the tariff breakeven point (the point at which $n\times$BRI is more expensive than $1\times$PRI) which varies from country to country. The PRI provides for $30\times B$ channels in Europe and $24\times B$ in North America in addition to a 64 Kbps D channel. Higher-order 64 Kbps ISDN channels are defined but are not commonly deployed. With PRI service deployed, a viable corporate network may be implemented at data rates from 64 Kbps to 1.9 Mbps (before compression). In many installations, one or more B channels may be dedicated to voice, fax, or CODEC-driven (H.261) videoconferencing. By 1997, carriers will provide for interworking between ATM and 64 Kbps ISDN within the central office, though some standards for this interworking function are still being finalized. Ultimately, the technology will be very successful at those sites requiring bandwidth no greater than 2 Mbps. It will be interesting to see if 64 Kbps ISDN ever does become a factor in the residential market if ATM-like services, to include voice, are offered by the public service providers.

6.2.2 Frame Relay

As with N-ISDN, Frame Relay is not in competition with ATM at higher data rates, but should still be mentioned as corporations will use a number of services, to include Frame Relay, in implementing enterprise networks. A reason for this will be the less than universal deployment of ATM over the coming years along with the lack of applications in the access environment justifying bandwidth over 2 Mbps. An enterprise network may easily include Frame Relay at access sites, connected to an ATM-based headquarters site via a Frame Relay to ATM interworking service (described in Chapter 4). This service, possibly even offering voice internetworking, will help ensure ATM's success in the backbone. Though Frame Relay is deployed at 2 Mbps, and has been demonstrated to operate effectively at T3/E3 data rates, its most common deployment is at speeds from 64 to 256 Kbps. The technology itself is based on many of the lessons learned in deploying X.25 but, in contrast to X.25's link-by-link flow control and retransmission, the protocol assumes that the end-systems are capable of performing this functionality via transport protocols (TCP, and so on). Frame Relay, operating at the frame layer (Layer 2), therefore does not provide for a networking stack in the same manner as the Layer 2 and 3 within X.25. Because of this, switching systems are simpler and latency is reduced. A factor in increasing throughput is providing for variable-length frame sizes equal to that of the LAN protocol. Frame Relay will also see use as a voice transport, with carriers providing voice interworking to ATM. Just as with SMDS/CBDS, the Frame Relay service definition may be decoupled from the underlying technology, in that currently deployed ATM switching systems and edge-devices (for example, routers) support the Frame Relay over ATM encapsulation and service. Therefore, the Frame Relay service will continue to exist even after dedicated Frame Relay switching systems are phased out in some locations, replaced by ATM switches providing for Frame Relay transport and interworking.

6.2.3 Distributed Queue Dual Bus (DQDB)

The DQDB was a technology standardized by the 802.6 group at the end of the 1980s for use in high-speed **Metropolitan Area Networks (MANs)**. Because of this, it is also known as a MAN and, in technical circles, **Queued Packet Switched Exchange (QPSX)**. DQDB is a viable technology for supporting the SMDS and CBDS service requirements. An advantage of DQDB is its ability to operate over many physical transmission systems – E1/DS1 through E4 and SDH. Note that this 34 or 155 Mbps transmission rate is the total bandwidth available in the system, or ring, since it is based on a shared medium. This contrasts with the increased scalability offered by switched technologies. SMDS addressing is based on E.164 international ISDN addressing, providing for ease of international connectivity. The technology, due to its use of fixed-length units known as **slots** (equivalent to ATM's cells) is also suitable for isochronous traffic (though manageability and scalability of this service was never proven). Higher-layer data frames are delivered to a convergence sublayer carrying out identical functions to those described under ATM AAL3/4, identical to the extent that code within SMDS and within SMDS over ATM end-systems may be re-used. This data is then delivered into the DQDB sublayer for processing, where it is segmented into 53-byte slots. Though the technology is con- nectionless, the header does contain a VCI used to identify segments comprising part of the same data frame. This header, also containing fields for synchronization and maintenance, is 4 bytes. At this point the technology diverges from ATM.

Two buses (A and B), each transport data in opposite directions. A slot generator at the head of each bus (HOB) generates empty 53-byte slots. Two types of slot may be created: **pre-arbitrated** for a specific node, and used for isochronous traffic, and **queued arbitrated**, used for normal data traffic via the DQ MAC procedure. A node wishing to transmit must signal its intent, and will then be provided with the next available slot. Depending upon destination, the node will transmit this data on the upstream or downstream bus. Data is transmitted as follows. Using Bus A as an example, a device which has no data to transmit will monitor Bus B for slot requests less the number of empty slots. This count, stored in the **request counter**, will determine the number of slots on Bus A which the node must allow to pass when it does have data to transmit. The node now signals its intent to transmit on Bus B, thus informing other nodes of its request, and copies the contents of the request counter into a **waiting counter**. With each passing empty slot, the node now decrements this waiting counter (along with the request counter). When this counter reaches zero, the node may transmit. These exact operations are mirrored on Bus B, resulting in full-duplex operation. DQDB supports four priorities via the use of three bits in the cell header, though these levels are not supported in existing equipment. One potential problem with DQDB involves lack of fairness caused by propagation delay influencing the timing of requests. Bandwidth balancing, whereby a transmitting node inserts empty slots during transmission, was proposed as a solution. A second limitation with the technology as deployed is that slots are not re-used by the DQDB protocol even if data has been delivered. Consider a node transmitting on Bus A to the next downstream node. Though the slot has been freed, it is unavailable for use by other downstream nodes and the empty slot must pass unchanged to the HOB.

A feature of the DQDB technology is its self-healing. If the system is originally configured in a physical ring, as most are, one node will be elected as the HOB and frame (slot) generator. Since all nodes if suitably equipped with hardware are capable of generating frames, backup is automatic if the default frame generator fails. This same holds true during link failure, as the ring will reconfigure. Yet another feature of the technology is its inherent support of closed user groups and broadcast/multicast traffic. A shared technology delivering a data frame to all potential recipients may very efficiently filter data at the ingress to or egress from the network. By the same token, broadcasting and multicasting results in no additional overhead on the ring. These are reasons why the DQDB technology was suitable as a base for the SMDS. Still, bandwidth is ultimately limited. As a way around this limitation, carriers that have deployed MAN rings will feed this traffic into a regional ATM backbone. This still does not solve the multiservice problem, in that slots allocated for isochronous traffic may not be used for connectionless data traffic. For a 34 Mbps DQDB system, only 14 slots are initially available. Slot management (for example, designating a slot as isochronous for a period of time) occurs at a central management station, not at the customer site. Therefore, the viability of DQDB for voice or CODEC-based video is questionable, relegating the DQDB hardware to data-only service. For this reason, carriers will phase out the equipment over the coming years while preserving the SMDS/CBDS service over ATM.

Initially, data transport over DQDB was via proprietary bridging modules. Thus, all traffic was bridged over the network as opposed to routed. Routers could of course be placed at the periphery of the system. This technique was replaced by 1992 with the deployment of SMDS. Now, all users would connect to the network via a router, normally running the SMDS-DXI protocol to an SMDS-DSU which would generate the 53-byte DQDB cells. The interface between the DSU and the SMDS interface at the MAN node is known as the **Subscriber Network Interface (SNI)**. If a router was co-located with the MAN equipment, the SMDS-DSU could often be eliminated, as the DQDB equipment would provide this functionality. Though the overhead across the SNI, equal to that within AAL3/4, may be acceptable at T1/E1 and above, it was deemed unnecessary at lower access speeds. Therefore, a hybrid architecture is widely deployed consisting of SMDS concentrator nodes co-located with MAN equipment. These nodes service many 64 Kbps and above connections to user CPE over the SMDS-DXI, eliminating the need for the SMDS-DSU. The SNI only appears at the T3/E3 connection between the concentrator and the MAN node. The deployment of these devices is probably the one factor which has led to acceptance of SMDS by end users and service providers.

6.2.4 Layer 1 technologies

Although we have focused on link layer technologies as alternatives to ATM in the local and wide areas, the real alternative to ATM in the wide area is offered by the transmission infrastructure. To understand the relationship between these Layer 1 technologies and ATM, we must first divide the reference model into sublayers; these may then be associated with the functions performed by the various WAN technologies. For example, X.25 resides at Layers 2 and 3, while Frame Relay operates only at Layer 2. The physical layer, Layer 1, may be divided into three sublayers: **media dependent**, responsible for timing, coding, and jitter correction, **media access**, based on TDM for example, and an additional **cell sublayer** found in ATM. The functionality of most transmission technologies is a result of a TDM function residing at the media access sublayer. This results in a transmission infrastructure that may act as a carrier for suitably mapped higher-layer data. In fact, this direct mapping, especially over SDH or SONET, is suggested by many in the industry for the transmission of data traffic. Of the two transmission technologies, PDH and SDH/SONET, the latter is more suitable for a number of reasons. PDH tributaries at each level of the hierarchy are multiplexed in such a way that there is no way to identify an individual channel within a higher-order trunk. In addition, the transmission hierarchies differ between Europe and North America, with standardized data rates only to 140 Mbps (E4) and 45 Mbps (DS3) respectively. Any higher rates are based on vendor-specific multiplexing schemes. This of course has negative implications for high-speed trunking. Luckily, carriers are well under way in deploying SDH/SONET which eliminates all of the problems outlined above. Since individual data streams may now be identified and accessed within a higher-order trunk, demultiplexing is no longer required. The system is globally standardized at 155 Mbps and above (with the exception of some of the overhead fields within the header as described earlier), so service providers may deploy trans-oceanic trunks at 155 Mbps and above.

PDH

User data mapped directly over **Plesiochronous Digital Hierarchy (PDH)** links is one of the most common ways of building dedicated wide-area networks. Where data only is required, routers may connect via DS1/E1 or DS3/E3 links. Either HDLC or PPP provides framing for this higher-layer data traffic. Voice and video service are integrated through the use of multiplexing equipment, breaking out the DS1 or E1 into 64 Kbps channels or DS3/E3 into DS1/E1 channels, and allowing for channel switching and redundancy. PDH is often deployed in a channelized configuration, where individual channels may be managed within a single physical link. For example, a channelized E1 contains 30 user channels of 64 Kbps. In this environment, a central location may use all 30 channels of the E1 service, while each branch office will require only a single channel. Multiplexing equipment within the service provider's domain will perform the required distribution function. This exact scenario may be repeated at E3 but at higher bandwidths.

SDH/SONET

The **Synchronous Digital Hierarchy/Synchronous Optical Network (SDH/SONET)** provides the ideal infrastructure for the support of higher-layer voice and data services due to sophisticated network management capabilities and scalable mapping mechanisms. Lower-speed streams may be directly mapped into higher-order frames via **Add-Drop Multiplexers (ADMs)**. In this way, a deterministic amount of bandwidth may be provided to end users on the SDH network. Though ATM user interfaces and trunks use SDH as a transport in both the local and wide areas, standards do exist for the direct mapping of data into the SDH/SONET frame structure based on PPP (Simpson, 1994). As a result of this mapping, we eliminate the intermediate ATM cell structure with its associated SAR overhead. Products actually exist which perform this function. One advantage of this direct mapping for data is that flow and congestion control is inherent to the system, as an SDH/SONET payload may never be oversubscribed and thus all data entering the network will be delivered to the destination. As with ATM, SONET/SDH transport includes network management functionality, including health and status monitoring, statistics gathering, and configuration control.

On a wider scale, most carriers deploy SONET/SDH as their baseline transmission architecture. ATM, N-ISDN, multiplexer, and datagram traffic are all mapped into SDH, in contrast to mapping all traffic types into ATM. This relates to the question of ATM voice traffic to N-ISDN interworking, in that voice traffic over the wide area will often be gatewayed from ATM to dedicated N-ISDN trunks and not vice versa. Following this line of thought, SONET/SDH will provide the universal infrastructure while ATM will be one of many services. This is unless placing all services on an ATM platform is proved to be more effective from the standpoint of OAM costs.

One group supportive of alternatives to ATM for data are some of the Internet service providers. They see no technical or business-driven reason at the moment to combine their router-based IP network into their voice backbones; both types of traffic may be transported over the same SONET/SDH infrastructure. In this data-only environment (notwithstanding that voice and video may be transported over the IP datagram service) the additional overhead of ATM and associated complexities in buffering and congestion avoidance make direct mapping of the PPP (or an equivalent) into SDH/SONET quite attractive. For wide-area connectivity, the PPP, first at 155 Mbps and then at 622 Mbps, may be the solution. However, SONET/SDH does introduce some disadvantages. Consider the various DS1/E1 and above tributaries combined into a trunk. The SONET/SDH ADM acts as a TDM in this respect, with the bandwidth available within any unused tributary wasted. This lack of flexibility is a factor working in favor of ATM.

6.2.5 Analysis

The future of wide-area networking is almost easier to predict than that for the local area. Carriers, which began to deploy commercial ATM services in 1995, will increase the rate of investment in this technology. It will become the service of choice for high-speed multiservice interconnection. Two services described above, Frame Relay and SMDS/CBDS, will continue to exist as part of an ATM-based service offering after carriers phase out dedicated Frame Relay and DQDB-based switching platforms. For an intermediate period, high-speed leased lines based on SDH/SONET will co-exist. The ultimate question in the wide-area is whether to go with a single multiservice switching platform above the transmission system or continue to improve the discrete voice and data systems (Figure 6.4). If the case can be made that a single platform will reduce costs and/or increase efficiency, then ATM will be the system of choice. However, this is not yet proven, and the service providers will continue to implement separate voice and data systems. In fact, in the Internet, we will see combinations of ATM over SONET/SDH and direct encapsulation across the same.

The decision for ATM may be a bit more clear cut within private WANs, where ATM is predicted to replace many TDM networks in the coming years. For lower-speed connectivity, 'native' Frame Relay, N-ISDN, and X.25 will remain viable, with N-ISDN the service of choice where users want to integrate voice and data, although voice over Frame Relay will also become popular. Within two to three years, the number of new X.25 connections should taper off considerably except in those countries where alternative services do not exist. This does not imply that existing X.25 users will abandon the service in mass; on the contrary, many users currently implementing large X.25 networks may have no reason to change services. In the residential market, the ultimate architecture may be more of a hybrid, in that the actual ATM network may

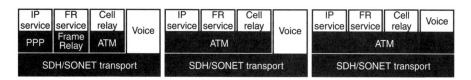

Figure 6.4 Multiservice deployment alternatives.

terminate at the central office or head into the home depending upon service provider and country.

With these choices, the ultimate acceptance of a service will depend on positioning by service providers via tariff structures. In a given geographic area, X.25, Frame Relay, ISDN, and even ATM may be deployed at T1/E1. A user subscribing to any one of these services must therefore have knowledge of application profiles and data flows, this knowledge influencing which service will be the most cost effective and most able to support the application.

6.2.6 Experimental

Parallel to the global deployment of ATM, many corporations have conducted research into high-speed alternatives, some of these based on one or more of the technologies passed over in favor of ATM. In more than one instance, these technologies are deployed internal to a given vendor's broadband offering, since only the user or inter-vendor interfaces need standardizing. This is no different to many X.25 and Frame Relay implementations even today, where switches rely on proprietary trunking mechanisms. Probably some of the most interesting research with long-term implications is that concerning lightwave networking. Some early networks based on this technology are already deployed. Very high-speed networking requires end-systems (see *Desktop area networks* in Section 5.2.5) and switching systems capable of handling data rates in excess of 1 Gbps. No longer will traditional copper and silicon-based switching be adequate. The next generation of ATM switches, with capacities of 1 Tbps and above, will be based on parallel architectures of optical matricies and wavelength-division multiplexing. One of the first examples of such a switch has been developed by Bell-Northern Research (Newsbytes, 1995). Others are sure to follow.

One experimental network, IBM's PARIS, opens the debate as to whether variable length packets or uniform cells are optimal. Within a network, small cells result in lower transit delays (important for voice), more easily managed queues, smaller I/O buffers and less data to retransmit if a cell is lost. This is at the expense of more processing on the end-systems (responsible for SAR), and increased overhead (5 bytes per cell). The opposite side of this argument is data loss under network congestion, where the loss of one 53 byte cell will invalidate an entire FDDI frame. As outlined in the previous section, some users and service providers question the merit of segmenting data traffic. Variable length packets do, however, add to switch complexity, though these switching functions may still be carried out in hardware, with the additional cost of switching more than balanced by lower costs due to elimination of the SAR function on every end-station. An often cited disadvantage of variable length packets is the delay introduced into voice traffic. If the frame size is limited, as in the 128-byte packets used within PARIS, echo cancellation devices may be used with no loss in quality. Of course, limiting the network to 128 bytes still does not eliminate segmentation. For this reason, variable length cells are not widely implemented, and end-systems will either be frame-based or will use the standard 53-octet cell (IBM, 1993b).

As a fitting close to the discussion of alternative technologies to ATM, it may be worth looking at some of the future alternatives to ATM as a switching technology and even SDH as a transmission infrastructure. One such network, known as Rainbow 2 is currently in operation at the Los Alamos National Laboratory and was developed by IBM. Rainbow 2 is an outgrowth of earlier research (Rainbow 1) conducted internally by IBM. Application traffic on this earlier 32-user network consisted of 270 Mbps digital video, 100 Mbps FDDI, and 44.1 k-sample/s CD quality audio. Though the purpose of Rainbow 1 was more to gain experience with the optoelectronic components, the goal of Rainbow 2 is an understanding of supercomputer interconnection and of the implications of optical networking on higher-layer protocols. As with the first network, Rainbow 2 is based on optical switching and wavelength division multiplexing. Each host is connected to the network via an **Optical Node (ON)** which converts the host HIPPI to 1 Gbps full-duplex WDM. The actual protocol between nodes is the **Optical Transport Protocol (OTP)**, based on fixed-length headers, a large packet size, and no flow control or packet fragmentation/reassembly. Between the actual host and the ON the **Simple Host Intersocket Protocol (SHIP)** offloads TCP/IP from the host. This offload solves some of the problems with TCP outlined earlier in the book, where a substantial proportion of available processor cycles may be required to service a very high-speed TCP session. Protocol-wise, SHIP provides for very large packet sizes (up to 1 Gbyte), fixed-length headers, simple flow control, but no checksum error control.

As with Rainbow 1, this network supports a maximum of 32 nodes connected via optical star couplers. Note that although the theoretical bandwidth of the network is 32 Gbps full duplex, in reality only a small proportion of this bandwidth will be in use at any given time if the computing environment consists of one supercomputer and multiple workstations since only one workstation will have access to the supercomputer at any given time. Current research is aimed at developing the components necessary to construct a full multi-access (switched) optical network (Rainbow 3) eventually leading to wavelength routing in the WAN environment (Green, 1994). With users always looking for the Next Great Networking Technology, the question to ask may be: is ATM already obsolete? From our perspective, the answer is a resounding 'No.'

Appendices

Technical

The following tables outline the various ITU, ATM Forum, IEEE, ANSI, ETSI, IETF, and Bellcore documents current at the time of writing. Many of these standards, specifications, and recommendations are referenced elsewhere within this book.

Table A.1 ITU standards.

CCOTT/ITU-T recommendation

1.113	Vocabulary of Terms for Broadband Aspects of ISDN, November, 1994 (A vocabulary baseline text to avoid confusion.)
I.121	Broadband Aspects of ISDN (Rationale and principles concerning ATM.) July, 1991
I.150	BISDN Asynchronous Transfer Mode Functional Characteristics, November 1993 (Basic ATM principles, the ATM cell structure, and the meaning of the fields within the cell header.)
I.211	BISDN Service Aspects, November, 1993 (A classification of broadband services and concepts.)
I.311	BISDN General Network Aspects, December, 1993 (Principles for the layering of network connections, traffic control, and initial guidelines for signaling.)
I.321	BISDN Protocol Reference Model and its Applications, July, 1991 (An extension of the I.320 ISDN reference model to include BISDN when referencing the OSI model.)
I.327	BISDN Functional Architecture (An extension of the I.324 ISDN functional architecture to include BISDN entities
I.356	BISDN ATM Layer Cell Transfer Performance
I.361	BISDN ATM Layer Specification, February, 1995 (A more detailed description of the information in I.150.)
I.362	BISDN Asynchronous Transfer Model Adaptation Layer, October, 1993 (The principles of the AALs corresponding to the BISDN service classes.)
I.363	Asynchronous Transfer Mode Adaptation Layer Specification, February, 1994/1996 (A more detailed description of the AALs from I.362, including the division of the AAL into the Segmentation and Reassembly sublayer and the Convergence Sublayer.)
I.364	Support of Broadband Connectionless Data Service on BISDN, October, 1993 (SMDS/CBDS support across the ATM-UNI in combination with a CLSF.)
I.365.1	Frame Relaying Service Specific Convergence Sublayer (FR-SSCS), November, 1994 (Frame Relay support across the ATM-UNI.)

	CCOTT/ITU-T recommendation
I.371	Traffic Control and Congestion Control in BISDN, November, 1993 (Defines basic public network reference configurations and traffic control capabilities.)
I.413	ISDN User–Network Interface with Broadband Capabilities, December, 1993 (Reference configuration for the UNI including interface function and OAM.)
I.432	B-ISDN User–Network Interface: Physical Layer Specification, January, 1994 (UNI interface structures, physical media, transmission, and OAM.)
I.432.1	General Characteristics (1996)
I.432.2	UNI Physical Layer at 155 and 622 Mbps (1996)
I.432.3	UNI Physical Layer at 1.544 and 2.048 Mbps (1996)
I.432.4	UNI Physical Layer at 51.8 Mbps (1996)
I.555	Frame Relay Bearer Service Interworking, November, 1994
I.580	General Arrangements for Interworking Between B-ISDN and 64 kbit/s Based ISDN, 1995
I.610	BISDN Operations and Maintenance Principles and Functions, January, 1994 (References M.20 in defining OAM requirements across the UNI and as they apply to a complete BISDN network.)
E.164	Numbering Plan for the ISDN Era, November, 1991
F.310	(Broadband Videotex, 1996)
F.811	Broadband Connection-Oriented Bearer Services, March, 1993
F.812	Broadband Connectionless Data Bearer Service, March, 1993
F.813	Virtual Path Service for Reserved and Permanent Communications (VPRPC Service), August, 1995
F.821	(Broadband TV Distribution, 1996)
F.822	(Broadband HDTV Distribution, 1996)
G.652	Characteristics of Monomode Optical Fiber Cables, February, 1994
G.xxx	(ATM Equipment Types and Characteristics)
G.702	Digital Hierarchy Bit Rates, June, 1990
G.703	Physical/Electrical Characteristics of Hierarchical Digital Interfaces, September, 1991
G.704	Synchronous Frame Structures Used at Primary and Secondary Hierarchical Levels, November, 1995
G.706	Frame Alignment and Cyclic Redundancy Check (CRC) Procedures Relating to Basic Frame Structures Defined in Recommendation G.704 August, 1991
G.707	Synchronous Digital Hierarchy Bit Rates, August, 1993 (1996)
G.708	Network–Node Interface for the Synchronous Digital Hierarchy, August, 1992 (1996)
G.709	Synchronous Multiplexing Structure, December, 1993
G.751	Digital Multiplex Equipment Operating at the 3rd Order Bit Rate of 34.368 Kbit/s and the 4th Order Bit Rate of 139.264 Kbit/s using positive justification, June, 1990
G.803	Architectures of Transport Networks based on the Synchronous Digital Hierarchy, November, 1993
G.804	ATM Cell Mapping into Plesiochronous Digital Hierarchy, 1994
G.832	Transport of SDH Elements on PDH Networks: Frame and Multiplexing Structures, October, 1994
Q.51	(ATM Equipment Function and Performance)
Q.921	ISDN User–Network Interface; Data link layer specification, November, 1994
Q.931	Digital Subscriber Signaling System No. 1 (DSS1); ISDN User–Network Interface Layer 3 Specification for Basic Call Control, October, 1994
Q.2010	B-ISDN overview. Signaling Capability Set 1, Release 1 August, 1991
Q.2100	B-ISDN Signaling ATM Adaptation Layer (SAAL) – Layer Management for the SAAL at the Network Node Interface, December, 1995
Q.2100	B-ISDN Signaling ATM Adaptation Layer (SAAL) Overview Description, February, 1995

CCOTT/ITU-T recommendation

Q.2110	B-ISDN SATM Adaptation Layer Service Specific Connection Oriented Protocol (SSCOP), April, 1995
Q.2119	B-ISDN ATM Adaptation Layer Protocols – Convergence Function for the SSCOP above the Frame Relay Core Service (1996)
Q.2120	B-ISDN meta-signaling protocol September, 1995
Q.2130	B-ISDN SAAL Service Specific Coordination Function (SSCF), April, 1995
Q.2140	B-ISDN ATM adaptation layer – Service-specific coordination function for signaling at the network–node interface (SSCF at NNI) November, 1995
Q.2210	B-ISDN Signaling Network protocols. Message Transfer Part level 3 functions and messages using the services of ITU-T Recommendation Q.2140 (1996)
Q.2610	B-ISDN Usage of Cause and Location in B-ISDN User Part and DSS 2, July, 1995
Q.2650	Broadband-ISDN, interworking between Signaling System No. 7 broadband ISDN user part (B-ISUP) and Digital Subscriber Signaling System No. 2 (DSS 2) September, 1995
Q.2660	Interworking between Signaling System No. 7 broadband ISDN user part (B-ISUP) and narrowband ISDN user part (N-ISUP) September, 1995
Q.2721	Section 1: Broadband-integrated services digital network (B-ISDN) user part. Overview of the B-ISDN Network Node Interface (NNI) Signaling Capability Set 2, Step 1 (1996)
Q.2722	Section 1: Broadband-integrated services digital network (B-ISDN) user part. Network Node Interface (NNI) specification for point-to-multipoint call./connection control (1996)
Q.2723	Broadband integrated services digital network (B-ISDN), BISDN User Part – Support of Additional Traffic Parameters, July, 1995 (1996)
Q.2724	Section 1: Broadband-integrated services digital network (B-ISDN) user part. Overview of the B-ISDN Network Node Interface (NNI) Look-ahead without state change for the network node–interface (NNI) (1996)
Q.2725	Section 1: Broadband-integrated services digital network (B-ISDN) user part. Modification procedures (1996)
Q.2726	Section 1: Broadband-integrated services digital network (B-ISDN) user part. ATM end system address for calling and called party (1996)
Q.2726	Section 2: Broadband-integrated services digital network (B-ISDN) user part. Network generated session identifier (1996)
Q.2726	Section 3: Broadband-integrated services digital network (B-ISDN) user part. Overview of the B-ISDN Network Node Interface (NNI) Signaling Capability Set 2, Step 1 (1996)
Q.2721	Broadband-integrated services digital network (B-ISDN) user part. Support of frame relay (1996)
Q.2730	Broadband integrated services digital network (B-ISDN), Signaling System No. 7 B-ISDN user part (B-ISUP), supplementary services August, 1995
Q.2761	Broadband integrated services digital network (B-ISDN), Signaling System No. 7 B-ISDN user part (B-ISUP). Functional description of the B-ISDN user part (B-ISUP) of Signalling System No. 7, October, 1995
Q.2762	Broadband integrated services digital network (B-ISDN), Signaling System No. 7 B-ISDN user part (B-ISUP). General functions of the messages and signals of the B-ISDN user part (B-ISUP) of Signaling System No. 7, November, 1995
Q.2763	Broadband integrated services digital network (B-ISDN), Signaling System No. 7 B-ISDN user part (B-ISUP). Formats and codes, 1994 (1996)
Q.2764	Broadband integrated services digital network (B-ISDN), Signaling System No. 7 B-ISDN user part (B-ISUP). Basic call procedures, 1994 (1996)
Q.2931	B-ISDN Digital Subscriber Signaling System No. 2 (DSS2) User–Network Interface (UNI) Layer 3 Specification for Basic Call/Connection control, 1995 (1996)

CCOTT/ITU-T recommendation

Q.2932   B-ISDN Digital Subscriber Signaling System No. 2 (DSS2); Generic Functional Protocol, 1996

Q.2932.1 Broadband-integrated services digital network (B-ISDN). Digital subscriber SS No.2 (DSS2). General functional protocol. Core functions (1996)

Q.2933   Broadband-integrated services digital network (B-ISDN). Digital subscriber SS No.2 (DSS2). Signaling specification for frame relay service (1996)

Q.2951   Stage 3 Description for Number Identification Supplementary Services Using B-ISDN Digital Subscriber Signaling System No. 2 (DSS2) Basic Call, October, 1995

Q.2957   Stage 3 description for additional information transfer supplementary services using B-ISDN Digital Subscriber Signaling System No. 2 (DSS 2), basic call, August, 1995

Q.2959   Broadband-integrated services digital network (B-ISDN). Digital subscriber SS No.2 (DSS2). Call priority (1996)

Q.2961   B-ISDN DSS2 Negotiation/Modification: Additional Traffic Parameter Indications, 1995 (Provides support for VBR traffic descriptors (comparable to UNI 3.1 descriptors) December, 1995

Q.2962   Broadband-integrated services digital network (B-ISDN). Digital subscriber SS No.2 (DSS2). Connection characteristics negotiation during call/connection establishment phase (1996)

Q.2963.1 Broadband-integrated services digital network (B-ISDN). Digital subscriber SS No.2 (DSS2). Connection modification – Peak all rate modification by the connection owner (1996)

Q.2964.1 Broadband-integrated services digital network (B-ISDN). Digital subscriber SS No.2 (DSS2). Basic look-ahead (1996)

Q.2971   B-ISDN DSS2 UNI Layer 3 Specification for Point-to-Multipoint Call/Connection Control, December, 1995

X.3fi   (Interworking with Frame Relay, 1994)

X.6   Public Data Networks Services and Facilities: Multicast Service Definition, November, 1993.

Table A.2 ATM Forum specifications. Source: ATM Forum.

ATM Forum specification		Description
UNI 3.0	ATM User–Network Interface (UNI) Specification, Version 3, August, 1993	Defines signaling, physical interfaces, and management between an ATM-connected end-system and an ATM switch; Q.93B based
UNI 3.1 AF-UNI-0010	ATM User–Network Interface (UNI) Specification, Version 3.1, 1995	Update of UNI 3.0 for compliance with ITU-T signaling; Q.2931 based
UNI 4.0 (95-1434)	ATM User–Network Interface (UNI) Specification, Version 4.0, 1996	Update of UNI 3.1 supporting additional signaling modes AF-UNI-0011 ILMI Version 3.0/3.1 AF-UNI-0012 Differences between UNI 3.0 and 3.1
	ILMI Version 4.0, 1996	Interim Local Management Interface (ILMI)
AF-PNNI-0026	Interim Interswitch Signaling Protocol, December, 1994	Defines an interswitch trunking protocol supporting SVCs; precursor to the PNNI
AF-PNNI-0055	Private Network–Node Interface Version 1.0, March, 1996	Defines an ATM Layer hierarchical routing protocol between ATM switches

ATM Forum specification		Description
B-ICI v1, v1.1	BISDN Inter Carrier Interface (B-ICI) Specification, August, 1993	Defines a service interface interconnecting ATM networks
B-ICI v2	BISDN Inter Carrier Interface	Defines additional features B-ICIv3 (TBD)
AF-BICI-0013	(B-ICI) Specification, 1995	when interconnecting ATM networks
DXI (93-590)	ATM Data Exchange Interface, 1993	Defines a frame-based access to ATM
AF-LANE-0021	LAN Emulation Over ATM Version 1.0, January, 1995	Defines a LANE service across ATM
AF-LANE-0050	LANE 1.0 Addendum, August, 1995	Fixes to LANE v1
AF-LANE-0057	LAN Server MIBs	For management of LESs
(95-1081)	LAN Emulation Over ATM Version 2.0, LUNI, (1997)	Second release of the LANE service includes QoS and better PVC support
	LAN Emulation Over ATM Version 2.0, LNNI, 1997	Second release of the LANE service supports server–server communications
AF-LANE-0038	LAN Emulation Client Management Specification V 1.0, September, 1995	Defines a management frame work for LANE clients
(95-0824)	Multiprotocol over ATM, 1997	Optimizes multiprotocol routing and connectivity across ATM network
AF-SAA-0030	Circuit Emulation Service Interoperability Specification, June, 1995	Defines a CES across ATM supporting the interconnection of PABXs and video CODECS
AF-SAA-0032	Frame UNI (FUNI), 1995	Defines a frame-based UNI supporting signaling and QoS; replaces the ATM-DXI
AF-SAA-0048	Native ATM Services Semantic Description, 1996	
AF-SAA-0049	Audio/Visual Multimedia Services: Video on Demand Specification, 1995	Defines services available under VoD
(95-0446)	VTOA Trunking, 1996	Defines trunking for Voice and Telephony over ATM
(95-0917)	VTOA to the Desktop, 1996	Defines a VTOA end terminal
AF-TM-0056	ATM Traffic Management Specification, 1996	Supports ABR and QoS; supported in UNI 4.0, PNNI Phase 1, and the AMS
AF-PHY-0015	155 Mbps over UTP-5, September, 1994	Defines framing and physical characteristics for 155 Mbps over UTP-5 and STP Type 1
AF-PHY-0016	DS1 Physical Layer Specification, September, 1994	Defines framing and physical characteristics for the 1.544 Mbps interface
AF-PHY-0018	Mid-range Physical Layer Specification for Category 3 UTP, September, 1994	Defines framing and physical characteristics for 51.84 Mbps and sub-rates over UTP-3
AF-PHY-0040	Physical Layer Specification for 25.6 Mbps over Twisted Pair June, 1995	Defines framing and physical characteristics for 25.6 Mbps over UTP-3 based on the Desktop ATM25 standard

ATM Forum specification		Description
E3 UNI (1996)	50 Mbps over Plastic Optical Fiber (PDF) 155 Mbps over Plastic Optical Fiber (PDF)	Defines framing and physical characteristics for 34 Mbps
AF-PHY-0043	Cell-Based Transmission Convergence, August, 1995	Defines a transmission convergence based on clear channel interfaces
AF-PHY-0046	622 Mbps Optical, October, 1995	Defines framing and physical characteristics for 622 Mbps over fiber
AF-PHY-0047	155 Mbps over UTP-3, October, 1995	Defines framing and physical characteristics for 155.52 Mpbs over UTP-3
AF-PHY-0053	120-ohm Interface to 155 Mbps, (1996)	Additional physical layer specification
AF-PHY-0054	Revised DS3 Using Direct Mapping, (1996)	New mapping for DS3; replaces PLCP
AF-PHY-0029	6.312 Mbps UNI Specification	Defines framing and physical characteristics for J2
(95-1121)	ATM Inverse Mux (1996)	Transmission of higher bandwidth ATM trunks across $n \times DS1/E1$
(94-0422)	E1 Physical Layer Specification	Defines framing and physical characteristics for 2.048 Mbps over copper
AF-PHY-0017	UTOPIA, 1994	Defines an interface between the physical layer and the upper layer entitles (that is, ATM layer and management)
AF-PHY-0039	UTOPIA Level 2 Specification	Extensions to UTOPIA
(95-1185)	Nirvana (Serial Utopia) Level 1	Defines a UTOPIA-like interface based on a serial architecture
(95-0766)	WIRE (1996)	Defines an interface between the PMD and TC sublayers
AF-TEST-0022	Introduction to ATM Forum Test Specifications, December, 1994	Overview of ATM conformance, performance, and interoperability testing
AF-TEST-0023	PICS Proforma for the DS3 Physical Layer Interface, September, 1994	Vendor Q&A of conformance to standard
AF-TEST-0024	PICS Proforma for the SONET STS-3c Physical Layer Interface, September, 1994	Vendor Q&A of conformance to standard
AF-TEST-0025	PICS Proforma for 100 Mbps Multimode Fiber, September, 1994	Supplier Protocol Implementation Conformance Statement (PICS) for the 100 Mbps fiber interface
AF-TEST-0028	PICS Proforma for ATM Layer (UNI 3.0), 1995	Vendor Q&A of conformance to standard
AF-TEST-0030	Conformance Abstract Test Suite for the UNI 3.0 ATM Layer of Intermediate Systems, 1995	To verify interoperability of equipment from multiple vendors
AF-TEST-0035	Interoperability Abstract Test Suite for the ATM Layer, April, 1995	To verify interoperability of equipment from multiple vendors
AF-TEST-0036	Interoperability Test Suites for Physical Layer: DS-3, STS-3c, 100 Mbps MMF (TAXI), 1995	To verify interoperability of equipment from multiple vendors

ATM Forum specification		Description
AF-TEST-0037	PICS Proforma for DS1, April, 1995	Supplier PICS for the DS1 interface
AF-TEST-0041	ATM Layer Conformance Test Suite for the UNI 3.0 ATM Layer of End Systems, July, 1995	To verify interoperability of equipment from multiple vendors
AF-TEST-0042	PICS Proforma for AAL5, 1995	Vendor Q&A of conformance to standard
AF-TEST-0044	PICS for the 51.84 Mbps Mid-Range (UTP-3) Physical Layer, 1995	Vendor Q&A of conformance to standard
AF-TEST-0045	Conformance Abstract Test Suite for the UNI 3.1 ATM Layer of Intermediate Systems, 1995	To verify interoperability of equipment from multiple vendors
AF-TEST-0052	Conformance Test Suite for the AAL5 Sub-Layer, 1996	To verify interoperability of equipment from multiple vendors
95-1459	Conformance Test Suite for the SSCOP Sub-Layer for UNI 3.1, 1996	To verify interoperability of equipment from multiple vendors
95-0584, 95-0858, 95-1131	Conformance Abstract Test Suite for Signaling (UNI 3.1) for the User Side, 1996	To verify interoperability of equipment from multiple vendors
AF-TEST-0060	Conformance Abstract Test Suite for the UNI 3.1 Layer of End-Systems, 1996	To verify interoperability of equipment from multiple vendors
95-1145	Conformance Abstract test Suite for Signaling (UNI 3.1) for the Network Side, 1996	To verify interoperability of equipment from multiple vendors
AF-TEST-0051	PICS for the 25.6 Mbps over Twisted Pair Cable (UTP-3) Physical Layer, 1995	Vendor Q&A of conformance to standard
AF-TEST-0059	PICS for ATM Layer (UNI 3.1), 1996	Vendor Q&A of conformance to standard
M3CNM Update	SNMP MIB Network Element (1996) M4, 1996	Visibility into public network from customer NMS
AF-NM-0058	M4 Public Network View Requirements, 1996 M4 Public Network View SNMP & CMIP MIB 1996 M5 Carrier Interface Power Management, 1996	
(95-1416)	Baseline text for the Residential Broadband Working Group, 1996	Physical interfaces for residential access networks
Security 1.0 1997	AF-NM- 0019 CNM for ATM Public Network Services (M3) AF-NM-0020 M4 Interface Requirements and Logical MIB AF-NM-0027 CMIP Specification for the M4 Interface	Security framework for ATM

Note: The left column us a document number for completed specifications or a contribution number for work in progress. Some earlier specifications have not been assigned document numbers (that is, DXI). Dates in parentheses are predicted. Current status available via Spec Watch page at www.atmforum.com. Some documents available at: ftp://atmforum.com/pub/contributions.

Table A.3 ANSI recommendations.

ANSI recommendations	
T1.102	Digital Hierarchy – Electrical Interfaces, 1990
T1.105	Digital Hierarchy – Optical Interface Rates and Format Specifications (SONET), 1991
T1.107	Digital Hierarchy – Formats Specifications, August, 1988
T1.107a	Digital Hierarchy – Supplement to Formats Specifications (DS3 Format Applications), 1990
T1.624	Broadband ISDN User–Network Interface: Rates and Formats Specifications, 1993
T1.635	Broadband ISDN – ATM adaptation layer type 5 common part functional specification, 1994
T1.637	Broadband ISDN – ATM Adaptation Layer – Service Specific Connection Oriented Protocol (SSCOP), 1994
T1.	Broadband ISDN ATM Aspects – ATM Layer Functionality and Specification,
T1.CBR	Broadband ISDN ATM Adaptation Layer for Constant Bit Rate Service; Functionality and Specification, February, 1993

Table A.4 IEEE standards.

IEEE standards and descriptions	
802.1	Higher-Level Interfaces, 1990 (ISO 8802-1)
802.1d	Local and Metropolitan Area Networks: Media Access Control Bridges, 1990
802.1h	MAC Bridging of Ethernet V2.0 in IEEE Local Area Networks, 1995
802.1i	Local Area Networks MAC Bridges FDDI Supplement, 1993
802.1p	Traffic Class Expediting and Dynamic Multicast Filtering, in progress (Specifies filtering on the basis of MAC frame information to enable better support for multicast traffic.)
802.1q	Virtual LANs based on frame tagging (in-progress)
802.2	Local Area Networks – Part 2: Logical Link Control, 1989, 1993 (ISO 8802-2)
802.3	Local and Metropolitan Area Networks – Part 3: Carrier Sense Multiple Access with Collision Detection (Ethernet) access method and physical specifications, 1993 (ISO 8802-3)
802.3u	MAC Parameters, Physical Layer, and Medium Attachment Units and Repeater for 100 Mb/s Operation, 1995 (Adds 100Base-T support using same CSMA/CD mechanisms; adds Media Independent Interface – MII.)
802.3x	Specification for 802.3 Full Duplex Operation, 1995 (Both 10 and 100 Mbps) Physical Layer Specification for 100 Mb/s Operation on Two Pairs of Category 3 or Better Balanced Twisted Pair Cable (100Base-T2), in progress
802.4	Token-Passing Bus Access Method and Physical Layer, 1990 (ISO 8802-4) (ARCNET; revision in progress)
802.5	Token Ring Access Method and Physical Layer, 1995 (ISO 8802-5)
802.6	Distributed Queue Dual Bus (DQDB) Subnetwork of a Metropolitan Area Network (MAN), 1990 (ISO 8802-6)
802.6i	Remote LAN Bridging Using the 802.6 MAN, 1990
802.7	IEEE Recommended Practices for Broadband Local Area Networks, 1989 (ISO 8802-7)
802.8	802 Recommended Practice for Fiber Optic Local and Metropolitan Area Networks, 1992
802.9	Integrated Services (IS) LAN Interface at the Medium Access Control (MAC) and Physical (PHY) Layers, 1994 (ISO 8802-9)
802.9a	Supplement to IS LAN Interface at the MAC and PHY Layers: Specification of ISLAN 16-T, 1995 (IsoENET)

IEEE standards and descriptions

802.9e	Supplement to IS LAN Interface at the MAC and PHY Layers: ATM Cell Bearer Mode, in progress (Designed to support transport of ATM cells to the desktop in the isochronous information stream of an IEEE 802.9 interface.)
802.10	Interoperable LAN/MAN Security (SILS), 1992
802.10f	Supplement to SILS: Recommended Practice for SDE on Ethernet V2.0 in IEEE 802 LANs, 1993
802.11	Standard for Wireless LAN Medium Access Control (MAC) and Physical Layer (PHY) Specification, in progress
802.12	Demand Priority Access Method, Physical Layer and Repeater Specification for 100 Mb/s Operation, 1995 (VG-AnyLAN)
802.12a	Supplement to above: Operation at Greater Than 100 Mb/s, in progress
802.12b	Supplement to above: Two-Pair Balanced Cable Physical Medium Dependent (2-TPPMD), Medium Dependent Interface (MDI), and Link Specifications, in progress (operation of VG-AnyLAN over 2-pair CAT5)
802.12c	Supplement to above: Full Duplex Operation, in progress
802.13	Not Assigned
802.14	Standard Protocol for Cable-TV Based Broadband Communication Network, in-progress (Will define MAC and PHY for support of different QoSs over cable with HFC as first topic; goal of compatibilty with ATM)

Note   Not every 802.xy standard is listed, only those referenced within this book

Table A.5 IETF RFCs.

IETF request for comments and relevant drafts	Description
826	Address Resolution Protocol (Std 37)	MAC to IP address
1112	Host extensions for IP multicasting	resolution Internet
1122	Host Requirements – Communications (Std 3)	multicasting and IGMP
1123	Host Requirements – Applications (Std 3)	
1190	Experimental Internet Stream Protocol, Version 2 (ST-II)	(see RFC-1819)
1191	Path MTU Discovery	End-to-end MTU negotiation
1209	The Transmission of IP Datagrams over the SMDS Service, 1991	Defines a protocol for the transmission of IP and ARP packets over a Switched Multi-megabit Data Service Network configured as a logical IP subnetwork
1213	Management Information Base for Network Management of TCP/IP-based internets: MIB-II	For SNMP For SNMP
1293	Inverse Address Resolution Protocol, 1992	Describes additions to ARP that will allow a station to request a protocol address corresponding to a given hardware address
1406	DS3/E3-MIB DS3/E3 Interface Type	For SNMP
1407	DS1/E1-MIB DS1/E1 Interface Type	For SNMP
1483	Multiprotocol Encapsulation over ATM Adaptation Layer 5, 1993	Describes encapsulations for carrying network interconnect traffic over ATM AAL5
1490	Multiprotocol Interconnect over Frame Relay, 1993	Describes an encapsulation method for carrying network interconnect traffic over a Frame Relay backbone

IETF request for comments and relevant drafts	Description
1573 Evolution of the Interfaces Group of MIB-II	For S
1577 Classical IP and ARP over ATM, 1994	Defines an initial application of classical IP and ARP in an ATM network environment configured as a Logical IP Subnetwork (LIS)
1595 MIB SONET/SDH Interface Type	For SNMP
1620 Internet Architecture Extensions for Shared Media	Relaxation of local/remote rule
1626 Default IP MTU for use over ATM AAL5, 1994	Specifies a default IP MTU.
1633 Integrated Services in the Internet Architecture: an Overview, 1994	Discusses a proposed extension to the Internet architecture and protocols to provide integrated services
1695 ATM Management Version 8.0 using SMIv2	For SNMP
1735 NBMA Address Resolution Protocol (NARP), 1994	Defines a method for a source terminal (host or router) connected to an NBMA link layer network to find out the NBMA addresses of the destination terminal provided that the destination terminal is connected to the same NBMA network
1754 IP over ATM Working Group's Recommendations for the ATM Forum's Multiprotocol BOF, 1995	Initial list of requirements submitted to the ATM Forum's Multiprotocol BOF for the operation of IP over ATM networks
1755 ATM Signaling Support for IP over ATM, 1995	Describes the ATM call control signaling exchanges needed to support Classical IP over ATM implementations as described in RFC 1577
1819 Internet Stream Protocol Version 2 (ST-2) Protocol Specification – Version ST2+	Application QoS support
1821 Integration of Real-time Services in an	Discussion of real-time application support
IP-ATM Network Architecture	Host multicast support
IGMP2	
Gateway Requirements (Std 4)	Router requirements
NBMA Next Hop Resolution Protocol (NHRP) (draft-ietf-rolc-nhrp-0x.txt, 1995)	Describes a protocol which can be used by a source station (host or router) connected to an NBMA subnetwork to determine the IP and NBMA subnetwork addresses of the 'NBMA next hop' towards a destination station.
1901– SNMPv2 (1996) 1908	Introduction, SMI, Textual Conventions, Conformance Statements, Protocol Operations, Transport Mappings, MIB-II, and co-existence with SNMPv1.
1932 IP over ATM: A Framework Document	Describes the various proposals of mapping IP into ATM.

IETF request for comments and relevant drafts	Description
Protocol Independent Multicasting (PIH) (draft-idmr-pim-dm-spec-ox.ps, 1996) (draft-idmr-pim-spec-ox.ps, 1996) (draft-ietf-rsvp-spec-ox.ps, 1996)	Multicast routing
Resource Reservation Protocol (RSVP) (draft-ietf-rsvp-spec-ox.ps, 1996)	Application QoS Support
Specification of Guaranteed Quality of Service (draft-ietf-intserv-guaranteed-svc-0x.txt, 1995) Controlled Delay (...control-del...) Controlled Load (...ctrl-load...) Predictive (...predictive...)	Describes the network element behavior required to deliver guaranteed service in the Internet
Support for Multicast over UNI 3.1 based ATM Networks.(draft-ietf-ipatm-ipmc-0x.txt, 1996)	Describes a mechanism to support the multicast needs of Layer 3 protocols; introduces the MARS and MCS
Classical IP and ARP over ATM Update (Part Deux) (draft-ieft-ipatm-classic 2-0x.txt, 1996)	Updates RFC 1577 and RFC 1626
RFC 1937 'Local/Remote' Forwarding Decision inSwitched Data Link Subnetworks	Describes extensions to the IP architecture which allow hosts in different IP subnets to directly communicate over an NBMA network.

Note   RFCs and Internet Drafts available via any IETF reflector (see Appendix C)

Table A.6 ETSI standards.

ETS 300 337, August, 1993	Transmission and Multiplexing (TM); generic frame structures for the transport of various signals (including ATM cells) at the CCITT Rec. G.702 hierarchical rates of 2048 kbit/s, 34, 368 kbit/s and 139,264 kbit/s
ETS 300 246, February, 1993	Business Telecommunication (BT); Open Network Provision (ONP) Technical Requirements; 2048 kbit/s Digital Unstructured Leased Line (D2048U) Interface Presentation
ETS 300 247, February, 1993	Business Telecommunication (BT); Open Network Provision (ONP) Technical Requirements; 2048 kbit/s Digital Unstructured Leased Line (D2048U) Connection Characteristics
ETS 300 248, February, 1993	Business Telecommunication (BT); Open Network Provision (ONP) Technical Requirements; 2048 kbit/s Digital Unstructured Leased Line (D2048U) Terminal Equipment Interface
prETS 300 167	Functional Characteristics of 2.048 Kbps Interfaces
prETS 300 300	SDH based User Network Access, Physical Layer Interfaces for B-ISDN Applications
prETS 300 478	CBDS over ATM, Framework and Protocol Specification at the UNI, Version 10/94
prETS 300 479	CBDS over ATM, NNI Protocol Specification, Version 10/94

Table A.7 Bellcore documents.

Bellcore requirements/advisories

GR-1248-CORE	Generic Requirements for Operations of ATM Network Elements, Issue 2, September, 1995.
TR-NWT-000253	Synchronous Optical Network (SONET) Transport Systems: Common Generic Criteria, Issue 2, December, 1991
TA-NWT-001110	Broadband ISDN Switching Systems Generic Requirements, Issue 2, August, 1993
TR-NWT-001112	Broadband-ISDN User to Network Interface and Network Node Interface Physical Layer Generic Criteria, Issue 1, June, 1993
TA-NWT-001117	ATM Customer Network Management, September, 1993
TA-NWT-001248	Generic Requirements for Operations of Broadband Switching Systems, Issue 1, October, 1992
TR-TSV-000772	Generic System Requirements in Support of Switched Multi-megabit Data Service, Issue 1, May, 1991
TR-TSV-000773	Local Access System Generic Requirements, Objectives, and Interfaces in Support of Switched Multi-megabit Data Service, Issue 1, June, 1991
TR-TSV-001060	Switched Multi-megabit Data Service Generic Requirements for Exchange Access and Intercompany Serving Arrangements, Issue 1, December, 1991, Revision 1, August, 1992, Revision 2, March, 1993
TR-TSV-001063	Operations Technology Generic Criteria in Support of Exchange Access SMDS and Intercompany Serving Arrangements, Issue 1, December, 1992, Revision 1, March, 1993
TA-TSV-001238	Generic Requirements for SMDS on the 155.520 Mbps Multi-services Broadband ISDN Inter-Carrier Interface (B-ICI), Issue 1, December, 1992
TR-NWT-000063	Network Equipment-Building System (NEBS) – Generic Equipment Requirements, Issue 5, September, 1993
TR-NWT-000078	Generic Physical Design Requirements for Telecommunications Products and Equipment, Issue 3, December, 1991
TR-NWT-001089	Electromagnetic Compatibility and Electrical Safety Generic Criteria for Network Telecommunication Equipment, Issue 1, October, 1991
TR-TSY-000487	Generic Requirements for Electronic Equipment Cabinets, Issue 1, June, 1989

Table A.8 Useful assigned numbers.

ATM Forum OUI	00-A0-3E	Multicast bit is the low-order bit of the '00'
ATM Forum well-known prefix	470079	
ATM Forum well-known group prefix	C50079	
ATM Name Server	C5.00.79.00.00.00.00.00.00.00 00.00.00.00.A0.3E.00.00.02.00	UNIT 3.x
LECS well-known NSAP	47.00.79.00.00.00.00.00.00. 00.00.00.00.A0.3E.00.00.01.00	UNIT 4.0
IFMP and GSMO	VCI=15	Ipsilom drafts
ILMI	VCI = 16	
LANE signaling	VCI = 17	
PNNI PTSP	VCI = 18	
FTTC upstream sign-on	VCI = 21	(proposed by DAVIC)
Reserved	VCI = 0-31 in all VPIs	

NHRP	Internet Protocol 54	Next Hop Resolution Protocol
MARS data messages (short)	PID = 0001	Within IANA OUI (00-00-5E)
Reserved for NHRP use	PID = 0002	With IANA OUI (00-00-5E)
MARS/NHRP control messages	PID = 0003	With IANA OUI (00-00-5E)
MARS data messages (long)	PID = 0004	With IANA OUI (00-00-5E)
IPv6	PID = 0800	Within LLC/SNAP header AA-AA-03 00-00-00
AppleTalk	PID = 809B	Within LLC/SNAP header AA-AA-03 00-00-00
Banyan Vines	PID = 80C4	Within LLC/SNAP header AA-AA-03 00-00-00
DECnet	PID = 6003	Within LLC/SNAP header AA-AA-03 00-00-00
Novell IPX	PID = 8137	Within LLC/SNAP header AA-AA-03 00-00-00
NSAP	3	IETF address family
E.164	8	IETF address family
E.164 with NSAP format subaddress	15	IETF address family (proposed)
B-LLI Information Element PID	0000	Reserved
	0001	LANE Control Direct VCC
	0002	LANE 802.3 Data Direct VCC
	0003	LANE 802.5 Data Direct VCC
	0004	LANE 802.3 Multicast VCC
	0005	LANE 802.5 Multicast VCC
	0006	CES DS1/E1 Basic
	0007	CES E1 W/CAS
	0008	CES DS1 SF W/CAS
	0009	CES DS1 extended SF W/CAS
	000A	P-NNI PGL to PGL
B-HLI Information Element PID	00000001	ATM Name Server

Note   IETF assigned numbers maintained at: ftp://ftp.isi.edu/in-notes/iana/assignments

Table A.9 Alignment of ATM Forum and ITU standards.
Source: ATM Forum, 1994.

Description	ITU-T	ETSI	ATM Forum
User Network Interface (UNI)	I.413	pr ETS 300 299	UNI 3.1/4.0
Physical layer	I.432	pr ETS 300 300	UNI 3.1/4.0
ATM layer	I.150	pr ETS 300 298-1	UNI 3.1/4.0
	I.361	pr ETS 300 298-2	
Resource management and traffic control	I.371	DE/NA-52807 pr ETS 300 301	UNI 3.1/4.0
ATM Adaptation Layer	I.362	DE/NA-52617 (AAL 1)	UNI 3.1/4.0

Description	ITU-T	ETSI	ATM Forum
(AAL)	I.363	DE/NA-52618 (AAL 3/4)	
		DE/NA-52619 (AAL 5)	
		DE/NA-52620	
Operations and	I.610	DE/NA-52209	
Maintenance (OAM) and		DTR/NA-52204	
network management		DE/NA-52806	
Signaling (UNI)	Q.93B (basic call)	DE/SPS-5024 (basic)	UNI 3.0
	Q.2931(basic call)		
	Q.93 (sup. services)	DE/SPS-5034 (sup.)	UNI 3.1/4.0
Signaling AAL5	Q.SAAL0		UNI 3.0
	Q.SAAL1 (SSCOP)	DE/SPS-5026-1	UNI 3.1/4.0
	Q.SAAL2 (SSCF)	DE/SPS-5026-2	UNI 3.1/4.0
Connectionless data	I.364	DTR/NA-53203	B-ICI 1.0
service over ATM		DE/NA-53205	
		DE/NA-53206	
Frame Relay over ATM	I.555	DE/NA-53204	B-ICI 1.0
	I.365.1		

In this next table (Table A.10), we compare difference in overhead between SDH and SONET at 155 Mbps and 622 Mbps. This information is relevant when verifying equipment from a given vendor for operation within either of these transmission systems. Note that many of the overhead bytes are identical between the two standards.

Table A.10 Differences between SONET and SDH overhead at 155 and 622 Mbps. Source: ATM Forum, 1995a.

Overhead byte	Function	SONET coding	SDH coding	Note 7
A1	Frame alignment	11110110	11110110	R
A2	Frame alignment	00101000	00101000	R
C1 (STM-1)	Identification	00000001-00000010-00000011	00000001-00000010-00000011	R
C1 (STM-4)	Identification (Note 1)	00000001-00001100 (bytes 1-12)	00000001-00000100 (bytes 1-4)	R
B1	Section error monitoring	BIP-8	BIP-8	R/O
B2	Line error monitoring	BIP-24/BIP-96	BIP-24/BIP-96	R/O
H1 (bits 1–4)	New data flag, Path AIS (Notes 2, 3)	0110 (nominal) or 1001 (actual)	0110 or 1001	R
H1 (bits 5–6)	SS bits, path AIS (Notes 2, 3)	00	10	R
H1 (bits	Pointer, path AIS	0000000000-1100001110	0000000000-1100001110	R

Over-head byte	Function	SONET coding	SDH coding	Note 7
7–8); H2				
H1*	Concatenation	10010011	10010011	R
H2*	Concatenation	11111111	11111111	R
H3	Pointer action			
K1, K2 (STM-4 only)	APS	Per T1.105	Per G.783	O
K2 (bits 6–8)	Line AIS, line RDI, removal of line RDI	111, 110, any non-110	111, 110, any non-110	O
Z2	Line FEBE	B2 error count	B2 error count	O
J1	Path trace	Note 4	Note 5	O
B3	Path error monitoring	BIP-8	BIP-8	R
C2	Path signal label	00010011	00010011	R/O
G1 (bits 1–4)	Path FEBE	B3 error count	B3 error count	R
G1 (bit 5)	Path RDI	1 (Note 6)	1 (Note 6)	R

Note 1 Receivers should not use this for frame alignment identification; SDH does not use bytes 8–12 and should therefore be set to a balanced value

Note 2 H1 and H2 are the first of three (155 Mbps) or 12 (622 Mbps) H1 and H2 bytes while H1* and H2* are the 2nd through 3rd or 2nd through 12th H1 and H2 bytes

Note 3 Path AIS is indicated by an all 1s condition in H1, H2, H1*, and H2*

Note 4 For SONET, this will consist of a 64-character Common Language Location Identifier (Bellcore)

Note 5 SDH interfaces may use a 64-byte string or the 16-byte E.164 address

Note 6 I.432 specifies the path RDI in response to a Loss of Pointer (LOP), path AIS, and Loss of Cell Delineation (LCD)

Note 7 R – Required; O – Optional

B

Rollouts

As an example of the widespread interest in and deployment of ATM among service providers, we look at three regions of the world: the US, Europe, and the Far East. On a more global basis, we look at a number of the multinational service providers and their offerings. This is not intended to be a complete list of service providers or services, as both change on a monthly basis. Also, space does not permit coverage of other areas of interest such as Central Europe, Russia, Southeast Asia, and South Africa.

North America

By 1995, most RBOCs and long-distance providers within the US had launched or announced ATM services. Initially, services offered by RBOCs were limited to their area of operations; interconnection was later provided via the long distance companies (AT&T, MCI, Sprint, Wiltel, MFS, and so on). The range in both service offerings and geography of many of these providers is expected to change with increasing deregulation. We summarize current and planned ATM services in Table B1.

Table B.1 North American public ATM offerings.

Service provider	Service name	Availability	Contact
Ameritech	Ameritech ATM	USA – Ameritech service area	+1 800 TEAM DATA +1 708 248 2000
AT&T	AT&T InterSpan ATM Service	USA	+1 800 248 3632
ATMnet	ATM Cell Service and others	USA – California	info@atmnet.com

Service provider	Service Name	Availability	Contact
Bell Atlantic	ATM Cell Relay Service	USA – Bell Atlantic Federal Systems	+1 202 392 4720
BellSouth Business Systems	Fast Packet Transport Services	USA – BellSouth Service Area	+1 205 444 0595 +1 404 982 7000
GTE Telephone Operations	ATM	USA – Primarily GTE service areas	+1 214 718 5600 ahoakes@gtetel.com
MCI Telecommunications	HyperStream ATM	USA	+1 800 933 9029 +1 202 872 1600
MFS Datanet	MFS Datanet ATM Service	USA, Europe	+1 408 975 2200, info@mfsdatanet.com
NYNEX	ATM Cell Relay Service	USA – NYNEX service area	+1 800 722 2300
Pacific Bell	FasTrak ATM Cell Relay Service	USA – PacBell service area	+1 510 823 2558, jmverge@pacbell.com
SBC Communications	Southwestern Bell ATM Cell Relay Service	USA – SBC service area	+1 314 235 9800
Sprint	Sprint ATM Service	USA	+1 800 736 1130 +1 703 318 7740
Stentor Alliance		Canada	+1 613 781 8798
Teleport Communications Group	TCG Switched Data Services	USA	+1 718 983 2000, rkbailey@aol.com
Unitel Communications	Canarie Network	Canada	+1 416 345 2000
US West	Interprise Networking ATM Service	USA - US West service area	+1 303 965 9271 +1 303 965 9286
WilTel (LDDS WorldCom)	LAN Connection Services	USA	+1 918 588 3210 +1 918 561 6098

Europe

Early trials

Broadband pilots in Belgium, France, Germany, and Spain were representative of the types of experiment which were conducted in the late-1980s and early-1990s. The Belgian project included early ATM switching equipment, subscriber concentrators, and customer premises equipment. This project was based on 'classical' public ATM devices (Network Termination, Sb Bus, and so on). The French experiment, targeted at business communications, consisted of ATM (VP) cross-connects connected by E4 (140 Mbps) or STM-1 links, with subscribers connected via the two. At the customer premises, the service would be broken out to either 30B + D ISDN and Ethernet connections via a provider-owned Network Termination or into 2 Mbps and 155 Mbps clear channels via a CPE or remote ATM subscriber concentrator. As in France, the Spanish trial consisted of CO ATM switching equipment and ATM subscriber concentrators, either co-located with the switch or remote. The user interface to this system was via an Sb Bus connected to a network termination (NT2), then connected upstream via the Tb to an NT1. The functions of the NT2 and NT1 may be combined in a single unit. Objectives of the network included testing the interconnection of network elements, testing ATM-delivered services, and analysis of the effect of ATM multiplexing on QoS. In addition, the network provided an interconnection with ISDN (De Prycker *et al*, 1990).

In Germany, tests were conducted as part of the BERKOM trial in Berlin. The first phase of this project was quite interesting in that it made use of a pre-ATM structure whereby an STM-1 physical interface was divided into pre-allocated channels. These channels included 140 Mbps (H4) video, 4×2 Mbps (H1) audio, data, and clear channel, and a $2B + D + Sync$ for ISDN services and control. As is obvious, bandwidth decisions were made before the advent of cost-effective high-quality video compression. Users connected to the network via CPE consisting of end-systems and a multiplexer; at the CO, the channels were demultiplexed into switching elements capable of handling the H4, H1, and ISDN signals. A feature of the BERKOM trial is that it implemented a D channel signaling protocol allowing users to select services and programming (Domann, 1990). BERKOM was later upgraded to BERKOM II.

European MOU

The European ATM Pilot, officially launched in November, 1994, provided the first international testbed for application, signaling, and management testing. Including 16 PTTs, the pilot provided the opportunity for the testing of hardware, ETSI standards, ITU-T recommendations, and EURESCOM specifications. The intent was to use the testbed as a base to develop specifications which may be used to procure interoperable ATM equipment and lay the foundation for commercial services. The operators included: Austrian PTT, BELGACOM (Belgium), Tele Danmark, Tele and Helsinki Telephone (both in Finland), France Telecom, Deutsche Telekom (Germany), British Telecom, Telecom Eireann (Ireland), Telecom Italia, PTT Telecom Nederland, Norwegian Telecom, Portugal Telecom, TELEFONICA (Spain), Telia AB (Sweden), and Swiss Telecom PTT.

Initial services over this network included Frame Relay, CBR, SMDS/CBCS, and what is known as **Virtual Path Bearer Service** providing ATM service to the customer premises. Due to the cooperative nature of the pilot, users worked closely with each other across national boundaries and with their respective PTTs to test various applications utilizing the services outlined above. A major result of this two-way information exchange was the determination of what QoS standards will be expected as part of a commercial service.

The pilot network consisted of one international node in each country (see Figure B.1), connected via 34 Mbps and/or 155 Mbps trunks to nodes in other countries as well as to additional national nodes (if deployed). The nodes support ATM VP cross-connect functionality with a minimum of 256 VPs per port. Initially, only point-to-point connections were supported; this was expected to migrate to point-to-multipoint over time.

Though the project has been a success, some problems identified early on concerned circuit management (initially conducted as out-of-band as one can get – via phone and fax) and the problems of interworking first generation ATM products from over a dozen manufacturers. Though initial testing concentrated on leased-line functionality (CBR), over the course of the pilot it had evolved to limited bandwidth-on-demand (VBR, UBR) and SVC testing. The first true trunking interface based on the ITU X-interface, as well as management interfaces based on the 'Q' series, were not implemented until 1995. Two problems identified with the equipment installed concerned the implementation of the policing function, which regulates traffic entering the network, and the E3 physical interface, found in two versions: an older PLCP-based mechanism (G.751) and a newer ATM mapping (G.804). This last problem also appears when end users wish to deploy private ATM networks over the wide area; they must be aware of the local E3 offering. Though the intent of the network was non-commercial, many participants have evolved their parts of the network into commercial services. As a follow-on to the

Figure B.1 European ATM pilot.

MOU, the James project was inaugurated at the end of 1995 for a two-year period. Participants include the consortium as above with the addition of Greece and Luxemburg. Planned service offerings include VP bearer, IP over ATM, CES, SMDS, switched VCs, and LAN interconnection.

Tariffed services

European ATM rollouts parallel those of the US. Almost every service provider and competitive access provider (CAP) has either introduced an ATM service or announced their intent to do so. As of the beginning of 1996, the information in Table B.2 was valid for the nations which participated in the MOU.

In addition to the traditional service providers in each European country, a number of alternative providers have been established in anticipation of increasing deregulation during the 1996–1998 timeframe.

Table B.2 European public ATM offerings.

Service provider	Service name	Availability	Contact
Austrian PTT	Internal trials	1995 (pilot)	www.telecom.at
BELGACOM	Tectris VoD Trial	1996 (pilot)	customer.services@is. belgacom.be
Tele Danmark	Datacom	1995	tdk@tdk.dk
Tele Finland	Datanet ATM	1994	+358 2040 2964
Helsinki Telephone (Finland)	VoD Trial	1996	+358 0 606 4803
France Telecom	Transrel ATM	1994	+33 1 44 44 53 14
Deutsche Telekom	ATM Service	1995	+49 228 1810
British Telecom	Internal trials	1996	+44 1473 642459
Telecom Eireann (Ireland)	Trials in Dublin	1995	postmaster@telecom.ie
Telecom Italia	Atmosfera	1996	webmaster@telecomitalia.it
PTT Nederland	Internal trials	1994 (pilot)	www.ptt-telecom.nl
Telenor (Norway)	Internal trials	1995 (pilot)	oslo 22772500
Portugal Telecom	Internal trials	1995 (pilot)	www.telecom.pt
TELEFONICA (Spain)	Internal trials	1994 (pilot)	www.telefonica.es
Telia AB (Sweden)	Telia City Services	1995	+46 8 713 1975
Swiss Telecom PTT	SwissWAN		+41 31 338 7393
Luxembourg	P&T	1995	
MFS Datanet (Europe)		1994	
Colt (UK)		1996	
Fibernet (UK)		1995	
Finnet (Finland)	LAN link ATM	1994	
Corporate Network Services (France)		1996	
Racal (UK)		1996	
Energis (UK)		1996	

Note   Table does not list involvement in European ATM Pilot or ATM-based national academic networks

Many of these organizations, formed from partnerships between cable companies, energy providers, railroads, and even some Telcos, are expected to offer ATM services during the coming years. Some of the better positioned in the business market may be the cable companies due to their installed base. We summarize ways of re-utilizing the coaxial and fiber plant as part of an ATM service offering in Section 4.4.

For historical completeness, it may be worth mentioning that the first European service provider to offer a nationwide ATM service was Telecom Finland, launching their service in September, 1994. Ten cities were interconnected, and a cross-border connection to Stockholm, Sweden, was installed as well. Tariffing was set to be competitive, as opposed to some offerings in other countries during the end of 1994 and into 1995 which were definitely priced not to compete with existing services. One PTT in particular, France Telecom, though offering a competitively-tariffed offering, avoided the difficult issue of whether or not to offer a native ATM service (with its possibilities for voice cannibalization) by offering a LAN interconnection service across the ATM backbone. This offering, supporting Connectionless Broadband Data Service (CBDS), made use of routers as CPE and CLSFs at the core ATM switches. An interesting study completed as a business case for this service showed two million LANs in France in 1995, doubling every two to three years. Pricing under this service is in fact competitive for major customers in comparison to high-speed leased lines.

Pacific Rim

Table B.3 summarizes Pacific Pim public ATM offerings.

Table B.3 Pacific Rim public ATM offerings. Source: Data Communications.

Service provider	Service name	Availability	Contact
Australia – Telstra Corp. Ltd.	ATM Test Network	Australia	www.telestra. com.an
Telecom New Zealand	ATM Test Network	New Zealand	
Singapore Telecom	ATM Test Network	Singapore	www.singtel.com
Hongkong Telecom	ATM Test Network	Hong Kong	www.hkt.net
Japan – NTT	Commerical Cell Relay	Japan	www.ht.jp
Japan – Kokusai Denshin Denwa (KDD)	International trial	Japan and various other countries	www.kdd.co.jp
South Korea – Korea Telecom Corp	ATM Test Network	Korea; planned connection to Japan	www.kotel.co.kr
Taiwan – Directorate Generale of Telecommunications	ATM Network	Taiwan	
China – Guangdong Post and Telecommunications Bureau	ATM Test Network	Guangdong	www.gz.gdpta. net.cn

Multinational service providers

Although we have considered multinational offerings by providers such as Sprint and MFS within North America and Europe, there is a separate class of global providers not easily associated with a given region. These service providers, growing out of the data service (for example, SITA) or computer (for example, IBM) industries, are able to offer ATM services on a global basis. For corporations spread throughout the globe, they therefore have a great deal of appeal. In addition to the service providers active within each country, other major global players include CompuServe, GEIS, the IBM Global Network, Infonet, and SITA. Current and planned offerings are summarized in Table B.4.

Table B.4 Global service providers public ATM offerings. Source: Communications Week International Dataquest.

Service provider	Service name	Availability	Contact
AT&T		No information	www.att.com
GlobalOne		1996	www.global-one.net
(FT, DT, Sprint)			
Cable & Wireless		1994 (pilot)	www.cwix.com
CompuServe		December, 1996	www.compuserve.com
Concert (BT/MCI)		1996	
IBM Global Network	IBM Business Port	US, Canada, Europe	+33 1 41 88 60 00
Infonet		No information	www.info.net
SITA		1997	www.sita.int
Unisource		1996	+41 31 688 8111
LDDS/Worldcom		No information	www.wiltel.com

C

Sources

International standards organizations

ITU (International Telecommunication Union)
General Secretariat – Sales Section, Place des Nations, CH-1211
Geneve 20, Switzerland
ITUDOC E-mail service: itudoc@itu.ch with HELP in body
http://info.itu.ch
E-mail: helpdesk@itu.ch

ISO (International Standards Organization)
ISO Sales, Case Postale 56, CH-1211 Geneve 20, Switzerland
http://www.iso.ch/welcome.html
E-mail: sales@isocs.iso.ch

ATM Forum
The ATM Forum, 2570 West El Camino Real, Suite 304, Mountain
View, CA, 94040 USA
Tel: +1 415 949 6700
Fax: +1 415 949 6705
http://www.atmforum.com
E-mail: info@atmforum.com

European Office:
The ATM Forum, Boulevard Saint-Michel 78, 1040 Brussels,
Belgium
Tel: +32 2 732 8505
Fax: +32 2 732 8485

Asia-Pacific Office: Hamamatsucho Suzuki Bldg 3F, 1-2-11
Hamamatsucho, Minato-ku, Tokyo 105, Japan
Tel: +81 3 3438 3694
Fax: +81 3 3438 3698
kyb01621@niftyserve.or.jp

IETF (Internet Engineering Task Force)
IAB (Internet Activities Board)
IRTF (Internet Research Task Force)
http://www.ietf.cnri.reston.va.us/home.html
RFC/Internet Draft Repositories:
Africa: ftp.is.co.za (196.4.160.8)
Europe: nic.nordu.net (192.36.148.17)
Pacific Rim: munnari.oz.au (128.250.1.21)
US East Coast: ds.internic.net (198.49.45.10)
US West Coast: ftp.isi.edu (128.9.0.32)
IETF Working Group minutes and archives
ftp://ietf.cnri.reston.va.us/ietf-mail-archive/*name of group*/

Technology-specific vendor and standards organizations

100VG AnyLAN Forum
Multivendor alliance to promote 100VG AnyLAN standard
Tel: +1 916 348 0212

Astral (Alliance for Strategic Token-Ring Advancement)
Multivendor alliance to guarantee interoperability among switched, full-duplex, and LAN emulation token-ring products

ADSL Forum
Multivendor forum to advance ADSL and VDSL technology and markets
303 Vintage Park Dr, Foster City, CA, 94404
Tel: +1 415 378 6680
Fax: +1 415 525 0182
E-mail: ADSLForum@ADSL.com
http://www.sbexpos/sbexpos/associations/adsl/index.html

AIW (APPN Implementers Workshop)
Industry consortium of venders developing APPN and SNA-related standards
http://www.raleigh.ibm.com/app/aiwhome.htm

DAVIC (Digital Audio Visual Council)
International consortium of 300+ cable TV, telecommunications, and computer firms working on a standard for digital video and audio
Tel: +1 201 966 4612
Fax: +1 201 377 2018
http://www.cnm.bell-atl.com/davic/davic.html

Desktop ATM25 Alliance
> Alliance for the 25 Mbps ATM standard which was chosen
> Tel: +1 408 383 1355

DVB (Digital Video Broadcasting)
> International project within European Broadcasting Union
> working to standardize digital broadcasting
> Tel: +41 22 717 2719
> Fax: +41 22 717 2727
> E-mail: dvb@pax.eunet.ch

Fast Ethernet Alliance
> Multivendor alliance to promote 100 Mbps Ethernet technologies
> Tel: +1 408 486 6832

Fiber Channel
> Fibre Channel Association (FCA)
> E-mail: fca@amcc.com
> http://www.amdahl.com/ext/CARP/FCA/FCA.html
> Telephone: +1 512 328 8422

Frame Relay Forum
> http://www.frforum.com
> 303 Vintage Park Dr, Foster City, CA, 94404
> Tel: +1 415 578 6980
> Fax: +1 415 525 0182
> E-mail: frf@sbexpos.com

Quantum Flow Control Consortium
> Multivendor alliance to promote a credit-based congestion
> avoidance mechanism in support of ABR
> c/o Ascom Nexion Inc., 1807 Park 270 Drive, Suite 350 Saint
> Louis, Missouri, 63141
> Tel: +1 314 579 6510
> Fax: +1 314 542 0495
> E-mail: folkerts@nexen.com

SATURN
> Multivendor group defining low-cost ATM hardware

SIG (SMDS Interest Group)
> http://www.zdexpos.com/zdexpos/associations/smds/home.html
> E-mail: smdstc@nsco.network.com

ESIG (European SMDS Interest Group)
> Merlin House, Station Road, Chepstow, NP6 5PB
> Tel: +44 291 620425

SONET Interoperability Forum
> http://www.adc.com/~don/sif/remote.html

TINA-C (Telecommunications Information Networking Architecture Consortium)
> http://www.tinac.com
> Tel: +1 908 758 2214
> Fax: +1 908 758 2865

Versit
> Standards for computer/telephone integration.
> Tel: +1 800 803 6240/+1 201 327 2804
> Fax: +1 800 803 6241/+1 201 327 4981
> http://www.versit.com

Standards bodies and professional organizations

ACM (Association for Computing Machinery)
> http:/www.acm.org

ANSI (American National Standards Institute)
> Attention: Customer Service, 11 West 42nd St, New York, NY 10036, USA
> http://www.ansi.org

CEPT
> Liaison Office, Seilerstrasse 22, CH-3008 Bern, Switzerland

ECMA (European Computer Manufacturers Association)
> 114 Rue du Rhone, CH-1204 Geneva, Switzerland
> http://www.ecma.ch

ETSI (European Telecommunications Standards Institute)
> F-06921 Sophia Antipolis CEDEX, France
> http://www.etsi.fr/infocentre
> Tel: +33 92 94 42 00

EURESCOM (European Institute for Research and Strategic Studies in Telecommunications)
> http://www.eurescom.com
> Tel: +49 6221 9890
> Fax: +49 6221 989 209

IEE (Institution of Electrical Engineers)
> PO Box 96, Stevenage, Herts SG1 2SD, UK
> http://www.iee.org.uk/
> gopher://gopher.iee.org.uk/
> Tel: +44 1438 313311
> Fax: +44 1438 742792

IEEE (Institute of Electrical and Electronic Engineers)
http://info.computer.org
gopher://stdsbbs.ieee.org:70/0/pub/ieeestds.html
Tel: +32 2 770 2198
Fax: +32 2 770 8505
E-mail: euro.ofc@computer.org
E-mail: cs.books@compmail.com

ISOC (Internet Society)
Tel: +1 800 468 9507/+1 703 648 9888
Fax: +1 703 648 9887
http://www.isoc.org
E-mail: membership@isoc.org or org-membership@isoc.org

Interoperability and performance test laboratories

Bradner
www.snci.com

EANTC
Tel: +49 30 314 21540
E-mail: herbert@prz.tu-berlin.de

Tolly Group
Tel: +1 908 528 3300
Fax: +1 908 528 1888
E-mail: info@tolly.com
http://www.tolly.com

UNH (University of New Hampshire InterOperability Lab)
Tel: +1 603 862 4532
http://www.iol.unh.edu
Also links to UNH consortiums: ATM, Fast Ethernet, and so on.

Some representative network contacts

The Canadian Network for the Advancement of Research, Industry and Education (CANARIE)   www.canarie.ca/ntn

Trans European Research and Education Network Association
www.terena.nl
Includes links to all European academic/research networks

United States Information Infrastructure Task Force (IITF)
iitf.doc.gov
Includes links to other US high-speed ATM testbeds

Other Global Information Infrastructure (GII) links via
www.spp.umich.edu/telecom/gii.html

Advanced Technology Demonstration Network (ATDnet)
disa11.disa.atd.net/disacfe/atdnet.arpa.html
US DoD ATM over SONET Test Network

MAGIC Gigabit Testbed   www.cse.ucsc.edu/research/baynet-atm

ATM-related corporate Web servers

This is not intended to be an exhaustive list of vendors involved with the
design, manufacture, or sales of ATM hardware, software, and test
equipment. We suggest www.*companyname*.com or www.*companyname*.
co.*country* for firms not listed here. Note that most phone numbers are
in the US. Corporate Web servers usually include a contact section
listing contact numbers by country. Note that the author has tried not to
use 1-800 numbers even if they are available.

3COM:	www.3com.com	+1 408 764 5000
Adaptec:	www.adaptec.com	+1 408 945 8600
ADC Kentrox:	www.kentrox.com	+1 503 526 6153
Agile Networks:	www.agile.com	+1 508 263 3600
Alantec:	www.alantec.com	+1 408 955 9000
Alcatel:	www.alcatel.com	+1 703 689 5047
Apple:	www.apple.com	+1 408 996 1010
Ascom Timplex:	www.timeplex.com	+1 201 391 1111
ATM Limited:	www.atml.co.uk or www.atminc.com	+44 1223 566 919
Bay Networks:	www.baynetworks.com	+1 508 436 3706
Cabletron:	www.ctron.com	+1 603 332 9400
Cascade:	www.cascade.com	+1 508 692 2600
Cellware:	www.cellware.de	+49 30 467 0820
Centillion (Bay):	www.baynetworks.com	+1 415 969 6700
Chipcom (3COM):	www.3com.com	+1 508 460 8900
Cisco Systems:	www.cisco.com	+1 408 526 4000
Com21:	www.com21.com	+1 415 335 1715
Connectware:	www.connectware.com	+1 214 997 4439
Digital:	www.digital.com	+1 508 692 2562
Digital Link:	www.dl.com	+1 408 745 4115
DSC:	www.dsc.com	+1 214 519 5644
Dynatech:	www.dynatech.com	+1 703 550 0011
Efficient:	www.efficient.com	+1 214 991 3884
Ericsson:	www.ericsson.com or ericsson.se	+46 8 719 0000
Fastcomm:	www.fastcomm.com	+1 800 521 2946
First Virtual:	www.fvc.com	+1 408 748 2219

Fore:	www.fore.com	+1 412 772 6600
Fujitsu:	www.fujitsu.co.jp or www.fujitsu.com	+1 919 790 2100
GDC:	www.gdc.com	+1 203 574 1118
GTE:	info.gte.com	+1 617 455 2058
Hewlett Packard:	www.hp.com	+1 514 856 6691
Hitachi:	www/hitachi.co.jp	+1 770 446 8820
IBM:	www.ibm.com	+1 919 254 2163
Insoft:	www.insoft.com	+1 717 730 9501
Intel:	www.intel.com	+1 503 264 7354
Interphase:	www.iphase.com	+1 214 919 9000
Ipsilon:	www.ipsilon.comu	+1 415 846 4600
Lannet: (Madge)	www.madge.com	+1 714 752 6638
Larscom:	www.larscom.com	+1 408 988 6600
Litton Fibercom:	www.fibercom.com	+1 540 342 6700
Lucent:	www.lucent. com	
Madge:	www.madge.com	+44 1753 661 000
Motorola:	www.motorola.com	+1 508 261 4000
MPR Teltech:	www.mpr.ca	+1 604 293 5122
National Semiconductor:	www.nsc.com	+1 408 721 5000
NEC:	www.nec.co.jp	+1 415 965 6476
NET-Adaptive:	www.net.com	+1 415 366 4400
Net2Net:	www.net2net.com	+1 508 568 0600
NetEdge:	www.netedge.com	+1 919 361 9000
Network General:	www.ngc.com	+1 415 473 2000
Network Systems:	www.network.com	+1 612 391 1145
Newbridge:	www.newbridge.com	+1 703 834 3600
Nokia:	www.nokia.com	+1 817 491 5800
NORTEL:	www.nortel.com	+1 919 992 4576
Novell:	www.novell.com	+1 415 616 7400
Oki:	www.oki.com or www.oki.co.jp	+81 3 3454 2111
Olicom:	www.olicom.dk	+1 214 423 7560
OnStream Networks:	www.onstream.com	+1 408 986 4243
Optical Data Systems:	www.ods.com	+1 214 234 6400
Optivision:	www.optivision.com	+1 415 855 0200
PMC-Sierra:	pmc-sierra.bc.ca	
Premisys:	www.premisys.com	+1 510 353 7681
Proteon:	www.proteon.com	+1 508 898 2800
Racal-Datacom:	www.racal.com	+1 305 846 1601
RAD:	www.rad.co.il (note: not rad.com)	+972 3 645 8118
Scorpio:	www.scorpio.com	+972 3 5339654
Siemens:	www.siemens.de	+49 89 722 25700
Silicon Graphics:	www.sgi.com	+1 800 800 7441
Standard		

Microsystems:	www.smc.com	+1 516 435 6000
Stratacom:	www.stratacom.com	+1 408 294 7600
Sun:	www.sun.com	+1 415 960 1300
SysKonnect:	www.syskonnect.de	+1 408 437 3840
Telco Systems:	www.telco.com	+1 510 490 3111
Thompson-CSF:	www.thomflex.fr	+33 1 4130 3091
Toshiba:	www.toshiba.com or www.toshiba.co.jp	+1 714 583 3000
Trillium:		+1 310 479 0500
Tut Systems:		+1 510 682 6510
UB:	www.ub.com	+1 408 496 0111
Wandel & Goltermann:	www.wg.com	+1 919 941 5730
Whitetree:	www.whitetree.com	+1 415 855 0855
Whittaker Communications:	www.whittaker.com	+1 408 565 6000
Xyplex:	www.xyplex.com	+1 508 952 4936
Xylan:	www.xylan.com	+1 818 880 3500
ZeitNet:	www.zeitnet.com	+1 408 986 9100

Telecom Web servers

Ameritech:	USA	www.aads.net
AT&T:	USA	www.att.com
Austria PTT:	Austria	www.telecom.at
Belcom:	Russia	www.belcom.net
Belgacom:	Belgium	www.belgacom.be
Bell Atlantic:	USA	www.ba.com
Bell Canada:	Canada	www.bell.ca
Bellcore:	USA	www.bellcore.com
BellSouth:	USA	www.bst.bls.com
British Telecom:	UK	www.bt.net
CrossComm:		www.crosscom.com +1 508 481 4060
CSELT:	Italy	www.cselt.stet.it
Deutsche Telekom:	Germany	www.dtag.de
France Telecom:	France	www.cnet.fr/somm_e.html
Helsinki Telephone:	Finland	www.hpy.fi
Hong Kong Telcom	Hong Kong	www.hkt.net
KDD:	Japan	www.kdd.co.jp
MCI:	USA	www.mci.com
MFS Communications:	USA	www.mfsdatanet.com
NetStar		www.netstar.com +1 612 943 8990
NTT:	Japan	www.ntt.jp/index.html
Nynex:	USA	www.niyp.com/corp.html

Pacific Bell:	USA	www.pacbell.com
Portugal PTT:	Portugal	www.telcom.pt
PTT Telecom:	Netherlands	www.ptt-telecom.nl
SBC:	USA	www.sbc.com
Singapore Telecom:	Singapore	www.singtel.com
Sprint:	USA	www.sprintlink.net
Stentor:	Canada	www.stentor.ca
Swiss PTT:	Switzerland	www.vptt.ch
Tampere Telephone:	Finland	www.tpo.fi
Tele Danmark:	Denmark	www.teledanmark.dk
Telecom Australia:	Australia	www.tansu.com.au
Telecom Eireann:	Ireland	www.telecom.ie
Telecom Finland:	Finland	www.tele.fi
Telecom Italia:	Italy	www.telecomitalia.interbusiness.it
Telefonica:	Spain	www.telefonica.es
Telenor:	Norway	www.telenor.no
Telkom South Africa:	South Africa	www.telkom.co.za
Teleglobe Canada:	Canada	www.teleglobe.ca
Telepost:	Norway	web.telepost.no
Telia:	Sweden	www.telia.se
Telstra:	Australia	www.telstra.com.au
Turku Telephone:	Finland	www.ttl.fi
Unisource:	Netherlands	www.unisource.nl
US West:	USA	www.uswest.com
Wiltel/LDDS:	USA	www.wiltel.com

Other on-line resources

Web search engines

Alta-vista	http://www.altavista.digital.com
Excite	http://www.excite.com
Inktomi	http://inktomi.berkeley.edu
Lycos	http://www.lycos.com
Yahoo	http://www.yahoo.com

ATM-related

Searchable list of ATM documents:
    http://www.research.att.com/biblio.html
Reference list of ATM standards documents:
    http://www.ipps.lsa.umich.edu/thumper.bellcore.com/pub/smq
Standards-FAQ:
    ftp//rtfm.mit.edu/pub/usenet/news.answers/standards-faq

ATM chip data at the Technical University of Chemnitz, Germany:
http://www.infotech.tu-chemnitz.de/~paetz/atm/
ATM At Work – sponsored site with ATM information:
http://www.atm.at-work.com/
ATM Knowledgebase
http://www.npac.syriedu/users/dpk/ATM-knowledgebase/ATM-
technology.html

Telecom-related

Meta-list of telecom information resources:
http://www.spp.umich.edu/telecom-info.html
Standards, search engines, FAQs, Internet data, publishers,
policy, standards bodies, laboratories, associations, testbeds,
corporations, and mailing list – links to most other sites
Meta-list of telecom and ATM sources:
http://www.cmpcmm.com/cc/
Source of organizations, corporations, standards, and projects
Meta-list of networking:
http://einstein.postech.ac.kr/people/qkim/qkim.html
Protocols, gigabit networks, ATM, communications, multimedia,
computer science, call for papers and participation, and so on.
ANSI Guide to Standards Organizations:
http://hsdwww.res.utc.com/std/gateway/orgindex.html
Links to other standards organizations
Reference list of standards documents:
http://www.cmpcmm.com/cc/standards.html
Frame Relay documents:
http://frame-relay.indiana.edu
Forum newsletters, implementation agreements, membership
listing, upcoming activities
ftp://frame-relay.indiana.edu:/pub/frame-relay
frame-relay-request@indiana.edu
SMDS documents:
http://www.cerf.net/smds.html
Ethernet Quick Reference Guide:
http://www.ots.utexas.edu/ethernet/ethernet.html
Includes 100BaseT

Internet-related

Searchable list of Internet mailing lists:
http://www.neosoft.com/internet/paml
Virtual library:
http://info.cern.ch/hypertext/datasources/bysubject/overview.html

Ipv6 (IPng)
   http://playground.sun.com/pub/ipng/html/ipng-main.html

Bookstores

Computer literacy
   http://www.clbooks.com

Periodicals and newsletters

Inter@ctive Week
   On-line publication covering multimedia, on-line services,
   broadband infrastructure, and politics.
   http://www.ziff.com/~intweek/web/iawhp1.html
   Phone: +1 516 229 3700
Broadband Communications News
   Newsletter covering business news and analysis of ATM, SMDS,
   and Frame Relay
   Publisher: Philips Business Information
   US Phone: +1 301 424 3338
   Fax: +1 301 309 3847
   E-mail: jwhalen@phillips.com
   UK Phone: +44 1438 742 424
   Fax: +44 1438 740 154
ATM Report
   Newsletter covering ATM standards, vendors, and developments
   Publisher: Broadband Publishing
   Phone: +1 301 816 7858
   Fax: +1 301 816 3021
   E-mail: 74551.1064@compuserve.com
ATM User
   Newsletter covering ATM standards, vendors, and developments
   Publisher: Jeffries Research
   Phone: +1 805 934 1056
   Fax: +1 805 934 2320
   E-mail: info@atm-user.com
ConneXions
   Newsletter covering internetworking/Internet/IETF issues and
   developments
   Publisher: Interop
   Phone: +1 415 578 6900
   Fax: +1 415 525 0194
   E-mail: connexions@interop.com

Madge ATM News Digest
   Daily digest of ATM industry
   Publisher: Madge
   E-mail: atmdgst@madge.com
Network World
   Phone: +1 508 875 6400
   E-mail: nwcirc@world.std.com
CMP Publications
   http://www.wais.com/techweb/corporate

Internet mailing Lists

ATM Forum discussions lists
   af-xpnni@atmforum.com (PNNI)
   af-xmpoa@atmforum.com (MPOA)
   af-xsecurity@atmforum.com (security)
ATM/Cell Relay
   Topics: Cell relay/ATM, general
   E-mail: cell-relay-request@indiana.edu
   Subscribe:
   Archives: http://cell-relay, indiana.edu
   cell-relay/archives/cell-relay.CellRelay.html
ATM Contributions
   Topics: ATM contributions
   E-mail: atm_contrib@sun.com
   Subscribe: atm_contrib-request@sun.com
Routing over Large Clouds – IETF
   Topics: Methods to optimize routing over NBMA - i.e., NHRP
   E-mail: rolc@nexen.com
   Subscribe: rolc-request@nexen.com
   Archive: ftp://ietf.cnri.reston.va.us/ietf-mail-archive/rolc/
   ftp://ftp.nexen.com/pub/rolc/
IP Over ATM – IETF
   Topics: IP over ATM – data models
   E-mail: ip-atm@nexen.com
   Subscribe: majordomo@nexen.com
   http://cell-relay.indiana.edu/cell-relay/archives/IPATM/
   IPATM.html
   http://www.com21.com/pages/ietf.html
RSVP
   Topics: Resource Reservation, Integrated Services
   E-mail: rsvp@isi.edu
   Subscribe: rsvp-request@isi.edu

Integrated Services
>   Topics: Integrated services over the Internet
>   E-mail: int-serv@isi.edu
>   Subscribe: int-serv-request@isi.edu

Obtaining organizational names

United States

To obtain an organization name for use in constructing a US DCC format
NSAP, request a registration packet from ANSI at the following address:
>   ANSI
>   11 West 42nd Street, 13th Floor
>   New York, New York, 10036
>
>   Tel: +1 212 642 4884
>   Fax: +1 212 398 0023
>   E-mail: MMAAS@ansi.org;

Canada

>   COSIRA Administrator
>   CGI Group Inc.
>   275 Slater St, 19th Floor
>   Ottawa, Ontario K1P 5H9
>   Tel: +1 613 236 7803
>   Fax: +1 613 234 6934
>   E-mail: (X.400) c=ca; admd=attmail; prmd=cgigroup; o=cosira;
>   s=administrator

United Kingdom

>   Administered by the UK Registration Authority (UKRA). Send
>   form DCC1 (Annex G of BS 7306) to:
>   Mr R Elliot
>   Secretary to UK DCC Committee
>   FEI, Russell Sq. House,
>   10–12 Russell Square, London, WC1B 5EE

Glossary (ATM from A to Z)

The ATM Forum has an acronym handbook available at http://www.atmforum.com as well as a glossary in the *ATM User Network Interface (UNI) Specification Verson 3.1* (ATM Forum, 1995a). Some of the Web sites referenced in Appendix C also contain extensive glossaries.

Words in *italics* in this glossary refer to other entries elsewhere in the glossary.

100 BaseT A 100 Mbps Ethernet technology based on the 10 Mbps CSMA/CD mechanism.

100 VG-AnyLAN A 100 Mbps LAN technology supporting both Ethernet and Token Ring applications. The VG-AnyLAN incorporates a priority switching scheme which allows a network administrator to set a priority for an end-system.

802.1q A VLAN mechanism for shared or switched media based on frame tagging.

802.3 (Ethernet) A LAN standard based on the Carrier Sense Multiple Access/Collision Detection (*CSMA/CD*) mechanism whereby an end-station will attempt to send when it has data. If it detects a collision on the network, it will cease transmission for a certain interval.

802.5 (Token Ring) A token-based LAN where each end-station will wait for receipt of the 'token' before transmitting.

802.6 (Distributed Queue Dual Bus) IEEE standard for a DQDB-based MAN. See *DQDB*.

802.10 A shared-medium security mechanism which may be used to implement closed user groups over *FDDI*, and other shared media, supporting *VLANs*. Each data frame is prepended with a data link identifier unique to the closed user group.

802.14 A physical layer and *MAC* standard for use over hybrid fiber-coax networks found within the cable TV industry.

ABR (Available Bit Rate) An ATM service class where the network makes a 'best effort' to meet the application's bandwidth requirements. It differs from *UBR* in that it uses a feedback mechanism whereby the network informs a source of an acceptable transmission rate. If the source complies, the network guarantees a low *CLR*.

ACR (Allowed Cell Rate) The rate at which an end-system is permitted to send, determined by the rate contained within the *ABR RM* cells.

AHFG (ATM Host Functional Group). ATM-connected host within MPOA.

ANSI (American National Standards Institute) A US standards organization. ANSI may submit proposals to the ITU.

API (Application or ATM Programming Interface) A defined programming interface between an application and the system internetworking software or hardware. The ATM Forum's SAA SWG is responsible for defining the semantics of an API.

APPN (Advanced Peer-to-Peer Networking) IBM's internetworking architecture to replace SNA. APPN is more suited to dynamic, multiple-media networks.

ATM (Asynchronous Transfer Mode) A switching and multiplexing technology based on the segmentation of voice, video, and data traffic into equal length cells which are then interleaved over a physical connection in a time-asynchronous manner. This contrasts with *TDM* where different traffic sources are assigned fixed timeslots.

ATM address An end-system identifier based either on the ISDN-format E.164 address for public ATM networks or on an NSAP-format address for private ATM.

ATM ARP The address resolution mechanism between an ATM end-system and an RFC 1577 (Laubach, 1993) ATM address resolution server. The ATM ARP is used to resolve IP network layer addresses to ATM addresses. ATM ARP servers will evolve to *NHRP* servers.

ATM DSU (Data Service Unit) A unit external to an ATM end-system used to convert between the HDLC-based ATM DXI and the ATM UNI by segmenting data frames into ATM cells.

ATM Forum A multivendor organization with the task of adapting international standards into implementation agreements, or developing standards where none exist. The organization consists of equipment vendors, service providers, research organizations, and end users.

ATM layer The layer between the *AAL* and the physical layer containing ATM cells. This is where switching of ATM cells is accomplished.

ATM switch Intermediate system optimized to switch ATM cells. Divided into four classes: workgroup, campus/enterprise, central office access, and central office. The latter three classes are usually equipped with multiservice interfaces, such as circuit, video, Frame Relay, *SMDS*, and possibly LAN.

B-ICI (Broadband Inter-Carrier Interface) The ATM trunking interface between two service providers.

B-ISDN Broadband ISDN. A high-speed network providing voice, data, and video services which evolved from ISDN. ATM was chosen by the ITU-T as the technology to deliver B-ISDN.

BECN (Backward Explicit Congestion Notification) Bit in the Frame Relay header set by a switch in frames traveling in the reverse direction of any network congestion. This allows quick action by the source.

Bellcore (Bell Communications Research) Research organization originally associated with the Regional Bell Operating Companies (RBOCs) in the US.

Bridging Used to interconnect two of the same or dissimiliar LANs at the link layer. Bridging is transparent to the network layer and above and does not segment the broadcast domain.

Broadcast media An environment in which one network layer host address is reserved for broadcast to all members of the *LIS*.

BT (Burst Tolerance) The number of cells which an ATM source may send back-to-back. When discussing *CAC*, this is the depth of the second leaky bucket.

BUS (Broadcast and Unknown Server). A component within *LANE* which receives and then retransmits all broadcast, multicast, and unknown traffic over the ELAN.

CAC (Connection Admission Control) Actions taken by the ATM network to accept or reject a connection request based on its *QoS* requirements, and then to route this connection across the network.

CAP (Competitive Access Provider) Alternate service provider competing with the traditional PTT/Telco.

CAS (Channel Associated Signaling) Voice signaling based on bits taken from voice timeslots, used by many PABXs.

CAT-3 (Category 3 UTP) Unshielded Twisted Pair standard for supporting voice and low-bandwidth data.

CAT-5 (Category 5 UTP) Unshielded Twisted Pair Standard for supporting high-bandwidth data.

CBR (Constant Bit Rate) An ATM service class providing for the support of constant bit streams such as those generated by PABXs. The CBR class specifies a *PCR*, *CDV*, and *CLR*, thus guaranteeing bandwidth and QoS.

CCITT (Comite Consultatif Internationale de Telegraphique et Telephonique) Consultative Committee on International Telegraphy and Telephony. See *ITU*.

CCR (Current Cell Rate) The currently acceptable transmission rate for an end-system as defined by *RM* cells within *ABR*.

CCS (Common Channel Signaling) Voice signaling based on use of a separate signaling channel, used by ISDN PABXs.

CDDI (Copper Distributed Data Interface) Original name for the FDDI TP-PMD.

CDV (Cell Delay Variation) A QoS parameter specifying the variance in delay between ATM cells. The maximum acceptable CDV is referred to as the Cell Delay Variation Tolerance, or CDVT.

Cell The 53-byte basic information unit within an ATM network. An ATM cell consists of a 5-byte ATM header containing address information and a 48-byte ATM payload which contains the user data.

CER (Cell Error Ratio) Ratio of errored cells to total cells across a *VCC* or *VPC*.

CES (Circuit Emulation Service) ATM Forum service supporting *VCCs* which emulate a *CBR* dedicated circuit.

CIR (Committed Information Rate) The average transmission rate which a user is provided with for Frame Relay service.

Circuit Steering Redirection of ATM traffic to a port for monitoring. Also known as 'snooping'.

Classical IP and ARP over ATM A standardized model where ATM acts as a high-quality link layer transport for higher-layer protocols. The Classical model is defined in RFCs 1577 (Laubach, 1993)and 1483 (Heinanen, 1993), and was the first deployed ATM architecture.

CLP (Cell Loss Priority) A one-bit field in the ATM cell header specifying whether or not the cell is more (CLP = 1) or less (CLP = 0) likely to be discarded by an ATM network experiencing congestion.

CLR (Cell Loss Ratio) Ratio of lost cells to total cells transmitted across a *VCC* or *VPC*.

CLSF (Connectionless Server Function) The server within an *SMDS/CBDS* over ATM network which maintains address mappings for data forwarding and emulates the broadcast/multicast function.

CMIP (Common Management Information Protocol) Standard for the message formats and procedures used to exchange management information within the OSI environment. In most internetworks, *SNMP* is used in place of CMIP.

CMIS (Common Management Information Services). Provides management services to CMIP.

CNM (Customer Network Management). Ability of a customer to monitor and possibly control a VPN.

Congestion control A method by which congestion across the ATM network is reduced. Congestion control schemes may be based on fields within the ATM cell header (*CLP*, *EFCI* within the *PTI*) or may be based on more sophisticated mechanisms between ATM end-systems and ATM switches. The ATM Forum has developed a mechanism based on rate control for *ABR*-type traffic.

Congestive collapse A state where the throughput across a congested ATM network drops towards zero due to retransmission of data. This is avoided by deploying ATM switches with effective buffering and traffic control mechanisms.

Connectionless service A service where no end-to-end connection is established. Instead, all data is sent over a *VC* to a connectionless server which then establishes a connection to the destination. Switched Multimegabit Data Service (*SMDS*) and Connectionless Broadband Data Service (*CBDS*) over AAL3/4 are two examples of this service.

Connection-oriented services An end-to-end connection is signaled and established prior to data transmission. Classical IP over ATM using AAL5 is an example of a connection-oriented service.

CPCS (Common Part Convergence Sublayer) A sublayer within the ATM *AAL* providing for packet framing and error detection. Used by all services which use the specific AAL.

CPE (Customer Premise Equipment) A term for the networking equipment located at the customer's site.

CRC (Cyclic Redundancy Check) A checksum appended to *CS-PDUs* to ensure that the upper-layer data has not been corrupted.

CRS (Cell Relay Service) Most basic of ATM services supporting the exchange of cells between ATM-connected end-systems.

CS (Convergence Sublayer) The sublayer of the ATM AAL where traffic is adapted based on its type before undergoing segmentation into cells (*SAR* process). The CS includes the *CPCS* and the *SSCS*.

CS-PDU (Convergence Sublayer Protocol Data Unit) The information frame generated by the *CS* before undergoing *SAR*.

CSMA/CD (Carrier Sense Multiple Access/Collision Detection) See *802.3*.

CTD (Cell Transfer Delay) Average transit delay of cells across a *VCC* or *VPC*.

D*BW (Delay Bandwidth Product) The amount of data in flow across a link, influenced by the delay and bandwidth of the connection. Used to calculate necessary buffer sizes for flow control. Also RTT*BT, since we actually refer to the Round Trip Time for Delay.

DAN (Desktop Area Network) Term used to describe an ATM network interconnecting elements of a workstation or PC (for example, processor, disk storage, display).

DE (Discard Eligibility) One bit field in Frame Relay header. When set to 1, frames are more likely for discard under network congestion.

DFFG (Default Forwarder Functional Group) Responsible for default path forwarding of intra-IASG data within MPOA. Paired with the ICFG, MARS/MCS.

DHCP (Dynamic Host Configuration Protocol) Allows end systems to automatically set parameters such as IP addresses from a server.

DQDB (Distributed Queue Dual Bus) A networking technology based on the transmission of cells (known as slots) on two buses. Defined as IEEE 802.6, and used for non-ATM *SMDS* networks.

DS-0 (Digital Signal Level 0) 64 Kbps level of North American Digital Hierarchy.

DS-1 (Digital Signal Level 1) 1.544 Mbps level of North American Digital Hierarchy, supporting 24 DS-0 signals. Sometimes called T1.

DS-3 (Digital Signal Level 3) 44.736 Mbps level of North American Digital Hierarchy, supporting 28 DS-1 signals. Sometimes called T3.

DTE (Data Terminal Equipment) Equipment at the customer end of a circuit. The network end is sometimes called the DCE.

DTL (Designated Transit List) PNNI-generated list of ATM switches to be transited across an ATM network.

DXI (Data Exchange Interface) An HDLC-based ATM interface defined between a packet-based ATM end-system and an external *ATM DSU* supporting the *ATM UNI*.

E.164 Public network addressing standardized by the ITU. Used by both N-ISDN, *SMDS*, and public ATM networks.

E1 (European Signal Level 1) 2.048 Mbps transport rate within the European *PDH* hierarchy, supporting 32 x 64 Kbps channels.

E-2 (European Signal Level 2) 8.192 Mpbs transport rate within the European *PDH* hierarchy, supporting 4 E-1 signals. E-2 is not widely deployed.

E-3 (European Signal Level 3) 34.368 Mbps transport rate within the European *PDH* hierarchy, supporting 16 E-1 or 4 E-2 signals. At high data rates, E-4 at 140 Mbps is also defined.

EDFG (Edge Device Functional Group) Multilayer LAN switch within MPOA.

EFCI (Explicit Forward Congestion Indication) Bit in *PTI* field of the ATM cell header which may be set by a switch under times of congestion. The EFCI is one form of *ABR* service.

EIA (Electronic Industries Association) US standards organization.

ELAN (Emulated LAN) The ATM segment of a Virtual LAN (*VLAN*)based on the ATM Forum *LANE* standard. A VLAN consists of an ELAN segment along with traditional (sometimes called 'legacy') LAN segments.

End-system ITU/OSI terminology for a system capable of sending or receiving data. An end-system will normally implement all seven layers of the protocol stack. End-systems are connected via intermediate-systems (see *IS*).

EPD (Early Packet Discard) A mechanism by which ATM switches discard AAL5 frames when network congestion is imminent. This avoids unwanted congestion which may prevent a switch supporting existing connection and helps avoid *congestive collapse*. (See also *TPD*).

ER (Explicit Rate Mode) One form of feedback under ABR service which defines the rate at which the end-system may transmit. A switch supporting this mode will indicate this rate in either forward or backward Resource Management cells.

ESI (End System Identifier) The 6 octet field within the ATM NSAP format address which identifies an end system. Equivalent to the MAC address of the device.

ETSI (European Telecommunications Standards Institute) Develops standards for use by service providers within Europe.

Fast Ethernet Generic term for 100 Mbps Ethernet technology, although it normally refers to 802.3u.

FDDI (Fiber Distributed Data Interface) ANSI-standardized 100 Mbps networking technology capable of LAN and *MAN* distances.

FECN (Forward Explicit Congestion Notification) Bit in Frame Relay header set by a congested switch in frames traveling in the direction of the congestion.

Firewall router or firewall A router which is configured to block certain traffic in order to provide security to systems internal to the management domain of which the router is a member.

Flow control A congestion control mechanism that results in an ATM system implementing flow control.

Frame Relay Forum Organization composed of Frame Relay vendors, service providers, and users. Relevant efforts include standardizing FR-ATM interfaces and services.

FUNI (Frame UNI) Frame-based interface to ATM supporting signaling and QoS. Replaces the ATM-DXI.

GCAC (Generic Connection Admission Control) A form of CAC used by PNNI when routing a connection request.

GCRA (Generic Cell Rate Algorithm) Traffic shaping algorithm based on a *VC*'s traffic parameters to shape the traffic within a VC while enforcing traffic limits.

GFC (Generic Flow Control) A four-bit field within the ATM cell header which may be used to identify whether or not an ATM system implements congestion control. At present, the GFC field is unused.

Header The first five bytes of an ATM cell containing a *VC* identifier consisting of a *VPI* and a *VCI*, along with fields for *HEC, CLP, GFC, CRC,* and *PTI*.

HEC (Header Error Check) A one-byte field within the ATM cell header providing for error detection. If an error is detected, the cell will be discarded before undergoing reassembly.

Host An end-system which will originate traffic and act as a destination but will not forward traffic.

IASG (Internetwork Address Sub-Group) A LIS, LAG, or other Layer 3 subnet within MPOA. Not necessarily a MAC broadcast domain.

ICFG (IASG Coordination Functional Group) Registers IASG members and runs the DFFG within MPOA. Paired with the DFFG, MARS/MCS.

ICR (Initial Cell Rate) The rate at which an *ABR* end-system will begin transmitting before receiving the *ER* via *RM* cells.

IEEE (Institute of Electrical and Electronic Engineers) US electronics industry standards body. IEEE projects include the 802.x series of recommendations.

IETF (Internet Engineering Task Force) TCP/IP-focused international standards organization.

IISP (Interim Interswitch Signaling Protocol) Formerly known as PNNI Phase 0. An ATM Forum standardized multivendor trunking protocol supporting signaling and simple rerouting. The IISP does not support topology discovery, hierarchical addressing, or *QoS*.

ILMI (Interim Local Management Interface) ATM Forum *SNMP*-based network management interface between an end-system and an ATM switch for status and configuration reporting as well as registering/de-registering ATM addresses.

IP address resolution protocol A protocol which provides a mapping (or the inverse mapping) between an IP address and a media-specific address.

I-PNNI (Integrated Private Network–Network Interface) Use of PNNI for both ATM and Layer 3 routing.

IP routing protocol A protocol operating at Layer 3 which maps IP addresses to the best forwarding addresses; in most cases the final destination may not be reached directly. A routing protocol (IS-IS, OSPF, BGP4, and so on) will react quickly to topology changes. Counterparts to IP routing exist at other layers of the reference model (see *PNNI*).

IPX (Internetwork Packet Exchange) Novell-developed Layer 3 protocol.

IS (Intermediate system) ITU/OSI terminology for a system capable of relaying data between end-systems. An intermediate-system may implement only those layers of the protocol stack critical to its function (that is, Layers 1, 2, and 3).

ISDN (Integrated Services Digital Network) International digital network supporting voice, video, and data over multiples of 64 Kbps circuits.

ITU (International Telecommunications Union) International standards body including all PTTs under UN treaty. The group responsible for communications standards is the ITU Telecommunications Standards Sector (TSS), formerly the CCITT.

J-2 (Japanese signaling level 2) Second level of the Japanese *PDH* hierarchy, supporting 36.312 Mbps.

JPEG (Joint Photographic Experts Group) Industry organization focusing on the storage and transmission of still images. See *MPEG*.

LAG (Local Address Group) Defines a set of ATM-connected systems which may establish direct connections between each other.

LAN switch A Layer 2 switching system using the contents of the frame MAC header to perform forwarding decisions. Packets between different source and destination ports may be switched quite rapidly in parallel. LAN switches may be extended to include multilayer functionality.

LANE (LAN Emulation or LAN Emulation Service) An ATM Forum standard providing for the support of native LAN protocols across an ATM network by emulating the *MAC* protocol. LANE defines a single Virtual LAN (*VLAN*) consisting of traditional LAN segments and an Emulated LAN (*ELAN*) segment across the ATM network. Routers will connect multiple VLANs. LANE provides for ATM-attached systems acting as *LECs* communicating with an *LECS*, *LES*, and *BUS* across an ELAN.

Leaky bucket algorithm A flow control algorithm whereby a 'bucket' receives credits at a rate equal to a user's traffic-shaping parameters (that is, a VC's average rate). Overtime, credits will be used at this average rate, though the bucket provides for bursts.

LEC (LAN Emulation Client) The *LANE* process residing in LAN switches, routers, PCs, and workstations attached to the LAN Emulation Service. This provides *VLAN* functionality to non-ATM-aware end-systems residing on traditional LAN segments connected to LAN switches and routers.

LECS (LAN Emulation Configuration Server) A component within *LANE* providing basic configuration information for a *LEC* that wishes to participate in LANE, allowing network administrators to control which *LECs* may join which *VLANs*. The most basic information returned to the LEC is the location of the *LES*.

LES (LAN Emulation Server) A server function within *LANE* providing for *LEC* registration, *MAC* to ATM address resolution, and security management of a *VLAN*.

LIS (Logical IP Subnetwork) Used to describe a network where all devices have direct connectivity with each other while adhering to the IP subnet model. See *LAG*.

LLC (Logical Link Control) The upper half of the data link layer (Layer 2) often used to identify different Layer 3 protocols sharing a common medium.

LNNI (LAN Emulation Network-to-Network Interface) The interface between two *LANE* domains.

LUNI (LANE User-to-Network Interface) The interface between an *LEC* and the server processes (*LECS*, *LES*, and *BUS*) within the LAN Emulation Service (see *LANE*).

MAC (Media Access Control) The lower half of the data link layer (Layer 2) defining topology independent access control.

MAN (Metropolitan Area Network) A network spanning a city or region, usually providing *SMDS* or ATM speed services.

MARS (Multicast Address Resolution Server) Registry within the Classical model and MPOA for ATM NSAP to Layer 3 multicast address mappings.

MBS (Maximum Burst Size) The number of cells at the peak cell rate which may traverse an ATM *VC*.

MCR (Minimum Cell Rate) The minimum transmission rate which the network guarantees to an *ABR* end-system. This equates to a field in the *RM* cell below which the *ER* may not be set.

MCS/MCS+ (Multicast Server) Device for efficient forwarding of multicast data within the Classical model and MPOA.

MCTD (Mean Cell Transfer Delay) The average delay for ATM cells across an ATM connection.

MIB (Management Information Base) A database of device configuration and performance information which is acted upon by SNMP or CMIP.

MPEG (Motion Picture Experts Group) Industry organization standardizing methods of coding and transmitting video. The international standard for broadcast coding is known as MPEG-2. See *JPEG*.

MPOA (Multiprotocol over ATM) Standard which defines how routers, LAN switches, and hosts running multiple Layer 3 protocols may optimize forwarding paths and multicasting across ATM while taking advantage of ATM *QoS* capabilities.

Multilayer switch A switch capable of performing both Layer 2 and Layer 3 forwarding of data but not generally including the processing which generates the forwarding information. Instead, the switch will obtain this data from a central processor (often located on a router) via a route distribution protocol.

Multiprotocol Encapsulation over ATM RFC 1483 (Heinanen, 1993) defines a method of encapsulating multiprotocol network layer data over ATM via one of two formats: LLC/SNAP or virtual circuit multiplexing where a given network layer protocol is assigned a *VC*. RFC 1483 provides the encapsulation basis for the Classical model defined in RFC 1577 (Laubach, 1993).

NBMA (Non-Broadcast Multiple Access Network) A network where direct access from any member of one LIS to any member of any other *LIS* is possible, but broadcast is not possible or practical due to scaling issues. NARP and *NHRP* are two methods of optimizing routing over NBMA networks. See *LAG*.

NDIS (Network Driver Interface Specification) Industry standard interface between higher layer networking software and the network interface card.

NEBS (Network Equipment Building Standards) Defines physical requirements for equipment installed in US Telco central offices.

NHRP (Next Hop Resolution Protocol) A protocol optimizing routing across *NBMA* networks, allowing end-systems to open *VCs* across *LIS* boundaries.

NIC (Network Interface Card) Interface hardware allowing a host to connect to a network.

NMS (Network Management System) The hardware and software supporting network management (*OAM&P*) functions.

NNI (Network-Node Interface or Network-to-Network Interface) The NNI is better characterized as a switch-to-switch interface. The ATMF has defined a Private-NNI (*P-NNI*) to connect switches within a single management domain. The *B-ICI* may also be considered as a class of the NNI, though between service providers.

NRZ (Non-Return to Zero) Line signal encoding of 1s and 0s to avoid generating a DC component.

NSAP (Network Services Access Point) OSI standard for network addressing based on a 20-octet hierarchical address structure. ATM uses this structure for private network and some public network addressing.

NVoD (Near Video on Demand) Technique of offering video programs to users at preset times. Also known as 'staggercasting.' See *VoD*.

OAM (Operation Administration and Maintenance) Management framework defined by the ITU. OAM cells are special purpose ATM cells exchanged between an ATM end-system and an ATM switch providing for network fault and performance management, analysis, and fault isolation.

OAM&P (Operations, Administration, Maintenance, and Provisioning) Describes the functions, services, and protocols used to operate and maintain an internetwork.

OC (Optical Carrier) The transmission unit within *SONET*, based on an optical signal of $n \times 51.84$ Mbps. OC-3c ('c' for concatenated) is interoperable with *SDH's* STM-1.

Octet Eight bits, most of the time referred to as a 'byte.'

ODI (Open Datalink Interface) Standard interface between Novel Netware software and the network interface card.

OSI reference model A seven-layer reference model for internetworking. Each layer interacts only with the layers directly below and above it; layers interact virtually between *end-systems* which are connected by intermediate systems (see *IS*). The layers include: physical, data link, network, transport, session, presentation, and application.

OSS (Operation Support System) Management Systems in conformance with the TMN model providing for element, network, service and business management.

Payload The 48-byte segment of the ATM cell containing user data. Any adaptation of user data via the AAL will take place within the payload.

PBX (Private Branch Exchange) A CPE telephone exchange which may be connected to the traditional N-ISDN network or to an ATM *CES*.

PCR (Peak Cell Rate) The maximum cell transmission rate within a VC.

PDH (Plesiosynchronous Transmission Hierarchy) A public transmission hierarchy based on a non-synchronous alignment of *octets* at different levels of multiplexing. PDH is only bit-synchronous. PDH networks are in the process of being replaced with SDH networks. Examples of PDH transmission rates include E1 and E3.

PDU (Protocol Data Unit) The basic unit of information at a layer of the networking stack which is exchanged with a peer entity which contains control information and user data.

PGL (Peer Group Leader) ATM switch within a PNNI peer group which summarizes reachability within the group and sends this information up the routing hierarchy.

PHY (Physical Layer) The layer of the protocol stack where the ATM layer is encapsulated for transmission over a given physical medium. The physical layer consists of a medium-independent sublayer providing convergence and a medium-dependent sublayer tied to a given physical medium type and rate.

PICS (Protocol Implementation Conformance Statement) Document prepared by vendors outlining compliance to ATM Forum standards.

PIM (Protocol Independent Multicast) Internet protocol providing for efficient routing of multicast data across an internetwork.

PLCP (Physical Layer Convergence Protocol) The protocol within the *TC* sublayer defining the method by which ATM cells will be formatted for a given transmission facility. Also, a specific method to map ATM and *DQDB* cells into *PDH* frames.

POH (Path Overhead) Header in the payload of a *SONET* or *SDH* frame which defines the structure and content of the *STS* or *STM* payload.

PMD (Physical Media Dependent) The *TC* sublayer relating to the actual transmission rate and technology. The PMD defines encoding techniques, optical wavelengths, fiber types, and so on.

PNNI (Private Network–Network Interface) The interswitch interface within a private ATM domain. The PNNI trunking protocol providing for hierarchical ATM-layer routing and *QoS* support. (See *IISP*.)

Point-to-Multipoint (pt-mpt) A unidirectional ATM connection with one root end-point and multiple destinations, or leaves.

Point-to-Point (pt-pt) A uni- or bi-directional ATM connection with only two end-points.

Policing An ATM switch will police the data on an incoming *VC* to determine whether it is in compliance with the user's service contract (which specifies a *QoS*).

PTI (Payload Type Identifier) A three-bit field within the ATM cell header indicating the AAL used, whether congestion has been experienced (*EFCI*), and whether or not the cell contains *OAM* information. When an AAL5 frame passes through *SAR*, the PTI within the last cell identifies the end of this AAL5 frame.

PTT (Postal Telegraph and Telephone Company) Term used to describe a government-operated phone and postal provider in many countries. When deregulated, a PTT may be known as a Telco or public service provider.

PVC (Permanent Virtual Connection) A pre-configured logical connection between two ATM systems. This contrasts with *SVCs*.

Q.2931 ITU-T signaling standard for *B-ISDN* and used by the ATM Forum's UNI 3.1/4.0 to signal *SVCs*.

Q.931 ITU-T signaling standard for ISDN which provides the basis for both Frame Relay and *Q.2931* signaling.

Q.933 ITU-T signaling standard for Frame Relay *SVCs*.

Q.93B Older ITU-T draft signaling standard for *B-ISDN* and used within the ATM Forum's UN 3.0. Replaced by *Q.2931*.

Quality of Service (QoS) The requirements of an ATM *VC* in terms of bandwidth, cell loss, delay, and jitter.

RBB (Residential Broadband) Group within ATM forum developing physical layer standards for ATM delivery to homes and small businesses.

RDF (Rate Decrease Factor) The amount by which an *ABR end-system* is told to decrease its transmission rate via *RM* cells.

RFC 1209 (The Transmission of IP Datagrams over the SMDS Service) Specifies the encapsulation of multiprotocol data for transmission over an *SMDS* network. *SMDS/CBDS* over ATM uses this encapsulation in combination with AAL3/4 and a Connectionless Server Functionality (*CLS*).

RFC 1483 (Multiprotocol Encapsulation over ATM Adaptation Layer 5) Specifies the encapsulation of multiprotocol data for transmission over an ATM network. RFC 1483 makes use of AAL5 in the support of *PVCs* and *SVCs*. The two methods defined in this RFC are *VC* muxing (each protocol uses its own VC) and LLC/SNAP encapsulation (different protocols are identified by a different LLC/SNAP header and are sent over the same VC).

RFC 1490 (Multiprotocol Interconnect over Frame Relay) Specifies the encapsulation of multiprotocol data for transmission over Frame Relay. Frame Relay over ATM uses this encapsulation in combination with AAL5.

RFC 1577 (Classical IP and ARP over ATM) Specifies an architecture for the support of IP over ATM, also defining an ATM *ARP* server. RFC 1577 relies on RFCs 1483, 1626, and 1755.

RFC 1626 (IP MTU over ATM AAL5) Defines a 9180-octet Maximum Transmission Unit (MTU) over ATM.

RFC 1755 (ATM Signaling Support for IP over ATM) Specifies the method of signaling SVCs within the Classical model.

RFFG (Remote Forwarder Functional Group) Responsible for default path forwarding of inter-IASG data within MPOA. Paired with the RSFG, ICFG/DFFG/MARS/MCS.

RFI (Request for Information) Document prepared by a potential user to gather vendor product, price, and service data.

RFP (Request for Procurement) Extends upon the *RFI* by requesting contractually binding product capabilities and pricing information.

RIF (Rate Increase Factor) Amount by which a source may increase its transmission rate under ABR.

RM (Resource Management Cell) Special ATM cell used to regulate traffic flow within the *ABR* service.

ROLC (Routing over Large Clouds) Group within IETF developing standards to optimize routing across NBMA networks.

Router An intermediate system within an internetwork capable of generating Layer 3 (network layer) forwarding information by running a routing protocol (IS-IS, OSPF, E-IGRP, and so on) and then forwarding data packets based on this information.

Routing Layer 3 (network layer) forwarding of datagrams based on a calculated routing table.

Routing table Information generated by the Layer 3 path calculation function in routers to determine the proper route for a datagram.

RR (Relative Rate Mode) A mode within *ABR* whereby an ATM switch sets a bit within a forward or reverse *RM* cell to indicate congestion. Effective for *end-systems* which have not implemented the Explicit Rate (ER) mode.

RSFG (Route Server Functional Group) Runs Layer 3 routing protocols and forwards reachability information to MPOA EDFGs (sometimes known as Multilayer Switches). Paired with the RFFG, ICFG/DFFG/MARS/MCS.

RSVP (Resource Reservation Protocol) Allows PCs and workstations to request QoS from a network. RSVP requests may be mapped to ATM signaling requests.

RTT (Round Trip Time) The amount of time required for flow control information to traverse the route from the source to the destination and then back to the source. See $D*BW$.

SAP (Service Access Point) Reference point between the networking stack and applications within an *end-system*.

SAR (Segmentation and Reassembly Sublayer) The sublayer where *PDUs* are segmented and rebuilt into/from ATM cells.

SAR-PDU (Segmentation and Reassembly Protocol Data Unit) Information which has been segmented by the *SAR* sublayer.

SCR (Sustainable Cell Rate) The maximum burst rate which a *VC* may maintain.

SDH (Synchronous Digital Hierarchy) A transmission hierarchy based on a synchronous alignment of bits at different levels of multiplexing. Though originally deployed in public networks as a replacement for the older *PDH*, SDH is now deployed within local ATM networks. An example of an SDH transmission rate is *STM-1*.

SDU (Service Data Unit) Information payload within a *PDU*.

SEAL (Simple and Efficient Adaptation Layer) ATM AAL5 was originally defined as SEAL, providing adaptation with no additional cell payload overhead for data traffic.

SG (Study Group) A technical working group within the ITU-T, with each SG identified by a unique number.

SIG (SMDS Interest Group); also ESIG Organization composed of vendors, service providers, and end users to promote *SMDS* use and standards. The European group is known as ESIG.

Signaling The procedure used to establish a connection over the ATM network. Signaling within ATM is based on *Q.2931*; this has been adapted by the ATM Forum as UNI 3.1./4.0. Some signaling implementations are also based on UNI 3.0 derived from an earlier ITU draft.

SIP (SMDS Interface Protocol) The layering model within the SNI. SIP1 is physical, SIP2 is cell and *DQDB*, while SIP3 is the DXI.

SMDS (Switched Multimegabit Data Service) A connectionless public data service developed by Bellcore for multimegabit data rates. SMDS when operated across ATM is also known as CBDS.

SNI (SMDS Network Interface) All layers of the interface between an end user and the *SMDS* network.

SNMP (Simple Network Management Protocol) Management protocol for the *OAM&P* of internetworks. Originally designed for TCP/IP devices but now extended to other products and functions.

SONET (Synchronous Optical Network) The North American variant of the *SDH*. An example of a SONET transmission rate is *STS*-3c.

SSCS (Service-Specific Convergence Sublayer) A sublayer within the AAL relating to the type of data traffic. The resulting PDU will be service (for example, SMDS or Frame Relay) dependent.

Staggercasting Transmission of a video program at set times to allow multicasting to many destinations. See *NVoD* and *VoD*.

STM (Synchronous Transfer Mode) A transmission technology whereby different data streams always receive the same bandwidth when combined over a single physical connection. STM is Time Division Multiplexing (*TDM*).

STM-n (Synchronous Tranport Module) The framing structure within *SDH*, where $n = 1$, 4, 16, and so on equating to multiples of 155.52 Mbps.

STP (Shielded Twisted Pair) Cable consisting of a pair of twisted wires surrounded by a metallic shield. See *UTP*.

STS-n (Synchronous Transport Signal) The framing structure within *SONET*, where $n = 1$, 3, 12, and so on, equating to multiples of 51.84 Mbps. A concatenated signal will be equivalent to its equal bandwidth *STM* frame (for example, STS-3c = STM-1).

Subnetwork or subnet A set of hosts or routers sharing a common contiguous address prefix, and able to communicate with one another without the need of a *router*. See *LIS*.

SVC (Switched Virtual Circuit) A logical ATM connection established via signaling. *End-systems* transmit their UNI 3.1, or 4.0 signaling request via the Q.2931 signaling protocol.

Switched LAN Replacement of a shared hub by LAN switches where each user or segment is provided with the full LAN bandwidth. Requires no *end-system* changes.

T-1 A North American physical transmission system consisting of two twisted wire pairs to support 1.544 Mbps. See *DS-1*.

T-3 A term used to refer to any *DS-3*-capable transmission system.

TAXI (Transparent Asynchronous Transmitter/Receiver) Physical layer specification for 100 Mbps across multimode fiber with 4B/5B encoding. One of the ATM Forum's physical layers.

TC (Transmission Convergence Sublayer) A sublayer within the physical layer where cells are prepared for transmission by the *PMD* sublayer.

TCP/IP (Transmission Control Protocol/Internet Protocol) US DoD-developed protocol suite providing for Layer 3 internetworking (IP) and Layer 4 reliable transport (TCP) based on windowing and retransmissions.

TDM (Time Division Multiplexing/Multiplexer) Method of combining multiple lower-speed signals into a higher rate by placing each channel within a known timeslot. TDMs form the core of many enterprise internetworks, and are being replaced by ATM.

TINA (Telecommunications Information Networking Architecture) An emerging application environment to interconnect management platforms and applications from multiple vendors and service providers.

TM (Traffic Management) Act of managing congestion across an ATM network by buffering, adjusting transmission rates, and policing connections. *ABR* is a part of ATM Forum traffic management.

TPD (Trail Packet Discard) A mechanism whereby ATM switches discard the remaining cells of an AAL5 frame if one or more have been lost due to congestion. This helps avoid *congestive collapse*. See *EPD*.

Traffic policing Mechanism whereby any traffic which violates the traffic contract agreed to at connection setup is detected and discarded.

Traffic shaping Control by an *end-system* of originating traffic parameters such as average bandwidth, peak bandwidth, burst, and CLP in order to meet the traffic contract.

UBR (Unspecified Bit Rate) Service type where user requests a *PCR* but has no guarantees as to throughput, latency, or *CLR*. UBR is 'best effort' service. A form of UBR where switches implement *EPD* or *TPD* is sometimes known as UBR+.

UNI (User–Network Interface) The interface between an ATM switch and an ATM-capable *end-system*. Requirements for the UNI are defined by the ATM Forum in a series of standards, the most recent being UNI 4.0.

UPC (Usage Parameter Control) Actions taken by an ATM network to monitor and control traffic. This protects the network and its service guarantees from sources which unintentionally or intentionally violate their traffic contract.

UTOPIA (Universal Test and Operation Physical Interface for ATM) A physical layer interface between ATM devices.

UTP (Unshielded Twisted Pair) Cable consisting of two cable pairs which are not surrounded by shielding. See *STP*.

VBR (Variable Bit Rate) Traffic containing bursts but centered around an average bandwidth. VBR, divided into real-time (rt-VBR) and non-real-time (nrt-VBR) traffic requires the same service guarantees (that is, delay, cell loss, and timing) are provided by CBR.

VC (Virtual Channel or Virtual Connection) A connection between two ATM systems. When used for data, a single VC may support one or many network layer protocols. Multiple Virtual Channels share a Virtual Path, and may be concatenated into a VCC.

VCC (Virtual Circuit Connection) An end-to-end connection consisting of a concatenation of two or more Virtual Channels between two endpoints. VCCs may be bundled into a VPC.

VCI (Virtual Channel Identifier) Used to identify each VC across the *UNI* or *NNI*. The VCI is a 16-bit field within the ATM cell header.

VLAN (Virtual LAN) A network architecture which allows geographically distributed users to communicate as if they were on a single physical LAN by sharing a single broadcast and multicast domain. ATM Forum LAN Emulation supports VLANs (see ELAN, LANE).

VoD (Video on Demand) Transmission of video programs based on individual user requests. Multicasting is normally not possible under VoD. See *NVoD*.

VP (Virtual Path) A grouping of virtual channels (*VCs*), important between ATM switches to facilitate management. Multiple VPs form end-to-end VPCs.

VPC (Virtual Path Connection) An end-to-end connection consisting of two or more Virtual Path links *(VPs)*.

VPI (Virtual Path Identifier) Used to identify each VP across the *UNI* or *NNI*. The VPI is an 8-bit field at the UNI; 12 bits at the NNI (no *GFC*).

VPN (Virtual Private Network) Public network service where a customer is provided a network which appears as if it were a private network.

VTOA (Voice and Telephony over ATM) ATM Forum group developing standards for voice trunking, signaling, and N-ISDN interworking.

Acronyms

AAL	ATM Adaptation Layer
ABR	Available Bit Rate
ACR	Allowed Cell Rate
ADSL	Asymmetric Digital Subscriber Line
AFI	Address Format Identifier
AHFG	ATM Host Functional Group
AIM	ATM Inverse Multiplexing
AIS	Alarm Indication Signal
AME	ATM Management Entity
AMS	Audio/Visual Multimedia Services
ANSI	American National Standards Institute
API	Application or ATM Programming Interface
APPN	Advanced Peer-to-Peer Networking
ARP	Address Resolution Protocol
ATM	Asynchronous Transfer Mode
AU	Administrative Unit
B-ICI	Broadband Inter-Carrier Interface
B-ISDN	Broadband Integrated Services Digital Network
B-NT	Broadband Network Termination
B-TA	Broadband Terminal Adaptor
B-TE	Broadband Terminal Equipment
BECN	Backward Explicit Congestion Notification
BT	Burst Tolerance
BUS	Broadcast and Unknown Server
CAC	Connection Admission Control
CAS	Channel Associated Signaling
CBR	Constant Bit Rate
CCITT	Comite Consultatif Internationale de Telegraphique et Telephonique
CCR	Current Cell Rate
CCS	Common Channel Signaling
CDDI	Copper Distributed Data Interface
CDV	Cell Delay Variation
CDVT	Cell Delay Variation Tolerance
CER	Cell Error Ratio

CES	Circuit Emulation Service
CIR	Committed Information Rate
CLNAP	Connectionless Network Access Protocol
CLP	Cell-Loss Priority
CLR	Cell Loss Ratio
CLSF	Connectionless Server Function
CMI	Cluster Member Identifier
CMIP	Common Management Information Protocol
CMIS	Common Management Information Services
CNM	Customer Network Management
CPCS	Common Part Convergence Sublayer
CPE	Customer Premise Equipment
CRC	Cyclic Redundancy Check
CRS	Cell Relay Service
CS	Convergence Sublayer
CS-PDU	Convergence Sublayer Protocol Data Unit
CSMA/CD	Carrier Sense Multiple Access/Collision Detection
CTD	Cell Transfer Delay
DAN	Desktop Area Network
DAVIC	Digital Audio Visual Interactive Council
DCC	Data Country Code
DE	Discard Eligibility
DFFG	Default Forwarder Functional Group
DFI	Domain Format Identifier
DHCP	Dynamic Host Configuration Protocol
DLCI	Data Link Connection Identifier
DQDB	Distributed Queue Dual Bus
DS-0	Digital Signal Level 0
DS-1	Digital Signal Level 1
DS-3	Digital Signal Level 3
DSP	Domain Specific Part
DSU	Data Service Unit
DTE	Data Terminal Equipment
DTL	Designated Transit List
DXI	Data Exchange Interface
E1	European Signal Level 1
E2	European Signal Level 2
E3	European Signal Level 3
E-IGRP	Enhanced Interior Gateway Resolution Protocol
E-SIG	European SMDS Interest Group
EDFG	Edge Device Functional Group
EFCI	Explicit Forward Congestion Indication
EIA	Electronic Industries Association
ELAN	Emulated LAN
EOM	End of Message
EPD	Early Packet Discard
ER	Explicit Rate
ESI	End System Identifier
ETSI	European Telecommunications Standards Institute
FDDI	Fiber Distributed Data Interface
FECN	Forward Explicit Congestion Notification
FUNI	Frame UNI

GCAC	Generic Connection Admission Control
GCRA	Generic Cell Rate Algorithm
GFC	Generic Flow Control
HAN	Home Access Network or Home Area Network
HEC	Header Error Check
HO-DSP	High Order Domain Specific Part
IAB	Internet Architecture Board
IASG	Internetwork Address Sub-Group
ICD	International Code Designator
ICFG	IASG Coordination Functional Group
ICR	Initial Cell Rate
IDI	Initial Domain Identifier
IDP	Initial Domain Part
IE	Information Element
IEC	Interexchange Carrier
IEEE	Institute of Electrical and Electronic Engineers
IETF	Internet Engineering Task Force
IGMP	Internet Group Management Protocol
IISP	Interim Interswitch Signaling Protocol
ILMI	Interim Local Management Interface
I-PNNI	Integrated Private Network–Network Interface
IP	Internet Protocol
IPmc	IP Multicast
IPv6	IP Version 6
IPX	Internetwork Packet Exchange
IS	Intermediate-System
IS-IS	Intermediate-System to Intermediate-System Routing
ISDN	Integrated Services Digital Network
ISO	International Organization for Standardization
ISOC	Internet Society
ITU-T	International Telecommunications Union – Telecommunications Sector
J-2	Japanese Signaling Level 2
JPEG	Joint Photographic Experts Group
JTC	Joint Technical Committee
L-NNI	LAN Emulation Network-to-Network Interface
L-UNI	LAN Emulation User-to-Network Interface
LAG	Local Address Group
LANE	LAN Emulation or LAN Emulation Service
LEC	LAN Emulation Client
LECS	LAN Emulation Configuration Server
LES	LAN Emulation Server
LGN	Logical Group Node
LIS	Logical IP Subnetwork
LIJ	Leaf Initiated Join
LLC	Logical Link Control
LSU	Link State Update
MAC	Media Access Control
MAN	Metropolitan Area Network
MARS	Multicast Address Resolution Server
MBS	Maximum Burst Size

MCR	Minimum Cell Rate
MCS	Multicast Server
MCTD	Mean Cell Transfer Delay
MIB	Management Information Base
MID	Message Identifier
MPEG	Motion Picture Experts Group
MPOA	Multi-Protocol over ATM
NARP	NBMA Address Resolution Protocol
NBMA	Non-Broadcast Multiple Access Network
NEBS	Network Equipment Building Standards
NDIS	Network Driver Interface Specification
NHRP	Next-Hop Resolution Protocol
NHS	Next-Hop Server
NIC	Network Interface Card
NLPID	Network Layer Protocol Identifier
NLSP	Novell Link State Protocol
NMS	Network Management System
NNI	Network-to-Node Interface or Network-to-Network Interface
NRZ	Non-Return to Zero
NSAP	Network Service Access Point
NVoD	Near Video on Demand
OAM	Operations, Administration, and Maintenance
OAM&P	Operations, Administration, Maintenance, and Provisioning
OC	Optical Carrier
ODI	Open Datalink Interface
OSI	Open Systems Interconnection
OSPF	Open Shortest Path First
OSS	Operations Support System
PACE	Priority Access Control Enabled
PBX	Private Branch Exchange
PCR	Peak Cell Rate
PDH	Plesiosynchronous Transmission Hierarchy
PDU	Protocol Data Unit
PGL	Peer Group Leader
PHY	Physical Layer
PICS	Protocol Implementation Conformance Statement
PIM	Protocol Independent Multicast
PLCP	Physical Layer Convergence Protocol
POH	Path Overhead
PMD	Physical Media Dependent
PNNI	Private Network–Network Interface
POH	Path Overhead
PTI	Payload Type Identifier
PTSP	PNNI Topology State Packet
PTT	Postal Telegraph and Telephony Company
PVC	Permanent Virtual Circuit or Connection
PVP	Permanent Virtual Path
QFC	Quantum Flow Control
QoS	Quality of Service

RBB	Residential Broadband
RDF	Rate Decrease Factor
RDI	Remote Defect Indication
RED	Random Early Detection
RFFG	Remote Forwarder Functional Group
RFC	Request for Comment
RFI	Request for Information
RFP	Request for Procurement
RIF	Rate Increase Factor
ROLC	Routing over Large Clouds
RM	Resource Management
RR	Relative Rate
RSFG	Route Server Functional Group
RSVP	Resource Reservation Protocol
RTT	Round Trip Time
SAAL	Signaling ATM Adaptation Layer
SAP	Service Access Point
SAR	Segmentation and Reassembly Sublayer
SAR-PDU	Segmentation and Reassembly Protocol Data Unit
SCR	Sustainable Cell Rate
SDH	Synchronous Digital Hierarchy
SDU	Service Data Unit
SEAL	Simple and Efficient Adaptation Layer
SEL	Selector
SG	Study Group
SIG	SMDS Interest Group
SIP	SMDS Interface Protocol
SMDS	Switched Multimegabit Data Service
SN	Sequence Number (AAL3/4)
SNAP	Sub Network Access Point
SNI	SMDS Network Interface
SNMP	Simple Network Management Protocol
SOH	Section Overhead
SONET	Synchronous Optical Network
SRTS	Synchronous Residual Timestamp
SSCF	Service-Specific Coordination Function
SSCOP	Service-Specific Connection Oriented Protocol
SSCS	Service-Specific Convergence Sublayer
ST-II	Streams II
STM	Synchronous Transfer Mode
STM-n	Synchronous Transport Module
STP	Shielded Twisted Pair
STS-n	Synchronous Transport Signal
SVC	Switched Virtual Circuit or Connection
T-1	See DS-1
T-3	See DS-3
TAXI	Transparent Asynchronous Transmitter/Receiver
TC	Transmission Convergence Sublayer
TCP	Transmission Control Protocol
TDM	Time Division Multiplexing/Multiplexer
TINA	Telecommunications Information Networking Architecture
TM	Traffic Management
TPD	Trail Packet Discard

TULIP	TCP and UDP over Lightweight IP
TUNIC	TCP and UDP over Nonexistent IP Connection
UBR	Unspecified Bit Rate
UNI	User-Network Interface
UPC	Usage Parameter Control
UTOPIA	Universal Test & Operation Physical Interface for ATM
UTP	Unshielded Twisted Pair
VBR	Variable Bit Rate
VC	Virtual Channel, Circuit, or Connection
VCC	Virtual Channel Connection
VCI	Virtual Channel Identifier
VLAN	Virtual LAN
VoD	Video on Demand
VP	Virtual Path
VPC	Virtual Path Connection
VPI	Virtual Path Identifier
VPN	Virtual Private Network
VT	Vritual Tributary
VTOA	Voice and Telephony over ATM
WFQ	Weighted Fair Queuing
WIRE	Workable Interface Example
WWW	World Wide Web:)

Bibliography

ATM Forum contributions, identified by the 9x-xxxx numbers are not publicly available. They are archived and available via the ATM Forum ftp server, atmforum.com, to all members of the ATM Forum. Due to the fast pace of ATM development, these contributions are the only way to document a number of the proposed standards, and should be considered as 'work in progress.' Some of the more critical contributions are made available to the general public. These are identified below. In addition, many ATM Forum documents, identified by the AF-xxx-xxxxxx numbers are also available in the same way, though they are also available for sale via the Forum's Web site (www.atmforum.com). However, documents are expected to be available as publications or on the public directory of the ATM Forum ftp server. IETF RFCs are available at a number of RFC repositories (ftp://ds.internic.net, nic.nordu.net, ftp.isi.edu, or munnari.oz.au). The same applies to IETF drafts, though these are subject to removal or updating. Thus, some of the draft references may no longer be available, may be available as newer versions, or may have been converted to RFCs. The current status of all IETF drafts is contained in 1id-abstracts.txt available on the above ftp servers. ITU recommendations are available for sale via the ITU's Web site (www.itu.ch).

3COM and Microsoft (1990). *LAN Manager: Network Driver Interface Specification.*

Adams M. (1994). *Network Design and Implementation of a large-scale, ATM, Multimedia Network.* Time Warner Cable Advanced Development, December, 1994 *Interop '95 Las Vegas Engineer Conference.*

ADSL Forum (1995). *VDSL: Fiber-Copper Access to the Information Highway.*' Draft, available through ADSL Forum.

Ahmed M. and Tesink K. (1994). *RFC 1695: Definitions of Managed Objects for ATM Management, V. 8.0.*

Alles A. and Finn N. (1994). *Architectural Overview for a Layer 3 Route Distribution / Query Protocol.* Contribution to ATM Forum PNNI SWG (Multiprotocol Over ATM BOF). 94-1206. ATM Forum.

Alles A. and Traina P. (1994). *Proposal for a Work Effort on a Layer 3 Route Distribution Protocol.* Contribution to ATM Forum Multiprotocol over ATM BOF. 94-0803. ATM Forum.

Anderson T., Owicki S., Saxe B., and Thacker C. (1992). *High speed switch scheduling for local area networks.* In *Proc. of ASPLOSV*, Boston, September, 1992.

ANSI (1993). *A Technical Report on A Comparison of SONET and SDH.* ANSI Working Group on Digital Transmission Network Architecture. Document T1X1.2/93-024R2.

ANSI (1995). *T1.646-1995, Telecommunications – Broadband ISDN and DS1/ATM User-Network Interfaces: Physical Layer Specification.*

Armitage G. (1996). *Support for Multicast over UNI 3.0/3.1 based ATM Networks.* Internet Draft: draft-ietf-ipatm-ipmc-12.txt.

Arora V. and Civanlan S. (1995). *Multicasting in LAN Emulation.* Contribution to ATM Forum LANE SWG. 95-1490R2. ATM Forum.

AT&T News Release (1995). *New Chip Platform for Interactive Services Over Copper Wire'* Berkeley Heights NJ: AT&T Microelectronics.

Atkinson R. (1994). *RFC 1626: IP MTU over ATM AAL5.*

ATM Forum (1993). *ATM Data eXchange Interface (DXI) Specification.* Version 1.0. 93-590R1.

ATM Forum (1993). *BISDN Inter Carrier Interface (B-ICI) Specification.* Version 1.0.

ATM Forum (1994). *PICS Proforma for the 100 Mbps Multimode Fibre Physical Layer Interface.* AF-TEST-0025.

ATM Forum (1994a). *'DS1 Physical Layer Specification.* AF-PHY-0016.

ATM Forum (1994b). *Mid-range Physical Layer Specification for Category 3 Unshielded Twisted-pair'* AF-PHY-0015.

ATM Forum (1994c). *Mid-range Physical Layer Specification for Category 3 UTP.* AF-PHY-0018.

ATM Forum (1994d). *Interim Inter-switch Signaling Protocol (IISP) Specification.* Version 1.0. AF-PNNI-0026.

ATM Forum (1994d). *UTOPIA, An ATM-PHY Interface Specification Level 1.* AF-PHY-0017.

ATM Forum (1994e). *UTOPIA, An ATM-PHY Interface Specification Level 2..*AF-PHY-0039.

ATM Forum (1994f). *Introduction to ATM Forum Test Specifications.* AF-TEST-0022.

ATM Forum (1994g). *Draft Phase I Security Extensions.*

ATM Forum (1994h). *Mock ATM RFI White Paper.* ATM Forum Enterprise Management Roundtable.

ATM Forum (1994i). *ATM Standards and Specifications – A Progress Report.*

ATM Forum (1995). *PICS Proforma for the DS1 Physical Layer Interface.* AF-TEST-0037.

ATM Forum (1995). *Specifications for 155 Mb/s Plastic Optical Fiber Links.* Contribution to ATM Forum PHY SWG. 95-1200. ATM Forum.

ATM Forum (1995a). *ATM User Network Interface (UNI) Specification Version 3.1.* Englewood Cliffs NJ: Prentice Hall.

ATM Forum (1995b). *Circuit Emulation Service Interoperability Specification.* AF-SAA-0032.

ATM Forum (1995c). *LAN Emulation Over ATM Version 1.0.* AF-LANE-0021.

ATM Forum (1995d). *622.08 Mbps Physical Layer Specification.* AF-PHY-0046.

ATM Forum (1995e). *DS3 Direct Mapped Physical Layer Interface Specification and Text as an Annex for DS3 PLCP Version.* AF-PHY-0054.

ATM Forum (1995f) *155.52 Mb/s Physical Layer Specification for Category-3 Unshielded Twisted Pair.* AF-PHY-0047.

ATM Forum. (1995g). *Proposal of 155 Mbps Plastic Optical Fiber PMD Sublayer for Very Low Cost Private UNI.* Contribution to ATM Forum Physical Layer and RBB SWGs. 95-1469. ATM Forum.

ATM Forum. (1995h). *50 Mbps Plastic Fiber PMD Sublayer for Home UNI.* Contribution to ATM Forum Physical Layer and RBB SWGs. 95-1472. ATM Forum.

ATM Forum (1995i). *A Cell-Based Transmission Convergence Sublayer for Clear Channel Interfaces.* AF-PHY-0043.

ATM Forum (1995j). *BISDN Inter Carrier Interface (B-ICI) Specification.* Version 2.0. AF-BICI-0013.0002.

ATM Forum (1995k). *LAN Emulation Client Management Specification.* AF-LANE-0044.

ATM Forum (1995m). *Frame-based User-to-Network Interface (FUNI) Specification.* AF-SAA-0030.

ATM Forum (1995n). *ATM Layer Conformance Test Suite at the UNI for End Systems.* JAF-TEST-0041.

ATM Forum (1996). *ATM User Network Interface (UNI) Specification Version 4.0.* AF-UNI-4.0.

ATM Forum (1996a). *Private Network–Network Interface Specification Version 1.0;* AF-PNNI-0055

ATM Forum (1996b). *ATM Forum Traffic Management Specification Version 4.0.* AF-TM-0056.

ATM Forum (1996c). *LAN Emulation over ATM Version 2-LNNI Specification.* 95-1032. Atm Forum.

Baker F. and Watt J. (1993). *RFC 1406: Definitions of Managed Objects for the DS1 and E1 Interface Types.*

Bassett, B and Hsia, A., *NOAA Setup Notes, http://www.erl.noaa.gov/noc/atm/setup.notes,* Feb 1996.

Bellcore (1995). *Generic Requirements for Operations Interfaces Using OSI Tools: ATM/Broadband Network Management.*

Berry W. (1994). *ENR comments of Flow Control.* Contribution to ATM Forum MA&E SWG. 94E-0008. ATM Forum

Berson (1995). RSVP over ATM, Presentation to December, 1995 IETF.

Birman A., Firoui V., Guerin R., and Kandlur D. (1995). *Provisioning of RSVP-Based Services over Large ATM Networks.* IBM Research Report No. RC 20250, October 1995, http://www.watson.ibm.com: 8080/.

Bonomi F. and Fendick K. (1995). The rate-based flow control framework for the available bit rate ATM service. *IEEE Network,* March/April, 25–39.

Borden M., *et al.* (1995). *RFC 1821: Integration of Real-time Services in an IP-ATM Network Architecture.*

Borman D., Braden R., and Jacobson V. (1992). *RFC 1323: TCP Extensions for High Performance.*

Braden R. (1989a). *RFC 1122: Requirements for Internet hosts – communication layers.*

Braden R. (1989b). *RFC 1123: Requirements for Internet hosts – application and support.*

Braden R. and Jacobson V. (1988). *RFC 1072: TCP extensions for long-delay paths.*

Braden R., Clark, D., and Shenker S. (1994). *RFC 1633: Integrated Services in the Internet Architecture: an Overview*.

Braden R., Postel J. and Rekhter Y. (1994). *RFC 1620: Internet Architecture Extensions for Shared Media*.

Braden R., Zhang L., Berson S., D., Herzog S. and Jamin S. (1996). *Resource ReSerVation Protocol (RSVP) – Version 1 Functional Specifications*. Internet Draft: draft-ietf-rsvp-spec-07.ps.

Bradley T. and Brown C. (1992). *RFC 1293: Inverse Address Resolution Protocol*.

Bradley T., Brown C., and Malis A. (1993). *RFC 1490: Multiprotocol Interconnect over Frame Relay*.

Brazdziunas C. (1994). *IPng Support for ATM Services*.

British Standards Institute (1995). *The operation of the UK scheme for the allocation of ISO DCC format OSI Network Layer Addresses (including the operation of the associated UK Registration Authority) (BS 7306)*. London: BSI.

Broadband Networking News (1995). 8 August.

Broadband Networking News (1995). *ATM Service Supplement*.

Brown C. (1996). *Baseline Text for MPOA*. Contribution to the ATM Forum MPOA SWG. 95-0824R6. ATM Forum.

Brown T. and Tesink K. (1994a). *RFC 1694: Definitions of Managed Objects for SMDS Interfaces using SMIv2*.

Brown T. and Tesink K. (1994b). '*RFC 1595: Definitions of Managed Objects for the SONET/SDH Interface Type*.'

Byers B. (1995). *A Simple Guide to ATM Traffic Shaping*. Edinburgh University Computing Service. http://www.ed.ac.uk/~bill/.

Callaghan R. (1995). *Native ATM Services: Semantic Description*. Contribution to ATM Forum SAA API *ad hoc* Work Group. 95-0008R4. ATM Forum.

Callon R. and Salkewicz B. (1995). *An Issue with Restricted-Transit PNNI Nodes*. Contribution to ATM Forum PNNI SWG. 95-1069. ATM Forum.

Callon R. *et al.* (1996). *The Relationship between MPOA and Integrated PNNI*. Contribution to MPOA and PNNI SWGs. 96-0352. ATM Forum.

Callon R. et al (1996a). *Overview of PNNI Augmented Routing*. Contribution to PNNI SWG 96-0354. ATM Forum.

Carpenter B., Katz D., Thomas S., and Sklower K. (1995). *Mechanisms for OSI CLNP and TP over IPv6*. Internet draft-carpenter-ipv6-osi-01.txt.

Castillo R. (1994). More operators sold on fiber. *Communications Week International*, 24 October, page 32.

CCITT (1992). *CCITT Recommendation M.3010, Principles and Architectures for the TMN*.

Chimento P. *et al* (1993). *Broadband Network Services for High-Speed Multimedia Networks*. IBM.

Cisco Systems (1995a). *Interface Queue Management*.

Cisco Systems (1995b). *How much routing is needed in a Network*? Private Correspondence.

Cole R., Shur D., and Villamizar C. (1996). RFC 1932: *IP over ATM: A Framework Document*. Internet Draft: draft-ietf-ipatm-framework-doc-06.

Cox, T. and Tesink K. (1993). *RFC 1407: Definitions of Managed Objects for the DS3/E3 Interface Type.*

Crocker D. (1993). *Making standards the IETF way. StandardView.* 1(1). Association for Computing Machinery.

Crowcroft J. (1994). *Why Lossy Internetworking and Lossless ABR ATM Services Do Not Go Together.*

Crowcroft J. (1995). *Packet Discard vs Flow Control.* E-mail to IP over ATM IETF working group. Archived at: http://cell-relay.indiana.edu/cell-relay/archives/IPATM/IPATM.html. Private correspondence.

Crowcroft, J. (1996a). *Re: Action ASAP: IEEE Internet 2001.* Private correspondence.

Crowcroft J. (1996b). *Re: Lightweight Signaling and RRS.* Private correspondence

De Prycker M., Paul J. L., and Campos A. (1990). Broadband national experiments in Belgium, France, and Spain. *Alcatel Electrical Communication,* 64(2/3), 218–228

Deering S. (1989). *RFC 1112: Host extensions for IP multicasting.*

Deering S. *et al.* (1996). *Protocol Independent Multicast (PIM): Motivation and Architecture.* Internet Draft.

Delgrossi L. and Berger L., eds (1995). *RFC 1819: Internet Stream Protocol Version 2 (ST-2) Protocol Specification – Version ST2+.*

Dellaverson L. (1995). *Wireless ATM Networking and Selected Service Aspects.* Contribution to ATM Forum Technical Committee. 95-1569. ATM Forum.

Digital Audio Visual Council. (1995). *DAVIC 1.0 Specification.* Revision 3.0.

Dobrowski G. (1994). *Technical Committee Overview.* ATM Forum.

Dobrowski G. (1996). *Anchorage Accord Contribution to ATM Forum Technical and ME&A Committees.* 96-0535. ATM Forum.

Domann G. (1990). BERKOM field trial: operational results and services. *Alcatel Electrical Communication,* 64(2/3), 269–275.

Duault M. and Caves K. (1995). *Baseline Text for Voice and Telephony over ATM – ATM Trunking for Narrowband Services.* Contribution to ATM Forum SAA SWG. 95-0446R3. ATM Forum.

Dudley G. (1995). *HPR Extensions for ATM Networks.* Document ATM-01. IBM.

Dunbeck P. (1993). *Digital's ATM Solutions.* Digital Equipment Corporation.

Dupraz J. and De Prycker M. (1990). Principles and benefits of the asynchronous transfer mode. *Alcatel Electrical Communication,* 64(2/3), 116–123.

DVB Project Office. (1995). *Digital Video Broadcasting: Television for the Third Millennium.*

Dwight T. (1994). *Re: ATM Flow Control Clarification.* E-mail to IETF IP over ATM WG.

Dwight T. (1995). *IP Address as a form of ATM End-System Address.* E-mail to IP over ATM WG.

EIA/TIA (1994). *Commercial Building and Wiring Telecommunications Wiring Standard.* Standards Proposal No. 2840-A, EIA/TIA-568-A.

Engel A. and Mobasser B. (1990). New standards in relation to broadband ISDN. *Alcatel Electrical Communication,* 64(2/3), 177–185.

Esaki *et al* (1995a). *Necessity of an FEC Scheme for ATM Networks*. Contribution to ATM Forum Plenary and SAA SWG. 95-0325R2. ATM Forum.

Esaki *et al* (1995b). *Draft Proposal for Specification of FEC-SSCS for AAL Type 5*. Contribution to ATM Forum Plenary and SAA SWG. 95-0326R2. ATM Forum.

Estrin, D., Farinacci D., and Jacobson, V. (1996) *Protocol Independent Multicast – Devise Mode (PIM-DM) Protocol Specification:* Internet Draft: draft-ietf-idmir-PIM-DM-spec-01p5.

Evagora A. (1995). Standards old guard ready to welcome forum specs. *Communications Week International*, 22 May.

Fang C. and Lin. A. (1995a). *A Simulation Study of ABR Robustness under Binary Switch Modes*. Contribution to the ATM Forum TM SWG. 95-1019. ATM Forum.

Fang C. and Lin A. (1995b). *A Simulation Study of ABR Robustness with Binary-Modes Switches: Part II*. Contribution to the ATM Forum TM SWG. 95-1328R1. ATM Forum.

Farinacci D. (1995). *IGMP over ATM*. Internet Draft: draft-ietf-farinacci-igmp-over-atm-00.

Fedorkow G. (1994). *Technical Approach to Providing Circuit Emulation over ATM Networks*. LightStream Corporation.

Fenner, W. (1996). *Internet Group Management Protocol, Version 2*. Internetdraft: draft ietf-idmr-igmp-vz-oz.txt.

Finn N. (1995). *LLC Multiplexing for LAN Emulation*. Contribution to ATM Forum LANE and MPOA SWGs. 95-0577R2. ATM Forum.

Fluckiger F. (1996). *Understanding Networked Multimedia*. Prentice-Hall.

Flugstad P. (1994). *Comments on IP over ATM Signaling Draft*. E-mail to IETF IP over ATM. Archived at: //ftp.hep.net/ftp/lists-archive/atm.

Focus Data Survey by Focus Data in 10/9/95 Network World.

Fore Systems (1993). *SPANS NNI: Simple Protocol for ATM Network Signaling (Network-to-Network Interface)*. Release 2.3.

Fore Systems (1993). *SPANS: Simple Protocol for ATM Network Signaling*. Release 2.3.

Fowler H. (1995). TMN-based broadband ATM network management. *IEEE Communications*, March, 74–79.

Frame Relay Forum (1993). *Multiprotocol Encapsulation over Frame Relaying Networks Implementation Agreement*. Document Number FRF.3.

Frame Relay Forum (1994). *Frame Relay/ATM PVC Network Interworking Implementation Agreement*. Document Number FRF.5.

Frame Relay Forum (1995). *Frame Relay/ATM PVC Service Interworking Implementation Agreement*. Document Number FRF.8.

Frame Relay Forum (1996). *Data Compression over Frame Relay Implementation Agreement*. Document Number FRF.9.

Fujimori T. and Scheel R. (1995). *An Introduction to an IEEE1394 Based Home Network*. Contribution to ATM Forum RBB SWG. 95-1378. ATM Forum.

Gaddis M. (1994). *Re: Multicasting over ATM draft*. E-mail to IETF IP over ATM WG.

Garrett M. (1994). *ATM Service Architecture: From Applications to Scheduling*. Contribution to ATM Forum TM SWG. 94-0846. ATM Forum.

Gibbons M. *et al.* (1995). *Clarifying the Definition of FTTC*. Contribution to ATM Forum RBB SWG. 95-1037. ATM Forum.

Goguen M. (1993). *AN2: A Self-Configuring Local ATM Network*. Palo Alto CA: DEC Systems.

Goode C. (1990). Broadband services and applications. *Alcatel Electrical Communication*, 64(2/3), 124–138.

Green Jr. P. (1994). Toward customer-useable all-optical networks. *IEEE Communications*, December, 44–49.

Heinanen J. (1993). *RFC 1483: Multiprotocol Encapsulation over ATM Adaptation Layer 5.*

Heinanen J. and Govindan R. (1994). *RFC 1735: NBMA Address Resolution Protocol (NARP).*

Hinden R. (1995). IP next generation overview. *Connexions*, 9(3), 2–18.

Hoelzle J. (1995). *E1 ATM UNI Specification (R3)*. Contribution to ATM Forum PHY SWG. 94-0422R3. ATM Forum.

Hoffmann T., Mueller D., and Vogt C. (1993). Video Compression Techniques for Multimedia Communications. *Alcatel Electrical Communication*, 4th Quarter, 402–410.

Howat G., Gillman D., and Wang B. (1995). *Discussion Paper on ATM Addressing*. University of Edinburgh.

Huitema C. (1994). *RFC 1715: The H Ratio for Address Assignment Efficiency.*

Hummel H., Petri B., and Nemeth K. (1994). *Interworking between Narrowband- and Broadband-ISDN*. Contribution to ATM Forum UNI-SIG and PNNI SWGs. 94-0347. ATM Forum.

IBM (1993). *Intelligent LAN Concentrators Evolution to ATM – Hub Update Presentation*. La Gaude, France: IBM.

IBM (1993a). *IBM Submissions to ATM Forum Focus on Reaching the Desktop*. IBM Fact Sheet, 9 March.

IBM (1993b). *IBM High-Speed Networking Technology: An Introductory Survey*. Publication GG24-3816-01, June, 209 ff.

Ikeda C. *et al.* (1995). *Is FEC really effective to the data transmission?* Contribution to ATM Forum Technical Committee. 95-1481. ATM Forum.

InfoWorld Publishing Company (1994) *LAN Talk – Are hyped, high-tech LAN products of value to your operation?*

Ipsilon (1996). *IP Switching: The Intelligence of Routing, The Performance of Switching*. Ipsilon Corporation. www.ipsiolon.com.

Institute of Electrical and Electronic Engineers (1989). *Information Processing Systems – Local Area Networks – Part 2: Logical Link Control.*

Institute of Electrical and Electronic Engineers (1990). *IEEE Standard 802.6: Distributed Queue Dual Bus (DQDB) Subnetwork of a Metropolitan Area Network (MAN) Standard.*

Institute of Electrical and Electronic Engineers (1991). *Information Technology – Local and Metropolitan Area Networks – Part 5: Token Ring access method and physical layer specification.*

Institute of Electrical and Electronic Engineers (1993). *Information Technology – Local and Metropolitan Area Networks – Part 3: CSMA/CD access method and physical specifications.*

Institute of Electrical and Electronic Engineers (1995). *IEEE1394 Standard for a High Performance Serial Bus*. IEEE Draft 8.0v2.

Institute of Electrical and Electronic Engineers (1995). *IEEE Standard 802.12: Demand Priority (VG-AnyLAN)*.

Institute of Electrical and Electronic Engineers (1995a). *IEEE P 802.14 Cable-TV Functional Requirements and Evaluation Criteria*.

Intel (1995a). *Windows Sockets 2 Application Provider Interface*. http://www.intel.com Revision 2.0.8.

Intel (1995b). *Windows Sockets 2 Service Provider Interface*. http://www.intel.com. Revision 2.0.8.

ISO (1987). *Informational processing systems, interface connector and contact assignments for ISDN basic access interface located at reference points S and T*. (ISO 8877).

ISO/IEC DIS 11801, JTC1/SC25 N106 (1992). *Generic Cabling for Customer Premises*. Draft Ballot.

ITU (1991a). *Recommundation G.704: Synchronous Frame Structures Used at Primary and Secondary Hierarchical Levels*.

ITU (1991b). *Recommendation G.703: Physical/Electrical Characteristics of Hierarchical Digital Interfaces*.

ITU (1994a). *Recommendation G.804: ATM Cell Mapping into Plesiochronous Digital Hierarchy*.

ITU (1994b). *Recommendation G.832: Transport of SDH Elements on PDH Networks: Frame and Multiplexing Structures*.

ITU-T (1993). *Recommendation G.957, Optical Interfaces for Equipments and Systems Relating to the SDH*.

ITU-T (1993a). *Recommendation I.432, B-ISDN User-Network Interface – Physical Layer Specification*.

ITU-T (1993b). *Recommendation I.364, Support of Broadband Connectionless Data Service on B-ISDN*.

ITU-T (1995). Q.2931: *Broadband Integrated Services Digital Network (B-ISDN); Digital Subscriber Signalling System No. 2 (DSS2); User-Network Interface (UNI) Layer 3 Specification for Basic Call/Connection Control*.

ITU-T (1995a). Q.2951: *Stage 3 Description for Number Identification Supplementary Services using B-ISDN Digital Subscriber Signalling System No. 2 (DSS2), Basic Call*.

ITU-T (1995b). Q.2957: *Stage 3 Description for Additional Information Transfer Supplementary Services using B-ISDN Digital Subscriber Signalling System No. 2 (DSS2), Basic Call*. Q.2957-1995.

ITU-T (1995c). Q.2971: *Broadband Integrated Services Digital Network (B-ISDN); Digital Subscriber Signalling System No. 2 (DSS2); User-Network Interface (UNI) Layer 3 Specification for Point-to-Multipoint Call/Connection Control*.

ITU-T (1995d). I.610 *B-ISDN Operation and Maintenance Principles and Functions*. International Telecommunication Union.

ITU-T (1996). Q.2932 *Broadband Integrated Services Digital Network (B-ISDN); Digital Subscriber Signalling System No. 2 (DSS2); Generic Functional Protocol*.

Jain R. (1995). *Congestion Control and Traffic Management in ATM Networks: Recent Advances and a Survey*. Ohio State University.

Jain R. and Nagendra B. (1995). *Performance Benchmarking of ATM Switches*. Contribution to ATM Forum. 95-1662R1. ATM Forum.

Jamin S., Shenker S., Zhang L., and Clark D. (1992). An admission control algorithm for predictive real-time service. Extended abstract in *Proc. Third International Workshop on Network and Operating System Support for Digital Audio and Video*, San Diego CA, November 1992, 73–91.

Jeffrey M. (1994). Advanced technology tutorial: ATM signaling. Supplement to *Communications Standards News*, Philips Business Information, 21 September.

Katz D., Piscitello D., Cole B., and Luciani J. (1995). *NBMA Next Hop Resolution Protocol (NHRP)*. Internet Draft: draft-ietf-rolc-nhrp-07.

Keene J. (1995) *LAN Emulation over ATM Version 2 – LUNI Specification – Draft 1*. Contribution to ATM Forum LANE SWG. 95-1081R1. ATM Forum.

Keene J. (1995). *LAN Emulation SWG Future Scope and Requirements*. Contribution to ATM Forum LAN Emulation SWG. 95-0259R5. ATM Forum.

Kercheval R. (1994). *ATMARP: An Architectural Proposal*. Xerox Palo Alto Research Center.

Kobayashi T. (1995). *Clarification on D.11 of AF/95-0810R1(H.320 over AAL5)*. Contribution to ATM Forum SAA SWG. 95-1660. ATM Forum.

Kuhn M. (1994). *Standards-FAQ*. ftp://rtfm.mit.edu/pub/usenet/news.answers /standards-faq.

Kumar S. (1995). *SAA/VTOA Voice and Telephony over ATM to the Desktop*. Contribution to the ATM Forum SAA SWG. 95-0917R2. ATM Forum.

Kwok T. (1995). *Residential Broadband Applications Requirements*. Contribution to ATM Forum RBB SWG. 95-1336. ATM Forum.

Laubach M. (1993). *RFC 1577: Classical IP and ARP over ATM*.

Laubach M. (1995). *RFC 1754: IP over ATM Working Group's Recommendations for the ATM Forum's Multiprotocol BOF Version 1*.

Laubach M. (1995b). *Classical IP and ARP over ATM Update (Part Deux)*. Internet Draft: draft-ietf-ipatm-classic2-00.txt.

Laubach M. (1995). *Using ATM over Hybrid Fiber-Coax Networks*. Com21, Inc. Paper presented to the Society of Photo-Optical Instrumentation Engineers. Available at: http://www.com21.com.

Laubach M. and Perkins D. (1994). *Internet Engineering Task Force (IETF) IP over ATM Working Group's Requirements for the ATM Multiprotocol BOF*. Contribution to ATM Forum Multiprotocol over ATM BOF. 94-0954. ATM Forum.

Leinwand A., Fang-Conroy K. (1996). *Network Management*. A Practical Perspective Second Edition. Addison-Wesley.

Leland W., Taqqu M., Willinger W., and Wilson D. (1994). On the self-similar nature of Ethernet traffic (extended version)' *IEEE/ACM Transactions on Networking*, 2(1), 1–15.

Lippis N. (1994). *Virtual LANs: Real Drawbacks*. Data Communications International 23–24.

Luciani J. (1996) *Server Cache Synchronization Protocol (SCSP)-NBMA*. Internet Draft: draft-luciani-rolc-scsp-01.text.

Lyles B. (1994). *Class-Y Baseline Document*. Contribution to T1 Committee. Document Number: T1S1.5/94-005R1.

Lyon T., Liaw F., and Romanov A. (1992). *Network Layer Architecture for ATM Networks*. Contribution to IETF IP over ATM WG. Sun Microsystems.

Maher M. and Mankin, A. (1996). *ATM Signaling Support for IP over ATM-UNI 4.0 Update*. Internet Draft: draft-ietf-ipatim-sig-uni-v4.

McCloghrie K. (1994). *Lan-Emulation's Needs for Traffic Management*. 94-0533. ATM Forum.

McCloghrie K. and Kastenholz F. (1994). *RFC 1573: Evolution of the Interfaces Group of MIB-II*.

McCloghrie K. and Rose M. (1991). *RFC 1213: Management Information Base for Network Management of TCP/IP-based internets: MIB-II*.

Mitchell R. (1995). *Security ad hoc group minutes*. Contribution to ATM Forum Technical Committee *Ad Hoc* Security Group. 95-1086. ATM Forum.

Mogul J. and Deering S. (1990). *RFC 1191: Path MTU Discovery*.

Newman, P. *et al*. (1996). *Ipsilon Flow Management Protocol Specification for IPv4 Version 1.0*. Internet Draft: draft-rfced-info-flowman-00.txt.

Newman, P. *et al*. (1996a). *The Transmission of Flow Labelled Ipv4 on ATM Data Links Version 1.0*. Internet Draft: draft-rfced-info-flowlabel-00.txt.

Newman, P. *et al*. (1996b). *General Switch Management Protocol Specification Version 1.0*. Internet Draft.

Newsbytes (1995). Bell-Northern claims switching breakthrough. *Newsbytes*, 27 April.

Noah M. (1995). *Voice Compression Algorithms for ATM*. Contribution to ATM Forum SAA/VTOA SWG. 95-1063R1. ATM Forum.

Novell (1992). *Open Data-Link Interface Developer's Guide*.

Onvural R. and Srinivasan V. (1996). *A Framework for Supporting RSVP Flows over ATM Networks*. Internet Draft: draft-onvural-srinivasan-rsvp-atm-atm-øøtxt.

Palka M. (1994). FDDI – finally, there's money to be made. *Business Communications Review*, August, 14–22.

Partridge C. (1992). *RFC 1363: A Proposed Flow Specification*.

Perez M. *et al*, (1995). *RFC 1755: ATM Signaling Support for IP over ATM*.

Perkins D. and Liaw F. (1994). *Beyond Classical IP – Integrated IP and ATM Architecture Overview*. Contribution to ATM Forum Multiprotocol over ATM BOF. 94-0935. ATM Forum.

Phelan S. (1994). *The bottom line: ATM when, where, and at what price*. Presentation Yankee Group Europe.

Piscitello D. and Lawrence J. (1991). *RFC 1209: The Transmission of IP Datagrams over the SMDS Service*.

Plummer D. (1982). *RFC 826: Ethernet Address Resolution Protocol: or converting network protocol addresses to 48 bit Ethernet address for transmission on Ethernet hardware*.

Postel J. (1981). *RFC 793: Transmission Control Protocol*.

Ratta G. *et al* (1995). *On the Proper Place for FEC*, Contribution to ATM Forum Technical Committee. 95-1548. ATM Forum.

Raychaudnuri R. *et al* (1995). *Rationale and Framework for Wireless ATM Specification*. Contribution to ATM Forum Technical Committee. 95-1646. ATM Forum.

Reeves J. (1995). Low-speed access: extending the reach of ATM. *Telecommunications*, February, 23–29.

Rekhter Y. (1995). *NHRP for Destinations of the NMBA Subnetwork*. Internet Draft: draft.ietf-rolc-r2r-nchrp-01.txt.

Rekhter Y. and Farinacci D. (1996). *Support for Sparse Mode PIM over ATM*. Internet Draft: draft-ietf.rolc-pim-atm-00.txt.

Rekhter Y. and Kandlur D. (1995). *IP Architecture Extensions for ATM*. Internet Draft: draft-rekhter-ip-atm-architecture-01.txt.

Rekhter Y. and Kandlur D. (1996). *RFC 1937 Local/Remote Forwarding Decision in Switched Data Link Subnetworks*.

Rooholamini R. and Cherkassky V. (1995). ATM-based multimedia servers. *IEEE Multimedia*, Spring, 39–52.

Roberts E. (1996). *Gigabit LAN standards – It takes Two to Tangle*. Data Communications, March 21.

Rooholamini R., Cherkassky V., and Garver M. (1994). Finding the right ATM switch for the market. *IEEE Computer*, April, 16–28.

Rose M. (1993). *The Simple Book: An Introduction to Management of TCP/IP-based Internets*. Englewood Cliffs NJ, Prentice Hall.

Ross T. (1995). ATM APIs: the missing links. *Data Communications*, September, 119–124.

Sass, F. (1996). *The New Cooperation Agreement with ETSI*. Contribution to ATM Forum Technical Committee. 96-0378. ATM Forum.

Saunders S. (1995). Next-generation routing: making sense of the marketectures. *Data Communications International*, September, 52–64

Schneier B. (1994). *Applied Cryptography: Protocols, Algorithms and Source Code in C*. New York: John Wiley and Sons.

Shelef N. (1995). SVC signaling: calling all nodes. *Data Communications International*, June, 123–130.

Simcoe R. and Roberts L. (1994). The great debate over ATM congestion control. *Data Communications International*, September 21, 75–80.

Simpson W. (1994). *RFC 1619: PPP over SONET/SDH*.

Smith A., Luciani J., and Halpern J. (1996). *Proposed Restructuring of LNNI to use IETF's Server Synchronization*. Contribution to LANE and MPOA SWGs. 96-0407. ATM Forum.

Smith T. and Armitage G. (1995). *IP Broadcast over ATM Networks*. Internet Draft: draft-ieft-ipatm-bcast-02.

Sourbes H. *et al* (1993). *Intelligent LAN Concentrators Evolution to ATM*. La Gaude, France: IBM Networking Systems Development Laboratory.

Stodola K. (1995). *DS3/E3 CBR Baseline Proposed Text*. Contribution to ATM Forum SAA and CES SWGs. 95-0278R1. ATM Forum.

Swallow G. (1994). PNNI: weaving a multivendor ATM network. *Data Communications International*, December, 102–110.

Sweeney T. (1995a). Copper loop breaks 50-mbps barrier. *Communications Week International*, 7 August, 1.

Sweeney T. (1995b). ATM Forum cedes API work. *Communications Week International*, 27 November, 4.

Takigawa Y., Terada N., and Kanada T. (1995). *The ATM-PON system – technologies and applications*. Contribution to ATM Forum RBB SWG. 95-1102. ATM Forum.

Taylor K. (1995). Assessing ATM analyzers. *Data Communications*, December, 93–100.

Telecommunications Industry Association (1995). *Multimedia Premises Reference Architecture, Draft 1.0.* ANSI/TIA (tbd).

Terdoslavich, W. (1994). CMP Publications.

Tesink K. and Brunner T. (1994). (Re)configuration of ATM virtual connections with SNMP. *The Simple Times*, 3(2), 24 August.

Topolcic C. (1990). *RFC 1190: Experimental Internet Stream Protocol, Version 2 (ST-II)*.

UIA (1994). *Virtual LAN's over ATM*.

UNIX International (1991). *Data Link Provider Interface (DLPI) Specification*. Revision 2.0.0. OSI Work Group.

Vallee R. (1995). *Baseline text for ATM Inverse Multiplexing Specification*. Contribution to ATM Forum PHY SWG. 95-1121. ATM Forum.

Van Der Putten F. *et al* (1995). *FTTC System Description*. Contribution to ATM Forum RBB SWG. 95-1356. ATM Forum.

Villamizar C. and Song C. (1994). *High Performance TCP in ANSNET*. Advanced Network & Services, Inc. and Advantis.

Waldbusser S. (1993). *RFC 1513: Token Ring Extensions to the Remote Network Monitoring MIB*.

Waldbusser S. (1995). *RFC 1757: Remote Network Monitoring Management Information Base*.

Wang Z. and Crowcroft J. (1994). *QoS Routing for Supporting Resource Reservation*. London: Department of Computer Science, University College London.

Wetzel G. (1995). *Registration Process for NSAP US DCC Organizational Name*. Contribution to ATM Forum Signaling SWG. 95-0624. ATM Forum.

Whitby-Strevens C. (1995a). *50 Mbit/sec UTP-5 PHY for RBB*. Contribution to ATM Forum RBB SWG. 95-1187. ATM Forum.

Whitby-Strevens C. (1995b). *Nirvana (Serial Utopia) Level 1*. Contribution to ATM Forum RBB SWG. 95-1185. ATM Forum.

Wired (1995). Align and conquer. *Wired*, February, 110ff.

Wojnaroski L. (1995) *Requirements/Criteria for the Home UNI*. Contribution to the ATM Forum RBB SWG. 95-1075R1,. ATM Forum.

Wojnaroski L. (1995a) *Baseline text for the Residential Broadband Working Group*. Contribution to ATM Forum RBB SWG. 95-1416. ATM Forum.

Wright S. (1995a). *SAA Audio-visual Multimedia Service (AMS) Implementation Agreement*. Contribution to ATM Forum SAA SWG. 95-0012R1. ATM Forum.

Wright S. (1995b). *SAA AMS Phase 2 Work Items from ATM Forum/95-0012R2 Annex D*. Contribution to the ATM Forum SAA SWG. 95-0810R1. ATM Forum.

Wurster S. *et al* (1995). *WIRE Specification*. Contribution to ATM Forum PHY SWG. 94-0766R2. ATM Forum.

xbind project Homepage: http://www.ctr.columbia.edu/comet/xbind/xbind.html.

Zhang L., Deering S., Estrin D., Shenker S., and Zappala D. (1993a) RSVP: a new Resource
ReSerVation Protocol. *IEEE Network*, September.

Index